The WORLD of CRIME

To Ruscha

The WORLD of CRIME

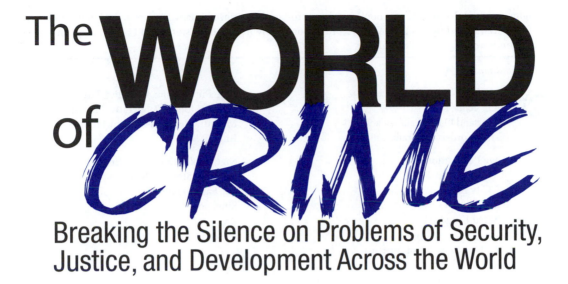

Breaking the Silence on Problems of Security, Justice, and Development Across the World

WITHDRAWN

Jan Van Dijk

International Victimology Institute, Tilburg University, The Netherlands

SAGE Publications

Los Angeles • London • New Delhi • Singapore

For information:

Sage Publications, Inc.
2455 Teller Road
Thousand Oaks, California 91320
E-mail: order@sagepub.com

Sage Publications Ltd.
1 Oliver's Yard
55 City Road
London EC1Y 1SP
United Kingdom

Sage Publications India Pvt. Ltd.
B 1/I 1 Mohan Cooperative Industrial Area
Mathura Road, New Delhi 110 044
India

Sage Publications Asia-Pacific Pte. Ltd.
33 Pekin Street #02-01
Far East Square
Singapore 048763

Printed in the United States of America.

Library of Congress Cataloging-in-Publication Data

Dijk, Jan van. The world of crime : breaking the silence on problems of security, justice and development across the world / Jan Van Dijk.
    p. cm.
Includes bibliographical references and index.
ISBN 978-1-4129-5678-9 (cloth)
ISBN 978-1-4129-5679-6 (pbk.)
    1. Crime. 2. Crime prevention. I. Title.

HV6025.D54 2008
364—dc22   2007040209

This book is printed on acid-free paper.

07 08 09 10 11 10 9 8 7 6 5 4 3 2 1

Acquisitions Editor:	Jerry Westby
Editorial Assistant:	Melissa Spor
Production Editor:	Karen Wiley
Copy Editor:	Cheryl Rivard
Typesetter:	C&M Digitals (P) Ltd.
Proofreader:	Kevin Gleason
Indexer:	Kirsten Kite
Cover Designer:	Candice Harman
Marketing Manager:	Jennifer Reed

Contents

Preface

This book gives a comprehensive and up-to-date overview of the new generation of survey-based statistics on both common crimes and on emerging global threats. Following the example of Transparency International's rankings of countries on levels of corruption, the book presents "league tables" on various types of crime. Using information from a wide range of sources, over 150 countries, from both the developed and developing world, are benchmarked on their levels of crime, violence, sexual violence, organized crime, trafficking in persons, petty and grand corruption, and terrorism. All information is presented in easily understandable tables and graphs, depicting levels of crime in world regions and individual countries. Statistics on the most important types of crime are depicted also in the form of color-shaded world maps. The book offers a first-ever World Atlas of Crime.

Part I of this book explains why it had to be written. Crime is rapidly becoming global in its various manifestations. Terrorist attacks are funded, planned, prepared, and executed across borders. Chemical drugs are shipped from Asia through Europe or Australia to end up in discos in North America. Cocaine goes from South America through the Caribbean or Africa to Europe. Young women are trafficked for sexual exploitation from countries in Asia, Africa, and Eastern Europe to the European Union, North America, and Australia. Billions in criminal assets are moved around the world by money launderers and stashed away in safe havens. Every year millions of naïve people fall victim to Internet-based frauds emanating from Nigeria: Their savings end up in banks in, for example, China within seconds.

The international community is slowly rising to the challenge of global crime. More and more people have started to realize that no American or European judge, however dedicated, can arrest a scam artist in Lagos, Nigeria, or freeze and confiscate assets hidden in Beijing. Something needs to be done to protect the victims of global crime. Governments appreciate that more international cooperation in criminal justice is needed. They understand that the strengthening of criminal justice agencies in poorer countries is the first line of defense against global crime. In recent years, the first global treaties against organized crime, human trafficking, corruption, and terrorism have entered into force. Both the United States and some European countries are detaching some of their best law enforcement experts and prosecutors abroad to assist local colleagues in countering global threats.

The question is whether criminology has also risen to the challenge of globalizing crime. Strangely enough, most research and most courses in criminology have maintained a distinctly domestic focus. We learn about the operations of domestic law enforcement and justice systems and about the characteristics of local offenders and local victims. Prevailing criminological theories are almost exclusively tested in national settings, using national or city data. The comparative approach, prevailing in economics and so many other advanced fields of study, remains conspicuously absent in criminology. Some textbooks offer a brief section on international or comparative issues for curiosity's sake, often using statistics on crime from Interpol. Ironically, even these statistics are no longer available. In 2006, Interpol made the decision to remove all crime statistics from its public Web sites. After publishing international figures of crime for 50 years, Interpol has discontinued its series precisely at a time when international information on crime makes more sense than ever.

In this book, I will argue that Interpol's decision is criminologically sound and its director should be commended. Statistics of police-recorded crimes reflect the performance of the police rather than levels of crime. Where police forces are incompetent or corrupt, fewer victims report crimes and recorded crime rates will consequently be low. Where police forces are more effective, levels of reporting are higher and rates of recorded crimes go up. This mechanism explains why according to international statistics, rates of recorded crime are highest in Sweden and New Zealand and lowest in Albania and Colombia. As measures of the levels of crime across countries, police figures of crime are a source of disinformation. Fortunately, new sources of information on crime in an international perspective have become available. The International Crime Victim Survey, a standardized survey on victimization experience, was carried out in 1988 for the first time in a dozen countries. It has since been repeated once or more in 78 countries. For many countries, including the United States, Canada, England and Wales, Australia, and the Netherlands, comparable survey-based data on victimization are available from five sweeps of the ICVS, the latest from 2005. Similar new sources of information have been created regarding organized crime and corruption.

Comparative surveys on various types of crime such as the ICVS have been given a clean bill of health by leading crime survey experts such as American scholar Jim Lynch. And yet the execution of the ICVS has remained a vulnerable undertaking, receiving more criticism than support. Its results have not been widely distributed through the UN or other international channels. In fact, many governments are opposed to international crime statistics, which they regard as a potential threat to their national sovereignty. They are unwilling to see their "dirty laundry" of crime and violence exposed in the international arena. As promoter of the ICVS and senior official within the United Nations Office on Drugs and Crime, responsible for crime issues, I have witnessed several instances where governments thwarted efforts to collect international statistics on crime, corruption, or terrorism. In 2004, for example, I coauthored a lengthy report on trends on crime and justice for the occasion of the 11th UN Crime Congress in Bangkok. This report was generally well received—and even praised in the Political Declaration adopted at the end of the Congress. And yet it never evolved into a full-fledged UN publication. At the United Nations' Crime Commission in Vienna later in the year, the executive director of UNODC, Antonio Maria Costa, tossed to the commission the idea of a biannual World Crime Report of the United Nations. This obvious proposal was, at the prompt initiative of the

U.S. delegation, summarily rejected. The consensus among the diplomats and experts convening in Vienna was that crime statistics are too politically sensitive for the United Nations.

In the current era of globalization, crime problems often have "spillover" effects across national borders. Governments can no longer treat crime problems as domestic affairs. The current book can be seen as an attempt to break the "conspiracy of silence" around international crime information. It is the personalized version of the kind of report that the Crime Commission voted down in Vienna 3 years ago.

Part II presents available data on common crimes, such as burglaries, robberies, and assaults based on the ICVS and on homicides based on police and health statistics. A special section is devoted to results on violence against women based on other international research. Subsequent chapters discuss the main causes of common crime at the macro level. The most important determinants of crime appear to be (rapid) urbanization, extreme poverty/economic inequality, overrepresentation of young males, discrimination of women, alcohol abuse, and availability of guns. Scatterplots depict the statistical links between national scores on known macro causes and national rates of crime. This visual presentation of the data allows the reader to see at a glance how individual countries are placed on, for example, beer consumption or gun ownership and rates of assaults. The plots also reveal which countries are outliers (e.g., score high on alcohol consumption but low on assaults). Readers can see for themselves whether the statistical relations look strong enough to be convincing. All data used in the analyses are also put in appendices, which makes them easily available for secondary analyses by the reader. The information on the causes of crime provides several entry points for strategies to prevent crime at the national or local level. Governments in Europe and Africa are, for example, alerted to the role of alcohol abuse in youth violence. Governments in the Americas will be informed on the links between gun ownership and various forms of serious violent crime.

The trend data on common crime, presented at the end of Part II, show that levels of crime are declining not just in the United States but in nearly all developed countries. This finding makes it important to find explanations for the drops in crime that are applicable across countries. In the United States, lower crime rates are often attributed to wider use of imprisonment. The international information shows that similar drops in crime have occurred in countries such as Finland and France where rates of imprisonment have remained stable or declined. Results of the ICVS and other studies demonstrate that in all Western countries, middle-class families and businesspeople have responded to increased losses from crime with massive investments in self-protection. This phenomenon of "responsive securitization" is presented as the main driving force behind the near-universal drops in common crime. Chapter 7 discusses the fact that poorer countries as well as low-income groups in richer ones cannot afford to invest as much in self-protection as those better off. This factor of security affordability explains why public safety is increasingly unequally distributed both between countries and within. While risks of crime have gone down in the North, many developing countries in the world's South are still struggling with rising rates of violence and crime. Within Western nations, risks have gone down steeper among high- and middle-income groups than among less well-protected low-income groups.

In Part III of this book, the focus is shifted from common crimes to the emerging global crime threats such as organized crime, corruption, and terrorism. Official statistics on organized crime are shown to be of little use. Harnessing information from a variety of sources such as surveys among business executives, risk assessments by security experts, and country rates of unsolved murders, a composite index is made of the prevalence of organized crime in countries. Unsurprisingly, this index is found to correlate strongly with a composite index of grand corruption. Organized crime and high-level corruption are shown to be two of a kind. Terrorism indices, however, point at a distribution that is very different, with a concentration in the Middle East.

In Part IV, countries are ranked according to the performance of their police forces, the independence and integrity of their courts, and their use of imprisonment. As before, results are presented in the form of tables and graphs, indicating differences between countries and regions. The results point at a major "justice deficit" in developing countries: In the world's South, police forces and courts are seriously underfunded and often perform poorly. As expected, the United States comes out as world leader in imprisonment. Perhaps more surprisingly, data from surveys among business leaders show confidence in the integrity of courts to be declining in both developing and developed countries, including western Europe and North America.

In Part V, the final part, police performance and judicial integrity are linked to levels of organized crime. The results reveal that institutional failures to uphold the rule of law are root causes of organized crime and grand corruption as well as of terrorism. In countries where police forces are not performing and the rule of law is not assured, organized crime and grand corruption can flourish and terrorist groups are more likely to attack. The analyses also show that such lawlessness is closely linked to economic stagnation. In the short term, national economies may receive a boost from criminal activities such as drug production and trafficking. But our analyses suggest that, on balance, the organized crime–corruption complex is a major obstacle for economic growth. Several developing countries are in the grips of vicious circles of institutional failure, generalized lawlessness, and economic stagnation. Crime emerges as a vitally important development issue.

Over the past years, the member states of the United Nations have adopted international legal instruments to strengthen the fight against organized crime, corruption, and terrorism. Insiders are unimpressed by the pace and scale of implementation of these treaties. The book ends with a plea for global reform in the justice and security sector. International cooperation in law enforcement and criminal justice should no longer be just preached over conference tables but practiced in police stations and criminal courts. In order to generate reliable partners in developing countries, a large-scale transfer of skills and equipment to the South is required. This book hopes to convince readers that functioning police and justice systems can do much to improve the quality of life and prosperity of those living in the poorest countries and would simultaneously serve the interests of the world community in its fight against international terrorism.

The book is important for students who want to put domestic crime and justice issues and criminological theories in an international perspective. The many tables, graphs, and scatterplots will induce advanced students to engage themselves in secondary analyses of the unique data contained in the appendices. The book should also appeal to readers professionally or privately interested in issues of crime, corruption, terrorism, law enforcement, criminal justice, and sustainable development. It puts, as said, the security and justice problems of over 150 countries on the map and formulates proposals for remedial action both at home and overseas. The many detailed world maps of crime, violence, and police performance will also be of use to those planning trips abroad for business or pleasure. This book, in sum, puts available international knowledge on crime in the public domain, regardless of national sensitivities.

Acknowledgments

This book builds on the sustained efforts of a large group of persons. The United Nations Office on Drugs and Crime published in 1999 a *Global Report on Crime and Justice,* edited by Graeme Newman. Work has since been ongoing on the collection and analysis of crime and justice statistics. A document on *Trends in Crime and Justice* was prepared by me and colleagues at UNODC/UNICRI for the occasion of the United Nations Eleventh Congress on Crime Prevention and Criminal Justice in Bangkok, Thailand, 2005.

Over the years, I have had the pleasure to collaborate on the International Crime Victim Surveys with a dozen or more colleagues involved in quantitative criminology. Their work is quoted widely throughout this book and I won't mention them here by name. I want to make use of this occasion to thank them all for two decades of shared commitment and friendship. One person deserves to be named here. John van Kesteren, now at Tilburg University, the Netherlands, has for more than a decade been the master of the ever-growing ICVS data set. Without his knowledge and dedication, all users, including myself, would be lost in numerical translation.

Since comparative work on crime and justice is underfunded wherever it is undertaken and most certainly at the United Nations, most of the hard work was done by interns. It is my pleasure to thank and name them here: Kleonika Balta, Fabrizio Sarrica, Michaela Messina, Alicia Burke, Linda Geradts, Resham Mantri, Mila Versteeg, and Tonia Strachey. In the Netherlands, Marisca Brouwer and Jaap de Waard of the Ministry of Justice and Fanny Klerx of Tilburg University helped me with the necessary updates. You were all Excel—lent.

I want to thank Marcus Felson for introducing me to Sage and Evelyn Rubin and Ineke Haen-Marshall for support in the preparation of the manuscript. Finally, I wish to express my sincere gratitude to my former colleagues at UNICRI and present colleagues at Tilburg University for having been with me in this undertaking.

The following reviewers are gratefully acknowledged:

Robert Homant, University of Detroit

Nick Larsen, Chapman University

Wayne Pitts, University of Memphis

Pamela Jean Preston, Penn State Schuylkill

Tilburg, March 2007
Jan Van Dijk

PART I

The Challenge of Measuring Crime Internationally

1

The Need for Better Crime Diagnostics

The Uses of International Crime Statistics

Reliable cross-national information on crime patterns allows governments to see how their domestic crime problems compare with other relevant countries (e.g., neighbors) and regional and global averages. Such objective diagnosis can provide a useful antidote to prevailing conceptualizations of crime and criminal justice based on sensationalist, media-led notions. If comparative crime statistics are used properly, they can help to inform countercrime policies. Specifically, they provide a benchmark of crime control policies to identify which policies do better than others and areas that can be improved.

In our global village, crime problems are no longer a domestic concern. Many types of crime have international dimensions, and trends in crime and justice in different countries are increasingly interdependent. The international nature of markets for drugs, sexual services, and illicit firearms is generally recognized. Less well understood is the international nature of many other criminal markets such as that for stolen cars with an estimated half million stolen cars transported from developed to less developed countries annually. More and more criminal groups operate internationally through loose networks of partners in crime. Similar to legitimate businesses, criminal organizations tend to operate from an established home base. Criminal groups that are able to operate with near impunity in their home countries show a tendency to branch out internationally. The United States, for example, is confronted with violent gangs from the former Soviet Union and the Caribbean (International Crime Threat Assessment, 2000). Countries in the Caribbean are coping with serious criminality committed by career criminals deported by the United States and the United Kingdom in large numbers. The European Union is confronted with influxes of criminality from Eastern Europe, for example, human traffickers from Albania, Bulgaria, and Kosovo

(EUROPOL, 2004). Southern Africa is struggling with an ongoing influx of Nigerian criminal networks (Shaw, 2003). At the global level, countries with dysfunctional justice systems provide safe havens for criminals to launder money, execute computer-facilitated scams, otherwise expand their criminal business, or plan terrorist attacks. In order to build lines of defense in appropriate places, national crime prevention requires reliable international intelligence on domestic crime across the world.

Information on the risk of crime and corruption must be considered by the international corporate world when deciding on where to invest and deploy human resources for profit. Information on governance is also key for policies aimed at sustainable development and poverty reduction. In the absence of reliable information on crime, decision makers of large corporations and funding agencies may make fundamentally wrong decisions. They may invest in countries where resources are covertly but systematically looted by well-camouflaged criminal elites. Or they may, conversely, abstain from investing in certain foreign countries or regions that have a bad reputation on false grounds.

At a more private level, international crime information is eminently relevant for all those who travel abroad for either business or pleasure. Travelers are especially vulnerable to all sorts of crime. Key considerations of potential travelers in selecting destinations are prices, cleanliness of accommodation, and safety. Just as foreign travelers are duly informed in travel guides about the threat of contagious diseases or the quality of swimming water, they would like to know more about the state of local crime. In the current situation, no reliable information on crime risks abroad is available to the common traveler (Pelton & Young, 2003).

International crime statistics serve several important public functions for governments, corporations, and individual citizens alike. In addition, such information provides the evidence base for testing assumptions on the macro causes of crime and on the macro long-term impact of countercrime policies. International statistical indicators belong to the empirical foundations of most modern sciences. A solid and broad knowledge base on the global epidemiology of crime would contribute greatly to criminological theory formation. For example, it would allow American criminologists to understand the recent drops in violent crime in the United States from an international perspective, rather than from a purely domestic one. It would allow criminologists to better understand which features of domestic crime are unique to their country and which are driven by forces that are universal. There can be no doubt about the scientific importance of more and better international crime information.

International Crime Statistics: The Sorry State of the Art

In recent years, the international community has seen a rapid growth in the production of international statistics. International organizations such as the World Bank and the International Monetary Fund (IMF) publish annually a wealth of detailed indicators of economic and financial activity (World Bank, 2005). Specialized agencies such as the World Health Organization (WHO), United Nations Development Program (UNDP), and Food and Agriculture Organization (FAO) regularly release comparative statistics on a wide range of topics such as diseases, infant mortality, educational attainment, and agricultural issues (UNDP, 2002b; WHO, 2005). There are also comparative statistics on the consumption of illegal drugs (UNODC, 2005), forced labor (ILO, 2005), and many other global social issues. It is not an overstatement to say that the world is experiencing an "information explosion" on cross-national issues.

In contrast, international statistics on crime and criminal justice are few and far between. As rightly observed by Kaufmann (2005), the leading researcher on governance issues at the World Bank Institute, metrics play hardly any role in the international discourse on security and justice. For many of the largest developing countries, no comparative statistical information on either crime or justice is available at all. Since 1987, an international poll has been conducted among the public of more than 70 countries about their recent experiences of crime (the International Crime Victim Survey [ICVS]). Based on results of this survey, new information has become available on experiences of the public of common crime in many developed countries and some cities in developing countries. In many parts of the world, ICVS results are the only source of reliable and up-to-date information on crime (for Southern Africa, see, for example, Naudé & Prinsloo, 2003; Naudé, Prinsloo, & Ladikos, 2006). But reliable crime information on some of the largest developing countries including Brazil, China, Egypt, India, Indonesia, Nigeria, Pakistan, and Russia is still conspicuously missing. Surprisingly, there are no signs that this situation is likely to improve in the near future.

In 1999, the United Nations Office on Drugs and Crime (UNODC) in Vienna, Austria, published the Global Report on Crime and Justice, which contained data that were at the time 5 years old (Newman, 1999). The publication was launched almost stealthily, without press releases or any other communication strategy, and has not become widely known in government circles. This pioneering report has not been followed up with any subsequent comprehensive UN reports on crime since. In fact, at the 14th session of the United Nations Commission on Crime Prevention and Criminal Justice in Vienna, Austria, in 2005, Antonio Maria Costa, the current executive director of UNODC, stressed in his opening speech the need for quantitative research as a foundation for policymaking on crime.

> The international community has considerable respect for the annual World Economic Report, World Development Report, World Trade Report, and World Drug Report . . . and similar publications. But here is the real question: Is the Crime Commission ready to deliberate policy on the basis of a World Crime Report?

The commission's short answer to this invitation was a firm no. The delegate from the United States was the first to express reservations about the production of such reports. Crime, in the view of his delegation, was a "more subtle" issue than drug trafficking. Production of and trafficking in drugs involves only a handful of countries, while each and every country has to struggle with domestic and international crime problems. Without further debate, the commission adopted a resolution requesting expert consultations on the feasibility and desirability of such a report rather than on the development of a report. No UN report on global crime and justice issues has since appeared or is likely to appear in the foreseeable future.

Since the 1950s, the international police organization (Interpol) has published biannually comparative police statistics on crime based on data provided mainly by its worldwide network of national liaison officers. In more recent years, these statistics were also available on their public Web site. Although frequently consulted and widely cited, the series has met with increasingly fierce methodological criticism (Rubin, 2006). In 2006, Interpol removed all crime statistics from their public Web site, and it is far from certain that an upgraded version of the series will ever be relaunched.

At the regional level, the situation is not much better. A UN-affiliated research institute in Finland (HEUNI) has published a series of high-quality reports on crime and justice in Europe and North America from a comparative perspective. In the fifth issue of the series, the authors admit that available data sources do not permit any firm conclusions about trends or correlates of crime. The project seems to have run out of steam (Aromaa et al., 2003). In the framework of the European Council's Permanent Committee on Crime Problems,[1] comparable data on crime and justice on its 46 member states have been collected twice (*European Sourcebook,* 2003). A third report was prepared with sponsoring of the Ministry of Justice of the Netherlands (*European Sourcebook,* 2006). Surprisingly, no funds for subsequent work have been made available by the Council of Europe itself. In fact, the Council of Europe, for decades a premier meeting place for young European and Canadian criminologists, seems bound to shelve its comparative criminological research program altogether.

The Eurostat Division of the European Commission, producing comparative statistics on a wide range of topics, once piloted a small "Eurobarometer of crime" (Van Dijk & Toornvliet, 1996). This survey among the public modeled after the ICVS was conducted a few times but failed to develop into a full-fledged crime survey. More recently, the European Commission has, within the framework of its research program, allocated ad hoc funds for the conducting of the International Crime Victim Survey among the 15 old member states of the European Union in 2005 (Van Dijk, Manchin, Van Kesteren, & Hideg, 2007). The development of a regular and comprehensive set of Eurostatistics on crime and justice has been under consideration in Brussels for some time. Several committees have been established to consider the feasibility and contents of such data-gathering instruments, but the issue is politically contentious. Building on the work done by the European Council, Eurostat has recently taken some initial steps toward the development of full-fledged European crime statistics, including an ICVS-type European crime survey. In the summer of 2007, the legality of these efforts under EU law was reportedly contested by at least one of the member states. The future fate of plans for standardized European crime statistics remains uncertain.

Crime as a Social Construct

Given the evident utility of reliable and comparative information on international crime patterns, how are we to explain that so few data are available or will soon become available? Some criminologists will be inclined to reply that comparative crime information is not produced because intrinsic technical-methodological problems render such production impossible. In their view, international crime statistics are a chimera, because universal definitions of crime do not exist. Crime, they assert, is a dynamic social construct reflecting the unique characteristics of societies, their cultures, and their histories.

It cannot be denied that legal definitions of criminal offenses show significant variation across countries and across time. One needs to think only of such culture-bound crimes as blasphemy and adultery. Behavior seen as offensive or reproachable in one country may constitute a serious offense across the border. Antinarcotics laws are also known to show great international variation. However, the cultural relativity of crime definitions should not be exaggerated. The criminal codes of most countries include similar definitions of core crimes such as murder, rape, theft, or robbery. In fact, the majority of countries across the world adopted either the British common-law system or one of the existing criminal codes of other European countries in the 19th or 20th century. The common-law and civil law systems prevail in most regions of the world. More recently, member states of the United Nations have adopted several criminal law treaties that oblige state parties to introduce well-defined crimes in their domestic criminal laws such as money laundering, trafficking in persons for exploitation, or the offering and acceptance of bribes. There is considerable uniformity in definitions of both common and emerging crime in national legislations across the world.

Parallel to the process of legal harmonization, the general public's perception of crime has also become increasingly universal because of globalization. More and more people are exposed to the same international media messages of crime, spend considerable time abroad every year, and make use of the same cyberspace. Personal experiences of crime are rapidly becoming more uniform across countries. For example, hundreds of millions of people across the world are exposed on an almost daily basis to the same "advance fee" scams emanating from Nigeria or elsewhere.

In the "global village," the common ground of citizens' experiences and perceptions of crime is substantial and rapidly expanding. This is especially true of inhabitants of large cities, which now make up more than half of the world population. Shared public perceptions of crime and justice across countries can be harnessed for the production of international crime statistics through survey research among the general public or special target groups of crime.

Although the production of comparative crime statistics is admittedly difficult and will never be easy, there seems to be sufficient communality in legal definitions and public perceptions to allow for the production of a core set of credible international crime statistics based on survey research such as the ICVS-based rates of victimization by common crime. There are, in my view, no a priori methodological reasons why this would not be possible, if serious and sustained efforts are made. It should also not be forgotten that many other topics about which widely used international statistics are collected suffer from a similar lack of universally recognized definitions, including, for example, unemployment, GDP, or educational attainment. There are many "best practices" in the development of international statistical indicators on social issues that can be transferred to the domain of crime.

International Crime Statistics as Controversial Knowledge

Committed criminologists can find ways to overcome the methodological reservations that some of their colleagues harbor concerning the production and use of international crime statistics. Yet there are powerful external forces restricting the international criminal justice community from actually producing uniform crime statistics. In my view, the single most important impediment is simply that governments do not want to be exposed to statistics that may show their countries in an unfavorable light in this extremely sensitive domain. Crime statistics are generally seen by governments as their nation's "dirty laundry," something not to be flaunted in the public arena. They are also seen as a threat to the sovereignty of the country in matters of crime and criminal justice as is apparent in the opposition to the development of EU-based statistics on crime.

One of the first statisticians to compare crime statistics across countries was the 19th-century French geographer André-Michel Guerry. He saw national crime figures as reflections of the moral state of a country, which he called "moral statistics." As is now generally understood, crime figures say much more about the demographic, social, and economic conditions in a society and perhaps about the performance of its police forces or crime-prevention systems than about the morality of its people. But public opinion still tends to agree with Guerry that high crime rates reflect badly on the moral state of a country and, more specifically, on the moral standing or leadership of those in power. Politicians always want to look good, of course, which means that their party and their country have to look good. "There are plenty of guides that talk about price and quality," says Robert Pelton in the fifth edition of *The World's Most Dangerous Places* (2003), "but how come they never talk about safety?" His blunt answer was, "Well, stupid . . . publicizing that information is bad for tourism." One could add that in the eyes of many governments, it is not only bad for tourism but, much worse, for the reputation of the country generally and the party in office.

In the late 1990s, domestic and international media reported on the extraordinary high level of violent crime in the new South Africa, dramatically labeled the "murder capital of the world." In response to this media hype, the government of South Africa decided to shoot the messenger. It imposed a total ban on the publication of crime statistics in 2000 that lasted for several years. Although crime statistics on South Africa have now reappeared in official publications, they are less detailed and available at longer intervals.

Many governments clearly have a vested interest in not disseminating reliable international crime information. Even though such knowledge could be used to perform several important public and private functions, especially for high-crime countries, a World Crime Report will probably never be welcomed by countries struggling to get their domestic crime and criminal justice problems under control. The messengers of such information cannot expect to be popular with governments, not even, as has surfaced at the meeting of the UN Crime Prevention Commission in 2005, with governments of the most open and democratic ones such as the United States.

Twenty Years of Thwarted Efforts

Are there grounds to believe in an international "conspiracy of silence" of governments to repress knowledge on crime? This seems to be a preposterous idea, but in my view, the historical facts point to an affirmative answer. First of all, corroborating evidence can be found in the history of the United Nations Crime Prevention Programme's efforts to collect global statistics on crimes recorded by the police. The opposition to a World Crime

Report that surfaced at the UN Crime Commission in Vienna in 2005 is far from unprecedented. In 1977, the UN started to collect official crime statistics from its member states. Ever since the UN launched its Survey on Crime and the Operation of Criminal Justice, member states have been suspicious of the objectives of the survey and reluctant to share their crime- and justice-related statistics. To encourage countries to share their crime figures, the UN initially promised to report on only regional aggregates and not to publish data on individual countries.[2] National crime statistics were at the time deemed to be too sensitive for consumption by the international community. To put this taboo in perspective, it should be remembered that in countries belonging to the Soviet bloc, crime statistics were regarded as state secrets—not to be published even for domestic consumption (Reichel, 1994). Countries such as China and most Arab countries are still reluctant to make statistical information on crime available to their own people. Such countries can be expected to be even more suspicious of attempts to develop internationally comparable crime statistics.

In 1983, American criminologist Freda Adler, one of the early protagonists of the UN efforts to collect official crime statistics, published her pioneering comparative book *Nations Not Obsessed With Crime*. It describes and compares the crime situation of seven *low-crime* countries such as Switzerland (Adler, 1983). It is worth noting here that her original draft included a description of seven *high-crime* countries as well. This darker flipside of the study had to be dropped because of political opposition of the countries involved. Another, more recent example of repressed knowledge on crime in a comparative perspective is a UNDP-sponsored book on the illegal drugs industry in Colombia, Peru, and Bolivia. In order not to embarrass the new, cooperative administrations of these countries with references to illegal drugs industries and drugs-related corruption in the past, the UNDP's head office stopped the publication of the planned publication (Thoumi, 2002).

In the United Nations Global Report on Crime and Justice of 1999, the editors, Graeme Newman and Gregory Howard, have the following to say about crime statistics:

> One need only to observe the ways in which countries behave internationally as entities—the ritual and care with which they make statements in the international arena—to realize that a country's open announcement in the international arena of its crime problems and its processing of offenders through the justice system is a major political event. (p. 8)

Their global report contained crime statistics of about 90 individual countries, but these were largely hidden in appendices. Some fragmentary information on crime at the country level was also reported about the years 1998 to 2000 in a UN-based journal (Shaw, Van Dijk, & Rhomberg, 2003). Otherwise, full-fledged global crime statistics have never been officially released in printed form by the United Nations.

In recent years, the number of member states participating in the UN crime surveys has declined rather than increased. In 2004–2005, only about 50 of the 190 member states of the UN shared comprehensive sets of their crime statistics with UNODC, with a clear overrepresentation of countries from the industrialized world. In a period of growing transparency on many issues, the willingness to "announce domestic crime problems in the international arena," in the words of Newman and Howard (1999), has apparently dwindled rather than grown.

The comparison of police-recorded crime data is fraught with methodological difficulties, as mentioned before and as will be amply discussed later in Chapter 2. Arguably, governments in the past had sound reasons to be cautious about comparative statistics on crime. However, in recent years, more reliable sources of information on various types of crime, based on independent research, such as the ICVS, have become available. This new generation of survey-based crime information has not been met with a more welcoming reception by governments either. The suspicious and often negative responses to this new generation of crime statistics reveal even more clearly the entrenched opposition to the gathering and dissemination of such sensitive knowledge.

Since 1998, Transparency International, the Berlin-based NGO (nongovernmental organization), has published a Corruption Perception Index (CPI), reflecting levels of corruption in the public sector as perceived by businesspeople, country analysts, and ordinary citizens. The CPI is a composite index, using data from over 15 different sources. In 2004, ratings were given for 146 countries. The results of this "poll of polls" have been met with fierce opposition from many governments featured at the bottom of the list (indicating rampant corruption). When South African president Mbeki in May 2005 dismissed the TI ranking of his country as "just based on perceptions," in a response to journalists, he echoed what many other politicians of countries with bad scores on the TI index have said before (cited in *The Economist,* June 2, 2005). In 1999, for example, the then prime minister of Malaysia, Mahathir Mohamed, dismissed those who believed the bad corruption ratings of his country as people with a colonial mind-set (*The Straits Times,* June 5, 1999). As we will now discuss, the reception of the International Crime Victim Surveys has not been more welcoming.

ICVS: Bringing the Bad News

The International Crime Victims Survey, mentioned above, does measure actual experiences of crime and street-level corruption, independently of police records. Through my prolonged involvement in the work on this survey, I have had firsthand experience with the reluctant reception of international crime victimization rates across the world. A few case histories on countries' responses to the ICVS will suffice to make the point.

The first release of the survey's findings on 13 industrialized countries in 1989 created a moral panic in the Netherlands, my home country, which found itself unexpectedly at the top of the league for household burglary and some other property crimes. The Dutch Parliament initiated a full-fledged parliamentary debate that lasted for several hours. The survey was lambasted in the media for weeks by politicians and fellow criminologists alike as fundamentally flawed and biased against the Netherlands. The Prosecutors General of the country tried—to no avail, fortunately—to persuade the Minister of Justice to discredit and discontinue the study, which in their view served no other purpose than making the Netherlands look bad.

The reception of the survey was hardly more favorable in the other high-crime countries. In Spain, researchers who planned to publish the high crime rates of Barcelona were advised that legal action would be taken against them with possible serious consequences for their careers. The Spanish results were eventually published as part of the general report, but Spain abstained from the subsequent three rounds of the survey. The government initiated its own crime survey of which the methodology was never shared with the academic community. The Minister for Police of New Zealand suggested at a press conference that the country's Maori minority was to blame for the country's comparatively high rates of violence. The ensuing public outcry forced him to resign, and New Zealand withdrew its support for the survey for the coming 10 years. It did not rejoin the ICVS until 2005.

In Canada and Australia, the first report resulted in a search by government officials and researchers for methodological shortcomings that could "explain away" the comparatively high national violence rates. Ironically, concern in the United States was focused on the unexpectedly low crime rates, which apparently did not match the American self-image of being the most dangerous country on earth. These rates were wrongly (as was later found) attributed by American experts to a possible undersampling of inner-city blacks. In all these instances, the ensuing debates were full of emotional undertones. Faced with crime rates of their countries in an international context, even some of the most critically minded and detached criminologists adopt the sort of nationalistic attitudes normally associated with sports commentators or war correspondents.

The first results of a pilot study in Seoul, South Korea, in 1992 showed comparatively high rates of sexual violence against women. The president of the country felt compelled to intervene, and the report was never officially released. Results of a UN-funded pilot study in Beijing in 1992 were duly published. The results of the subsequent full-fledged survey of 1996 were never released or even shared with the coordinators of the ICVS. Sadly, the People's Republic of China had to be added to the black list of countries that carried out the survey without ever publishing the apparently politically unwelcome results.

Many more examples could be given of the problematic reception of ICVS results over the years. In 2005, the republication of older ICVS results in UNDP's Human Development Report 2005 triggered a media hype in Scotland, which found itself topping "the world league table for violent crime." The validity of the findings were immediately put in doubt by the Scottish police (*Sunday Times,* September 18, 2005; BBC News, September 19, 2005).[3]

When the results of the European component of the ICVS 2005 were published in February 2007, Ireland and the United Kingdom appeared to have the highest rates of victimization by common crime in Europe. In Ireland, a politician of the leading party asserted on national television that the study was methodologically flawed and that the results should not be taken seriously. In the United Kingdom, the Minister of Police dismissed the results as being "three years out of date" (*The Times,* February 6, 2007). The latest British crime survey data available at that time related to 2005. The ICVS 2005 results cover experiences of the public during 2004 and were therefore less out of date than asserted.

After almost 20 years, criticism of the ICVS methodology has somewhat abated. Favorable reception of the results in some Western countries including the Netherlands, Poland, and Estonia has probably been aided by the downward trend in levels of burglary and other common crimes across the region. The ICVS is finally bringing some governments the long-awaited "good news" on crime, namely, that it is falling. Overall, the brief history of the ICVS confirms that comparative crime statistics are politically explosive and provoke furious denials from governments whose crime-reduction policies are put into an unfavorable light. It confirms what the organizers of the original UN crime surveys on official crime statistics had found out before: Comparative crime statistics are not popular with the authorities, especially not in countries whose crime rates are comparatively high, rising or not falling as steeply as elsewhere. Those comparing unfavorably with others in terms of crime or justice will always try to obstruct the collection of such information and, if this strategy fails, to discredit the source.[4]

Breaking the Silence

Those convinced of the utility of collecting and analyzing comparative crime statistics for political and academic reasons find themselves in a quandary. Because of the intrinsic opposition of many governments, the production of international crime statistics is chronically underfunded. As a result, the case for such statistics must be made on the basis of fragmentary, dated, and, in some respects, imprecise statistics. Anyone publishing such data can count on close scrutiny of their methodological soundness and, if any flaws are detected, on stridently critical reviews. In this situation, many experts are inclined to stay on the scientifically safe side: The few available international crime statistics are presented to illustrate their methodological weakness rather than their potential to inform policy-making and advance grounded theories of crime. Looking back at his own involvement in analyzing official crime data of the United Nations Crime Surveys, Joutsen (2004) disqualifies it with hindsight as "comparing what shouldn't be compared."

From a scientific perspective, such a cautious approach might be commendable, and indeed, as we will argue in the next chapter, it is sometimes better to abstain from comparisons altogether. However, this does not warrant the attitude of smug negativism concerning international crime statistics so often encountered among criminologists. As Aebi, Killias, and Tavares (2001) rightly point out, such an attitude plays into the hands of those officials who prefer such information not to be, or ever become, available for self-serving, political reasons. It means capitulating to political forces that would prefer comparative criminology to remain "statistically challenged" forever. In the current era, criminology owes the world better international crime data. To quote Jeremy Travis, past director of the National Institute of Justice in Washington, D.C., and current dean of John Jay College of Criminal Justice in New York: "In this global age the world needs an infrastructure for building knowledge about crime and justice" (Travis, 2000).

In our opinion, the availability of new sources of survey-based information on various types of crime has brought new and challenging opportunities for comparative criminology. The time has come for criminologists to break the politically inspired "conspiracy of silence" of politicians and policymakers concerning comparative crime and justice statistics. The new generation of criminologists is well traveled and intellectually more internationally oriented than their predecessors. They will hopefully revolt against the conspicuous absence of credible international statistics in their chosen field of study.

SUMMARY POINTS/IN CONCLUSION

• This book seeks to break the vicious circle of political opposition and scientific caution regarding international crime information. It will present the "state of the art" of comparative crime and justice statistics, documenting not just their well-known weaknesses but their actual and potential strengths as well. A careful selection is made of the best international crime statistics available. These metrics will allow us to put domestic crime problems in an international perspective. They will also allow us to take a fresh look at different schools of thought on the macro causes of crime.

• Our overview of international crime statistics will hopefully also serve political purposes. Following the example set by Transparency International, the book will not shy away from ranking countries on several sensitive criteria regarding crime, corruption, and justice. It is clearly in the interest of the world community to enhance international transparency on these issues in order to improve domestic and international policies. It is also morally imperative that crime risk information available to intelligence agencies and major corporations should be disseminated to ordinary citizens traveling abroad for pleasure, business, or study or for selecting a retirement location. For several obvious reasons, the statistical truth about crime, terrorism, and justice should be put on the table in the public domain.

• The first, introductory part of this book, consisting of two chapters, introduces the reader to the problems and prospects of international crime statistics. The second and third parts of the book present and discuss the statistics themselves. Detailed overviews are given of the state of common crime and emerging global crimes, respectively. Using information from a wide range of survey-based, commercial, and official sources, more than 150 countries will be ranked according to their levels of property crime, violence, sexual violence, organized crime, trafficking in persons, grand and petty corruption, and terrorism. Special chapters will analyze the main correlates of these types of crime across the world.

• In the fourth part, countries will be ranked according to the performance of their police forces, availability of special victim services, integrity of the courts, and use of imprisonment to punish offenders, again using a broad selection of sources, many of which have never been tapped by criminologists before.

• In the fifth and final part, composite indices of crime and justice will be presented that can be used to diagnose the state of crime and justice of individual countries comprehensively. In this final analysis, countries will be ranked according to their overall degree of lawfulness, based on indices of conventional crime, organized crime, corruption, police performance, and adherence to the rule of law. We will use these metrics to explore the overall impact of crime and justice on sustainable development and to underpin an agenda for global reform and action in the security and justice domain.

• Admittedly, the quality and comprehensiveness of the statistical data presented here is still far from ideal. Those who take issue or disagree with our findings are invited to be as fierce in their criticisms as we will be regarding conventional police figures of crime in the next chapter. However, be prepared to show concrete ways for improvement, preferably by bringing your own superior metrics to the debate. Our ultimate goal is to persuade democratic governments everywhere to step up their efforts to contribute to the collection of international crime information, so as to better inform their own and others' countercrime policies and better serve the information needs of the public. We hope to give a push to the development and wider use of quantitative crime diagnostics. If that happens, this book will have achieved its strategic aim.

Notes

1. The Council of Europe is an international organization in Strasbourg, France, focusing on the promotion of human rights across Europe. It predates the European Union and includes former countries of the Soviet Union including Russia among it members.

2. Member states are increasingly recognizing the importance of comparative work for cross-national purposes but require reassurance that the data reported will not be used for any international numerical "ranking" (UN Crime Prevention and Criminal Justice Branch, Vienna, Austria [A/CONF.144/6]).

3. Fife Chief Constable Peter Wilson, president of the Association of Chief Police Officers, questioned "whether useful comparisons could be drawn between various countries with different reporting practices." He had apparently missed the point that the ICVS circumvents the problem of differences in reporting by interviewing the general public about their experiences rather than consulting police administrations.

4. In 2003, researchers of UNODC presented preliminary findings of a database on documented cases of trafficking in persons sponsored by the governments of Norway and Belgium (Kangaspunta, 2003). Several of the most affluent, developed countries were listed among those cited most often as destination countries of human trafficking for sexual exploitation. Although such a listing only confirms the concentration of profitable sex markets in more-affluent countries, several of the governments involved made official objections to the listing of their country among the main destination countries. The ensuing debate has delayed publication of the full results by almost 3 years (UNODC, 2006).

Mismeasuring Crime

A Technical Note With Far-Reaching Implications

International Crime Figures Available

The traditional source of information on levels and trends of crime are court statistics on convictions for criminal offenses. In the 20th century, these court statistics were supplemented by statistics of crimes known to the police. Since around 1950, most industrialized countries regularly publish statistics on the numbers of various types of crime recorded by their national police. In most countries, crime recording is in the hands of different police forces, each applying its own definitions and counting rules. This institutional factor has made standardization of these statistics at the national level a difficult process. To overcome such problems, the United States introduced the so-called Uniform Crime Reports. National statistics are collected for a core set of well-defined crimes only. In the United Kingdom, a government committee advised in 2002 the introduction of a similar system of "index crimes" (Maguire, 2002).

The comparison of police-recorded crime data is beset with even greater problems at the cross-national level. Scandinavian countries have made serious efforts to standardize their crime statistics but never succeeded to agree on full standardization. Work on the standardization of European crime statistics has in recent years been promoted by the Council of Europe. A committee of experts drafted a set of definitions of the major categories of crime and subsequently brought together statistics from the member states that seemed roughly in line with the agreed-upon definitions. This admirable exercise resulted in the *European Sourcebook of Crime and Criminal Justice Statistics* (2003, 2006). The *European Sourcebook* provides the groundwork of what could evolve into a European system of "index crimes." As yet, no legal decisions by the

Council of Europe—or of the European Union—on the standardization of crime statistics have been taken. To our knowledge, no initiatives have been taken to standardize crime and justice statistics in any other world region either. While crime is being globalized at a high pace, the production of crime statistics has remained a strictly domestic, nation-based exercise.

The United Nations has from the outset been interested in comparative crime statistics. As early as 1947, the General Assembly commissioned the Secretary-General to determine the impact of World War II on levels of recorded crime. In the 1970s, the United Nations started the United Nations Survey on Crime Trends and the Operations of Criminal Justice Systems. This regularly conducted survey collects, among other things, data on the incidence of police-recorded crime from the member states. To this end, a questionnaire is used, outlining the types of crimes for which statistics should be shared. The survey has been repeated eight times. The sixth, seventh, and eighth surveys have been carried out at regular intervals. The UN publishes the data received on its Web site, and incidental results have been analyzed and published in reports or articles by staff (Newman, 1999; Shaw, Van Dijk, & Rhomberg, 2004). Although the UN's data set is indisputably the most important resource of global crime data, its coverage of countries is far from satisfactory. The response of member states to the UN crime surveys is rather low—below 50%—and shows a declining trend. Developing countries, about which little or no information from other sources is available, are especially sadly underrepresented. Many countries report to the survey only incidentally and partially. The irregular response pattern to the survey generates many gaps in the data set that prohibit trend analyses, especially concerning developing countries.

Another historical source of information on police-recorded crimes has been the international policing organization Interpol in Lyon, France, which has published numbers of recorded crimes biannually since 1950. The numbers given by Interpol do not always coincide with those collected and published by the UN (Rubin, 2006; Rubin & Walker, 2004). In a careful analysis, Killias et al. (2000) found that even the relative position of countries in the Interpol statistics on different types of crime does not or only weakly correlate with the position according to the Council of Europe statistics. One reason could be that the Interpol statistics come directly from the police without screening by statistical agencies or otherwise. A review of the UN statistics on crime has cast similar doubts on the credibility of some of the replies (Rubin, 2006).

A further source of information on one particularly important form of crime, homicides, is the World Health Organization. The WHO statistics on homicide are collected through medical channels, which do not necessarily follow the same definitions as police forces. This issue, one of many besetting international crime information, will be revisited below. A major source of statistical and other information on criminal violence, including domestic violence from a health perspective, is the World Report on Violence and Health published by the WHO in 2002.

A Crime Is a Crime?

Most of the data available on the crime situation of countries in an international perspective relate to the number of recorded crimes overall and numbers of main categories such as theft, burglary, robbery, rape, and murder. In criminological litera-ture, such crimes are often referred to as "common," "volume," or "conventional" crime and distinct from "complex crime" or "nonconventional crime" such as organized crime, corruption, and other economic and financial crimes.

The questionnaires of the UN and Interpol use broad definitions that seek to capture the common elements of the various national legal definitions of common crimes found in the world. It is well known, however, that different criminal codes and criminal justice administrations define most crimes in different ways. Even a seemingly straightforward concept such as "burglary" is actually defined differently across countries. In common-law countries, the concept traditionally refers to the breaking and entering of premises with the intention to commit a serious crime. The defining element is the act of illegally accessing a home. In civil law systems, "burglary" refers to an act of theft under aggravat-ing circumstances. In many continental European countries, thefts from cars are included under the numbers of "burglaries." Crimes other than thefts committed after break-ins are not counted. In other words, the concept of burglary has hardly any meaning in an international discourse. Variations in the definitions of violent and sexual crimes in national criminal codes are even considerably larger (Rubin & Walker, 2004).

Because of the broad, open definitions used, the UN and Interpol statistics of police-recorded crimes will inevitably reflect what national legislators, law enforcement officers, and courts consider as crimes under these labels. In some central European countries, minor thefts are counted as misdemeanors and are not included in statistics on criminal offenses. In some countries, traffic incidents are included, and in others, they are not or only partially included. The same is true for contraventions of tax laws. League tables of numbers of police-recorded crimes in many respects compare apples and oranges. Comparisons can be made only by approximation (Joutsen, 2004).

Recording Practices of the Police

International comparisons of data on recorded crimes are not compromised just by the use of different legal, judicial, and law enforcement definitions of criminal offenses across countries. In addition, the reporting of crimes by the public and recording prac-tices of police forces vary hugely across countries and even within countries (Maguire, 2002; Mayhew, 2003b). We will first discuss recording practices. The British Crime Survey has repeatedly shown that the police record only about half of the crimes reported to them (Kershaw et al., 2001). Dutch research has shown that the proportion of all crimes reported to the police by victims and officially recorded by the police var-ied between less than 50% for vandalism and assaults to 60% for pick pocketing and bicycle theft to over 70% for burglary and car theft (Van Dijk & Steinmetz, 1980). Overall, one third of all reports by victims were not officially recorded as crimes. In some European countries, research has shown that less than 30% to 40% of violent crimes reported to the police are actually recorded (Aebi, Killias, & Tavares, 2003). In China, only one in three reported incidents is thought to be recorded by the police (Reichel, 1992). Recording rates clearly show significant variation across types of crime and across countries. In no country can victims rely on their crime reports being duly recorded by the police as a matter of routine.

There can be several legitimate reasons for less than optimal recording of crime reports by the police. In many countries, notably in the Arabic regions, the police have formal discretion to mediate an informal settlement between the parties concerned to avoid a formal record of the case. In many other countries with a more legalistic approach, the police are duty bound to record all reported crimes but in practice apply discretion in their recording of reports. Reported cases may be deemed not to constitute crimes or to be too trivial to deserve official recording and follow-up.

Importantly, police chiefs also often have institutional stakes in the numbers of crimes recorded by their forces. In the United States, for example, the Federal Crime Control Act of 1994 allocates more funds to states with higher levels of crime as recorded by the police. This provides an incentive to do more accurate recording. In the 1980s, the Chicago police, believing that their superiors wanted a low crime rate, were discarding many more crime reports than were police in other large city departments (Reichel, 1992).To an increasing extent, police forces are held accountable for the percentages of crimes cleared up by them. In many jurisdictions across the world, the percentages of crimes for which a perpetrator is arrested by the police are used as a performance measure. The use of such "clearance rates" as performance indicators invites the introduction of higher thresholds for recording reports of crimes that seem difficult to clear up. In several eastern European countries, the police maintain clearance rates above 80% for most types of crime. This miraculously successful performance is achieved through the systematic dismissal of reports of crimes that at face value look hard to solve.

As will be discussed in more detail in Chapter 9 on police resources, police departments in developing countries are often grossly understaffed and overloaded with work. Nonrecording of crime reports may in such situations largely be the result of system overload. Such departments may therefore be even less ready to record crimes than those in more developed countries. It can be expected that recording rates in such countries are therefore systematically lower than in more developed countries with better-funded police departments. This factor of available resources alone introduces a major bias in international police figures of crime.

Reporting Patterns

The key factor, besides recording practices, in determining the proportion of crimes recorded by the police remains the propensity and capacity of citizens to approach the police about their victimization in the first place. For the recording of most categories of conventional crimes, police forces are wholly dependent on whether the individual victim decides to report the crime, which may depend on social and cultural differences. In this respect, too, major differences exist across world regions and countries (Goudriaan, 2004; Skogan, 1984).

Victims in various countries may have different perceptions about what constitutes a crime and may also have different levels of tolerance of some behaviors that—irrespective of their being criminalized by domestic law—may be culturally considered acceptable in some societies or groups. This is the case, for example, with domestic violence, with women in some parts of the world enduring violence from their partners and relatives at home without daring to go out and report it. It may also be the case with other types of interpersonal violence, such as vendettas and honor killings.

In many developing countries, the police are generally disliked or feared by large segments of the public, and approaching them in case of victimization may not be perceived as the obvious step to gain access to justice. The police may also be seen as corrupt and/or biased against minorities or women. In these countries, citizens try to avoid contact with law enforcement and instead turn to traditional justice or private security firms or private detectives. Also, in many countries, citizens may not be able to approach the police because of practical impediments, including the distance from the police station or language difficulties. Individuals may report with more frequency if this is made easier for them, in particular by developing practical and social conditions that facilitate the access of citizens or victims to the authorities mandated with the task of receiving their reports.

For the reasons mentioned above, in most countries only a small proportion of all crimes committed are reported to and consequently recorded by the police. The largest proportion remains hidden from the official records (known in all European languages as the "dark numbers of crime"; in French, "le chiffre noir"). Police figures, as it is often expressed, show just the tip of the iceberg of real crime. Variation in the number of crimes recorded by the police across countries may reflect either variation in the number of crimes committed or variation in the proportion of crimes reported and recorded. Increases in police-recorded crime can mean that the actual number of crimes committed has gone up or, alternatively, that victims are more willing to report crimes to the police.

Which proportions of actually committed crimes end up in the official police statistics and which parts remain hidden have for two centuries been the subject of much criminological speculation and debate. The ensuing uncertainty about the validity of official crime statistics has traditionally cast a shadow over the use of police-recorded statistics for scientific or policy purposes. New international research into the crime experiences of the general public has finally brought this crucially important issue into focus. The main findings will be given consideration in the following section.

The Breakthrough of Crime Victimization Surveys

In order to circumvent the many uncertainties concerning police-recorded crimes as measures of crime, since 1973 the United States has pioneered crime victimization surveys among households and businesses focusing on rates of victimization by offenses as defined in the domestic criminal codes (Reichel, 1994). The Netherlands started its series of fixed national crime victimization surveys, including sets of questions on public attitudes, in 1976 (Van Dijk & Steinmetz, 1980). England and Wales and other western European countries soon followed suit (Maguire, 2002). The results of these surveys provide an alternative and, in many respects, a more comprehensive source of information about crime to what the police record. It provides a count of many forms of volume crime to which ordinary citizens are exposed, regardless of whether they have been reported to the police and recorded or not. It also provides information on relevant public attitudes regarding crime and policing.

If the research methodology used is standardized, the surveys can also offer opportunities for the collection of statistics on the level of crime as experienced by the public across different countries. Since such information is not affected by differences in definitions in criminal codes, reporting rates, or police-recording practices, it is well suited for comparative analyses. This seems especially true for surveys along the model developed in the Netherlands in the 1970s whereby crimes are defined in plain-language terms rather than in terms of local, criminal law definitions. Rather than using legal terms for burglary or aggravated theft, the questionnaire asks respondents, for example, whether someone has entered their house without permission to steal or to try to steal something.

Using the questionnaires of the Dutch, English, and Swiss national crime surveys as its basis, the International Crime Victims Survey was launched in 1989 by a group of European criminologists with expertise in crime surveys (Van Dijk, Mayhew, & Killias, 1990). Since its initiation 18 years ago, surveys have been carried out one or more times in 78 countries. Surveys among samples from the national population were conducted in 35 countries, including all member states of the European Union and a broad selection of other developed nations including the United States, Canada, Australia, New Zealand, Switzerland, Norway, and Japan. In addition, surveys have been carried out in capital cities of 43 developing countries and countries in transition (Van Dijk, Van Kesteren, & Smit, 2007).[1] More than 320,000 citizens across the world have to date been interviewed with the same questionnaire, translated in at least 30 languages. The ICVS has branched out to the most far-flung corners of the world, including Papua New Guinea, where local staff interpreted the questionnaire into the different languages of each valley (Zvekic & Weatherburn, 1994).

The core questions in victimization surveys relate to recent experiences of the population with crime and corruption. Answers to these questions form the hard core of the chapters in Part II on the epidemiology of common crime. Victim surveys also collect information on the rate of reporting to the police by victims and on reasons why many crimes are not reported. These results can shed light on the "dark numbers of crime."

The first empirical question concerning dark numbers to be addressed is whether the proportions of actually committed crimes that remain hidden do indeed, as suggested above, vary across world regions. Figure 2.1 shows which percentages of those who had experienced victimization are said to have reported the incident to the police.

Globally, less than half of conventional crimes are reported to the police (40%). The rates of reporting to the police show considerable variation across world regions. In western Europe, North America, and Oceania, those experiencing victimization are more likely to report to the police than those in other regions. Roughly speaking, the proportion of such crimes brought to the attention of the police is *twice as* high in Western, developed countries as in developing countries and countries with economies in transition. These results suggest that in global comparisons, the police figures of developing countries should be increased by a factor of two or more to correct for underreporting. At the country level, the variation is even larger. Countries with the lowest rates include the Philippines (15%), Mozambique (21%), Mexico (16%), and Albania (18%). Much higher rates are found in, for example, New Zealand (59%),

❖ **Figure 2.1**   Percentage of Victims Reporting Any Crime[2] to the Police, by World Region

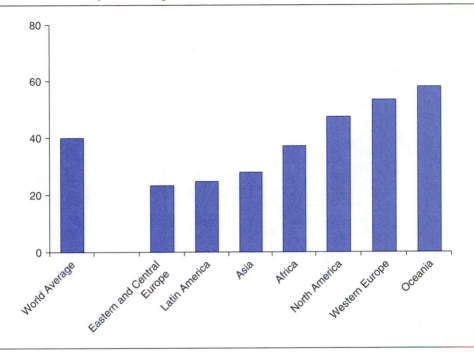

Source: ICVS, 2005, or latest data available.

Belgium (63%), England and Wales (59%), and the United States (48%). For more comparable results, the official crime figures of individual countries would need to be corrected with country-specific correction factors based on ICVS data on reporting.

As can be seen in Figure 2.2, reporting rates vary across different types of crime. In all regions, household burglary is the most frequently reported crime (apart from car theft that is almost universally reported). Burglary was most frequently reported in western Europe, North America, and Oceania. Important factors determining reporting are insurance coverage (the requirement for making a claim for compensation being dependent on having reported the incident to the police) and the ease of reporting (determined by factors such as access to the local police and/or availability of telephones). Robbery was also frequently reported in western Europe, North America, and Oceania but was reported much less in the other regions, with a record low in Latin America, where only one robbery victim out of five reported to the police. Robbery, as will be discussed later, is rampant in many Latin American countries. It seems that in countries where robberies are most prevalent, victims are less likely to report. In the case of robberies, reporting seems to be dependent on confidence in the police. Those refraining from reporting often have no trust in their local police. This is borne out by

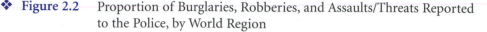

❖ **Figure 2.2**   Proportion of Burglaries, Robberies, and Assaults/Threats Reported
to the Police, by World Region

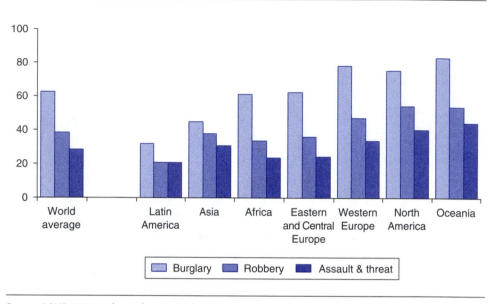

Source: ICVS, 2005, or latest data available.

the responses to the ICVS survey showing that more than 50% of the Latin American
victims of robbery who did not report to the police said that they did not do so
because "the police would not do anything," and approximately 25% said that they
feared or disliked the police (Van Dijk, 1999).

Finally, assault or threat was the least frequently reported type of crime. Globally,
less than one in three of all victims of criminal violence report to the police. Women
are least likely to file a complaint of threat or assault. Reporting of violent incidents is
most common in North America and Oceania/Australia. Reporting rates are, again,
lowest in Africa, eastern Europe, Asia, and Latin America: In these regions, one in five
victims of violence notifies the police. Globally, the most vulnerable categories of victims of violence—women in the poorest countries—are the least likely to seek and
receive assistance from the police. Only a tiny part of violence against women shows
up in official measures of crime, especially so in the South.

The pattern of distribution of reporting rates presents almost the exact reversal
of that of crime victimization rates, to be shown in Chapters 3 and 4 (Part II). In the
regions where more crimes occur, fewer are reported to the police, and vice versa. The
proportion of reporting of robbery and violence is lowest in Africa and Latin
America, regions where victimization rates are highest. This global pattern suggests
that the public is less inclined to report to the police in regions where levels of crime

are high and confidence in the police is consequently low. Reichel (1994) some time ago rightly summed up the ongoing debate on the uncertain meaning of police figures on crime:

> High rates of recorded crime in some countries may reflect the "real" crime occurring, or it may reflect efficient and thorough systems for reporting and recording crime. Similarly, countries reporting low crime rates may actually have little crime, or the low rates may simply reflect system inefficiency. (p. 38)

ICVS-based data on reporting rates show that police statistics on crime are not unreliable in merely a random way. They prove to be *systematically* biased in the sense that in high-crime countries, victims report fewer crimes, most likely out of mistrust of the police. If this hypothesis is confounded by other data, it would fundamentally alter our understanding of international police figures. This hypothesis therefore merits closer empirical scrutiny, by using ICVS data on attitudes toward the police and reasons for nonreporting.

Victim Satisfaction and Trust Levels

A special section of the ICVS deals with the assessment of general police performance by the public at large. The question is, "Taking everything into account, how good do you think the police in your area are at controlling crime? Do you think they do a very good job, a fairly good job, a fairly poor job, or a very poor job?" Results of the survey confirm that residents of Latin America, eastern Europe, and Africa are most skeptical about the capacity of the police to prevent and control crime. The percentage of respondents satisfied with the job that the police were doing was much lower in these regions (Figure 2.3). As a general rule, satisfaction with local policing is inversely related to the level of crime. In line with this rule, the judgment on the effectiveness of local police has in recent years become more positive in Western countries where crime rates have dropped (Van Dijk, Van Kesteren, & Smit, 2007). Police competence is assessed more favorably in the United States, Australia, and several western and central European countries than it was 10 years ago.

As a next step in our inquiry, we looked at the relationships between national levels of satisfaction with the police and national rates of reporting to the police for various types of crime. In all cases, the correlations were statistically significant. In the case of assault or threat, which are, as just mentioned, the least reported types of crime, the statistical correlation is fairly strong ($r = 0.47$, $p < .05$, $n = 47$). Goudriaan (2004), using data of the 2000 ICVS, found in multi-level analyses that country-level variables such as confidence in the competence of the police account for a substantial amount of the cross-country variation in reporting property crimes. In another secondary analysis of ICVS data, corruption experts found a strong, inverse correlation between the level of corruption in a country and the level of crime reporting, suggesting that victims in high-corruption countries refrain from reporting out of mistrust in the integrity of the local police (Soares, 2005). In other words, the less competent and ethical the police are perceived to be, the less people are inclined to report victimizations to them.

❖ **Figure 2.3**   Satisfaction With the Police in Controlling Crime, by World Region

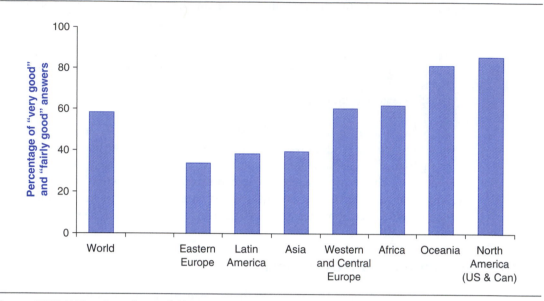

Source: ICVS, 2005, or latest data available.

The empirical evidence shows that, as we assumed, high levels of crime (and corruption) go together with low confidence in the police, reduced willingness to report crimes, and resulting high dark numbers. Low levels of crime are accompanied by high confidence in the police and higher reporting, which drives up police figures of recorded crime. This empirical finding leads us to formulate a theoretical model of the production of police figures that sees crime reporting and recording as a function of police performance. The problem with international crime figures of the police goes deeper than differences in definitions. The problem originates in the different capacities of police forces to process cases of crime. This model puts to bed any hopes that standardized police figures can ever be used as a measure of the level of crime in an international perspective.

The More Recorded Crime, the Less Crime?

Police forces across the world routinely present official statistics of crime as evidence of good performance. Recorded crime rates that are declining or that are lower than in other countries are presented by police chiefs as the result of effective policing. In reality, comparatively low or declining levels of police-recorded crime in a country should not necessarily be taken as a positive sign. In some countries, low police figures may, to the contrary, reflect extraordinarily poor performance of the police, resulting in a low level of trust among the public, limiting the proportion of crimes reported to the police. A country like Albania can serve to make the point. In this former Stalinist country, using figures of police-recorded crimes, the Ministry of Justice registered stable and even slightly declining levels of crime in the period 1990 to 1995. ICVS surveys carried out in the country showed increases in most types of crime instead as well as a total lack of confidence in the police (only 25% percent of the population was satisfied with their local policing in 1995) and very low reporting (Hysi, 2000). If the Albanian chief of police would at the time have proudly presented his relatively low and declining crime figures to the national media, his report would have met with derision. It was common knowledge in Albania at the time that the system of controlling and recording crime had broken down and that actual levels of crime were booming.

In light of the global ICVS results presented above, a severe verdict on the comparability of international police statistics seems warranted. In our view, there is evidence for a strong, systematic bias in police-recorded crime rates. This bias is not, as in the case of Albania, the result of unique circumstances in individual countries but of built-in mechanisms operating in police administrations worldwide. Leaving aside political interference, criminal justice systems can, within existing budgets and organizational means, respond adequately to only a given number of crimes per year. If more crimes enter the system than can be processed by police, prosecutors, courts, and prison departments, system overload generates an institutional need for reducing input. The most efficient way to achieve such reduction is refusing to make official records of reported crimes that seem less important. Since most victims of crime are powerless individuals without much understanding of their rights, their reports can easily be defined as irrelevant for the system. If their reports refer to the kind of incidents that would hopelessly clog the system in any subsequent stages, these are duly ignored.

Earlier reference was made to the recording practices of the British and Dutch police in the 1980s, showing that only about half of victim reports were officially recorded at the time. Analyses of the nonrecorded cases in the Netherlands showed that the police systematically left unrecorded those incidents for which the prosecutors would be unlikely to initiate prosecution. Cases of minor theft of property with a value below $500 were at the time not deemed worthy of scarce law enforcement and prosecutorial resources. Such cases, if presented by the police to the prosecutors, were systematically dismissed on grounds of expediency. To prevent the investment of police time on recording and investigating cases that would surely be dismissed, police forces refrained from recording thefts with values below roughly $250. The Dutch police, acting as gatekeepers of the justice system, informally applied a structural form of discretion. Victims, in turn, were found not to be naïve and to anticipate nonrecording by the police. In order to prevent pointless reports that would not have any follow-up, they refrained from reporting thefts with values that did not reach the threshold. Victim reporting and police recording seemed, as expressed in the title of a report on these findings, a "function of prosecution policies" (Van Dijk, 1982).

There can be little doubt that police forces across the world apply similar discretion in their crime recording (Sanders & Young, 2002). This selective recording by the police, whether formalized in guidelines or not, will not go unnoticed by the public. Victims whose reports have not been officially recorded show significantly higher levels of dissatisfaction with their treatment by the police than other victims (Van Dijk &

Steinmetz, 1980). And, as has been found in global ICVS data, dissatisfied victims are more likely to refrain from reporting similar incidents on future occasions (Van Dijk, 2000). Dismissals of victim reports by the police due to overburdening of the policing system—or of the criminal justice system further down the line—appear to offer powerful feedback to the clients of the systems. If they sense that their reports are dismissed routinely, they subsequently adjust their reporting behavior downward. A case in point is reporting rates for bicycle theft that are decreasing in many countries in recent years. In this way, the criminal justice system ingeniously manages to control its input and thereby its workload. The system does not acknowledge the existence of any more crime than what it can properly handle within existing resources. Crime is recorded by the system to the extent that resources permit.

The phenomenon of selective recording has important implications for the use of police figures of recorded crimes as policy information in a local or national context. It has even more far-reaching implications for the usefulness of international crime figures. From this theoretical perspective, the number of police-recorded crimes must primarily be seen as an indicator of the capacity of national law enforcement systems to process crime cases through the system. Since the available means of police systems and criminal justice of countries are generally scarce and are determined by factors other than the volume of crime, such as tax revenues and spending priorities, the relationship between police-recorded crimes and the level of crime will always be tenuous at best. More recorded crime in a country is likely to reflect availability of more resources to tackle crime rather than more crime. By comparing statistics of police-recorded crime of countries with results of the ICVS, this hypothesis can be put to the test.

Police-Recorded Crime and Victimization Rates Compared

As discussed above, the absolute number of crimes committed is several factors larger than the number of police-recorded crimes. Thanks to crime victimization surveys, the fact that police-recorded crimes form only a part of the total volume of crime is now generally acknowledged. Police figures can thus not be used as a measure of the absolute volume of crimes. There is still room for debate as to whether police-recorded crimes can perhaps still be used to rank countries on a dimension of low to high crime levels. According to the optimistic school of thought, differences in reporting and recording may exist but not to the extent that they significantly influence the relative positions of countries in terms of crime levels. The optimists, in other words, assume that in spite of different proportions between reported and recorded crimes, countries where more than the average number of crimes is committed will always end up at the top of the list of crimes recorded, and those with fewer actual crimes end up at the bottom. Rankings of countries in terms of police figures are supposed to be roughly similar to rankings in terms of actual victimization.

The correlation between country ranks in terms of ICVS victimization rates and recorded crime rates has previously been examined for a limited number of Western countries (Van Dijk, Mayhew, & Killias, 1990). Strong correlations were found for car theft but only moderately strong ones for household burglary and robbery. No correlations were found concerning violent crimes, including sexual crimes. For the categories of property crimes, the correlations became significantly stronger if the victimization rates were corrected for reporting rates. The latter finding was to be expected, since by adjusting for reporting rates, one of the major sources of error in the police figures had been eliminated.

In a subsequent analysis using data from a broader and less homogeneous group of countries from Europe and North America, the convergence between relative positions in victimization rates and recorded crime rates was weaker (Mayhew, 2003b). For example, Russia and the Ukraine featured in the top quartile for victimization and in the lowest for recorded crime, while Finland scored in the top quartile for recorded crime but in the lowest for victimization. As in the previous study, a higher correspondence was found between recorded crime rates and victimization rates after adjustments were made for varying reporting rates.

Aebi, Killias, and Tavares (2003) analyzed the correlation for 12 mostly western European countries between the 2000 ICVS victimization rates for all crimes with the total police-recorded crime rates of the *European Sourcebook* project, adjusted for reporting (using ICVS data). An analysis of the correlation between ICVS victimization rates and police-based crime rates of a larger group of European countries showed the same results (Gruszczynska & Gruszczynski, 2005). These findings confirm those of Van Dijk, Mayhew, and Killias (1990) and Mayhew (2003b), in the sense that robust correlations are found only after adjustment for differences in reporting.

Using results of the ICVS 2005 and more recent police figures, Van Dijk, Manchin, Van Kesteren, and Hideg (2007) found once again that among 18 European countries, the number of crimes recorded by the police bears hardly any relationship to the ICVS-based measure of overall crime. The police figures were highest for Sweden, a country with average victimization rates. The lowest police figures were reported by Ireland, the country where victimization by overall crime was highest.

A repeat of this analysis with results of a larger number of developed countries confirmed that recorded crime rates and victimization rates correlated better if account was taken of different reporting rates (Van Dijk, Van Kesteren, & Smit, 2007). Unadjusted rates of recorded crime for specific types of crime showed no correlation with victimization rates except for car theft. Results thus show that even among developed countries, recorded crime rates cannot be reliably used as indicators of even the relative level of crime. In order to be used for such comparative purposes, recorded crime rates must first be corrected for reporting and, ideally, if at all possible, for recording practices as well.

Finally, Howard and Smith (2003) looked at the relationships between police figures of the UN Crime Survey, *European Sourcebook,* and Interpol and between these three official measures of crime and ICVS victimization rates. Their analysis was limited to Europe and North America. Their conclusion was that "official measures of recorded crime are mostly consistent in their depictions of crime rates while official measures and victimization measures were typically in disagreement." Their results show that for the group of countries under study, official measures collected by the UN, the *European Sourcebook,* and Interpol are reasonably consistent among themselves but show little or no resemblance to rankings based on crime survey research among the public. They also concluded that analyses of the social correlates of crime showed fundamentally different, even opposing, results, depending on the data sources used. The last finding puts in doubt most of the existing knowledge on the macro causes of crime, which is based almost exclusively on police data.

A further test of the usefulness of recorded crime as a measure of the relative level of crime should include data on countries from all regions of the world and not just from Europe and North America. Both the UN crime survey and the ICVS contain a measure for "total crime." For 39 countries data are available on the overall ICVS victimization per 100 respondents in 2000 and the total number of crimes per 100,000 recorded by the police in 2002. Figure 2.4 depicts both the number of recorded crimes per 100,000 inhabitants and the percentage of the public victimized by crime according to the ICVS.[2] Although the picture is made somewhat artificial by combining two scores with different scales on the same vertical axis, visualizing how these two measures of crime relate to each other can be helpful.

As can be seen at a glance, there is absolutely no correlation between the actual level of victimization by crime and the rates of crime recorded by the police among these 39 countries ($r = 0.212$, $n = 39$, n.s.). Some countries with exceptionally high numbers of recorded crimes also show comparatively high victimization rates (South Africa), but many others such as Finland, Canada, and Switzerland do not.

In the 39 countries with information from both sources, on average 28% of the respondents to the ICVS were victims of at least one of the crimes included in the survey. Victimization rates in the majority of countries (23) were close to the average (between 23% and 33%), while six were well below the average (Azerbaijan, the Philippines, Croatia, Japan, Spain, and Portugal) and ten were markedly above. Among them, the countries where citizens were most frequently victimized were Colombia, Swaziland, Estonia, Uganda, South Africa, Zambia, and the Czech Republic.

In contrast, the highest levels of police-recorded crime were observed in Sweden, the United Kingdom, Finland, Belgium, Denmark, the Netherlands, and Canada, while in Colombia, Uganda, and Zambia, which as just mentioned appeared in the group of countries with the highest rates of victimization, police-recorded levels of crime are comparatively low.

It can be observed that four out of six countries with the highest victimization rates were in Africa, while among the six countries with the highest levels of police-recorded crime, five belong to the 15 member states of the European Union before enlargement.

The comparison between country rankings according to ICVS victimization rates and police-recorded crimes was repeated for different types of crime. The results showed positive correlations for robbery ($r = 0.663$, $n = 37$) and car theft ($r = 0.353$, $n = 34$), while no correlations were found for any other type of crime.

The case of fraud statistics is especially illuminating.[3] According to the UN Crime Survey data on police-recorded fraud, this type of crime is most prevalent in Europe, the Americas, and Asia (see Figure 2.5). However, ICVS results show exactly the opposite: The percentage of people who were victimized by consumer fraud (cheating) is highest in Africa.[4] The discrepancy between information of police records and surveys of citizens' experience is particularly striking in this instance.

❖ **Figure 2.4**   Total Crime, by Countries

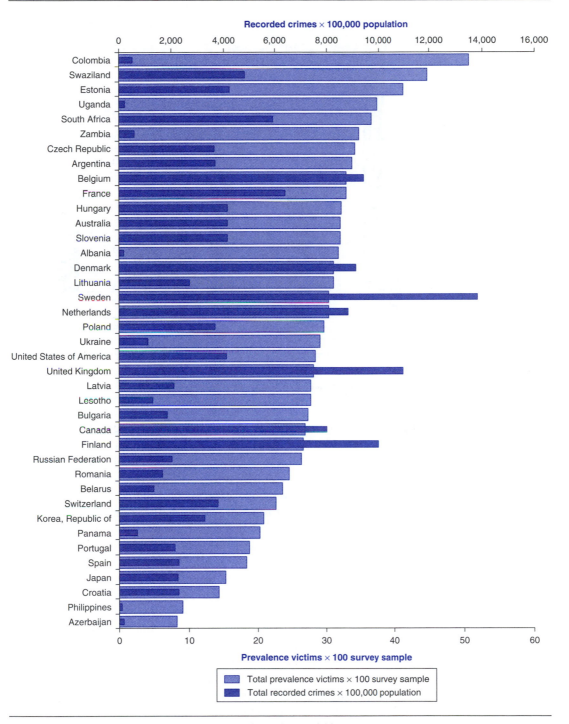

Sources: ICVS, 2000, and UN Crime Survey, 2002, or latest data available.

❖ **Figure 2.5**   Fraud, by World Region

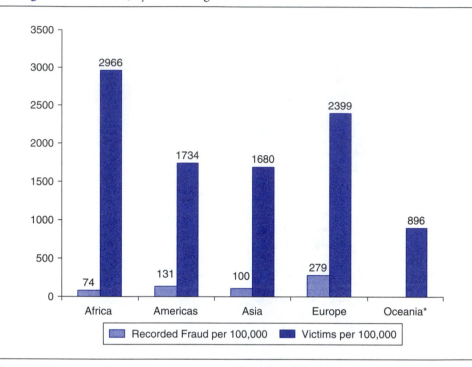

Sources: ICVS, 2002, and UN Crime Survey, 2002, or latest data available.

*No comparable data on recorded fraud from Oceania available.

Surprisingly, regional police statistics on fraud provide the perfect mirror image of regional fraud victimization rates. This result could be just a statistical coincidence but the negative correlation is strong enough to look for a possible theoretical interpretation. In our view, comparatively high rates of police-recorded cases of fraud reflect the operation of well-functioning police forces and a high trust level among the public. This feature of societies tends to go in tandem with a range of other institutional arrangements including those regulating economic activities, such as consumer protection. In such well-regulated countries, there seems to be less scope for common forms of consumer fraud.

If this interpretation is correct, police-recorded fraud statistics can, ironically and paradoxically, be used as an inverse proxy indicator of the actual prevalence of fraud: Countries showing below-average police-recorded fraud can safely be considered as countries where fraud is more common, due to poor consumer protection. In countries showing comparatively high rates of police-recorded fraud, this form of crime is probably in reality reasonably well under control.

A second example of the "perversity" of official crime statistics is provided by statistics on corruption, shown in Figure 2.6 below.[5] Both the UN Crime Survey and the ICVS refer to bribery of public officials in their definitions of corruption. As is the case with fraud, there is a major discrepancy between citizens' experiences and the official figures. African countries score high on actual experiences of people with officials asking for bribes but not on the actual numbers of corruption cases recorded. There is also a major discrepancy between the two data sets regarding west-central Europe: While this is one of the top-ranking subregions regarding police-recorded corruption, the average victimization among the old EU-15 was extremely low (0.9%). Among the new EU members, the average victimization rate for corruption was much higher (11%) but was still lower than the other subregions.

❖ **Figure 2.6**   Corruption, by World Region

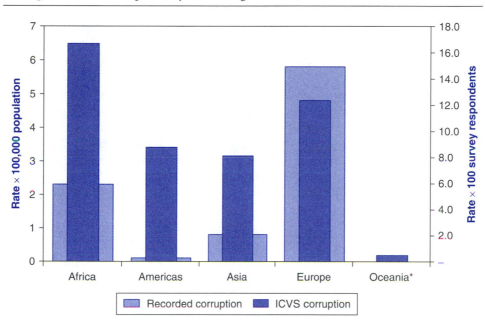

Sources: ICVS, 2000, and UN Crime Survey, 2002, or latest data available.

*No comparable data on recorded crime from Oceania available.

These findings, taken together, show that in a global perspective the recorded crime rate per 100,000 inhabitants of a country provides no useful information on the actual level of crime compared to other countries. To determine countries' *relative* levels of crime, throwing dice seems as good as—or even better than—consulting their official measures of police-recorded crime. Recorded crime rates cannot and should not be used as an indicator of the absolute or relative level of crime in a country. This seems to be the case for rates of both total crimes and specific categories of crime. In some exceptional cases such as fraud and other "economic" crimes," police recorded crimes may in fact be used as *inverse* proxy indicators of criminal reality. The lower the police figures, the higher the actual prevalence of those crimes is likely to be.

As a general rule, the use of police figures for cross-national comparative purposes seems warranted only if the recorded crimes can be adjusted for reporting. In view of such adjustments, it has often been said that police-recorded crime statistics and victimization survey results can supplement each other. This is not our view. Police-recorded crime rates can indeed be used as proxy indicators of volume crime if adjusted for differential reporting rates. But in countries where data are available for such adjustment, the ICVS or another victimization survey has been executed. It is, then, more economical to rely on the victimization prevalence rates themselves as indicators of crime than on adjusted police figures. In our opinion, police figures as indicators of the level of crime should simply be replaced by the results of standardized crime surveys where available. Where no victimization surveys have been executed, the level of conventional crime is anybody's guess.

As will be discussed in greater detail in Chapter 5, the rates of victimization by any crime were negatively correlated with the Human Development Index ($r = -.321$, $p < 0.05$, $n = 45$), while no correlation was found between rates of police-recorded total crime and the HDI. This combined finding confirms that victimization is higher in less-developed countries but remains largely hidden because police recording is dependent on the level of funding of police organizations. In poorer countries, even remotely sufficient funding is rarely available. Only in developed countries can police forces afford to give sufficient priority to investigation of crimes reported and to accurate recording of volume crime. If, for example, high victimization countries such as Colombia, Swaziland, and Uganda achieved the same crime-recording accuracy as Sweden, their recorded crime rates would boom. These findings also put into perspective the consistent failure of most developing countries to fill in the UN's crime surveys. Police administrations that lack resources to adequately record crimes and produce meaningful crime statistics can hardly be expected to allocate scarce resources to answer international questionnaires about information they know to be fundamentally flawed. A much better proposition would be the international funding of annual ICVS-type surveys in these countries and expedient dissemination of international results.

Our analysis of the production of police-recorded statistics reveals how victim reporting of crimes is responsive to police recording practices, which are in turn responsive to decisions of prosecutors and judges in a context of scarce resources. The behavior of the police in their interactions with crime victims is not just a matter of "police culture" but is contingent on available resources for police investigations and for the other elements in the criminal justice system. These complexities can help to explain the slowness of improvements in the rates of recorded crime in newly emerging democracies.

Although levels of crime in central Europe no longer differ much from those in the West, the levels of police-recorded crime remain incredibly low (*European Sourcebook*, 2003, 2006). In 2000, the European countries recorded on average 4,333 crimes per 100,000 people. Albania, our favorite showcase of dubious crime statistics, recorded 149 crimes per 100,000 people in 2000. This was 24% less than in 1995. If one believes these statistics, Albania seems to be on its way to becoming a crime-free country. Most eastern European countries show crime rates far below the European average. The highest rates among the European countries in transition are registered by Hungary (4,445), Estonia (4,037), and the Czech Republic (3,811), not coincidentally the most economically advanced countries of the group and early entrants into the enlarged European Union. Even the last three countries still show rates of police-recorded crime vastly below those of the United Kingdom, the Netherlands, or Sweden, although their ICVS victimization rates are in the same range. Limited availability of resources for the police and the criminal justice system at large should be blamed first and foremost for this lagging behind in police figures of crime by the new members of the European Union.

According to criminological modernization theory, levels of common crime go up together with modernization, due to concurrent breakdowns of traditional social controls (Neapolitan, 1995; Shelley, 1981). This theoretical school was grounded in analyses of statistics on police-recorded crimes across countries. In view of our present knowledge, modernization theory still seems valid but should be reformulated as a theory not on crime but mainly on crime recording. The number of crimes officially recorded by the police goes up with modernization because of the strengthening of the official systems of social control, including their capacity to record crime and invite victim reporting. Countries record more crimes to the extent that they are more "modern." This theory can make sense of the otherwise puzzling fact that police figures of crime are the highest in Sweden, Finland, and New Zealand. Cross-sectional research into the determinants of the levels of crime in society is a different matter altogether. Such research requires data collected independently of the police such as the results of victimization surveys.

Other Uses of Police-Recorded Crime Statistics

Our bleak conclusions on the usefulness of police figures as measures of the level of crime raise the question whether there remain other purposes for which police-recorded crime statistics can be used in a comparative perspective. In Part IV, "International Trends in Criminal Justice," we will address the issue of how police figures of recorded crime can be successfully used in analyses of the productivity or efficiency of criminal justice systems. Here we will focus on their use in the epidemiology or geography of crime.

One type of crime for which police figures can probably (with some caveats) still be used as a rough prevalence indicator seems to be homicide (LaFree, 1999; see also Reichel, 1994). Although police-recorded rates of homicide are not without methodological problems of their own (Rubin & Walker, 2006), levels of reporting and recording seem sufficiently high almost universally to warrant their use for comparative analyses of actual levels of serious violence. Especially in developed countries, the reporting and recording of homicides is close to 100% and thus leaves little scope for variation.

Some serious attempts have been made to combine ICVS results and police-recorded crime statistics from Europe and North America into composite indices for certain types of crime (Aromaa et al., 2003; Kangaspunta, Joutsen, & Ollus, 1998). The justification for such data integration was found in robust correlations between these two sets of data among countries of the Euro-American region. Although the indices of violent crime seem especially robust, the mixing of ICVS data with police-recorded statistics will often reduce the validity and reliability of the measure at hand and compromise the outcomes of subsequent analyses. Our current preference is to restrict analyses of the social causes of volume crime to pure ICVS data, even if this means working with data from a smaller number of countries. We will pursue this purist approach ourselves in Chapter 5 on the determinants of crime.

Police Figures as Trend Indicators

Some authors have argued that police-recorded crime statistics could still be used for the measurement of change over time across countries under the assumption that reporting and recording rates remain more or less stable over the years in each country (Bennett, 1991). For comparative trend analyses, changes in police figures can be expressed in percentage point changes compared to the rates in a certain index year. Even if the absolute numbers show huge variation, the trends can be usefully expressed in such an indexed way. Uncertain is whether such percentages of increases or decreases in crime since a given date reflect the actual movements of crime in a comparative perspective or changes in reporting or recording.

In some Western countries, including the United Kingdom, crime victim surveys have recently shown decreasing levels of violence, while levels of police-recorded crimes of violence have gone up. A comparison of victimization rates, police figures of recorded crimes, and data from injury surveillance systems in England and Wales show that police figures are out of line with congruent crime survey data and medical data on violence. Both crime survey data and medical data confirm declining trends resulting from better prevention and surveillance. Increasing numbers of police-recorded crimes are prompted by better surveillance and targeting of potential offenders and better recording (Shepherd & Sivarajasingam, 2005). Such findings suggest that police figures of recorded crime cannot be reliably used as trend indicators.

Several European textbooks on criminology interpret the 500% or more changes in police-recorded crime in many western European countries from 1950 to 1990 as evidence of actual, postwar booms in crime (Van Dijk, Sagel-Grande, & Toornvliet, 2000). Indeed, it seems hard to imagine how such long-term significant increases can be fully accounted for by improvements in reporting and recording. In general, however, trend data on police-recorded crime should be interpreted with great caution, and using them for comparative purposes seems hazardous. Factors undermining their use for trend analyses are the same as those preventing their use in cross-sectional analyses. Legal definitions, recording practices, and the willingness of the public to report have been found to change significantly over time (Maguire, 2002). Recorded crime rates, for example, tend to go up to the extent that recording processes are computerized. For this practical reason alone, more technologically advanced countries are bound to show comparatively stronger increases (or smaller decreases) in recorded crime than others.

Data on drug offenses are collected through, among other methods, the UN Crime Surveys. These offenses showed an average increase of 47% between 1995 and

2002, a sharper increase than any other type of crime. The police figures show that only Japan among the observed countries had a stable trend in the period 1995–2002. In other countries, including South Africa, Canada, Germany, and Poland, a rise in recorded drug offenses was observed. As can easily be imagined, trends in official measures of drug offenses may reflect changes in legislation and/or law enforcement priorities rather than in the actual number of offenses committed. In Canada, for example, possession counts for the majority of drug-related offenses, followed by trafficking and other offenses, including importation and cultivation. Possession showed the biggest fluctuations over time, while a moderate but steady increase was observed for trafficking and other offenses. Arresting policies for the possession of drugs are in a state of flux in many countries, including Canada. Changes in the number of recorded drug offenses are more likely to be caused by changes in policing priorities than in actual possession.

The Human Security Report 2005 shows an upward trend in the number of police-recorded rapes in the world since 1977. However, as criminologist Graeme Newman dryly observes in his commentary on these statistics: "With respect to sexual violence, determining whether the apparent increase in the world rape rate is due to better reporting and recording, or is due to a real increase in the incidence of rape, or to both, is simply impossible."

Police-recorded crime generally can be expected in the medium to long term to undergo an upward trend in developing countries due to improvements in service-oriented policing and computer-aided recording practices. Solely as a result of these changes, police-recorded crime rates of many developing countries could well go up by several hundred percentage points in the decades to come without any increase in the level of actual crime.

If comparisons are limited to developed countries, some of these problems may be less severe. Farrington, Langan, and Tonry (2004) compared results of national victimization surveys with police-recorded crimes of eight Western countries for the period 1980 to 2000. With regard to the similarity between the trends in the two measures over time, their results are mixed. For burglary, the two trends were correlated for six of the eight countries. For robbery, only two countries showed similar trends in police figures and victimization rates. Reviewing the available data, Cook and Khmilevska (2005) observed that recorded data and survey results exhibited very different growth rates.

For some countries, comparisons can be made between the trends in ICVS victimization rates and the trends in total recorded crime. Figure 2.7 presents the trends of police statistics and ICVS victimization for total crime in five countries between 1988 and 1999, with observations corresponding to the years covered by the four repetitions of the ICVS (1988, 1991, 1995, and 1999, the calendar year preceding the interviews). Both victimization rates and police figures are indexed at 100 for 1988. If we take 1988 as the starting point, the trends on the left and on the right show amazing symmetry. To a large extent, the two trends mirror each other in each country.[6] With the exception of one country in which police data were stable and survey data showed a steady decrease, in the other countries crime went up between 1988 and 1991, stabilized or decreased between 1991 and 1995, then further decreased between

1995 and 1999. Trend analyses of several other countries for which fewer observations are available have confirmed that as a rule the two trends go in the same direction. Some differences between the two trends could be attributed to changes in reporting patterns. For example, the ICVS showed drops in reporting to the police in the early 1990s in both the Netherlands and England and Wales, and this factor explains the flatter trend in police figures.

As can be seen in the graph, police-recorded crimes show, as a rule, less-marked variation than victimization rates. The trend analyses indicate that police figures tend to deflate rather than inflate changes in actual crime. The explanation might be that in years of sudden increases in the number of crimes reported to the police, police administrations and prosecution services will be clogged. Reporting victims will have to wait longer, and responsible officers will be inclined to increase thresholds for recording at least in the short term. These processes may in turn discourage (repeat) victims from reporting. Police figures will reflect crime surges in a deflated way. In years of sudden decreases of crimes reported to the police, available human resources will be freed, and larger proportions of reported crimes will subsequently be timely recorded, inviting more reporting by victims. Decreases in crime will thus partly be offset by better recording and more reporting, resulting in a deflated reflection of the decrease in police statistics of crime. In the case of England and Wales, recent decreases

❖ **Figure 2.7** Police and Survey Crime Trends, Five Countries 1988–1999 (Index 1988 = 100)[7]

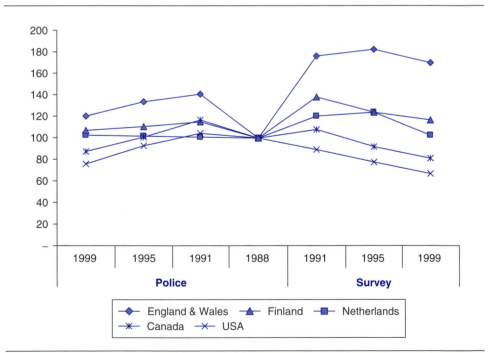

Source: Van Kesteren, Mayhew, & Nieuwbeerta, 2000.

of overall crime may have freed resources for targeted investigations of violent crimes. This factor may have caused an increase in police-recorded crimes of violence.

Incremental introduction of ICT technology in reporting and recording of crimes facilitates both reporting by victims and recording of reports by the police. These mechanisms can help to explain why the dramatic decreases in crime according to crime surveys in North America and western Europe are not always fully and timely reflected in police statistics. A recent analysis of the congruence between trends in ICVS rates and recorded crime rates in 20 developed countries showed mainly negative results between 1988 and 2004 (Van Dijk, Van Kesteren, & Smit, 2007). In Chapter 6, our discussion of trends in crime over time will therefore be largely based on results of the ICVS.

A Moratorium on International Police Figures?

In recent years, more and more researchers publishing or using recorded crime statistics have added "health warnings" to these data, for example, stating that these data should be interpreted with caution. In *The Economist*'s World in Figures (*The Economist*, 2005), statistics are given on serious assault and on theft. The countries leading the list for serious assaults are Australia and Sweden. Those who believe this top ranking reflects reality will be surprised to know that Zimbabwe, Jamaica, and the Ivory Coast are placed much lower on this league table for violent crime. On the ranking for theft, the top place is taken by Australia, with the Netherlands and the United Kingdom in second and third place, respectively. Much lower placed in this ranking are, to name just two, South Africa and Uruguay. It is explained in a footnote that these crime statistics are based on offenses recorded by the police and "therefore may not be strictly comparable." In view of the data on the levels of victimization by crime in these countries that will be presented in the next chapters, this seems to be an understatement. In our view, such crime statistics would more appropriately be called strictly incomparable.

In Fitzroy Dearborn's *Book of World Rankings* (2000), a league table is given for country rates of larceny, comprising robbery and burglary. Sweden and Denmark find themselves leading the larceny league table of 86 countries, followed by the United Arab Emirates, the Netherlands, and the United States. At the bottom are Kenya, Burundi, Senegal, and the Congo. In an introductory note the authors admit "that there is no way of verifying whether a greater crime rate is simply the result of better enforcement and a better reporting system" and finish with the lame observation that "it is not clear whether Interpol has grappled with this problem." As discussed, Interpol has not. It has instead at the advice of criminologists decided to take its crime statistics off its public Web site.

The 2003 *European Sourcebook* warns in its opening remarks that "police statistics do not always provide a good measure of crime" and cautions that "the data contained in this document should not be used for country by country (level) comparisons." The experience with the actual use of the recorded crime statistics has taught us that such health warnings will not keep the readers from smoking. When made available, such statistics will always be used to misleadingly compare levels of crime across countries. This will be done not just by journalists but by criminologically less-informed analysts as well. Many economists' publications on crime in a comparative perspective are, although theoretically refreshing, based on sloppy data uncritically taken from police administrations. They therefore can contribute little to the body of knowledge about crime or justice. Any hypotheses confirmed will have to be retested with better data. Worse, even dedicated crime prevention experts can be caught presenting police figures as if they are measures of crime. At an international conference on crime prevention hosted in Paris in 2004, one of the keynote speakers extensively presented and interpreted statistics on assaults taken from the *European Sourcebook*. Commenting on these police figures, the expert concluded, with a straight face, that the Scandinavian countries (Sweden and Finland) were the most violent countries in Europe, more violent than Russia or other eastern European countries. One could add, facetiously, that, according to these figures, problems of violence in the United Kingdom are in fact 100 times worse than in eastern Europe and 10 times worse than in Italy. According to the *Sourcebook,* by far the most peaceful country in Europe is, no surprises here, Albania, followed by Georgia and Moldova. As a nice detail, violent crimes seem to have remained stable in Georgia and Moldova recently, in spite of enduring civil strife, whereas in England and Wales, France, and the Netherlands, in contrast, violent crimes went up by 50% in the course of just 2 years.

The picture emerging from all these recycled police figures is, of course, completely erroneous. ICVS results on actual victimizations by assaults, to be presented in Chapter 4, show, for example, a different picture altogether. The comparatively high number of recorded assaults in Finland and Sweden largely reflects superior and accurate reporting and recording of such crimes by the authorities (e.g., recording a single report of domestic violence as several individual cases of assault) rather than a more prevalent use of violence among the population. Statistics of police-recorded crimes such as the ones presented at the international conference in Paris on assaults present a blatantly distorted picture of criminal reality. In such cases, police figures do not provide a "mirror image" of the real face of crime but rather a wildly distorted one. Police recording practices seem to act here as a funhouse mirror, called in the Dutch language: a mirror-of-laughs (*Lachspiegel*). Tables with such police figures indeed make a mockery of crime statistics. One of the most hilarious examples, cited in Lauw and Schonteich (2001), provides the Human Development Report of the United Nations Development Programme of 2000. Using the UN Crime Survey data, the UNDP reported that Canada has the highest rape rate in the world and that the rate of drug crimes in Switzerland is more than 10 times that in Colombia. Was there no one at the statistical unit of UNDP who doubted the validity of these statistical facts?

The computerization of police administrations will in the coming years make police-recorded crime figures more readily available in more and more countries than ever before. This new supply of police statistics on crime is likely to lead to a flood of comparative crime overviews in the media. Already in France and other countries in western Europe more and more articles appear in local newspapers comparing crime rates of cities and counties using computerized police statistics. The production of such statistics provides a sad example of what is known in the world of computers as "garbage in, garbage out." The availability of such statistics, often presented as multicolor maps for greater impact, will create an explosion of misinformation about the levels of crime across geographical areas. It will not lead to a better understanding of crime problems of the public by any means but will only enhance confusion and possibly fear. Evidence for the inbuilt distortions in geographical crime data based on police figures of recorded crimes can be found in a national victimization survey executed in Jamaica (UNODC, 2007a). The results showed that reporting rates were systematically lower in areas where victimization rates were higher. As the authors note: "Official data are biased downwards for higher crime areas." This inbuilt bias in official crime data is even larger in intercountry comparisons.

Considering the current state of knowledge, it would seem worthwhile to consider a worldwide moratorium among criminologists on the publication of comparative, international police-recorded crime statistics. Experts who feel compelled to publish such statistics should explain exactly for what purposes they can and, more importantly, cannot be used. Arguably, statistics on police-recorded crimes should be used only as input indicators of police forces and criminal justice systems. They are important for analyzing the productivity and efficiency of such systems. Authors should explain in the most unambiguous terms that they cannot and should not be used to make any statements on the absolute or even relative level of crime in a country or trends in crime. Experts can no longer in good faith attach the usual "health warnings" to their tables and then leave it to the reader to use them as they want at their peril. They should clearly state that the use of police figures as measures of the level of crime is wrong and that any attempt to use them in such a way will cause fatal misunderstandings.

Chiefs of police see themselves as the quintessential experts on the state of crime in their city or district. This is also how they are seen by the public and how, up to a point, they should, at least in democratic societies, be seen. In the eyes of the public, the police are the institutional "owners" of the crime problem and therefore the obvious agencies to know and tell the truth about crime. It will take time before the public understands that statistics on crime collected by this specialized institution itself provide little or no useful information on the realities of crime in a comparative perspective. It will also be difficult for senior police officers to refrain from expressing opinions about the state of crime on their watch based on data from their own administrations. However, as we have argued, geographical crime comparisons, especially international ones, based on police statistics, provide a fundamentally distorted picture of criminal reality. By knowingly presenting such gross misinformation on crime, police forces will ultimately undermine their credibility with public opinion. It is in the best interest of the international police community to fully convert to crime surveying as the method of data collection on crime. They should discontinue the practice of announcing drops in crime or crime rates that compare favorably with those of neighboring areas, using faulty police figures.[8] The decision of Interpol in 2006 to remove its historical series of crime statistics from its public Web site is to be applauded and should serve as a model for the police community.

The Political Context of Crime Surveying

The replacement of police figures by crime survey results as the main source of crime information must be understood against the background of new concerns about violence and crime over the past three decades. Policymakers in the United States and later elsewhere understood that police figures could not be used as reliable indicators of the levels and trends of crime. The launch of national crime victimization surveys reflects the growing understanding of governments that crime as a social problem had become too serious to be left to the security and justice sector alone. Crime issues were reconceptualized as social problems of great immediate concern to the public at large, determining the outcomes of national and local elections. Parallel to this, a powerful movement came into being at the grassroots level demanding more services for victims of crime. To respond to these demands, criminal policies had to be based on statistics reflecting the experiences of the victims rather than those of the officials and lawyers working for the institutions involved. Experiences of crime of the public at large and crime victims in particular were introduced as the ultimate standard of the success or failure of state policies in this domain. Criminal policies had become more people and victim centered. At the advice of statisticians, the decision was subsequently made to collect data directly from the public, as happens with the indicators of many other social problems. From this perspective, the statistical innovation of "crime surveying" resulted from the politicization of crime and justice issues in the 1970s and 1980s across the Western world. Methodological innovation was driven by politics and related social theory. Both countercrime policies and crime statistics were revolutionized by a newly emerged victimological consciousness and victim-centered criminal justice agenda.

As mentioned before, the discourse on crime and justice is now becoming more and more global in orientation. Both perpetrators and victims are increasingly borderless. Crime itself as well as its many repercussions has acquired global dimensions. This development generates a new demand for comparative, *global* crime information. The ICVS as a standardized survey instrument launched in 1989 was ahead of its time in a period when crime problems were still regarded as mainly domestic in nature. In the current era, the ICVS and its twin sister, the International Crimes Against Businesses Surveys, are, with their established methodologies, well positioned to satisfy the newly felt need of international information on crime.

In the meantime, NGOs such as Transparency International as well as the World Bank in its Investment Climate Surveys have started to collect information on crime, violence, and corruption. In the commercial sphere, several consultancy companies offer international crime information as part of risk assessments (e.g., MIG in the United Kingdom, The PRS Group in the United States, and AON and PricewaterhouseCoopers worldwide). The new method of choice is surveys among business executives and/or security consultants about their experiences and perceptions of crime. An important source of global crime information is the global Executives Opinion Surveys repeated annually by the World Economic Forum. These polls among executives are funded by the private sector because information on global crime problems, including the performance of relevant institutions dealing with them, informs strategic investment decisions of the increasingly internationally oriented business community. Once again new demands for reliable information on crime have created an innovative supply of such information. Once again the information is based on the experiences of newly emerging victim groups, in this case, international companies and their employees.

The information on crime presented in this book is largely taken from surveys among either the public or among business executives, conducted in the framework of the ICVS or otherwise. Little use will be made of official crime statistics. This methodological preference for consulting the potential victims rather than the officially assigned crime fighters is not only informed by methodological considerations. It also stems from the political belief that today's crime problems can no longer be "owned" by domestic institutions in the security and justice sector. Current crime problems constitute sources of human misery and economic waste spanning the world. The fight against these problems should serve the interests of the world community of private citizens and businesspeople rather than of nation-states. The new global threats require broad-based and well-coordinated interventions from governments across the world, and these ought to be based on metrics reflecting the experiences of world citizens. With the publication of this book we seek to fuel the international debate on victim-centered anticrime policies with victim-based statistics on problems of crime and justice.

❖

SUMMARY POINTS/IN CONCLUSION

- For years, those interested in comparative crime statistics have indulged in using statistics of police-recorded crime as collated and disseminated by Interpol and the UN. The comparability of these police figures across countries is compromised by three sources of error: differences in legal definitions of crime, differences in reporting of crimes by the public, and differences of recording by the police.

- In order to protect themselves against the criticism of comparing oranges and apples, authors routinely warn their readers to exercise due caution in interpreting the data. In this chapter, I have argued that criminologists can no longer hide behind such "health warnings." They should take full responsibility for the soundness of their data themselves. Comparative work on levels of or trends in crime should no longer be based on statistics taken from police administrations. It would be useful to follow the example set by Interpol, which has withdrawn its police figures from its public Web site, and to impose a global moratorium on the publication of police-recorded statistics as comparative measures of crime.

- The International Crime Victims Surveys and similar surveys among the business community provide a source of information on crime that is more credible than police figures. By using universally common definitions of main types of crime, it offers information on crime as perceived by ordinary people that is not colored by domestic legal definitions. Crime survey results are also unaffected by reporting patterns of the public or recording practices of the police. Such surveys provide an estimate of the true level of crime experienced by victims, including the so-called dark numbers. This information can be used as a rough but reliable comparative indicator of the level of crime. Where surveys have been carried out over a longer period, they can also provide information on trends in crime.

• Analyses of the ICVS data on reporting and recording of victimization incidents have provided new insights in the way police-based statistics on crime are systematically distorted. As a general rule, police forces act as gatekeepers of the criminal justice system. They are inclined to use their discretion in recording as a mechanism to prevent overburdening of their own capacities as well as those of prosecution, courts, and corrections. Priorities in recording are introduced that prevent cases that would increase backlogs and overload from entering the system. Victims experiencing the thresholds of recording adjust their own reporting and refrain from reporting incidents that stand little chance of being recorded.

• For this reason, police forces in poorer, developing or transitional countries, facing both comparatively high levels of crime and comparatively limited resources for law enforcement and criminal justice, are more economical in crime recording. The selectivity in recording discourages victims of crime in these countries from reporting less serious victimizations to the police. Rates of recorded crime of developing countries are therefore strongly and systematically *deflated* compared to those of more affluent countries.

• The systematic and resources-related nature of deflated crime statistics from the South erodes any hope that additional efforts from international organizations to standardize international police statistics will ever result in credible information on the true levels of crime in countries. It should not come as a surprise that police authorities in developing countries have little interest in cooperating with the United Nations Crime Surveys. Their experts know that their police figures say nothing about the true level of crime in their country in a global perspective and see little point in sharing such information.

• The production of global statistics on police-recorded crimes cannot be separated from the way law enforcement and justice systems are funded and operate. Only when law enforcement and justice systems meet with minimum international standards can statistics on crime be made roughly comparable. Standardization of police figures cannot therefore be undertaken in isolation but should instead be part of structural reforms in justice and security sectors of developing and transitional countries.

• In the meantime, the conduct of standardized victimization surveys in as many countries as possible should be chosen as a strategic priority by the international donor community. The regular repeat of the ICVS will allow governments of developing countries as well as international organizations to monitor not just trends in real crime but trends in the public's access to justice and satisfaction with law enforcement as well. In Part II of this book, we will give a foretaste of the kind of policy-relevant information that standardized surveys can provide at comparatively modest costs. In Part IV, we will show how survey results can also be harnessed to monitor performance of the justice and security sector. In Part V, finally, we will demonstrate the importance of such knowledge for a variety of pressing political agendas.

Notes

1. The first ICVS took place among 13 developed countries and one city each in Indonesia and Poland. The second survey was carried out in a selection of developed and developing countries with the involvement of the United Nations Interregional Criminal Justice Research Centre (UNICRI) funded by the Dutch Ministry of Foreign Affairs (Alvazzi del Frate, Zvekic, & Van Dijk, 1993). The ICVS was repeated in 1996, and again in 2000. The fifth survey was carried out in 2004/2005 among a total of 32 countries, including 18 member states of the

European Union, with cofunding from the Directorate of Research, Technology, and Development of the European Commission. Results of the EU component, called the EU/ICS, were reported in Van Dijk, Manchin, Van Kesteren, & Hideg, 2007, and results on the 5th sweep of the ICVS in Van Dijk, Van Kesteren, & Smit, 2007. The integrated 1989–2005 ICVS database is currently maintained at Gallup/Europe in cooperation with the International Victimology Institute at Tilburg University, the Netherlands (see www.europeansafetyobservatory.eu or www.intervict.nl).

2. A similar picture appeared in the unpublished UNICRI/UNODC report prepared for the occasion of the Eleventh Congress on Crime Prevention and Criminal Justice in Bangkok, Thailand, on April 17–27, 2005.

3. The definition provided by the UN Crime Survey referred to "the acquisition of another person's property by deception." The corresponding ICVS question asked whether the respondent had been the victim of a consumer fraud over the past year. In particular, reference was made to cheating in commerce or delivering a service.

4. A similar picture appeared in the unpublished UNICRI/UNODC report prepared for the occasion of the Eleventh Congress on Crime Prevention and Criminal Justice in Bangkok, Thailand, on April 17–27, 2005.

5. A similar picture appeared in the unpublished UNICRI/UNODC report prepared for the occasion of the Eleventh Congress on Crime Prevention and Criminal Justice in Bangkok, Thailand, on April 17–27, 2005.

6. In Bulgaria, the execution of the ICVS in 2001 and 2004 produced a series of victimization rates that confirmed the downward trend in recorded crime (Bezlov et al., 2005).

7. Figure reproduced from Van Kesteren, Mayhew, & Nieuwbeerta (2000).

8. In the United States, the United Kingdom, and the Netherlands, results of crime surveys are now finally seen by the media as the primary source of information on levels and trends of crime. In the United Kingdom and the Netherlands, the national crime victimization surveys are carried out annually among samples of the public in all regional police districts. These mega-surveys are used to collect comparable information on crime and fear of crime as well as on the performance of the police in rendering services to the public, including victims of crime.

PART II

Common Crimes Across the World

The Burden of Property Crime

Introducing the ICVS

As discussed above, the International Crime Victims Survey will be used here as the principal source of information on the level of common crime across countries (also referred to as volume crime). Most of the data used are from the 1996, 2000, and 2005 sweeps of the ICVS. Where appropriate, data from other sources, such as from official police administrations, will be added on an ad hoc basis. In this chapter, the focus will be on frequently occurring property crimes. Violent crimes will be the topic of the next chapter. Chapter 5 will look at the determinants of common crimes and in Chapter 6, we will discuss global and regional trends in crime over time.

The ICVS collects information on experiences of crime for 10 "common crimes." Among the 10 types of crime, some are "household crimes," that is, those that can be seen as affecting the household at large. For these crimes, respondents are asked to report on all incidents experienced by the family. The first group of crimes deals with the vehicles owned by the respondent or his or her household: theft of car, theft from car, theft of bicycle, and theft of motorcycle.[1] The second group refers to burglary and attempted burglary. The third group of crimes refers to victimization experienced by the respondent *personally:* robbery, theft of personal property, threat or assault, and sexual offenses.

The ICVS provides an overall measure of victimization by common crimes: the percentage of those ages 16 or over who experienced, over the previous 12 months, one or more of the 10 main types of common crimes covered by the questionnaire. These percentages are called the *one-year victimization prevalence rates.*

Cross-validation of crime survey findings with information on police-recorded crimes has proven to be problematic. Estimates of the total number of crimes committed based on extrapolations of survey results are typically much higher than the number of crimes recorded by the police. As explained, crimes are filtered out through nonreporting by victims and nonrecording by the police. The one type of crime least affected by such filtering is, besides homicide, theft of car. Most car thefts are reported to the police and duly recorded. Concerning this type of crime, the estimated total of crimes committed according to survey research should be roughly the same as the officially recorded number. Studies comparing the estimated number of car thefts according to crime victimization surveys with number of car thefts recorded by the police have indeed shown a high level of agreement (Van Dijk & Steinmetz, 1980). This concurrence suggests that interviewing samples of the public can indeed yield reliable estimates of the true levels of common crime.[2]

Although crime victimization surveys possess their own specific limitations and methodological weaknesses, they are by now generally regarded as the best available source of information on the level of common crimes.[3] Topical methodological issues concerning national surveys such as the National Crime Survey in the United States and the British Crime Survey in England and Wales are discussed in Hough and Maxfield (2007). Discussions on key methodological issues concerning the ICVS can be found in various reports (e.g., Block, 1993; Kury, 2001; Mayhew & Van Dijk, 1992; Nieuwbeerta, 2002; Van Dijk, Van Kesteren, & Smit, 2007; Van Kesteren, Mayhew, & Nieuwbeerta, 2000). Recurrent concerns relate to the quality of methods and techniques of data collection employed and the extent of standardization achieved. In a recent review of international crime surveying, Lynch (2006) came to the conclusion that nation-specific surveys, which are typically better funded, produce higher-quality data on individual nations but that the ICVS provides more comparable data across countries. A brief description of some of these technical issues is included in Appendix A.

Through standardization of the questionnaire and basic features of the sampling design, the ICVS indeed produces victimization rates that can reliably be compared across countries. In many developing countries, the ICVS has for logistical and cost reasons been carried out only in the capital city (for example, in Johannesburg, Buenos Aires, and Djakarta) usually with samples sizes of 1,000 people. In developed countries, the surveys were usually carried out among samples of the national population of 2,000 per country. For the purpose of cross-country comparisons, we have calculated the victimization rates of inhabitants of capital or other main cities of developed countries.[4] In the ICVS 2005, booster samples were drawn from inhabitants of capital cities of around 1,000 per country. Cross-country comparisons made in this chapter pertain to the percentages of inhabitants of capital or other main cities who were victimized by crime over the past 12 months (one-year urban victimization prevalence rates).

Comparing urban victimization rates of countries brings the additional advantage that the impact of different degrees of urbanization on national crime rates (to be discussed in Chapter 5) is eliminated. On the downside, the comparison of urban rates ignores victimization in rural areas, which might show a different picture. In most countries, levels of crime are significantly lower in rural areas. However, it should be borne in mind that currently more than half of the world's population lives in urban areas and that this proportion keeps increasing. These demographic facts support our focus on urban victimization rates in international comparisons. National rates are used in Chapter 6 to illustrate trends of crime over time in selected countries.[5]

Only a few countries have taken part in all five rounds of the ICVS conducted so far. For the comparisons, we have included the results of the latest surveys available for each country from 1996 onward. Data presented are from countries where ICVS-based surveys were last carried out in either 2005 or 2000, supplemented with some data of 1996 surveys. In the tables with victimization rates of individual countries and in the various maps, we have added the results of five countries that took part only in 1992 (China, Egypt, Tunisia, Tanzania, and Papua New Guinea). Since these rates fall outside the chosen reference period of 1996–2005, they are marked with an asterisk in the tables. ICVS data are available on 78 countries, but the total numbers vary per variable because of missing data values (e.g., overall victimization rates cannot be calculated for countries that have changed one of the questions on the 10 different crime types). Comparisons are primarily made between the rates of world regions. North America is represented by Canada and the United States and Oceania by Australia and New Zealand. Western Europe is represented by 20 countries and eastern/central Europe by 18. For Latin America, regional rates were calculated using data from seven countries in South America, including Brazil and Argentina and two from Central America (Mexico and Costa Rica).[6] Asia is represented by eight countries, including Japan, Hong Kong/China, and Indonesia. The data set for Africa comprises seven countries including South Africa and Nigeria. For an overview of all participating countries and/or cities, see Appendix A.

Overall Levels of Crime

Figure 3.1 shows the regional distribution of one-year prevalence rates of victimization by any of the 10 mentioned crimes among people living in capital cities (typically with 1,000,000 inhabitants or more).

The results of the ICVS 1996–2005 show that on average, one in four citizens (25%) living in urban areas was the victim of at least one form of crime over the 12 months preceding the interview. This result confirms that real levels of crime are several times higher than those recorded by the police because of nonreporting by victims or nonrecording by the police. In selected Western countries, analyses have shown real crime level to be four to five times larger than police-recorded crime, especially violent and sexual crime (Van Dijk & Steinmetz, 1980). The gap between actual and recorded crime is much larger in developing countries since reporting and recording rates are considerably lower, as discussed in the previous chapter. Globally, the number of real volume crimes committed can be roughly estimated as at least 10 times higher than those recorded. Global recorded crime can rightly be described as just the tip of the iceberg.

Regional rates do not differ more than 10 percentage points from the global average. Victimization rates are highest for city dwellers in Latin America (34%) and Africa (33%) and lowest in Asia (21%). Variation in overall victimization among regions consisting mainly of developed countries is minimal.

As we will see below, variation between regional rates is significantly larger for specific types of crime. Lower rates for some types of crime seem to be offset by higher rates in other criminal domains. As a result, regional rates vary within the range of 21% to 34%. No world region is immune from high levels of volume crime in urban areas.

❖ **Figure 3.1**   Overall Percentages of General Public in Urban Areas Victimized by Any of 10 Types of Common Crime During the Past 12 Months, by World Region

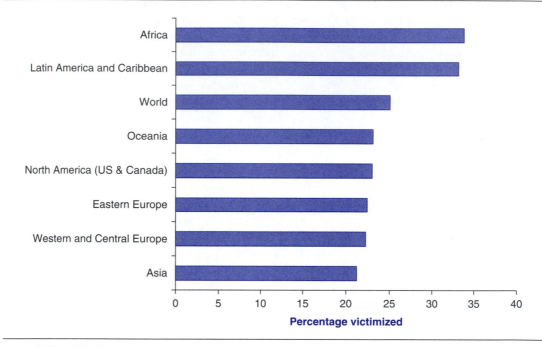

Source: ICVS, 1996–2005.

It is noteworthy that the variation in regional rates does not fully conform to the commonly held notion that levels of crime are driven by poverty. The low crime rate in Asia is clearly at odds with this notion. The fact that the level of crime in eastern Europe is identical to that of more affluent central and western European countries also belies easy generalizations about the relationships between poverty and crime. We will return to this issue in Chapter 5 on the determinants of crime.

For methodological reasons, ICVS survey questionnaires ask about victimization experiences during the past 5 years before asking detailed information on incidents during the past 12 months. Rates on most recent experiences are known to be more reliable and are therefore used as the basis for calculating victimization rates. Information on the 5-year reference period provides a rough indication of the prevalence of criminal victimization over a longer period of time. Globally, over a 5-year period, two out of three inhabitants of big cities were victimized by a crime at least once. In Europe and North America, roughly one in two are victimized once or more in the course of 5 years according to the latest available data (Van Dijk, Van Kesteren, & Smit, 2007). This finding confirms that criminal victimization is no longer a rare event for those living in the big cities of today's world. To be confronted with crime has become an almost normal feature of life for those living in an urban setting anywhere in world.

As previously stated, this book aims to present statistics on the levels of crime *in* all world regions as well as in as many individual countries possible. Table 3.1 shows

❖ Table 3.1 World Ranking of Countries According to Victimization of the Public in Urban Areas by any Crime in the Course of One Year, Rank Number, and Percentage of Victims per Year

Fifteen Countries With the Highest Rates								
1	Colombia	48.7	6	Peru	41.0	11	Tunisia*	35.9
2	Zimbabwe	46.8	7	Mongolia	40.6	12	Namibia	35.1
3	Costa Rica	43.5	8	Bolivia	38.9	13	Paraguay	34.5
4	Swaziland	43.4	9	Mozambique	37.7	14	Zambia	34.4
5	Cambodia	41.3	10	Tanzania*	37.6	15	Slovak Republic	32.4
Fifteen Countries With Medium-High Rates								
16	United Kingdom	32.0	30	Ireland	25.7	39	Norway	21.5
19	Argentina	31.2	31	New Zealand	25.9	46	China*	21.6
21	India	29.7	34	South Africa	25.7	51	Switzerland	20.1
26	Lesotho	27.3	37	United States	23.3	53	Canada	19.1
28	Netherlands	27.0	38	Russian Federation	23.1	56	Brazil	18.4
Fifteen Countries With the Lowest Rates								
58	Turkey	17.9	63	Italy	16.6	68	Japan	10.8
59	France	17.8	64	Spain	13.7	69	Portugal	9.7
60	Austria	17.2	65	Greece	13.5	70	Philippines	9.1
61	Australia	16.9	66	Croatia	12.9	71	Hong Kong, China	7.8
62	Korea, Rep.	16.7	67	Hungary	12.6	72	Azerbaijan	7.7

Source: ICVS, 1992, 1996–2005, latest survey available.

*Countries with data from ICVS, 1992.

the ranking of countries on the basis of one-year overall victimization rates, based on results of ICVS surveys carried out in the period 1996–2005. For three countries, data were included from the 1992 survey (indicated by an asterisk).

In interpreting countries' rates, it must be borne in mind that they are based on relatively small samples with an average size of 1,000 respondents. The actual rates among the population may deviate from the ones given here. As a general rule, there is less than a 10% chance that the overall victimization rates of the city population deviate more than three percentage points from the rates of the samples. Individual countries' rates, then, cannot be seen as exactly right but provide a reliable indicator of which countries have relatively high, moderately high, or relatively low rates of victimization among their urban populations. Full details of all country prevalence rates are given in Appendix B, and underlying sample sizes are given in Appendix A.

The countries with the highest prevalence rates for common crime are mainly from Latin America or sub-Saharan Africa, with the exception of Mongolia, Cambodia, and Estonia. Very high prevalence rates for most types of crime were also found in Papua New Guinea (overall rate not available).[7]

Europe and North American countries are almost without exception situated in the middle category. Contrary to common perception, overall rates of volume crime—such as burglary, robbery, and assault and threats—are not higher in the United States than in most parts of western Europe. In fact, U.S. rates are significantly lower than those of, for example, England and Wales and the Netherlands. Ireland and Iceland also stand out as European countries with relatively high crime rates. The overall rate of Canada is somewhat below the means of the European Union and the United States. In the latest round of the ICVS, Australia, represented by Sydney, emerged as a relatively low-crime country.

Countries with the lowest rates form a fairly mixed group with a strong representation of eastern European and affluent Asian countries (Japan, South Korea, Hong Kong), middle-income ones (China), and poor ones (Philippines, Indonesia, Azeabaÿan). Switzerland and Norway used to be countries with the safest main cities in western Europe, but according to the latest ICVS round, this position has been taken over by Austria, Italy, Spain, and Greece.

Figures 3.2 and 3.3 show the world and European maps of victimization by common crimes around 2000.

❖ **Figure 3.2**   World Map of Victimization by Any Common Crime (around 2000)

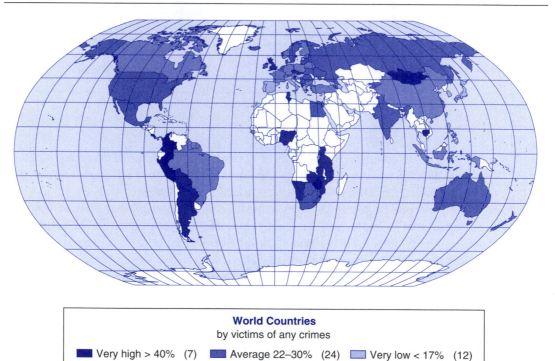

World Countries
by victims of any crimes

- ■ Very high > 40% (7)
- ■ High 30–40% (14)
- ■ Average 22–30% (24)
- ■ Low 17–22% (17)
- □ Very low < 17% (12)
- □ No data (120)

Source: ICVS, 1992, 1996–2005.

❖ **Figure 3.3**   European Map of Victimization by Any Common Crime (Around 2000)

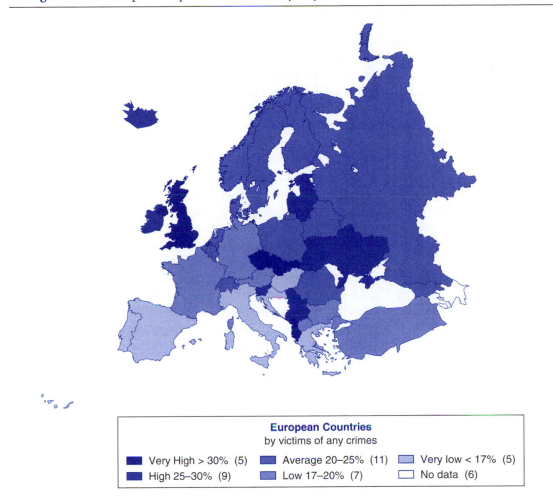

European Countries
by victims of any crimes

■ Very High > 30% (5)	■ Average 20–25% (11)	■ Very low < 17% (5)
■ High 25–30% (9)	■ Low 17–20% (7)	□ No data (6)

Source: ICVS, 1996–2005.

Other Measures of the Crime Burden

The victimization prevalence rates are the percentages of those ages 16 years and older who experienced any crime once or more. It provides a rough measure of exposure to common crime, disregarding both the number of victimizations per respondent (one or more times during the year) and their seriousness (ranging from bicycle thefts to car thefts and sexual violence). Critics have pointed out that comparing overall prevalence rates of countries may lead to erroneous conclusions on the comparative burdens of crime of respective national populations.

In previous reports on the ICVS, overall prevalence rates (percentage of population victimized at least once by any of the 10 types of crime) have been supplemented by incidence rates (total numbers of victimizations of crime experienced per 100,000 people). The prevalence and incidence rates appeared to show similar rankings of the countries. Countries scoring the highest on prevalence rates scored equally high on incidence rates (Van Kesteren, Mayhew, & Nieuwbeerta, 2000). One of the few exceptions is the somewhat higher rank number of the United States on incidence rates than on prevalence rates. The comparatively higher rank on incidence rates suggests that in the United States, there is more concentration of crime among certain subpopulations. However, incidence rates of the United States are also lower than those of several western European countries. The observation that the United States can no longer be regarded as a high-crime country in terms of overall victimization by common crime still stands.

Perhaps more to the point than the issue of victimization frequencies is the criticism that overall prevalence rates may imply comparing minor crimes such as bicycle thefts or cases of pickpocketing with more serious crimes such as robberies or sexual assaults. In previous publications, we have looked into this issue as well. In the surveys, the seriousness of different types of crime was assessed through special follow-up questions to all respondents reporting being victimized ("How seriously would you rate this incident?"). As expected, sexual assaults and car thefts were deemed more serious than simple thefts. Incidence rates were recalculated for each country taking into account the seriousness of each type of crime as judged by the victims. In other words, victimization experiences were weighed for perceived seriousness per type of crime. The results showed that most countries kept exactly the same rank number in the weighted incidence rates as in relation to overall incidence rates (Mayhew & Van Dijk, 1997). In conclusion, the unweighted overall prevalence victimization rate presented here, however rough, stands as a reasonable comparative indicator of the overall burden of common crime of countries.[8]

Burglary

In this chapter, the focus will be on victimization by property crime. The first topic is burglary. The ICVS questionnaire asks respondents whether anyone did actually get into their house or flat without permission and steal or try to steal something. Figure 3.4 shows the regional, one-year victimization rates for household burglary in urban areas.

ICVS results show that households in urban Africa, Latin America, and Oceania (Australia, New Zealand) are most at risk. The European, Asian, and North American regions showed risks below the global average.[9]

The distribution of rates for attempted burglary shows a similar pattern with highest rates in Africa and Latin America (see Appendix B). In many developed countries, there are, however, more attempted burglaries than completed burglaries, and in many developing countries, completed burglaries are more common (Alvazzi del Frate & Van Kesteren, 2001). One explanation for this difference is the higher prevalence of security measures against burglaries in many Western countries, especially in the United Kingdom, Australia, and the United States (Van Kesteren, Mayhew, & Nieuwbeerta, 2000). In these countries, investments in security precautions such as

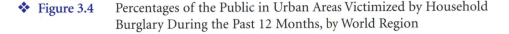

❖ **Figure 3.4**   Percentages of the Public in Urban Areas Victimized by Household Burglary During the Past 12 Months, by World Region

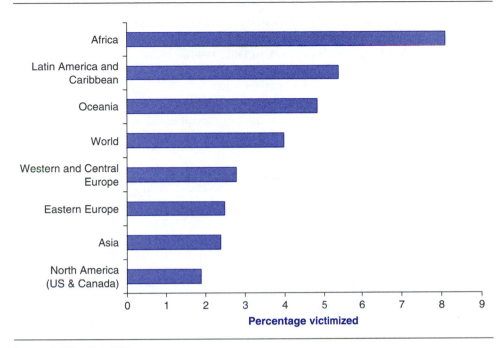

Source: ICVS, 1996–2005.

burglar alarms seem to result in higher proportions of *failed* burglaries. The topic of crime prevention and its impact on levels and trends of crime will be discussed in more detail in Chapters 5 and 6.

A new and worrisome crime trend in some countries is *home invasions,* whereby burglars enter occupied houses with the use of force to steal property (Hicks & Sansfacon, 1999). This type of crime combines elements of burglary with those of robbery. It is one of the types of crime that instill great fear among urban communities in Africa. Many home invasions are recorded by the police as residential robberies. In the United States, residential robberies account for 13.5 % of all recorded robberies. They have been analyzed as a specialty of Asian gangs, usually targeting families in their own communities (Dunlap, 1997). In South Africa, house robberies recorded by the police have continued to increase to a rate of 21.7 per 100,000 people in 2005 (www.Institute for Security Studies).

The consequences of burglary in terms of monetary value may vary widely in different contexts. While in the industrialized world burglars frequently steal objects of a high value, such as audio/video equipment, jewelry, or computers, burglary in developing countries is often aimed at stealing food, household appliances, linen, or cutlery. Regardless of the economic losses, victims regard burglaries as very serious since it is a violation of their privacy in the domestic sphere. It is therefore a crime with high psychological impact and is well remembered by survey respondents (Mawby, 2001).

Since people universally keep a large part of their properties in their homes or apartments, household burglary is a crime to which inhabitants of all countries are similarly exposed. Researchers tasked to estimate the level of property crime with just one indicator are well advised to choose victimization by domestic burglary. Burglary victimization rates have proven to be the best statistical predictors of overall victimization by common crime (Van Dijk, 1999).

❖ **Table 3.2**   World Ranking of Countries According to Urban Victimization Rates for Household Burglary in the Course of One Year, Rank Number, and Percentage of Victims per Year

Fourteen Countries With the Highest Rates								
1	Cambodia	15.8	6	Swaziland	9.4	11	Bolivia	7.7
2	Papua, N. G.	14.4	7	Costa Rica	8.5	12	Tunisia*	7.2
3	Mozambique	12.6	8	Paraguay	8.2	13	Peru	6.8
4	Zambia	10.8	9	Namibia	8.1	14	Botswana	6.8
5	Zimbabwe	10.7	10	Mongolia	8.0	15	Czech Republic	6.7

Fifteen Countries With Medium-High Rates								
19	South Africa	5.4	37	Switzerland	2.7	47	Netherlands	2.1
22	Turkey	4.6	41	Georgia	2.6	48	Sweden	2.1
24	United Kingdom	4.5	42	Belarus	2.6	52	Norway	1.9
29	Slovenia	3.5	44	China*	2.3	54	Canada	1.9
30	Mexico	3.5	45	Australia	2.2	55	United States	1.9

Fifteen Countries With the Lowest Rates								
57	Poland	1.8	62	Croatia	1.3	67	Spain	1.1
58	Russian Federation	1.8	63	Brazil	1.3	68	Japan	0.7
59	Greece	1.7	64	Hungary	1.2	69	Portugal	0.7
60	Italy	1.5	65	Philippines	1.2	70	Azerbaijan	0.6
61	Romania	1.5	66	Germany	1.1	71	Hong Kong, China	0.6

Source: ICVS, 1992, 1996–2005, latest survey available.

*Countries with data from ICVS, 1992.

Cambodia and Papua New Guinea stand out as the countries with the highest burglary rates together with several southern African countries, including South Africa. A question on domestic burglary in the Afrobarometer indicates similarly high rates in other sub-Saharan countries, not just in southern Africa but in Kenya and Uganda as well (Afrobarometer, 2004; UNODC, 2005). The comparatively high levels of burglaries in Costa Rica (8.5%), Mongolia (8%), Bolivia (7.7%), Tunisia (7.2%), the Czech Republic (6.7%), and the United Kingdom (4.5%) are also worth mentioning.

Figures 3.5 and 3.6 show the world and European maps for household burglary around 2000.

❖ **Figure 3.5**   World Map of Household Burglary (Around 2000)

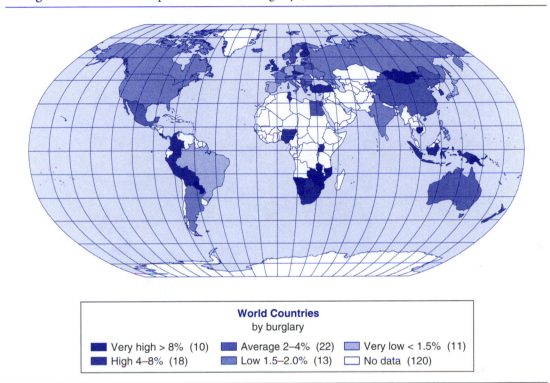

World Countries
by burglary

■ Very high > 8% (10)   ■ Average 2–4% (22)   ▨ Very low < 1.5% (11)
■ High 4–8% (18)   ■ Low 1.5–2.0% (13)   ☐ No data (120)

Source: ICVS, 1996-2005.

Theft and Frauds

The ICVS contains a question on experiences with personal theft such as theft of purses, wallets, clothing, or equipment. Victims of such thefts are asked whether they were carrying what was stolen. Those answering in the affirmative are classified as victims of pickpocketing. Figure 3.7 shows the regional rates.

The distribution of regional rates is somewhat exceptional. The crime of pickpocketing seems comparatively rare in North America and Australia and New Zealand. The countries of eastern Europe find themselves in an unusual high-rate place, at the same level as Latin America, Asia, and Africa. Pickpocketing is three times more common in eastern Europe than in western Europe with rates in central Europe lying somewhere in between. This high-rate position of eastern Europe differs from the more modest positions of the region on the world rankings for other types of property crimes. A possible explanation for the unusual distribution

❖ **Figure 3.6**   European Map of Household Burglary (Around 2000)

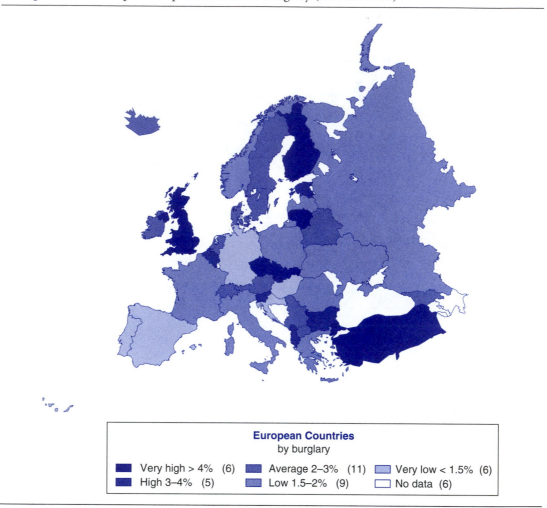

European Countries
by burglary

■ Very high > 4% (6)	■ Average 2–3% (11)	■ Very low < 1.5% (6)
■ High 3–4% (5)	■ Low 1.5–2% (9)	□ No data (6)

Source: ICVS, 1996-2005.

of pickpocketing is common modes of mass transportation. In regions and countries that rely heavily on public transportation such as trains and city trams, there are more opportunities for pickpocketing than in countries where cars are the dominant form of transportation. Another explanation could be that pickpocketing, as a sophisticated form of property crime, requires the development of skills that are transferred within local criminal subcultures from generation to generation. Such subcultures might be more prevalent on the European continent than in the Anglo-Saxon world by tradition.

National victimization rates for pickpocketing seem to show little variation within regions (see Appendix B).

❖ **Figure 3.7**   Percentages of the Public in Urban Areas Victimized by
Pickpocketing During the Past 12 Months, by World Region

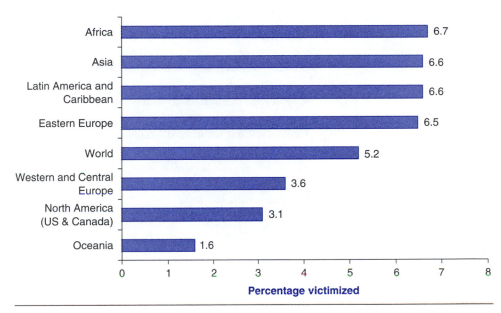

Source: ICVS, 1996–2005.

Consumer Fraud

The ICVS asks whether the respondent has been the victim of a consumer fraud over the past year, focusing on cheating in commerce or the services industry. The most common frauds occurred in shops or during construction or repair work or in a garage. Globally, less than 1% of the cases had been reported to the police or any other authority. Figure 3.8 shows the regional prevalence rates for consumer fraud.

Consumer fraud shows more variation across regions than any other type of crime. Thirty eight percent of the respondents from eastern Europe actually experienced a consumer fraud of this type, followed by 30% in Asia and 26% in Africa (Figure 3.8). In Australia and New Zealand, consumer fraud is comparatively rare. The high rates in eastern Europe have been interpreted as a side effect of the transition from a planned economy—coupled with a huge black market—toward a regulated market economy (Svekics, 1998). The extent of consumer fraud seems to be higher in newly emerging market economies where consumer protection is poor. Regulation of markets can be expected to be weaker in countries where the size of the informal sector is large. The victimization rates for fraud were found to be related to the size of the informal economy as perceived by business executives ($r = .42$, $p < 0.005$, $n = 80$).[10]

Within regions, variation is limited (see Appendix B for the country rates). Almost all countries in the highest category are either in eastern Europe, Asia, or in northern

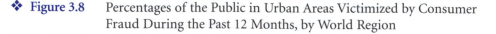

❖ **Figure 3.8**   Percentages of the Public in Urban Areas Victimized by Consumer Fraud During the Past 12 Months, by World Region

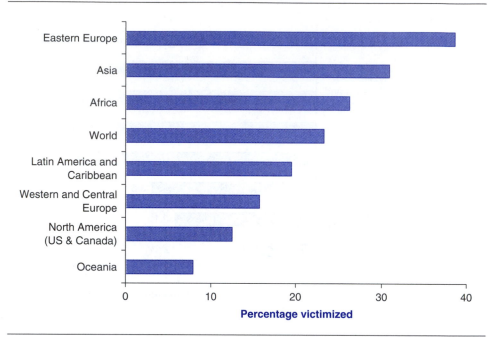

Source: ICVS, 1996–2005.

or sub-Saharan Africa. Lowest rates were found in Japan, South Africa, several EU countries, Canada, and Switzerland.

Victims of consumer fraud were asked in which type of situation the incident had taken place. In the 2005 wave of the ICVS, victims were specifically asked whether the fraud had been Internet based. On the country level, 45% of victims said the fraud had taken place in a shop. Eleven percent mentioned either building or construction work or a garage. Nine percent mentioned shopping on the Internet. This implies that 1% of the national respondents have been victimized by a fraud on the Internet. Among city inhabitants the victimization rate was 1.5%. Internet-based frauds have reached prevalence rates that are similar to those of common crimes such as car theft or pick-pocketing. The topic of Internet-based crimes will be revisited in Chapter 8.

Car Crimes

The ICVS interview screener inquiries open with a question about whether the house-hold owns one or more cars and whether any of these cars have been stolen. Subsequent questions ask about theft from cars (both items left in the car and car parts) and car vandalism. In the 2005 round of the ICVS, the question about car vandalism was deleted to shorten the interview. The ICVS also contains questions on theft of bicycles and motorcycles, but for brevity's sake, these results will not be presented here in full (see Appendix B for results). Some analytical findings on the relationship between vehicle ownership rates and vehicle-related thefts will be taken up in Chapter 5.

Car Theft and Joyriding

While a number of cars are stolen for the purpose of joyriding, others are sold in domestic or transnational markets for stolen vehicles or are dismantled. In Australia and North America, around 80% of the stolen cars are eventually recovered. In these regions, most cases of car theft comprise joyriding. In most European and Asian countries, on average more than half of stolen cars are recovered. The recovery rate is lowest in developing countries, notably in Africa (45%) and Latin America (48%) and in Poland (34%) and Hungary (35%). In developed countries, recovery rates show a declining trend, indicating a shift toward more professional types of theft, probably in response to better protection (Van Dijk, Van Kesteren, & Smit, 2007).

It would be wrong to assume that cases of joyriding are not serious. In many cases, cars recovered after being stolen had been seriously damaged. In the judgment of victims, both car theft and joyriding are judged to be among the most serious forms of common crimes covered by the ICVS (Van Dijk, 1999). In fact, victim respondents in Africa, Latin America, Asia, and central and eastern Europe consider both car theft and joyriding to be the most serious types of crime, more serious even than sexual violence or robbery. Respondents in Australia, North America, and western Europe rank the seriousness of car thefts lower than sexual violence and robbery with a weapon but higher than household burglary and any other crime. Apparently, many owners are much attached to their cars and resent losing them due to a criminal act.

Figure 3.9 shows the regional rates of victimization by car theft, including joyriding. Regional rates for car theft show a distribution across regions that is almost the mirror image of overall victimization by any crime or of burglary. Rates in North America and Oceania (Australia and New Zealand) are among the highest. Lowest rates are found in eastern Europe, and Asia. Obviously, the level of car theft, as it is for other car-related crimes, is strongly dependent on national rates of car ownership. Where more households own cars, the prevalence of such crimes is higher. Car crimes are a prime example of how affluence-related opportunities of crime can drive up the volume of common crime. In recent years, better antitheft protection of cars seems to have reduced the availability of easy targets for car theft and joyriding in more-affluent countries. We will return to this issue in Chapters 5 and 6 when discussing the macrosocial causes of crime and trends in common crime, respectively.

To give a better picture of the risks for owners, rates were calculated for the percentages of owners victimized by these crimes in the course of a year. Figure 3.10 shows the results.

Car owners' victimization rates for car theft are, of course, higher than the general population's victimization rates for car theft. The differences are most marked in regions where car ownership is comparatively low (Africa and Latin America). The ranking of regions in terms of car owners' risks is almost the reverse of that of general victimization risks and resembles that of overall victimization rates. The risks to owners of cars—and to those renting a car abroad—are 50% higher in Africa and Latin

❖ **Figure 3.9**   Percentages of the Public in Urban Areas Victimized by Car Theft
or Joyriding During the Past 12 Months, by World Region

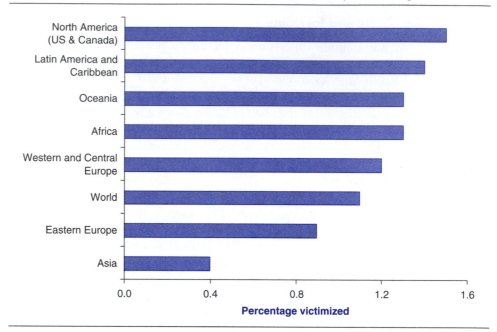

Source: ICVS, 1996–2005.

❖ **Figure 3.10**   Percentages of Car Owners in Urban Areas Victimized by Car Theft
or Joyriding During the Past 12 Months

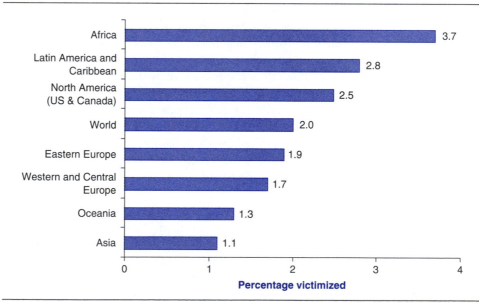

Source: ICVS, 1996–2005.

❖ **Table 3.3**   World Ranking of Countries According to Victimization of Car Owners in Urban Areas by Theft of a Car in the Course of One Year, Rank Number, and Percentage of Victims per Year.

Fifteen Countries With the Highest Rates

1	Papua New Guinea*	9.8	6	Tanzania*	5.7	11	Colombia	3.5
2	Mozambique	7.5	7	Tunisia*	4.6	12	Albania	3.5
3	South Africa	7.1	8	Argentina	3.9	13	Ireland	3.5
4	Swaziland	6.3	9	Italy	3.7	14	Zambia	3.2
5	Brazil	6.0	10	Czech Republic	3.5	15	Slovak Republic	3.0

Fifteen Countries With Medium-High Rates

18	United States	2.7	34	United Kingdom	2.0	49	Norway	1.2
19	Mexico	2.6	35	New Zealand	1.9	50	Belgium	1.1
20	Portugal	2.6	36	Latvia	1.9	51	Iceland	1.1
26	Belarus	2.2	42	Peru	1.5	55	Netherlands	1.0
27	Ukraine	2.2	48	Zimbabwe	1.2	56	Canada	1.0

Fifteen Countries With the Lowest Rates

58	India	0.9	63	Germany	0.6	68	Switzerland	0.3
59	Slovenia	0.8	64	China	0.6	69	France	0.3
60	Indonesia	0.8	65	Austria	0.5	70	Japan	0.2
61	Australia	0.8	66	Macedonia, FYR	0.5	71	Romania	0.2
62	Hungary	0.6	67	Korea, Rep.	0.4	72	Hong Kong, China	0.0

Source: ICVS, 1992, 1996–2005, latest survey available.

*Countries with data from ICVS, 1992.

America than globally. Risks of losing one's car to a criminal act are by far the lowest in Asia and Australia. Table 3.3 shows national rates.

As can be seen in Table 3.3, ownership risks are highest in Papua New Guinea (1992), Mozambique, and South Africa. Risks for owners in Europe are highest in Italy, the Czech Republic, Slovakia, Ireland, Portugal, and the United Kingdom.

Car Hijacking

In recent years, some countries, most notably in Africa, have been increasingly confronted with the very serious crime of car hijacking, a hybrid of car theft and robbery. In the African version of the ICVS, carried out in 2000, a question was added about experiences with this type of crime (Prinsloo & Naudé, 2001). More than 1% of the ICVS respondents in African countries indicated they were victims of car hijacking.

This brings the actual victimization rate in Africa to an even higher level. In South Africa (Johannesburg) and Swaziland (Mbabane), the victimization rates for car hijacking was above 2% per year.[11] According to police figures, car hijacking has reached a plateau in South Africa recently, probably as a result of focused policing.

Robbery

Robbery is a property crime that involves the use of violence. In the ICVS, robbery is defined by the question, "Has anyone taken something from you by using force or threatening you or tried to do so?" It is a well-established fact that robberies at gun- or knifepoint are especially traumatizing for victims, much more so than cases of pickpocketing. We will focus our discussion on these most severe cases of robbery.

Figure 3.11 shows regional victimization rates for robbery.

Many robberies are committed by groups of perpetrators. On average, about 6 in 10 said that more than one offender was involved. Something was actually stolen in about half of the cases. Robbery victims were asked whether the offender(s) carried a weapon of some sort. In the fifth round of the ICVS, on average, more than a third of victims (38%) in main cities said the offender(s) did—an increase compared to the

❖ **Figure 3.11**   Percentages of the Public Victimized by Robbery in the Course of One Year, by World Region

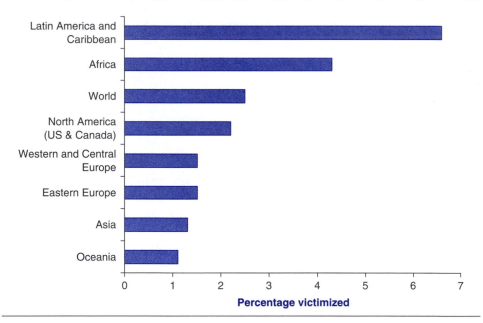

Source: ICVS, 1996–2005.

findings in previous sweeps (Van Dijk, Van Kesteren, & Smit, 2007). In 18.6% of robberies, a knife was carried, and in 12.4% of robberies, the perpetrator carried a gun.

By far the highest rates for robbery were observed in Latin America (7% on a yearly basis). The risk for individual citizens to be victimized by robbery is three times higher in this region than the global average. This makes the crime of street robbery one of the defining elements of the crime profile of Latin America. Robberies in Latin America are often carried out with the use of a gun. In Brazil, for example, more than half of all robberies are at gunpoint, and in Mexico, a third are. In Argentina, 13% of robberies were at gunpoint. In Latin American countries, so-called "express robberies"—named after American Express credit cards—have become a significant new trend: In such cases, victims are held at gun- or knifepoint until they provide some form of ransom, often by drawing money from an automatic bank teller machine (e.g., using their American Express cards).

Robbery risks are also comparatively high in urban areas in Africa. In Johannesburg (South Africa), almost half of robberies were at gunpoint. The overall prevalence of robberies is lower in Africa than in Latin America. As said, in Latin American countries, robberies are more commonly carried out with the use of guns. Availability of guns across Latin America may explain higher rates of robberies in the region. In North America, robbery rates are twice as high in the United States (2.3%) as they are in Canada (1.0%). A quarter of robberies in New York (United States) are at gunpoint, compared to 13% in Canada in urban areas. Differential gun ownership might be one of the factors determining these differences.

In Europe, Asia, and Oceania, the risk of being robbed remains below 2% per year everywhere and can therefore be regarded as a rare event. On average, 5% of robberies in cities in these regions are at gunpoint. The typical case of robbery in these regions is a case of bag snatching. These low rates of robbery, especially of robberies at gunpoint, in Europe, Asia, and Oceania coincide with moderately low rates for violent crimes, such as assaults or homicides, as will be shown in the next chapter. Table 3.4 shows country rates for robbery.

Robbery has reached crisis levels in the main cities of Costa Rica, Argentina, Colombia, Paraguay, Bolivia, and Brazil with more than 5 in every 100 persons victimized per year. People living or staying in several southern and eastern African cities are also especially at risk to be robbed. Moderately high levels of robbery are found in southern Europe (Spain and France). The latter two countries are the main holiday destinations in Europe. High prevalence of robberies should be of concern to tourists, who happen to be prime targets of street robberies around sights and recreational areas. Moderately high rates are also observed in central eastern Europe (Estonia, Poland, and Russia). In these countries as well, tourists are especially at risk. Countries with low robbery rates can be found in northern Europe, including the Netherlands and Austria and across Asia. Inhabitants' risk of being robbed in most Asian countries seems comparatively remote. Figures 3.12 and 3.13 show the global and European maps.

❖ Table 3.4   World Ranking of Countries According to Victimization of the Public in Urban Areas by Robbery in the Course of One Year, Rank Number, and Percentage of Victims per Year

Fifteen Countries With the Highest Rates								
1	Tanzania*	16.4	6	Colombia	8.6	11	Bolivia	6.6
2	Tunisia*	13.8	7	Egypt, Arab Rep.*	8.4	12	South Africa	5.5
3	Costa Rica	10.0	8	Mozambique	7.6	13	China*	5.3
4	Argentina	10.0	9	Peru	7.4	14	Brazil	5.2
5	Papua, New Guinea	9.8	10	Paraguay	6.7	15	Namibia	5.0

Fifteen Countries With Medium-High Rates								
22	Albania	2.9	46	Slovak Republic	1.2	51	New Zealand	1.1
25	Belgium	2.5	47	France	1.2	54	Netherlands	1.1
28	Russian Federation	2.4	48	Denmark	1.2	55	Australia	1.1
29	United States	2.3	49	Germany	1.2	56	Norway	1.0
36	Cambodia	1.8	50	Macedonia, FYR	1.1	57	Canada	1.0

Fifteen Countries With the Lowest Rates								
58	Panama	0.9	63	Iceland	0.7	68	Czech Republic	0.5
59	Turkey	0.9	64	Sweden	0.7	69	Hong Kong, China	0.4
60	Romania	0.8	65	Greece	0.7	70	Japan	0.4
61	Austria	0.8	66	Croatia	0.6	71	Korea, Rep.	0.3
62	Italy	0.7	67	Indonesia	0.5	72	Philippines	0.3

Source: ICVS, 1992, 1996–2005, latest survey available.

*Countries with data from ICVS, 1992.

Kidnapping

The phenomenon of kidnapping has reportedly grown considerably in the past decade, most notably in Latin America but also in parts of the Middle East, Asia, and Africa. The practice of kidnapping itself, which consists of unlawfully detaining one or more persons against their will for the purpose of demanding for their liberation an economic gain or other material benefit, or in order to oblige someone to do or abstain from doing something, has traumatic implications for victims and their families. A growing tendency is for organized-crime groups to resort to kidnapping, especially kidnapping for the purpose of extortion, as a method of accumulating capital or collecting debts.

While it remains difficult to give a clear indication of the overall level of kidnappings across the globe, reports from several countries most affected by the crime suggest that there may be an estimated 20,000 to 30,000 kidnappings every year, with notable increases in several countries.[12] It is estimated that serious cases of kidnapping reported across the globe have increased significantly over the past several years.[13] In

❖ **Figure 3.12**   World Map of Street Robbery (around 2000)

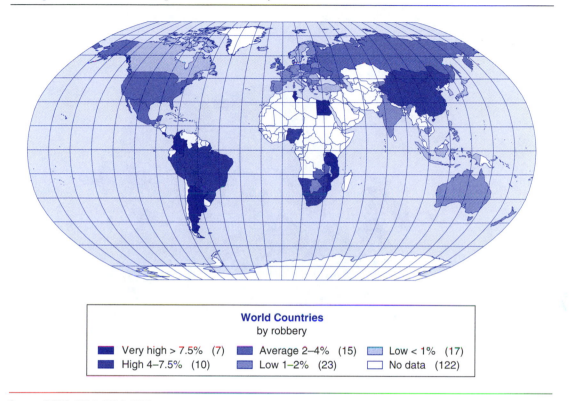

World Countries
by robbery

■ Very high > 7.5% (7)	■ Average 2–4% (15)	■ Low < 1% (17)
■ High 4–7.5% (10)	■ Low 1–2% (23)	□ No data (122)

Source: ICVS, 1992, 1996–2005.

Colombia, where kidnapping with extortion has assumed dramatic proportions over the past decade, successes in countering the problem are now being reported. There was a decline from 1,468 reported cases in 2003 to 746 reported cases in 2004.[14]

Lack or inaccuracy of reporting is a key impediment to assessing the true extent and nature of the problem. There are various reasons including the following three: (1) Many victims do not report their kidnapping because they are afraid of potential retaliation or they suspect that local police are implicated (Pelton, 2003). (2) A substantial percentage of kidnappings in some jurisdictions is conducted between or within organized-crime groups and thus are not brought to the attention of the authorities. (3) Finally, in many circumstances, kidnappings are resolved quietly through the payment of the ransom under the condition of not reporting the incident to the authorities.

Data on kidnapping have been collected by the Eighth UN Crime Survey, collecting data on 2001 and 2002. Thirty-five countries reported on such crime, thus showing the limited availability of official statistics in this respect. Furthermore, some additional statistics on kidnapping were available through a survey conducted by UNODC in 2003, thus bringing the total of responding countries to 49.[15]

❖ **Figure 3.13** European Map of Street Robbery (Around 2000)

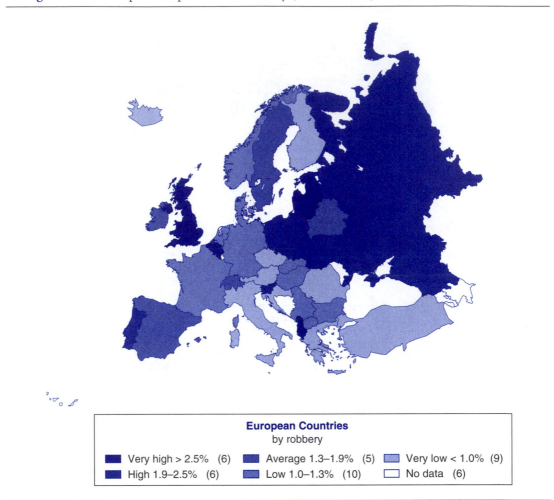

European Countries
by robbery

■ Very high > 2.5% (6)   ■ Average 1.3–1.9% (5)   □ Very low < 1.0% (9)
■ High 1.9–2.5% (6)   ■ Low 1.0–1.3% (10)   □ No data (6)

Source: ICVS, 1996–2005.

As with all police-recorded crime statistics, kidnapping statistics can at best give a tentative impression of regional distribution of risks that ought to be followed up by further research. At the regional level, the highest rates were observed in Africa, followed by the Americas, Europe, and Asia. Fourteen countries showed rates of police-recorded kidnappings of above 1 per 100,000 people. According to media reports, kidnapping has reached crisis levels in Haiti, where ordinary middle-class families and their children have increasingly become targets (*The Economist*, June, 18, 2005).

The Heavy Crime Burden of the Business Sector

Victimization through common crimes is usually associated with the public at large. In reality, the business sector is a prime target group of many forms of property crime.

Crimes committed against businesses are not accurately reflected in police figures for the same reason as other crimes. To collect better information on commercial victimization across countries, a special survey was launched. The International Crime Business Survey (ICBS) was carried out in 1992 among, initially, samples of retailers in nine European countries, Australia, and South Africa (Mirrlees-Black & Ross, 1995; Naudé, 1994; Naudé, Prinsloo, & Martins, 1999; Van Dijk & Terlouw, 1996; Walker, 1994). The questionnaire was modeled after the ICVS and contained a similar range of common crimes.[16] Table 3.5 presents an overview of the main findings of the first survey with regard to retailers.

The results show that most retail businesses are regularly victimized by common crime. Victimization percentages vary across countries. Rates are significantly higher in South Africa (not included for technical reasons). The lowest rates are found in Switzerland and Italy.

The corporate victimization percentages are many times higher than those of private persons. This is not only true for theft (e.g., shoplifting) but for burglary as well. On the basis of the survey, Mirrlees-Black and Ross estimated that the retail and manufacturing industries in the United Kingdom suffered some 148,000 burglaries in 1993 (Mawby, 2001). Studies of the total costs of crime have indicated that the total damages resulting from property crime of the corporate sector surpass those of the public at large in the Netherlands (Van Dijk, Sagel-Grande, & Toornvliet, 2002). Using Australian data, Mayhew (2003) estimated that commercial burglaries account for 18% of all burglaries and 32% of the total costs.

The ranking of countries according to level of private victimization and that of commercial victimization is largely in agreement (Van Dijk & Terlouw, 1996). Car thefts, for example, are more common in South Africa, the United Kingdom, Australia, and Italy on both counts. Both domestic and commercial burglaries are most

❖ **Table 3.5**   Percentages of Retailers Victimized by Common Crimes Over the Past Year in Eight Countries

Country	Burglary	Theft of Company Vehicles	Total Theft by Persons	Fraud by Personnel	Fraud by Outsiders	Robbery	Assault
Netherlands	34.7%	3.0%	66.4%	3.0%	11.3%	4.4%	11.0%
Germany	28.7%	3.1%	63.5%	3.1%	27.6%	4.6%	5.7%
France	31.6%	9.4%	61.3%	1.3%	42.3%	5.2%	7.3%
Switzerland	24.9%	1.5%	60.5%	1.3%	13.6%	1.5%	3.4%
Czech Republic	40.0%	4.7%	72.3%	6.0%	21.2%	5.6%	10.3%
United Kingdom	36.9%	10.0%	61.7%	2.5%	21.0%	4.0%	17.6%
Hungary	35.9%	1.5%	83.0%	2.9%	11.2%	4.2%	22.6%
Italy	14.4%	9.1%	44.5%	1.6%	24.7%	1.4%	1.0%

Source: ICBS, 1992–1993.

prevalent in South Africa, the Czech Republic, Australia, and the United Kingdom. Italy is a comparatively nonviolent country according to both the ICVS and the ICBS. This is an important finding since it suggests that country rankings based on ICVS results can be generalized to rankings of volume crime across the board.

With funding from the Dutch Ministry of Development Cooperation, the surveys were replicated among small and medium-sized businesses in nine central-eastern European cities in 2000, including but not limited to retailers.[17] In order to enhance the significance of the study for the region, the questionnaire was revised and extended with questions focusing on complex crimes such as corruption of public officials. Results on complex crimes will be presented in Chapter 5 and Chapter 7. The results of the survey on common crimes in eastern Europe cannot be compared with those of the first ICBS due to changes in the questionnaire. Victimization rates in eastern Europe seem generally somewhat lower than in western Europe, with the exception of fraud by employees. Twelve percent of businesses reported fraud by employees, a much higher rate than what was found in the western European countries and Australia. The highest fraud-by-employee rates were found in Minsk, Belarus (24%), and Tirana, Albania (18%).

Recently international accounting firms have taken an interest in crime surveying. The most recent victimization survey of companies across the world indicates that 45% of all respondents had suffered from some form of economic crime in the course of the past 2 years. These global results indicate an increase on previous surveys, which holds across regions (PricewaterhouseCoopers, 2005).[18] Prevalence rates remained the highest by far among companies in Africa. A similar survey of global companies in 2004 found that just under one half of respondents (47%) had experienced a significant fraud in the past year (Ernst & Young, 2004). According to these two surveys, half or more of the perpetrators of economic crimes are company insiders (managers or staff). Where the perpetrator could be established, organized-crime groups were believed to be responsible in 6% of such cases.[19]

Costs for Businesses

Victimization surveys among households are increasingly supplemented by business victimization surveys, but the latter have not yet yielded much internationally comparable data on a global scale. The surveys among business leaders of the World Economic Forum provide a subjective indicator of the extent of business victimization by common crime through the inclusion of a question about the business costs of common crime and violence: Do common crime and violence (e.g., street muggings and firms being looted) impose significant costs on businesses? The item covers the business sector's equivalent of the household questions on burglary and street violence in the ICVS.

The results show that business executives in Latin America and Africa are most concerned about common crime. Medium to high rates of concern are found in Europe and Asia. Concerns about crime are lowest in North America and Oceania. The perceptions of business leaders of risks to their businesses roughly mirror those of individual persons concerning the risks to their households, as measured in the ICVS. The ranking of countries on both rates is very similar. Somewhat surprising is the comparatively high concern among Asian business executives, given the relatively low crime rates in most Asian countries according to the ICVS.

Results from surveys among the business sector demonstrate how critically important they are to obtaining a comprehensive picture of the total burden of property crime of society. The results of commercially conducted surveys also point to the need for more standardization of instruments and greater transparency regarding country results (data are often not publicly available). Having said this, the growing interest of the business and financial services sector in funding surveying victimization by crime across countries is a boon for the epidemiology of crime, to be welcomed by the community of criminologists. In Chapters 7 and 8, surveys among business executives will be used extensively as a principal novel source of information on organized crime and other complex types of crime.

In the next chapter, an overview will be given of the levels of violent crimes across the world. And in Chapter 5, some general conclusions will be drawn on the determinants of common crimes across the world. In Chapter 6, we will discuss trends in common crime over time and regional profiles.

SUMMARY POINTS/IN CONCLUSION

• Results of the ICVS 1996–2005 on 78 countries from all world regions show that globally, one in four inhabitants of urban areas are hit by common crime once or more per year. Over a 5-year period, the average victimization risk is two in three. Criminal victimization must be regarded as a statistically normal aspect of life in today's world. The numbers reported by the public in the surveys are more than 10 times higher than those recorded by the police. Only a small part of these billions of victimizations per year ever show up in police statistics of recorded crime.

• According to the surveys, levels of common crime are highest among the urban population in Africa and Latin America and lowest in Asia. Rates of the other parts of the world are near the global average. Overall victimization rates in the United States, Canada, and Australia are lower than in many western European countries.

• Victimization rates for specific types of property crime show more variation across regions and countries. Burglary rates vary between a high of 8% per year in Africa and a low of less than 2% per year in North America (Canada and the United States). In defiance of common perceptions, burglary rates in the United States are much below those in most western European countries and even lower than those in Asia. In terms of household burglary, the United States has become a low-crime country.

• The distribution of robbery rates across world regions also shows huge variation. Rates of robbery are the highest by far in Latin America (6.5% per year) and Africa (4.5%). Robbery rates are below 2% in Australia, Asia, eastern Europe, and western and central Europe. The rate of North America is close to the world average of 2.5% (United States: 2.3%).

• A small minority of robberies are committed by perpetrators carrying weapons: On average, 18.6% of perpetrators carry a knife, and 12.4% carry a gun. Robberies are most often carried out at gunpoint in Latin American countries (Brazil, over 50%; Mexico, 30%) and in South Africa (47%). Among developed countries, the United States stands out with 27% of robberies at gunpoint in New York City, compared to 13% in Canadian cities and even lower percentages in western European and Asian cities (on average, 5%).

• Rates of pickpocketing and consumer fraud each show uniquely different distributions. For pickpocketing, rates are highest in Africa (6.7%),

Asia (6.6%), Latin America (6.6%), and eastern Europe (6.6%). Rates are considerably lower across the rest of the Western world (Australia, 1.6%; North America, 3.1%; and western and central Europe, 3.6%). For pickpocketing, the high rates of Asia and eastern Europe and the low rates in North America and Australia stand out. The low rate of pickpocketing in the United States contrasts with its comparatively high rate of robbery.

- Rates for consumer fraud are by far the highest in eastern Europe and the lowest in Australia, North America, and western and central Europe. The distribution of rates suggests special problems with consumer fraud in countries with economies in transition where free markets are not yet well regulated and consumer protection is underdeveloped.

- The distribution of car-related crime is the reverse of that of other types of property crimes, with the highest rates found in Australia and North America. However, if rates are recalculated for car owners only, the familiar distribution reappears with rates highest in Africa and Latin America. The high rates of victimization among the general public in Australia and North America are obviously related to the higher prevalence of car ownership in these countries. This issue will be taken up again in Chapter 5.

- Levels of victimization for all types of property crime except pickpocketing are comparatively low in Asia. This is true for both developing countries in the region such as Indonesia and Cambodia and for developed countries such as Japan and Hong Kong/China.

- Rates of victimization by crime of the business sector found in special surveys among this target group show distributions similar to the ones found in the ICVS, suggesting that the ranking of regions and countries on the basis of the ICVS results concerning households can be generalized to common crime in general. Asian businesspeople, however, perceive relatively large losses from common crime.

- One of the most worrying trends is the increase in several developing countries of new types of property crime with the use of force besides robberies at gunpoint. These new types of violent property crime include car hijacking, home invasions, and kidnapping for the purpose of extortion.

Notes

1. In the first four sweeps of the survey, a question was included about car vandalism. To shorten the questionnaire, this item was deleted in 2005. Overall victimization rates of surveys conducted up to 2000 refer to victimization by any of 11 crimes. In comparisons with results of later surveys, overall victimization rates have been recalculated for 10 crimes only.

2. Analyses have also confirmed, as discussed in Chapter 2, the broad agreement between the ranking of countries according to rates of victimizations, adjusted for reporting to the police, and rankings on the basis of police-recorded crimes (Van Dijk, Mayhew, & Killias, 1990).

3. One of the most straightforward methods to validate victimization survey results is the reverse record check whereby incidents reported by respondents to interviewers are subsequently traced back in police records. In studies in the United States and the Netherlands, 68% and 81%, respectively, could be traced back in the police records (Schneider, 1978; Van Dijk, 1992).

4. Rates for the United States in 2005 are based on a booster sample of the population of New York City ($n = 1,000$). Australia is represented by a booster sample of Sydney ($n = 1,500$) and Switzerland by a booster sample of Zurich ($n = 500$). Canadian rates are based on a a subsample of 765 respondents residing in cities with 100,000 or more inhabitants. Similarly rates of New Zealand, Japan, Mexico, and Bulgaria are based on urban samples (see Appendix A).

All other countries, samples were used from the capital city, except in Brazil, where samples from Rio and São Paulo were used.

5. In the older sweeps of the ICVS, no booster samples were drawn from capital cities of developed countries, and trend analyses are therefore possible using only the national data.

6. Brazil is represented with rates from Rio de Janeiro and São Paulo.

7. Data on Papua New Guinea are available only in printed form and cannot be used for special computations.

8. As will be discussed in later chapters, different pictures emerge when the prevalence of homicides and uncommon crimes such as organized crime and corruption are included in the equation.

9. Police-recorded burglary, as recorded by the UN Crime Surveys, was highest in Oceania, while the ICVS results indicate that the most affected regions were Africa and Latin America, which in turn showed the lowest rates in police data. As discussed in the previous chapter, rates of police-recorded burglaries give no useful information on the actual prevalence of crimes such as burglary across regions or countries.

10. Surveys of the World Economic Forum (2003).

11. Car hijacking rates were much lower in Botswana (0.3%) and Namibia (0.1%).

12. See the report of the UN Secretary-General, *International Cooperation in the Prevention, Combating, and Elimination of Kidnapping and in Providing Assistance to Victims,* Commission on Crime Prevention and Criminal Justice, 13th Session, Vienna, May 2004, E/CN.15/2004/7.

13. This is according to insurance company reports.

14. Consolidated results for 2004 of the Democratic Security Policy as presented by the Minister of Defense. (Data supplied by the Colombian Permanent Mission in Vienna, January 2005)

15. Based on Ecosoc resolution 2002/16. See E/CN.15/2003/7, *International Cooperation in the Prevention, Combating, and Elimination of Kidnapping and in Providing Assistance to Victims.*

16. A more detailed description of the history and methodology of the ICBS is given in Appendix A.

17. The survey was conducted by UNICRI in nine central-eastern European cities within the framework of the project Assessing Violence, Corruption, and Organized Crime in Eastern-Central European Countries (see the Methodology section in Appendix A for details).

18. PricewaterhouseCoopers (2005), Global Economic Crime Survey 2005, in collaboration with Martin Luther University, Economy and Crime Research Center. Comparisons with previous surveys are hazardous due to significant changes in both the sampling design and questionnaires used. No results on individual countries are in the public domain.

19. Ernst & Young (2004), *Fraud: The Unmanaged Risk.*

Patterns of Violent Crime

Homicide

For many people, murder or homicide is the quintessential crime. In times of peace, homicides in most parts of the world are very rare events. In some African countries, surveys have started collecting information on murders that have occurred in the family and/or that the interviewed person may have witnessed. Fourteen percent of respondents to the National Victims of Crime Survey in South Africa (2003) said they had at least once during their lifetime witnessed a murder (Burton, Du Plessis, Leggett, Louw, Mistry, & Vuuren, 2004). In most other parts of the world, percentages of the public exposed to homicide are much smaller.

Homicide during times of peace can be subdivided into two broad categories: those committed as a result of interpersonal conflicts, often under the influence of alcohol, and those committed for instrumental purposes by gangs or organized-crime groups.

It goes without saying that data on committed homicides are not available through victim surveys. Fortunately, and as discussed in Chapter 2, homicide represents one of the few types of crime for which data from police and health administrations are available and can be used for tentative comparisons at the international level. This is due to a relatively uniform definition and to relatively high reporting and recording rates across all countries (Zimring & Hawkins, 1997). As pointed out by Altbeker (2005), police-recorded homicide rates suffer to some extent from the same flaws of underreporting and poor recording as other police-recorded crime statistics. In countries where security forces are among the main perpetrators of violent crimes, reporting and recording will be low. In many developing countries, administrative systems and communication infrastructures of police services preclude proper recording of even the most serious types of crime.

Statistics on police-recorded homicides are recorded through the United Nations Crime Surveys. The other main source of information is the health statistics collected by the World Health Organization through hospital surveys (WHO, 2002). The WHO statistics reflect the views of medical doctors on the causes of death of hospitalized patients and are independent from police administrations. Comparisons of the country rates according to the UN surveys and the WHO revealed a reasonable degree of agreement (Rubin & Walker, 2004).

However, an analysis of rates over a 16-year period showed WHO rates to be on average 15% higher (Shaw, Van Dijk, & Rhomberg, 2003). The explanation for this higher count of the WHO might be that hospitals classify as homicides cases of assault resulting in death whereby the perpetrator did not intend to apply lethal force. Further analysis revealed that the higher counts of WHO do not occur in developed countries. The discrepancies are limited to middle-income countries (WHO numbers 19% higher) and developing countries (WHO numbers 45% higher). The latter finding suggests that the main reason for the differences is that in developing countries, even for as serious a crime as homicide, a significant proportion of crimes committed is never reported to the police or never recorded. In many developing countries, even police-recorded homicides have their dark numbers.

The UN surveys of police-recorded homicides show a global average of 7 homicides per 100,000 inhabitants per year in recent years. The WHO counted for 2000 over half a million homicide-related deaths, or 8.8 per 100,000. Males account for 77% of all homicides and have rates that are three times those of females (13.6 and 4, respectively). The highest rates are found among males ages 15–29 years (19.4 per 100,000).

For the purpose of this publication, the latest available national homicide rates were taken from the sixth, seventh, and eighth UN surveys, covering the period 1990 to 2002 (most rates relate to the period 1998 to 2002). To increase coverage of countries, data were added from the WHO data set for 12 countries not participating in any of the UN surveys. In the cases where these were rates of middle- or lower-income countries, statistical adjustments were made to achieve better comparability with the UN rates of police-recorded homicides. Through this procedure, homicide rates could be calculated for 110 countries.

Figure 4.1 shows subregional rates for committed homicides. Homicide rates are highest in southern Africa, which in this respect is in a category of its own with rates above 30 per 100,000 population or three times the world average. Southern Africa is followed by Central America, South America, the Caribbean, and Eastern Europe, while other regions show much lower rates.

The lowest levels reported were in North Africa, the Middle East/Southwest Asia, western and central Europe, and East and Southeast Asia. Homicide rates in North Africa appear to be the lowest on earth with many countries maintaining rates below 1 per 100,000 inhabitants (see for country details below).[1] Apart from North Africa, such low rates can be found only in some parts of western Europe.

The differences between different parts of the Western world are particularly noteworthy. North America, here represented by the United States and Canada, stands out with higher rates than both western Europe and Oceania (Australia and New Zealand). In terms of homicides, Canada is more similar to western Europe than to the United

❖ **Figure 4.1**   Homicides per 100,000 Population, per World Subregion (2002)

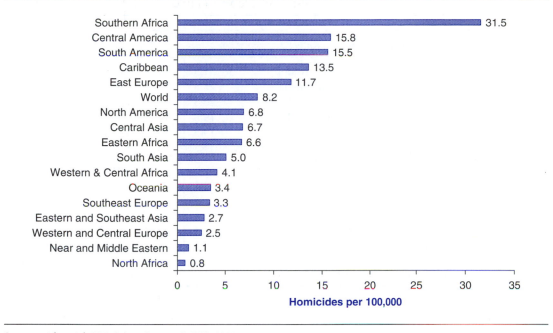

Sources: 6th to 8th UN Crime Surveys; WHO, 2002.

States and Mexico. If Mexico were included in the rates for North America, the regional rate would be even higher. Eastern Europe contrasts starkly with western Europe, with countries such as Russia (19.8) showing extremely high rates. High homicide rates in the former Soviet countries have also been observed in previous statistical overviews (Aromaa et al., 2003).

Previous analyses of data from Europe and North America have shown that the levels of various forms of violent crime are intercorrelated, although not strongly (Van Dijk, 1999). The high homicide rates observed in (sub-Saharan) Africa and the Americas are accompanied by high levels of robberies, assaults, and sexual assaults (see below).

National Homicide Rates

Country rates for homicides are collected through the UN crime survey, supplemented by data from the WHO report on Health and Violence (WHO, 2002). Table 4.1 shows results for selected individual countries.

Figures 4.2 and 4.3 show the full data set in the form of world and European maps of homicide. The European map reveals a consistent increase of homicide rates from the west to the east. The only outliers are Portugal and Switzerland.

❖ Table 4.1   World Ranking of Countries According to Rates of Homicide per 100,000
Population in 2002 or Latest Available Year (110 countries)

Fifteen Countries With Highest Homicide Rates								
1	Swaziland	88.6	6	El Salvador	31.5	11	Bahamas	14.9
2	Colombia	62.7	7	Guatemala	25.5	12	Kazakhstan	14.5
3	South Africa	47.5	8	Puerto Rico	20.6	13	Mexico	13.0
4	Jamaica	33.7	9	Russian Fed.	19.8	14	Ecuador	13.0
5	Venezuela, RB	33.1	10	Brazil	19.5	15	Paraguay	12.0
Fifteen Countries With Medium-High Homicide Rates								
16	Estonia	10.4	56	Turkey	3.3	80	Canada	1.7
26	Thailand	8.5	56	Switzerland	2.9	89	Italy	1.1
44	United States	5.6	59	Australia	2.8	90	Germany	1.1
46	Cuba	5.3	67	Sweden	2.5	92	Indonesia	1.0
53	India	3.7	73	United Kingdom	2.0	96	Netherlands	1.0
Fourteen Countries With Low Homicide Rates								
97	Bahrain	1.0	102	Austria	0.8	107	Israel	0.5
98	Jordan	1.0	103	Greece	0.8	108	Morocco	0.5
99	Saudi Arabia	0.9	104	Oman	0.6	109	Cyprus	0.3
100	Singapore	0.9	105	Hong Kong	0.6	110	Myanmar	0.2
101	Luxembourg	0.9	106	Japan	0.5			

Sources: 6th to 8th UN Crime Surveys; WHO, 2002.

Assault

The crime category of assault and threat is defined in the ICVS as personal attacks or threats, either by a stranger or a relative or friend, without the purpose of stealing. It is another "contact" crime, and although physical consequences may be minor in most cases, it may very well have important emotional repercussions for victims, especially if a weapon was used. Threats include both verbal threats, which are seen as less serious by the victims, and threats with the use of a weapon, which are seen as very serious.

Assault on women is more likely to be domestic in nature than assault on men. In a third of the cases of violence against women, the offender was known at least by name to the victim. In one of five of the cases, the crime was committed in the victim's own house. Figure 4.4 shows the regional rates of victimization for assaults. Threats have been excluded because of their heterogeneous composition, ranging from mere verbal threats to threats with the use of guns or knives.

❖ **Figure 4.2**   World Map of Homicide (Around 2000)

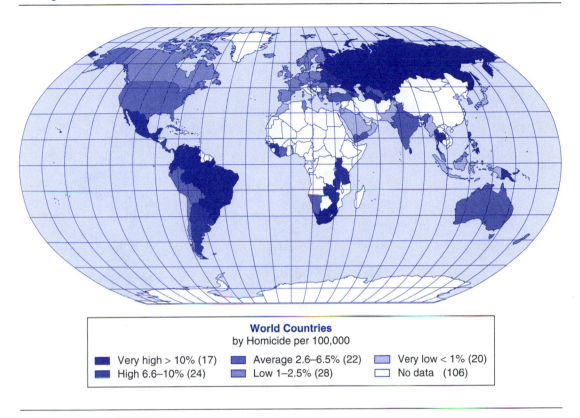

World Countries
by Homicide per 100,000

- ■ Very high > 10% (17)   ■ Average 2.6–6.5% (22)   ■ Very low < 1% (20)
- ■ High 6.6–10% (24)   ■ Low 1–2.5% (28)   □ No data   (106)

Sources: UNODC and WHO, 2002.

The region showing the highest risks on this question is Africa. Levels used to be comparatively high in Latin America in previous rounds, but this is no longer true for the countries participating in 2005. Moderately high rates are found in Oceania and North America. Relatively low rates are shown by Europe, Asia, and eastern Europe.[2] The distribution of rates of assault does not match that of homicide rates, which are, besides in sub-Saharan Africa, the highest in Latin America and eastern Europe and comparatively low in Oceania (see Figure 4.1).

In the fifth ICVS, 22.6% of the perpetrators of threats and assaults in main cities had used a weapon: in 9.4%, a knife; in 5.7%, a gun (Van Dijk, Van Kesteren, & Smit, 2007). The percentage of gun attacks was highest in the Brazilian cities Rio de Janeiro and São Paulo (39% and 35%, respectively), in Mexico (16%), and in South Africa (Johannesburg, 13%). The percentage of gun attacks was 10% in New York City, which compares unfavorably with percentages, on average, below 3% in cities in western Europe, Canada (4%), and Australia (3%). The distribution of gun attacks across countries mirrors that of robberies at gunpoint.

❖ Figure 4.3   European Map of Homicide (Around 2000)

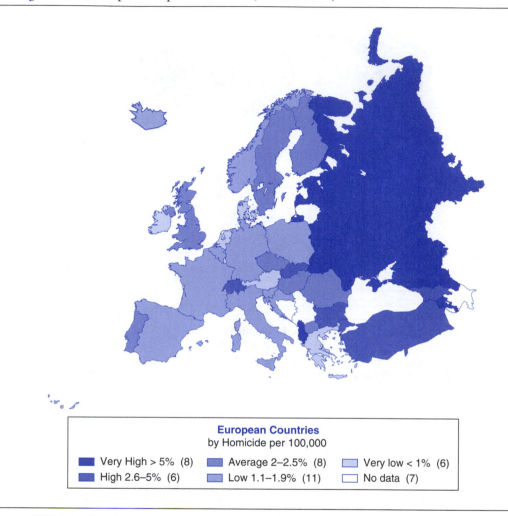

European Countries
by Homicide per 100,000

◼ Very High > 5% (8)   ◼ Average 2–2.5% (8)   ◻ Very low < 1% (6)
◼ High 2.6–5% (6)   ◼ Low 1.1–1.9% (11)   ◻ No data (7)

Sources: UNODC and WHO, 2002.

Hate Crimes in Western Europe

In several countries, concerns have been raised about the extent and possible increase of ideologically motivated personal violence ("hate crimes'"). In the international media, incidents of hate crime against new immigrants have been reported from Moscow in Russia to Los Angeles in the United States. Racial tensions were also at the root of severe riots in French inner cities in the winter of 2005. In the European component of the ICVS 2005, respondents of the 15 old EU member states were asked whether in 2004 they or family members had fallen victim to any crime

❖ **Figure 4.4**   Percentages of the Public Victimized by Assaults in Urban Areas, by World Region

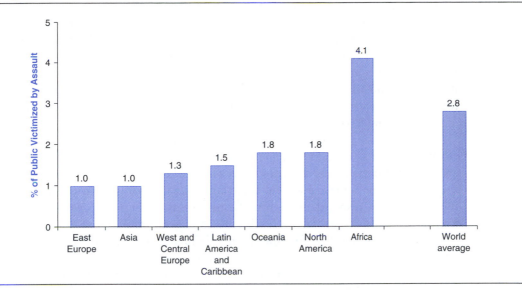

Sources: ICVS, 1996–2005.

❖ **Table 4.2**   World Ranking of Countries According to Victimization by Assault

Fifteen Countries With the Highest Rates					
1	South Africa	5.6	6	Mozambique	2.9	11	New Zealand	2.4
2	Zimbabwe	5.0	7	Colombia	2.9	12	Serbia and Montenegro	2.3
3	Swaziland	3.8	8	Namibia	2.5	13	Mongolia	2.1
4	Zambia	3.1	9	Kyrgyz Republic	2.5	14	Lesotho	2.0
5	Iceland	3.0	10	United Kingdom	2.5	15	Latvia	2.0

Fifteen Countries With Medium-High Rates					
17	Canada	1.9	28	Nigeria	1.5	38	Czech Republic	1.1
18	United States	1.7	31	Estonia	1.3	39	Poland	1.1
20	Finland	1.7	35	Russian Federation	1.1	44	India	0.9
21	Costa Rica	1.6	36	France	1.1	47	Georgia	0.9
25	Denmark	1.6	37	Spain	1.1	48	Argentina	0.8

Fifteen Countries With the Lowest Rates					
50	Austria	0.7	55	Greece	0.6	60	Hong Kong, China	0.3
51	Albania	0.7	56	Korea, Rep.	0.5	61	Italy	0.2
52	Romania	0.6	57	Hungary	0.5	62	Turkey	0.2
53	Indonesia	0.6	58	Azerbaijan	0.4	63	Philippines	0.1
54	Slovak Republic	0.6	59	Portugal	0.3	64	Mexico	0.1

Source: ICVS, 1996–2005.

"because or partly because of their nationality, race or color, religious belief, or sexual orientation."

The results allow a first rough assessment in comparative perspective of the extent of such hate crimes in the EU as perceived by respondents (Van Kesteren, 2006). On average, 3% of the European inhabitants have experienced hate crimes. The extent of hate crime per country shows great variation. Percentages of such victims are highest in France, Denmark, the United Kingdom, and the Benelux countries. Lowest rates are found in Italy, Portugal, Greece, and Austria. The level of hate crimes is about average in Germany and Sweden.

Although the definition of "hate crimes" is not limited to crimes motivated by ethnic hatred, its prevalence in countries might be related to the presence of immigrant communities. Respondents were asked whether they consider themselves, their parents, or someone else in their family as immigrants. In the 15 countries together, 7% of respondents define themselves as immigrants, 5% as children of immigrants, and 3% as having family members who immigrated. In total, 15% of the respondents qualified for the broadly defined status of immigrant. We subsequently looked at victimization by hate crimes among immigrants. The results of our analysis confirm that victimization by hate crimes is strongly related to immigrant status. Of those indicating they are immigrants, 10% report that they have fallen victim to hate crimes. The victimization rate among nonimmigrants is 2%. Countries with proportionally larger immigrant communities tend to show higher rates of hate crimes ($r = .46$).

The analysis of victimization rates of those indicating a religious affiliation showed insignificant results. Those practicing a religion showed similar victimization rates for hate crimes as those who do not. Within the immigrant communities, however, religion was positively related to victimization. Of those of immigrant status who are religious, 12% had been victimized, compared to 9% of those who are not. This result indicates that in the European Union, Muslim immigrants are especially exposed to victimization by hate crimes.

Sexual Assault/Rape

Victimization by sexual violence is a gendered phenomenon. Women are more at risk to be victimized by both intimate partners and nonpartners. In the first four rounds of the ICVS, the question on sexual victimization was put only to female respondents because male respondents had responded frivolously to it in pilot tests run in the Netherlands. In the ICVS 2005, the question was asked from all respondents in the European Union, Canada, Australia, and the United States but not elsewhere. The results confirm that victimization by sexual incidents is three to four times more common among women than among men. Victimization by rapes or physical sexual attacks was rarely reported by male respondents at all (less than 0.1%, on average).

One of the most prevalent subcategories of sexual victimization by nonpartners is sexual harassment in the workplace, educational institutions, and in sports. A subcategory of the most serious forms of sexual violence against women is rapes in the context of armed conflicts. It is estimated that between 250,000 and 500,000 women were raped during the 1994 genocide in Rwanda, between 20,000 and 50,000 in Bosnia in the early 1990s, and around 200,000 during the conflict in Bangladesh in 1971 (United Nations, 2006).

Sexual crime is one of the types of crime with the largest dark numbers. Measuring sexual incidents is also extremely difficult in victimization surveys, since perceptions as to what is unacceptable sexual behavior may differ significantly across countries, even in the current era of increasingly globalized norms and values. Willingness to disclose such experiences to interviewers is also likely to be culture bound. The ICVS results on sexual incidents or assaults therefore cannot be taken at face value.

Analyses of ICVS data on violence, including sexual violence, against women have shown that the level of such violence shows, curiously, a curvilinear relationship with measures of gender equality. The highest rates of violence against women are found in developing countries where the social position of women is still weak. Among developing countries, a negative relationship was observed between measures of gender equality and victimization by sexual violence (Alvazzi del Frate & Patrignani, 1995). In a more comprehensive analysis of ICVS data, Finnish anthropologist Kristiina Kangaspunta found that in countries that stand at the top end of the gender equality scale, for example, countries such as the United States, Canada, Finland, and New Zealand, women report somewhat *higher* proportions of (relatively minor) incidents than the average (Kangaspunta, 2000). This finding suggests that more liberated women perceive sexually loaded incidents more often as criminal and/or are more willing to report them to interviewers in the context of a survey on criminal victimization. In light of this finding, rates of victimization by sexual incidents/crimes from developing countries should probably be seen as somewhat deflated compared to those of Western countries. ICVS data on sexual incidents must be interpreted with due caution for this possible bias.

The ICVS question on sexual offenses/incidents reads as follows: "People sometimes grab, touch, or assault others for sexual reasons in a really offensive way. This can happen either at home or elsewhere, for instance, in a pub, the street, at school, on public transport, in cinemas, on the beach, or at one's workplace. Over the past five years has anyone done this to you?" (for the calculation of victimization, only incidents occurring in the past year are considered, as explained earlier).

The ICVS question on sexual offenses is formulated fairly broadly, thus including both the most serious incidents such as rape, attempted rape, and sexual (physical) assault as well as less serious incidents. Also, the supposedly less serious sexual incidents are regarded by most victims as fairly serious—more serious than offenses such as simple thefts (Van Dijk, 1999). Globally, 2.7% of women had been victims of sexual incidents as defined in the questionnaire. The global percentage of women victimized by rapes, attempted rapes, or sexual assaults was roughly half of that.

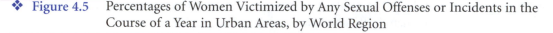

❖ Figure 4.5   Percentages of Women Victimized by Any Sexual Offenses or Incidents in the Course of a Year in Urban Areas, by World Region

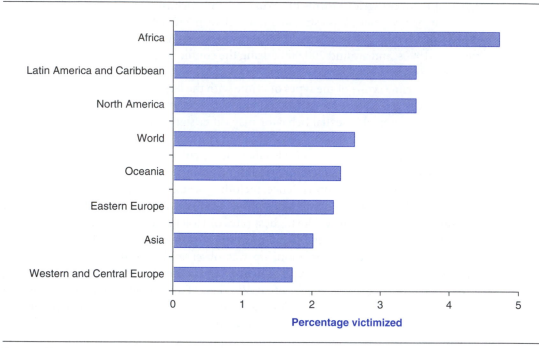

Sources: ICVS, 1996–2005.

Figure 4.5 shows the regional distribution of sexual incidents as measured by the ICVS, including the less serious incidents.[3] Victimization rates are above average in Latin America and Africa. As said, rates in Africa and Latin America, although comparatively high, might in fact be deflated by cultural attitudes among women in those countries, condoning forms of abuse by intimate partners or preventing disclosure to interviewers. The surprisingly high rates in North America (United States and Canada) might have been inflated for the opposite reason: Women in these countries might be more sensitive to such victimization and report more (minor) incidents. Table 4.3 presents details at the country level.

All countries in the top 10 are characterized by low gender equality. Other countries with relatively high rates include Finland, Denmark, the United States, the Netherlands, Canada, Switzerland, the United Kingdom, Germany, and New Zealand. Their position above many developing countries as well as southern and eastern European countries flies in the face of gendered perspectives. These countries show the highest scores on measures of gender equality. This confirms the hypothesis of Kangaspunta (2000) that ICVS-based victimization rates for sexual violence are probably somewhat inflated in countries where gender equality is most advanced compared to other countries. The measurement of sexual offenses in the framework of the ICVS is unquestionably superior to that of police statistics—which show, as discussed in Chapter 2, Canada on top—but it remains flawed and unsatisfactory.

❖ **Table 4.3**   Ranking of Countries According to Sexual Offenses or Incidents Against Women

Fifteen Countries With the Highest Rates								
1	Papua, New Guinea	11.8	6	Swaziland	6.2	11	Namibia	4.8
2	Colombia	10.2	7	Lesotho	5.7	12	Peru	4.7
3	Nigeria	8.8	8	Costa Rica	5.5	13	Serbia and Montenegro	4.6
4	India	7.0	9	Zambia	5.4	14	Finland	4.3
5	Albania	6.7	10	Botswana	5.0	15	Denmark	3.8

Fifteen Countries With Medium-High Rates								
16	United States	3.5	28	Germany	2.5	45	Austria	1.3
20	Netherlands	3.2	29	New Zealand	2.4	46	Brazil	1.3
21	Canada	3.1	36	Bolivia	1.8	49	Hong Kong, China	1.2
22	Switzerland	3.1	39	Mexico	1.7	51	Greece	1.1
25	United Kingdom	3.0	40	Japan	1.7	52	Italy	0.9

Fifteen Countries With the Lowest Rates								
58	Turkey	17.9	63	Italy	16.6	68	Japan	10.8
59	France	17.8	64	Spain	13.7	69	Portugal	9.7
60	Austria	17.2	65	Greece	13.5	70	Philippines	9.1
61	Australia	16.9	66	Croatia	12.9	71	Hong Kong, China	7.8
62	Korea, Rep.	16.7	67	Hungary	12.6	72	Azerbaijan	7.7

Sources: ICVS, 1996–2005.

Violence Against Women Revisited

In several countries, special in-depth surveys using very extensive questionnaires with more prompts to assist the respondent in remembering and reporting incidents have been carried out on violence against women, including sexual violence, following the groundbreaking Canadian survey of 1993. Several other countries have followed suit (Tjaden & Thoennes, 2000). Such dedicated surveys aim to collect information on a wider range of specific violent acts and consequently show higher victimization rates among women than the ICVS (Kangaspunta, 2000). Such surveys have now been carried out in 70 or more countries across the world in the period 1994 to 2004. Missing in this group of countries are the Arab countries except two (Egypt and Israel among its population of Palestinians).

The dedicated surveys show that between 10% and 70% of women report they have been physically assaulted by an intimate partner at least once during their life (United Nations, 2006; WHO, 2002). Globally, on average, an estimated 30% of women have been victimized by male partner violence at least once in their lifetime. One in 10 women has been a victim of intimate partner violence in the course of the past year. In a majority of cases, women are victimized by both ordinary violence and sexual violence by the same intimate partner.

Results of independently conducted, nonstandardized surveys on violence against women cannot be reliably used for comparative purposes. Problems with comparing the results of stand-alone general victimization surveys are compounded by the use of highly divergent definitions of violent behavior against women, including unwanted sexual behavior. Some questionnaires include nonphysical sexual harassment; others do not or do include it to a lesser extent. Since the methodologies used vary within world regions as much as across regions, a comparison of regional rates can still give a tentative insight into the epidemiology of violence against women across world regions. Figure 4.6 presents an overview of regional rates of women victimized by intimate partner violence over the past 12 months according to nonstandardized, dedicated surveys.

The regional rates for intimate partner violence show huge variation. Rates are highest in Arab countries ($n = 2$) and in Latin America ($n = 11$). Given low overall rates of crime and violence in the Asian region, the medium-high rates of intimate partner violence are striking. Rates are lowest in North America and western and central Europe.

❖ **Figure 4.6**   Percentages of Women, 15 Years and Older, Victimized by Violence From Intimate Partners Over the Past 12 Months

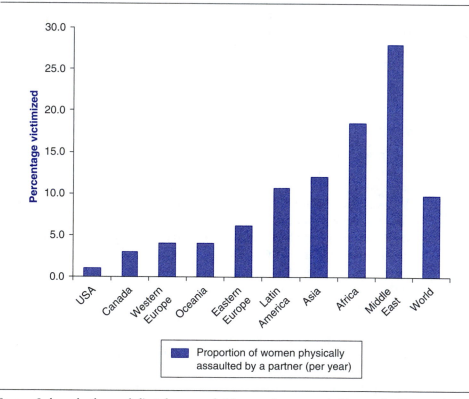

Sources: Independently run, dedicated surveys of violence against women in 72 countries (UN, 2006).

The distribution of regional rates of violence against women by intimate partners suggests that dedicated surveys about this type of crime succeed in eliminating the bias in ICVS-based results caused by underreporting in developing countries. There appears to be an even stronger negative correlation between development (and related gender equality) and violence against women than previously found in the ICVS-based results.

Toward Further Standardization

In order to develop better comparable information on violence against women, the International Violence Against Women Survey (IVAWS) has recently been launched in 10 mostly developed countries by a consortium of researchers including those from the United Nations (Nevala, 2003). The report of Switzerland's team showed that in Switzerland, 10% of women had experienced violence from partners or ex-partners over their lifespan. Comparable lifetime prevalence rates were 23% in Denmark and 37% in the Czech Republic (Killias, Simonin, & Du Pay, 2005). The Australian team reported a lifetime prevalence rate for partner violence of 32% (Mouzos & Makkai, 2004). The lifetime rate of victimization by any male violence was 57%. Results of other countries are currently being analyzed.

In 2005, the WHO published results of another standardized international survey on violence against women carried out in 10 developing countries, unfortunately using a different questionnaire than the IVAWS (WHO, 2005). Lifetime prevalence rates for partner violence in the latter study were 61% in Peru (province), 49% in Ethiopia (province), 47% in Tanzania (province), 43% in Brazil (province), 42% in Bangladesh (province), 41% in Samoa, 34% in Thailand (province), 31% in Namibia (city), 23% in Serbia (city), and 13% in Japan (city). In most cases, women experiencing physical violence had also been sexually abused.

Although their results are not strictly comparable, the two standardized surveys on violence against women confirm that globally, at least one in three women suffer from violence by a partner over their lifetime. The results also confirm our tentative conclusion that male violence against women is more prevalent in developing countries. In all countries where standardized surveys were carried out in both provincial areas and cities, prevalence rates were found to be higher in provincial areas than in cities. In this respect, violence against women seems to differ fundamentally from other types of common crime, which, as will be discussed in Chapter 5, is more prevalent in urban settings. The higher rates of intimate partner violence in provincial areas in developing countries lend support to the political position of the United Nations that violence against women is an expression of gender inequality (United Nations, 2006). Available evidence suggests that violence against women is more prevalent in less-developed countries where women possess lower social status, especially in rural areas of such countries where gender inequality is most extreme.

Child Abuse and the Cycle of Violence

No global data are available on the extent of child abuse.[4] The WHO estimates that there were 57,000 deaths attributed to homicide among children under 15 years of age in 2000 (WHO, 2002). Dedicated surveys have been carried out in 2000 in Germany among 11,000 teenagers between 14 and 16 years of age about their experiences with domestic violence. Seven percent of the sample reported to have been beaten by parents. Eight percent had seen violence between their parents, usually but not exclusively by their father against their mother (Pfeiffer, 2004). German children of divorced or separated parents reported on average even higher percentages (30%). Significantly higher percentages of violence against mothers were reported by children of immigrants, 9% among Greeks, 32% among Turks, 25% among immigrant families from Yugoslavia, and 20% among Russians. The percentages of immigrant families experiencing such violence was higher to the extent that they had resided longer in Germany, suggesting growing tensions between spouses after a longer exposure of women to German norms and values concerning gender equality.

Several studies have found links between childhood experiences with domestic violence and violent offending at later stages (National Crime Prevention, 1999). The phenomenon of second-generation effects is so common that it has been dubbed the "cycle of violence." The high percentages of teenagers who have experienced domestic violence as a child among second-generation German immigrants deserve mentioning in this respect. The WHO study, cited above, also observed that many perpetrators had witnessed the use of violence against their mothers in their youth.

In a separate report of the World Health Organization on the economic dimensions of interpersonal violence, the total costs of intimate partner violence in the United States is estimated at $12.6 billion (WHO, 2004). Child abuse is estimated to result in annual costs to the economy of $94 billion or 1% of the gross domestic product of the United States (WHO, 2004). Results on developing countries are scarce, but costs of intimate partner violence have been estimated to amount to 2% of the GDP in Chile and 1.6% in Nicaragua. In these calculations, "multiplier effects" caused by the cycle of violence are not taken into account.

SUMMARY POINTS/IN CONCLUSION

• Police and hospital records provide reasonably reliable estimates of the numbers of homicides committed. With some adjustments of the somewhat deflated rates from developing countries, comparable homicide rates per 100,000 inhabitants have been calculated on 110 countries. The global risk of homicide is fairly low (7 per 100,000 per year). Significantly higher rates are found in southern Africa (32 per 100,000), Central America (6 per 100,000), South America (15 per 100,000), the Caribbean (13 per 100,000), and eastern Europe (12 per 100,000). In the United States, homicide rates have plummeted over the past 10 years, but the current rate of 5.6 per 100,000 is still the highest of all developed countries. In Europe, the homicide rates fluctuate within a narrow range of 0.5 to 2 per 100,000.

• Rates of common assault as measured by the ICVS show a distribution that is different in some respects from that of homicide. The region showing the highest risks on this question is again Africa, but a moderately high rate is also found in Australia, where homicides are rare. Relatively low rates are shown by eastern Europe, where homicides are relatively common. Curiously, rates of assault in the United States are below those in Canada and the United Kingdom.

- In 22.6% of all threats or assaults, weapons were used: in 9.4%, knives, and in 5.7%, guns. The percentage of gun attacks was highest in Brazil, Mexico, and South Africa. Among developed countries, the United States stands out with a percentage of gun attacks/threats of 10%.

- The measurement of violence against women, including sexual abuse, is admittedly the Achilles' heel of the ICVS. Although female respondents of developing countries—where women possess a low social status—report the highest ICVS-based rates of sexual offenses, rates are also relatively high in some developed countries where gender equality is most advanced, including the United States and northern European countries. This paradoxical result suggests that female respondents in the latter countries hold stricter opinions about what constitutes an act of violence against them than women elsewhere. For this reason, the rates of developing countries provide an undercount from a Western perspective.

- In many countries, dedicated surveys have been conducted on violence against women, employing specially designed methodologies. These more in-depth studies show that intimate partner violence is rampant almost universally. One in three women experiences such victimization during her lifetime, and one in 10 experienced it in the course of the past year. To the extent that these surveys are comparable, they confirm that violence against women is most prevalent in developing countries, where rates of homicide and other violence are generally high and gender equality is comparatively low. Violence against women appears to be more prevalent in rural areas than in urban ones. The available evidence suggests that this type of violence must indeed, as claimed by the United Nations in many resolutions and other documents, be understood as an expression of gender inequality and discrimination of women.

- Statistics on victimization by violence largely confirm the existence of the Asian exception in criminological epidemiology. This exception, however, does not apply to violence against women by intimate partners, which is comparatively high. Asia cannot be regarded as a low-crime region for its female inhabitants.

Notes

1. Homicide data on Algeria are not available.
2. See Appendix A for details on the methodology of the ICVS.
3. The most recent data available on Australia are from 2000.
4. Data on missing and sexually exploited children in the 25 member states of the European Union have been collated by a Belgian research team (Vermeulen, 2004).

Determinants of Common Crimes

Comparative Perspectives

Traditionally, crime experts have based their theories of the macro causes of crime on data from police records or courts. In the late 19th and early 20th centuries, criminologists generally related national or regional levels of crime to climate, extreme poverty, demographic composition, urbanization, secularization, social disorganization, and a wide range of other macro characteristics of societies (Beirne, 1993). Comparative criminology was part of mainstream criminology. In later years, diminished confidence in the reliability of official crime statistics as measures of crime led to a decline in epidemiological studies. Cross-country comparisons, using police figures, continued to be made but did not receive much attention. In many textbooks on criminology, results of such studies were not discussed at all. In the second half of the 20th century, criminological research in many countries focused exclusively on characteristics of individual offenders and methods of treatment or rehabilitation. The epidemiology of crime went into hibernation.

The development of alternative methods of data collection, such as sample surveys among populations of actual and potential victims, has opened new avenues for analyzing levels of crime across countries and over time. Victimization survey research has put epidemiological criminology on a new methodological footing by providing data that are collected independently of the police. These data allow cross-country comparisons that are less influenced by differences in legislation or institutional practices.

This chapter will begin with a discussion of the relationship between common (volume) crimes and a core set of social factors at the macro level (e.g., affluence, urbanization, inequality). Some of these correlates of crime at the macro level will be revisited when discussing trends in crime in the next chapter. To optimize the transparency of our analyses, most relationships are presented in the form of scatterplots depicting the position of each country on two dimensions (e.g., GDP and level of crime). The key conclusions about relationships have been retested in multivariate analyses. Although for many countries fresher data are available from the fifth round of the ICVS, cross-sectional analyses are done mainly on data from around 2000. Correlates of crime are unlikely to have changed much in the meantime. The economical, social, and institutional contexts of organized crime, corruption, and terrorism will be discussed separately in Chapter 12.

Urbanization and Crime

A consistent finding in traditional analyses of police-recorded crime rates was that recorded crime is more prevalent in large cities than in rural areas (Beirne, 1993). These studies confirmed the general 19th-century stereotype of cities as hotbeds of vice and crime. More recent statistics on police-recorded crime generally confirm the urban-rural divide. In many European countries, for example, the number of police-recorded crimes is at least twice as high per 1,000 inhabitants in the larger cities as in the countryside (United Nations, 1995). In the Netherlands, urban crime rates are four times higher in the largest cities than in villages (Van der Heide & Eggen, 2003). In central and eastern European countries, crime is traditionally the problem of urban areas. For instance, in Hungary in 2000, 50% of the Hungarian population lived in urban settlements, where 70%–75% of all registered crime was committed.

Higher urban crime rates according to police administrations may also reflect limited opportunities of inhabitants in underpoliced, rural areas to report incidents to the police. Victimization surveys can shed new light on the issue. Data from national crime victimization surveys have confirmed the urban-rural crime divide. The recent national crime victim survey of South Africa, for example, found victimization risks for both theft and violence to be 50% higher in metropolitan areas than in traditional urban and farming areas (Burton et al., 2004). Victimization surveys also confirm the concentration of fear of crime in the big cities of countries. This was, for example, confirmed in a survey carried out among the population of Poland in 2003 (Polish Public Opinion, 2003).

ICVS-based studies found similar results, which are presented below. In developing countries, the ICVS is for cost reasons normally conducted among samples of persons living in the capital city only. This restriction precludes an extensive comparison between urban and nonurban victimization rates at the international level using the ICVS database. At present, sufficient victimization data on urban and rural areas are available for only three world regions: western Europe, North America (United States and Canada), and Oceania (Australia and New Zealand).

Figure 5.1 shows victimization rates of those living in cities of different population sizes (six categories) in these world regions. The rates show how many of the respondents living in each of the six urban categories were victimized by crime per world region.

As can be seen in Figure 5.1, the rate of victimization per 100,000 inhabitants increases steadily as city size increases. Limited results concerning respondents from Asia where the survey was carried out at the national or state level in Cambodia, Indonesia, the Philippines, and India (larger Bombay) do not conform to the general

❖ Figure 5.1   Percentages of the Public Victimized by Any Crime, by Town
Size, for Western Europe, North America, and Oceania

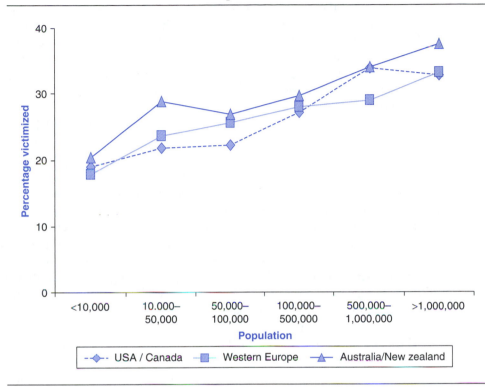

Source: ICVS, 1996 and 2002.

pattern in which levels of crime relate to city size. Since levels of crime in Asia are, as
reported in Chapters 3 and 4, comparatively modest, the present findings may indicate
that large Asian cities have maintained levels of safety more typically found in rural
areas elsewhere in the world. The "Asian exception" relates to the lack of urban crime
problems. It may be caused by the preservation in urban settings of mechanisms of
social control more typically found in rural communities. The results found in
Cambodia may have been affected by large-scale resettlement policies of the previous
communist regime whereby large groups of city dwellers were forced to migrate to rural
areas. This is likely to have destabilized rural communities.

In Europe, the link between living in large cities and high victimization risks is
strong and nearly universal (Van Kesteren, Mayhew, & Nieuwbeerta, 2000). The international crime victimization surveys have found that in Europe, 28% of urban residents felt insecure in their neighborhoods at night, while the comparable percentage
in rural areas was 15%. In addition, the use of self-protection measures such as
antiburglary devices is most prevalent among those living in the largest cities.

Multivariate analyses of previous ICVS data confirm that countries with higher proportions of people living in big cities show higher national victimization rates regardless of other characteristics (Van Dijk, 1999; Van Wilsen, 2003). The ICVS, as mentioned, has now been conducted among the national populations of more than 30 mostly Western countries. Within this group the degree of urbanization of countries and the national level of crime were found to be weakly but statistically significantly correlated ($r = .34$, $p > 0.05$, $n = 25$). Degree of urbanization and victimization by contact crimes were found to be even more strongly correlated ($r = .59$, $p > 0.05$, $n = 28$) (Van Dijk, Van Kesteren, & Smit, 2007).

The fairly consistent relationship between urbanization and levels of volume crime at both individual and country levels calls for further theoretical reflection. According to routine activity theory, crime rates are determined by the confluence in space and time of pools of motivated offenders and viable opportunities to commit crimes (Cohen & Felson, 1979). This perspective can help to explain the urban–rural crime divide. Although average levels of affluence tend to be higher in cities, rapid urbanization in many developing countries has resulted in a concentration of very poor, unemployed young males in big cities. While poverty by itself may not be a major cause of crime—in Asia, rates of property crimes remain low in even the poorest countries—the propensity to offend is higher among young, disenfranchised males than among other groups. Other factors possibly contributing to higher levels of offending in large cities are weakened family ties and other forms of social cohesiveness and the concentration of people from different cultures. Multivariate analyses of ICVS data at the national regional level have confirmed that the urbanization–crime link is mediated by weaker social cohesiveness (Van Dijk, 1994b).

At the same time, and perhaps more importantly, targets of crime such as cars and other luxury goods are abundantly available in large cities, while the daily routines of urban dwellers may leave these targets of crime less "socially well-guarded." Typical for large cities, for example, are shopping malls and large-scale school complexes where natural surveillance is weak. City life generally brings people into contact more often with strangers, including potential offenders.

This confluence of criminogenic push-and-pull factors in large cities goes a long way to explain the higher crime rates in big cities (Felson, 1997). As mentioned, violence against women is not more but less prevalent in cities. The anonymity of public space in urban settings seems less relevant for types of crime of violence committed in the domestic sphere. The higher social status that women enjoy in urban environments may act as a shield against this special type of criminal victimization, for example, in the workplace.

Regional Patterns and Future Trends of Urbanization

Urbanization has represented one of the most significant worldwide social transformations of the past century. In recent decades, rapid urbanization in many parts of the world has definitely been a major driving force behind the growth in volume crime. The urbanization factor can account partly for the above-average crime rates in South and Central America, currently one of the most highly urbanized regions in the world.

It can also account for rising crime in Africa, a region urbanizing at a higher pace than the global average (UNODC, 2005).

The above-average levels of crime in some Western countries can also be partly explained by the comparatively high percentages of people residing in cities with 100,000 or more inhabitants. This is, for example, the case in Australia, where 69% of the population resides in a large city. Australia is one of the few countries where national rates are as high as urban rates, for example, those of Sydney. It is also worth pointing out in this context that in the ICVS database, the percentage of residents living in a place of more than 100,000 inhabitants is lower in the United States (21%) than in several countries of the European Union, Canada (43%), and Japan (39%). Compared to other industrialized nations, the United States is less highly urbanized. The comparatively low proportion of big-city dwellers in the United States may partly explain its moderately low level of volume crime according to the ICVS.

Presently, about half of the world population resides in urban areas (UN, 2004). Urbanization is forecasted to continue in the coming two decades with the share of population living in urban areas expected to reach two thirds by 2025. The projected pace of urbanization differs across regions, with urbanization in western Europe, North America, Latin America, and Oceania expected to level off. In contrast, rapid further urbanization is forecasted for Asia and Africa. In the latter regions, the share of inhabitants living in cities is forecasted to increase by 40% in the coming two decades (United Nations, 1995).

These regional trends will have important implications for the levels of volume crime and violence in Asia and Africa. The expansion of big cities in developing countries, although conducive to economic growth and modernization, may have a downside in the form of higher levels of volume crime. In Asia, increasing urbanization may eventually generate more serious crime problems in the coming decades and challenge the Asian exception. It is possible that violence against women decreases when women acquire a stronger position in societies with urbanized cultures. In African countries undergoing further rapid urbanization, crime problems may become ever more serious and violent, and governments will be hard-pressed to raise sufficient funds to address these issues successfully and may need foreign aid for institution building.

Demographics and Crime

Thefts, burglaries, assaults, and other forms of volume crime are, to a large extent, youth-related phenomena. In all countries, the majority of offenders as well as a disproportionately large proportion of victims are males between 15 to 30 years of age (Adler, Mueller, & Laufer, 1998). The ICVS database allows comparisons of the victimization rates of various age groups for different types of crime. Universally, younger people (24 years of age or less) are markedly more at risk than older ones, defying the stereotypical notion of offenders preying on the elderly. Related to the age factor, those who go out more frequently in the evening are more at risk, particularly for contact crimes (Van Kesteren, Mayhew, & Nieuwbeerta, 2000).

Findings on offending show the same age-related patterns and profiles.[1] Among 12- to 18-year-olds in many countries, engagement in forms of juvenile delinquency is very common, especially among boys. Across countries and cultures, most people involved in criminal activities significantly reduce their involvement in crime after reaching young adulthood. Many studies report steep declines in criminal involvement after the age of 25 for property crimes and after 30 for violent crime (called the "aging out" phenomenon). Self-reported delinquency surveys from different countries show that the peak of young people's criminal activities lies between 15 and 18 years (Barberet et al., 2004). Overrepresentation of young males among offenders is attributed by criminologists to weak social integration during the transition from childhood to adulthood (Wilson & Hernnstein, 1995).

The overrepresentation of young males among offenders leads to the epidemiological hypothesis that societies with relatively large proportions of young males will show higher levels of crime. This hypothesis was confirmed by LaFree and Tseloni (2006) in a multivariate analysis of homicide trends. As shown in Figure 5.2, ICVS data on victimization by common crime confirm that overall victimization rates are significantly higher in societies with more young males.

The data in Figure 5.2 reveal a moderately strong relationship between demographic compositions of populations and levels of crime ($r = .37$, $p > 0.05$, $n = 62$). The age structure of the countries or cities included in the analysis explains 25% of the variation in victimization rates. The above-average crime rates in countries such as

❖ Figure 5.2　Scatterplot of Percentages of Young Males in Country or City Populations by Overall Rates of Victimization (Ranked Variable)

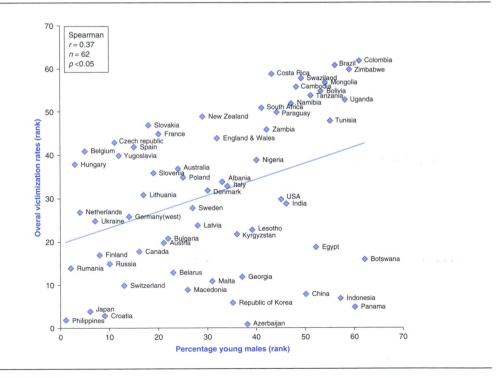

Source: ICVS, 1996–2000.

Brazil, Colombia, Zimbabwe, Uganda, and Costa Rica are partly explained by the over-representation of young males in their (urban) populations. Outliers include several Asian countries (China and Indonesia) as well as Botswana. Considering the skewed age structure of their populations, higher levels of crime were to be expected in these countries. Among the (mainly Western) countries participating in the fifth wave of the ICVS at the national level, the correlation between age composition and overall victimization was not significant (Van Dijk, Van Kesteren, & Smit, 2007). However, the correlation between age composition and victimization by contact crimes was fairly strong ($r = .59$, $p < 0.05$, $n = 28$).

Previous analyses of global ICVS victimization data have shown that the macro factors of urbanization and age structure combined explain half of the variation in national victimization rates (Van Dijk, 1999). Put differently, if all world populations were roughly similar in degree of urbanization and age structure, national differences in levels of crime would be reduced by half.[2]

Future Demographic Trends

Countries show great variation in age structure. The proportion that young males make up of the world population is currently 15%. Their share of the population is roughly twice as high in Africa (20%) as in Asia, western Europe, and North America (10% or less). Africa currently hosts the world's youngest population (43% under the age of 15) (UNDP, 2004). Higher crime rates in African countries can, to a fairly large extent, be attributed to the overrepresentation of young males in their national populations.

Many Western countries have undergone the social and economic impact of a significant "baby boom" since the end of World War II. The overrepresentation of young people in the national populations from 1960 to 1980 was an important factor behind the crime booms in those years in North America and western Europe. The subsequent stabilization of crime rates since 1990 in these countries can be seen as partly an effect of the aging of their populations.

World populations are currently undergoing an unprecedented, rapid demographic transition. Due to lower fertility and mortality, national populations are aging rapidly in many countries across the world. The young–old balance is shifting with the proportion of young people declining. The world's median age of 26 is forecasted to increase to 36 by 2050 (United Nations, 2004). This aging trend is expected to be enduring and irreversible in the foreseeable future and to pose many economic and social challenges, for example, for the funding of welfare benefits of the elderly. However, one of the rarely mentioned advantages of the aging trend might be a reduction of youth-related forms of volume crime, a trend that is already in evidence in North America, Europe, and Australia.

In the coming decades, the pace of the aging trend is forecasted to increase in many developing countries so that youth-related crime problems, especially in the African region, might at a later point be somewhat alleviated. However, since older people tend to be more concerned about personal security, feelings of insecurity are likely to increase globally, even in countries where levels of actual victimization are stable or declining. The elderly will make up an increasingly important segment of the electorate in developed countries. From this "gray vote," more political pressure will be brought to bear on governments to ensure protection against real or perceived security threats. Paradoxically, declining rates of volume crime may be accompanied by increasing fear of crime and demands for "super security." The first sign of such trends is the growing concern among the public in several European countries, including the United Kingdom and the Netherlands, about minor incivilities and diminished concerns about burglaries or other forms of serious crime.

Affluence and Crime

From an economic perspective, it seems self-evident that the opportunity costs of committing offenses for potential offenders are lower if their levels of licit income are low. For those living in extreme poverty, a life of crime presents a tempting escape route. Empirical studies do not confirm, however, any straightforward relationship between poverty and crime at the macro level (Belknap, 1989; Van Wilsem, 2003). The Human Development Index (HDI), published annually by the UN, ranks nations according to their citizens' quality of life using criteria such as life expectancy, educational attainment, and adjusted real income. An analysis of the relationship between country rates of victimization as reported in the ICVS and the Human Development Index shows inconclusive results. As expected, crime rates tend to be on average somewhat higher in poor, less-developed countries, but the differences in overall crime levels between poor and rich countries are fairly small.

For a proper understanding of crime rates, the prevalence of poor or unemployed young people in a population is not the only relevant factor. The prevalence of potential *victim* populations and of situational factors facilitating crime must also be taken into consideration (Felson and Clarke, 1989; Van Dijk, 1994a, 1994b). Many other factors in society besides the income of potential offenders determine the level of crime. Some of these factors are positively related to affluence. One such factor is, as mentioned above in the discussion of the city–crime link, the availability of suitable targets of property crime. As countries become more affluent, more people own commodities that may become easy targets of crime. This by itself may drive up levels of crime, regardless of the income situation among local pools of potential offenders.

An obvious example of the affluence-driven supply of suitable targets for crime is the automobile. Motor cars are suitable targets for joyriding and car theft and are also important tools for the commission of other crimes such as armed robberies. Figure 5.3 shows the relationship between car ownership rates per country and national victimization rates for three types of car-related crime (car theft, theft from a car, and car vandalism). It shows the strong relationship between the rates of car ownership in a country and the total rates of such car-related crimes per household ($r = .71$, $p > 0.05$, $n = 65$).

If more cars are available in a country, more people are engaged in car-related crimes. The rates of car-related crimes per 100,000 people are higher in countries where more people own cars. As discussed in Chapter 3, the picture changes when rates are calculated for car owners only. However, even car owners' victimization rates are partly driven by national rates of car ownership. Individual car owners run higher risks of being the victim of car theft in the United Kingdom than in other European

❖ **Figure 5.3** Percentages of Car Ownership and Rates of Car-Related Crimes per 100,000 Population (Households)

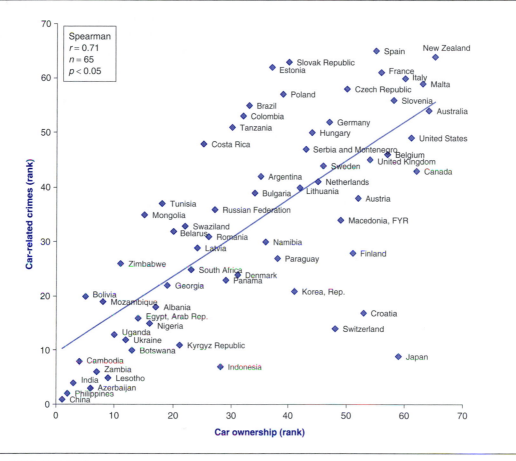

Source: ICVS, 1996–2000.

countries where cars are much scarcer (Van Dijk, Mayhew, & Killias, 1990). Japan and Hong Kong/China provide an interesting exception to the rule: Although cars are widely available, rates of car-related thefts have remained low.

Mass Transportation and Crime

Countries that rely predominantly on private cars for transportation are at the top of the list for car crimes. In such countries, car-related crimes make up a substantial part of the total costs of volume crime. For example, in Australia, thefts from cars and car thefts are responsible for 8% of the total costs of crime (Mayhew, 2003). High rates of car-related crimes can be seen as a hidden cost of national transportation systems relying mainly on the use of private cars. Countries with better-developed public transport will suffer less from such car-crime losses.

Countries relying more on public transport systems, however, may incur additional crime costs in another domain. As discussed earlier, public transport systems provide ample opportunities for theft from the person through pickpocketing. Countries relying more on trains, buses, and trams for transportation than on cars, such as Spain, France, the Netherlands, Poland, and the Czech Republic, experience markedly higher levels of pickpocketing than the United Kingdom, Australia, or the United States (Mayhew & Van Dijk, 1995).

In several European and Asian cities, bicycles are among the most important modes of transportation. Figure 5.4 provides yet another example of how the levels and nature of crime are shaped by the dominant modes of transportation in a country. It shows the strong relationship between bicycle ownership rates as measured by the ICVS and bicycle theft, with rate of ownership explaining 63% of variation in national

❖ Figure 5.4   Percentages of Bicycle Ownership and Bicycle Theft

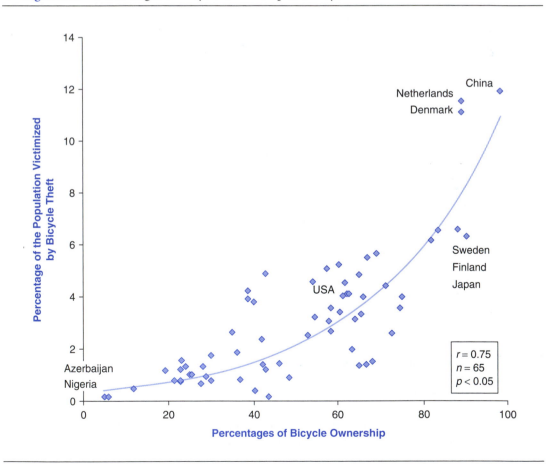

Source: ICVS, 1996–2000.

victimization rates related to bicycle theft ($r = 75$, $p < 0.05$, $n = 65$). Indonesia is among the outliers, but Japan and China conform to the pattern.

The results on bicycle theft confirm the theory that levels of property crime are determined by criminal opportunity structures (Felson & Clarke, 1989). Bicycle theft, as with car theft, appears to be clearly driven by availability. Even in otherwise low-crime countries such as China and Japan, the general availability of bicycles generates high rates of bicycle theft as "crimes of expediency." The analysis reveals an *exponential* relationship between bicycle ownership and theft. If bicycle theft surpasses critical levels, a chain reaction seems to be set in motion by victims committing themselves to stealing—or to knowingly buying from "fences"—to replace the stolen bicycle. This phenomenon of "compensatory stealing" of bicycles has been well documented among student populations in the Netherlands (Van Dijk, 1986) and probably also occurs in Denmark, China, and Japan.[3] It is an example of the kind of multiplying mechanisms that cause affluence-driven crime epidemics.

Equally strong relationships have been demonstrated between motorcycle ownership and motorcycle theft. Motorcycle theft also provides an interesting example of how the introduction of new safety regulations and ensuing changes in behavioral patterns yield an unexpected crime prevention bonus. In the 1970s, several countries introduced safety laws requiring motorcyclists to wear helmets. Offenders wanting to steal a motorcycle now had to go equipped with a helmet or they would be spotted quickly. The enactment of the new helmets legislation has led to dramatic declines in motorcycle thefts in several countries, including the United Kingdom, the Netherlands, Germany, and India (Mayhew, Clarke, & Elliot, 1989).

Patterns of Vehicle Theft at Second Sight

The impact of vehicle ownership goes further than the fact that more cars drive up car theft and more bicycles drive up bicycle theft. Previous analysis of ICVS results has shown a strong *inverse* relationship between rates of car theft/joyriding and rates of bicycle theft, controlling for urbanization, affluence, and levels of other crime (Van Dijk & Mayhew, 1992). Thus, in countries where bicycle ownership is high and bicycle theft is therefore relatively common, stealing cars occurs less often. For example, low car theft rates are found in Finland, Germany, and the Netherlands, countries where almost all households own one or more bicycles. Motorcycle ownership seems also to be inversely related to car theft, with Greece and Italy being two cases in point.

A broad explanation of the links between bicycle/motorcycle ownership and car theft is that young people in North America, Australia, the United Kingdom, and Ireland are more accustomed to driving cars. In Sweden, the Netherlands, and Germany, young people tend to be more attuned to the use of bicycles, and in Italy and Greece, to motorcycles, although car ownership rates are comparatively high as well. These general patterns of preferred vehicle use among young people are reflected in national patterns of vehicle theft. Patterns of vehicle theft in Europe provide a neat example of how crime patterns are shaped by routine activities of the population.

The strong inverse relationship between bicycle ownership and car theft/joyriding also suggests that those looking for illegal, short-distance transportation will make do with a bicycle or motorcycle if there are plenty available and young people are used to riding such vehicles. Consistent with this interpretation is that in typical low-bicycle-ownership countries, such as the United Kingdom and France, a larger proportion of all car thefts qualify as cases of joyriding (because the car is eventually recovered) than elsewhere, for example, in Germany and the Netherlands. This finding led Van Dijk, Mayhew, and Killias (1990) to hypothesize that "On the market of illegal transportation, bicycles could be a substitute for cars, if bicycles are in sufficient supply."

Over the past 10 years, improved anti-theft security has reduced opportunities for car theft and joyriding, especially in countries where such crimes were relatively common (e.g., the United Kingdom). In the next chapter, results will be presented showing pronounced decreases in many developed countries in rates of joyriding. According to the hypothesis of bicycles acting as "substitute goods," this reduction in opportunities for joyriding should have increased the vulnerability of available bicycles and motorcycles as targets of theft. The ICVS 2005 shows indeed a sharp increase in motorcycle thefts in the United Kingdom in recent years (2000–2005), and stable rates of bicycle theft decreasing elsewhere. This result suggests that two-wheelers have acted as substitute goods for (better-protected) cars as targets of theft for illegal transportation.[4] Improved security of motor cars has arrived at a moment when the use of bicycles has become more popular and is actively promoted for environmental reasons. The unintended side effect of these two trends might well be a displacement from joyriding of cars to thefts of two-wheelers.

More Affluence, Less Crime?

It is widely believed that economic and social development will automatically result in decreasing rates of crime by eliminating its social root causes. According to conventional criminological "strain" theories, for example, fewer people will be motivationally inclined to engage in offending if societies become more prosperous. Unfortunately, crime trends in developed countries over the past 50 years have failed to conform to this optimistic model of crime prevention through economic development. Trends in crime over time are strongly and *positively* related to levels of affluence. Almost everywhere, crime rates start rising as soon as the economy starts to grow. All developed countries experiencing "economic miracles" in the 1960s after recovering from World War II saw their crime rates surging, with crime rates multiplying fivefold or more in some countries (Laycock, 2001; Van Dijk, 2000).[5] Several central European countries have likewise experienced crime booms in tandem with healthy economic growth over the past two decades. More recently, Ireland, where economic growth was delayed, stands out with a boom in crime, whereas levels of volume crime have reached a plateau in most other developed countries.

The trend data on crime and affluence seem to point to a dynamic interplay of push-and-pull factors at the macro level that is not easy to understand. While high levels of crime in poor countries seem to require no explanation—opportunity costs of offending are, as said, comparatively low due to poverty and massive unemployment—the curvilinear relationship between affluence and crime in most Western countries over the past 50 years poses a theoretical puzzle. According to routine activity/criminal opportunity theory, mentioned earlier, the impact of affluence on crime in societies is not limited to a reduction of the pool of potential offenders. Affluence brings into mass circulation goods that fit the acronym CRAVED: Concealable, Removable, Available, Valuable, Enjoyable, and Disposable (Clarke, 1999). Affluence is also often accompanied by urbanization and related weakening of social cohesiveness. As affluence levels rise, fewer people may be driven toward crime by economic deprivation, but more are driven toward it by the presence of abundant suitable targets. Car theft has been mentioned as a prime example of a type of crime driven by opportunity. A neat, topical example of supply-driven crime effects is the recent upsurge in robberies and thefts caused by the massive distribution of mobile phones (Mayhew, 2003). In conclusion, the crime-reducing effects of fewer people with a poverty-driven propensity to offend are more than offset by the increased availability of opportunities to commit profitable crimes with near impunity. The dual impact of affluence on levels of crime is described in Figure 5.5.

❖ **Figure 5.5**   Graphic Description of the Dual Impact of (Growing) Affluence on Crime

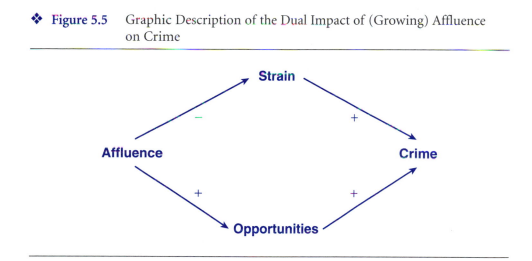

If losses from crime increase, investments in crime prevention and criminal justice become more and more economically rewarding. Sooner or later, inhabitants of affluent societies respond to higher crime rates with increased expenditures on counter-crime measures. As a general rule, more effective crime prevention measures are put in place if losses from crime outweigh the costs of effective prevention. High crime rates automatically generate market demand for crime prevention. Examples are security measures against household burglary, robberies of post offices and banks, and check fraud (Laycock, 2001). As crime prevention and criminal justice reach sufficient levels, the costs of offending will increase and crime rates are likely to start falling. Increased affluence leads to a "crime harvest" in the medium term. Eventually, sufficient measures are put in place by potential victims to counter increased losses from crime, and crime rates will stabilize at a lower level. We will return to this hypothesis of equilibrating forces on the market of crime in our discussion of the trends in crime over time in the next chapter.

Development and Crime Revisited

There are clear indications that among the most developed countries, rates of volume crime such as burglaries and car thefts have started to fall, after four decades of increases. In this context, evidence will be presented of the significantly increased investments in crime prevention and criminal justice in countries enjoying drops in crime. With a time lag of several decades, the most developed countries have finally counterbalanced increased opportunities of crime with better protection and more effective deterrence. Western societies are finally reaping the delayed benefits of the crime prevention measures that their higher affluence has allowed them to put into place.

From an economic perspective, the criminological outlook for developing countries is less positive. Rapid urbanization, demographics producing a "youth bulge," and high unemployment have already driven up crime rates. For the reasons explained above, economic growth, however welcome for other reasons, is unlikely to produce crime reductions as an automatic side effect. In developing countries, poverty alleviation by itself is no remedy for crime, at least not in the short or even medium term. The experiences of developed countries, including most recently those in central and eastern Europe and Ireland with affluence-driven crime booms, leaves little room for optimism about the immediate future of urban security in developing countries, even if they experience robust economic growth. Within sub-Saharan Africa, levels of crime are the highest in the more affluent countries (e.g., South Africa). As other African countries approach similar levels of affluence, their crime rates may soon surge to South African levels. According to high-ranking Chinese police authorities, levels of common crime are stable but are rising in the economically most advanced areas (personal communication to the author).

Decreases in crime in developing countries with expanding economies can be expected only if both private and public investments in crime prevention and criminal justice are brought up to the standards of developed countries or to levels even higher. Such catching up will require much larger investments in countercrime policies than currently available or planned for. As with other public goods, many developing countries, especially in sub-Saharan Africa, lack the resources to bring crime prevention and criminal justice up to par. Failure to address crime problems may in turn negatively affect development. This issue will be further discussed in Chapters 12 and 13, which deal with the impact of the justice and security sector on sustainable development and the need of global reforms.

Correlates of Violence

Many comparative studies of crime levels have shown levels of violent crime to be related to sets of social factors other than those of property crimes (Howard & Smith, 2003). Bennett (1991) has specifically maintained that development serves to decrease crimes of violence but simultaneously acts to increase crimes of theft. Similarly, analysis of older ICVS data showed that violent crime is related to indicators of poverty and inequality, while property crime is associated with opportunities of offending created by affluence (Van Dijk, 1999; Van Dijk & Kangaspunta, 2000).

Poverty and Inequality

Analyses of older ICVS data on 50 countries have shown that a measure of poverty-related "strain"—percentage of young males dissatisfied with their income—was strongly related to levels of contact crimes (robbery and threats/assaults, sexual offenses). In multivariate analyses, the strain factor emerged as the strongest predictor of levels of violence (Van Dijk, 1999). In other secondary analyses of ICVS data on fewer countries, income inequality emerged as the most important correlate of common violent crime (Van Wilsem, 2003). This finding has been contested by Pare (2006), who argues that not income inequality but infant mortality, which is a measure of poverty, is the best predictor of common violence. Since income inequalities tend to be larger in poorer countries, where more people suffer from extreme poverty, the impact of poverty and inequality on violence is difficult to disentangle. Arguably, income inequality and various measures of perceived or objective poverty are two sides of the same coin. In many countries, both are measures of the forms of severe deprivation conducive to violence.

The statistical linkage between income inequality and violence is confirmed in the results of the ICVS 2000 for both threats/assaults and robbery. Figure 5.6 shows the relationship between income inequality, as measured by the Gini coefficient (a measure of inequality in a population) and the levels of robbery as measured in the ICVS. The relationship between income inequality and rates of victimization for street robbery appears to be moderately strong ($r = .62$, $p < 0.05$, $n = 50$). In the upper right quarter, which indicates where these problems are most severe, are mainly Latin American and African countries as well as Russia and Estonia.

In several epidemiological studies of levels of police-recorded criminal violence, including domestic violence, statistical relations have been found with income inequalities (Fajnzylber, 1997; Fajnzylber, Ledermann, & Loayza, 2000; LaFree, 1999; LaFree & Tseloni, 2006). According to Neumayer (2003) and Pare (2006), other measures of deprivation are more important. As said, the distinction may not matter much in developing countries. Many countries in Africa (Swaziland, South Africa, Zimbabwe) and Latin America (Brazil, Colombia, Bolivia) where homicide rates are high show high scores on both income inequality and on many measures of poverty/deprivation. As South African president Thgabo Mbeki argued in response to the UNDP 2000 Human Development Report: "Poverty is not only expressed in shortage of food, shelter and clothing. It is also expressed in high levels of crime, including violence among the poor themselves, especially against women and children, in many instances accompanied by substance abuse."

Criminal Victimization and Gender Inequality

Analyses of the ICVS data at the level of individuals reveal a fairly even gender distribution of risks of victimization for property crimes. Burglary victimization rates are just about the same for males and females. For other property crimes in general, male–female differences are slight, with males experiencing somewhat higher robbery

❖ **Figure 5.6**   Income Inequality and Rates of Victimization by Robbery

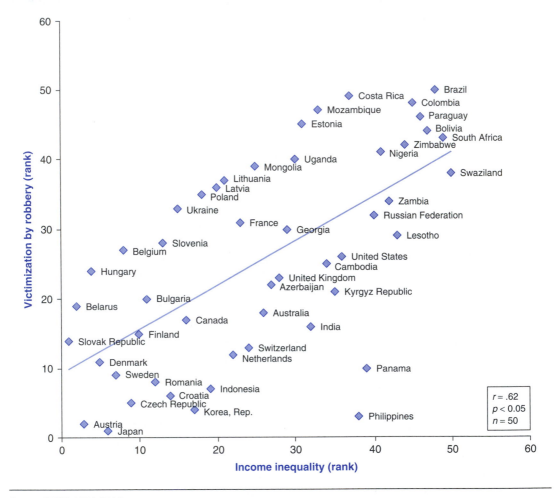

Source: ICVS, 1996–2000.

victimization rates. As discussed before, violent crime is more clearly gendered. Violence of males against females, including sexual violence, is prevalent in many societies (United Nations, 2006; WHO, 2002; WHO, 2005). Since the measurement of these forms of violence has many methodological problems, all available results should be regarded as tentative. Analysis of ICVS data has shown that violence against women, measured independently of the police, is linked to gender inequalities. Rates of victimization by violence among females are higher in countries where women are less educated (Alvazzi del Frate & Patrignani 1995; Van Dijk, 1999). Results of dedicated surveys on violence against women showed developing countries experiencing a higher prevalence of partner violence than developed countries. Such violence is also more common in provincial areas than in urban ones (United Nations, 2006). These results indicate the existence of a link between gender equality and violence against women. Violence against women is also, like all forms of criminal violence, linked to deprivation among males, as correctly assumed by President Mbeki (Van Dijk, 1999).

If ICVS-based data on victimization by sexually motivated violence (sexual harassment and rapes) are combined with data on other violence (assaults), a comprehensive index of violent crime shows females to be somewhat more at risk of violence than males. The gender ratio for violence shows a highly differentiated pattern across regions. In Europe and North America, males show higher rates of victimization by violence than do females. But in the other regions, the difference goes in the other direction. In Africa, South and Central America, and Asia, the percentage of women victimized by any kind of violence is 50% or more above that for males. In Asia, female victimization by violence is even twice as high as male victimization (Van Dijk, 1999). The generalized notion that Asian countries are low on violence must be qualified with respect to gender. For Asian women, the risks of being violently victimized are not much lower than for women in Western countries.

The distribution of the risk of being lethally wounded differs from the risks of being victimized by nonlethal violence. As just mentioned, women are more at risk of being victimized by violence if sexually motivated violence is included in the measures used, especially in many developing countries. Homicide, however, appears universally to victimize predominantly (young) males. WHO homicide data show the risk for homicide to be the highest for young males (19.4 per 100,000) and young adult males (18.7 per 100,000) (WHO, 2002). Risks for females are significantly lower in all age groups (4.5 per 100,000).

Although high levels of violence, including violence against women, are clearly linked to poverty and inequality, other factors such as alcohol consumption and gun ownership play an important role, independent of affluence. These special determinants of levels of crime and violence are discussed below.

Drugs and Alcohol Abuse

Many drug addicts finance their addiction at least partly through predatory crime. A significant percentage of arrested offenders in many countries test positive for illicit drug use. In Australia, for example, $3.7 billion of the cost of property and violent crime stems from drug-attributable crimes, according to the findings of the Drug Use Monitoring in Australia program (Makkai & McGregor, 2003). This amounts to almost 20% of the total crime bill of the country (Mayhew, 2003). Nonetheless, research has not provided much support for the theory that young drug users turn to crime solely to pay for drugs. Those who commit crimes frequently and over a longer period of time are often those who began offending at a young age, then moved to illicit drug use, and then increased the scope of their criminal activities. As it is often expressed, illicit drug use is just one element of a delinquent lifestyle (UNDCP, 1997).

Though not necessarily causally linked, the two phenomena—drug use and crime—often occur in tandem. In the United States, for instance, the current use of cocaine among the general population decreased by 35% between 1988 and 2002. Over the same period, total recorded crime fell by 15%, the number of murder victims declined by 22% (those related to the drug law offenses declined by more than 50%), and property crime fell by 28% (National Drug Control Strategy Reports, 2004; UNODC, 1996). Similarly, the "heroin drought" in Australia (2002), following an initial hike, resulted in crime rates falling overall as large numbers of heroin addicts left the market. Although the continuous drop in property crime in Australia can only partly be attributed to the heroin drought, it seems to have assisted the downward trend (Moffatt, Weatherburn, & Donnelly, 2005).

A component of the I-ADAM study dealt with self-reported sources of illegal income of arrested drug users over the past 12 months in a selection of countries (Bennett, Holloway, & Williams, 2001). The majority admitted income-generating property crime (theft, burglary, robbery, handling, and fraud/deception). Furthermore, drug-using arrestees reported higher levels of illegal income than non-drug-using arrestees.

Drug scenes can by themselves, regardless of their association with property crime, be perceived as constituting a public nuisance or incivility problem by the public at large. A question in this respect has been addressed to EU citizens in the framework of the Eurobarometer (Van Dijk & Toornvliet, 1996).[6] The results for 2002 are presented in Figure 5.7.

❖ **Figure 5.7**   Contact With Drug-Related Problems in the Area of Residence (in %) in 15 European Union Countries (2002)

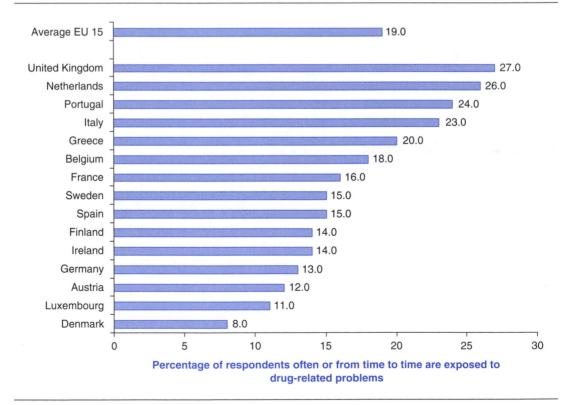

Percentage of respondents often or from time to time are exposed to drug-related problems

Source: Eurobarometer, 2003, adapted.

On average, 19% of the respondents said that they had been in contact with drug-related problems either often or from time to time during the past 12 months. Five countries, namely, the United Kingdom, the Netherlands, Portugal, Italy, and Greece, were above the average while the others showed lower percentages. The high percentages of exposure in the United Kingdom and the Netherlands tie in with the current political debates in these countries about "incivilities." Feelings of unsafety in the street were found to be strongly correlated with perceived exposure to drug problems ($r = .79$). The same question has been introduced in the ICVS 2005 for European countries. The results indicate that concerns about drug-related incivilities have continued to go up in most EU member states (Van Dijk, Manchin, Van Kesteren, & Hideg, 2007).

Alcohol Abuse and Violence

Alcohol abuse is a major cause of fatal traffic accidents across the world. Most countries have therefore introduced laws prohibiting driving under the influence of alcohol. In the United States, 4 out of 10 fatal motor vehicle accidents involve alcohol (Bureau of Justice Statistics, 1998). The dramatic consequences of drunk driving have led to campaigns for more stringent action against drunk drivers (Mothers Against Drunk Driving, MADD). For individuals, the link between alcohol abuse and violent behavior is equally well established. Alcohol consumption often precedes violent events, and the amount of drinking is related to the severity of the subsequent violence (WHO, 2002). Alcohol use is known to reduce restraints and relax antiviolence norms. In some situations, alcohol-related violence is facilitated by norms condoning or prescribing such behavior (WHO, 2002).

Studies across the world have consistently shown the close association of alcohol and violent crime. In the United States, almost half of all offenders convicted for violent crimes were under the influence of alcohol during the crime (Adler, Mueller, & Laufer, 1998). Among attacks committed by current or former intimate partners, two out of three perpetrators had been drinking prior to the attack. In homicide cases, alcohol involvement of both offenders and victims is even higher than in less serious crimes (Adler, Mueller, & Laufer, 1998). Very similar statistics have been reported from South Africa. According to recent victim surveys, in just over 70% of all assault cases, either the victim or the offender, or both, were under the influence of alcohol. The contributing role of excessive alcohol consumption goes some way to explain the seasonal patterns of violence in South Africa, showing clear peaks during holidays (Shaw, 2002).

At the macro level, time series analysis has consistently shown clear relationships between alcohol consumption and homicide rates in northern European and central European countries, while such relationships in southern European countries tend to be weak (Lenke, 1990; Rossow, 2001).

In analyses of ICVS rates of victimization, rates of beer and liquor consumption have been found to be related to rates of victimization by assaults and threats among Western countries. Figure 5.8 shows the results of the analysis of the relationship between beer consumption according to World Drink Trends (2004 and 2005) and victimization by threats and assaults, using data of the ICVS 2005 for developed countries and Mexico.

❖ **Figure 5.8** Rates of Victimization by Threats/Assault in 1996–2005 and Beer Consumption (Liters per Head) in Developed Countries (2004)

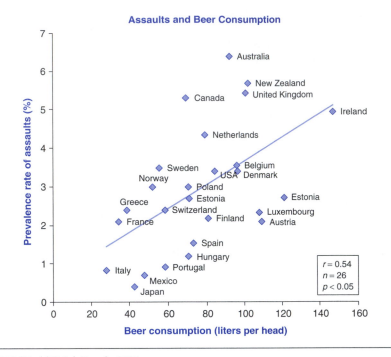

Sources: ICVS, 2005; World Drink Trends, 2004.

As is shown in Figure 5.8, levels of assaults or threats are moderately correlated to levels of beer consumption per 100,000 population ($r = .54$, $p > 0.05$, $n = 26$). Countries combining comparatively high rates of beer consumption and levels of violence include Ireland, Australia, New Zealand, the United Kingdom, and the Netherlands. In a multivariate analysis of correlates of violence, using the ICVS 2005 data, levels of beer consumption emerged as the strongest independent predictor of levels of assault or threats. Degree of urbanization and beer consumption together explained 47% of the variance in the 30 countries included in the analysis (multiple $r = .69$). Beer consumption was found to be strongly correlated with wealth ($r = .54$). The latter finding suggests that among developed countries, alcohol-induced violence can be seen as an affluence-driven social problem.

Within northern Europe and Australia, excessive beer drinking is commonly associated with rowdy behavior by young adolescents (so-called "lager louts"). Manifestations of this phenomenon consist of different forms of street violence including vandalism. Analyses of older data from ICVS 2000 confirm the linkage between beer consumption and rates of vandalized cars, which can be seen as a proxy for hooliganism. Countries scoring high on both beer consumption and vandalism included Austria, Australia, the United States, Belgium, and the Netherlands.

We finally looked at the relationship between hard liquor consumption and homicide in Europe. Again, a clear correlation between alcohol and violence was found after the deletion of two outliers (Estonia, Ukraine) of which the data on liquor may be deflated ($r = .35$, $p < 0.05$, $n = 24$) (see Figure 5.9).

Trends in Alcohol Consumption

Total alcohol consumption is higher in the more affluent world regions, with Europe and Australia clearly on top. Trends in alcohol consumption are different for the three main types of alcohol (hard liquor, wine, and beer) and are divergent across regions and countries. Over the past 10 years, total alcohol consumption has declined in many of the more affluent regions and increased elsewhere. Several middle-income countries such as Mexico, Brazil, Russia, and South Africa have experienced significant

❖ **Figure 5.9**   National Rates of Consumption of Hard Liquor (Liters per Head) and Rates of Homicide in Europe (Ranked Variables)

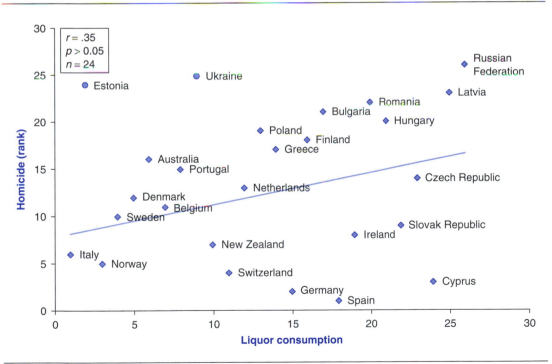

Sources: World Drink Trends, 2004; 6th–8th UN Crime Surveys; WHO, 2002.

increases in beer consumption over the past 20 years (World Drink Trends, 2004). Total alcohol consumption has also increased by 12% in the United Kingdom since 1997. This increase, in conjunction with more liberal licensing rules, is blamed by experts for the increase of attacks on strangers in British cities as measured by the British Crime Surveys (*The Economist*, August 1, 2004). Especially worrying from a criminological perspective are reports of increasing consumption of alcohol by very young people in the United Kingdom, the Netherlands, and elsewhere in Europe. By contrast, underage drinking is more successfully addressed in the United States mostly as a result of pressure from groups such as MADD. In his detailed analysis of the famous crime drop of New York in the 1990s, Karmen (2000) identifies decreases in the use of hard liquor as one of the key factors. Publication of the ICVS 2005 results in Europe in February 2007 has fueled a political debate about alcohol abuse among youngsters in the United Kingdom, Ireland, and the Netherlands (e.g., *Daily Telegraph*, February 6, 2007).

Availability of Guns

In many regions of the world, the easy availability of firearms is seen as another important contributing factor of violent crime, and the ongoing proliferation of small firearms worldwide is a cause for grave concern for many governments. The danger of readily available weapons, especially in combination with alcohol abuse, has been recognized since time immemorial. In the epic poem, "The Odyssey," written about ancient Greece over three millennia ago, the hero, Odysseus, explains his removal of weapons from a hall where young noblemen are bound to feast as a measure of crime prevention. He observes that they may otherwise, "drunken from wine," start wounding each other: "because iron has that attraction to men."

In the current era, guns are the "tools of choice" for serious crimes of violence committed across the world. At least 200,000 non-conflict-related firearm deaths occur each year worldwide, most of them classifiable as firearm homicides (Small Arms Survey, 2004). Firearm homicides appear to be concentrated in South America and the Caribbean (40% of global cases). This region loses between 73,000 and 90,000 victims by firearms annually, overwhelmingly through homicides. Another 20% of the world's firearm homicides take place in Africa. Guns are also widely used in the commission of nonlethal crimes such as threats, aggravated assaults, robberies, and, to a lesser extent, sexual crimes.

The ICVS questionnaire includes an item on ownership of firearms that allows an estimate of national or city ownership rates, independent of official registration. Since ownership of firearms is illegal in some countries, the responses may be somewhat deflated. Reported ownership may also be deflated in countries where governments and NGOs are actively campaigning against ownership. Figure 5.10 shows the ownership rates for firearms and handguns specifically in urban areas. Ownership rates of firearms and of handguns are strongly correlated at the country level.

Globally, one in 10 households owns one or more firearm. Firearm ownership rates are highest in North America (United States and Canada, weighted for population), Latin America, and eastern Europe. The proportions of firearms that are handguns are largest in Latin America and Africa. The ownership rate in Africa for handguns is slightly above the global mean.

❖ **Figure 5.10**   Percentages of Households in Urban Areas Possessing One or More Firearms and Handguns, by Region

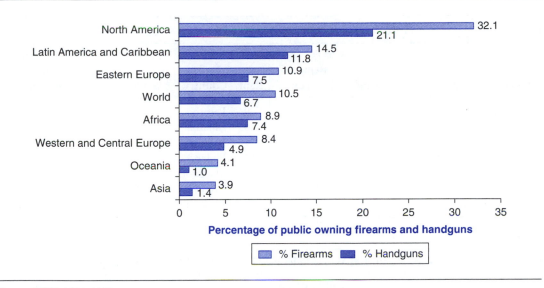

Source: ICVS, 1996–2000.

Reasons for firearm ownership were asked about in the ICVS, starting from the third sweep of the survey (1992). The most common primary reason in that survey given was hunting or sport. The percentages of owners who mentioned protection are highest in Africa (79%) and Latin America (65%). In the United States, 39% mentioned protection as reason. The percentage is much lower in western Europe (9%).

Table 5.1 shows the national firearms ownership rates in urban areas, also indicating the proportion of hand guns.

The ICVS survey confirms that firearm ownership in the United States is very common: Firearms are present in over 30% of households and are mainly handguns. Other countries with high firearm ownership rates among city dwellers are some of the Latin American countries, such as Paraguay and Costa Rica. High rates are also found in some countries in eastern Europe (Serbia, Albania) and some countries in Africa (South Africa, Namibia). Switzerland's high rate is largely explained by mandatory ownership of a military weapon by all male adults. Low ownership rates are found in Asian countries such as China, India, and Japan and western Europe (the Netherlands and the United Kingdom).

Firearms and Violent Crime

International cross-sectional studies find that gun ownership levels are associated with overall homicide rates (Hepburn & Hemenway, 2004; Killias, 1993; Killias, Van Kesteren & Rindlisbacher, 2001). In South Africa, the increased availability of firearms in recent years has not only increased the percentages of homicides committed with

❖ **Table 5.1** World Rankings According to Firearm Ownership and Proportion of Handguns in Urban Areas

Fifteen Countries With Highest Rates of Gun Ownership							
Rank	Country	% Firearms	% of Firearms Being Handguns	Rank	Country	% Firearms	% of Firearms Being Handguns
1	United States	34.4	67.6	9	Lesotho	15.0	100.0
2	Paraguay	31.9	93.7	10	Albania	14.3	39.3
3	Serbia & Montenegro	28.4	86.4	11	Belgium	14.1	30.6
				12	Finland	13.1	37.6
4	Switzerland	27.4	37.2	13	Macedonia	12.8	65.4
5	Namibia	22.1	100.0	14	Croatia	11.8	88.2
6	Costa Rica	19.2	64.0	15	Panama	11.8	86.8
7	South Africa	18.3	85.7				
8	Malta	17.4	8.9				

Fifteen Countries With Moderately High Rates of Gun Ownership							
Rank	Country	% Firearms	% of Firearms Being Handguns	Rank	Country	% Firearms	% of Firearms Being Handguns
16	Canada	11.5	17.8	29	Bulgaria	7.3	77.3
18	France	11.0	32.1	31	Austria	7.1	60.8
20	Colombia	10.8	81.8	33	Indonesia	6.5	12.6
21	Argentina	10.2	84.4	36	Hungary	5.6	74.3
22	Brazil	9.0	97.4	38	Denmark	4.7	25.5
25	Czech Republic	8.7	74.5	39	Poland	4.6	37.6
26	Russian Federation	8.5	49.3	40	Australia	4.1	24.6
28	Sweden	7.5	15.8				

Fifteen Countries With Low Rates of Gun Ownership							
Rank	Country	% Firearms	% of Firearms Being Handguns	Rank	Country	% Firearms	% of Firearms Being Handguns
41	Botswana	4.0	20.8	49	Nigeria	1.6	43.8
42	Latvia	3.9	54.4	50	Korea, Rep.	1.6	84.4
43	Slovak Republic	3.9	43.8	51	United Kingdom	1.3	24.0
44	Mozambique	3.0	93.3				
45	Philippines	2.9	90.9	52	Netherlands	0.9	36.3
46	Zimbabwe	2.8	19.8	53	India	0.8	14.2
47	Romania	2.0	88.8	54	Azerbaijan	0.7	11.1
48	Uganda	1.9	57.9	55	Japan	0.1	0.0

Source: ICVS, 1996–2000 or latest available.

firearms but has also, even more dramatically, increased firearm use in serious rob-beries, including car hijackings (Shaw, 2002).

The comparison of the United States to other industrialized nations underscores the role of guns as facilitators of homicide, aggravated assault, and gun robberies. Homicide and other serious violence rates in the United States are many times higher than compa-rable rates in western Europe. This is not because the United States is a more criminal or violent society generally. In fact, as discussed, rates of overall volume crime, including common assaults, are at the same level or lower than in many other Western countries, including Canada and the United Kingdom. Rather, the much higher homicide rates of the United States may result from the widespread availability of handguns, which means that the opportunity to carry out a quick but dangerous attack is much greater, even when the victim is stronger than the attacker (Felson & Clarke, 1998).

Sloan et al. (1988) compared homicide rates of Seattle, Washington, in the United States, and Vancouver, British Columbia, in Canada. Although these two cities are comparable in terms of age, race, and income, homicide rates were 50% higher in Seattle probably because of greater availablity of handguns. Across U.S. regions and states, where there are more guns, there are more firearm homicides. The association continues to hold after accounting for poverty, unemployment, urbanization, and alcohol consumption (Miller et al., 2002). Several studies have also found that the more guns there are, the more that women become victims of homicide, usually com-mitted by intimates (Small Arms Survey, 2004). Higher levels of gun ownership are also related to higher levels of gun robberies, the most dangerous category of robberies (Cook, 1987). The link between gun availabity and serious violence has been con-firmed in field experiments. Interventions to reduce gun availability in Kansas City, New York, and Boston have proven to result in lower violence (Wintemute, 2005).

Previous analyses of global ICVS victimization rates have found positive relation-ships between gun ownership and rates of assaults or threats with guns as well as gun robberies, which held after controlling for other determining factors (Van Dijk, 1999). Analyses using data from later sweeps of the ICVS confirm the existence of these sta-tistically significant, though not always very strong, associations. Gun ownership was found to be statistically unrelated to rates of threats or assaults.

Figure 5.11 presents results of the analysis of ICVS 1996–2000 data on the rela-tionship between firearm ownership rates and assaults with firearms. Countries where firearm ownership—and especially handgun ownership—is more common tend to show, on average, higher rates of firearm-related assaults ($r = .26$, $p < 0.05$, $n = 56$). This relationship was once again confirmed in an analysis of ICVS 2005 data ($r = .62$, $p < 0.05$, $n = 30$). Obvious examples of countries where high ownership of guns goes together with high rates of gun-related violent crime are the United States, South Africa, Albania, Colombia, and Costa Rica. The case of Switzerland is sometimes men-tioned as evidence that high levels of gun ownership are not linked to high levels of serious violence. It should be recalled, though, that most of the Swiss firearms are mil-itary weapons owned by reservists and do not easily lend themselves for concealed possession in public and are ususaly locked away at home.

Supporters of defensive gun use have pointed out that gun availability might actu-ally save lives and prevent crime by deterring would-be offenders from attacking or

❖ **Figure 5.11**   National Rates of Firearm Ownership and Rates of Assaults Involving Firearms

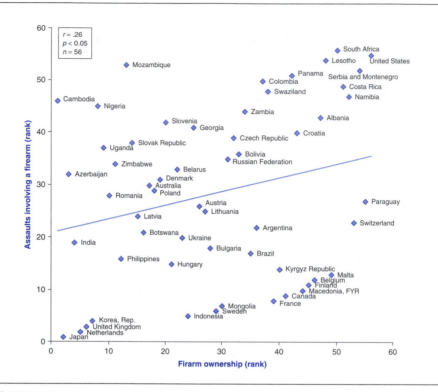

Source: ICVS, 1996–2000.

from entering premises for burglary. The economist John R. Lott argued in his book *More Guns, Less Crime* that violent crime has decreased in areas where law-abiding citizens are allowed to carry concealed guns (Lott, 1997). There seems, however, to be little supporting empirical evidence for this hypothesis (Wellford, Pepper, & Petrie, 2004).

In a paper presented at the American Society of Criminology, Felson, Pare, and Haber (2006) show that across American states, gun possession is related to rates of homicide but is unrelated to rates of common assault. In southern states, homicide rates are comparatively high and assault rates comparatively low. In their view, the presence of firearms discourages violence because fear of armed adversaries may lead offenders to avoid fistfights. This mechanism may also explain the consistent finding of ICVS surveys that rates of common assaults are comparatively low in gun-ridden societies with high homicide rates such as the United States and Brazil and are comparatively high in gun-free societies such as England/Wales, Australia, Canada, and the Netherlands, where homicide rates are low. It seems worth noting that in typical high-gun-ownership countries such as the United States and South Africa, rates of pick-pocketing are also comparatively low.

At the national level, more guns are related to higher levels of serious violence, including homicide. On the positive side, however, more guns are not related to higher levels of common assault. A high prevalence of guns might even discourage potential attackers from initiating violent interactions or pickpocketing. It seems possible, as argued by Lott, that gun possession in some respects results in less crime. The preventative effect on common assaults, however, comes at the price of higher levels of serious and lethal violence including gun robberies. On balance, the crime-related impact of guns on societies looks to be a distinctly negative one.

Guns and Violence in Developing Countries

The recent boom in lethal violence in Costa Rica illustrates the importance of both inequalities and gun ownership as determinants of serious violence. Homicide rates per 100,000 inhabitants in Costa Rica remained stable in the 1990s, fluctuating around 4 per 100,000. From 1992 onward, homicide rates suddenly started to rise, and were at 7 per 100,000 of the population in 2003. The rise in homicides coincided with a general rise in recorded crime rates, including robberies and kidnappings. According to staff of the United Nations Research Institute in Costa Rica (ILANUD), two social factors seem to be related to the upward surge of homicides: increased income inequalities and greater availability of firearms (Caranza & Solana, 2004).

Inequality in income distribution as expressed in the Gini coefficient has risen in Costa Rica from 0.374 in 1990 to 0.425 in 2003. The variations in the Gini coefficient scores show a strong positive correlation with the increase in the homicide rate ($r = 0.62$) (see Figure 5.12).

Figure 5.12 shows that homicide rates in Costa Rica have risen in tandem with income inequality in recent years. The percentage of homicides committed with a firearm has risen 17 points since 1989: from 35.6% that year to 52% in 2003. The percentages of firearm killings and the increase in homicide rates were found to be closely related. The results show that the rise in the overall homicide rate in Costa Rica over the past 10 years was caused by an increase in male-to-male violence, which is typically committed with the use of firearms and often in the context of other criminal activities against the background of gross socioeconomic inequalities.

The results confirm the conclusion reached in the latest Small Arms Survey (2004) that availability of firearms in households is more likely to increase the risks of being victimized by serious crime than of being protected against strangers. Although it is obvious that firearm availability by itself cannot explain rates of serious violent crime—social causes are at least equally and probably even more important—the results are consistent with a policy position against widespread availability of firearms.

Several countries, including Australia, Brazil, and South Africa, have recently introduced tighter gun legislation or regulations seeking to reduce the availability of firearms. In several postconflict countries, for example, in western Africa and Central America, special programs have been carried out to control the availability of weapons. The program developed by the city government and the church in Bogota, Colombia, to buy back weapons in exchange for cash represents a promising effort in this regard. It also illustrates the added value of collaboration between the administration

❖ **Figure 5.12** Homicide Rates per 100,000 Inhabitants and Income Distribution by the Gini Coefficient, Costa Rica 1990–2003

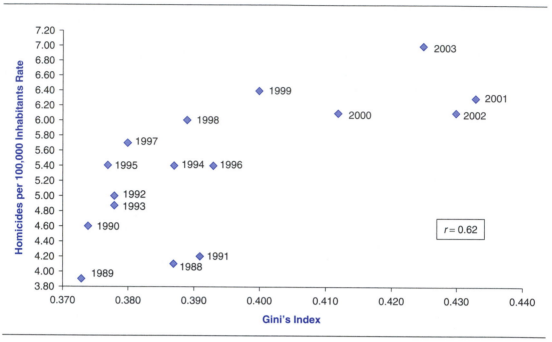

and the private sector. Between 1993 and 2001, the number of murders in Bogota decreased from 4,452 to 1,993, whereas national rates of homicide in Colombia declined only marginally (Waller, 2006). Another interesting experience in handgun control in Colombia comes from Cali, where the carrying of handguns was prohibited on high-risk weekends and is held partially responsible for lowering Cali's homicide rates (Buvinic, Morrison, & Shifter, 1999).

In 2004, Brazil's President Lula undertook systematic attempts to come to grips with one of the worst social problems and deterrents for investors in Brazil, violent crime. The government adopted a two-pronged strategy. First, a gun amnesty, launched in July 2004, has had more success in taking arms off the streets than had been expected. In the first month alone, 57,000 weapons had been turned in. Second, the president pushed legislation through Congress to limit the issuing of permits on weapons to anyone except those in dangerous professions.

In a report on "reducing gun violence through the UN process on small arms control," Justice and Security Sector Reform (JSSR) is recommended as part of the solution, especially in postconflict situations (Missing Pieces, 2005). In postconflict situations, disarmament requires a functioning, nonmilitary, restrained police who instill trust in law-abiding citizens.

The observation on the conditionality of gun control on "generalized trust" brings us back to the conventional wisdom expressed in Homeros' verse about the need to remove weapons from places where young men are going to party and drink. However sensible and wise such preventive measures may be, in the case of Odysseus it was a devious ruse to make his rivals defenseless against his planned retaliatory attack on his wife's suitors. Possession of firearms increases the risks for serious violence within communities and should therefore be reduced. But in the debate on gun control, the primary function of firearms, to offer a defense against enemies, must not be overlooked. The reduction or elimination of guns requires a social context of general lawfulness and trust. In postconflict societies, gun control measures have a better chance for lasting results when introduced as part of comprehensive reforms of the justice and security sector.

❖

SUMMARY POINTS/IN CONCLUSION

• The most important general risk factors in the epidemiology of common crimes are age composition (proportion of young males in the population), degree of urbanization, and affluence. The combined factors of age composition and urbanization can explain a large part of the variation in crime rates across countries. The impact of affluence on levels of crime is more complex. On the one hand, more affluence reduces extreme poverty and inequalities, factors linked to the level of some property crimes and, more strongly, contact crimes including homicides and violence against women. On the other hand, more affluence creates opportunities for property crimes such as vehicle-related crime. From a criminological perspective, economic growth is a mixed blessing. Economic growth can not be seen as a fix for crime problems of developing countries. As the experience of Western countries over the past three decades

has proven, economic growth in the short and even medium term spurs rather than reduces overall levels of common crime.

• Governments have limited capacity to influence factors such as urbanization and age-composition, and no government will be ready to slow down development in order to prevent some types of property crime. To control crime at the global level and prevent a widening of the gap in security between the affluent North and the poor South, developing countries will need to invest more of their scarce resources in types of crime prevention and control that have proven their cost-effectiveness in the developed countries. The range of policies and interventions available will be discussed in Chapter 9 in Part IV.

• Risk factors for violence include economic deprivation of young males, gender inequality, alcohol abuse, and availability of guns. Governments of developed and developing countries have the option to introduce policies that can help to reduce these three risk factors and thereby contribute to making their societies safer. Politically, such policies are often controversial or opposed by special interest groups. In western Europe, powerful lobbying from beer companies and their associates in the leisure industry prevents governments from tackling binge drinking by not being able to raise age levels for alcohol consumption to above 16. In the United States, legislation to reduce availability of guns consistently meets with fierce opposition of the National Rifle Association.

• Comparative information on the links between risk factors and crime across countries can inform ongoing policy debates. Reviews of best practices in crime prevention provide several examples of successful actions to reduce violence by measures against gender inequality, alcohol abuse, and the possession of firearms (see Chapter 9 for details).

Notes

1. Self-report studies among samples of juveniles are another method for collecting information on crime rates independently of the police. Through standardization of instruments, comparative results can be obtained. The first International Self-Report Delinquency Study (ISRD) was launched in 1992 by the Dutch Research and Documentation Center (WODC). The study was based on data collected in 11 mostly EU countries, Nebraska (United States), and New Zealand (Josine Junger-Tas, Gert-Jan Terlouw, & Malcolm W. Klein [1994]: *Delinquent Behavior among Young People in the Western World – First Results of the International Self-report Delinquency Study,* Kugler Publications; Josine Junger-Tas, Ineke Haen Marshall, & Denis Ribeaud [2003]: *Delinquency in an International Perspective –The International Self-Report Delinquency Study,* Criminal Justice Press and Kugler Publications). A small steering committee coordinates the ongoing project. Contact person is Josine Junger-Tas (Jungertas@xs4all.nl).

2. Urbanization and age composition together explain 27% of the variance in overall victimization rates of the 30 mainly Western countries participating in the ICVS 2004/2005.

3. Similar "crime chains" may also apply to the theft of other personal items associated with affluence such as Walkmans, laptops, mobile phones, and other electronic gadgets among student populations (Felson & Clarke, 1998).

4. In 1988, the United Kingdom showed one of the lowest rates of victimization for motorcycle theft of all Western countries. In the 2005 sweep of the ICVS, the UK's owners' motorcycle theft victimization rate was second only to that of Italy (Van Dijk, Manchin, Van Kesteren, & Hideg, 2007).

5. In her inaugural lecture as director of the Jill Dando Institute of Crime Science in London, Laycock commented on the rise of recorded crime in the United Kingdom since World War I: "The rise was not caused by an increase of poverty—we are, by any measure, better off now than we have ever been. Nor was it caused by a lack of education, even the worst educated members of our population spend more time in formal education than did the average child of the early 20th century. Nor is there any evidence that "parenting" has been in catastrophic

decline throughout the period (. . .) All these factors may, in combination have played their subtle part, but there is one factor, which we do not hear about, and that is opportunity" (Laycock, 2001).

6. The item on contact with drugs-related problems follows the methodological strategy of the ICVS to interview people about real-life experiences rather than about beliefs and perceptions: "Over the last 12 months, how often were you personally in contact with drug-related problems in the area where you live? For example, seeing people dealing in drugs, taking or using drugs in public spaces, or by finding syringes left by drug addicts? Was this often, from time to time, rarely, or never?"

Global Trends and Regional Profiles

Global Trends in Common Crimes

The analysis of global trends in crime over time is handicapped even more than cross-sectional comparisons by a lack of reliable data. The Interpol data on police-recorded crime go back to 1950 but cannot be reliably used to analyze trends for the reasons discussed in Chapter 2. International trend data based on crime victimization surveys are available only since the inception of the International Crime Victim Surveys in 1988.

With the release of the results of the fifth sweep of the ICVS, some conclusions can now be drawn about trends in crime based on survey research among populations over a time span of almost 20 years. Data are now available from ICVS studies of 1988, 1992, 1996, 2000, and 2005 for England and Wales, the Netherlands, Finland, the United States, and Canada. These countries participated in all five rounds of the ICVS. Some other countries, mainly from the Western world, participated in all four rounds of the ICVS since 1992. Some trend data are also available from Argentina (Buenos Aires) and South Africa (Johannesburg). Figure 6.1 shows the trends in overall victimization rates of selected countries from different world regions in the period 1988–2005. To maximize comparability with data from previous ICVS sweeps, the trend analyses regarding developed countries are based on data from national samples and not, as in the cross-sectional analyses presented in previous chapters, on city samples.[1] As a consequence, the country rates are lower than the rates presented in Chapters 3 and 4 that are based on samples from capital or other main city populations.

The rates of victimization of North America, Australia, and the nine European countries for which ICVS-based trend data are available show distinct downward trends. In the United States, the drop in crime was already in evidence between 1988 and 1992. In Canada, the turning point came somewhat later, similar to what

❖ **Figure 6.1**   Trends in Crime Experienced by National or City Populations During 1988–2005; Overall Victimization Rates in South Africa (Johannesburg), Argentina (Buenos Aires), Australia, Canada, the United States, and Europe (nine countries)

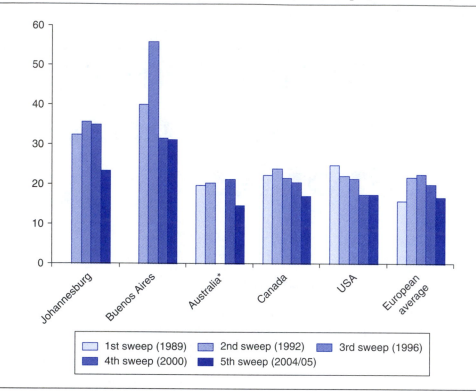

Source: ICVS, 1988–2005.

Notes: Trends in overall victimization rates are based on 10 crimes that are consistent over time.
*Australian trend is based on 9 crimes consistent over time.

happened in most European countries and Australia. Since data on sexual offenses are missing, the overall victimization rate of Australia is an approximation based on the rate for nine other offenses and results in previous years. Nevertheless, Australia shows without any doubt the same curvilinear trend as the European countries with an all-time peak around 2000 and a sharp drop thereafter.

In the course of the past 10 years, the level of crime in the Western world seems to have converged. Differences between the United States, Canada, Australia, and western and central Europe seem to have narrowed down. Although trend data are available from only two middle-income cities in the developing world, these too point to a downturn in overall victimization since 1996 (Buenos Aires) or 2000 (Johannesburg). Crime trends across the developed and middle-income countries, then, show remarkable uniformity. ICVS results show an increase in general crime between 1988 and 1991 and a downward trend since 1996 or 2000 across the developed world.[2] The ICVS seems to have been initiated just in time to register the rise in volume crime, its peaking around 1995, and its subsequent decline.

Based on police statistics of recorded crime, some European commentators have observed a continuing rise in violent crime in contrast to declining rates of property crime (*European Sourcebook,* 2006). As can be seen in Figure 6.2, such a diverging trend in violent crime is not evident in our survey-based data.

Over the period 1988–2005, levels of contact crime have gone down in the United States. In Canada and Europe as well as in Johannesburg and Buenos Aires, levels of contact crime show a curvilinear trend. Increases in the 1990s were followed by a drop. The picture confirms the gap in levels of contact crime between the two developing countries and the others. Although rates in large cities such as Johannesburg and Buenos Aires cannot be directly compared with the national rates of other countries, the level remains comparatively very high. Contact crimes are somewhat more prevalent in the United States than in Europe and Canada, but the differences have become smaller since 1988. Australian rates do not include data on sexual violence and are therefore not strictly comparable. Rates of nonsexual violence in Australia indicate a clear downward trend, but they remain high compared to some other Western countries.

❖ **Figure 6.2**   Trends in Contact Crime (Robberies, Threats/Assault, Sexual Offenses) Experienced by National or City Populations During 1988–2005; Overall Victimization Rates in South Africa (Johannesburg), Argentina (Buenos Aires), Canada, the United States, and Europe (nine countries)

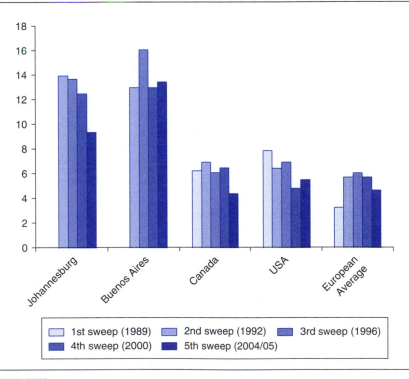

Source: ICVS, 1988–2005.

European Trends in Focus

In all European countries for which sufficient trend data are available, with the exception of Belgium, rates of victimization in 2005 are lower than 10 years before. In Estonia, France, the Netherlands, Poland, and the United Kingdom, crime leveled off since 1996. In Finland and Sweden, the turning point came after 2000. Figure 6.3 shows the results.

❖ **Figure 6.3**   Trends in Crime Experienced by National Populations in Nine European Countries During 1988–2005

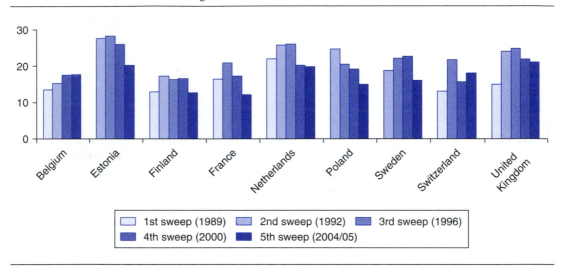

Source: ICVS, 1988–2005.

Because of the uniform downward trends, the *ranking* of countries in Europe in terms of overall victimization by common crime has not changed much, with Estonia, the United Kingdom, and the Netherlands still on top. Poland, for which ICVS-based national data are available since 1990, shows a clear and consistent downward trend. From a European perspective, Poland has turned from a high-crime into a medium-crime country. In Sweden, decreases in crime seem to have been somewhat delayed. The 2000 survey still showed a small increase for Sweden, putting it in the category of high-crime countries. Between 2000 and 2004, Swedish crime dropped steeply, and the level has now returned to the medium range.

Belgium is, as mentioned, the only European country where levels of crime have not shown a decrease. In 1988, Belgium was recorded by the ICVS as a comparatively low-crime country. Since crime has dropped elsewhere, the country has now moved into the category of countries with levels of crime above the European mean.

No historical ICVS data are available on Ireland, but as shown in Chapter 3, the 2005 rates are now among the highest in Europe. According to results of stand-alone Irish surveys, crime has indeed gone up steeply since 1998 (Central Statistical Office

Ireland, 2004). In Northern Ireland, part of the United Kingdom, overall victimization rates have also increased markedly in recent years (see Appendix B for details). The level of overall crime has climbed up to the level in England and Wales and has overtaken that of Scotland. This steep rise is reflected in the perception of a large majority of the public that crime has been on the rise in recent years (Freel & French, 2006). Ireland and Northern Ireland seem to experience, somewhat belatedly, the crime epidemic that hit other Western countries 10 or 20 years earlier. They can no longer be regarded as traditional rural countries blessed with few crimes. In the case of Northern Ireland, the reduced role of the IRA in informal policing may have created a vacuum of social control in certain areas.

Finally, Figure 6.4 presents data on trends in contact crimes in the European countries.

❖ **Figure 6.4** Trends in Victimization by Contact Crime Experienced by National Populations in Nine European Countries During 1988–2005

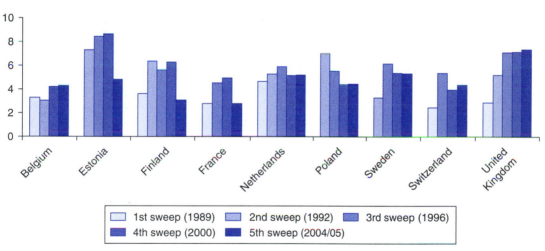

Source: ICVS, 1988–2005.

Trends in contact crime are less consistent in Europe than those in property crimes. The ICVS data set indicates significant decreases in contact crimes in Estonia, Poland, Finland, and France. In the other six countries, levels of robberies, threats or assaults, and sexual offenses have gone up between 1988 and 1992 and thereafter remained more or less stable.

Trends in Police-Recorded Crimes

As discussed in Chapter 2, global crime trend data based on police administration data must be interpreted with great caution since reporting and/or recording patterns may have changed over time. Global trend analyses of police-recorded crime are further complicated by fragmentary data. Since police-recorded rates on homicide are generally regarded as useful indicators of the volume and trends of actual homicides, these police statistics merit further examination. As reported by LaFree and Drass (2001), homicide rates among the Western, industrialized countries showed converging trends between 1965 and 1994, with smaller, low-crime countries in Europe catching up with the others. Divergence on the global scale was due to declining or stable rates among Asian industrialized nations. More recently, a clear downward trend was observed in the United States, where homicide rates decreased to its present 5 per 100,000 population from 10 in the early 1990s. South Africa has also witnessed a consistent decline in homicide over the past 10 years, bringing down the rate of total intentional homicides committed from 68 to 47 per 100,000 population around 2000. In 2005–2006, the murder rate in South Africa had declined further to 39.5 per 100,000 population. The steepest declines were recorded in parts of the country previously most afflicted by postconflict violence.

In the period 1988 to 2000, homicide trends of individual countries remained more or less stable in the majority of countries. It is likely that levels of homicide would not fluctuate much in such a short time span. The data show an increase in some countries in Latin America, for example, from 7 per 100,000 population in 1998 to 9 in 2000 in Argentina, from 4 per 100,000 in 1992 to 7 in 2003 in Costa Rica, and from 4 per 100,000 in 1998 to 6 in 2002 in Uruguay.[3]

According to data from the Pan American Health Organization, the homicide rate for the Americas rose over 44% during the period 1984–1994 (Buvinic, Morrison, & Shifter, 1999). If rates have been stabilizing somewhat in recent years, this should be seen against the background of steep increases over a longer time period.

Explaining the Drop in Crime

Nearly all developed countries, including the United States, Australia, Canada, and most EU member states, show a curved trend of volume crime since the mid 1980s with all-time peaks situated between 1995 and 2000 and steep declines of up to 50% or more thereafter. The only difference between American and European crime trends is that the drop in crime in the United States started 5 or more years earlier than in Europe. These strikingly uniform, curvilinear crime trends cannot be coincidental. The data suggest that a similar set of factors has been pushing crime up until 1995–2000 and pulling it down afterward across the Western world. Possibly similar factors are also at play in the middle-income cities Buenos Aires and Johannesburg. To which universally operating set of determining factors can the universal crime curves be attributed?

American crime drops have been ascribed to the crack epidemic, quadrupling of prison population, and enhanced police deployment (Blumstein & Wallman, 2006). In addition, economist Levitt has imaginatively linked the crime drop to the legalization of abortion by the U.S. Supreme Court ruling in *Roe v Wade* in 1973 (Levitt & Dubner, 2005). According to Levitt, crime started to drop in the United States in the early 1990s when the first cohort of children not wanted by their mothers was missing among the subgroup of criminally active youngsters. The American crime drop, then, has been ascribed to the aforementioned four main factors.

The impact of the increase in sheer numbers of police officers on American crime rates has been contested by Eck and Maguire (2006), and the impact of legalized abortion on crime has been disputed by Blumstein and Wallman (2006). Whatever may be the final verdict in this ongoing debate, the identification of these four putative determinants of the American crime drop is exclusively based on analyses of American data. It would seem natural in an epidemiological debate to test the significance of putative key factors in other countries, especially since, as we have seen, all Western countries have experienced similar drops in crime.

In a European context, two of the four hypotheses can be eliminated right away. Few if any European countries have ever experienced a crack epidemic, and reductions in this factor cannot have played a role in European crime drops. Abortion was formally or de facto legalized in some European countries such as England and Wales (1967), Finland (1970), and the Netherlands (c. 1970), that is, years before *Roe v Wade.* And yet crime in these countries started to decrease 5 or more years *later* and definitely not sooner than in the United States. In other European countries such as Portugal and Poland, abortion has never been legalized. Drops in crime in these countries are as large as elsewhere. It seems very unlikely that legalization of abortion can have been a key factor behind the European crime drops.

The impact of police resources and incarceration rates on Europewide crime drops merits closer scrutiny. Canadian analysts have found no evidence that the Canadian crime drop in the 1990s can be explained with these two factors. Government spending on policing and more severe punishment did not appear to have a similar effect on crime rates in Canada (Ouimet, 2002; Welsh & Irving, 2005). The same can be said about Europe. Trends in expenditures on policing and imprisonment show huge variation across European countries. Since the early 1990s, prison populations in countries such as Finland, France, and Poland have gone down or fluctuated rather than gone up (*European Sourcebook,* 2006; Tornudd, 1997). As in Canada, resources for policing show no consistent trend across western Europe over the past 10 years (*European Sourcebook,* 2006).

None of the four factors highlighted in American analyses of the U.S. crime drop can convincingly explain the curvilinear trends in volume crime across the Western world. More police resources and wider use of prisons may have been decisive factors behind the crime drop in the United States, but generalizations to other countries are unwarranted. The issue of what factors have caused the crime drop in all major Western countries must be revisited from an international perspective. This international analysis should, we think, not be focused on the decreases in the last 5 to 10 years but rather should seek to explain the curvilinear trends between 1970 and 2005; in other words, it should seek to understand both the rise and the fall of common crime as resulting from specific factors.

Responsive Securitization and the Drop in Crime

According to the theory of criminal opportunities discussed in Chapters 3 and 5, crime trends across countries are driven by the availability of suitable targets of crime or criminal opportunities. The theory was initially developed to explain the rise of crime in industrialized societies. Crime booms were portrayed as undesirable side effects of economic growth (Cohen & Felson, 1979; Felson, 1997; Van Dijk, 1994). The recent rise of crime in Ireland is a case in point. Ireland entered the European Union in 1971 and received major incentives for its economy that since has grown from one of the weakest into one of the most powerful in Europe. Higher crime rates appear to be the downside of the belatedly acquired affluence. Iceland, Norway, and Switzerland provide other examples of countries whose rising levels of crime seem to be a side effect of growing prosperity. But opportunity theory, in our view, cannot explain only increases in crime. It seems also well placed to explain the near universal crime drops of recent years. It seems likely that opportunities for crime that have since the 1970s expanded, together with the economic booms, have subsequently shrunk due to improved self-protection of households and businesses against crime in response to increased losses from crime. According to this elaboration of criminal opportunity theory, potential victims react to higher crime rates with increased concerns about crime losses and subsequently with additional investments in measures to avoid or protect themselves from crime risks.

In a study using data from the United States in the period 1984 to 1994, it was found that for every 100 burglaries per 100,000 population, there was a 3% increase in the demand for alarm systems (Philipson & Posner, 1996). Somewhat higher proportions of persons protected by burglar alarms will not affect rates of burglary because sufficient suitable targets will remain. But when collective levels of self-protection surpass certain thresholds, risks and costs of offending for local offenders will go up. Increasingly, local offenders will be discouraged from engaging in criminal activity by changed costs-gains trade-offs.[4] Ultimately, levels of crime will go down (Cusson, 1990; Philipson & Posner, 1996; Van Dijk, 1994a; Van Dijk, 1994b). This assumed feedback loop of private security efforts in response to rising crime has been dubbed "reflexive securitization'" by British criminologist Hope (Hope, 2007). Since potential victims are supposed to mobilize against their risks on the basis of costs-benefits assessments, responsive securitization would perhaps be the most fitting name. Figure 6.5 depicts the causal mechanisms at play in crime epidemics according to the hypothesis of responsive securitization derived from criminal opportunity theory.

ICVS data on fear of crime and the use of self-protection measures lend empirical support to the notion of responsive securitization. Cross-sectional analyses have shown strong statistical links between levels of burglary victimizations in countries or regions, levels of fear of burglary, and the use of antiburglary measures (Van Dijk, 1994b). Where objective burglary risks are high, more citizens are concerned about their victimization risks, and those concerned are more ready to invest in security measures. Trend data from the ICVS confirm the links between objective risks, perceived risks, and investments in security as well. In nearly all developed countries, the level of concern about burglary increased from 1989 to 1992 and fell significantly thereafter. Trends in the United States, Canada, Australia, and Europe show the same curved patterns.[5] These trends in subjective feelings mirror trends in actual victimization by burglary.

❖ **Figure 6.5**   Schematic Representation of the Dynamics of Crime Epidemics in Western Countries

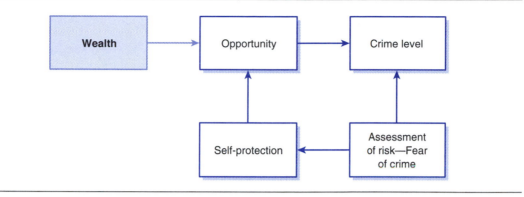

Investments of individual households in home security are difficult to assess in a comparative perspective since types of security show great variation across countries. In some countries (such as France and Canada), concierges or caretakers in high-rise apartment buildings are traditionally more common than elsewhere (Van Kesteren, Mayhew, & Nieuwbeerta, 2000). Special grills on doors and windows are more common in the United Kingdom and Australia, and these features may reflect national design traditions rather than topical concerns about crime. According to ICVS data, across the world one in two households protects itself against burglary with special locks. Such precautions are almost universal in Australia and New Zealand and also comparatively common in Africa. Within western Europe, two out of three households in many countries had installed special locks in 2005; in the Netherlands, the coverage is 80%. The use of such locks shows an upward trend almost everywhere. This universal boom in precautionary measures can be seen as evidence for responsive securitization.

Another useful indicator of responsive securitization is the installment of burglar alarms. The use of this measure requires serious investments that will not be made spuriously. It has become more common over the past two decades in almost all affluent countries, especially among the middle classes. Figure 6.6 shows regional trends in the use of burglar alarms since 1990.[6]

The results in Figure 6.6 show that the use of burglar alarms by households has gone up in the more affluent parts of the world. In the United States, for example, it went up from 16% in 1989 to 28% in 2005. As observed above, levels of precaution at the national level were positively related to national burglary risks; that is, those in countries facing higher risks were generally more likely to have installed alarms. This

❖ **Figure 6.6**   Percentages of Households Protected by Burglar Alarms

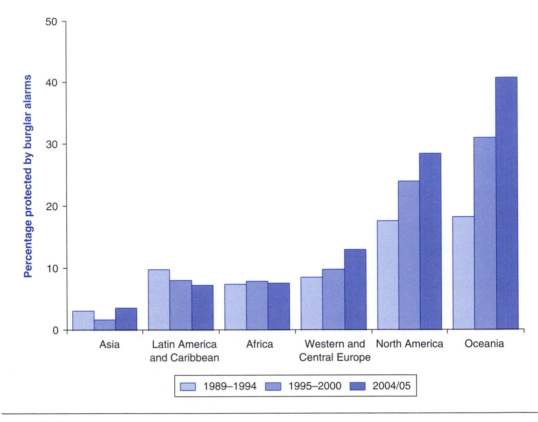

Source: ICVS, 1992–2005.

is demonstrated in particular by the low rates in Asia. The use of such precautionary devices would, in all likelihood, be much higher in Africa and Latin America and the Caribbean if more households could afford them. In a middle-income city like Johannesburg, 10% of the households possess a burglar alarm. In South Africa, the use of such precautions is near universal among the most affluent, many of which live in highly secured, "gated communities."

The rate of burglar alarm use is clearly driven by levels of burglary and perceived risks. At both the household and national levels, burglary experiences, fear of burglary, and use of alarms are strongly linked. The increase in their use therefore represents a clear example of the widespread mobilization of civil society against crime, including increased readiness of households to invest in expensive self-protection devices, especially in affluent and middle-income countries.

Responsiveness to crime risks can also be expected from the profit-oriented business sector. If marginal benefits of prevention in terms of reduced losses are larger than the extra costs, prevention will be stepped up to increase profits. The total value of the global private security market was estimated at $75 billion in 2000. It shows annual growth percentages of 7% to 8% worldwide. In Chapter 9, statistics will be presented on the explosive growth of private security across the world over the past two decades. In the United States, estimates of the 1970s indicated less than half a million private security staff. The current staffing is estimated at between 1.5 million and 2 million (Manning, 2006). The use of private security is massive and has quadrupled in recent years. In the European Union, staff employed by private security firms has gone up from 0.5 million to 1 million since 1996 (Van Steden & Sarre, 2007). In South Africa, the private security industry has expanded rapidly since 1980: Initially it expanded at a rate of 30% a year, slowing to 10%–15% more recently (Shaw, 2002).

The ICVS trend data provide clear evidence that the use of household security measures and other forms of "target hardening" has increased significantly over the past 20 years across the Western world. There has also been more attention to "designing out" crime through the introduction of environmental, architectural, and product designs that offer better protection against crime. Indicative of large-scale securitization of public spaces is the expansion of closed-circuit television (CCTV) cameras in the United Kingdom from 40 in 1990 to over 40,000 in 2002 (Farrington & Jolliffe, 2005).

Security Measures and Trends in Burglary Victimization Rates

The hypothesis of responsive securitization outlined above assumes that the countermovement of private securitization ultimately discourages offending and reduces crime. Previous analyses of ICVS data have confirmed that households with alarms installed have significantly lower risks of having burglars enter the house than those without alarms. For those in selected developing countries with alarms installed at the time of the offense, 1.1% had a burglar enter the house, as against 1.8% without alarms (Mayhew & Van Dijk, 1997). In the United Kingdom, home security protection and membership of neighborhood watch schemes appear as significant predictors of lower likelihood of burglary and household theft (Tseloni, 2006). In the Netherlands, national victim surveys have shown that of houses without any special preventive measures, 8% were entered by burglars compared with less than 1% of those with five or more special measures such as burglar alarms, special lights, and so on (Van Dijk, Toornvliet, & Sagel-Grande, 2002). It has also been demonstrated in several analyses that the proportion of unsuccessful burglaries is higher in countries where more houses have installed preventive measures (Van Dijk, 1994b).

It is difficult to demonstrate the impact of better household security on levels of burglary at the country or city level because levels of security, as discussed above, tend to be higher where burglaries are more prevalent. As also mentioned, households invest more in expensive security measures to the extent that they are more affluent, regardless of actual risks. In a secondary analysis of the ICVS data set on the 12 (Western) countries for which sufficient historical data are available, the hypothesis was tested whether since 1988, coverage by security measures has gone up more substantially among higher-income than among lower-income families. This hypothesis was fully supported by the data. Across North America, western Europe, and Australia, high-income groups have improved security more than lower-income groups, and consequently, gaps in security levels between income groups have become wider. The differences are most marked in the use of burglar alarms. On average, the use of burglar alarms in the 12 countries went up from 18% in 1988 to 33% in 2004 among the upper quartile and from 11% to 17%

in the lowest quartile. In the United States, inequality in security has increased the most. The use of burglar alarms went up from 19% to 40% among the upper-income quartile and from 8% to 12% among the bottom quartile.

Subsequently, the hypothesis was tested whether since 1988, rates of victimization by burglary in the 12 countries have gone down more steeply among (increasingly better protected) high-income families than among low-income families. The results confirmed this hypothesis as well. On average, burglary rates between 1988 and 2004 went down from 2.4% to 1.7% among the upper quartile (a decrease of 30%) and from 2.6% to 2.3% among the lowest quartile (a decrease of 10%). Between 2000 and 2004, the rate for the upper quartile decreased *from 2.2%* to 1.7%, but the rate of the lowest quartile remained stable at 2.3%. Since 1988, the other quartiles show trends in between those of the upper and lower quartiles. In the United States, the divergence in risk trends is especially striking. Since 1988, burglary rates dropped from 4.1% to 1.7% among the upper quartile and increased from 3.9% to 5.9% among the lowest quartile (for details, see Appendix B).

The results of this analysis suggest that the overall drop in burglaries in Western countries since 1988 was at least in part the result of improved self-protection of higher-income groups. It also suggests that improved security has resulted in the unintended side effect of greater inequality in levels of actual security across income groups. Possibly, improved security in better-off neighborhoods has resulted in displacement of burglaries to less protected, poorer neighborhoods.

Security Measures and Trends in Car Theft and Joyriding

The widespread introduction of antitheft measures installed in cars such as steering column locks, alarms, and electronic ignition systems are known to have brought down overall levels of car theft in Germany, the United Kingdom, and the United States (Webb, 1997). If decreasing levels of car theft witnessed across the Western world since 1990 are in part or largely caused by better security, it can be expected that decreases have been steeper in the subcategory of thefts for joyriding, committed by amateurs, than in the subcategory of professional car theft. The ICVS data set allows a disaggregation of car thefts into these two categories. A closer analysis of the drop in car theft revealed that cases of joyriding in North America, Australia, and western Europe have plummeted by 50% since 1990 but that thefts whereby the car is never recovered have, on average, remained stable over the years. In the United States, for example, the rate of joyriding dropped from 1.7% in 1988 to 0.7% in 2004, and in England and Wales, from 2.8% in 1992 to 1.2% in 2004. Over the same period, rates of car theft remained at 0.4% in the United States and decreased slightly from 0.8% to 0.6% in England and Wales. These results suggest that reductions in car theft have been restricted to thefts by opportunistic nonprofessionals who can easily be discouraged by improved technical protection (for country details, see Appendix B).

Although evidence that improved security has actually brought down levels of burglaries, car thefts, and other types of crime at the country level is still inconclusive, there is abundant evidence for the effectiveness of technical or situational crime prevention at the level of individual premises or neighborhoods. Several examples of "proven practices" in technical or situational crime prevention will be presented in Chapter 9. In light of the ICVS-based findings concerning upward trends in self-protection and its relationship to crime drops across the Western world presented above, it seems plausible that the feedback mechanisms of increased investment in self-protection including private security have indeed helped to stabilize rates of property crime over time. The affluent West seems to have finally arrived at the point where the costs–benefits ratio of offending have deteriorated so much that committing offenses has become an unprofitable and therefore unappealing option. These countries may now have reached the "tipping point' where fewer young people are tempted to a criminal lifestyle by successful criminal role models in their social environment. In neighborhoods or cities where opportunities of crime have shrunk, young delinquents may no longer be perceived as local heroes but as losers.

While the academic and public debate on crime in many countries focused on the role of governments as managers of crime in society, private citizens and businesspeople have responded to growing victimization risks with improved self-protection. The invisible hand of responsive securitization may have contributed more to the current drop in crime than the official crime-reduction strategies of governments (Hope, 2007). The large-scale introduction of self-protection measures by households and companies amounts to a formidable grassroots movement against crime. Although investments in the security of individual households and businesses are motivated by self-interest, the collective effect of these investments has also served the wider community by providing lower rates of crime and reducing the caseload of law enforcement and criminal justice. On the downside, responsive securitization seems to have increased inequalities in victimization risks across income groups.

The Growing North–South Security Divide

There are no regions or countries where victimization by common crime is a rarity for people living in big cities. The risk for inhabitants of big cities—comprising more than half of the world population—to be victimized is at least 15% annually everywhere. Notwithstanding the universality of crime victimization risks, regional variation is significant. Developing countries in sub-Saharan Africa and Latin America suffer by far the highest rates of crime. Distribution is most skewed toward sub-Saharan Africa and Latin America with regard to the most serious forms of violent crime, including homicide, violence against women, and property crime with the use of violence, such as robbery at gunpoint, violent car theft, and kidnapping. Sub-Saharan Africa leads in the number of homicides, sexual assaults, and violence against women. Latin America tops the rates for street robberies and kidnappings.

The levels of public safety in Africa and Latin America are incomparably lower than in the developed countries of the North. While levels of all types of volume crime have been falling steadily and significantly in North America, western Europe, and Australia since around 1995–2000, levels of contact crimes, especially robberies, are still rampant in many parts of Africa and Latin America. It seems no exaggeration to speak of a "security divide" between the North and the South. The gap in urban security between the developing and developed countries is huge and in some respects is still widening.

The lack of security in developing countries is first and foremost a grave humanitarian problem. The security divide is also of great economic relevance for many developing countries. Lack of security is a factor that determines foreign investment. Rarely mentioned is the impact of security concerns on foreign tourism. The number of people visiting other countries as tourists is nearing one billion per year. Developing countries have experienced an especially significant growth in tourism. In particular, sub-Saharan Africa is now regarded as the fastest-growing tourist market in the world. At the present, 6% of employment and 7% of the GDP in the region is tourism related (WTTC, 2004). A recent report of the World Tourism Organization predicts that "current growth levels can be maintained across the African continent, which has the potential to triple the number of foreign tourists, *provided security for such visitors is improved*" (italics added). Because of the importance of tourism in spreading wealth from the North to the South, the security issue, which determines the extent of tourist victimization, merits more attention.

The Asian Exception

As striking as the high victimization rates in Africa and Latin America are the consistently low rates in Asia. This is as true for affluent Japan, Hong Kong, and South Korea as it is for countries with emerging economies such as China and India. It is also true for poorer developing countries such as the Philippines, Indonesia, and Cambodia. Levels of petty theft are remarkably low in the megacities of all these countries. Although car ownership is widely common in Japan, Hong Kong, and South Korea, car theft is still rare. Poverty-driven crimes such as robberies are rare across the region. To the extent that data are available, levels of juvenile delinquency seem also comparatively modest. Homicide rates in Asia are below the world average as well. According to the latest WHO studies, violence against women is more common in Asia than in western Europe but yet less common than in Africa or South America. The "Asian exception" with regard to crime levels seems to hold across all types of common crime.

Crime and Conflict

Pertinent for understanding regional crime trends in developing countries are recent booms in violence and crime in postconflict or post-transitional situations (ICHRP, 2003). Three main world regions, Africa, eastern Europe, and Latin America, have over the past two decades undergone fundamental changes in their political and economic makeup. Each of them has been confronted with law and order crises, jeopardizing their transformations into peaceful democracies.

Comparative studies suggest that crime increases markedly during periods of radical political transition coupled with instability and violence. In many countries in transition, common crime and violence are endemic. This is especially true for countries experiencing the effects of modern wars on the population. According to Collier and Hoeffler (2001), homicide rates increase on average by 25% in the 5 years following a civil war. As Nelson Mandela writes with his usual frankness in the preface to the WHO World Report on Violence and Health: "We often talk about how a culture of violence can take root. This is indeed true—as a South African who has lived through apartheid and is living through its aftermath, I have seen and experienced it" (WHO, 2002).

In Africa, a substantial increase in crime was experienced in Botswana in the 1980s and in Namibia in the run-up to and just after the independence as well as more recently in post apartheid South Africa (Shaw, 2002). Although almost no statistics on crime in Nigeria are available, experts are unanimously of the view that crime, especially violent crime, and robberies have increased after the transition from military to civil rule in 1999 (ICHRP, 2003). Many of the world's bloodiest and lengthiest recent conflicts have taken place in sub-Saharan Africa. In many parts of Africa, countries are now experiencing crime booms in postconflict situations, especially in the Great Lakes Region (UNODC, 2005). In the final stages of these conflicts, insurgents and organized-crime groups often collaborate in the extraction and smuggling of local commodities such as diamonds in exchange for weapons. Criminal and politically motivated groups intermingle and are hard to distinguish from each other. Humanitarian disasters are perpetuated through these postconflict, predatory coalitions.

In the absence of reliable crime statistics, very little is known about crime trends in Africa generally. In his well-documented case study of South Africa, Shaw (2002) links the indisputable crime boom in the country to a decline of community bonds being forged during the resistance against apartheid; interethnic political violence—purposefully fueled by the former apartheid regime—abundant availability of firearms; a lost generation of poorly educated, unemployed youth; and morally discredited and ineffective law enforcement. These factors taken together are conducive to creating a boom in violence and crime, including violence against women.

Many of these elements can be found in other countries in sub-Saharan Africa as well (UNODC, 2005). According to the World Bank in Africa, "Civil war creates a cadre of young people experienced in the use of deadly weapons who, in the process of unconventional terrorizing war, develop a 'mercenary mentality' that would underpin criminality" (World Bank, 2004). In his analysis of postconflict South Africa, Shaw (2002) explains how the government in this newly emerging democracy has been challenged to address the crime issue. The government also faces the challenge of striking a balance between the need to respect human rights and civil liberties and calls from the public to "deliver" public safety in response to rising rates of crime and violence. The experiences of the new South Africa are far from unique. In Nigeria, loss of confidence in the police has resulted in the emergence of violent vigilante groups with the tacit or even open support of local government. Human rights gains achieved through demilitarization of the police have been offset by a rise in violent vigilantism. Large parts of central and eastern Europe and Latin America seem to go through very similar processes whereby precious gains in civil liberties are put at risk by booms in common crime and subsequent authoritarian responses. Law and order crises seem to be an inevitable part of the "traumas of transition" of emerging democracies.

During the transition period after the fall of the Iron Curtain, the crime problem was growing in all central and eastern European countries. In the former Soviet Union, for example, the number of crimes recorded by the police rose from 1.8 million in 1987 to 2.8 million in 1990, a rise unlikely to be caused by improved reporting or recording. In the former Czechoslovakia, crime rates swelled by 200% in the years immediately following the Velvet Revolution in 1989. In Poland, the greatest increase in recorded crime occurred in the 1990s. In 1999, the recorded crime rate was double that of 1990. In the Baltic countries, recorded crime also doubled since the early 1990s. ICVS data have confirmed the increase of volume crime in eastern Europe in the early 1990s (Gruszczynska, 2001).

The upward trend that began in 1990 after the collapse of the communist bloc seems now to have reached a plateau. As discussed above, data on Poland and Estonia indicate a decrease of crime over the past 5 years. The overall recorded crime rates are now beginning to decline in the region (*European Sourcebook,* 2006). In the wider European context, crime levels in central Europe seem to have leveled with those of the West. Eastern Europe currently shows comparatively low levels of property crimes but comparatively high levels of serious violence. Violent crime is a persistent problem in the countries of the former Soviet Union. Across the region, the proportion of crimes recorded by the police per 100,000 population is still lagging far behind those of western Europe, indicating a limited capacity of the police to adequately record reported crime incidents.

After a relatively short period of liberal crime-control policies shaped by expert advice, ideas of more punitive crime-control policies became increasingly popular among politicians and the media in the region, according to Krajewski (2004). American slogans like "zero-tolerance," "three strikes and you're out," and similar concepts have been increasingly applauded as examples of successful policies that have brought political success for their promoters, and more security for citizens, according to Hungarian criminologist Kereszi (2004). In Russia, fear of crime and the need to fight crime have been central issues in political campaigns of reactionary political parties ever since the breakup of the Soviet Union (ICHRP, 2003). The "new penal climate" has been reinforced by media-induced fear of crime, fueling a public demand for harsher punishments and increased effectiveness of the police, prosecutors' offices, and the court system. Across the region, it has resulted in changes in sentencing policies of the courts and in the restriction of parole policies. After 2000, the prison population in these regions has once again gone up.

Difficult social, political, and economic transitions in central and eastern Europe have, in addition, generated tensions that find expression in xenophobia and racism. Often the Roma people, or gypsies, are the first targets of such social discontent. Three broad categories of human rights violations are affecting Roma people: (1) racially motivated violence by skinheads and others, (2) violence by law enforcement officers, and (3) systematic racial discrimination. The incidence of hate crimes is widespread in the region. From Bulgaria to the Czech Republic and Yugoslavia, young toughs who hold extremist views commit hate crimes against Roma people, who make up sizable minorities in these countries.

Latin America: The Price of Democracy

In the 1980s and 1990s, many South and Central American countries experienced remarkable transitions from authoritarian rule and civil strife to democratic governments and more stable political regimes. Despite these transitions, there remains a great deal of political instability in the region, as well as human rights violations, particularly violations of civil and social rights, which continue to be structural in the region. Yet, in addition to the challenges of economic and social development, the main concern in the region seems to be not the consolidation of democracy but rather the rise of crime and violence (De Mesquita Neto, 2004). While the confidence in democratic regimes has increased and the fear of democratic breakdown and civil wars has receded, the fear of crime and violence, particularly urban crime, organized crime, and terrorism, has gone up significantly in the past decade.

As in Africa, the limitations of criminal justice statistics and victimization surveys represent a major problem for researchers and policymakers seeking to analyze crime trends and find solutions for crime problems in Latin America. Yet the information available, particularly on homicides and robberies, shows that there have indeed been significant increases in violent crime in the past two decades in Latin America, most notably in Argentina and Brazil (ICHRP, 2003).

Criminal justice reforms in the region aim toward the objective of making criminal justice institutions (the police, the courts, and the prisons) more independent from the military and the government, more accountable to the law and the public, as well as more effective, efficient, and impartial. They also aim to build criminal justice institutions whose structure and function are more compatible with international norms and standards. Finally, criminal justice reforms have had the objective of expanding the participation of civil society in crime prevention and the administration of justice, specifically by means of community policing, special courts, informal means of conflict mediation and resolution, alternative (noncustodial) sentences, and rehabilitation programs for criminal offenders.

A major challenge, given the diversity of expectations and interests of the numerous groups involved in the reform process, has been the formation of stable coalitions and the establishment of a consensus regarding the objectives of the reform process and the strategies to achieve them. According to De Mesquita Nero (2004), democratic governments in Latin America have to face multiple policy debates and dilemmas in the course of the reform process.

In Latin America, there has been also a growing concern with domestic violence, intimate partner violence, sexual violence (Buvinic, Morrison, & Shifter, 1999), and, as in eastern Europe, violence against minority groups (including people of color, indigenous groups, and migrants). These types of violence have increasingly become the focus of policies and programs developed by governmental and nongovernmental organizations.

SUMMARY POINTS/IN CONCLUSION

- ICVS results show that since 1990, victimization by common crime has gone down in North America, Oceania, and central and western Europe. Risks in some European countries in transition were higher than in the most developed countries in the 1990s, but a rapid convergence seems to have taken place. Crime levels in the new members of the European Union such as Poland and Hungary are now at par with those in western Europe. Levels of crime in western Europe and North America are medium high. Risks in Asia remain by far the lowest, regardless of development.

• Trends in violent crime show a divergence between developed and developing countries, with rates falling in North America and across Europe and increasing in parts of Africa and Latin America, though not universally so. Rates have remained highest in Latin America and sub-Saharan Africa, creating a security divide between the North and the South.

• Asian countries, whether affluent or poor, enjoy lower levels of common crime including violence than anywhere else. The most plausible explanation is the retention in large cities of levels of informal social control normally found in rural environments. The only exception to the Asian difference seems to be violence against women, which shows rates comparable to those in Europe.

• Decreasing rates of volume crime in the Western world can partly be accounted for by changed demographics (aging), a more favorable economic climate, and changes in drug markets, notably the stabilization of the violence-prone markets for crack cocaine in the United States (Blumstein & Wallman, 2000). According to the same authors, better policing and reliance on incarceration as punishment are likely to have played a role as well. Expansions of criminal justice cannot, however, convincingly explain coincidental drops in crime of countries whose criminal policies show enormous variation, as will be shown in Chapters 9 and 10. At the global level, we find no statistical link between the size of police forces or severity of sentencing and crime trends. Many European countries as well as Canada have experienced drops in (violent) crime similar to that in the United States while using prison sentences much more sparingly. The costs of the prison model in both financial and humanitarian terms have recently become the subject of debate in the United States, especially in California. Global crime statistics suggest that crime can be successfully contained without imprisonment rates as high as in the United States.

• It seems likely that the near universal crime decreases in the developed world have resulted more from increased investments by private citizens, businesses, and governments in preventive measures in response to increased losses from crime than from more punitive criminal policies. The hypothesis that crime drops are caused by such responsive securitization is supported by ICVS-based findings. Analyses of trend data on 12 Western countries confirm that self-protection of households against crime has increased markedly since 1988, especially among higher-income groups. Analyses also confirm that rates of victimization by burglary have been most pronounced among better-protected middle- and higher-income families across Western countries. By stepping up their level of protection against crime, individual households seem to have indirectly contributed to lower rates of crime. Although overall rates of crime have dropped, the distribution of risks of victimization across income groups has become more skewed: Victimization risks among the lowest-income groups have decreased less steeply than average or remained stable.

• A disaggregation of ICVS data on car theft showed that among Western countries, drops of car theft are confined to less professional forms such as theft for joyriding, suggesting that opportunistic offenders have been discouraged by better protection rather than that professional thieves have been deterred by punishment.

• Macro factors external to criminal policies will continue to shape the volume and nature of crime in the future. Some countries in Africa and Asia are likely to benefit in the medium to long term from the crime-mitigating impact of the aging phenomenon. This positive impact will probably be more than offset by further processes of rapid urbanization in Africa and Asia. Economic growth is foreseen for many developing countries of Africa, Latin America, and Asia, but contrary to generally held beliefs, this will not necessarily lead to lower crime rates by itself. Experience in other regions suggests that affluence-driven crime booms are likely to appear in economically expanding urban areas in the developing world before decreases at national levels due to "responsive securitization" eventually set in. Within developing countries, gaps in levels of security between the rich and the poor are likely to become more and more pronounced.

• The key factor behind present and future crime problems of developing countries is their crime-prevention and criminal justice deficit. As shown in the data on burglar alarms, investments in private security measures are, understandably, much lower than in more affluent countries as are investments in collective arrangements for security (policing and courts). Developing countries seem to be lagging behind in their counter-crime efforts at both the individual and the collective levels.

• In the developed world, many countries report persistent concerns about crime and anti-social behavior, while actual rates of volume crime have fallen and continue to fall. In the current area, fear of crime is fueled by the threat of terrorist attacks. Another explanation for the discrepancy between objective and subjective security seems to be the demand for "super security" by economically well-off and aging populations in the "postmodern risk society" (Boutelier, 2004). While reliance on the help of the government or state in other domains has decreased, it has become stronger concerning human security. One of the major challenges for the future is to ensure that private parties continue investing in their own security, even when crime losses are dwindling (Eck, 2005). Technical or design-based measures will remain in place in periods of lower crime, but others, for example, hiring private security services, will prove to be more elastic. Investments will be scaled down if costs of crime have become lower. One of the risks in periods of decreasing crime is that common crime-control policies of the government will dissuade private parties from investing in their own self-protection. Especially in low-crime periods, expansions of public efforts to control crime may crowd out more efficient, private investments. The promotion of crime prevention should remain a priority of governments' strategies against crime, especially among low-income groups.

• Levels of crime in large parts of the world must be understood in the broader framework of political transition. In the final stages of protracted modern wars, insurgents and organized-crime groups tend to develop symbiotic relationships, prolonging the conflict. More generally, political transformations toward democracy and economic freedom are often accompanied by temporary surges in violence, including crimes in the domestic sphere, and other forms of common crime. Current crime booms in Latin America, eastern Europe, and sub-Saharan Africa can be compared with similar upward trends in crime in western Europe in the immediate aftermath of World War II. A temporary surge in volume crime including violent crime seems the price to pay for gaining democracy and economic freedom. Urban insecurity may perhaps, to some extent, be seen as the downside of (delayed) modernization.

• For new, vulnerable democracies, postliberation crime booms can pose serious political challenges. Ensuing fear of crime among voters can threaten support for the emerging democracy and raise the political stakes of its countercrime policies. Human rights activists can easily be put on the defensive in discussions about the lack of personal security. In both Latin America and South Africa, human rights defenders have been depicted as "advocates of criminality." Perceived or real crime booms often force governments to take urgent action by introducing repressive countercrime policies that curry favor with public opinion. In the process, hard-won advances in democracy and respect for human rights can be put in jeopardy. Such responses turn the clock back. What governments should do is to introduce evidence- and rights-based countercrime policies in collaboration with civil society, including human rights groups. Such broad-based responses have proven to be effective in the Western world. The alternative of regressing to repressive, neoauthoritarian policies will ultimately prove to be counterproductive. We end this part with another quote from Nelson Mandela: "Violence thrives in the absence of democracy, respect for human rights, and good governance." By implication, violence cannot be successfully tackled by sacrificing respect for human rights. The complex relationship between the rule of law and various types of crime will be revisited in more detail in Chapter 12.

Notes

1.   As explained, the ICVS was carried out among booster samples of the population of capitals or other main cities of developed countries for the first time in the 2005 sweep.

2.   The sharp downward trends in crime rates in the West over the past decade have been confirmed in national victimization surveys of several countries, including the United States, the Netherlands, and England and Wales (Farrington, Langan, & Tonry, 2004). In the United States, the percentage of households that experienced any crime declined from 25% in 1994 to 16% in 2000 (BJS, 2002). In the United Kingdom, overall victimization peaked in 1995 and has now fallen back to the level of the 1980s (sources: www.homeoffice.gov.uk/rds/pdfs05/hosb1105tab201.xls). In the Netherlands, the most common types of crime such as burglaries, car thefts, and pickpocketing have been reduced by 40% between 1993 and 2004, according to the annual Dutch National Victimization Surveys (www.wodc.nl).

3.   A study of homicide rates in Latin America in the 1980s and 1990s showed that homicide rates have increased among the entire population (including the youth) in 9 out of 14 countries in which data was available: Puerto Rico, Trinidad and Tobago, Argentina, Uruguay, Panama, Costa Rica, Venezuela, Ecuador, and Brazil. In El Salvador, Colombia, and Mexico, homicide is the main cause of violent death among the entire population (including the youth). In Brazil and Puerto Rico, homicide is the main cause of violent death among the youth. Considering the different age groups, the highest homicide rates are in the population of 20–24 years of age, but there has been a significant increase in the homicide rates among the 15–19 age bracket.

4.   In affluent societies with low unemployment, the motivation to engage in offending is comparatively low due to higher opportunity costs. This factor may explain why drops in crime can be very steep when criminal opportunities are shrinking.

5.   In the United States, percentages of the population who think a burglary next year is very likely went down from 31% in 1989 to 16% in 2005. In England, it went up from 35% in 1989 to 45% in 1992 and then down to 35% in 2005 (see Appendix B for more country details).

6.   Older data are incomparable because of a change in the item on alarms in the questionnaire. Insufficient trend data were available on eastern Europe.

PART III

Emerging Global Crime Threats

Assessing Organized Crime

The New Crime Threats

The crime data presented in the previous chapters related to common types of crime such as burglaries, thefts of cars, robberies, sexual offenses, and homicides. In most countries, common crimes remain the primary source of peoples' anxieties about crime. However, current political debates about homeland or global security are to an increasing extent centered on newly emerging, transnational types of crime such as organized crime, including trafficking in persons and money laundering, international terrorism, high-level corruption, and cybercrime. These types of crimes do not belong to the core offenses that universally make up common crimes. They are therefore labeled uncommon or nonconventional crimes (Buscaglia & Van Dijk, 2003). Just as nonconventional weapons do, "nonconventional" crimes constantly take on new, previously unknown forms and can be extremely serious in their humanitarian and economic consequences.

In the UN Secretary-General's High Level Panel on Threats, Challenges, and Change, six key security challenges are listed as the foremost challenges of the contemporary age (United Nations, 2004). These are economic and social threats, including poverty, infectious disease, and environmental degradation; interstate conflict; internal conflict, including civil war, genocide, and other large-scale atrocities; nuclear, radiological, chemical, and biological weapons; terrorism; and, last but not least, transnational organized crime. The panel concluded that now "threats are from non-State actors as well as States, and to human security as well as State security" (United Nations, 2004).[1] The single most important current threat is the potential use by international terrorists of nuclear weapons, possibly to be acquired with the help of organized-crime groups.

The primary international legal instrument to counter the new crime threats is the United Nations Convention Against Transnational Organized Crime that came into force in September 2003 and has now been ratified by over 100 member states

(Albrecht & Fijnaut, 2002). It is also significant to note its three attached supplementary instruments, which target specific manifestations of transnational organized crime: the Protocol on Trafficking in Persons, Especially Women and Children, which entered into force in December 2003; the Protocol on Smuggling of Migrants, which entered into force in January 2004; and the Protocol on Illicit Manufacturing of and Trafficking in Firearms, which entered into force in June 2005. More recently the member states of the UN adopted a Convention Against Corruption, which entered into force in 2005 as well. Several international instruments relate to the prevention and suppression of international terrorism (United Nations, 2001).

The new global security context, as described in the high-level panel, underscores the critical importance of effectively implementing these conventions and their protocols, most prominently in states and regions where state capacity is weak, either as a result of protracted conflict or political instability, and where a nexus has developed between organized crime, corruption, and terrorism. In the legal instruments just mentioned, governments have committed themselves to share information on trends in organized crime and corruption. In the current situation, such information is even less developed than information on common crime. In this chapter, available statistical information will be presented on organized crime, including trafficking in persons. In the next chapter, data will be presented on corruption, terrorism, and cybercrime. As in the previous chapters on common crime, little use will be made of data from police administrations. Our main sources are surveys among the public and among special at-risk groups, such as business executives, about their experiences of such crimes. Some fragmented data on cybercrimes were collected from open sources on the Internet. The latest round of the ICVS also provided some data on Internet-based frauds.

Defining Organized Crime

According to definitions of organized crime in criminological literature (Kenney & Finckenhauer, 1995; Levi, 2002), defining traits of organized crime include the use of extreme violence; corruption of public officials, including law enforcement and judicial officers; penetration of the legitimate economy (e.g., through money laundering); and interference in the political process. These elements are not only incorporated in national anti-Mafia laws in some countries, including the United States and Italy (Fijnaut & Paoli, 2004), but are also used as operational definitions by the international police community, among other things, through the so-called Falcone checklist (Levi, 2002).

The UNODC has collected information from police files on a geographically well-spread-out international sample of 40 organized-crime groups that were chosen as typical for their country by national experts. The results showed that most groups operate transnationally and are engaged in multiple criminal activities. Of the 40 groups analyzed, 30 used corruption and 33 employed violence (Van Dijk, Shaw, & Buscaglia, 2002). Of the 40 cases, 30 showed evidence of the investments of profits from illegitimate activities in legitimate business activity. Figure 7.1 presents an overview of these results.

Instrumental violence, corruption of officials, and penetration of the legitimate economy through money laundering or other activities appear to be near universal

❖ **Figure 7.1** Key Characteristics of Transnational Organized-Crime Groups

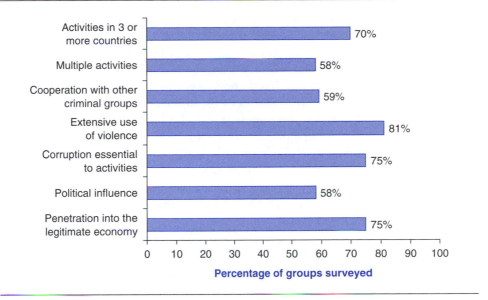

Source: Van Dijk, Shaw, & Buscaglia, 2002.

characteristics of organized crime. A majority of organized-crime groups seek political influence to promote their criminal activities.

The UNTOC convention, also known as the Palermo convention after the host city of the signing conference in 2002, contains provisions obliging state parties to criminalize membership in an organized group or conspiracy. The criminalization obligation extends to the laundering of ill-received money and offering of bribes to public officials (grand corruption). Governments are also encouraged to take action against the reinvestment of criminal assets in the legitimate economy through preventive means. The adoption of these additional treaty provisions reveals the convention's objective of tackling those forms of crime that are defined in both criminological literature and operational police practice as organized crime: stable groups that commit crimes for profit and that typically use violence and corruption to advance their criminal interests and reinvest their laundered gains in the legitimate economy.

The Changing Nature of Organized Crime

Although the criminological definition remains the point of departure of any serious analysis of organized crime, it would be wrong to focus exclusively on hierarchically structured criminal groups, that show all or most characteristics of a Mafia-type organization and disregard smaller, more loosely organized criminal groups that commit serious crimes that are transnational in nature. In some countries, for example, Italy, Russia, and Mexico, the Mafia-type organizations still prevail (Fijnaut & Paoli, 2004; Gonzalez-Ruiz, 2001). In eastern Europe as well, for example, Bulgaria and Albania, a limited number of major criminal groups seem to monopolize criminal activities in certain areas (Bezlov, 2005). The main criminal organizations are fairly stable, and their territories are known to the public.

In most other parts of the world, the organized-crime scene seems to be in a state of flux. Most notably in Colombia, the notoriously powerful Cali and Medellin cartels have long since been disbanded and superseded by hundreds of smaller, more flexible and more sophisticated cocaine-trafficking organizations. Nigerian organized crime is highly improvised and has therefore even been characterized as "disorganized organized crime" (Shaw, 2002). Much organized crime, including the smuggling of persons, in mainland China seems also to be in the hands of small to medium-sized, locally active groups that do not fit the traditional concept of the highly organized "triad" (Zhang, 2001; Zhang & Chin, 2001).

The fragmentation of organized crime seems to be a worldwide trend. Loose and often temporary alliances or associations may be formed around specific criminal "projects," not unlike high-risk ventures in the licit economy. Organized-crime groups today resemble networks of entrepreneurs able to blend illegality with legitimate business. This new generation of "Mafias" does not conform to the hierarchical, static, and semi-bureaucratic structures, the cartels, cupolas, and the like. In many cases, territorially oriented groups have been replaced by criminal organizations that are smaller, less stable, and lighter on their feet. Their activities span many countries, where criminal opportunities exist, or where governments may have insufficient capacities and/or political commitment to combat global crime.

Illicit Markets

Traditionally, organized-crime groups maintain a parasitic relationship with the legitimate economy through racketeering, intimidation/extortion, and kidnapping (Fijnaut & Paoli, 2004). Extortion remains a fairly universal, but often overlooked, characteristic of Mafia-type groups across the world. It is known to be a common practice in the United States (Reuter, 1987), Italy (Jamieson, 2000), eastern Europe (Aromaa & Lehti, 1996), and among Chinese communities both at home and in the diaspora (EUROPOL, 2004; Lintner, 2002).

More recently, trafficking in cocaine, heroin, cannabis, or synthetic drugs has become the main activity of organized crime, especially in the main production and transit countries. While drug trafficking and racketeering remain the main source of profit for most criminal organizations, many have now diversified their activities and new organizations have arisen in several new and specialized sectors. While detailed information on changes in illicit markets is often lacking, the available evidence confirms the rapid expansion of criminal activity across a number of sectors besides drug trafficking. Most prominently, trafficking in human beings for purposes of sexual exploitation and smuggling of immigrants have in the past decade developed into a multibillion-dollar illicit enterprise (EUROPOL, 2003, 2004). The International Labor Organization estimates that at any given time, 2.5 million people are in forced labor as a result of trafficking, 42% of whom are in prostitution (ILO, 2005). The number of illegal migrants smuggled annually around the world is estimated by the International Organization for Migration (IOM) to range between 15 and 30 million.[2]

Environmental crime, including the trafficking of endangered species, is now estimated to be an important area of organized-crime activity as well. One prominent example of the involvement of organized-crime groups in this area is the trade in illegal caviar, both in terms of the severe threat that it poses to the species (stocks of sturgeon in the Caspian Sea) and the rich rewards it provides to criminal groups. Powerful criminal groups have thus become involved in the trade, making use of violence, corruption, and close links to state agencies. By the late 1990s, it was estimated that over 50% of the world trade in caviar was illegal, and that in some areas, less than one fifth of the actual sturgeon catch is thought to be officially registered.[3]

Other activities in which organized crime is now involved include trafficking in firearms and stolen cars, the trade in cultural artifacts and stolen works of art, and currency, as well as luxury goods counterfeiting. In some countries, cigarette smuggling remains an important illicit market as well. Organized-crime groups increasingly pursue multiple activities, using, for example, existing trafficking routes for different commodities (e.g., drugs and firearms) or combining trafficking activities with fraud and money laundering. This trend is likely to continue in conjunction with expanding globalization.

Advances in technology, including the rapid growth of the Internet and e-mail communication, have had a significant impact on illicit activities. Firstly, these have made criminal organizations more flexible and dynamic, with e-mail and mobile phones in particular allowing ease of communication among groups of people without regard to distance, excessive cost, or organizational hierarchy. Additionally, advances in technology have resulted in new opportunities for organized criminal activity.

Organized-crime groups have also taken advantage of the transnational nature of global finance to launder money. Money laundering is the process by which the proceeds of crime are disguised to conceal their criminal origins and make their future use appear legitimate. Money laundering provides organized crime with both cash flow needed for further operations and capital for reinvestments in the licit economy. Depriving the criminal of the crime's profit is a critical weapon, as the profit is the main incentive for committing most crimes. For both developed and developing countries, money-laundering activities hamper the stability and integrity of their financial systems and anticorruption efforts.

It is difficult to assess the exact scale of money laundering as these kinds of activities are very well disguised and accordingly do not reliably appear in official statistics. However, the Financial Action Task Force (FATF) estimated in 1996 that, roughly, the value of money laundered globally ranged between US$590 billion and US$1.5 trillion. Recently published data show a substantial increase in reported cases of money laundering in many jurisdictions including the European Union, although this may in part be the result of more stringent reporting regulations. The rise of the electronic banking sector can benefit organized crime as it allows for fast and anonymous transfer of huge amounts of money and thus facilitates money laundering. In the future, the Internet will be used more extensively to transfer money from jurisdiction to jurisdiction. Money laundering will then increasingly take place via online banking, cell-phone banking, and prepaid cards. Such transactions will be more difficult to trace—enhancing opportunities for organized crime and grand corruption.

There is also an increased involvement of organized-crime groups in the area of fraud, most specifically credit-card fraud and fraud on the Internet. As an example of the possible extent of the problem of fraud on the Net, a Canadian government paper notes that it is estimated that telemarketing fraud accounts for up to 10% of the US$500 billion in telemarketing sales each year in Canada and the United States. Nigerian criminal groups are heavily involved in the execution of advance-fee scams over the Internet, disguised as business proposals (Shaw, 2002). Numbers of perpetrators are estimated at 250,000 with an annual growth of 3%. Victims run into the ten millions with an estimated 650,000 in 2006. Total losses of victims of Nigerian letters have been estimated at $3 billion in 2006 alone (www.ultrascan.nl). Increasingly, the bogus proposals, called 419 scams in police jargon after the provision in the Nigerian code that prohibits the practice, are now sent from other more reputable locations, for example, South Africa.[4]

The Pressure to Measure

Collecting information on organized crime in a variety of jurisdictions presents a series of difficulties. The first is the conducting of cross-jurisdictional criminology, with all the issues of legal definition and varying interpretation discussed in Chapter 2. If comparing official police-based information on garden-variety crimes as burglary or street robbery seems no longer feasible, there is little hope for optimism regarding the comparison of police-based information on more complex crimes. At the global level, it is to be expected that the number of police-recorded cases of organized crime correlates inversely with the seriousness of the problem. Where organized crime rules, few such cases will ever be investigated, let alone brought before a court. Statistics on drug seizures can illustrate the point. Seizures of drugs by police or customs authorities of a country are likely to reflect law enforcement priorities and professional capacities rather than the global flow of drugs.

Comparative studies on organized crime contain additional challenges that are not present in other areas of criminological metrics (Finkenauer & Warring, 1998; Hobbs, 1995). One obvious obstacle is the fact that any study of international organized crime has to rely on information generated in individual states, while transnational organized crime, by definition, operates across national boundaries. Information obtained from any one state therefore may provide only a partial reflection of reality. Illustrating this point are, again, the difficulties of interpreting statistics of drug seizures by customs and police. High quantities of drugs seized in the world's largest seaports, such as Rotterdam or Singapore, cannot be taken as evidence of a high prevalence of local organized crime. Many of the groups operating in these ports have little or no connection with the countries at issue. Such seizure statistics can just as well reflect the activities of criminal groups from other countries using these ports as points of entry into regional markets.

For these and other reasons, the quantitative, comparative study of organized-crime groups as well as of specific illicit markets with global dimensions is not well developed. Literature on the subject is either very general, providing an overview of the key principles or defining features of organized crime per country or region, drawing on exemplary cases rather than on statistics (Fijnaut & Paoli, 2004), or it refers to the activities, history, and trends of specific criminal groups (Arlacchi, 1993). Comparative studies that examine the characteristics and correlates of organized-crime groups in a variety of societies, having collected standardized, primary data on these, are a rare species (Sung, 2004). The reviews of global organized-crime activity completed to date provide high-level overviews of transnational organized-crime trends but no quantification of the phenomenon in a comparative perspective (Adamoli et al., 1998; Fijnaut & Paoli, 2004; International Crime Threat Assessment, 2000; Van Duyne, Von Lampe, Van Dijk, & Newell, 2004). There is thus a significant gap in the available data on international organized-crime trends, limiting opportunities for fact-based theory formation, international policy analysis, and objective monitoring of international trends.

Victimization Surveys Among the Business Community About Organized Crime

As shown in the previous chapters, the level of common crime can be succesfully estimated through the administering of standardized victimization surveys among the public or samples of business executives. Through direct contacting of key groups of the public, bypassing the domestic legal institutions, at least some of the methodological problems can be avoided. There seem to be no a priori reasons why the same approach could not be followed to estimate the extent of organized crime in a country, for example, by interviewing business executives, the key target group of racketeering and extortion, traditionally one of the most important manifestations of local organized crime in many countries.

In Italy, surveys are regularly conducted by business associations among their members on experiences with extortion/protection. For example, a survey carried out in 1998 revealed that 70% of shops in Reggio Calabria and four out of five shops in Palermo and Catania were extorted (Jamieson, 2000). Extortion of local businesses is regarded as the "bread and butter" activity of the locally operating Italian Mafia groups, through which a steady flow of revenues can be secured.

As mentioned in the previous chapters, building on the methodology of the ICVS, some surveys were carried out in 1995 among samples of business executives from the retail industry in 10 developed countries (Van Dijk & Terlouw, 1996). In these surveys, respondents were asked about victimization by volume crime such as shoplifting, burglary, and corruption. They were also asked to assess the frequency of extortion and demands for protection money in their line of business in the country. In most western European countries, between 7% (UK) and 15% (Italy) of the respondents felt this was very or fairly common. Much lower percentages were found in France and Switzerland. The highest rates were found in two countries in central Europe, the Czech Republic and Hungary.

Between 1995 and 1999, ICBS surveys using the same methodology were replicated in St. Petersburg (Russia), Latvia, and Lithuania to address the issue of security of Finnish and other foreign businesses set up in the Baltic region (Aromaa & Lehti, 1996). From the surveys carried out in St. Petersburg and the Baltic countries, it became clear that extortion and corruption were among the central problems facing businesses in the region (Aromaa, 2000). During the year 1994, one out of two enterprises studied in St. Petersburg had become the victim of some kind of extortion, blackmail, or other kind of pressure from criminal groups.

An adjusted version of the ICBS questionnaire with more questions on organized crime and corruption was used in a UNICRI/Gallup-executed survey in 2000 among capital cities in nine countries in central and eastern Europe (for details, see Appendix A and Alvazzi del Frate, 2004). A revised version of the older question on extortion and protection was used. On average, 15% of the respondents said that intimidation and extortion are very or fairly common practices in their line of business. This finding cannot be compared to the previous rate, but it confirms that the perceived extent of "racketeering" is higher in eastern Europe than in most countries of western Europe but not necessarily dramatically so. An eastern European country that stands out with exceptionally high rates is Belarus (Minsk).

The ICBS questionnaire also asks about actual victimization by intimidation and extortion, which were defined to the respondents as follows: extorting money from the company; threatening and intimidating managers and/or employees; and threatening product contamination (such as poisoning of food, altering of colors, damaging of external packages, etc.). Furthermore, requests for protection money were defined as "somebody who requested money in exchange for his/their services to protect your company from robbery, extortion, acts of vandalism, or further requests of bribes."

On average, 9% of the businesses experienced intimidation and/or extortion over the past year, and 8% were requested to pay protection money. The city where intimidation occurred most frequently was Minsk, with 29% of businesses victimized. Percentages of risk above the average were also observed in Kiev and Bucharest (10%). Requests for protection money were also most frequent in Minsk (see Figure 7.2).

One third of the victims believed that local organized-crime groups were involved in intimidation (especially in Minsk and Vilnius, with 47% and 44%, respectively). Only two victims mentioned the likelihood of the involvement of international organized-crime groups. Twenty-three percent felt that intimidation was due to rivalry among businesses (especially in Sofia, 44%).

In the case of requests for protection money, 61% of the victimized businesses felt that local organized-crime groups were involved. This was especially true in Kiev (86%), Sofia (79%), and Moscow (74%). The involvement of international organized crime was mentioned by 8% of victims, while 13% mentioned rival businesses.

The results confirm the general view that organized crime has gained a strong presence across eastern and central Europe. The survey results provide a ranking of countries in the region according to the organized-crime prevalence, which can be used for setting policy agendas in the region for addressing the threat of organized crime. Regrettably, no repeat surveys of the ICBS have to date been conducted.

In 2005, the Center on Organized Crime in southeastern Europe gauged perception of organized crime among the general public in Bulgaria, Macedonia, Montenegro, and Serbia (Foglesong, 2005). The results of this pilot study reveal a

❖ **Figure 7.2**   Percentages of Respondents Who Experienced Requests for Protection Money and Intimidation/Extortion in 1999, Nine Central-Eastern European Cities

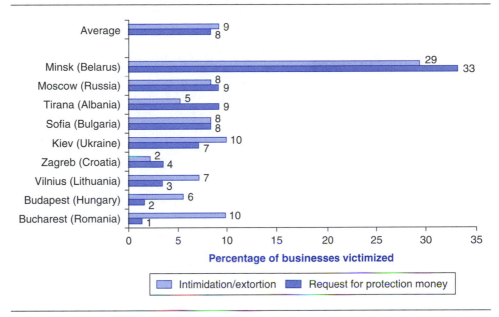

Sources: Alvazzi del Frate, 2004; ICBS, 2000.

general perception of widespread collusion between organized crime and politics. More than three fourths of respondents in all four countries believe that organized crime is a "network of persons that includes not only criminals but also people in power and that harms the society as a whole." It is widely believed in the region that politicians patronize people related to organized crime. The study in Serbia and Montenegro also inquired about whether respondents would be ready to report organized-crime activity to the police. In these countries, less than one fourth of respondents would be willing to report such activities to the police, a percentage much lower than the one found in a previous study in Northern Ireland.

In the Eurobarometer, a public opinion poll conducted among samples of the general population of EU member states, questions were included in 2002 about the perceived infiltration of national and local governments by organized crime. At that time, EU membership was still limited to 15 western European countries. Perceived levels of infiltration of national and local governments, respectively, were almost identical. The perceived levels showed considerable variation across the member countries with comparatively high levels in Italy (71%), Greece (62%), and Ireland (61%). Infiltration was perceived to be a problem by much lower percentages of the public in the Nordic countries and Luxembourg (Eurobarometer, 2003).

The results of the ICBS on victimization by organized crime of businesses as well as the explorative studies on organized-crime perceptions among both business executives and the general public demonstrate the untapped potential of crime surveying for the collection of information on the extent and nature of organized crime and other complex crimes.

Toward an Organized-Crime Perception Index

The ICBS or any other victimization surveys among businesses about their experiences of crime using a standardized methodology have not yet been conducted on a global scale and at regular intervals. The perception studies among the general public cited above have also been executed only regionally and incidentally. It would be a major breakthrough in epidemiological criminology if such business victimization surveys would be implemented regularly in a broad selection of countries. In the meantime, several omnibus surveys have been carried out gauging the perceptions of business leaders on the prevalence of business risks in various countries. Some of the risk-assessment studies include questions about the prevalence of crime and corruption in the work environment of businesses. Surveys done by and on behalf of the corporate sector are usually treated with suspicion by scholarly criminologists. Only a few criminologists have harnessed the results of these commercial surveys as a source of criminologically relevant information (Van Dijk, 2001, 2008; Van Dijk & Nevala, 2002; Sung, 2004). Although commercial surveys are not always very sophisticated methodologically, there is no reason to disregard their results. As Van Velthoven (2005) observes, the very fact that companies are prepared to pay for such information testifies to its "good enough" methodological quality. This argument seems especially strong for large-scale surveys that are repeated over longer periods of time. If donors or clients would find the results to be unreliable, such surveys would soon be discontinued.

Since 1997, the World Economic Forum has carried out surveys among CEOs of larger companies to identify obstacles to businesses in an increasing number of countries, reaching a total of 102 in 2003 (WEF, 2003, 2004, 2005).[5] From the onset, one of the questions in these "executives' opinion surveys" asked about the prevalence in the country of "Mafia-oriented racketeering, extortion (imposes or not serious costs on businesses)." An analysis was conducted of the patterns of answers given to this question on perceived Mafia prevalence from the seven annual rounds of WEF surveys conducted between 1997 and 2003. Considering the possible sampling errors in results based on sample sizes of no more than 100 business leaders per country, the answers on the racketeering question were found to be remarkably stable over the years. In a very few countries, the mean scores showed significant variation from year to year. To further reduce sampling error, the scores of the seven sweeps of the surveys up to 2003 were averaged. The resulting mean scores are based on sample sizes of 500 and over. They reflect the perceived prevalence of organized crime in the period 1997 to 2003 according to business executives operating in these countries.

The WEF scores were correlated with country rankings on organized-crime activity, based on a regional survey among business leaders in central and eastern Europe asking a similar question on the costs of organized crime for business, conducted by the World Bank and the European Bank of Reconstruction and Development (BEEPS, 1996). The two rankings were found to be correlated, though not strongly ($r = .36$, $p < 0.05$, $n = 27$).

Extortion of companies and other forms of racketeering belong, as said, to the core activities of organized-crime groups in many if not most parts of the world. If business leaders perceive these types of crime to be common in their country, this finding by itself indicates a high prevalence of organized crime generally. Likewise, if business executives in a country are little bothered by racketeering, the position of organized crime in the country is probably not pronounced. Theoretically, organized-crime groups in some countries will abstain from racketeering and exclusively focus on other types of criminal activities. To further explore this issue, the averaged WEF rates of organized-crime prevalence perception were correlated with an indicator of a broader range of Mafia-related activities, based on assessments of international security experts.

Risk analysts of The Merchant International Group Ltd (MIG), an internationally active security consultancy group with a background in intelligence, assess the extent of various risks including organized crime and corruption in over 150 countries on a quarterly basis (MIG, 2004; Poole-Robb, 2003). Their ratings of corruption are used as one of the regular sources to determine a country's state of corruption by Transparency International. The expert assessments of MIG of organized-crime prevalence are less well known. They are based on analyses of the prevalence of 10 different types or aspects of organized crime, including extortion, drugs, arms and people trafficking, kidnapping, money laundering, secret societies, and criminal activities in unions. Assessments are, as said, made on a quarterly basis. Quarterly and year to year changes in the scores given to countries were found to be very limited. The first quarterly rates for 2005, for example, deviated slightly from the former ones in only a handful of the 150 countries.

The four quarterly organized-crime ratings of MIG for 2004 were averaged. This mean score was correlated with the averaged WEF scores for the period 1997 to 2003. The correlation between the two ratings was fairly strong ($r = .63$, $p < 0.00$, $n = 102$). Considering the fundamentally different sources of information—the first, an opinion survey on racketeering among business leaders and the other ratings of the prevalence of 10 types of organized crime by security risk experts—the correlation between the two ratings lends credibility to both indicators as proxy measures of organized-crime prevalence. Equally high correlations were found between MIG assessments and WEF scores from earlier years (Buscaglia & Van Dijk, 2003).

In order to facilitate further statistical exploration, a composite index based on the averaged rankings of countries on the WEF surveys of 1997 to 2003 and the MIG assessments for 2004 was constructed, covering a total of 155 countries. Incorporated in the index were also the results of the BEEPS survey, which included Albania. In this way, a composite index of organized-crime perception was constructed covering 156 countries, based on three independent sources. The averaged rates per region and subregion are presented in Figure 7.3.

❖ Figure 7.3   Scores on Composite Index of Perceived Extent of Organized-Crime Activity, Based on Two Independent Surveys Among Business Leaders Conducted in 1997 to 2003 and Expert Opinions, per World Region (high scores indicating high prevalence)

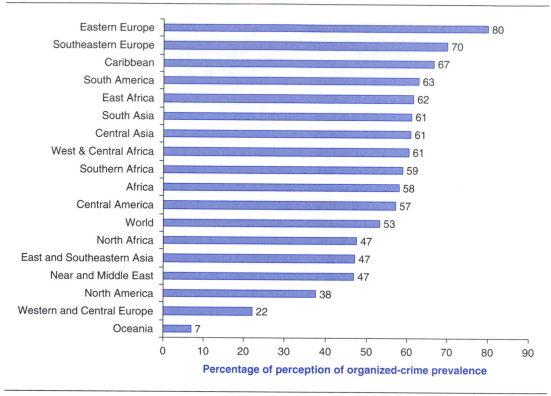

Sources: World Economic Forum, Global Competitiveness Reports, 1997–1998 to 2003–2004; Merchant International Group, 2004; BEEPS, 2002.

The scores on the Organized Crime Perception (OCP) Index allow the unprecedented, though still tentative, mapping of the extent of organized crime across the world. The highest subregional scores on this indicator of organized-crime prevalence, indicating a high perceived seriousness of the problem, were found in Central Asia and Transcaucasian countries and southeastern Europe. Above-average scores were found in Latin America, including Central America and in the Caribbean. Moderately high scores were found across Asia and sub-Saharan Africa.

Organized crime, like corruption, is perceived by business leaders and security experts to be most prevalent in developing and transitional countries. On the global North–South dimension, organized-crime prevalence is clearly concentrated in the South, although less heavily so than homicide and other types of serious violent crime. Within both America and Africa, the more affluent North is comparatively less affected by Mafia-type criminal activity. Within Europe, levels of racketeering tend to go up if one moves from the West to the East.

Other "Markers" of Organized-Crime Presence

The OCP Index refers to the level of different types of organized-crime activities such as extortion and drugs, arms, and people trafficking as perceived by potential victim groups and experts. The widespread perception among key persons that such activities are rampant in a country provides by itself no firm proof that this is actually the case, but it provides ground for further enquiries. It can be regarded as a "marker" of organized-crime presence, suggesting that further tests are called for. As mentioned above, instrumental violence, corruption of public officials, and money laundering are regarded as universal secondary characteristics of organized crime. It is hard to imagine a high level of organized crime in a country without a significant amount of these three systemic Mafia-related phenomena. Although high rates of criminal violence are not a unique characteristic of organized crime and some organized-crime groups may (at least temporarily) abstain from violent acts, a high prevalence of killings in a country can be used as a marker for Mafia-type criminal activity. Where homicide rates are high, organized-crime activity is likely to be significant, and vice versa.

Statistical indicators were selected for the prevalence of each of these three defining systemic characteristics or markers of organized-crime activity in countries: instrumental violence, high-level corruption, and money laundering.

Instrumental Violence

Statistics of recorded homicides often lump together different types of homicide. The common category of homicide consists of violence by spouses or other family members and violence resulting from interpersonal conflicts between people, for example, when frequenting pubs or discos. The level of these common homicides is determined by such factors as social inequality, gender inequality, alcohol abuse, and availability of guns, as discussed in Chapter 5.

The second main category of homicides in nonconflict situations is committed by members of organized-crime groups, including youth gangs engaged in drug peddling, to advance and protect their criminal activities: "Organized crime almost always generates violence because it has no way of resolving disputes except by mutual consent or settling of scores" (Gonzalez-Ruiz, 2001). In countries as different as the United States, Colombia, Mexico, and Italy, trends in overall homicide rates are closely related to the extent of organized-crime activity (Gonzalez-Ruiz, 2001; Orlando, 2001; Rubio, 2001). In Kosovo, homicide rates plummeted after the reconstruction of the justice and security sector by the United Nations and focused police action against the local Mafia. In Serbia, homicide rates went down after the disruption of the local organized-crime groups after the assassination of the prime minister in 2002 (Dulic, 2005).

Mob-related acts of violence typically are carefully planned and executed with professional skills and due caution. Such homicides are notoriously difficult for the police to solve. In some countries, police may also be reluctant to investigate for fear of retaliation and/or as a result of corruption. Police records do not normally differentiate between different types of homicide. If they do, such as those collected by the Jamaican Constabulary Force, they invariably show that domestic or conflict-related homicides show much higher clearance rates than homicides related to drugs or gang activity. In Jamaica in 2006, the clearance rate of drug-related homicides was zero and that of gang-related homicides, 27%. Clearance rates of conflict-related homicides and domestics were 69% and 61%, respectively (UNODC, 2007).

In an attempt to develop a proxy measure of "mob-related violence," rates were calculated of the number of police-recorded homicides per country minus the number of convictions for homicide. Both types of data were drawn from the 8th UN Crime and Criminal Justice Survey. The resulting rates of "unsolved homicides" can be used as a proxy indicator of mob-related homicide. Figure 7.4 shows the correlation between the Organized Crime Perception Index and the rate of police-recorded but unsolved homicides.

❖ **Figure 7.4**   Prevalence of Mafia-Type Activities as Perceived by Business Leaders and/or Security Experts and Rates of Unsolved Homicides (Ranked Variables)

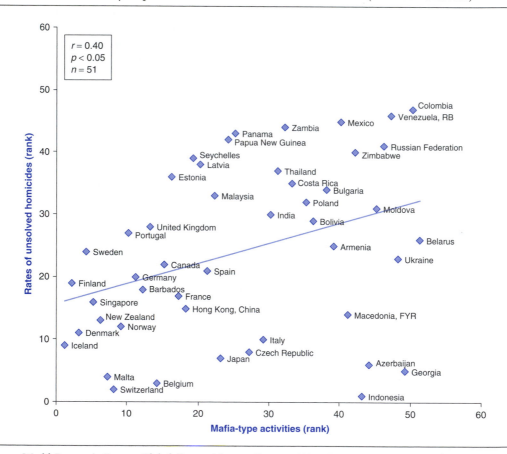

Sources: World Economic Forum, Global Competitiveness Reports, 1997–1998 to 2003–2004; Merchant International Group, 2004; BEEPS, 2002 , 2002; 8th UN Crime Survey.

As the results in Figure 7.4 show, perceptions of organized-crime prevalence are fairly strongly correlated with rates of unsolved homicides ($r = .40$, $p < 0.05$, $n = 51$). In countries where business leaders and security experts perceive high levels of racketeering and extortion, rates of (unsolved) homicides tend to be higher as well. This correlation suggests that in such countries, groups of criminals are indeed more frequently employing lethal violence to intimidate rivals and clients or discipline group members. The correlation between the subjective ratings of business leaders and risk analysts with official data on unsolved homicides from police and courts indicates that perceptions of the prevalence of organized crime of informed groups in society are concurrent with police records of mob-related serious violence. This result confirms that perceptions of organized-crime prevalence and rates of unsolved homicides can indeed be used as "markers" of organized crime. If a country shows high scores on both "tests," the combined results point to serious problems with organized crime and should give rise to grave concerns.

The Organized-Crime–Corruption Complex

The second defining characteristic of organized crime besides instrumental violence is corruption of relevant public officials including high-ranking police officers, appeals judges, and politicians. In Italian legislation, infiltration of the licit economy, the state, and the electorate process are defining traits of organized crime (Jamieson, 2000). "Buying" protection from the state is a necessary condition for the sustained growth of organized-crime activities. Such immunity is arranged at different levels of the public sector, starting from occasional bribing of police officers, having such officials on the payroll, to compromising heads of relevant agencies such as drug enforcement or customs departments. The highest level of infiltration encompasses the capture of the state's policies by criminal groups who are then able to unduly influence law making, policy setting, and crucial (appeals court) judicial decisions. This phenomenon has been called "state capture" in World Bank reports. A "culture of corruption" is a near universal concomitant of rampant organized crime.

An index was constructed to measure the extent of high-level corruption using existing survey research findings collated by the World Bank Institute from a variety of sources (Kaufmann, Kraay, & Zoido-Lobaton, 1999). The items in the index relate to distortions arising from lobbying groups, independence of policies from pressures of special interest groups, the likelihood of biased judicial rulings, perceptions of the relative value of public procurement contracts paid for by bribes, and the overall prevalence of state capture (Buscaglia & Van Dijk, 2003).

The WEF/MIG scores on organized-crime prevalence were correlated with scores on this composite index of high-level corruption, including judicial corruption. Figure 7.5 shows the results.

The index of organized-crime perception is strongly correlated to the index of high-level corruption ($r = .66$, $p < 0.05$, $n = 103$). Among the 67 countries included in the analysis, there are only a very few countries that suffer from organized crime without also suffering from rampant high-level corruption, and vice versa. High levels of grand corruption can also be regarded as a marker of organized crime.

❖ **Figure 7.5** Prevalence of Perceived Organized Crime and Regional Scores on Composite Index Measuring High-Level Corruption/State Capture

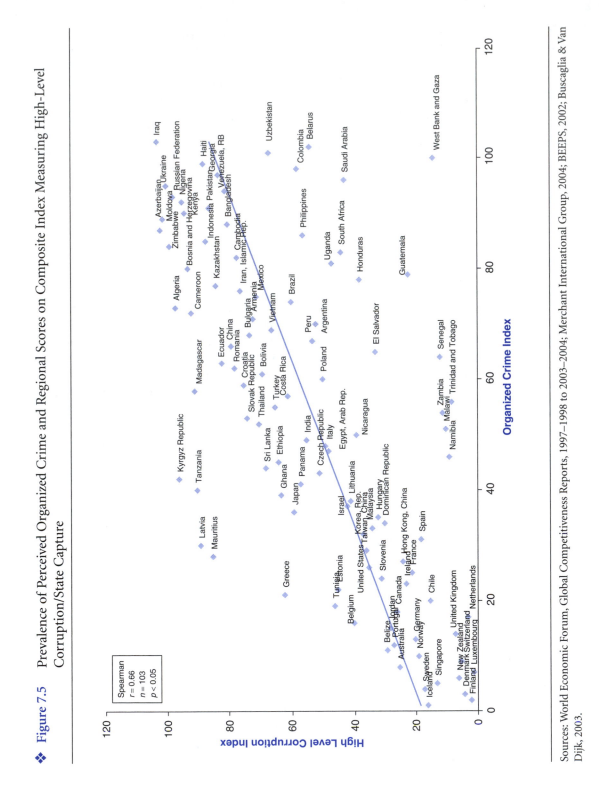

Spearman
r = 0.66
n = 103
p < 0.05

Sources: World Economic Forum, Global Competitiveness Reports, 1997–1998 to 2003–2004; Merchant International Group, 2004; BEEPS, 2002; Buscaglia & Van Dijk, 2003.

The results confirm that almost all organized-crime groups need and actively seek protection from powerful public officials, including police chiefs and senior judges. Cooperation with corrupt politicians and public officials also offers opportunities for profitable illegal "deals" in public procurement. In many countries, corrupted officials rely on their part in organized-crime groups to protect their interests against the scrutiny of journalists and investigators and to fix elections. The well-documented symbiosis between corrupt politicians and the Mafia in southern Italy is a case in point (Jamieson, 2000). Organized crime and corruption at high levels of government feed on each other. In many countries, the organized-crime–corruption complex is deeply rooted in society, exercising significant influence on economical and political decision making.

Money Laundering and the Black Economy

Successful organized-crime groups reinvest their profits in further criminal activities, whereas excess profits are typically reinvested in the legitimate economy (Naylor, 2002). This reinvestment of illegally acquired assets in the legitimate economy forces criminal groups to engage in financial operations that can help to hide the illicit origins of the funds (money-laundering schemes).

Money laundering used to be executed through the official banking system. Under the influence of international legal instruments and actions by international organizations, such assistance has been made more difficult through enhanced screening and reporting procedures. To an increasing extent, criminal gains are now laundered through informal, trust-based banking systems that leave little or no paper trail (called HAWALA banking in some countries).

The WEF business executives' opinion surveys of the later years included questions on the extent of money laundering (WEF, 2004). Respondents were asked to assess the extent of money laundering through both the official and non bank, informal financial channels in their country. The scores on these two items were found to be almost perfectly correlated ($r = .90$). If money laundering is common, it happens in both of these ways. The congruence between the level of the two forms of money laundering does not lend support to the notion that money laundering through official banks has been replaced by HAWALA systems as a result of effective anti-money-laundering measurses taken by the official banking system. Rather, it suggests that the extent of money laundering in a country is determined by local demand for such services. If local demand is significant, money laundering takes place by both banks and entities other than banks, regardless of the extent of security measures in place.

Scores on the two items were combined into a composite scale on money laundering. The scores on this money-laundering scale correlated very strongly with the scores on perceived prevalence of organized crime ($r = .82$, $p < 0.05$, $n = 101$). High volumes of money laundering seem also to be a universal concomitant (a marker) of organized-crime presence in countries.

Finally, organized-crime groups are also known to engage in conspicuous consumption financed with black money and to invest in shadow economies. In many parts of the world, the relative sizes of the shadow economies are on the increase as a result of crime and corruption (Schneider, 2004).[6] The link between corruption and crime and the size of shadow economies is empirically well established (Schneider & Enste, 2000; Sung, 2004). Especially in countries where organized crime is highly profitable, for example, where it controls major international illicit drug markets, informal or shadow economies can be expected to be comparatively large. Current examples are the Andean countries and Afghanistan.

The Organized Crime Perception Index was correlated against the perceived extent of the informal economy according to the WEF business executives' survey (2003/2004). The two factors were indeed found to be very strongly correlated ($r = .80$, $p < 0.05$).

The relatively large size of the shadow economies in high-crime countries does not point only to the need for organized-crime groups to somehow spend and invest their criminal gains outside the reach of the law. It may also point to possible interrelations between the size of the shadow economies, reduced tax revenues of the state, and resulting minimal resources available for countering organized crime and grand corruption through law enforcement and criminal justice. The operation of such nefarious circular interrelationships will be revisited in the final part of this book.

Composite Organized-Crime Index

The strong statistical relationships between the organized-crime perception index and four other indicators of secondary manifestations of organized-crime activity support the construction of a composite organized-crime index combining the five interrelated indicators (Van Dijk, 2008).[7] Considering the high correlations between the indicators, the composite index is not much different from the Organized Crime Perception Index. An important advantage of the composite index is the incorporation of at least one *objective* measure of organized-crime activity, the rate of unsolved homicides according to official administrations. Scores on this composite index cannot be dismissed by governments as being based on "just perceptions." The scores are corroborated by the official "body counts" of their own police authorities as reported to the United Nations in the crime and justice surveys.

Although ideally, large-scale crime victimization surveys should be carried out among business executives and other potential victim groups about their experiences with organized crime, the Composite Organized-Crime Index seems to be a useful step in the search for metrics on organized crime (Buscaglia & Van Dijk, 2003; Van Dijk, 2008; Van Dijk & Nevala, 2002). The strong correlations between primary indicators of organized crime such as perceived racketeering and unsolved murders and money laundering and the size of shadow economies point to the broader economic implications of organized crime, an issue to which we will return in the final part.

In our view, scores on the Composite Organized-Crime Index should not be taken at face value. Scores on the index and on the five source indicators should be used as a set of diagnostic tools. Just as medical doctors diagnosing complex pathological syndromes in individual patients apply independent tests measuring different markers of the disease, criminologists should try to arrive at evidence-based crime diagnoses of individual countries by looking at both the overall score and the scores on five different indicators. Table 7.1 depicts the regional distribution of the Composite Organized-Crime Index, based on data from over 150 countries. For diagnostic purposes, the picture presents both the

❖ Table 7.1   Regional Mean Scores on Composite Organized-Crime Index (COCI) and Data on Source Indicators: Perceived Organized-Crime Prevalence, Grand Corruption, Money Laundering, Extent of Shadow Economy, and the Rates of Unsolved Murders per 100,000 Population

Region	Average of the Composite Organized-Crime Index	Organized-Crime Perception Rank	Informal Sector Rank	Unsolved Homicides Rank	High-Level Corruption Rank	Money-Laundering Rank
Oceania	33	1	1	1	2	1
Western and Central Europe	35	2	2	2	4	3
North America	44	4	4	4	6	4
Eastern and Southeast Asia	45	5	3	7	3	6
Central America	50	4	13	3	8	13
Near and Middle East	50	7	6	11	1	2
World	*54*					
Southern Asia	54	14	8	8	7	11
North Africa	55	6	5	6		5
East Africa	55	12	9		11	9
Southern Africa	56	10	12	5	12	10
South America	58	11	14	10	13	12
Southeastern Europe	58	15	10	12	9	14
West & Central Africa	60	13	11	15	5	8
Eastern Europe	70	17	16	14	14	16
Central Asia and Transcaucasian Countries	70	16		13	15	
Caribbean	70	9	15		16	15

absolute scores on the composite index and the rank orders for the five source indicators used. Higher scores and lower ranks indicate more organized crime and corruption.

The regional scores of the composite index and those on its five constituting indicators show a high degree of consistency. Regions with the highest scores such as the Caribbean, central Asia, and eastern Europe also exhibit the highest scores on the source indicators, including the rates of unsolved murders. Data on the Caribbean are not available but murder rates are known to be the highest in the world (UNODC, 2007). Regions with the best overall scores—Oceania, western and central Europe, and North America—are also at the bottom of the list for the five source indicators. Deviations from the overall pattern include relatively high rank numbers on the informal sector and money laundering in the low-crime region of Central America. Among the high-crime regions,

West and central Africa show a relatively low rank number on homicides. This result could point to a shortcoming in the available statistics—homicide statistics for Nigeria are, for example, missing. It could also reflect that organized-crime groups in the region are less prone to the use of extreme violence. In any case, such deviations suggest the need for improving the criminological diagnosis through further focused research.

Country Scores

The combination of data from different sources allows the calculation of scores for a large number of countries. In some cases, the index score is based on just one source, resulting in a comparatively large margin of error. In the following presentation of country scores, we have included only countries for which more than one source was available. To facilitate assessments of the organized-crime situation of countries, the rank numbers of countries for each of the indicators/markers are included. In most cases, the rank numbers for different indicators are in the same range. Deviations of single indicators can point to specific features of organized crime or to deficiencies in some of the measures. In such cases, further research is indicated. In some cases, the diagnosis can only be very tentative due to insufficient information, for example, on the rates of unsolved murders. Details on individual countries are presented in Table 7.2 (for data on more countries, see Appendix B and Chapter 12).

Fifteen Countries With the Highest Scores

The rank numbers for different indicators are mostly in the same range as the rank on the composite index. For example, among the countries with the highest scores on the composite index are all three countries with the highest rates of unsolved murders (Colombia, Albania, and Kazakhstan). None of the 15 countries at the bottom show high scores on unsolved murders. Deviations of single indicators from the COCI rank can point to specific features of organized crime in the country or, alternatively, to deficiencies in the data. Scores on the source indicators of Colombia indicate a discrepancy in high scores on violence and relatively low scores on corruption and informal economy. Among the European countries, Italy stands out with a world rank of 69 out of 156. That country scores particularly unfavorably on corruption (35th in the world). The rank number of Italy on unsolved homicides is in the same range as the index score. The hypothesis that Italian organized crime has in recent years become more restrained in the use of lethal violence is not confirmed nationwide. Such restraint may be limited to the Sicilian Mafia only and may not include the Camorra in Naples or the 'Ndrangheta in Calabria.

Figures 7.6 and 7.7 show the global and European maps for organized crime, based on the organized-crime perception index which covers a larger number of countries.

Within Europe, organized-crime prevalence increases diagonally from the northwest to the southeast, with levels being low in England, Germany, and Scandinavia; higher in Spain and Italy; and by far the highest in Russia, Albania, Bulgaria, and Ukraine. In Asia, rates are the worst in parts of South Asia (Pakistan, Bangladesh). But China and India are also rated comparatively high on this composite index (higher than Italy). More research on the role of the organized-crime–corruption complex in these two emerging superpowers seems warranted. In the international literature on organized

❖ **Table 7.2**   World Ranking of Countries According to Scores on the Composite
Organized-Crime Index (156 countries)[8]

	Country	Composite Organized-Crime Index	Organized-Crime Perception Index Rank	Informal Sector Rank	High-Level Corruption Rank	Unsolved Homicide Rank	Money-Laundering Rank
	Fifteen Countries With the Highest Scores						
1	Haiti	100.00	2	1			10
2	Paraguay	95.74	20	2			4
3	Albania	93.90	1		19	2	
4	Nigeria	91.93	7	7	4		11
5	Guatemala	91.57	21	10			1
6	Venezuela	89.57	6	8	12		7
7	Russian Fed.	88.20	14	17	3	4	16
8	Angola	87.90	25	4			9
9	Ukraine	87.40	9	6	2	16	2
10	Colombia	86.81	3	41	26	1	5
11	Mozambique	86.54	42	5			3
12	Bangladesh	84.69	11	24			15
13	Kazakhstan	83.78	49		7	3	
14	Pakistan	83.71	8	9	6		52
15	Jamaica	83.42	17	16			22
	Fifteen Countries with Medium-High Scores						
22	Mexico	75.03	26	31	17		23
25	Indonesia	74.51	13	60	5		42
28	Peru	72.64	32	11	33	5	28
30	Turkey	72.08	55	15	22		26
33	Brazil	69.24	27	37	25		41
38	South Africa	66.07	16	39	38	8	54
48	Argentina	59.39	34	21	30	59	14
56	Egypt	56.17	58	46	36		59
59	China	55.48	35	54	10	46	51
64	India	53.79	56	38	29	33	43
69	Italy	46.81	57	59	35	52	49
81	United States	36.36	85	85	45	15	84
86	Japan	32.67	70	94	27	56	90
90	Chile	30.59	90	74	57	21	85
97	Canada	25.06	93	73	51	62	88

(Continued)

❖ Table 7.2 (Continued)

	Fifteen Countries With the Lowest Scores					
Country	Composite Organized-Crime Index	Organized-Crime Perception Index Rank	Informal Sector rank	High-Level Corruption Rank	Unsolved Homicide Rank	Money-Laundering Rank
99 United Kingdom	23.90	99	84	62		94
100 Norway	22.08	104	90	58	53	82
101 Luxembourg	21.11	107	102			81
102 Germany	20.21	101	89	56	57	92
103 Switzerland	19.98	105	97	65	54	66
104 Jordan	19.38	97	77		51	96
105 The Netherlands	18.91	95	92	66	41	93
106 Denmark	18.41	112	86	64	42	89
107 Sweden	18.30	111	80	60	44	98
108 Australia	16.79	106	101	54	37	99
109 Bahrain	15.28	89			49	
110 Singapore	14.10	110	99	61	58	97
111 New Zealand	12.83	109	93	63	48	100
112 Iceland	12.46	114	95			102
113 Finland	10.41	113	98	67	34	101

Sources: World Economic Forum, Global Competitiveness Reports, 1997–1998 to 2003–2004; Merchant International Group, 2004; BEEPS, 2002, 2002; 8th UN Crime Survey.

crime, India is rarely the focus of attention. Perhaps this is a serious oversight. The Public Affairs Centre, a Bangalore-based NGO, has recently reviewed the criminal background of all newly elected members of Parliament and found that just under one fourth of elected MPs faced criminal charges for crimes punishable by 5 years of imprisonment or more (*Financial Times,* October 2004). The support of Mafia dons by the electorate is explained as a rebellion of lower-caste voters against higher-caste elites. The concentration of parliamentarians with criminal backgrounds is largest in the northern states of India. Research on Chinese organized crime is mainly focused on Chinese expatriates. Limited available research findings on homeland China point to involvement in people smuggling in coastal areas and collusion between corrupt Communist Party members and local gangs in remote areas (Zhang, 2001).

In Africa, Nigeria, Angola, and Mozambique stand out with the highest scores. Nigerian organized-crime activity in both the country and the region has been well documented (Shaw, 2002, 2003; UNODC, 2005). A detailed account of how organized crime threatens to penetrate state and businesses in southern Africa, notably in Mozambique, is given in Gastrow (2003). In Latin America, Haiti, Paraguay, Guatamala, Venezuela, and Colombia show the highest scores. High scores are also observed in Jamaica.

As discussed above, data are available on the perceived infiltration of national governments by organized crime for the 15 old EU countries based on the Eurobarometer

❖ Figure 7.6   Global Map With Scores on Organized-Crime Perception Index (Around 2003)

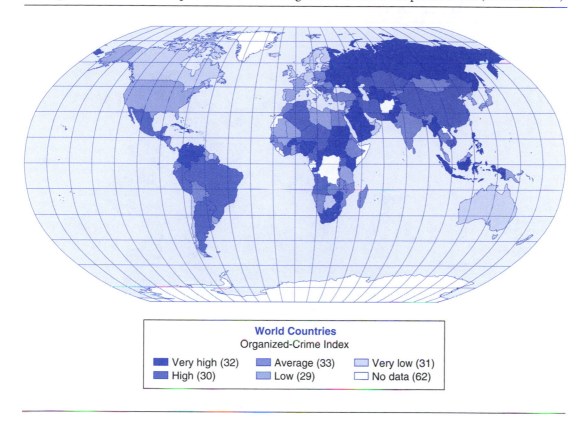

World Countries
Organized-Crime Index

■ Very high (32)	■ Average (33)	▢ Very low (31)
■ High (30)	▢ Low (29)	□ No data (62)

2002. We looked at the relationship between country scores on the Composite Organized-Crime Index and the perceived infiltration of organized crime according to the Eurobarometer. The two measures of organized-crime prevalence were strongly correlated ($r = .70$). Figure 7.8 shows results in the form of a scatterplot.

The results given in Figure 7.8 indicate that in terms of Mafia-related problems for the state, Italy and Greece are in a league of their own in western Europe.

Trends in Organized Crime

Since the data sources of the index are regularly updated, it seems feasible to produce updates of the composite index. This would allow international organizations such as Interpol and UNODC to monitor major trends in the level of organized crime per region or country. At this juncture, only trend data of the World Economic Forum on the costs of organized crime as perceived by business executives are available. The data cover the period 1997 up to 2005. According to these data, the perceived extent of organized crime has not changed much at the world regions level. Only the Caribbean shows a downward trend in recent years (data on the Dominican Republic, Jamaica, and Trinidad and Tobago).

❖ Figure 7.7   European Map With Scores on Organized-Crime Perception Index
(Around 2003)

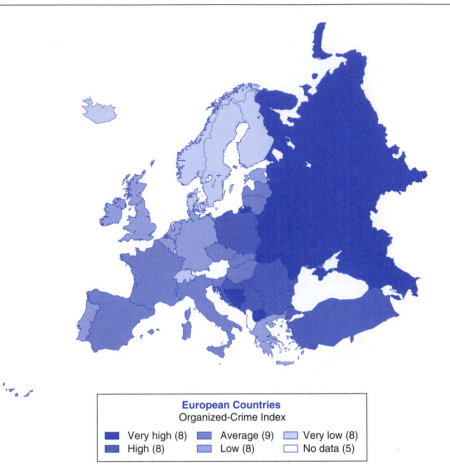

European Countries
Organized-Crime Index

■ Very high (8)   ■ Average (9)   ☐ Very low (8)
■ High (8)   ■ Low (8)   ☐ No data (5)

At the country level, there is more variation over time. As evidence for change in perceived prevalence of organized crime, we consider a consistent change of one point or more on the scale of seven points. According to this standard, problems with organized crime have gone up in Brazil, Romania, and Spain. Gradual improvements in perceived costs from organized crime have occurred in South Africa and Taiwan as well as in three new members of the European Union: Hungary, Latvia, and Lithuania.

Participation of National Organized-Crime Groups in Specific Criminal Markets

Organized-crime groups typically operate in one or more of the world's main criminal markets such as those in illicit drugs, the trafficking in persons for exploitation

❖ **Figure 7.8**   Country Scores of EU Countries on the Composite Organized-Crime Index and Percentages of the Public Agreeing That the National Government Has Been Infiltrated by Organized Crime

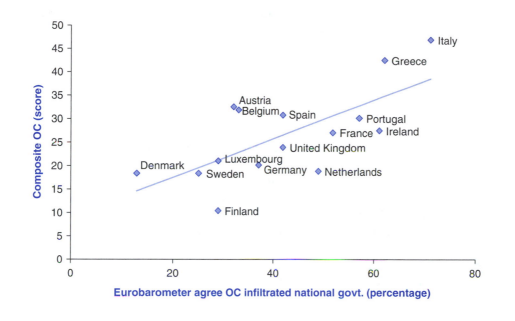

Source: Eurobarometer, 2002.

or illegal entry, and illicit trafficking in firearms, stolen cars, and cigarettes (Buscaglia & Van Dijk, 2003). Much of the organized-crime literature seeks to analyze the dynamics of these markets. Organized-crime groups in individual countries or regions tend to specialize in activities in one or more of these core criminal markets (EUROPOL, 2003, 2004). Organized-crime groups with headquarters in Colombia and Mexico, for example, are known to be heavily involved in the international trafficking of cocaine (Gonzalez-Ruiz, 2001). Russian groups tend to specialize in economic crimes and extortion, while ethnic Albanian and Bulgarian groups are notoriously active in the markets of human trafficking and sexual exploitation besides drugs (EUROPOL, 2003, 2004). Dutch and Belgian organized-crime groups play a major role in the production and wholesaling of certain types of synthetic drugs (Blickman, 2005). Many African organized-crime groups are actively involved in the trafficking of stolen cars (Shaw, 2002), and Chinese groups engage in the smuggling of migrants and extortion (Zhang & Chin, 2001).

Some databases have been developed to track the extent of specific criminal activities in different countries and/or the involvement of persons from those countries in these activities. If countries are prominently active in any of the main markets for illicit goods or services, a higher prevalence of organized crime in the country can be expected.

By the same token, nationals of countries with high scores on the organized-crime index can theoretically be expected to play a prominent role in some of the core markets.

Since drug trafficking is supposedly the largest global criminal market, heavy involvement in drug trafficking would seem to imply a high prevalence of organized crime. Our analyses of relationships between statistics on seizures of illicit drugs and the various indicators of organized-crime presence have consistently produced negative findings (Buscaglia & Van Dijk, 2003). The level of drug seizures in a country does not reflect the extent of local organized-crime presence. There are several explanations for this lack of congruence. As said before, statistics on drug seizures may reflect police performance rather than the actual level of drug trafficking. Large drug seizures in transit countries also do not necessarily point to the involvement of many nationals of the country in such activity. The main operators may be members of organized-crime groups from abroad. A better indicator of the involvement of national organized-crime groups in drug trade would be the number of nationals of countries arrested for such activities, either in their home country or anywhere else in the world. At this juncture, such data on drug traffickers are not available on a global scale. Considering the wealth of information on drug production and consumption, it is surprising to note how little quantitative information is available about the involvement of organized crime in drug markets.

Trafficking in Persons

The U.S. State Department has made worldwide estimates of the number of persons trafficked across international borders for the purpose of exploitation; these estimates fluctuate between 600,000 and 900,000 persons (OMCTIP, 2005). It is not clear on what methods this count is based. To gain better insight into the main flows of trafficking in persons for the purpose of exploitation, UNODC collects data from open sources about cases of trafficking in persons as defined in the UN protocol against trafficking in persons (Kangaspunta, 2003). Reports from police forces or national parliamentary committees on trafficking are supplemented with data from NGOs, international organizations, and, to a lesser extent, media reports.

As with all crime data from official registrations, the numbers may partly or wholly reflect investigative activities of the police or the lack of them rather than the true extent of criminal activity taking place. Not all countries are equally committed to or equipped to carry out investigations or prosecutions regarding such cases. In many countries, trafficking in persons is not criminalized as such, and possible prosecutions are counted under other offense categories. In the case of human trafficking, the distortions are at least partly neutralized by the possibility of using different types of sources. If governments deny or repress information on human trafficking, international media reports can be a useful alternative source. In addition, the transnational nature of the crime of trafficking in persons allows the collection of data about what happens in countries of origin from information collected in countries of destination, and vice versa. For example, reports on cases of human trafficking coming from destination countries often provide information about where the victims were recruited and through which countries they were transported. Even if the authorities of the latter countries are in denial, the involvement of their countries can be externally documented. In addition, media reports from foreign journalists sometimes provide information on trends in human trafficking in countries where awareness of the phenomenon is still absent or low. The inclusion of such reports in the database can help to counterbalance biases in the official data of some countries.

A comparison of the UNODC database results with those of regional databases on human trafficking flows in Europe and Africa, respectively, showed a high level of congruence (HEUNI, 2003; UNICEF/Innocenti, 2003). The UNODC database ranking of countries based on citations in public sources should not be viewed as an unbiased measure of the extent of the problem, but it certainly provides unique information on which countries are reportedly the most obvious origin, transit, and destination countries and thereby on the main global trafficking flows between them.

The majority of the cases in the UNODC database are about trafficking for the purpose of sexual exploitation (77%). Twenty-three percent refer to trafficking for labor exploitation. The majority of victims are women (54%) or minors (44%; mainly girls).

Table 7.3 presents an overview of countries most often cited in public sources as a country of origin, a transit country, or a country of destination.

In 2004, the SECI Regional Center, a regional law enforcement agency, coordinated a special regional action against human trafficking, labeled Operation Mirage 2004. During a period of 10 days, law enforcement authorities in southeastern Europe targeted both victims of and criminals involved in human trafficking. From the information received by the law enforcement authorities through international information exchange and from domestic sources, and as a result of special investigations, 601 women were identified as victims of international or domestic trafficking during the action. The largest contingent originated from Romania, Bosnia Herzegovina, Albania,

❖ **Table 7.3**   Most Frequently Cited Countries of Origin, Transit, and Destination of Trafficking in Persons (2002)

	Main Countries of Origin	Main Transit Countries	Main Destination Countries
1	Russian Federation	Albania	Belgium
2	Ukraine	Bulgaria	Germany
3	Thailand	Hungary	Greece
4	Nigeria	Poland	Italy
5	Republic of Moldova	Italy	The Netherlands
6	Romania	Thailand	Israel
7	Albania		Turkey
8	China		Japan
9	Belarus		Thailand
10	Bulgaria		United States
11	Lithuania		

Sources: Kangaspunta, 2003; UNODC, 2006.

and Moldova. Among the 117 victims that were domestically trafficked, 40 were minor victims (34%), and among the 484 victims internationally trafficked, 68 were minors.

As a follow-up to the Mirage campaign, the SECI Centre initiated regular data collection on human trafficking cases in the Balkan region (SECI, 2005). In the first half of 2005, 2,380 victims were identified, with the largest numbers originating from Romania, Moldova, and Bulgaria. Greece, Turkey, and Slovenia were identified as key destination countries in the region. These regional findings by and large confirm the geographical patterns emerging from the UNODC database.

Secondary analyses of the UNODC database showed that the numbers of citations of countries as country of origin were positively correlated to country scores on the Composite Organized-Crime Index. The countries with the highest scores for trafficking showed statistically significant higher average scores for organized crime than those with low or very low scores. Where recruitment for trafficking is more often reported, organized crime is more prevalent. A significant correlation was also found among the more affluent countries between the country scores on citations for destination and on the organized-crime index.

The UNODC database on trafficking in persons contains not only data on the number of times that countries are cited in open sources as countries of origin or destination but also some fragmentary data on the nationality of offenders in documented trafficking cases, regardless of the country of origin or destination. The ranking of countries in terms of citations of their nationals as offenders was found to correlate with the organized-crime perception index, though only weakly ($r = 0.27$, $p < 0.05$, $n = 57$). The correlation is largely based on the position of Nigeria, Albania, and Russia at the extreme high end of both variables.

These findings suggest that there are links between the presence of organized-crime groups in a country and its role on the global market for trafficking of humans for exploitation. However, the statistical links are not very strong. Strong correlations are not to be expected since the overall level of organized crime in a country is obviously dependent on involvement of residents in many other forms of crime besides trafficking in persons.

Organized Car Theft

High levels of car theft, especially of cars that are never recovered by the owners, point to the involvement of organized-crime groups arranging both the actual thefts and the transportation and sale in other places. Trafficking in stolen vehicles is cited by many African countries as one of the major activities of organized-crime groups (Shaw, 2002). In Europe, many countries reported either car theft or trafficking in stolen vehicles among the major organized-crime markets in 2002–2003 (Council of Europe, 2004).[9] A key aspect of this form of crime is the need to legalize stolen vehicles in order for the criminal to achieve a monetary gain. Interpol cites an estimate of US$19 billion generated by illicit trafficking of vehicles. The analysis of the relationship between prevalence of organized crime and the available ICVS-based data on rates of stolen cars that are not recovered did not provide significant correlations ($r = .14$). Finally, the correlation of the COCI scores with country rankings drawn from databases on cigarette smuggling was calculated (Buscaglia & Van Dijk, 2003). Moderately strong correlations were found between organized-crime prevalence and cigarette smuggling ($r = .33$), but available data were limited to few countries.

The Intercorrelates of Crime

The analysis has shown that available data from different surveys among business executives on perceived prevalence of racketeering and extortion correlate strongly among themselves and with country ratings of such activities by international security risk analysts. These subjective data also correlate fairly strongly with a proxy indicator of mob-related violence, based on official police and court data (rates of unsolved murders per 100,000). In addition, they strongly correlate to indicators of high-level corruption, money laundering, and the size of the informal sector. The overall prevalence of organized crime was found to be only weakly related to country ratings for different types of organized-crime activities such as drug seizures, trafficking in persons, and trafficking in cigarettes as well as car theft. Apparently, the ranking of countries in databases on cases concerning special forms of organized crime cannot by itself be used as an indicator of overall prevalence of organized crime.[10] It would seem worthwhile to explore further the potential of supplementing the Composite Organized-Crime Index with quantitative data from international police and customs organizations on other aspects of organized crime, including involvement in drug trafficking. This is clearly an area where more quantitative research needs to be done.

For both theoretical and policy reasons, it seems important to know whether our new comprehensive measure of organized crime correlates with the results of the ICVS on the distribution of common crimes. The analyses showed that the world map of organized crime emerging from the Composite Organized-Crime Index differs fundamentally from that of common crimes, as can be seen in Figure 7.9.

Some countries are confronted with high levels of both common crime and organized crime (e.g., Columbia, Mozambique, and Zimbawe). Other countries are low crime countries in both counts (e.g., Japan, Switzerland, and Finland). However, the perceived prevalence of organized crime and the overall ICVS rates of victimization by volume crime were found to be unrelated ($r = .18$, n.s.). The level of volume crime in a country says very little about the level of organized crime. This result suggests that levels of volume crime and of organized crime are determined by different factors at the macro level. There seems to be little room for generalized theories about the macro causes of crime. The determinants of common crime discussed in Chapter 5 are not necessarily related to organized crime as well. Country scores on the COCI are, for example, unrelated to known determinants of common crime like urbanization. Unlike common crime, organized crime seems unequivocally linked to underdevelopment both globally and within Europe. Common crime and organized crime seem to be driven by different macro factors and seem to call for different approaches and strategies (Van Dijk & Nevala, 2002).

Tentative Transnational Responses

In the late 1990s, criminal law finally broke out of its traditional domestic mold. Both regionally and internationally, new legal instruments were created that provided for legal interfaces between the operating criminal justice systems of countries.

❖ **Figure 7.9**   Country Scores on ICVS for Overall Victimization by Common Crime and on the Composite Organized-Crime Index (Ranked Variables, With Low Rank Numbers Indicating Low Levels of Crime)

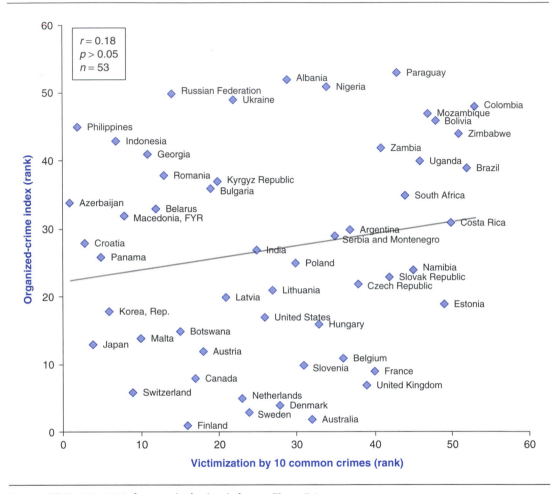

Sources: ICVS, 1992–2000; for organized-crime index, see Figure 7.4.

For the first time, the member states of the United Nations have recently agreed on two criminal law conventions, one against transnational organized crime, with three supplementary protocols, and one against corruption. The Convention Against Transnational Organized Crime was adopted by the General Assembly on November 15, 2000. In this section, we will look at the follow-up from member states to the UNTOC convention.

The UNTOC had on July 1, 2005, been ratified (or acceded) by 108 member states as well as by the European Commission and Cook Islands.[11] The statistics for the three protocols were 88 ratifications/accessions for the protocol against human trafficking, 80 for the protocol against smuggling of migrants, and 45 for the protocol against firearms, respectively. Of all member states, 57% had ratified the conventions, 46% the protocol against human trafficking, 42% the one against smuggling of migrants, and 24% the protocol against firearms.

Figure 7.10 shows the regional percentages of ratifications of UNTOC and the three protocols in July 2005. Ratification percentages are comparatively high in Europe and are below average in Asia, Africa, and Latin America, regions where problems of organized crime and corruption are particularly severe.

The European Union had in July 2005 ratified the convention, but three of its member states had not: Italy, host country of the UNTOC's signing conference in 2000, the Czech Republic, and the United Kingdom. Conspicuously absent on the list of state parties on July 2005 was also the United States. Surprisingly, some of the most ardent promoters of the convention had not yet ratified it 5 years after its adoption (the United States had ratified the convention in 2006). The overview indicates that there is little relation between

❖ **Figure 7.10**   Regional Percentages of Member States Having Ratified the UNTOC Convention and Its Three Supplementary Protocols (July 2005)

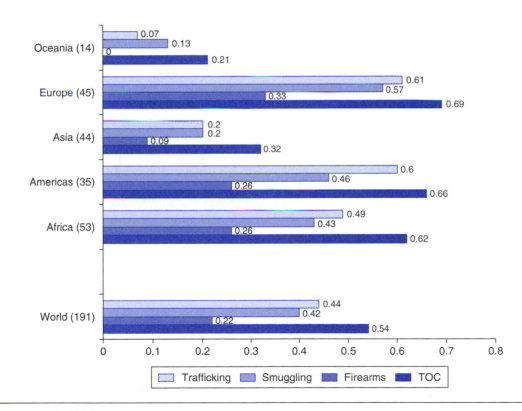

Source: www.UNODC.org.

the prevalence of organized crime in countries and ratification of the convention. Some developing or transitional countries most in need of bringing their law enforcement capacities up to international standards in order to tackle their domestic organized-crime–corruption problems seem to have been reluctant to ratify the convention.

Obviously, ratification of an international legal instrument is a necessary but far from sufficient condition for actual implementation. Since the state parties of the UNTOC convention have not yet reached agreement on a monitoring mechanism, at this stage no data are available on the implementation of this new UN legal instrument against organized crime. One indirect and, admittedly, tentative way of assessing the progress made by state parties in implementing the UNTOC convention is to look at the prevalence of organized crime in their country and their overall police performance.[12] The average score on our Composite Organized-Crime Index of the state parties to the UNTOC convention in 2005 is somewhat better (37.2) than that of the non–state parties (42.6), indicating that organized crime is somewhat less prevalent among state parties. Differences on the index for police performance are slight but go also in the right direction, in the sense that state parties on average perform somewhat better than the others. These differences cannot be seen as evidence that the UNTOC has already improved performance. More likely countries that are underperforming have, in the absence of external pressure, been reluctant to subscribe to international standards by ratifying the convention. In the coming years, the current scores on these indices can perhaps be used as benchmarks to measure progress in the fight against transnational organized crime by the state parties of the UNTOC convention. Scores of state parties should show greater improvements over time than those of non–state parties. Such shifts would indicate that the convention has had a real impact in the global and national fights against organized crime.

The U.S. Report on Trafficking in Persons

The U.S. State Department releases an annual report that assesses the efforts of foreign governments in tackling trafficking in persons for exploitation, as defined in the Trafficking Victims Protection Act (TVPA) of 2000 of the country. The report, using information from US embassies, meetings with governments, NGOs and, international organizations, qualifies countries in four tiers. Tier 1, refers to countries whose governments are in full compliance with the act's minimum standards. Tier 2 refers to countries not fully complying but making significant efforts. Tier 2 Watch List, refers to countries not complying but whose efforts are significant and deserve special attention (the watch list), and, finally, Tier 3 refers to countries neither complying nor making significant efforts. Countries placed in Tier 3 can become the target of sanctions by the U.S .government (online: www.state.gov/g/tip/rls/tiprpt/2004).

It must be stressed that the assessments are made with reference to the national legislation of the United States and not to the UN protocol and that they reflect nothing more or less than the opinions of the government of one member state of the UN.[13] Since there is broad agreement between the TVPA of 2000 and the UN protocol against trafficking in persons, the results are nevertheless worth examining as an indication of compliance with the UN protocol. For ease of reference, we have added to the U.S. qualifications information on ratification of the UNTOC convention and the

❖ **Figure 7.11** Percentages Ratifications of the UNTOC Convention and Its Antitrafficking Protocol, Mean Scores on the Composite Organized-Crime Index, and Police Performance Index of Countries Classified by the U.S. Government as Fully Complying With U.S. Trafficking Victims Protection Act of 2000 (Tier 1), Not Fully Complying but Making Serious Efforts (Tier 2), Not Complying and Making Serious Efforts but to Be Watched (Tier 2, Watch List), and Noncompliance (Tier 3).

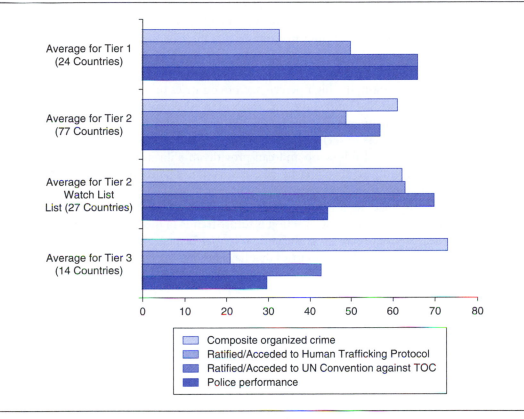

Sources: Online: www.state.gov/g/tip/rls/tiprpt/2004); www.unodc.org.

trafficking protocol as well as the country scores on the indices for organized crime and police performance. Figure 7.11 shows the overview of this information.

The information contained in Figure 7.11 shows, first of all, that the scores for the prevalence of organized crime are broadly in line with the classification in four tiers of the U.S. government. Scores are lowest among Tier 1 countries, almost twice as high among countries in Tier 2 and on the Tier 2 watch list, and higher still among those in Tier 3. The mean scores on police performance are equally in agreement with the classification, although differences between Tier 2 and the Tier 2 watch list are minute.

Surprisingly, the percentages of countries that have ratified the UN countertrafficking protocol are inconsistent with the U.S. classification. Of the Tier 1 countries,

66% had ratified the convention by July 2005 and 50% the protocol. Of the Tier 2 countries, 57% had ratified the convention and 49% the protocol. The ratification percentages of the UN protocol for these two groups of countries that are fully or at least intentionally in compliance with the U.S. 2000 Act seem surprisingly low. Of the Tier 2 watch list countries, 70% had ratified the convention and 63% the protocol. In July 2005, countries placed on the U.S. watch list for noncompliance with the U.S. legislative standards have more often ratified the UN convention and protocol than even the Tier 1 countries. This high rate of ratifications among watch list countries could in theory mean that their placement by the United States on a watch list was unjustified. The other, more plausible interpretation is that these countries have hastily ratified the protocol in order to make a good impression on the U.S. government without serious legislative preparation and/or operational follow-up.

In our opinion, the high percentage of countries on the U.S. watch list for noncompliance that had ratified the UN protocol in 2005 reveals the weakness of international legal instruments for which no functional monitoring mechanism has been put in place. The access to such instruments does not commit governments to real legislative or operational follow-up and can provide an alibi in the international political arena for countries unwilling to take real action against the Mafias of the world. International legal instruments without proper monitoring mechanisms run the risk of becoming mere fig leaves for noncooperative countries. The litmus test for the UN protocol against trafficking in action is future trends in the rating of countries both by our measures of organized crime and police performance and the ratings by the U.S. State Department. Those countries that have ratified the protocol should demonstrate more favorable trends than those that have not.

SUMMARY POINTS/IN CONCLUSION

• The growing concern of national governments and international organizations about new, transnational manifestations of organized crime has triggered a wave of studies into these phenomena. But the field is handicapped by an almost total lack of quantitative data. Both policy and theory formation are largely based on fragmented information from police and media reports.

• One fundamental obstacle to measuring organized crime is the absence of a universal definition. Another is its transnational nature. Besides, available statistics from police authorities on local organized crime reflect current law enforcement resources and priorities. For comparative purposes, police figures of the extent of organized crime can be very misleading indeed.

Due to corruption in police circles and the courts, arrests and convictions for Mafia-related activities tend to be low in countries most deeply affected by Mafia groups.

• To overcome methodological problems with interpreting police figures on organized crime, criminologists have to become creative. Pursuing the approach of victimization surveys on common crimes, information must be collected from groups most exposed to Mafia-type activities. Arguably, the segments of society most exposed to organized crime are professional groups such as lawyers and bankers as well as the business sector. To assess the extent of organized crime, the experiences of such groups should be harnessed.

- A possible source of information on organized crime is large-scale victimization surveys among the business sector or professional groups. So far such dedicated business victimization surveys have been carried out in only a small number of countries. The most readily available data on organized crime can be found in the global surveys among large samples of business executives carried out annually by the World Economic Forum in Davos. One of the recurrent items in these surveys is the perception of the costs for business of organized crime such as extortion and racketeering.

- Answers to this item from national samples of business executives were found to be strongly correlated with risk assessments from security experts. More to the point, these perceptions-based ratings were also found to correlate with country rates of *unsolved murders,* a proxy indicator of the prevalence of mob-related violence. Using a selection of such indicators, a first-ever composite index of organized crime was constructed that provides a ranking of over 100 countries.

- The ranking of world regions on the index shows a strong link between development and prevalence of organized crime. Mafia-type activities are most common in developing countries in the South. Within Europe, high levels in the East and South contrast with low levels in the West and North.

- Scores on the composite index show correlations with other estimates of a country's involvement in special types of organized crime such as trafficking in persons for the purpose of (sexual) exploitation. The correlations found, though, were not very strong. No correlations were found with existing data on drug trafficking. There seems to be ample scope for more quantitative research on different types of organized crime.

- Levels of organized crime are distributed quite differently from those of common crimes. Organized crime is not, for example, related to urbanization. It is strongly inversely related to the GDP. The lack of any clear association between the two types of crime suggests that they are driven by different sets of factors, a topic that will be addressed in Part V.

- In the meantime, governments of many countries have stepped up their efforts to contain organized crime and strengthen their international cooperation. In recent years, several international legal instruments have been elaborated and approved, such as the United Nations Convention against Transnational Organized Crime and its three protocols. The entry into force of this convention forms no guarantee that international cooperation will actually improve. State parties of the convention have so far failed to agree on independent monitoring of implementation, and no sanctioning of noncompliance is foreseen. In the absence of such follow-up, ratification of such legal instruments runs the risk of being nothing more than a shield behind which uncooperative countries can hide their lack of capacity and/or political will to tackle global crime threats in concert with others.

Notes

1. In the words of the UN Secretary-General, human security is "freedom from want, freedom from fear, and the freedom of future generations to inherit a healthy natural environment" (UNIS/SG/2555,9). In 2003, the UN's Commission on Human Security defined the concept as "safeguarding and expanding people's vital freedoms," that is, protecting people from threats to the vital core of all human lives (United Nations, 2003).

2. http://www.iom.int/en/who/main_service_areas_counter.shtml#chap1.

3. Submission by the United Nations Environment Programme to the UN Systems Chief Executive Board, June 2004. The figures are drawn from *Roe to Ruin: The Decline of the Sturgeon*

in the Caspian Sea and the Road to Recovery, Natural Resources Defense Council, Wildlife Conservations Society and SeaWeb, December 2000, pp. 2–3.

4. One Web site is devoted entirely to the topic (http://hom.rica.net). Several national police organizations are publishing information on the topic as well.

5. Online: www.weforum.org.

6. The shadow economy can be tentatively defined as market-based production of goods and services, whether legal or illegal, that escape detection in the official estimates of the GDP or other official registration (Schneider, 2004).

7. A factor analysis revealed high loadings of all five indicators on one component. The reliability of the scale is high (Cronbach's alpha is .81). We have decided against weighing the indicators because this would, for lack of a guiding theoretical framework, have been based on subjective assessments of their significance as a Mafia marker.

8. In the calculation of the Composite Organized-Crime Index, only the figures that are based on at least two values are shown. According to the GAD survey, however, perception of crime is very high in Iraq, the Congo, the West Bank, and Gaza (all in top five but not included in Table 7.2).

9. Austria, Belgium, Croatia, Germany, Estonia, Latvia, Lithuania, the Netherlands, and Poland.

10. It may prove possible in the future to construct a comprehensive index of organized-crime activities based on statistical databases on different types of organized crime, including drug trafficking, human trafficking, car theft, counterfeiting, to name just a few.

11. On February 1, 2007, the number of parties of the UNTOC had risen to 131 countries.

12. For the index on police performance, see Chapter 9.

13. The report provides no qualification of the policies of the United States, although the United States, according to UNODC data, is among the world's main destination countries of trafficking in persons.

8

Other Global Security Threats

Corruption, Terrorism, and Cybercrime

Defining Corruption

Corruption can be broadly defined as the abuse of public power for private gain. A distinction is often made between "grand" corruption and "petty" or "street-level" corruption. Grand corruption refers to corrupt practices that pervade the highest levels of government. Petty corruption involves the payment by individuals or companies of relatively small sums to gain preferential treatment from public officials in the conduct of their professional tasks (Langseth, 2002b). One of the most common forms of corruption is bribery, the bestowing of (financial) benefits in order to unduly influence an action or decision. A further distinction can be made between active and passive bribery. Active bribery refers to the offering or payment of bribes, and passive bribery refers to the seeking or receiving of bribes.

The United Nations Convention Against Corruption, which entered into force in 2005, does not provide a general definition of corruption (United Nations, 2005). The treaty obliges state parties to criminalize two specific types of corruption (active and passive bribery and embezzlement by a public official) and to consider criminalizing other types such as trading in influence, abuse of public functions, and illicit enrichment (defined as a significant increase in the assets of a public official that he cannot explain as resulting from his lawful income).

Corruption Indicators: Perceptions and Experiences

The most commonly cited statistical indicator of corruption is the Corruption Perception Index (CPI), designed and maintained by the Berlin-based NGO Transparency International, generally known as TI (Transparency International, 2004). The CPI is a composite index of the perceived extent of corrupt practices in countries, both grand and petty, drawing on over a dozen different surveys including the ICVS and expert assessments (Lambsdorff, 2000). Recent versions of the CPI are largely based on results of surveys among businesspeople and ratings made by risk analysts. The findings of the various surveys and risk analyses used show high correlations, which support the construction of a composite index (Lambsdorff, 2005).

Although the CPI has significant political impact, its methodology is increasingly criticized. One common criticism is that the sources used differ significantly across countries and years, thus compromising the comparability of the results. The incremental extension of the number of sources used for the CPI may not have strengthened but, rather, weakened the index. Conceptual clarity and comparability of results may have diminished as a consequence. Another criticism is that perceptions of business leaders and experts influence each other and that high rankings could therefore be based on the mere "echoing" throughout countries of unfounded, media-led beliefs. Perhaps the most salient criticism is that the CPI as an index measuring perceptions of a wide range of broadly defined corruption problems cannot accurately reflect changes in the actual extent of specific forms of corruption. Governments that have achieved hard-won victories in their fights against corrupt practices in specific institutions, for example, customs offices or traffic police, have reason to be annoyed if such successes do not show up in their CPI scores. The above criticisms also apply to other perception-based "catchall" indices of corruption such as those developed by the World Bank, which, although more stringently standardized, in essence follow the same methodology as TI's "poll of polls" (Kaufmann, Kraay, & Mastruzzi, 2004).

As mentioned in Chapter 3, the International Crime Victims Survey (ICVS) includes a question on the respondent's actual experiences with street-level corruption in the previous year ("During the past year, has any government official such as a customs officer, police officer, or inspector asked you or expected you to pay a bribe?"). In older versions of the CPI, the ICVS country rates of victimization by corruption were incorporated (TI, 2001). The ICVS-based data on actual victimization by corruption, although hardly noticed outside criminology, meets the standards of crime surveying and is arguably the most reliable source of truly comparative information on corruption prevalence.

In 2003, TI contracted Gallup to conduct a public opinion survey in 64 countries among a total of 50,000 people to assess not just perceptions of corruption but also personal experiences (Global Corruption Barometer, TI, 2004). The question used to measure actual victimization experiences reads: "In the past 12 months, have you or anyone in your household paid a bribe in any form?" The question resembles the one used in the ICVS but is not, unfortunately, identical because it focuses on just the actual payment rather than on solicitation ("were you asked or expected to pay"). In spite of this difference, the analysis of the relationship between the prevalence rates found in the ICVS and in the TI corruption barometer revealed a high degree of agreement. The two measures of victimization by petty corruption were found to be strongly correlated ($r = 0.75$). On average, ICVS rates are 9.9% higher than the Transparency International data, as was to be expected considering the wider scope of the question used in the ICVS.

In order to increase the coverage of the two studies and enhance the significance of the results, we have integrated the two data sets with an adjustment of the TI data to better match ICVS data (TI scores were multiplied by 109.9%). Through this operation, we were able to calculate corruption victimization rates for 92 countries.

Figure 8.1 shows the subregional prevalence rates for street-level corruption in the years 2000–2002. The results clearly show huge regional variation in levels of street-level corruption. Victimization by such corruption is almost unknown in western Europe, North America, and Oceania but is quite common everywhere else.[1] Secondary data from the ICVS show that across the world, police officers were the category of officials most often mentioned as receivers or seekers of bribes, followed by government officials, customs officers, and inspectors.[2] Only a very few victims reported the incident to the police or any other official authority. Compared to the common crimes included in the ICVS, corruption is by far the crime category with the highest amount of "dark numbers."

Table 8.1 shows the country rankings on corruption as measured by the ICVS TI barometer of petty corruption.

❖ **Figure 8.1** Percentages of the General Public Involved in Bribe-Giving During the Past Year, per World Subregion, 2000–2002

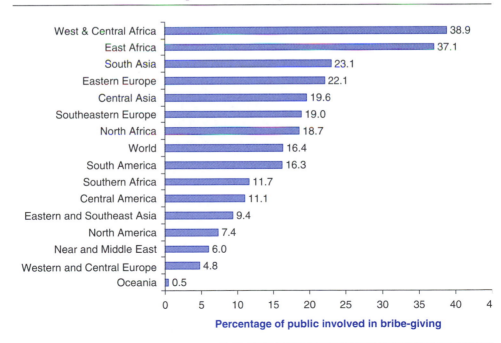

Percentage of public involved in bribe-giving

Sources: ICVS, 2000; TI, 2004.

❖ **Table 8.1**   World Rankings on Street-Level Corruption, 2000–2002 (88 countries)

"Over the past 12 months, has any government official, for instance, a customs officer, a police officer, or inspector in your country, asked you or expected you to pay a bribe for his or her services?" (% affirmative answers)

Fifteen Countries With the Highest Victimization Rates								
1	Albania	59.1%	6	Indonesia	32.9%	11	Cambodia	29.0%
2	Cameroon	57.2%	7	Mozambique	30.5%	12	Bolivia	25.9%
3	Kenya	39.6%	8	Nigeria	29.8%	13	India	23.1%
4	Moldova	35.2%	9	Ecuador	29.7%	14	Lithuania	22.9%
5	Uganda	34.7%	10	Ghana	29.7%	15	Mongolia	21.3%
Fifteen Countries With Average Victimization Rates								
17	Mexico	20.9%	33	Peru	15.4%	64	France	2.4%
21	Belarus	20.6%	42	Pakistan	9.9%	69	Italy	2.2%
22	Egypt	18.7%	49	Poland	8.6%	69	Spain	2.2%
24	Brazil	17.9%	52	Argentina	6.8%	70	Switzerland	2.2%
29	Russian Fed.	16.6%	63	South Africa	2.9%	73	Germany	1.1%
Fifteen Countries With Lowest Victimization Rates								
74	Hong Kong	1.1%	79	Botswana	0.8%	84	Canada	0.4%
75	Ireland	1.1%	80	United States	0.7%	85	Finland	0.4%
76	Singapore	1.1%	81	Belgium	0.6 %	86	England & Wales	0.3%
77	Taiwan	1.1%	82	Denmark	0.5%	87	Sweden	0.2%
78	Netherlands	0.9%	83	Australia	0.5%	88	Japan	0.1%

Sources: ICVS, 2000; TI, 2004.

The category of countries with the highest scores is composed of developing countries from across the world, with eastern Europe, sub-Saharan Africa, and Latin America all containing several countries in the group with the highest rates.

The excessively high figure of Albania, first observed in ICVS surveys and now confirmed by the TI barometer, should be interpreted against the background of the massive "pyramid scam" that bankrupted many Albanian citizens some years ago and in which government officials were believed to be involved. Equally remarkable is the high score of Cameroon. This score is based on the TI barometer. Other results of the TI survey also seem to point to rampant corruption among the police and other agencies in that country. Also, the people of Cameroon are among the most pessimistic in the region about the future trends in corruption (TI, 2004).

Almost all Western countries show comparatively low scores. Within western Europe, northern countries show lower scores than Mediterranean countries. In the ICVS 2005 (results not shown here), Greece, where the ICVS was conducted for the first time nationwide, came out with a percentage rate of 13%. Including this result in the table would have placed Greece among the 50 most corrupt countries worldwide.

The ICVS 2005 revealed a declining prevalence of corruption among the new entrants of the European Union, Poland and Estonia.

At the bottom end, Japan stands out with a rate of 0.1. Street-level corruption seems to be a rarity in Japan. Among the 15 countries with the best scores on corruption are Botswana, Hong Kong, Taiwan, and Singapore. These countries are all reputed to have made great efforts in curbing corruption. Their low scores on victimization by petty corruption demonstrate the success of their large-scale and sustained countercorruption campaigns.

Figures 8.2 and 8.3 show the corruption maps of the world and of Europe.

❖ **Figure 8.2**   World Map of Street-Level Corruption in 2000–2002

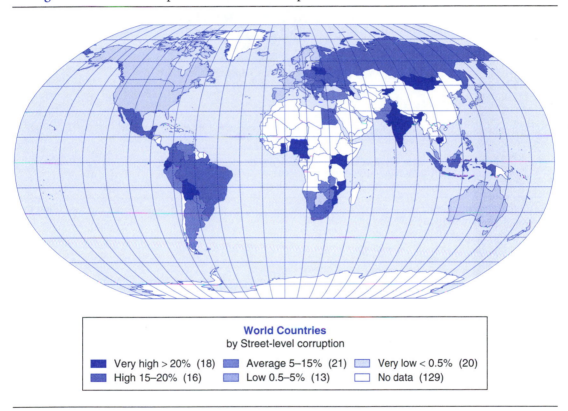

World Countries
by Street-level corruption

■ Very high > 20% (18)	■ Average 5–15% (21)	▫ Very low < 0.5% (20)
■ High 15–20% (16)	■ Low 0.5–5% (13)	☐ No data (129)

Sources: ICVS, 2000; TI, 2004.

Assessing the Merits of Objective and Subjective Indicators

The relatively simple victimization question used in the ICVS provides, in our opinion, a better, more valid indicator of the most common forms of corruption than any of the perceptional indicators or indices. This assumption is confirmed by the

❖ **Figure 8.3**   Map of Street-Level Corruption of Europe in 2000–2002

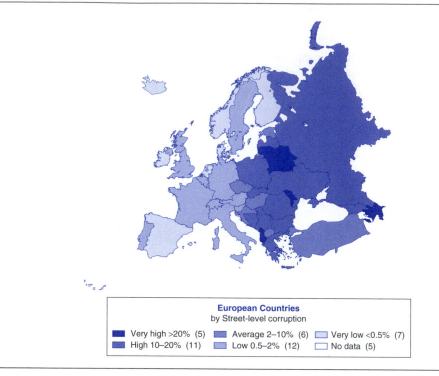

European Countries
by Street-level corruption

■ Very high >20% (5)	■ Average 2–10% (6)	☐ Very low <0.5% (7)
■ High 10–20% (11)	■ Low 0.5–2% (12)	☐ No data (5)

Sources: ICVS, 2000; TI, 2004.

time series data on corruption experiences, collected in Bulgaria by Coalition 2000, an NGO campaigning against corruption in cooperation with the government. The Bulgarian research team has carried out quarterly surveys among the Bulgarian public since 1998, asking about both actual participation in corrupt transactions and "corruption pressure" (having been asked to pay a bribe) as well as about perceptions of the extent of corruption. The percentage of respondents admitting to having actually paid a bribe during the past month declined from 1% in early 1999 to 0.5% in November 2004. The quarterly rates show a clear, linear downward trend. The corruption pressure indicator showed a similar downward trend (Coalition 2000, 2005). These trends seem to accurately reflect the positive effects of the huge efforts of the government to curb corruption in the country. The ICVS-type of question seems capable of monitoring movements in the actual level of corruption. Interestingly, the same research team did not register any changes in its index of perceived levels of corruption during the same period. Although actual levels of petty corruption had gone down significantly, the scores on the perception-based items remained more or less constant during the reference period. Perception-based indicators showed fluctuations linked to recent press releases, including those about actions against corruption by the government or Coalition 2000 itself.

Although Bulgaria's experience confirms the methodological vulnerability of perception-based data and the superiority of data on actual victimizations, it would be wrong to summarily dismiss TI's CPI or similar perception-based aggregated indices of the World Bank. Surveys on actual experiences with corruption may be the best option of measuring petty corruption, but they cannot measure forms of grand corruption, involving high-level public officials, politicians, and connected businessmen, collaborating in the theft of state resources. Ordinary people are not personally confronted with such hidden practices of "state capture." In this context, it should be pointed out that the medium-high position of Italy and Spain on the ICVS-based scale of corruption probably underestimates the seriousness of corrupt practices in high circles in these countries. Victimization surveys among households can only measure everyday petty corruption. Their results on corruption will therefore always have to be supplemented with data from other sources. Perception-based aggregate indices might at this juncture be the only viable option for gathering comparative information on grand corruption.

Our analyses have consistently shown that Transparency International's CPI and the rates of actual experiences of citizens with petty corruption are moderately strongly correlated ($r = -.45$, $p < 0.01$, $n = 40$). This finding goes some way in validating the CPI as a rough indicator of the comparative extent of actual corrupt practices across countries. Soares, analyzing the impact of rampant corruption on the willingness of people to report crime incidents to the police, found a strong statistical relationship between CPI and the proportion of crime victimizations reported to the police according to the ICVS (Soares, 2005). Where corruption is more prevalent, fewer people report crime victimizations to the police. Soares sees low reporting of crimes to the police as evidence of police corruption. He interprets the link between the CPI and low reporting as evidence supporting the use of perception data such as the CPI as a measure of actual corruption (in this case, within police forces).

Subjective indices of corruption should at any rate not be dismissed as "just reflecting perceptions," as is often done by politicians, embarrassed by the poor CPI rankings of their country. Perceptions of corruption are based on information from business leaders and risk analysts about what goes on in individual countries that seems solid enough to allow an indicative ranking of countries (Kaufmann & Kraay, 2005). However, perceptional indicators should be used cautiously. They cannot and should not be used to measure changes in corruption levels over time. The Bulgarian experience has demonstrated that the use of such indices by development aid agencies to monitor progress in curbing corruption is unfair to the recipient governments and therefore is irresponsible.

Corruption Victimizations in the Corporate World

Both the CPI's and the ICVS's questions on bribery aim to capture the extent to which public officials in a country ask or actually receive bribes for their services. Both measures focus on the prevalence of corrupt officials in a country (the demand side of corruption). Of special interest for the international fight against corruption is the payment of bribes by international companies to public officials in foreign countries. The Organization of Economic Cooperation and Development (OECD) adopted in 1997 at the urgent request of the U.S. government a Convention on Combating Bribery of Foreign Public Officials in International Business Transactions, which entered into force on February 15, 1999 (United Nations, 2005). The convention obliges state parties to criminalize the payment of such bribes in their domestic legislation and has been ratified by the majority of industrialized countries.

Since 1999, Transparency International has carried out global surveys among business experts in 15 emerging market countries on the relative propensity of international companies to pay bribes to win or retain business in their country. The sectors where bribery by foreign companies seeking contracts were most common included public works/construction, arms/defense, and oil/gas. The survey asked about the likelihood of companies offering bribes to officials in various sectors of the economy. A perfect score, indicating zero perceived propensity to pay bribes, is 10.0, and thus the ranking starts with companies from countries that are seen to have a low propensity for paying foreign bribes. Table 8.2 shows the results.

Australia and several northern European countries show comparatively low scores on bribe-giving by companies, in line with their low scores on the CPI and the ICVS/TI indices of bribe-taking. Russia and China, both non-OECD members, rank at the top of the bribe-givers list. Companies of several countries that have ratified the OECD convention such as South Korea, Italy, and Japan are seen by business leaders in emerging market countries as often engaging in activities prohibited by the provisions of the OECD convention.

It is worth pointing out that in many of the countries with high or moderately high scores on bribe-giving abroad, prevalence rates of corruption at home are fairly low. This is particularly striking in the case of Taiwan, Hong Kong, and Japan. Companies in these countries seem to be exporting to developing countries a vice that has with great effort been rooted out in their home countries.

A follow-up report by Transparency International on the enforcement of the OECD Convention in 2007 confirmed that compliance has to date remained unsatisfactory (see online: www.transparency.org). Of the major exporting countries, Canada, Japan, and the United Kingdom are singled out as countries with no or very few prosecutions. The highest numbers of prosecutions were initiated in the first half of 2007 in the United States (67), Hungary (18), the Netherlands (10), and France (9).

As mentioned before, the UN Convention Against Corruption entered into force in 2005. Ratification of the 2003 UN Convention Against Corruption reveals a puzzling distribution. The world map of countries that have ratified the convention (www.legacarta.org) is almost a copy of our world map of corruption prevalence. The earliest parties to this convention were almost exclusively developing countries and countries with economies in transition where corruption is rampant and anticorruption policies seriously flawed. The overrepresentation of highly corrupt countries among the first accessories begs the question whether ratification expresses a real commitment to tackle corruption or a wish to be seen as being committed for internal and/or international political purposes.

Several of the developed countries have up to February 2007 still not ratified the convention. These include Japan, South Korea, Malaysia, Italy, Singapore, Germany,

❖ Table 8.2   Ranking of Countries, Based on Responses to the Question: "In the business sectors with which are you most familiar, how likely are companies from the following countries to pay or offer bribes to win or retain business in this country?"

Ranking by Country

Rank	Country	Score
1	Australia	8.5
2	Sweden	8.4
3	Switzerland	8.4
4	Austria	8.2
5	Canada	8.1
6	Netherlands	7.8
7	Belgium	7.8
8	United Kingdom	6.9
9	Singapore	6.3
10	Germany	6.3
11	Spain	5.8
12	France	5.5
13	United States	5.3
14	Japan	5.3
15	Malaysia	4.3
16	Hong Kong	4.3
17	Italy	4.1
18	South Korea	3.9
19	Taiwan	3.8
20	People's Republic of China	3.5
21	Russia	3.2
22	Domestic companies	1.9

Source: Transparency International, Annual Report, 2003.

and Switzerland. One cannot avoid wondering whether the reluctance of these developed countries to ratify may be related to their high position on the bribe-givers ranking. Some developed countries may fear that the convention may make their industries more vulnerable to legal action from developing countries. They may also fear the "repatriation" of billions of corrupt moneys stashed away in Western banks to developing countries from where it was looted, as envisaged by the convention.

Business Crime Surveys

The International Crime Business Survey (ICBS), introduced in Chapters 3 and 7, interviews business executives on their companies' experience with crime and corruption. The questionnaire of the 2000 sweep included two questions on corruption

❖ **Figure 8.4**   Businesses Victims of Corruption in Nine Central-Eastern European Cities

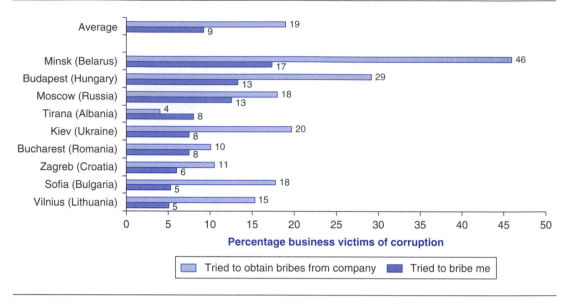

Source: ICBS, 2000.

experience, one dealing with personal experience ("Did anyone try to bribe you?") and the other one with bribes requested from the company ("Did anyone try to obtain bribes from the company?"). Figure 8.4 shows the results.

On average, 9% of the respondents mentioned having been offered bribes, with a minimum of 5% in Vilnius and Sofia and a maximum of 17% in Minsk. Nineteen percent mentioned that someone had tried to obtain bribes from the company, with a minimum of 4% in Tirana and a maximum of 46% in Minsk. Both types of corruption occurred most frequently in Minsk, followed by Budapest. As regards personal experience, the lowest rates were observed in Vilnius, Sofia, and Zagreb. Company risk of corruption was lowest in Tirana, Bucharest, and Zagreb. The comparatively high score for Belarus (Minsk) is in line with the ranking of the country on the ICVS/TI index of street-level corruption. The low ranking of Albania (Tirana) is at odds with high scores for street-level corruption.

Patterns and Trends in Terrorist Crimes

Terrorist incidents, due to their calculated use of demonstrative violence against noncombatants and innocent third parties, generate emotionally charged responses. The use of metrics in this discourse is not very common. Decision making on the prevention of future incidents should nevertheless not be informed by hasty generalizations from one of a few individual cases of catastrophic terrorism. Just as with decisions on other types of crime, decisions on how to prevent and tackle terrorism should be grounded in evidence-based, social science data on prevalence, trends, and root causes.

In research on terrorism, quantitative, epidemiological approaches are underdeveloped, but some international databases from independent organizations or scholars are available (Kaufmann, 2005; Schmid, 2004). Databases on terrorist incidents suffer from many of the same methodological problems as databases on crime in general, plus some that are unique to this special type of politically motivated crime. Databases on terrorism have to adopt purpose-made working definitions since no universal definitions have yet been formally agreed upon by the world community. Most of the existing databases focus on incidents where violence is used against civilians, but some also cover acts of sabotage against property. Most databases rely heavily on open source material, supplementing media reports with some government data. Since terrorist attacks typically take place against the background of political conflicts, both official and media reports can often be distorted by (self) censorship and deliberate disinformation.

Despite these obvious shortcomings, databases on terrorist incidents have much to say about the phenomenon of terrorism, especially if used cautiously and in combination with each other. As is to be expected, various databases come up with very different numbers due to different working definitions, sources utilized, and resource limitations of the monitoring agency. Databases on terrorism should therefore not be used to arrive at estimates of the size of the phenomenon. Rather, they should serve, like the UNODC database on trafficking in persons presented in Chapter 7, to gain a broad understanding of global trends in various sociopolitical contexts.

An important consideration in the design of databases on terrorism is the distinction between domestic and international terrorism. In the case of national terrorism, the country where the attacks take place is also the country of origin of the attacks. In the case of international terrorism, countries of origin, countries of destination, and perhaps transit countries must be distinguished. According to most databases, incidents of international terrorism in which the victim is not a national, the perpetrator is not a national, or the theater of the attack is foreign form only a small part of global (that is, national and international) terrorism. The database that will mainly be used here has been developed by RAND. The disaggregation of the RAND data shows that globally, slightly more than 10% of the incidents as recorded by RAND are international in nature. Most terrorist attacks are domestic in nature, carried out by local insurgent groups representing ethnic minorities or by groups of extremists with left- or right-wing political agendas. The international component is largest in the Middle East (20%). For a global analysis of terrorism, indices of terrorism in general can be used.

Dutch terrorism expert Alex P. Schmid, currently director of terrorism studies at St. Andrew's University in Scotland, maintained at UNODC a global database of terrorism incidents in the period 1999 to 2002, building on his previous work at Leiden University. This database was arguably the most rigorous and comprehensive of its kind. Regrettably, work on the database was discontinued in 2003 at the request of some UN member states who felt there was no need for UN-based statistics on terrorism.

The most readibly available and up-to-date database is the RAND/Oklahoma City National Memorial Institute for the Prevention of Terrorism database (RAND, National Memorial Institute for the Prevention of Terrorism [MIPT]). Updates are available at the following Web site: http://www.mipt.org/terrorismdefined.html. Also available are the perceptions of business executives of the "costs of terrorism for business" conducted by the World Economic Forum (WEF, 2004). The latter index measures the perceived costs of terrorism, without differentiating between national and international terrorism.

The rates of actual terrorist incidents according to the RAND/MIPT database showed a moderately strong correlation with the perceived costs of terrorist attacks for business as measured by the WEF survey 2004 ($r = .46$, $p > 0.000$, $n = 72$).[3] This correlation, though not very strong, validates the usefulness of the WEF perception scores as a proxy indicator of terrorism prevalence in global analyses. We will present below results of some analyses of the correlates of terrorism using the WEF data.

The Incidence of Terrorism

As the RAND/MIPT database provides counts of the real number of incidents, according to open sources, the RAND index seems the best possible measure of the extent of terrorism per country. Figure 8.5 shows the number of national and international terrorist incidents per region, included in the RAND database covering the period 1998 up to mid-July 2005. Figure 8.6 shows the mean number of incidents per country by region.

Terrorism incidents are most prevalent in the Middle East. On average, countries in the region experienced over 400 incidents. Other regions where countries are most at risk of terrorist attacks are South Asia and Europe. Africa, heavily afflicted by so many other types of crime, seems to be least affected by terrorism. Other databases show similar regional patterns.

The RAND database provides information on both the number of incidents and the number of fatalities. Table 8.3 shows the 20 countries victimized most often by terrorist attacks from 2000 up to July 2005, according to the RAND/MIPT database, as well as a selection of countries with medium to high rates and those with the lowest rates.

The countries most afflicted by terrorism as measured by number of incidents constitute a geographically mixed group. In terms of incidents, Israel and Iraq are most heavily affected. In the course of 2005 alone, 2,336 incidents of terrorism were counted in Iraq. In terms of fatalities, Iraq and the United States (after the 9/11 attacks) show the highest numbers, followed by Israel and Colombia.

Trends in Terrorism

According to Schmid (2005), the databases point to two important global trends. Terrorist incidents, although more or less stable in volume, have in recent years more often been lethal in their consequences. Older historical figures on global terrorism for the years 1968–1993 collected by the Interdisciplinary Research Programme on Causes of Human Rights Violations at Leiden University in the Netherlands support the

❖ **Figure 8.5**   Absolute Number of Terrorist Incidents by Region, January 1, 1998, to July 17, 2005

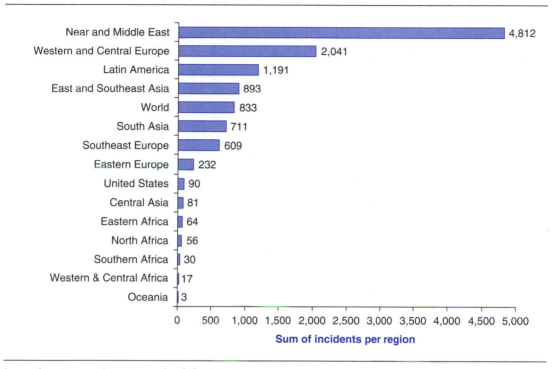

Source: http://www.mipt.org/terrorismdefined.html.

thesis of a rise in casualties. At the same time, more and more incidents have been committed by groups with a nonsecular agenda. Several sources have estimated the current component of nonsecular groups as 38% of the total (Pluchinsky, Armond, & Sprinzak, 2004). Percentages of nonsecular groups are even higher among those engaged in international terrorism. Since nonsecular terrorism more often results in lethal consequences, these trends seem to be interrelated. Terrorist attacks used to be and still are mainly domestic, motivated by local political agendas and not necessarily lethal. But more often they are becoming motivated by nonsecular agendas, more international and more lethal in their consequences.

Correlates of Terrorism

In our analyses of the correlates of terrorism at the macro level, we have used both the RAND/MIPT index and the WEF index of perceived terrorism prevalence. It is widely believed that poverty and lack of development are among the main root causes of terrorism (Gorman, 2001). Earlier statistical evidence was presented in Chapter 5, on the links between economic inequality and extreme poverty and common violent crime. Can similar links be found between poverty, inequality, and terrorism?

❖ **Figure 8.6**   Mean Number of Terrorist Incidents per Country by Region, January 1, 1998 to July 17, 2005

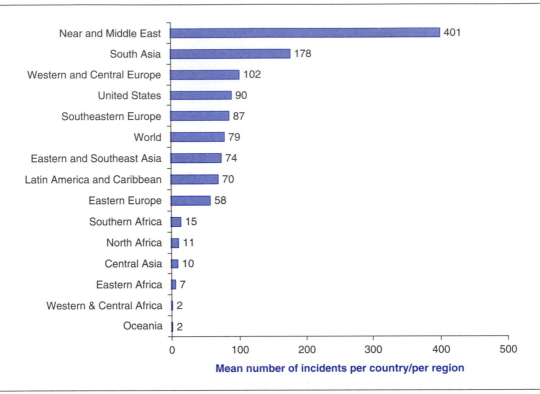

Mean number of incidents per country/per region

Source: http://www.mipt.org/terrorismdefined.html.

The regional distribution of terrorism with high prevalence in the comparatively affluent Middle East and low prevalence in Africa seems to go against this assumption. Correlation analysis between the human development index of UNDP and an index of terrorist incidents prevalence similar to the one of RAND/MIPT (Schmid, 2005) lends no support to the poverty-causes-terrorism hypothesis. Our own analyses confirmed that the WEF index of perceived terrorism threats was only weakly inversely related to the Human Development index ($r = .24$) and was not related to economic inequality. Links between the RAND index of terrorism incidents and development indices were weaker still. If links between underdevelopment and terrorism exist, they are certainly not as strong and straightforward as assumed. Similar conclusions were reached by Kaufmann analyzing WEF data on terrorism (Kaufmann, 2005). There is no empirical support for the notion that poverty or inequality is a root cause of terrorism.

Terrorism and Organized Crime

There is ample case-based evidence for the many links and crossovers of organized crime and terrorist groups across the world (Schmid, 2004). Many terrorist groups

❖ **Table 8.3**   World Rankings on Victimization by Terrorist Attacks, 2000 up to July 2005

Twenty Countries With Highest Scores on Terrorist Incidents								
	Country	Incidents	Injuries	Fatalities		Country	Incidents	Injuries	Fatalities
1	Israel	1,976	4,460	1,119	11	India	305	1,467	625
2	Iraq	1,928	8,859	5,222	12	Nepal	285	350	150
3	Colombia	981	1,757	1,035	13	Russia	217	2,716	916
4	Spain	680	1,031	241	14	Greece	215	6	1
5	United Kingdom	538	100	17	15	Philippines	192	1,559	464
					16	Indonesia	186	1,390	455
6	Thailand	458	670	210	17	Italy	123	73	3
7	Turkey	415	1,097	153	18	United States	90	14	2,990
8	France	410	70	14					
9	Afghanistan	395	877	490	19	Serbia & Montenegro	88	88	24
10	Pakistan	368	2,104	718					
					20	Bangladesh	74	1,545	147

Twenty Countries With Moderately High Scores on Terrorist Incidents								
	Country	Incidents	Injuries	Fatalities		Country	Incidents	Injuries	Fatalities
21	Venezuela	72	61	29	51	Uzbekistan	9	35	20
22	Lebanon	54	211	38	52	Argentina	8	0	0
24	Sri Lanka	47	612	195	55	Mexico	8	5	2
27	Algeria	38	158	90	57	Egypt	7	196	44
31	Uganda	25	294	411	60	Netherlands	7	0	2
32	South Africa	23	31	3	63	Morocco	6	0	35
34	Japan	19	1	0	64	Sweden	6	0	0
36	Germany	13	15	1	65	Switzerland	6	0	0
40	Brazil	11	2	1	77	Malaysia	3	2	5
47	China	9	12	5	86	New Zealand	2	0	0s

Twenty Countries With Lowest Scores on Terrorist Incidents								
	Country	Incidents	Injuries	Fatalities		Country	Incidents	Injuries	Fatalities
90	Australia	1	0	1	100	Mauritania	1	0	0
91	Belarus	1	0	0	101	Nicaragua	1	13	1
92	Burundi	1	0	1	102	Norway	1	0	0
93	Chad	1	0	1	103	Portugal	1	0	0
94	Costa Rica	1	0	1	104	Slovenia	1	0	
95	Cote d'Ivoire	1	0	1	105	Syrian Arab Republic	1	1	0
96	Djibouti	1	6	0					
97	Guinea	1	0	0	106	Taiwan, China	1	1	0
98	Hungary	1	0	0	107	Tunisia	1	20	15
99	Korea, Rep.	1	0	0	108	Turkmenistan	1	1	1
					109	Vietnam	1	132	0

Source: http://www.mipt.org/terrorismdefined.html; RAND, 2005.

engage in the trafficking of heroin, cocaine, or cannabis as well as in extortion practices and other criminal activities to raise funds for their terrorist activities. Examples include the PKK in Europe, the FARC in Colombia, The United Wa State Army in Myanmar, and the Tamil Tigers in Sri Lanka. From their side, many organized-crime groups provide services to terrorist groups for profit such as the sale of weapons. In several parts of the world, terrorist groups have over the years drifted into the execution of organized-crime activities for the sake of criminal gains, with the Colombian insurgents and paramilitaries being the most notorious examples. In Europe, parts of the IRA military wing are suspected of having "turned criminal" and of now controlling some of the most powerful criminal syndicates in the United Kingdom.

However, in spite of these connections, the regional distribution of terrorist attacks differs, fundamentally, as we have seen, from the regional distributions of both volume crime and organized crime. Terrorist incidents are most prevalent in the Middle East where rates of both volume crime and organized crime, as shown in previous chapters, are comparatively low. Prevalence is low in eastern Europe and sub-Saharan Africa, where rates of both volume crime and organized crime are comparatively high. Some of the countries most afflicted by terrorism score high on our index of organized crime, but far from all do.

At the aggregate level of countries, a weak relationship could be established between the prevalence of organized crime as measured by the Composite Organized-Crime Index (COCI) and the prevalence of terrorist incidents according to RAND/MIPT ($r = .22$, $p > 0.05$, $n = 82$). We found a somewhat stronger correlation between the perceived prevalence of terrorism (WEF rates) and our Composite Organized-Crime Index (COCI) ($r = .41$, $p < 0.05$, $n = 102$). Terrorist attacks, then, are somewhat more frequent in countries with high rates of organized crime (and, as we will discuss later, poorly performing police forces).

Although the two types of criminal behavior—one profit driven, the other mostly ideology driven—may in some respects share the same background, they should, in our view, analytically be clearly distinguished from each other. In Chapter 12, we will return to the issue of macro determinants of both organized crime and terrorism in a discussion on the impact of governance, including police performance and the rule of law, on both global threats.

Cybercrime: Trends in Information and Communication Technology (ICT) Crimes

Information and communication technology are increasingly being used for criminal purposes (Savona & Mignone, 2004). These new types of crime are generally known as cybercrimes. A distinction can be made between crimes in which ICT is the object of crime and crimes that use ICT as tools for the commission of other crimes such as fraud. The first category of crimes, which go against the confidentiality, integrity, and availability of ICT, is known as *computer crime*. The second category is often called *computer-related* or *computer-facilitated crime*.

Cybercrimes are the quintessential transnational crimes, committed in a borderless universe, requiring international cooperation in investigation and prosecution.

Cybercrime, more than any other crime, challenges the rules, traditions, and practices of national law enforcement and criminal justice systems. A first problem is that states have vastly different definitions of what constitutes a computer or cybercrime. A second and related problem is that traditional legal solutions cannot keep up with the rapid advances in ICT. Few countries have adequate national laws that address most of the issues (McConnell, 2000). Even those countries that do have adequate national laws are constantly faced by new legal issues. The best-known international legal instrument is the Council of Europe Convention on Cybercrime that provides future state parties with legal tools to assist in the investigation and prosecution of cybercrimes. The convention calls for criminalization of certain offenses related to computers, the adoption of new procedural powers, and the promotion of international cooperation (Angers, 2004).

Surveys among businesses on economic crimes often include questions on cybercrime (PricewaterhouseCoopers, 2005). Such crimes are among the most frequently reported types of economic crime. Available information on police-recorded cybercrimes reflects only a minute part of the offenses actually committed. Most cybercrime remains unrecorded or "hidden." The hidden nature of cybercrime is caused by several factors. First, sophisticated ICT, with its immense, compact storage capacity and speed, ensures that cybercrime is very difficult to detect. In contrast to most traditional areas of crime, unsuspecting victims are often informed post facto by law enforcement officials that they have been vicimized by a computer crime. Second, investigating officials often do not have sufficient expertise and skills to effectively deal with problems in the complex environment of ICT. An additional cause of the hidden nature of cybercrime is the reluctance of victims to report computer offenses once discovered. In the business sector, this reluctance is related to commercial concerns. Some victims may be unwilling to divulge information about their operations for fear of adverse publicity, public embarrassment, or loss of trust.

Computer-Facilitated Crime

The rapid increases in technology and expansion of the Internet have brought new opportunities for computer-facilitated economic crime. For example, the Internet Crime Complaint Center (formerly the Internet Fraud Complaint Center) in the United States, a joint initiative of the National White Collar Crime Center and the Federal Bureau of Investigation, has noted a marked increase in complaints received over the past 5 years (IC3 2005 Internet Crime Report, 2005). In 2005, the center received 231,000 complaints. This is an 11% increase over 2004 and a doubling since 2003. The largest category of complaints was auction frauds (67%), nondelivery (16%), and credit-card or debit-card fraud (7%). Fewer complaints were received about nonfraudulent incidents such as spam or child pornography. Of the 231,000 complaints, 190,000 were referred to enforcement agencies at the federal, state, or local level. The median loss per incident was $425. Total losses from reported cybercrimes in 2005 were $183 million. Twenty-nine percent of the perpetrators were located abroad, especially in Nigeria (8% of all complaints). The average loss in Nigerian incidents of Advance Fee Fraud was $5,000.

In Australia, annual victimization surveys are conducted among public and private organizations about cybercrimes and security (Auscert, 2006). Results of the 2006 survey pointed at a reduction in the numbers of electronic attacks on computer systems. One in five organizations experienced attacks that harmed the confidentiality, integrity, or availability of data or systems over the past 12 months. Total average annual losses from electronic attacks and computer-facilitated frauds increased, but fewer organizations were affected. Auscert expresses concern that investments in security are stagnant and may even be cut back.

Internet-Based Fraud and Credit-Card Fraud

As mentioned in Chapter 3, the latest round of the International Crime Victims Survey asked victims of consumer fraud about the specifics of their victimization. Nine percent of all victimizations by fraud had taken place while shopping on the Internet. This implies that on average, more than 1% of citizens of participating countries had experienced an Internet-facilitated fraud. In a separate question, fraud victims were also asked whether the case of consumer fraud had involved the use of a credit card. Nationally, 7% said that it had. In capital cities, 10% of fraud victims said it was credit-card fraud. This implies that victimization rates for credit-card fraud among the general public are, on average, 0.9% nationwide and 1.5% in capital cities. Over a quarter of all Internet-based fraud cases had involved credit cards (28%). A quarter of all credit-card frauds had taken place on the Internet. Table 8.4 shows details for national surveys and capital city surveys conducted in 2004 or 2005.

Victimization by Internet-based fraud is most common in the United States, Poland, Germany, Bulgaria, and the United Kingdom. In the United States, the annual victimization rate for Internet-based fraud is 3.3%. The victimization rate for credit-card fraud in the United States is 4%. In London, the financial capital of Europe, 7.5% of respondents were victimized by credit-card fraud in the course of 2004. These percentages are higher than those victimized by common property crimes such as pickpocketing or car theft. To some extent, the drop in volume crime, discussed in Chapter 6, is offset by the rise of new types of crime such as Internet-based and credit-card fraud.

Countries or cities with the highest rates of victimization by Internet-based frauds are a mixed group in terms of Internet use. It comprises both countries where the Internet is most widely used and countries that are technologically less advanced. Locations with low victimization rates also appear to be heterogeneous in terms of Internet use. For example, use of the Internet is very common in Iceland and Finland, countries where Internet-based fraud is rare. On the face of it, there is no strong relationship between use of the Internet by national populations and prevalence of Internet-based fraud. This lack of an obvious relationship between vulnerability and victimization flies in the face of criminal opportunity theory and merits further analysis. It is possible that levels of victimization by high-tech fraud are determined not just by the levels of use of such devices but more by levels of Internet and credit-card security.

❖ Table 8.4   One-Year Prevalence Rates for Victimization by Fraud While Buying Something on the Internet and Fraud Involving a Credit Card in Countries and Capital Cities

	Fraud With Shopping on the Internet	Credit-Card Fraud		Fraud With Shopping on the Internet	Credit-Card Fraud
United States	3.3	4.0	Lima (Peru)	10.7	
Poland	3.0		Berlin (Germany)	3.8	
Germany	2.7		New York (United States)	3.7	4.3
Bulgaria	2.6		London (England)	3.2	7.5
United Kingdom	2.4	1.8	Paris (France)	2.7	2.4
England & Wales	2.2	1.7	Copenhagen (Denmark)	1.5	0.1
Norway	1.5		Edinburgh (Scotland)	1.0	1.9
Denmark	1.4	0.3	Madrid (Spain)	1.0	1.3
New Zealand	1.3		Vienna (Austria)	0.9	0.4
Sweden	1.2	0.3	Hong Kong (SAR China)	0.9	
Northern Ireland	1.2	1.3	Amsterdam (Netherlands)	0.9	0.3
Austria	1.1	0.4	Dublin (Ireland)	0.7	1.6
Scotland	1.0	1.4	Stockholm (Sweden)	.7	0.2
Spain	0.7	0.9	Brussels (Belgium)	0.6	1.1
Ireland	0.7	1.3	Tallinn (Estonia)	0.6	
Canada	0.7		Belfast (Northern Ireland)	0.5	1.4
Estonia	0.6		Athens (Greece)	0.4	1.4
Portugal	0.5	0.4	Oslo (Norway)	0.4	
Luxembourg	0.5	0.3	Reykjavik (Iceland)	0.3	
Iceland	0.4		Greater Johannesburg (RSA)	0.3	
France	0.4	0.3	Lisbon (Portugal)	0.2	0.0
Belgium	0.4	0.4	Helsinki (Finland)	0.0	0.1
Netherlands	0.3	0.4	Budapest (Hungary)	0.0	0.1
Mexico	0.2	0.6	Rome (Italy)	0.0	
Greece	0.1	1.4			
Finland	0.1	0.0			
Italy	0.0	0.1			
Average	1.1	0.9	Average	1.5	1.5

Sources: ICVS, 2004–2005, and EUICS, 2005.

No Asian Exception

In recent years, a growing sensitivity to the problems of cybercrime has been shown by several technologically advanced countries/territories of Southeast Asia such as Japan, Taiwan, the Republic of Korea, and China. According to reliable forecasts, the region will soon become a dominant user of the Internet. It is not possible to generalize about the region as a whole since each country has formulated its own response to the information economy, depending on individual circumstances. Some countries have attempted to tightly control the introduction of new technology, while others have encouraged its penetration of their markets and societies.

Despite these differences, some general trends can be identified. The recorded number of incidents as well as criminal responses shows an upward trend with variations across types of cybercrime. Data from Hong Kong and the Republic of Korea illustrate these trends (Hong Kong Computer Emergency Response Team Coordination Centre (HKCERT). The total number of arrests related to cybercrimes in the Republic of Korea increased from 1,715 in 2000 to 41,900 in 2002. Analyzing the data for 2002, of all cybercrimes, 46% were for Internet fraud followed by hacking and the introduction of computer viruses. About 69% of all cybercrimes were committed by young people in their teens and twenties. These crimes include, for example, blackmail and cyberstalking.

Computers, Organized Crime, and Terrorism

Korean data may show that the majority of offenders arrested are in their teens, but new technology has also resulted in new and increased opportunities for organized-crime activity; for example, the fraudulent use of credit and debit cards by sophisticated organized-crime groups making use of advanced counterfeiting technologies has now become a truly globalized business. By making use of off-the-shelf technologies, data from genuine credit cards can be compromised in one country in the morning, counterfeit cards produced in the afternoon in another country, then used elsewhere again. The countries may not even be on the same continent. One of the latest trends in the Nigerian letter scams is that victims are invited to open secured bank accounts on (faked) Web sites of well-known British or Dutch banks. After the promised sums have actually been transferred to the newly opened, virtual accounts, payment of advance fees is requested for further transactions. Advance-fee scams are typically executed through computers in three or more different countries to frustrate investigations.

The Council of Europe's 2004 situation report on organized crime focuses in particular on the role played by criminal groups in relation to cybercrime. The report concludes that member states of the Council of Europe have found important links between organized-crime groups and cybercrimes, and it is feared that such links will continue to expand in the future, particularly in the area of computer fraud, computer-related forgery, child pornography, and copyright infringements. The report cites an analysis of larger cases of child pornography on the Internet conducted by the Swiss Federal Police Authorities, "according to which producers and distributors of child pornography are, as a rule, not themselves pedophiles but rather are interested in lucrative business opportunities. According to the study, this is true primarily for criminal organizations in Eastern Europe" (Council of Europe, 2004).

The Internet provides an increasing range of opportunities for criminal groups, most notably (but certainly not confined to) the area of fraud. The impact of the growing problem of identity fraud on business in many countries is now substantial. Identity fraud involves the collection of data on individuals and the counterfeiting of their identities, among other things, for credit purposes, and given the complexities involved, it requires a relatively high degree of organization (Levi & Maguire, 2004).

To an increasing extent, terrorist groups use the Internet to identify and recruit potential members, to collect and transfer funds, and to organize terrorist attacks, including the provision of training. Perhaps of most concern, terrorist groups successfully use the Internet to incite the commission of suicide attacks by targeting susceptible young people through propaganda Web sites and technical advice.

The use of the Internet is not linked to a physical locale. People intent on abusing the Internet for criminal purposes can do so virtually anywhere in the world. Rapid technological advances demand that governments and law enforcement officials address this issue as a matter of priority. More debate is required as to the most effective mechanisms to counter the use of cyberspace by transnational criminal and terrorist groups, including by building more effective forms of international cooperation and greater capacity to counter the problem in developing countries.

International information available suggests that cybercrimes against organizations may have reached a ceiling in some countries because of improved protection. Private Internet users seem increasingly at risk of being victimized by fraudulent crime in the course of ordinary transactions such as auctions or purchasing of goods as well as by Nigerian-type letter scams. There are signs of greater sophistication in modes of cybercrime including involvement of organized crime and terrorist groups.

SUMMARY POINTS/IN CONCLUSION

- On the world map of corruption, developing and middle-income countries in the South, including in Asia, show the highest scores. Within Europe, problems of corruption are most pronounced in the countries of the former Soviet Union. The mapping of corruption is very similar to the mapping of organized crime.

- Victimization by terrorist attacks is uniquely distributed across regions and countries. Numbers of attacks since 2000 have been highest in the Middle East (Israel, Iraq), Colombia, and some European countries (Spain, United Kingdom, France). In numbers of fatalities the United States stands at the second highest place, after Iraq.

- Cybercrime is an emerging type of crime about which only fragmented data are available. On the face of it, it is most common in technologically more advanced countries such as the United States and the United Kingdom. High-tech frauds on the Internet and/or with the use of

credit cards have in many countries reached the level of common crimes such as pickpocketing or car theft.

- At the end of Part II, Chapter 6, some broad generalizations were made on the global map of common crime. It was concluded that, by and large, common crime is still comparatively rare in most parts of Asia, has finally been brought under control in the developed world, but is reaching crisis levels in many of the urban areas in the developing countries of sub-Saharan Africa and Latin America. This global distribution is particularly disconcerting as citizens of the poorest countries are least able to cope with medical and economic consequences of violent, predatory crime. A veritable security gap between the North and the South has come into existence.

- In this broad-brush global picture of crime, some important adjustments must now be made, taking into account the data on emerging global crimes presented in Part III. The so-called Asian exception does not hold for the crime of corruption, which is rampant in many otherwise low-crime countries such as Indonesia and India. Apparently, the social forces that keep common crime in check in both poor and rich Asian countries do not operate as effectively with regard to corruption. It remains also to be seen if cybercrime will be controlled in Asia any better than elsewhere in the world. Domestic systems of social control may not prevail in cyberspace. Perhaps Internet-based types of crime will increasingly show regional distributions of their own, which will be largely technology driven, rather than culture driven. There may be more of these crimes where technical opportunities for committing them are plentiful, regardless of cultural constraints.

• A second amendment to our conclusions on the epidemiology of crime relates to North Africa and the Middle East. This is another region with comparatively low rates of common crimes including homicides—although more information on this would be useful for arriving at better-grounded conclusions. But evidently, rates of corruption and, to a lesser extent, organized crime are above the world average. This is also one of the regions most severely plagued by international and domestic terrorist attacks. Criminologically speaking, the Arab world is a hotbed of contradictions. More statistical data on crime in both North and sub-Saharan Africa should be made available through focused efforts.

• If in Europe common crimes have started to decline steeply, this is far from true in the domain of organized crime and corruption. Especially in eastern Europe and the Caucasus, both of these forms of uncommon crimes are rampant. The organized-crime–corruption nexus seems to have established strong roots across all countries of the former Soviet Union. The corruption engrained in the communist state systems has successfully adapted itself to market economies. Since these forms of crime impact deeply on the way societies are governed and run their economies, they are likely to compound the problems of further political and economic integration of Europe.

• Entry into the European Union and the required upgrading of justice systems seems to have helped several new members such as Poland and the Baltic countries to get a better grip on local organized crime. In fact, several of the 2004 entrants now show rankings lower than those of some of the old 15 member states such as Italy. With a view to further eastbound expansion of the Union, justice and security sector reform will need more attention. The central and eastern European countries that entered the European Union in 2004 are less affected by organized crime and corruption than the new entrants Bulgaria and Romania and aspiring candidates further to the east. The Union now possesses several candidate and neighboring countries where powerful local Mafias control large sectors of economic and political life.

• In one crucial respect, the global map of crime remains largely unchanged if emerging global crimes are added to the equation. Countries in Africa and Latin America are most severely affected not only by common but also by corruption and organized crime. Our composite index for organized crime and grand corruption reveals high scores for the Caribbean and South America as well as for all subregions of sub-Saharan Africa.

• The North–South security divide, postulated on the basis of metrics on common crimes, emerges even more clearly if information on organized crime and corruption is added to the equation. This of course, first of all, adds to the already comparatively heavy crime burden of the inhabitants of countries in the South themselves. But it would be naïve to think that the crime problems of the South will not increasingly, and in many yet unknown ways, spill over to the North. Besides international terrorism, there will be more and more border-crossing criminal attacks, similar to the fraudulent "business proposals" from Nigerian businessmen that continue to flood the Internet.

• In today's interdependent world, the wide and deepening security gap between the North and the South matters to the governments of all countries (Costa, 2002). It should also be acknowledged that activities of the North are at the root of some of the crime problems of the South. Drug markets in the developed world are at the root of problems of organized crime in countries such as Colombia, Mexico, and Afghanistan. In spite of the OECD Convention against bribery in foreign countries, international companies based in northern Europe and Asia continue unabated with their corrupting practices, thereby directly undermining good governance in the South. The blooming sex industries in the North generate demand for sexual services in slave-like circumstances from young women from the South and create opportunities for criminal traffickers in the source countries. Lack of due diligence in the banking systems of the North and ineffective international judicial cooperation provide safe havens for the criminal assets of kleptocrats in the South looting their own countries.

- In view of global interdependencies and spillover effects, regional crime problems can no longer be left to the countries most directly affected by them and to regional or international organizations alone. Governments of all major countries have to become part of the solution of these problems worldwide. This is not just a matter of humanitarian solidarity but of self-interest as well.

Notes

1. In the questionnaire used in 2000 in central and eastern Europe, respondents were also asked whether in their opinion it was likely that a given official of specific state institutions would ask for a bribe or would expect to be bribed. The large majority confirmed that in their experience, all types of officials mentioned would routinely accept bribes. Of the various categories, nurses and doctors, police officers, and customs officers were mentioned most often as ready receivers of bribes (Alvazzi del Frate & Van Kesteren, 2004).

2. Using several independent data sets, an international research team comprising Anand Swamy, Stephen Knack, Young Lee, and Omar Azfar investigated the relationship between gender and corruption across the world (Swamy et al., 2000). The findings consistently showed significant inverse relationships between female participation and the level of corruption in a country. Where women have a stronger position in the political and economic spheres, the prevalence of corruption tends to be lower. Subsequent analyses of the same data have not, however, confirmed these results (for an overview, see Sung, 2005). However, Swamy et al. rightly conclude that their evidence is fully consistent with prevailing criminological knowledge about the persistence of gender differences in delinquency and crime involvement (Heidensohn, 2002; Junger-Jas, Ribead, & Cruyff, 2004). It would indeed be surprising if corruption offenses were the exception to the gendered nature of most types of offending. More research into this issue seems warranted for both theoretical and policy reasons. As will be documented in Chapter 10, law enforcement in the majority of countries is an almost exclusively male profession. If the gender–corruption link exists, this would provide a strong additional impetus to seek a better gender balance in police forces. A positive side effect of better gender balances in police forces could be a reduction of corruption in their ranks.

3. The RAND database shows, as can be seen in Figure 8.5, a much skewed distribution of terrorist incidents with a small number of countries experiencing the bulk of the incidents. If scores are rank ordered on both indicators, the correlation is similar ($r = .38$).

PART IV

International Trends in Criminal Justice

Law Enforcement, Crime Prevention, and Victim Assistance

Trends in Criminal Justice Resources

The United Nations Surveys on Crime Trends and the Operations of Criminal Justice Systems seek to collect data on the incidence of (police-recorded) crime and the operations of criminal justice systems across the world. In the previous chapters, we have critiqued the use of police-recorded crime statistics as measures of the incidence or trends of crime. We will now turn our attention to the second and potentially more useful objective of the surveys: to collect data on the workload of criminal justice systems and the processing of cases through the system (Newman, 1999).

In the UN Crime Surveys, data are collected on all major stages of criminal justice from crime recording and investigation by the police to prosecution, sentencing, and execution of sentences. Besides these data, which allow an analysis of the attrition of cases in their flow through the main components of the system, the questionnaire contains a section on human and financial resources available for the four main components of the criminal justice system: police, prosecutors, courts, and prisons. Before looking at comparative performances of national criminal justice systems, we will examine the resources available across countries.

Allocation of Resources to Law Enforcement and Criminal Justice

Expenditures on policing, courts, and prisons are, not surprisingly, higher in more-affluent countries. The most complete expenditure data available are those on the police. The data on police expenditures in recent years show that more-affluent countries spend much more on policing per capita than do developing countries (Shaw, Van Dijk, & Rhomberg, 2003). This is an obvious result since more-affluent countries can afford to spend more on all state functions. A more informative way of comparing such expenditures is to look at the percentage of the gross domestic product (GDP) spent on it. On average, countries across the globe spend just under 1% of the GDP on policing, with some countries spending significantly more than that. The Middle East countries of Bahrain and Kuwait are on top, with 4% and 3%, respectively. According to the UN data, most developed countries spend less than 1% of the GDP on policing (United States, 0.6%; France, 0.7%; and Italy, 0.8%).

Among the larger countries worldwide, South Africa stands out with almost 2% of the GDP spent on policing. For a developing country, this level of expenditures is strikingly high. Less than 0.5 % of the GDP is spent on policing by several developing countries such as Rwanda, Venezuela, Guatemala, Madagascar, Honduras, Costa Rica, and Zambia (Shaw, Van Dijk, & Rhomberg, 2003). In South Africa, the percentage of the national budget allocated to criminal justice amounted to 10.3% in 2002 (Schonteich, 2003). The South African budget for criminal justice equals that for public health. These statistics indicate how serious the postapartheid South African government is in addressing the security problems of the country.

An important aspect of the allocation of financial resources to criminal justice is the relative distribution to police, prosecution services, courts, and prisons. As shown in Figure 9.1, the average among the countries reporting to the UN show just under two thirds of all expenditure was on the police (64%). The second largest budgets were for prison (on average, 16%), and the third largest budgets were for courts (14%). The prosection services receive just 6% of total criminal justice resources (data from 1998–2002).

Examination of the allocation of resources to policing, prisons, courts, or prosecutors within country budgets for the justice and security sector reveals significant differences. Since the operation of criminal justice systems is roughly similar across countries, significant differences in how the budgets are spent may point to divergent policy priorities in criminal justice. Developing countries tend to spend a larger chunk of their criminal justice budget on policing (see Figure 9.2). The emphasis on policing is most pronounced in southern Africa (see Figure 9.3), where expenditure patterns are strongly skewed toward the police (73% of the total criminal justice budget compared to 64% globally). Only 5% of the budget in southern Africa is spent on the courts and relatively little is spent on prosecution (3%). The part of available budgets spent on prosecution and courts is 60% below the world average. The defense of civil liberties through judicial procedure seems a luxury that developing countries struggling with rampant problems of violent crime can ill afford. Priority is given to spending on law enforcement.

❖ Figure 9.1   World Average Expenditures on Security and Justice

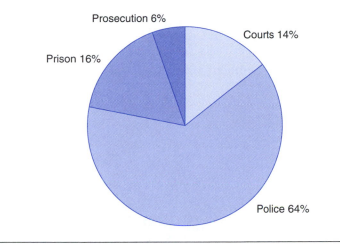

Source: www.unodc.org; 8th UN Crime Survey.

❖ Figure 9.2   Developing Countries' Expenditures on Security and Justice

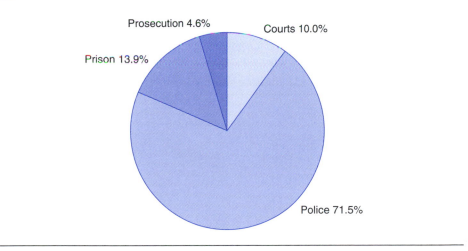

Source: www.unodc.org; 8th UN Crime Survey.

In North America and Europe, more is proportionally spent on courts. There are also significant differences between these two regions. In North America, the overall expenditure breakdown between the police, courts, prosecution services, and prisons is the most divided: 54% is spent on the police, 23% on prosecution and courts, and 23% on prisons (see Figure 9.4).

❖ **Figure 9.3**   Southern African Countries' Expenditures on Justice and Security

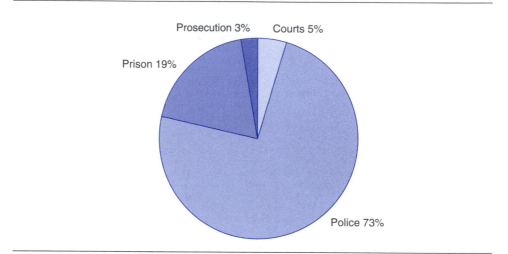

Source: www.unodc.org; 8th UN Crime Survey.

❖ **Figure 9.4**   Expenditures on Justice and Security in the United States

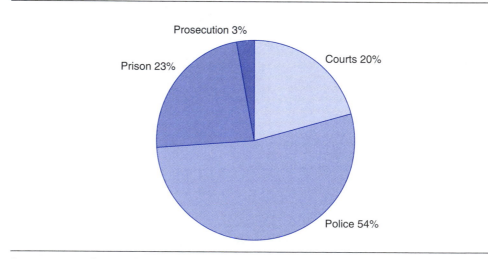

Source: www.unodc.org; 8th UN Crime Survey.

❖ **Figure 9.5** Expenditures on Justice and Security in Western Europe

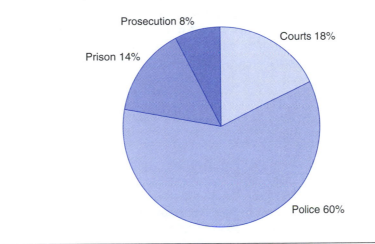

Source: www.unodc.org; 8th UN Crime Survey.

The 23% budget allocation to prisons in the United States goes far beyond the global mean of 16%. In the developing world, only 14% of the budgets is spent on prisons. Western European countries also spend much less on prisons than the United States (14% instead of 23% of their total justice and security budget), but, probably due to different procedural arrangements, they spend more on prosecution services (see Figure 9.5). Compared to the United States, European countries allocate somewhat larger proportions of the budgets to their police forces (60%, European countries, compared to 54%, United States).

From the limited data available, it appears that developing countries spend comparatively more on policing and less on the courts and prosecution services. The proportion of resources allocated to prisons in developing countries is also slightly below the global mean. Significant differences in allocation priorities have also emerged between the United States and Western Europe. Comparatively large chunks of the justice and security budget in the United States are spent on prisons, and comparatively less is spent on policing and prosecution.

Human Resources for Police and Private Security

Data on financial resources of the justice and security sector are available on few countries. Fortunately, more countries have provided data on numbers of police personnel and judges employed. Since criminal justice budgets are mainly spent on remunerations of personnel, the number of personnel per 100,000 inhabitants can be used as a proxy indicator of available resources. As an additional advantage, no complicated adjustments for currency fluctuations have to be made in comparisons of head counts.

International comparisons of the number of police are fraught with methodological problems since definitions of police or security functions differ across countries

(Mawby, 1999; Newman & Howard, 1999). Trend data from individual countries provided to the UN sometimes show sudden shifts in rates, suggesting the adoption of new, larger, or narrower definitions of "policing." Data on the number of police officers per 100,000 inhabitants, as shown in Figure 9.6, provide only a rough estimation of the regional variation in police personnel. Regional rates are often based on a limited and not necessarily representative selection of countries.

❖ **Figure 9.6**   Number of Police Officers per 100,000 Inhabitants per Region, 1999–2002

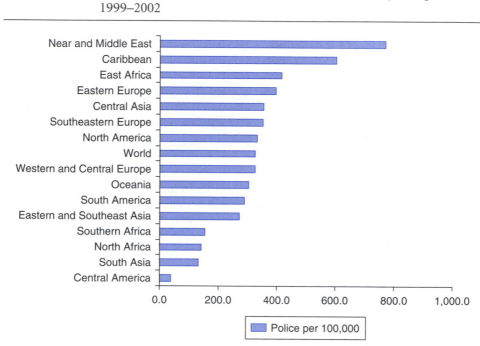

Source: www.unodc.org; 8th UN Crime Survey.

On average, there are just over 300 police officers per 100,000 inhabitants across the globe. Africa, although spending a relatively large part of its criminal justice budgets on policing, still has the lowest numbers of police officers per resident. Even high-crime, middle-income countries such as Nigeria and South Africa employ less than 250 officers per 100,000 population. The comparatively high rate of Mauritius is exceptional and drives up the rate of the sub-region of East Africa. Police per capita rates are also comparatively low in some countries in South and Central America, although the picture is far from complete because few countries of the Latin American region have provided data on their number of police officers in the UN survey.

Rates in Asia show great variation with India and Japan having only 110 and 130 officers per 100,000 residents, respectively, and Hong Kong/China, Singapore, Malaysia, and Thailand reporting rates of 300 or more. The average rate is also above

400 per 100,000 population in the former Soviet countries in central Asia. Within Asia, high rates of police officers seem related to more authoritarian regimes.

European and North American jurisdictions as well as Australia report rates of police officers of 300 or more per 100,000, with some of the Caribbean countries reporting 400 or more police per 100,000 residents. The number of police officers per 100,000 population was slightly lower in the United States (321) than in the European Union (370). As discussed above, a larger part of the total budget for criminal justice is spent on policing in western Europe than in the United States. Within Europe, the police presence is significantly higher in eastern and central Europe (e.g., Russia, Ukraine, Albania, Czech Republic, Latvia, and Croatia) than in western Europe. The high police density in transitional countries seems to form part of the heritage of the Soviet era. Within western Europe, rates are higher in the South (e.g., Italy, 560; Portugal, 450) than in the North (Sweden, 120, the Netherlands, 220). The higher rates in the South must be seen against the background of historical reliance on national police forces, answerable to different ministers, to maintain different aspects of public order.

Table 9.1 shows world rankings of countries according to the number of police officers per 100,000 population.

❖ **Table 9.1** World Rankings According to Number of Police per 100,000 Population Around 2000

Fifteen Countries With High Scores

1	Kuwait	1,116.1	6	Italy	559.0	11	Hong Kong	496.2
2	Mauritius	755.4	7	Argentina	558.6	12	Mexico	491.8
3	Bahamas, The	693.8	8	Uruguay	540.7	13	Macedonia, FYR	483.2
4	Cyprus	618.2	9	Panama	518.9	14	Ukraine	470.2
5	Dominica	605.0	10	Barbados	516.5	15	Kazakhstan	464.3

Fifteen Countries With Moderately High Scores

16	Czech Republic	458.5	32	United States	326.4	45	United Kingdom	257.6
18	Portugal	449.8	33	Singapore	324.2	51	South Africa	224
19	Croatia	446.2	37	Australia	304.2	56	Netherlands	212
21	Israel	424.8	38	Germany	303.2	57	France	211
27	Belgium	357.5	44	Poland	259	60	Denmark	192.1

Fifteen Countries With Low Scores

61	Korea, Rep.	191.9	66	Finland	160.1	71	Lesotho	101.9
62	Canada	186.3	67	Morocco	141.6	72	Tanzania	80.3
63	Japan	182.2	68	Philippines	141.3	73	Maldives	71.4
64	Sweden	181.0	69	Myanmar	141.0	74	Costa Rica	39.0
65	Zimbabwe	162.3	70	Zambia	129.5	75	Venezuela, RB	15.8

Source: **www.unodc.org**; 8thUN Crime Survey.

UN data sets allow trend analyses since 1973 for only a selection of countries. The size of police forces has increased worldwide, with the greatest increases shown by some developed countries (Newman & Howard, 1999; Reiner, 1995). International variation is significant, though. In western Europe and North America, the number of police officers went down slightly in the early 1990s and increased somewhat thereafter. Since 1990, the number of police officers has not gone up significantly in any developing country reporting to the UN surveys. Some countries such as South Africa and Chile show decreases since 1990. Such decreases in the face of increasing crime rates must probably be understood in the context of police reforms after political transitions, as discussed in Chapter 6, but may also reflect funding problems.

A weak positive relationship was found between national affluence as measured by the human development index and levels of policing. Higher state budgets seem to allow governments to invest more in the size of their police forces. The latter finding suggests that many developing countries may indeed have been unable for reasons of fiscal restraint to allocate the extra resources needed for law enforcement to cope with increases in crime. Resources for law enforcement in developing countries have generally failed to match increases in crime over the past 15 years.

Police Workloads

Since rates of crime have gone up in many developing countries over the past few decades, the finding that rates of police officers per 100,000 have not increased implies heavier workloads for the police. The overall number of crimes recorded by the police is greatly influenced by recording practices of the police forces themselves, as discussed in Chapter 2. If police forces feel overburdened by crime reports, they become more selective in recording. Numbers of total recorded crimes cannot therefore be reliably used to measure the workload of the police. This problem is, as previously discussed, less severe with the recording of homicides. Police forces have little discretion in the recording of this most serious type of crime. Since recorded homicides reflect both the levels of serious violent crime and the extent of organized crime, the number of homicides recorded by the police per 1,000 police officers provides a rough comparative indicator of the workload of the police. Figure 9.7 shows the number of homicides per 1,000 police for world regions, based on countries for which data are available.

In Figure 9.7, it can be seen that police forces in countries where rates of serious crime are high have significantly higher workloads (reported homicides per 1,000 officers) than low-crime countries. The most unfavorable ratios are found in South Africa. This finding points to the existence of a serious "justice and security deficit" in several developing countries, including South Africa, which invests a comparatively large part of its total state budget on law enforcement. Assessments of the crime and criminal justice situation in Central America have come to the same conclusion (UNODC, 2007b). It seems also worth noting that case loads are higher for police forces in North America than for those in western and central Europe.

❖ Figure 9.7   Number of Homicides Recorded per 1,000 Police Officers, per World Region

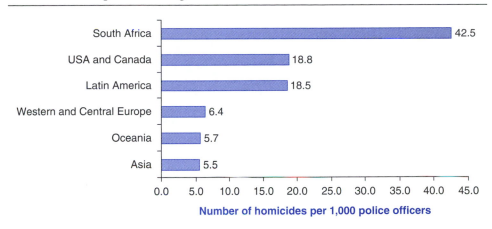

Number of homicides per 1,000 police officers

Source: www.unodc.org; 8th UN Crime Survey, 2002, or latest available year.

The Private Security Industry

Policing by public police forces is supplemented everywhere by surveillance and detective work carried out by private security companies. As discussed in Chapter 6, these forms of privately funded policing have been booming in many parts of the world in response to growing losses from crime. International data on private security are limited. Neither the UN Crime Survey nor Interpol has ever collected statistical information on resources for private policing. Collecting comparable statistics is complicated by the lack of international definitions of private security and the low quality of existing employment registrations. The Dutch Ministry of Justice has collected some international information that was recently updated by others (De Waard, 1999; Morre, 2004; Van Steden & Sarre, 2007). The available international information on numbers employed in private security is presented in Figure 9.8 for world regions (no data on Asia available). Rates of security personnel per 100,000 residents are combined with data on police officers per 100,000 residents to illustrate the relative sizes of private and public policing as well as the size of the total security force.

The data in Figure 9.8 show that the provision of security through surveillance is far from monopolized by the state. Worldwide, more people are employed as a private security officer (348 per 100,000) than as a police officer (318 per 100,000). Security markets are in most parts of the world, including North America, central Europe, South America, Oceania, and Africa, quantitatively dominated by private providers. Sizes of the total security market seem unrelated to the level of common criminality, which is, as previously discussed, highest in Africa and Latin America and fairly low in eastern Europe.

❖ **Figure 9.8**   Relative Number of Employees Within Private Security Services and Police Forces, per World Region or Country, 2003–2005

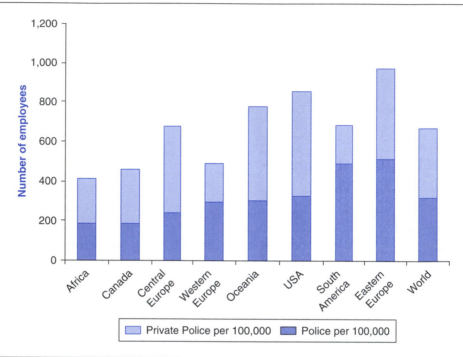

Sources: De Waard, 1999; Morre, 2004; Van Steden & Sarre, 2007; www.unodc.org; 8th UN Crime Survey.

Absolute and relative sizes of the private security industries show considerable variation across regions and countries. The proportion of private security employees is largest in Oceania, the United States, Canada, and central Europe, all comparatively affluent regions. The distribution suggests that businesses are readier to invest in security in more-affluent parts of the world. However, wealth is not the only determining factor because much lower rates are found in western Europe, especially in southern Europe. The proportion of the private security is relatively small in South America.

The highest rate of private police per 100,000 population was observed in Bulgaria (1,640), Hungary (784), Russia (578), Poland (523), South Africa (558), the United States (533), and Ireland (511). The ratio between police and private security is heavily skewed toward the police in Italy, Austria, Belgium, and the Scandinavian countries. Figure 9.9 shows details for western and central Europe (for more country details, see tables for Chapter 9 in Appendix B).

The number of private security personnel per 100,000 residents is not related to the number of police officers at the regional or country level ($r = .11$ and $.04$, respectively). Numbers of police officers seem to be dependent on other, economical and political factors than numbers of private security officers. In some countries, though,

❖ **Figure 9.9**   Relative Number of Employees Within Private Security Services and Police Forces in Europe, per Country, 2003–2005

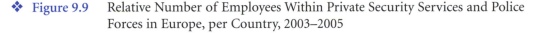

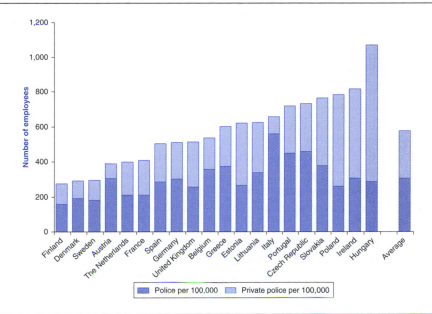

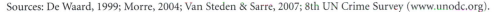

Sources: De Waard, 1999; Morre, 2004; Van Steden & Sarre, 2007; 8th UN Crime Survey (www.unodc.org).

private security firms seem to make up for a lack of public policing, for example, in Bulgaria (CSD, 2004).

Trends in Private Policing

As discussed in Chapter 6, the private security industry has been booming since the mid-1980s across the world and continues to grow steadily. The rapid growth of private security can be seen as a rational response of the business community and well-to-do households to their increased financial losses from criminal activity. The growth of private policing is part and parcel of "responsive securitization." To a large extent, the expanded supply of such services just matches increased demand from commercial and private parties seeking to shield their interests from growing crime. On the other hand, the strength of private security services is also determined by government policy, with some governments traditionally being reluctant to allow private policing, seen as an infringement on the state's "monopoly of violence." In some regions such as Central Asia, the aversion to private policing stemmed from the undemocratic impulses of oppressive, authoritarian regimes. On the other hand, private security can lead to abuses of power that compromise fundamental rights and freedoms of citizens. In most democratic countries, private security industries are therefore tightly regulated and monitored by the state.

In the Anglo-Saxon, common-law countries, private policing has traditionally been well established alongside public police forces. Civil law countries of the European continent tend traditionally to rely more exclusively on public police forces. In southern Europe, governments have until recently been suspicious that private security might undermine the sovereignty of the state. In these countries, policing tends to remain largely in the hands of the central government. Italy represents the clearest example of this tradition. In Spain and Portugal, expansion of the private security industry is a relatively new phenomenon that commenced only after democratic institutions were reestablished in the 1970s.

Significant growth in the number of private security personnel has been observed in central and eastern Europe as a consequence of increasing concern about personal and property safety after the breakup of the Soviet Union as well as a rollback of state monopolies in all domains. In several countries in this region, such as Russia, Hungary, and Poland, private security firms now employ many more people than the police forces. In several of these countries, including Russia, regulatory structures are still underdeveloped. According to a report from the Center for the Study of Democracy in Sofia, Bulgaria (CSD, 2004), "moonlighting" among police officers is rampant: Private security firms employ many officials from police or security services. Some private security companies in the western Balkans operate in the gray zones between organized-crime and state security agencies. In recent years, private security firms have also mushroomed in China, where by 1999, 250,000 such companies had been set up (Guo, 1999).

In Nigeria, private security is the second largest income earner after the oil industry. Private security is a major industry in Kenya also (Abrahamsen & Williams, 2005). In the context of South Africa, the growth of private security has been interpreted as a mixed blessing (Shaw, 2002). Although it has contributed to greater security for certain groups and created much needed low-skills jobs for others, its ascendancy could threaten citizens' rights and entrench a divide between those able to hire personal protection and those who cannot. Even more problematic is the recourse of poorer parts of the population to vigilantism or mob justice and the human rights abuses it inevitably entails.

There has been a significant growth of private security services in Latin America as well. In Brazil, one study shows that the number of people employed in private security firms increased much faster than those employed as police officers (De Mesquita Neto, 2004). In Brazil as in eastern Europe and Russia, private security agencies frequently employ off-duty police officers—a practice that is illegal but widely tolerated by police and government authorities. Public resources have been used by police officers for private security. Working in private security, police officers have become more exposed to violence and have become both victims and authors of homicides. In the state of São Paulo, Brazil, according to official statistics, the majority of police officers killed are killed off duty rather than on duty. The police and the government record the majority of homicides committed by police officers as justifiable homicides ("resistance followed by death"). However, there are reports, criminal inquiries, and judicial processes indicating the participation of police officers in vigilante groups and extrajudicial executions (De Mesquita Neto, 2004).

Market research forecasts significant further growth in the security industry almost universally, especially in its high-tech forms. This expansion should go hand in hand with improved regulatory structures to assure accountability and respect for civil liberties. Private security increasingly makes up a dominant part of the market in security but remains much under-researched, compared to policing. It is time for empirical criminology, and for statistical offices as well, to bring private security into focus.

More Police, Less Crime?

Different hypotheses can be formulated about the relationship between levels of policing and levels of crime. Higher crime rates tend to drive up levels of policing, which may subsequently result in lower rates of crime. According to this hypothesis, sustained high levels of policing would be inversely related to levels of crime. A case in point is Singapore, a country with low crime rates and high numbers of police officers (and of private security officials as well). Hungary might be another example of a country high on policing and low on crime. High levels of public policing may perhaps also contribute to low levels of crime in the Arab world, although statistical information on both factors is regrettably scarce.

In the 8th UN Survey of 2000, covering 80 or more countries, no clear relationship between levels of recorded crime and levels of public police resources can be detected. Furthermore, no relationship was found between levels of victimization (ICVS) and rates of police personnel either. In developed countries, a positive relationship was found between the level of serious crime and numbers of police officers per 100,000 population (Mayhew, 2003b). This positive relationship suggests that more police are put to work if crime is more of a problem without having much measurable, overall impact on crime. One explanation for this finding is that more police increases the official capacity to record crime as well as the willingness of victims to report crime.

Available international data do not lend unequivocal support to either the "more police equals less crime" or the "more crime equals more police" hypothesis. In the next section, focusing on the impact of police performance rather than of police resources per se on the level of crime, the issue will be revisited.

Homicide Conviction Rates as a Performance Measure

Traditionally, the most widely used indicator of criminal justice performance is the proportion of recorded crimes that are "solved" by the police, in the sense that a suspect is found (called the "clearance rate"). In most countries where volume crime has gone up, overall clearance rates have fallen significantly, often to levels as low as 10%. Overall clearance rates as a performance measure have been much criticized by the law enforcement community and for good reasons. They are, first of all, strongly influenced by the types of crime recorded. In the case of shoplifting, a report is usually made after a hot arrest by security guards. Such crimes are "solved" by the police almost by definition. The resulting high clearance rates for such offenses do not reflect police performance in any meaningful way. In cases of petty theft such as pickpocketing or bicycle theft, perpetrators are rarely detected. Most police forces no longer make any investigative effort in such "dead end" cases. If such crimes make up a larger component of total crime, overall clearance rates automatically drop. Again, such changes say nothing about police performance.

Clearance rates are not dependent on just the types of crimes recorded but also on how outcomes of police investigations are counted. If persistent offenders are arrested, they may, under prolonged interrogation, confess to tens or even hundreds of crimes committed over the past years. If all these crimes are counted as "solved cases," this significantly affects the overall clearance rate. Police recording methods and counting rules show large variation across forces and countries. For these reasons, overall clearance rates cannot be used to compare police performance across countries.

Homicides, as discussed in Chapter 4, are usually duly reported to the police. The police have limited discretion in recording, and some sustained efforts are normally made to find and arrest the perpetrator. Clearance rates for homicide therefore provide some indication of the effectiveness of criminal investigation departments of the police. If perpetrators are arrested, the suspects will usually be prosecuted and in most cases convicted. The percentage of recorded homicides resulting in a conviction provides a broad indication of the overall effectiveness of the criminal justice system including law enforcement.

Figure 9.10 shows regional proportions of police-recorded homicide cases where a conviction for homicide was obtained (the "conviction rate").

❖ **Figure 9.10** Comparative Homicide Conviction Rates (number of convictions for homicide as percentage of recorded cases), per World Region, 1999–2002

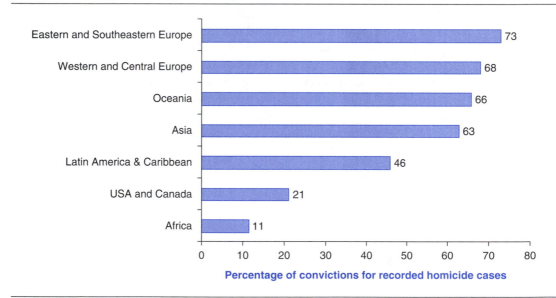

Percentage of convictions for recorded homicide cases

Source: www.unodc.org; 8th UN Crime Survey.

With respect to the proportion of convictions obtained for police-recorded homicides, the data show that a conviction is likely to be obtained in one out of every three reported homicides, worldwide. Africa appears to be in a poor position, with a conviction in only one of every 10 cases recorded by the police. In some African countries, the conviction rates are even much lower. Ethiopia, for example, reported conviction rates for homicide below 5% in 2001 and 2002 (UNODC, 2005). According to media reports in Guatemala, there were only 115 convictions out of 5,338 reported cases (a conviction rate of 2%) (UNODC, 2007).

Surprisingly, conviction rates in North America are also low. This finding requires further analysis and may be an artifact of different recording of homicides by the police and/or convictions for homicide. Possibly, North American police forces are more inclined to qualify cases of violence as homicide than elsewhere. A larger proportion of such cases might eventually be tried as aggravated assaults and therefore not show up under convictions for homicide. The low homicide conviction rate of the United States can also partly be explained by the relatively high acquittal rate for homicide prosecutions and a comparatively high case load for police officers.

The conviction rates for robbery are also much lower in developing countries (Shaw, Van Dijk, & Rhomberg, 2003). On average, one out of eight cases of robbery results in a conviction. In countries of sub-Saharan Africa for which data are available, only one in every 40 cases of reported robbery resulted in a conviction. Southeast Asia and the Pacific show equally low rates, with only one conviction for every 35 cases of recorded robbery. This is followed by Latin America and the Caribbean, with one conviction being recorded for approximately every 15 recorded cases. In these regions, even the most serious offenses can almost be committed with impunity. Conviction rates for robbery in both North America and Europe are significantly higher (Shaw, Van Dijk, & Rhomberg, 2003).

Given the remarkably high levels of both homicide and robbery in many developing countries, their low conviction rates should give cause for concern. In new democracies, the most pressing issues in police reform were the separation between the police and the military, the establishment of police accountability to democratic governments and common courts, the limitation and control of the use of force, and the protection of human rights. National and international human rights organizations have played an important role in supporting these police reforms. Arguably, the time has now come to request more resources and priority for the instrumental, crime-control function of the justice and security sectors. First and foremost, their capacity to bring offenders to court should be brought up to par.

Toward a Composite Index for Police Performance

For most crime victims, the police are the first agency with which they come into contact. Impressions of police reception are often decisive for victims' evaluation of the system's response to their victimization (Shapland, Willmore, & Duff, 1985). In the ICVS, several questions deal with the interactions of the victims with the police. The key question asked of those who have been victimized is whether anyone had reported the incident to the police. Other questions deal with the measure of satisfaction of victims with the treatment of the complaint by the police and the general opinion on the performance of the police in the area. The ICVS, then, provides three direct measures of citizen satisfaction with the police: one objective measure (the proportion of victimizations reported to the police) and two subjective measures (the degree of satisfaction of victims with their personal treatment by the police and the satisfaction of all respondents with police performance in their local area). The three indicators are fairly strongly correlated to each other (all correlations showed coefficients in the range of $r = 0.40$ to 0.71) If the police succeed in treating crime victims well, reporting rates are higher and overall performance is judged more favorably by the community. These indicators of police performance are all closely linked.

Another important source of police performance evaluations are results of surveys among business executives. Businesses experience higher rates of victimization than individual citizens, as discussed in Chapter 3. Although far from all victimizations are reported to the police, many executives frequently interact with their local police (Van Dijk & Terlouw, 1996). In many countries, business associations actively cooperate with the police to increase security. Business executives are therefore well placed to assess police performance. The survey of business leaders conducted by the World Economic Forum (WEF, 2002/2003; WEF, 2003/2004) asks to what extent police services can be relied upon to protect businesses against criminal activity. The reliability of the police as protectors of company property is perceived to be the best in Oceania and North America and the poorest in Caribbean, Latin American, and African countries. The low scores for the Caribbean are particularly striking, considering the comparatively high numbers of police officers per 100,000 residents in many countries in the region.

The police reliability ratings of the WEF surveys correlate strongly with the three ICVS-based measures of police performance (correlation coefficients are in the range from $r = .55$ to $.77$). Correlations were calculated between the four available police performance indicators and homicide conviction rates, the objective performance measure discussed above. The results showed that the proportion of victims reporting their victimizations to the police was positively correlated with the homicide conviction rate ($r = .45$). Victims are more inclined to report incidents of crime to police forces that better succeed in solving reported homicides. The assessments of citizens and business executives of police effectiveness were also correlated with the homicide conviction rates.[1]

Given these results, a composite index was constructed for the overall performance of the police, combining the two objective measures (victim reporting rate and homicide conviction rate) and three subjective measures (victim satisfaction, citizens' satisfaction, and business executives' satisfaction). Cronbach's alpha, a measure for the coherence of composite indices, was fairly strong (= 0.63). Figure 9.11 presents regional scores on this composite Police Performance Index (PPI).

Figure 9.11 shows large differences in police performance across regions. The justice and security sectors are performing poorly in developing countries, and the general public as well as the business community seems to be well aware of this. Police forces in developed countries in North America,[2] Oceania, and Europe are performing best and

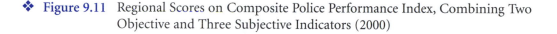

❖ **Figure 9.11**   Regional Scores on Composite Police Performance Index, Combining Two Objective and Three Subjective Indicators (2000)

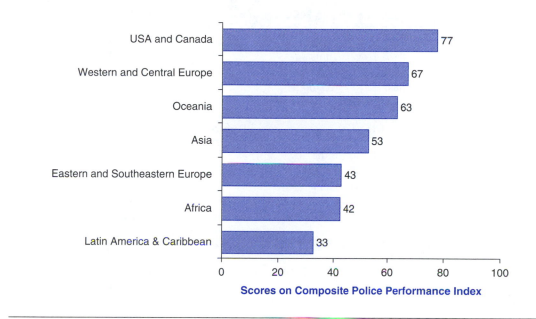

Sources: ICVS, 2000; WEF, 2002/2003, 2003/2004; www.unodc.org; 8th UN Crime Survey, 1997–2002.

those in developing countries in Africa, Latin America, and eastern Europe, worst. In Latin America, Africa, and eastern Europe, performance by the police evidently leaves much to be desired. Table 9.2 shows the national scores and rankings on this index.

Resources, Performance, and Integrity

Data was presented earlier on the number of police officers per 100,000 population. This data can be used as an indicator of the public resources made available for law enforcement across countries. It seems reasonable to expect a positive link between the level of resources and performance. This assumption is not confirmed by the data. The analysis of the relationship between public expenditures for policing and performance showed negative results, as can be seen in Figure 9.12.

The analysis shows that the number of police has little influence on performance scores. Higher numbers of police officers per 100,000 population do not necessarily result in better police performance as measured by our index. Countries such as the United States, Australia, and Denmark achieve higher scores on the composite Police Performance Index than Italy, although Italy employs almost twice the number of police officers per 100,000 population. Mexico also shows a relatively poor performance score, considering its high number of police officers.

One factor that may explain the lack of correlation between the number of police officers and performance is corruption within police forces. According to the Global

❖ Table 9.2   World Rankings According to Composite Index of Police Performance (2000)

Fifteen Countries With the Highest Scores on Police Performance Index								
1	Jordan	94.1	6	Luxembourg	85.6	11	United Kingdom	78.2
2	Australia	91.7	7	Tunisia	83.2	12	Korea, Dem Rep	77.7
3	Israel	90.6	8	Netherlands	83.0	13	United States	77.5
4	Denmark	88.6	9	Iceland	82.5	14	Finland	77.1
5	Switzerland	87.9	10	Barbados	79.6	15	Sweden	76.6
Fifteen Countries With Moderately High Scores on Police Performance Index								
16	Canada	76.4	46	India	56.2	79	Georgia	37.2
20	France	71.7	49	Croatia	54.0	85	Russian Fed.	33.6
31	Italy	67.2	51	China	53.5	88	Lithuania	31.5
34	Botswana	64.0	63	South Africa	45.7	96	Uganda	27.5
41	Japan	59.8	68	Philippines	40.6	99	Jamaica	26.7
Fifteen Countries With Lowest Scores on Police Performance Index								
100	Peru	26.7	105	Madagascar	16.8	110	Bolivia	11.1
101	Venezuela, RB	25.1	106	Trinidad & Tobago	16.8	111	Pakistan	6.9
102	Colombia	24.5	107	Mozambique	15.6	112	Chad	5.5
103	Mexico	19.9	108	Kenya	14.7	113	Bangladesh	3.0
104	Brazil	17.7	109	Ecuador	12.9	114	Haiti	1.0

Source: See Note 3.

Corruption Barometer of Transparency International, the police are seen as one of the most corrupt of all state sectors. In the following countries, the police are seen as the most corrupt of all sectors: Georgia, Ghana, Kenya, Malaysia, Nigeria, Pakistan, the Philippines, and Russia. In some other countries, the police tied with other sectors as the most corrupt: Cameroon, Guatamala, Mexico, Moldova, South Africa, and Ukraine (Transparency International, 2004b). In the latest Afrobarometer survey, 70% of Nigerians said they thought most or all of the police in their country were corrupt (Afrobarometer, 2004). Surveys in other African countries such as Kenya and Tanzania show similarly dismal results (UNODC, 2005). In the Ukraine, the traffic police were dismantled after the political transformation in 2005 on account of rampant corruption. Earlier, a dismantling of corrupt traffic police forces had been undertaken in Mexico City and Georgia.

Police corruption is not only a financial burden for the public, but it also undermines police effectiveness in several ways. Time and energy spent on "rent-seeking" reduces efforts to prevent and investigate crime. It also can easily result in collusion between police and local criminal groups, resulting in a reduction of clearance and conviction rates.

❖ Figure 9.12   Relationship Between Number of Police per 100,000 Population and the
Police Performance Index (ranked variables)

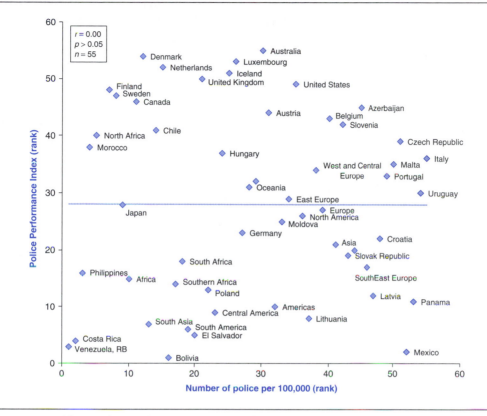

Sources: PPI; see Table 9.2; 8th UN Crime Survey (www.unodc.org).

Victim Empowerment and Support

One of the most fundamental and far-reaching reforms in the justice and security sector of the past three decades has been the acknowledgment of crime victims as stakeholders of the police and courts (Sebba, 1996). Victims are nowadays to an increasing extent regarded not just as providers of testimony in criminal trials but as clients or consumers of law enforcement and criminal justice with their own rights in criminal procedure and entitlements to specific services (Crawford & Goodey, 2000). In 1985, the General Assembly of the United Nations unanimously adopted the Declaration of Basic Principles of Rights of Victims of Crime and Abuse of Power. This declaration, although not legally binding in a formal sense, is seen as a hallmark by the international "victims' rights" movement because it lays down international standards for the treatment of victims.

The declaration carries the stamp of American legislation passed in the early 1980s such as the Victims of Crime Act of 1984. It has subsequently inspired legal reforms on behalf of crime victims across the world (Vetere & David, 2005). One of the rare pieces of European Union legislation on criminal justice procedure ever passed is the Framework Decision of the European Union's Council on the Standing of Victims in Criminal Proceedings of 2001. This legally binding decision obliges the 25 member states of the European Union to implement a set of provisions that duly reflects the UN's basic principles. Perhaps the most comprehensive law on the rights of victims influenced by the declaration is the recently adopted Fundamental Law for Crime Victims of Japan (Shikita & Morosawa, 2005). In the preamble to this law, the Japanese government acknowledges its responsibility for the prevention of crime and the realization of a safe and reliable society. In this context, it acknowledges its obligation to hear the voices of victims and to protect their rights and interests. The principles of the declaration have also found their way into the newly adopted UN conventions against transnational organized crime and corruption, discussed in Chapter 7. Several important victims' rights, such as the right to express views in court, have been incorporated into the Rome Statute, establishing the International Criminal Court in The Hague, where war criminals can be brought to trial (Van Dijk, 2005).

Although the elaboration and adoption by the General Assembly of the UN Victims Declaration is rightly seen as a major achievement, implementation of its principles in actual practice of various countries is far from assured. A first data-gathering exercise on its implementation by the UN secretariat showed disappointing results (Groenhuysen, 1999). In this section, we will use ICVS data as a source of information on the extent to which the standards of the UN Victim Declaration are put into practice across the world.

Victim Reception by the Police

One of the primary objectives of modern policing is, or should be, a considerate, helpful, and reassuring reception and treatment of people reporting their victimization by serious crime to their local police. There are many instrumental justifications for this, but the one overruling all others is that such services are, as stipulated in fresh Japanese legislation, a humanitarian duty of the state toward people who its specialized crime-control agencies have failed to protect.

As mentioned above, victims who reported their victimization by serious crime to the police were asked in the ICVS to assess their treatment by the police.[4] These evaluations have been incorporated into our composite police performance index, but they provide information important in its own right on the quality of service delivery to crime victims. The regional results are presented in Figure 9.13.

Among those who reported, less than half were satisfied with the way the police dealt with their case. Those least satisfied were the respondents from eastern Europe. Within Europe satisfaction was lower in eastern and central Europe than in western Europe (not shown here separately). Low satisfaction rates were also found in Latin America/Caribbean, Africa and Asia. It is noteworthy that the satisfaction level among crime victims in Eastern Europe is even below that in the developing world.

Only in western Europe, North America, and Australia did more than 60% of victims who reported to the police positively evaluate the treatment received. If police forces were service industries competing for "business" on a competitive market, they

❖ **Figure 9.13**   Percentages of Victims Satisfied With the Police After Reporting Serious Crimes, in Six Global Regions

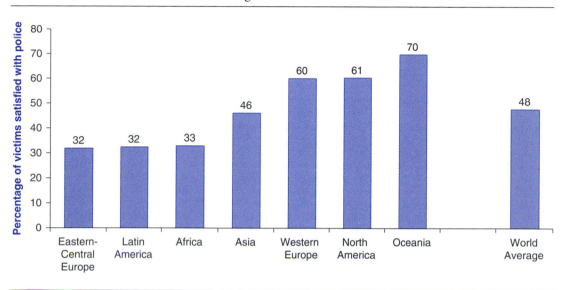

Source: ICVS, 1996–2000.

would, with such levels of customer satisfaction, face serious difficulties to stay in business. One of their key client groups, crime victims, is in majority fundamentally dissatisfied with their services. This low level of customer satisfaction might be one of the drivers behind the rise of private security services, including private detectives.

In most parts of the world, police agencies fail to meet the expectations of citizens reporting criminal victimizations in the majority of cases. In the ICVS 2005, the most common reason for dissatisfaction was that the police "did not do enough" (60%), "were not interested" (45%), or "did not find the offender" (42%). Roughly one in three unsatisfied victims was unhappy that the police had not kept them sufficiently informed (32%). Around 20% said the police had been impolite or incorrect.

Table 9.3 shows world rankings of countries on victim satisfaction with the police. The country scores on victim satisfaction show that police forces in Anglo-Saxon countries and in northern Europe provide the best services in the eyes of crime victims. Among the old 15 member states of the EU, the lowest rates are found in France, Italy, and Greece. In Greece, very few victims are satisfied with their treatment by the police. Newer members of the union (Hungary, Poland, Estonia, and Bulgaria) as well as Turkey also show rates significantly below the European mean. Victim satisfaction proved to be remarkably high in India. Similarly high victim satisfaction rates were also found in a stand-alone ICVS-type study carried out in the main cities in southern India (Chockalingham, 2003). One of the innovations introduced in the state of Tamil Nadu in southern India are all-female police stations that receive reports of female victims. Such gender-specific victim reception had been introduced earlier in some cities in Brazil.

❖ Table 9.3   World Rankings on Satisfaction of Crime Victims With Treatment
by the Police

Fifteen Countries With the Highest Rankings on Victim Satisfaction								
1	Finland	80.0	6	Netherlands	70.7	11	United States	64.7
2	New Zealand	78.8	7	Switzerland	70.6	12	India	58.0
3	Denmark	75.2	8	Sweden	68.6	13	*Papua New Guinea*	*57.0*
4	Canada	71.7	9	Germany	67.7	14	Azerbaijan	56.1
5	Australia	70.8	10	United Kingdom	65.0	15	Tunisia	55.2

Fifteen Countries With Moderately High Scores on Victim Satisfaction								
17	France	51.6	25	Austria	48.0	35	Japan	39.4
18	Nigeria	50.8	28	Czech Republic	46.1	39	*Egypt, Arab Rep.*	*35.4*
19	Belgium	49.6	31	Italy	41.2	42	Poland	34.6
21	Spain	49.0	33	South Africa	39.5	43	Brazil	34.3
23	Argentina	48.2	34	Hungary	39.5	47	China	31.9

Fifteen Countries With the Lowest Rankings on Victim Satisfaction								
52	Albania	29.3	57	Mozambique	26.7	62	Georgia	18.8
53	Panama	29.0	58	Zambia	26.6	63	Mongolia	18.0
54	Estonia	29.0	59	Russian Fed.	25.6	64	Korea, Rep.	17.1
55	Romania	28.4	60	Bulgaria	20.1	65	Ukraine	15.7
56	Colombia	27.0	61	Kyrgyz Republic	19.2	66	Bolivia	14.1

Source: ICVS, 1996–2000, or 1992 if in italics.

By and large, the distribution of victim satisfaction rates across regions and countries suggests that military-type police forces such as those in Latin America and eastern Europe perform less well in their interactions with crime victims than more service-oriented forces. The latter seem better placed to provide adequate services to crime victims as members of the local communities police forces are supposed to serve.

Trends in Victim Satisfaction

Figure 9.14 shows trends in victim satisfaction from selected countries for which data are available.

The country rates confirm that victim satisfaction is higher in the more-affluent countries of North America, Oceania, and western Europe. Rates of satisfaction among victims of serious crimes, however, show a remarkable downward trend in several developed countries. Between 1996 and 2005, victim satisfaction went down in the United States, the United Kingdom, the Netherlands, Canada, and Sweden. Nation-specific crime victim surveys in England and Wales and the Netherlands, using much larger samples, have also registered a decline in satisfaction in recent years (Allan et al., 2006; Veiligheidsmonitor, 2006).

❖ **Figure 9.14** Percentages of Reporting Victims Satisfied With Their Treatment by the Police

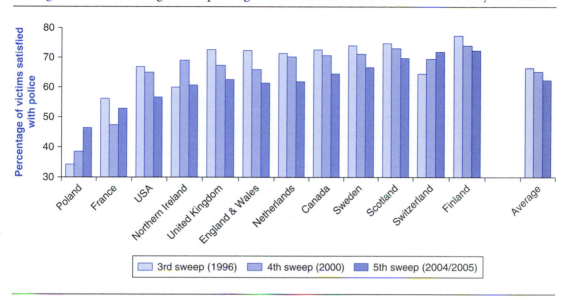

Source: ICVS, 1996–2005.

This intriguing result can be interpreted in different ways. One explanation is that victims are treated as professionally as before but that expectations among victims have been raised to the point that they can no longer be satisfied. Police forces may ask victims whether they would want to be informed about the investigation. If subsequently no information is given, victims might be more upset than if the issue had not been raised. A second possible interpretation is that police forces have bureaucratized the reporting of crimes.[5] Third, in countries where special provisions for victims outside the police have been set up, police forces may feel that victim needs are duly met if a referral is made to such agencies. It seems striking in this respect that in Europe, victims are more consistently satisfied with the police in countries where victim support outside the police hardly exists, such as Denmark (not depicted here), France, Finland, and Luxembourg. Police forces in the United States, the United Kingdom, and the Netherlands may be inclined to relegate the rendering of victim support to existing, well-functioning outside agencies. An incentive for such relegation might have been the shift in policing priorities in favor of terrorism prevention and zero-tolerance law enforcement and away from service delivery to the community.[6] Whatever may be the reasons, the fact that fewer victims than before are satisfied with their treatment by the police should give police chiefs in these countries food for thought. If the downward trend in victim satisfaction prevails, a subsequent decline in the readiness to report crimes to the police is to be expected.

Victim Support Services

In line with the UN Victims Declaration, more and more countries have introduced government-funded victim support schemes for all victims or for special vulnerable categories (Goodey, 2005; Lurigio, Skogan, & Davis, 1990).Victims of more serious crimes (burglaries or contact crimes, including robbery, threat/assault, and sexual offenses) who had reported to the police were asked in the ICVS surveys whether they had received support from a specialized agency, defined as "an agency helping victims by giving information, or practical or emotional support." Worldwide, 6% of victims of more serious crimes had received help. The highest rates were in North America (15%), western Europe (9%), and Oceania (New Zealand, 24%; Australia, 5% in 2000).

In many countries in these regions, levels of support for victims have gone up significantly from 1996 to 2005. In the United States, the percentage went up from 11% in 1996 to 16% in 2005, and in Canada, from 9% to 14%, in those years, respectively. In western Europe, the percentages of victims who received support went up in Austria, Belgium, the Netherlands, Scotland, and Northern Ireland. In 2005, the rates of victims of serious crimes receiving victim support were the highest in New Zealand (24%), the United Kingdom (16%), the United States (16%), the Netherlands (14%), Johannesburg /South Africa (14%), Belgium (13%), and Austria (13%).

In the United Kingdom, victim support is provided by trained volunteers under supervision of a National Association for Victim Support. Similar national organizations bundling voluntary work for victims are in operation in Scotland and Northern Ireland, the Netherlands, and Belgium. In Europe, victim support provided by volunteers is probably, institutionally speaking, the most developed. Victim support is provided and promoted in the United States by the National Organization of Victim Assistance and the National Center for Victims of Crime, which runs a helpline. Actual victim services are mainly provided by local organizations, including hospitals. In South Africa and Nigeria, some local projects exist, especially providing support to female victims of violent crime. In Japan, local NGOs providing services to victims have recently been expanding. Elsewhere in the world, outside Australia and New Zealand, operational victim support organizations are still nascent. In Russia, for example, a first initiative to promote support for crime victims was launched in 2007.

The figures of victims who received help vary across offense type. Of those who reported burglaries to the police, 4% had received help. Of all victims of contact crimes[7] who reported to the police, 7% had been given such help. Approximately 16% of female victims of sexual offenses who had reported to the police had received specialized support in North America and western Europe. Elsewhere, the percentages were lower. In all regions, only a small percentage of male victims of assaults had received specialized help (4%). In developing countries, very few male victims of violence indicated to have received any such help.

The finding that in, for example, the United States 16% of victims have received specialized help does not imply that the other 84% of victims were all in need of such help. Although the questions about victim support were put only to victims of comparatively serious crimes, it cannot be assumed that all such victims need to be given specialized assistance to cope with the consequences. Many of them may possess the resilience to fend for themselves. Victims who had not received help from a specialized agency were therefore asked whether they would have appreciated help in "getting information, or practical or emotional support." According to the survey, half of the reporting victims, who had not received specialized help, would have welcomed it. There are clearly unmet needs among a large proportion of victims of serious crime, especially among female victims of violence. Globally, three out of four victims of violence against women, including sexual violence, would have appreciated help.

The results indicate that the need of help among victims of serious crime is widespread though not universal. The percentages of victims who would have appreciated help but did not receive it were 50% or higher in Asia, Africa, Latin America, and eastern Europe. In developed nations, only 30% to 40% express such needs. The distribution of the need for help across regions is the reverse of that of its actual reception. In developing countries, many more victims would have wanted such help. This is caused partly by the fact that in those countries, such help is rarely offered and partly because fewer other general provisions of health care or social work are available. Among developed countries, the percentages of victims who would have liked to receive victim support tend to be smaller in countries with extended welfare states such as Iceland (23%), Austria (26%), Germany (27%), Canada (27%), the Netherlands (30%), and Denmark (30%). Higher percentages were found in the United States (38%), England and Wales (45%), and especially in some southern European countries (Spain, 68%; Portugal, 70%).

Figure 9.15 shows the regional rates of victims who received help together with the rates of victims who would have liked to receive it. The comparison between the regional percentages of victims of serious crimes who had received assistance and of those who would have appreciated receiving such assistance indicates a gap between supply and demand of such services. Everywhere there are more who would have liked to receive it but didn't than those who did. The "take-up rate" of victim support agencies can be calculated by dividing the number of victims who received help or would have liked to receive it by those who received it. Figure 9.16 shows regional take-up rates of victim support.

Only in North America and Oceania are a significant proportion of those in need of help served by the existing supply of such services (one in three).[8] Even in western Europe the take-up rate of victim support remains on average below 20%. Table 9.4 shows the take-up rates of victim support per country.

Across the world there clearly exists a huge gap between the need for help and its actual provision. Even in countries where victim support has become more common, the need for such help is still largely unmet. As said, some progress has over the years been made with the provision of special victim assistance in North America and western Europe, but elsewhere the extent of unmet needs of victims of common crime is as large as ever. Citizens in developing countries are more exposed to volume crime, including violence. They are the least equipped to cope with the consequences due to lack of insurance, free health services, or welfare provisions as well as of specialized victim support. This feature exacerbates the negative impact of violence and other common crimes on the human security conditions in the South.

❖ Figure 9.15   Percentages of Victims of Serious Crimes Who Have Received, or Would Have
Considered Useful, Specialized Victim Support, by World Region

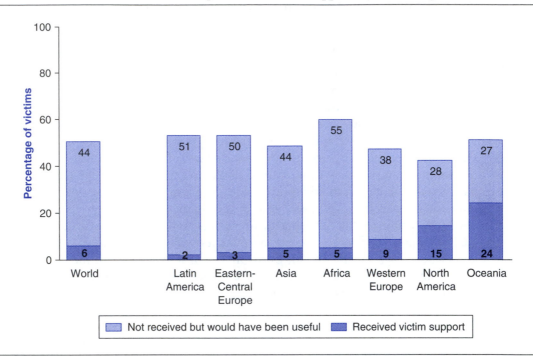

Source: ICVS, 2005 or latest available.

Implementing the UN Victims Declaration

In 1999, the UNODC published a collection of international best practices in victim support, the *Handbook of Justice for Victims,* available on the Internet (www
.victimology.nl). The ICVS findings on victim empowerment presented above show
that in most countries, the standards of the 1985 UN Declaration of Basic Principles
of Justice for Victims of Crime and Abuse of Power, even when duly incorporated in
national or supranational laws, have not yet become a reality. Especially in many developing countries and European countries in transition, policing and criminal policies
are still insufficiently victim centered. Many victims are consequently reluctant to
report their victimizations to the relevant authorities. This lack of confidence in the
police implies that crime victims often have no authority to turn to and feel alienated
from state institutions. The low rates of crime reporting, especially of more serious
crimes, are also an impediment to effective crime prevention and control. The chances
of arresting the offenders and getting a conviction are largely dependent on the information supplied by the victim. If many victims are not convinced, as is clearly the case

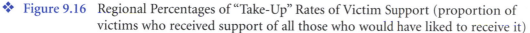

❖ **Figure 9.16**   Regional Percentages of "Take-Up" Rates of Victim Support (proportion of victims who received support of all those who would have liked to receive it)

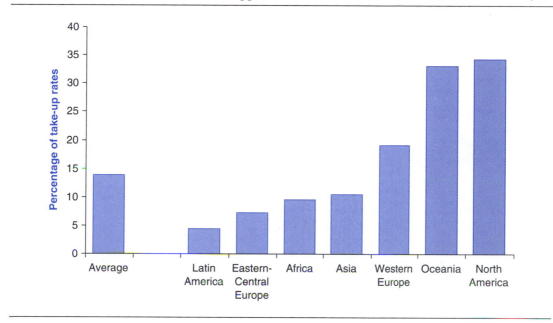

Source: ICVS, 2005 or latest available.

in most developing nations, that reporting to the police will do them good, the effectiveness of the police is severely undermined. For more effective criminal investigations, the cooperation of victims is essential. This is another reason why the proportion of satisfied victims—currently globally below 50%—is an important performance indicator for police forces across the world.

In this context, attention should be given to the outcome of an evaluation of the effects of better treatment of victims by the police, the prosecutors, and the courts in the Netherlands (Wemmers, 1995). The results of a field experiment show that victims who have been treated better by the police have a more positive attitude toward both the police and the criminal justice system generally. Even more to the point, they are also more inclined to feel an obligation to abide by the law and are therefore less likely to commit offenses themselves. This result confirms the notion that citizens as reporting victims are very sensitive to the treatment given to them by the police and the judicial authorities. If the police set the right example, respect for the law is reinforced. If the police treat victims disrespectfully or are uninterested, justice-related goodwill is lost.

Better services, besides more rights for crime victims, seems to be an obvious priority for national and international crime-prevention strategies. In developing countries and countries in transition, the consequences of criminal victimization are often very severe since financial support and adequate medical treatment are not available (UNODC, 2005). Better services for crime victims should be promoted with the

❖ Table 9.4   Percentages of Those in Need of Victim Support Who Actually Received Help, per Country (national take-up rates of victim support)

Fifteen Countries With the Highest Scores								
1	New Zealand	47.0	6	Netherlands	35.0	11	Belgium	28.0
2	Scotland	40.0	7	Albania	35.0	12	Denmark	27.0
3	Austria	38.0	8	United States	33.0	13	Hong Kong (SAR China)	25.0
4	Northern Ireland	37.0	9	Japan	30.0	14	Norway	23.0
5	Canada	37.0	10	United Kingdom	30.0	15	Iceland	22.0
Fifteen Countries With Moderately High Scores								
16	Sweden	21.0	27	France	11.0	46	Germany	8.0
17	Switzerland	18.0	33	Indonesia	10.0	47	Italy	7.0
21	Australia	16.0	36	Mexico	8.0	50	Portugal	5.0
22	Panama	16.0	38	Macedonia, FYR	8.0	51	Croatia	5.0
26	Ireland	13.0	29	Poland	8.0	52	Costa Rica	5.0
Fifteen Countries With Low Scores								
59	Spain	4.0	64	Argentina	3.0	69	Slovak Republic	2.0
60	Mongolia	4.0	65	Paraguay	3.0	70	Bolivia	2.0
61	Cambodia	4.0	66	Turkey	3.0	71	Serbia and Montenegro	1.0
62	Mozambique	4.0	67	Russian Federation	3.0	72	Hungary	1.0
63	Greece	4.0	68	Romania	2.8	73	Azerbaijan	0.0

Source: ICVS, 2005 or latest available.

support of the donor community and international organizations. The ongoing UNODC pilot project offering small grants for the launching of victim support initiatives in India and some other developing countries, including for victims of human trafficking, provides an example of what needs to be done. To this end, the World Society of Victimology, with the support of the International Victimology Institute–Tilburg, in the Netherlands, has started lobbying for a better follow-up to the UN Victims Declaration of 1985. A proposal has been launched to upgrade the declaration into a legally binding UN Convention on the Rights of Victims of Crime (and Terrorism) (for details, see www.tilburg.edu/intervict).

International Best Practices in Crime Prevention

In the discussion on resources for law enforcement, the issue was raised as to whether more police equates with less crime. Interestingly, statistical analysis did not confirm the hypothesis that more resources for police result in lower crime rates. In fact, many countries with high levels of police officers experience comparatively high levels of volume crime. The positive relationship between police resources and the level of recorded crimes may be the result of higher recording productivity of better-performing police forces and ensuing better reporting by victims.

Another hypothesis tested was whether police performance, as measured by the composite index described above, is associated with lower crime rates. The first relationship tested was that between the Composite Index of Police Performance and the number of police-recorded crimes per 100,000 residents. The analyses did not confirm the "better police equals less crime" hypothesis either. The police performance measure was in fact positively related to the total rate of recorded crimes. Better-performing police forces record higher numbers of crime, again indicating a greater capacity to make official records of crimes reported. The next step in the analysis focused on the links between policing and levels of actual crime. A weak negative correlation was found between the police performance index and the level of volume crime as measured by the ICVS ($r = -.32$, $p < 0.05$, $n = 56$). Countries with better-performing police forces tend to have somewhat lower rates of victimization by common crime, but the link is far from strong and may be spurious.

The absence of a clear relationship between police performance and actual levels of volume crime has also been found in multivariate analyses (Mayhew, 2003b). Volume crime seems to be shaped primarily by social causes of crime, such as urbanization, demographic composition, and social inequality, as well as affluence-related characteristics (e.g., the number of cars and other targets of property crime) and specific facilitators (gun availability and alcohol abuse). The impact of policing on crime levels must be viewed against the background of these powerful criminogenic forces. Even if police services are successful in reducing the number of certain types of crime locally—and there are many examples of such local successes (see below)—such efforts alone seem to have limited impact on overall, nationwide levels of volume crime. Investments in policing to improve performance and service delivery are a necessary component of any crime-reduction strategy. But for such efforts to actually bring down levels of crime, they must be supplemented by the actions of other institutional actors focusing on the causes of crime. As will be discussed below, many of the proven practices to reduce volume crime require the involvement of other players besides the police and the courts (Welsh, 2004).[9] The next section will provide an overview of proven practices.

Guidelines for the Prevention of Crime

In 2002, the United Nations Economic and Social Council adopted the United Nations Guidelines for the Prevention of Crime. The overarching aim of the guidelines is expressed in its first article: "Crime prevention offers opportunities for a humane and more cost-effective approach to the problems of crime." In the guidelines, crime prevention is defined as comprising all measures that seek to reduce the risk of crime occurring by intervening in its multiple causes. Criminal justice–type interventions can also, as just mentioned, perform preventive functions, but these fall outside the scope of the UN guidelines. The guidelines distinguish four main categories of crime prevention:

A. Social crime prevention, including early intervention

B. Community-based crime prevention

C. Situational and victim-oriented crime prevention

D. Reintegration of offenders

Social Crime Prevention

Social crime prevention seeks to reduce risk factors of criminality and enhance protective factors, for example, through early intervention in the development of socially problematic lifestyles. Techniques of intervention resemble those used to reduce demand of drugs: education and awareness-raising through youth networks. International best practices assembled by the UN-affiliated International Centre for the Prevention of Crime and the National Crime Prevention initiative in Australia offer several examples of effective, nonstigmatizing support programs for vulnerable families and children (National Crime Prevention, 1999).

According to Farrington and Welsh (2003), three types of family-based programs have been found to be effective in preventing crime:

1. Home visitation

2. Day care/preschool

3. Parent training (with younger children)

Programs offering support to single-parent families, including Nurse-Family-Partnership for pregnant women in vulnerable situations, have been found to be an excellent investment in preventing both child abuse and later involvement in delinquency and drug abuse by the child (Aos et al., 2004). Other types of targeted intervention promoting the development of self-control and social integration of children at risk, such as preschool programs, have consistently been found to yield the best returns on investment of all known responses to crime (Schweinhart, 2004; Sherman et al., 1997; Welsh & Farrington, 2000). Parent training including Parent Child Training Interaction Therapy has been shown to result in lower stress levels among parents, fewer cases of abuse, and better school performance and less involvement in delinquency of the child at a later age.

Community-Based Crime Prevention

Hope (1995) defined community crime prevention as "actions intended to change the social conditions that are believed to sustain crime in residential communities." Local social institutions (e.g., families, associations, churches, and youth clubs) are usually the medium by which these programs are delivered to address delinquency and crime problems. Recent reviews carried out to assess the effectiveness of community-based programs to prevent crime (Sherman et al., 1997; Sherman et al., 2002; see also Hope, 1995) have concluded that this approach does not, at the present time, demonstrate evidence of proven effectiveness in preventing crime. Disappointing as this result might be, it should be heeded in the planning of new programs.

Three new types of community-based programs focusing on youth at risk are considered to be promising in preventing crime:

1. Gang member intervention programs that are focused on reducing cohesion among youth gangs and individual gang members

2. Community-based mentoring of vulnerable youth (Waller, 2006)

3. After-school recreation (Welsh, 2003; Welsh & Hoshi, 2002)

Situational and Victim-Oriented Crime Prevention

An internationally known proverb says that "opportunity makes the thief." In Spanish, the same insight is formulated even more pointedly: *Puerta abierta, al santo tenta* (even saints are tempted by an open door). The origins of situational crime prevention are based in the larger body of opportunity theory that sees the offender "as heavily influenced by environmental inducements and opportunities and as being highly adaptable to changes in the situation" (Clarke, 1995; Felson, 1997).

Reducing the opportunities for crime is achieved essentially through some modification or manipulation of the environment and can take the form of a number of different measures:

- Increasing perceived effort (target hardening, access control, deflecting offenders, and controlling facilitators)
- Increasing perceived risks (entry/exit screening, police surveillance, surveillance by employees, and natural surveillance)
- Reducing anticipated rewards (target removal, identifying property, reducing temptation, and denying benefits)
- Inducing guilt or shame (rule setting, strengthening moral condemnation, controlling disinhibitors, and facilitating compliance) (Clarke & Homel, 1997)

Three types of place-focused programs, listed under the first and second items in the list above, have been found to be especially effective in preventing crime:

1. Nuisance abatement (the utilization of civil law to curtail drug dealing and related crime problems in private residential premises) (Eck, 2002)

2. Closed-circuit television (CCTV) surveillance cameras. In the case of CCTV, it was found to have a significant desirable effect on crime, with an overall reduction in crime of 21% in experimental areas compared with control areas (Welsh & Farrington, 2004)

3. Improved street lighting (Eck, 2002; Farrington & Welsh, 2002)

Targeted policing is largely focused on situational risks and therefore included here under situational crime prevention. A focus on crime risk factors is crucial to the effectiveness of the police in preventing crime. "The value of policing focused on risk factors is the most powerful conclusion reached from three decades of research. Simply hiring more police does not prevent serious crime. Community policing without a clear focus on crime risk factors generally shows no effect on crime. But directed patrols, proactive arrests and problem-solving at high-crime 'hot spots' have shown substantial evidence of crime prevention. Police can prevent robbery, disorder, gun violence, drunk driving, and domestic violence, but only by using certain methods under certain conditions" (Sherman & Eck, 2002).

Special mention should be made in this connection of advising victims of crime how to prevent repeat victimization, the phenomenon that some people are victimized more than once by the same type of crime in a short period of time. The topic of repeat victimization has recently drawn the considerable interest of the criminological research community, particularly in the United Kingdom (Farrell & Peace, 2001). One especially frightening cause of repeat victimization is the deliberate decision of burglars or perpetrators of other crimes to revisit the target of a previously successful "strike." The prevention of such repeats should be a police priority everywhere. Analyses of ICVS data have confirmed that many victims of crime are revictimized by the same type of crime within the same year and often even within weeks or months after their first victimization. Globally, more than 40% of those victimized by any common crime are revictimized the same year at least once (Van Dijk, 2000). The rates of repeat victimization are the highest for sexual and other violent offenses. Interventions in cases of domestic violence such as civil law injunctions can prevent further abuse and murder. Since victims of many types of property crime, including burglary and robbery, also run a much greater risk of being victimized again, advice on situational prevention for victims has proven to be highly cost-effective (Farrell & Pease, 2001).

Reintegration of Offenders

Finally, the guidelines advocate innovative approaches to reintegrate offenders, especially ex-prisoners, through corrections-related treatment programs. Detention as such does not reduce recidivism (McKenzie, 2002). Several types of correction-based programs have been found to reduce recidivism (Sherman et al., 2002). Of special value are training programs designed to enhance various life skills (Lipsey & Wilson, 2001).

Evidence-Based Approaches

Many people have strong opinions on how crime and juvenile delinquency should best be tackled. For the conservative minded, the best approach includes boot camps for juvenile delinquents, programs that confront youth at risk with the harsh realities of prison life (Scared Straight projects,) and "short sharp shocks" of imprisonment for spouse abusers. Unfortunately, carefully designed field experiments have proven that none of these "feel good" approaches reduces offending. They might even, as is the case with "scared straight" projects, be counterproductive and promote offending (Sherman et al., 1997).

Those with liberal persuasions tend to be in favor of softer approaches, such as more leisure-time facilities for kids at risk, job programs for young offenders, state-funded survival trips for juvenile delinquents, or counseling for spouse abusers. These types of interventions have not fared any better in experimental tests. None of such projects has ever been found to have a tangible impact on levels of offending or crime (Sherman et al., 1977).

Research on what works in preventing crime has long been of interest to criminologists. Thirty years ago, Lipton reviewed correctional treatment programs (Lipton, et al., 1975), and in the 1980s, numerous studies were carried out to determine the effectiveness of alternative forms of preventing crime, such as community crime prevention (Rosenbaum, 1986). This type of policy-oriented research continued into the 1990s, with several notable studies including Clarke's (1992) *Situational Crime Prevention: Successful Case Studies,* Tonry and Farrington's (1995) *Building a Safer Society: Strategic Approaches to Crime Prevention,* Sherman's report to the U.S. Congress, *Preventing Crime: What Works, What Doesn't, What's Promising* (Sherman et al., 1997*),* an update of that report, *Evidence-Based Crime Prevention* (Sherman et al., 2002), and, finally, Waller's book *Less Law, More Order,* a passionate plea for evidence-based alternatives to more cops, courts, and corrections (Waller, 2006).

In the late 1990s, the above-mentioned UN-affiliated International Centre for Prevention of Crime in Canada (ICPC) published a digest of successes and strategies for success. ICPC also identified 100 crime-prevention programs that illustrate what can be done to reduce crime (Gauthier et al., 1999) and conducted a comparative analysis of costs and benefits of prevention programs (Waller & Sansfacon, 2000; see also Welsh & Farrington, 2000). Cost-effectiveness is often the strongest argument politically for investment in prevention. The RAND Corporation estimated that in the mid-1990s, for a 10% reduction in crime through incarceration of more offenders, taxes in the United States would have to be increased $250 per household but that similar results could be obtained through school-based programs or parent training for $50 and $35 per household, respectively (Greenwood et al., 1996). The parent–child interaction therapy yields average benefits of $4.72 while average costs are $1.30, resulting in a net gain of $3.42 per child (Aos et al., 2004).

Support for evidence-based crime prevention is still growing and has been fostered by a number of recent developments, including a movement toward an evidence-based approach in other disciplines, such as medicine and education. Large-scale, government- and foundation-sponsored reviews of what works in crime prevention and, most recently, the establishment of the Campbell Collaboration and its Crime and Justice Group (Farrington et al., 2001) have further promoted evidence-based crime prevention (www.Campbellcollaboration.org).

In more recent studies, there has been an increased effort to improve the degree of confidence in claims about what works in preventing crime. This has come about through the use of (a) high-quality empirical evidence and (b) rigorous and transparent review methods to assess what works best. A common critique against this approach is that it favors discrete interventions with immediate effects, conducive to experimental testing. More complex and holistic measures with diffuse, long-term impacts fall outside the scope of experimental designs. In this connection, the evidence-based approach is also sometimes critiqued for introducing a Western bias in crime prevention theory since few developing countries can afford the expensive designs required for rigorous testing.

These points are well taken, and it would indeed be wrong to discard every crime-prevention measure that has not yet passed the "Campbell Cooperation test," especially those introduced with apparent success in the developing world but not tested because of lack of funds. Nevertheless, for the further development of crime prevention as an evidence-based discipline, we see no alternative to rigorous scientific testing of promising interventions. The analogy of modern medicine is illuminating here. Advances in medicine, available to the world community, have largely come from the application of scientific methods by research teams in the developed countries. This reliance on Western scientific methods has profited people across the globe and does not imply a bias against traditional medicine. There is a growing recognition in medical circles of the complementary value of forms of "alternative healing," often rooted in centuries-old traditions in non-Western cultures. Likewise, there is much for criminologists to learn from, for example, community-based, traditional mechanisms of dispute resolution (Braithwaite, 1989). In fact, some experimental evidence exists supporting the belief that indigenous forms of restorative justice can deliver better results than modern criminal justice (Strang & Sherman, 2004).

It is with due respect for "complementary crime prevention" that we recommend those interested in planning crime-prevention initiatives in any country to first and foremost consult the research inventories of Sherman, Farrington, and Welsh, highlighting the proven practices to prevent crime. Their overviews show that crime can be successfully prevented through family- and school-based programs, measures targeted at specific places, targeted actions by the police, and correctional interventions delivered in institutions and the community. There are also a number of new promising practices in preventing crime in communities. Furthermore, these reviews of the current state-of-the-art crime-prevention measures demonstrate that crime prevention can be successful in preventing juvenile delinquency and disorder, property crimes as well as violent crimes. Although experimental evidence is difficult to obtain in this area, there is ample case-based evidence of the effectiveness of preventive measures in the fight against organized crime as well (Hicks, 1998; Jacobs et al., 1999; Van de Bunt & Van der Schoot, 2003).

Planning and Implementation

As representatives of the state of "science" on proven practices to reduce crime, these overviews of the Campbell Group are impressive. However, making available scientific evidence on what works best to policymakers and practitioners and having these policies put into practice are two entirely different things. The implementation of a comprehensive crime-prevention strategy requires the organizational involvement and coordination of a large set of subsystems. The development of sustainable structures for such cooperation poses a formidable challenge. Figure 9.17 shows an overview of the main subsystems, provided by Hungarian criminologist and former state secretary for crime prevention Katharina Gonczol (2004).

❖ **Figure 9.17**   Crime Prevention Subsystems

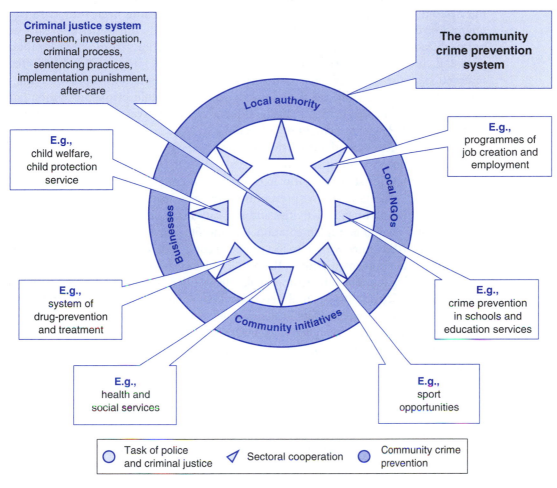

Source: Gonczol, 2004.

Unfortunately, the institutionalization of crime prevention has proven in many countries to be a slow-moving process with many setbacks (Sansfacon, 2004). Although many countries have initiated major crime-prevention initiatives or strategies over the years, organization and management of crime prevention have often been in the hands of ad hoc councils, task forces, steering committees, or private foundations (Gilling, 1997). Most of these structures were very much underfunded in view of their broad mandates to reduce levels of volume crime nationwide or in other large territories. This is most markedly the case with the much underfunded National Crime Prevention Council in the United States. The requirement of involving different parts of central and local governments, all with their own mandates, professional cultures, and political agendas, as well as representatives of the private sector, has in many instances resulted in unstable organizations without clear political leadership. Many of the fledgling organizations for crime prevention have therefore been subject to frequent restructuring. Underfunding, lack of organizational continuity, and unclear political leadership have together prevented these organizations from achieving their potential. In many countries, they have also failed to develop and maintain the required expertise about effective and sustainable implementation of proven crime-prevention measures. Although the knowledge base is available, crime prevention has so far been implemented on a shoestring. It has therefore not yet grown into a profession on par with law enforcement or corrections.

The UN guidelines render extensive attention to the planning and implementation of crime prevention. "Crime prevention," reads Article 10, "requires adequate resources, including funding for structures and activities." All too often in the past, governments have launched ambitious crime-prevention strategies while providing just limited funds for a few experimental activities and without due regard for the staffing needed for sustainable planning, implementation, and monitoring of results on a wider scale. In recent years, the United Kingdom has provided comparatively generous resources for crime-prevention implementation at the municipal level as well as to several specialized NGOs. An evaluation report by Homel et al. (2003), titled *Investing to Deliver,* critiques the lack of a sufficiently strong, multileveled structure ensuring accountable and effective implementation. Independent evaluation of crime-prevention implementation in other countries would probably arrive at similar or, more likely, even more critical judgments. The development of effective and sustainable implementation structures for crime prevention is still in its infancy everywhere (Waller, 2006).

The implementation of evidence-based crime prevention continues to present many challenges to the criminal justice communities of the world. Not the least of these challenges is the need to adapt proven practices designed in developed countries to the special circumstance in developing countries. Important platforms for such adaptation include the International Center for the Prevention of Crime in Montreal, Canada, as well as the Safer Cities Program of UN-Habitat (www.crime-prevention-intl.org). The UN-Habitat Program brought together African mayors in 1998, 2002, and 2003 to exchange experiences and build capacity. The center in Montreal is developing an international training institute. In 2004, UNODC initiated the South-South Cooperation for Determining Good Practices for Crime Prevention in the Developing World, in cooperation with the Institute for Security Studies in South Africa (UNODC, 2004). A valuable example of crime-prevention proposals tailored to local situations in the developing world can be found in a joint UNODC/World Bank report on crime and justice issues in the Caribbean (UNODC, 2007a).

Developing countries can learn much from the mistakes of the West. Rather than launching ambitious programs implementing a wide range of different measures and involving many institutions, governments in the South should focus their efforts on the large-scale implementation of a limited selection of "proven practices." Community-based crime prevention may seem politically appealing, but there is, as discussed above, little ground to believe that it will work better in Third World cities than it did in the West. More viable candidates for crime prevention in the South seem to be the provision of parental support to single parents in vulnerable communities or a selection of situational measures to address violent crime at "hot spots." The new generation of crime-prevention programs should be as technical as possible and follow the model of health programs focusing on the elimination of the well-established risk factors of specific illnesses rather than on promoting health in a general sense.

The implementation of such long-term programs requires, as the Western experience has taught, political commitment from the top and stable organizational structures at all levels of implementation. To have maximum impact, and avoid leakage of funds, crime-prevention efforts in developing countries should, to the greatest extent possible, go hand in hand with much-needed reforms in the security and justice sector. We will return to this crucial issue of security governance in the final two chapters.

❖

SUMMARY POINTS/IN CONCLUSION

- Law enforcement agencies across the world receive two thirds of budgets available for criminal justice in a broad sense. Police forces in developing countries are seriously underfunded considering below-average levels of resources and above-average levels of both common and complex types of crime in Africa, Latin America, and eastern Europe. This underfunding is reflected in comparatively poor performance of these forces as measured by a composite index of police performance combining objective- and perception-based ratings. This result reveals the existence of a serious justice and security deficit in the South.

- Private security firms have grown explosively almost everywhere in response to growing crime rates. Security guards now outnumber public police officers in most parts of the world. The rise of private security has changed the landscape of policing. Private security has the potential to contribute to better crime prevention and control, but in many parts of the world, lack of regulation and quality control make the booming private security industries a mixed blessing for society at large. Private security cannot replace state functions such as criminal investigation respecting fundamental freedoms and rights.

- Important other global trends besides the rise of private policing are the recognition of crime victims as clients of the police and the experimentation with nonpunitive interventions to reduce crime. In North America, western and central Europe, and Oceania, special victim assistance organizations have been set up that cater to the needs of victims of serious crime. Available statistics about their take-up of victims in need of help point to the need to further expand such services and to start introducing them in developing countries.

- Reception and treatment of victims by the police has improved but appears to be slacking in recent years in North America and western Europe. Satisfaction of crime victims with their treatment by the police shows downward trends in countries where specialized victim support is most developed. This trend begs the question whether special services outside the police may have weakened the commitment of the police to render services to victims themselves. Police chiefs in these countries should critically reexamine the quality of their treatment of crime victims.

- Methodologically rigorous testing of the effectiveness of conventional policing and innovative types of interventions has increased the knowledge base about what works and what does not work in reducing crime. Proven practices vary from early support for vulnerable families and their babies and young children to situational measures to prevent crime, including advice to victims for how to prevent repeat victimization. Interventions by police officers focusing on "hot spots" and the elimination of known risk factors have also been proven to be effective.

- Large-scale implementation of measures for which the cost-effectiveness has been demonstrated remains a political challenge. Crime-prevention programs are grossly underfunded and badly organized compared to the justice and security sectors at large. Much bigger improvements in effective crime reduction seem feasible if small parts of available budgets for crime control would be reallocated to the promotion of prevention.

• Efforts to enhance effective policing in developing countries can profit from the newly developed knowledge base on proven practices in crime prevention as well as from errors made in the West in their implementation without sufficient funding. Arguably, the best strategy would be to prioritize large-scale investments in the implementation of proven practices in specific areas such as family care among vulnerable communities or urban planning. A prerequisite for successful anticrime policies would be a sustained drive to enhance the professionalism and integrity of police officers, private security personnel, and crime-prevention practitioners alike.

Notes

1. Among Western countries, the subjective indicators—levels of satisfaction with police performance of the public and of business leaders—were found to be correlated with an objective indicator of police performance, the percentages of all recorded crimes resulting in a conviction (Mayhew, 2003).

2. The North American score on the Police Performance Index is somewhat deflated by the comparatively low homicide conviction rate.

3. The police performance index is, as explained, composed of five variables: (1) Reporting to the police of selected crimes, (2) Were victims satisfied with reporting to the police, (3) Satisfaction with how the police are dealing with crime (all three ICVS 1996–2000), (4) Reliability of police services (WEF, 2004), and (5) Homicide conviction ratio. The last is computed using number of intentional homicides minus number of convictions for intentional homicides (Source: 8th UN Crime Survey).

4. Serious crimes here include burglary, robbery, threats/assaults, and sexual offenses.

5. A factor behind the drop in satisfaction may be the gradual increase of victims reporting by phone or via the Internet. There is some evidence that in England and Wales, victims who have no face-to-face contacts with the police are somewhat less satisfied (Allan, 2005, 2006).

6. The Dutch crime victim survey shows, for example, that the provision of crime-prevention advice to reporting victims has gone down significantly since the 1990s.

7. Contact crimes here include robberies, sexual assaults, and threats/assaults.

8. Data from the records of victim support organizations on their numbers of clients confirm the ranking on percentages of victim/clients according to the ICVS 2005. In New Zealand, for example, about 100,000 victims are assisted annually (population, 4 million). Other countries with comparatively high numbers of victim/clients include England and Wales, Scotland, and the Netherlands.

9. I am indebted to Brandon Welsh (2004) for his exhaustive overview of crime-prevention literature in a paper commissioned by UNODC in the preparation of the report on Trends in Crime and Justice, submitted to the UN Crime Congress in Bangkok in 2005.

10

Courts and Sentencing

Judges and Magistrates

The UN Crime Survey provides information on the number of professional judges or magistrates employed (defined as officials authorized to hear civil, criminal, or other cases, including appeals courts). Functions of judges and magistrates vary across legal systems, and international comparisons must therefore be regarded as indicative only (Newman & Howard, 1999; Reichel, 1994). Figure 10.1 presents information on the number of professional judges/magistrates per 100,000 population per region.

On average, there were approximately nine judges or magistrates per 100,000 inhabitants, worldwide, in 2000. Globally, the number of judges is, just as the number of police officials, positively related to levels of affluence. Well-funded judiciaries seem to be collective goods that only affluent countries can afford. There is significant variation in the number of professional judges per 100,000 inhabitants, from a low of 3 in Africa to a high of 18 in Europe. The results for Africa and parts of Asia indicate that there are comparatively few judges and magistrates per 100,000 inhabitants in these regions, regardless of the legal systems in place. Latin America and the Caribbean also have comparatively fewer judges and magistrates. All subregions in Europe, including eastern Europe, as well as North America have comparatively a large number of judges and magistrates.

Available data from a limited number of countries indicate contrasting trends in the sizes of judiciaries in developing and developed countries. While the number of judges per capita has been stable or declining in many developing countries, the rates have gone up since the 1990s in many developed countries, including transitional countries in Europe.

❖ **Figure 10.1**   Number of Judges per 100,000 Population, by Region, 1997–2002

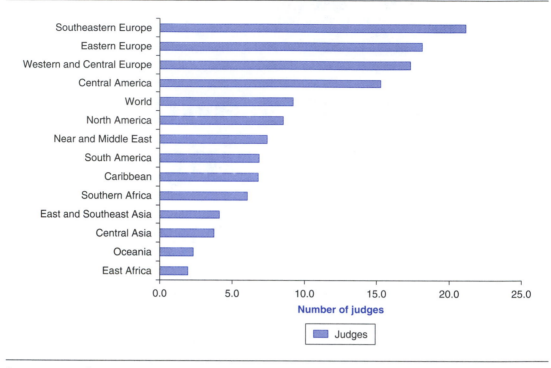

Source: www.unodc.org; UN Crime Survey, 2002, or latest available.

Table 10.1 shows world rankings on number of judges per 100,000 population. Several countries with the highest number of judges apply or have, until recently, applied socialist law modeled after the legal system of the Soviet Union. In the framework of the socialist law system, judges have a comparatively low status as civil servants and receive very modest remuneration. Among Western countries, the lowest rates of judges and magistrates are found in countries practicing common law (United Kingdom, United States, Australia, and New Zealand) as opposed to codified, civil law.[1] The judiciary of Germany is also comparatively extended. This feature can be seen as a deliberate move to break away from the lawlessness under the Nazi regime. Globally, most of the countries with the lowest rates of judges were those with common law, for example, the United Kingdom, Singapore, Malaysia, and Zimbabwe. These low rates are not accounted for by higher rates of lay judges in common-law countries. On the contrary, lay judges tend to be more common under the civil law system. Lay judges are particularly prominent in many African judiciaries.

Separate data have been collected in the same UN surveys about the number of prosecutors per capita. The vastly different roles of prosecutors across types of legal systems preclude a useful comparison. Prosecutors are most numerous in the countries of eastern and central Europe where they had an important, wide-reaching role in the former

❖ Table 10.1   World Ranking of Countries According to Number of Judges per 100,000 Population

Fifteen Countries With High Scores								
1	Russian Fed.	46.7	6	Czech Republic	26.6	11	Greece	20.5
2	Croatia	40.2	7	Germany	25.3	12	Poland	20.5
3	Slovenia	39.4	8	Hungary	25.1	13	Bulgaria	20.0
4	Andorra	35.2	9	Slovak Republic	23.6	14	Sweden	19.1
5	Macedonia, FYR	31.4	10	Belgium	23.0	15	Lithuania	18.3
Fifteen Countries With Moderately High Scores								
18	China	15.9	38	Colombia	9.4	52	Thailand	4.8
21	Portugal	13.5	40	Turkey	8.7	54	Argentina	4.7
25	Finland	13.1	42	Spain	8.4	55	South Africa	4.4
28	Italy	11.8	46	Israel	6.8	57	Chile	4.2
32	United States	10.4	49	Canada	6.6	61	Guatemala	3.4
Fifteen Countries With Low Scores								
62	Saudi Arabia	3.2	67	United Kingdom	2.2	72	Namibia	0.7
63	Ireland	2.8	68	Hong Kong	2.1	73	Zimbabwe	0.6
64	Venezuela, RB	2.6	69	Singapore	2.1	74	Tajikistan	0.5
65	Japan	2.4	70	Philippines	2.0	75	Papua New Guinea	0.3
66	Myanmar	2.4	71	Malaysia	1.5	76	Ethiopia	0.2

Source: www.unodc.org, 8th UN Crime Survey.

socialist legal system. Prosecutors are also more common in civil law than in common-law countries where law enforcement traditionally carries out many prosecution functions. In this respect, the U.S. system of district attorneys is more similar to the civil law system of continental Europe. Available trend data once again indicate steep increases since the 1970s in the developed countries and more or less stable rates elsewhere.

The judicial systems of many developing countries are vastly understaffed. One important indicator of judicial overburdening is the percentage of inmates "awaiting trial." In Africa, about one third of inmates are awaiting trial, a significantly higher percentage than in most other parts of the world (UNODC, 2005). These high percentages of inmates in pretrial detention are largely the result of delays in court proceedings, due to lack of judges or even of material resources such as office supplies (Schaerf, 2003).

Gender Balance in the Courts

Information is collected in the UN Crime Surveys on the extent to which women participate in the criminal justice workforce as police officers, prosecutors, judges, or corrections officers (Mayhew, 2003; Newman & Howard, 1999). The number of countries providing information on this issue in the 8th Survey was unfortunately rather low. Three general trends can be observed in the data. First, the percentage of women is higher in developed countries than in developing countries. Second, female participation is generally on the increase; and third, female participation everywhere is highest in judiciaries and prosecutorial offices (globally, around 25%–30%) and lowest in police forces (around 10%), with percentages in corrections in between (15%).

The overall conclusion cannot be other than that, globally, justice and security sectors are still a male-dominated sector (Mayhew, 1998). If there is truth in the assumption that female officials are less likely to support corrupt practices, as discussed in Chapter 7, the almost exclusively male composition of police forces in many countries might be an impediment to improving professional integrity. Following this logic, the traffic police in Mexico City was some years ago transformed into an all-female force in an attempt to curb petty corruption.

The data in Table 10.2 data show the regional percentages of female judges in the period 1997 to 2002.

❖ Table 10.2   Proportion of Female Judges (2002 or latest available year)

World	25%
Sub-Saharan Africa	15%
Americas	42%
Asia	21%
Europe	50%
Oceania	17%

Source: www.unodc.org, 8th UN Crime Survey.

The data over the years 1997 to 2002 show fairly stable proportions of female judges. Within Europe, the proportions are higher in central and eastern Europe, where judges are relatively poorly remunerated compared to those in western Europe. The highest proportions of female judges were reported by Latvia (70%) and Romania (69%). Many countries in southeastern and central Europe reported percentages above 60%. Exceptionally low percentages of female judges were reported by some African countries and by the United Kingdom (12% in 2002) and Malta (4%).

Perceived Independence and Integrity of the Judiciary

The United Nations, as well as regional organizations and human rights organizations, has focused attention on the reform of the courts in developing countries. They have stressed the crucial importance of strong and independent courts for the consolidation of the rule of law and the protection of human rights, and particularly for provision of justice for the underprivileged. Judges also play a crucial role in tackling organized crime and high-level corruption by ensuring unbiased rulings in trials against powerful defendants (Jamieson, 2000).

In the WEF surveys, discussed before, business leaders are asked to rate the extent to which the judiciary in their country is "independent from political influence of members of government, private persons or firms." In the same survey, respondents are asked about the extent that "firms make undocumented extra payments or bribes connected with getting favorable judicial decisions." Business executives are, in other words, probed about the prevalence of judicial corruption. The country scores on "judicial independence" and "judicial corruption" were almost perfectly correlated in the data set of 2003–2004 ($r = .92$, $n = 102$). In countries where the judiciary is not seen as independent from undue political pressure, it is invariably also perceived to be financially corruptible. We have therefore decided to focus our analyses on the item of "political independence." The scores on this single item can also be used as a proxy indicator of corruptibility. Regional scores for 2003 are given in Figure 10.2.

❖ **Figure 10.2**   Political Independence of National Judiciaries From Undue Pressure According to Business Executives, by World Region (high scores indicating high independence)

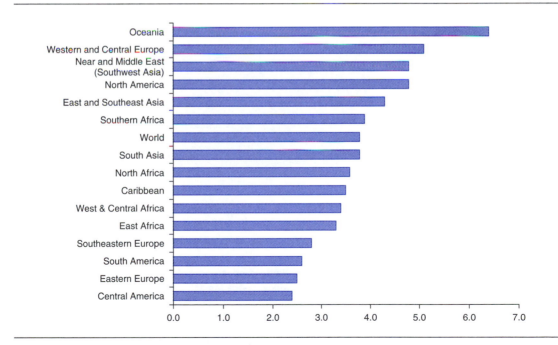

The regional distribution of the scores is similar to that of the composite Police Performance Index presented in Figure 9.12 in Chapter 9. The best-performing judiciaries are those in Oceania, Western Europe, the Middle East, and North America. In many developing countries, the independence of the judiciary—as well as its incorruptibility—is perceived as fairly low, especially in the Caribbean, Africa, and Latin America. Confidence in the judicial systems is also very low in Eastern Europe.

Data on perceived independence of the judiciary have been collected by the World Economic Forum since 1999. The trend data indicate that trust in the independence of the judiciary is declining almost everywhere. Kaufmann reported significant improvements in the industrialized countries of East Asia and deteriorations among many developing countries and countries with economies in transition (Kaufmann, 2004). When the latest data are added, the picture becomes even bleaker. Figure 10.3 shows trends for the period 1999–2005.

❖ **Figure 10.3**   Regional Scores for Perceived Judicial Independence

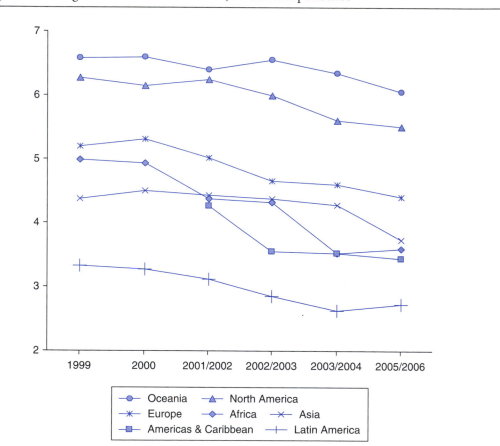

Source: Results of the WEF Business Opinion Surveys, 1999–2005; WEF, 2005. Reprinted with permission of Oxford University Press.

Confidence in the integrity of the judiciaries shows a worldwide deterioration. Even in both Europe and North America, confidence in the judiciaries has slipped since 2000. Particularly striking are the steep downward trends in the Caribbean and Asia. Trust in the judiciary has remained low in Latin America but has not declined further. The average scores of African countries are also lower in the last two WEF surveys than was previously the case, but this is partly explained by the inclusion of more poor African countries in the samples of the last rounds.

The perceived extent of bribery in the judiciary as measured by the WEF surveys also reflects deteriorating rates since 1998 in many developing countries, confirming a negative trend in judicial integrity.

Table 10.3 shows national scores on judicial independence according to business executives. In the category of the 15 countries with the lowest scores on perceived independence of the judiciary, 11 are countries in Latin America. In particular, the judiciaries of Latin America seem to have lost the confidence of the business sector. Other public opinion polls show that only 33.8% of the population in Latin America is reasonably confident in the judiciary, against 65% in Europe and 50% in the United States (Biebesheimer & Payne, 2001). Recent opinion polls in Argentina confirm the

❖ **Table 10.3**   World Ranking of Countries According to Perceived Judicial Independence/Incorruptibility

Fifteen Countries With the Highest Scores								
1	Israel	6.5	6	New Zealand	6.3	11	Botswana	5.9
2	Denmark	6.4	7	Finland	6.1	12	Switzerland	5.9
3	Australia	6.4	8	Germany	6.1	13	United States	5.7
4	Iceland	6.3	9	Sweden	6.0	14	Portugal	5.7
5	Netherlands	6.3	10	United Kingdom	6.0	15	South Africa	5.6
Fifteen Countries With Moderately High Scores								
18	Canada	5.5	43	France	4.4	66	Indonesia	3.2
24	Singapore	5.2	44	Italy	4.4	71	Colombia	3.1
25	Jordan	5.2	52	Brazil	3.9	77	Pakistan	2.8
26	India	5.2	57	Spain	3.8	80	Russian Fed.	2.5
35	Japan	4.7	64	Mexico	3.3	85	Romania	2.4
Fifteen Countries With the Lowest Scores								
87	Macedonia, FYR	2.3	92	Ecuador	1.9	97	Bolivia	1.7
88	Guatemala	2.2	93	Peru	1.9	98	Nicaragua	1.6
89	Panama	2.2	94	Chad	1.8	99	Paraguay	1.4
90	Angola	2.0	95	Argentina	1.8	100	Venezuela, RB	1.2
91	Honduras	1.9	96	Zimbabwe	1.7	101	Haiti	1.1

Source: WEF, 2003-2004. Reprinted with permission of Oxford University Press.

❖ Table 10.4   Percentages of the General Public in Buenos Aires, Argentina, Expressing
Much/Fairly Much, Little, or No Trust in Key Institutions, $n = 300$, August 2004

	Much/Fairly Much	Little	No	Don't Know
Federal Police	15	55	29	1
Supreme Court	13	45	42	
Judiciary	10	53	36	1
BA Police	8	35	55	2
Chamber of Deputies	6	44	49	1
Senate	6	48	46	

Source: David, 2004.

lack of public confidence in the country's security and justice sector (David, 2004). Table 10.4 shows the public's ratings of key institutions in Buenos Aires, the capital of Argentina.

Table 10.4 shows that the general public in Buenos Aires has little or no trust in the federal police and even less in the judiciary and the local police. Trust in the main democratically elected political bodies is almost equally low.

In the Global Corruption Barometer, an international opinion survey commissioned by the Berlin-based NGO of Transparency International, respondents were asked to rate the various key state institutions in terms of corruption. Of the 15 sectors mentioned, judiciaries were, together with the police, seen as the third most corrupted sector after political parties and Parliament. In four countries, Afghanistan, Croatia, Macedonia, and Venezuela, the judiciaries were seen as the most corrupted sector, even before political parties (Transparency International, 2004).

Toward an International Code of Conduct for Judges

A group of chief judges from common-law countries, The Judicial Group on Strengthening Judicial Integrity, expressed at a meeting convened by UNODC during the 10th UN Congress on Crime Prevention and the Treatment of Offenders in Vienna the need for a code against which the conduct of judicial officers could be measured (Langseth, 2002). In a subsequent meeting in Bangalore, India, the group agreed on a code identifying the core values and principles. This code was later amended at a meeting co-organized with UNODC at the Peace Palace in The Hague, the Netherlands, with greater participation of judges from civil law countries. It was approved by the Commission on Human Rights in Geneva. The full text of the document can be consulted at the Web site of UNODC (www.unodc.org). In Nigeria, UNODC carries out a multiyear program to strengthen the integrity of the judiciary that has recently been extended (Langseth & Mohammed, 2002). The federal government has established a national commission to reform the judiciary.

Public Attitudes Toward Sentencing

In the area of criminal justice, one of the crucial roles of the judiciary is the sentencing of offenders. Sentencing tariffs vary significantly across countries with great implications for the size of the prison populations, as will be discussed in the next chapter. Analyses have shown that the severity of sentencing tariffs of national judges tends to be broadly in line with public opinion on the sentencing of offenders (Van Dijk, Mayhew, & Killias, 1990). In countries where sentences are stiffer, the public is more punitive in its attitudes toward offenders. Trends in public attitudes toward sentencing determine to some extent the range of sentencing options available to judges. Monitoring and analysis of such attitudes is therefore of importance for policy making in criminal justice.

In the ICVS, respondents are asked what sentence they consider most appropriate for a recidivist burglar—a man age 21 who is found guilty of burglary for the second time, having stolen a color television. Across regions, community service orders, fines, and prison were the preferred options. Figure 10.4 shows available trends in regional and national percentages of the public in favor of the sentencing option of imprisonment.

Regions show a fairly wide divergence in opinions on the most appropriate punishment for burglars. Prison sentence is the preferred option in Africa, Asia, and, to a lesser extent, Latin America and North America. In Europe and Australia, those favoring imprisonment are in the minority. Community service orders and fines are more often deemed the most appropriate punishment in these countries. Within Europe there is huge variation in support for imprisoning recidivist burglars. Support is most widespread in the United Kingdom (52% in 2005). In many other European countries, less than 20% of the general public opts for imprisonment (e.g., France, 13%; Spain, 17%; Germany, 19%). These intercountry differences in punitiveness have proven to be consistent over time and to be unrelated to demographics. Analyses have shown that popular support for imprisonment is generally somewhat stronger in countries with higher burglary rates. The relationship is not strong, though, with Asian countries showing a distinct preference for imprisonment without experiencing high burglary rates.

The first four rounds of the ICVS showed a general hardening of attitudes toward punishment, especially in Europe and Canada. Support for imprisonment had increased, along with a general decline in support for the sentencing option of community service. No changes were observed in the United States and Australia or in any developing or transitional countries between 1992 and 2000. A hardening of attitudes toward offenders in Europe has been confirmed in national trend studies of public attitudes toward sentencing, for example, in Hungary (Kereszi, 2004). In many countries, an increasingly louder call for tough, punitive action against offenders could be heard since the 1980s. This trend in public attitudes can be seen as another example of the spontaneous mobilization of public opinion in high-crime societies against crime. Those investing private money in self-protection also demand extra efforts against crime from their governments, including more severe sentencing.

Interestingly, this trend has not continued since 2000. According to the ICVS 2005, lower percentages are favoring imprisonment in 2005 than in 1996–2000 in the United

❖ **Figure 10.4** Percentages Favoring Imprisonment for Recidivist Burglar, per World Region and Countries and per Year

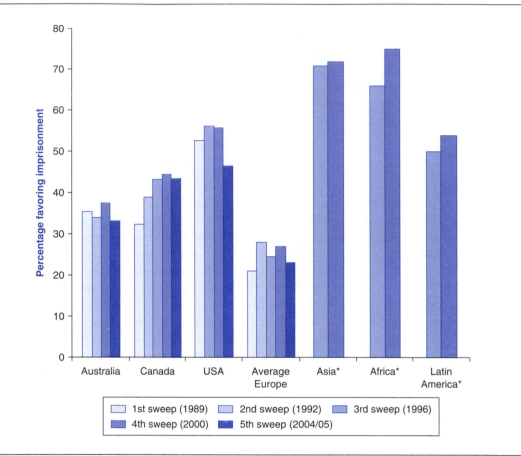

Source: ICVS, 1992–2005.

*Trends for the developing countries are not fully available.

States, Australia, and Europe, as can be seen in Figure 10.4. Public attitudes toward sentencing in Canada and the United States have consequently converged. The gap between North America and Europe remains enormous, though. Figure 10.5 shows the trends in punitiveness of selected European countries for which trend data are available.

The steepest fall in percentages favoring imprisonment has happened in Estonia and Poland. In these country, the public seems to have increasingly distanced itself from the punitiveness that was typical for the communist era. Other European countries with diminished support for imprisonment are Australia, Finland, Belgium, Portugal, and the Netherlands. No changes are shown in public support for imprisonment in the United Kingdom and Sweden. Respondents who opted for a prison sentence were asked

❖ Figure 10.5   Percentages of the Public Favoring Imprisonment in Selected European Countries

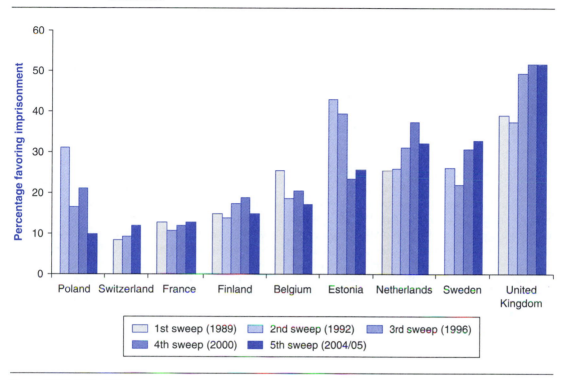

Source: ICVS, 1989–2005.

asked how long this sentence should be. The length of sentence recommended is correlated to the rate of respondents per country who opt for a prison sentence: At the country level, a more punitive attitude also translates into support for longer sentences. A downward trend in public support of imprisonment does not necessarily go together with a more lenient "tariff." The results for the United States are therefore the more striking. Where support for imprisonment went down from 53% in 1989 and 56% in 2000 to 47% in 2004–2005, the recommended length of prison sentences went down from 37 months in 1989 to 28 months in 2004–2005 (Van Dijk, Van Kesteren, & Smit, 2007). If both measures are taken together, the U.S. public has become markedly less punitive over the past two decades, especially since 2000.

The reversal in public attitudes toward sentencing in the United States, Australia, and several European countries may reflect the fact that concerns about burglary and common crime generally have gone down in response to lower rates of actual victimization. This change in public opinion points to a growing willingness to accept the imposition of noncustodial sentences for the offense of burglary.

❖

SUMMARY POINTS/IN CONCLUSION

• Judiciaries perform the crucially important functions of defending civil liberties through due process and adjudicating cases predictably and fairly. Worldwide, the number of judges per 100,000 inhabitants is nine. In developing countries, the rate is considerably lower (two or three). In most countries, the total group of judges comprises no more than a thousand professionals. The comparatively small number of judges in developing countries points to the existence of a justice deficit in the South.

• Most judiciaries of the world are not only poorly resourced and overburdened but professionally challenged as well. In formerly communist countries, judges have low social status. In many developing and transitional countries, judges are deemed to be corrupt by both the business community and the public at large. Loss of confidence in the judiciaries is most striking in South America.

• In spite of a worldwide trend toward more democratic government, in many parts of the world, the professional quality and integrity of judiciaries seem to have deteriorated, at least in the public eye. This is also true for North America and Europe. Deteriorations have taken place most clearly in the Caribbean and in Asia.

• One of the crucial roles of the judiciary in criminal justice is the imposition of criminal sentences. Especially in countries where judges are elected, sentencing tariffs are influenced by public opinion. ICVS results on sentencing preferences of the public show great variation across countries, with respondents in developing countries being more often in favor of imprisonment. Among Western nations, the United States, Canada, Australia, and the United Kingdom stand out with the greatest support for imprisoning the average offender (a recidivist burglar). In these countries, one in two favors imprisonment. In many European countries, including France and Germany, less than one in five opt for such a sentence. In these countries, the majority favors other options such as community service.

• Between 1989 and 2000, attitudes have become more punitive in many European countries. Results of the latest round of the ICVS point to a change in sentencing opinions in many Western countries: In 2005, more people expressed a preference for noncustodial sentences than in 2000. This turnaround in public opinion is most pronounced in formerly communist Estonia but is also in evidence in the United States, Australia, the Netherlands, Belgium, and Portugal, among others. If this trend prevails, public opinion may become less opposed to the use of noncustodial sentences for serious property offenses than was the case over the past decades.

Note

1. For a succinct description of the world's main legal systems, civil law, common law, socialist law, and Islamic law, refer to Newman, 1999.

Corrections

A Global Perspective

Trends in Imprisonment Rates

On the basis of the latest available figures of the World Prison Population List, collated by British criminologist Roy Walmsley, the world imprisonment rate was approximately 147 per 100,000 population in 2004–2006. This figure indicates that at that time, over 9 million people were being held in penal institutions around the world, either as pretrial detainees or after having been convicted.[1] According to informed estimates, the Chinese numbers exclude 610,000 people in "administrative detention" ordered by the prosecutors outside court procedures and another 400,000 people in pretrial detention (Walmsley, 2007). If these estimated dark numbers of Chinese prisoners are added, the world total of inmates can be estimated at 10.2 million. This amounts to the total population of a medium-size country such as Belgium or Portugal. It means that the real global imprisonment rate is about 166 per 100,000 people.

Since many prisoners stay in prison for less than a year, the total number of persons admitted into a prison in the course of a year (admission rate) is higher than the number incarcerated at any date. In many countries, the prison admission rate is three times higher than the imprisonment rate. The total number of people admitted to prisons per year can be estimated at over 20 million worldwide.

Over the past 3 years, prison populations have continued to grow in many parts of the world. Prison populations have risen in 73% of countries included in the World Prison Population List. The largest prison populations according to now-available data are to be found in China (2.55 million, including pretrial detainees and those in administrative detention), the United States (2.19 million in 2005), the Russian Federation (0.87 million in 2006), Brazil (0.36 million in 2005), India (0.33 million in 2004), Mexico (0.21 million in 2006), Thailand (0.16 million in 2005), South Africa (0.15 million in 2005) and Iran (0.15 million in 2006).

Figure 11.1 shows the regional and subregional variation in prison population rates per 100,000 inhabitants. Imprisonment rates per 100,000 residents show modest

❖ **Figure 11.1** Annual Imprisonment Rate per 100,000 Inhabitants per Region and Subregion (2004–2006; latest available)

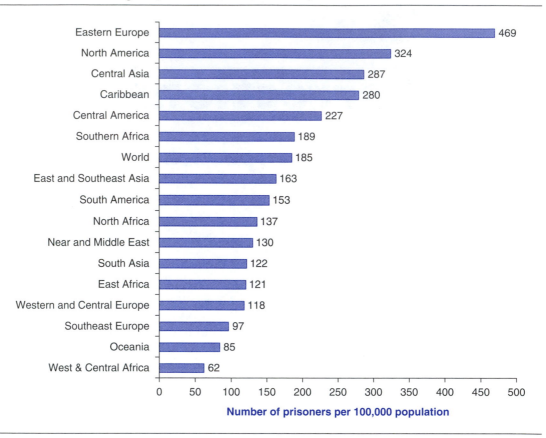

Source: World Prison Population List, UK, 2007.

variation across world subregions with exceptionally high rates in eastern Europe and North America. Above-average rates are also found in central Asia/Caucasus and the Caribbean. The lowest regional rates of imprisonment are found in west and central Africa, Oceania, and southeast Europe.

National Prison Populations

Imprisonment is, besides capital punishment, the most severe form of punishment. The rates of imprisonment per 100,000 population reflect the seriousness of national crime problems but can also be used as a proxy indicator of the punitiveness of national criminal justice systems. We will return to this issue of interpretation below. Table 11.1 shows the national imprisonment rates per 100,000 population of countries.

At the country level, rates per 100,000 population are highest in the United States. Other categories of corrections show equally high figures in the United States. In 2004,

❖ Table 11.1   World Ranking According to Number of Prisoners per 100,000
Population (2004–2006; latest available)

Fifteen Countries With High Rates								
1	United States	701	6	Belize	459	11	Bahamas, The	410
2	Russian Fed.	606	7	Suriname	437	12	South Africa	402
3	Belarus	554	8	Dominica	420	13	Thailand	401
4	Kazakhstan	522	9	Ukraine	415	14	Kyrgyz Republic	390
5	Turkmenistan	489	10	Maldives	414	15	Singapore	388
Fifteen Countries With Moderately High Rates								
18	Estonia	361	68	Mexico	156	75	Spain	138
27	Cuba	297	70	New Zealand	155	108	Germany	98
33	Tunisia	252	74	United Kingdom	141	130	Sweden	73
38	Iran	226	91	China (est. at 166)	117	134	Finland	70
39	Poland	218	92	Canada	116	151	Japan	53
Fifteen Countries With Low Rates								
164	Congo, Rep.	38	169	Mali	34	174	Comoros	30
165	Guinea	37	170	Micronesia	34	175	Indonesia	29
166	Iceland	37	171	Nigeria	33	176	India	29
167	Sudan	36	172	Gambia, The	32	177	Nepal	29
168	Angola	36	173	Solomon Islands	31	178	Burkina Faso	23

Source: World Prison Population List (Seventh Edition), King's College, London, UK, 2007.

a total of 7 million people were in prison or jail or under another form of correctional supervision such as parole or probation (Uggen, Manza, & Thompson, 2006). High rates of imprisonment are also found in countries of the former Soviet Union such as Russia (606), Belarus (544), Kazakhstan (522), and Turkmenistan (489) as well as in Southern Africa (e.g., South Africa, 402) and the Caribbean (e.g., Bahamas, 410). In Asia, Thailand and Singapore stand out with comparatively high rates. At the low end stand countries in western and central Europe, southern Europe, South-Central Asia (e.g., India, 29; Indonesia, 29) and, more surprisingly, West Africa (e.g., Nigeria, 33).

Expanding Use of Imprisonment

Prison populations grew since the late 1980s in most parts of the world. Growth figures vary from 20% in western Europe to 60% or more in the United States, Mexico, Brazil, and Colombia. In the United States, the number of people incarcerated rose by 290% since 1980 (Waller, 2007). Rising crime rates may explain in part these movements in prison populations. In many countries, rates of serious crimes have, however, been fairly stable or decreasing over the past 10 years, as was the case in the United

States and most European countries. Part of the rise in the prison population is therefore attributed by experts to an increasing belief among sentencing decision makers that prison is preferable to its alternatives or perceived to be so by the public (Blumstein, 1993; Waller, 2006). Reviews of factors behind recent major increases in prison populations indicate that the growth is mainly the result of changes in sentencing policies: greater use of imprisonment, longer sentences, and more restricted use of parole or conditional release (Walmsley, 2003b).

In eastern and central European countries, there was, as discussed in Chapter 6, a marked increase in crime after the political transformations in the early 1990s, and this seems to have resulted in the increased use of imprisonment. Since the mid-1990s, crime rates have been mainly stable, whereas the imprisonment rate continues to rise. One of the reasons for this could be that the public, the media, and, subsequently, the politicians were alarmed not just by the rise in crime but by its changing nature. Media reporting on transnational organized crime, corrupt practices, and other economic crimes may have increased a climate of anxiety and indignation, which caused a generalized toughening of public attitudes toward offenders.

An important distinction in prison statistics is between the number of persons incarcerated and the number of persons incarcerated who are convicted (convicted prisoners). In 2002, worldwide 75% of all prisoners were convicted. In some subregions, approximately a third to half the prison population was not convicted (Africa, South America, Central America, Near and Middle East). The low proportions of convicted prisoners indicate that many of those imprisoned in developing countries are awaiting trial. This in turn is, as said earlier, an indication of backlogs in the criminal courts, due to understaffing and heavy workloads.

Interpreting Imprisonment Rates

Imprisonment rates are determined by the level of serious crime in countries and national capacities to investigate and prosecute offenders as well as by sentencing tariffs applied by the courts. Countries with high rates may have especially punitive sentencing tariffs, but this is not necessarily always the case.[2] High rates of imprisonment may be the result of higher levels of serious crime and/or the outcome of more effective action in solving and bringing to justice those who have committed serious crimes on national territory.

The comparative "punitiveness" of national criminal systems—the degree to which they inflict painful punishment on people convicted for crime—is difficult to determine in a global perspective. Such assessment would require a detailed comparison of the processing of cases through the system and specifically of the proportion and average length of custodial sentences and actual time served for equivalent cases of crime. Such comparisons have been made for eight Western countries (Farrington, Langan, & Tonry, 2004). The results show that the United States, although not experiencing higher rates of burglaries and robberies than the other seven countries, has higher conviction rates for arrested burglars and robbers and more often imposes custodial sentences in such cases. Mean actual months served in custody of these groups of convicts are the highest in the United States as well. In terms of punitiveness, Australia seems to come in second place after the United States on this criterion.

The available global statistics do not allow a replication of such refined analysis on a global scale. Previous studies have found that in the Western world, levels of imprisonment are fairly closely linked to the level of serious, violent crime (Haen-Marshall, 1998). In order to put the national imprisonment rates in perspective, we decided to relate the imprisonment rates per 100,000 population to the rates of homicides per 100,000 population. As we have argued above, homicide rates are a reliable indicator of the overall level of violent crime. Homicide rates also reflect reasonably well the extent of organized crime in a country. Homicide rates can therefore be used as a proxy indicator of the overall level of crime punishable by imprisonment in countries in a comparative context. This indicator is especially relevant in a policy assessment of current imprisonment rates since public opinion usually feels that imprisonment should target first and foremost dangerous, violent offenders.

In our data set, the imprisonment rates and homicide rates of countries from 2002 are moderately strongly correlated with each other ($r = .40$, $p < 0.00$, $n = 120$). Countries where imprisonment rates are above average tend to have above-average homicide rates as well. The correlation is, however, only moderately strong. Many countries do not conform to the general pattern. Several countries incarcerate more people per 100,000 inhabitants than the global average, while their domestic levels of serious crime are comparatively modest. High rates of imprisonment seem to be to a fairly large extent the result of discretionary policy choices of governments. This raises the issue of which policy considerations are driving imprisonment rates.

Costs and Limits of Imprisonment

As discussed in Chapter 9, in the section "International Best Practices in Crime Prevention," prison sentences have no proven ability to rehabilitate offenders if not accompanied by treatment or training programs. Recidivism rates are higher than 50% across the Western world. In the United Kingdom, it is estimated that more than half of prisoners commit another crime and more than one third are sent back to prison on another sentence within 2 years of release (Centre for Crime and Justice Studies, 2005). In the United States, two thirds of prisoners are rearrested within 3 years of their release (Langan & Levin, 2002). The support for wider use of imprisonment is no longer based on the belief that prisons are effective houses of rehabilitation. It is more often based on the belief that prison sentences will serve as a deterrent for potential offenders and/or prevent those incarcerated from victimizing members of the community during their stay in prison.

As just mentioned, the number of prisoners per 100,000 inhabitants shows no strong relationship with levels of crime across countries. To the extent that there is a relationship, it is a positive one: Where more people per 100,000 population stay in prison, crime rates tend to be higher and not lower. This positive relationship at the country level does not by itself support the notion that an extensive use of imprisonment reduces overall levels of serious crime. Analyses of trends in imprisonment rates and crime data from the United States have supposedly lent support to the hypothesis that high imprisonment rates reduce crime (Levitt, 1996). Since such studies typically use police-recorded crime data as measures of crime, the results must be interpreted with caution. As explained in previous chapters, trends in police-recorded crime are strongly influenced by recording policies. In some circumstances, increased use of imprisonment may go together with cuts in resources for policing or prosecution, resulting in decreased recording of crimes. Such effects can be ruled out only if the level of crime is measured independently from the police data.[3] To our knowledge, no analyst using crime survey data instead of police data on recorded crimes has demonstrated a negative link between the use of imprisonment and the level of crime, controlling for external factors.

Using data on homicides, Spelman (2006) concludes that the threefold increase in the number of prisoners in the United States may account for 27% of the recent drop in serious violent crime in that country. Current imprisonment rates in Australia are estimated to prevent a quarter additional burglaries through incapacitation (Weatherburn, Hua, & Moffatt, 2006).[4] Although such an impact is considerable in terms of the avoided pain and suffering of victims, it would seem wrong to see it as evidence that "prison works." Similar or greater and more lasting gains could possibly have been obtained with other, more cost-effective means. Decreasing crime rates are occurring across the board in the West, regardless of specific sentencing policies of the countries involved, as discussed in Chapter 6. The Scandinavian countries are a case in point. Levels of all types of common crime are falling, while prison populations have remained modest from a global perspective, and in the case of Finland, they have even significantly declined.

Crime-reducing effects of imprisonment certainly come at a very high cost. In the United States, for example, the costs of prison systems totaled $60 billion in 2001 (Bauer & Owens, 2004), up from $9 billion two decades ago. On a per-prisoner basis, the cost of incarceration averages $22,650 a year. The costs of imprisonment are still growing. A debate is currently ongoing in California and elsewhere in the United States on the optimal cost of punishment, particularly when considering the need for more expenditures on other collective goods such as health care.

The costs of imprisonment extend beyond the expenses reflected in prison budgets. The number of people ever imprisoned exceeds 6 million in the United States (Uggen, Manza, & Thompson, 2006). This group represents 2.9% of the population, 5.5% of the adult male population, and 17% of the black adult male population. For each person sent to prison, family members are left behind and must adjust to new challenges, including loss of income generated by the individual now in prison, new parenting responsibilities, loss of spousal support, and other shifts in social networks. When these costs are examined at a community level, particularly in societies experiencing high levels of imprisonment, these disruptions to normal social functioning can weaken precisely those forces of informal social control that are known to be effective in preventing crime.

A sure consequence of incarceration is the phenomenon of prisoner reentry (Travis, 2005). With the exception of prisoners who die of natural causes or are executed, all individuals sent to prison eventually return to live in free society. Around the world, several million prisoners are released from prison each year. Those societies that have experienced significant increases in rates of incarceration have also witnessed increases in the population of returning prisoners. In the United States, for example, the fourfold increase in incarceration rates over the past quarter century has resulted in a quadrupling of the reentry population, from approximately 150,000 in 1977 to 630,000 in 2002 (Travis, 2005; Travis et al., 2001). The individual, familial, and social challenges of reconnecting large numbers of returning prisoners to the networks of support are significant costs of incarceration policies that are not reflected in simple financial calculations.

The phenomenon of prisoner reentry presents a wide variety of challenges to the returning individuals, members of their families, local communities, and the government. In many countries, those returning from prison are very likely to return to a life of crime. Individuals leaving prison are often highly likely to be unemployed. This, coupled with the stigma attached to a criminal conviction, can hinder returning prisoners as they attempt to gain employment and become productive members of society. Incarcerated individuals are much more likely than others to suffer from a communicable disease, including HIV/AIDS (WHO, 2004). They are liable to be a source of further contamination upon release.[5] Mental health and substance-abuse problems can also plague returning prisoners and prevent their full reintegration into society.

Increases in prison populations often result in overcrowded prison facilities if prison construction does not keep pace with demand. Data collected through the UN Crime Survey show very high occupancy rates in South Asia, sub-Saharan Africa, and Latin America in particular (UNODC, 2005). In Brazil, due to overcrowding of the penitentiary system, approximately 75% of the prison population are in the penitentiary system and 25% are in cells in police stations, which do not have minimum conditions for the incarceration of prisoners (Human Rights Watch, 2004).

These overcrowded facilities may, then, be more difficult to manage, more conducive to violence, more likely to provide opportunities for prison rape, and generally result in further dehumanizing of the prison experience. In the Dominican Republic, for example, deaths in custody are recorded to have gone up from 48 per 10,000 inmates to 68 in 2005 (UNODC, 2007). In the United States, according to a survey in seven prisons, 21% of adult prisoners had experienced rape at least once (Pelton, 2003). In 2003, a first-ever piece of national legislation to address the issue of prison rape was enacted in the United States at the federal level. The law calls for data collection to assess the extent of the problem; the development of national standards for the prevention, treatment, and reduction of prison rape; and the creation of grants for individual states to use to address the problem of prison rape.

In 2005, a select committee of the United Kingdom's House of Commons published a report on an inquiry into the Rehabilitation of Prisoners, partly based on an analysis of prisoners' diaries (UK House of Commons, 2005). One of its main conclusions is that "overcrowding is having a hugely damaging impact on the delivery of rehabilitative regimes across the prison estate, both in terms of quality and quantity of appropriate interventions." The report criticizes the high proportions of prisoners engaged in little or no purposeful activity or work. It recommends better assessments of prisoners' potentials on admission and greater use of day release schemes enabling prisoners to experience work in the community prior to release.

The Search for Alternatives

To address a variety of issues related to increasing incarceration rates and prison over-crowding, many countries have embarked on initiatives to create alternatives to incarceration programs. Some of these initiatives are geared toward providing judges with community-based options that will serve as appropriate sanctions for the crime. Some operate as diversions from the formal criminal justice system. Others, such as halfway houses, temporary-release programs, and furloughs, operate at the back end of the prison system and provide nonincarcerative options for use by correctional administrators and parole boards. Some countries, for example, Finland and Poland, have in recent years successfully embarked on sustained national policies of decreasing the use of incarceration as a response to crime.

It is often assumed by politicians and judges that public opinion will not accept less severe sentencing. As discussed in the previous chapter, the ICVS data on attitudes toward sentencing show that percentages favoring imprisonment as punishment for a recidivist burglar vary greatly across countries and are in recent years decreasing in many. Within the Western world, those countries where the public favors imprisonment, such as United States and the United Kingdom, tend to have higher imprisonment rates. Worldwide, as Figure 11.2 shows, no relationship was found between public attitudes toward sentencing and actual imprisonment rates.

❖ **Figure 11.2** Percentage of Public Favoring Imprisonment of Recidivist Burglars and Actual Imprisonment Rates Around 2000

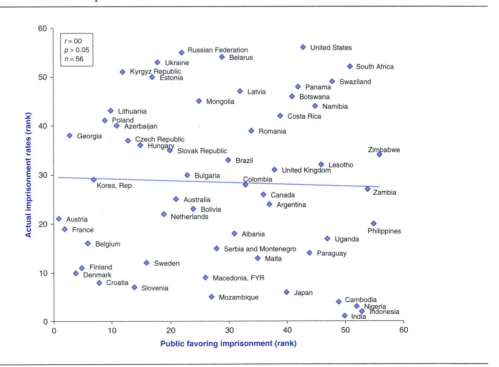

Sources: ICVS: 1996–2005 (national rates), World Prison Population List (Seventh Edition), King's College, London, UK, 2007.

Public opinion survey research supports the broad proposition that the public, when considering whether hypothetical cases should result in a sentence to prison, is more likely to favor a noncustodial sentence when that option is fully developed. Information at the country level has shown that public attitudes are influenced by available sentencing options. If alternative, noncustodial sentences are introduced in a country, the proportion of respondents favoring this option usually goes up sharply in the aftermath. For example, the percentage opting for a community service sentence in Finland increased markedly after 1989, when it was first introduced in the country. In this regard, it is worth pointing out that noncustodial sentences are not widely available in developing countries. Reliance on prison sentences in developing countries seems partly determined by the lack of viable alternatives for which new institutional arrangements would have to be put in place.

Imprisonment rates are very high in Russia and Belarus, while public opinion as measured in the ICVS is comparatively mild. In several central and eastern European countries such as Poland, Ukraine, and the Baltic states, imprisonment rates are comparatively high, while the majority of the public favors noncustodial sentences. The discrepancy between public opinion and sentencing tariffs has grown in recent years since public support for imprisonment has remained stable or has fallen between 2000 and 2005 (Estonia is a case in point). High imprisonment rates seem to be part of the inherited vestiges of the former Soviet Union. In this region, in particular, there seems to be scope for a significant reduction of imprisonment rate without antagonizing public opinion, following the trend set by Finland in the 1990s as well as, more recently, Poland (Krajewski, 2004). In contrast, in some developing countries, imprisonment is the public's punishment of choice but not often implemented in practice, partly because governments cannot afford the resources needed for extended prison systems.

Benchmarking Imprisonment Rates

As discussed above, the statistical link between levels of homicides and imprisonment rates is positive but not very strong. There are countries with high imprisonment rates that do not suffer from high levels of serious crime. The great financial and human costs involved in the use of imprisonment justify a closer examination of these incongruities. The relationship between the two rates can be analyzed in more detail by looking at differences between country rankings on both homicide and imprisonment. For the purpose of benchmarking, countries were classified according to their position in the quintiles of imprisonment rates and of homicide rates, respectively. The Russian Federation, for example, finds itself in the first quintile (top 20%) for both imprisonment rates and homicide rates. Japan is in the fifth quintile on both scores.

Table 11.2 shows an overview of the results, presenting the country's rank numbers on both indicators. This overview allows governments of countries with comparatively high imprisonment rates—those classified in the two columns at the left—to identify at a glance, countries with similar homicide rates but significantly lower imprisonment rates by turning to the right in the same row. To mention a few examples, it may benefit South Africa and Russia to study in more detail the criminal

❖ Table 11.2 Classification of Countries in World Quintiles for Imprisonment Rates and Homicide Rates per 100,000 Population: First rank number refers to imprisonment rate and the second rank number refers to homicide rate (high to low)

	High Imprisonment Rates (top 20%)		Above-Average Imprisonment Rates		Average Imprisonment Rates		Below-Average Imprisonment Rates		Low Imprisonment Rates	
High Homicide Rates (top 20%)	Swaziland	17 1	Jamaica	37 4	Colombia	58 2	Sri Lanka	80 18	Venezuela, RB	90 5
	South Africa	10 3	Brazil	44 8	El Salvador	47 6	Uganda	82 22	Guatemala	94 7
	Puerto Rico	14 9			Mexico	48 14			Ecuador	101 12
	Russian Federation	2 10			Argentina	67 21			Paraguay	91 16
	Kazakhstan	4 11								
	Bahamas, The	9 13								
	Trinidad and Tobago	20 15								
	Estonia	16 17								
	Belarus	3 19								
	Panama	18 20								
Above-Average Homicide rates	Latvia	19 23	Lithuania	24 29	Tajikistan	46 27	Philippines	77 32	Papua New Guinea	97 24
	Ukraine	7 25	Seychelles	32 37	Nicaragua	51 31				
	Turkmenistan	5 26	Guyana	39 40	Zambia	60 34				
	Thailand	11 28	Uruguay	31 41	Tanzania	61 35				
	Kyrgyz Republic	12 30	Costa Rica	26 42	Zimbabwe	45 38				
	Moldova	21 33	Namibia	23 43	Armenia	55 39				
	Barbados	15 36								
	Cuba	22 44								
Average Homicide Rates	United States	1 46	Georgia	34 47	Bulgaria	56 52	Albania	81 45	Cote d'Ivoire	99 51
	Maldives	8 60	Uzbekistan	35 50	Australia	59 59	Andorra	86 48	India	109 54
	Dominica	6 61	Azerbaijan	28 62	Portugal	54 66	Peru	70 49	Nepal	110 55
			Slovak Republic	42 63			Yemen, Rep.	87 53	Switzerland	96 57
			Romania	33 65			Turkey	79 56	Finland	95 64
							Bolivia	71 58	Sweden	92 67

266

	High Imprisonment Rates (top 20%)	Above-Average Imprisonment Rates	Average Imprisonment Rates	Below-Average Imprisonment Rates	Low Imprisonment Rates
Below-Average Homicide Rates		Czech Republic 40 70 Mauritius 29 71 Hungary 41 75 Poland 27 76 Chile 30 82 Tunisia 25 88	Malaysia 59 68 United Kingdom 52 73 Korea, Rep. 57 74 Canada 63 80 Fiji 66 81 New Zealand 49 86 Spain 53 87	Tonga 68 72 France 78 79 Belgium 83 84 Italy 73 89	Macedonia, FYR 100 69 Slovenia 105 77 Croatia 102 78 Malta 93 83 Iceland 108 85
Low Homicide Rates	Singapore 13 100	Hong Kong, China 36 105 Israel 43 107 Morocco 38 108	Bahrain 50 97 Saudi Arabia 65 99 Myanmar 62 110	Germany 76 90 Ireland 84 94 Kuwait 72 95 Netherlands 74 96 Jordan 69 98 Luxembourg 85 101 Austria 75 102 Greece 89 103 Oman 88 104	Norway 103 91 Indonesia 111 92 Denmark 98 93 Japan 106 106 Cyprus 107 109 Pakistan 104 111

Sources: www.unodc.org; 8th UN Crime Survey; World Prison Population List (Seventh Edition), King's College, London, UK, 2007.

and correctional policies of several major Latin American countries. Some of these countries may have been more successful in introducing noncustodial sanctions and forms of mediation. This issue might also be of interest to Puerto Rico. From the countries with high imprisonment rates and above-average homicide rates, Thailand may benefit from learning more about a country like the Philippines, whose ranking on homicide is very similar (32, compared to Thailand, 28) but whose imprisonment rate ranks 77 while that of Thailand is 11. Which factors have allowed the Philippine government to maintain relatively low imprisonment in the face of its high murder rates?

The United States, a country housing almost a quarter of the world's total prison population, ranks first on imprisonment rates and 46th on homicide rates. Possible candidate countries for a benchmarking exercise would be Australia and Finland, whose homicide rates are roughly similar (rankings of 59 and 64, respectively) but whose rankings on prisoners rates are incomparably lower (64 and 95) than the top position of the United States. Homicide rates are not dramatically lower in the United Kingdom or Spain either, two other countries with much lower imprisonment rates. Benchmarking with these countries might provide useful insights for the United States. If the United States would move somewhat in the direction of the imprisonment rates of a country such as the United Kingdom, such a policy would potentially produce savings of several tens of billions of dollars of government expenditures per year. The benchmarking will, among other things, reveal that levels of (serious) crime are falling in these referenced countries as fast as in the United States. They seem as successful as the United States in reducing crime while maintaining much lower imprisonment rates.

Such benchmarking might also be of interest to countries with medium-high imprisonment rates such as the United Kingdom. It seems interesting to examine in more detail and depth why the United Kingdom ranks 52 on imprisonment rates and Sweden ranks 92, while the UK homicide rates are lower than those of Sweden.

For a quick assessment of countries' positions in the two-dimensional universe of homicide and imprisonment, Figure 11.3 shows the relative positions of countries on both indicators in the form of a scatterplot. Countries showing above-average imprisonment rates without above-average or even with below-average homicide rates are depicted in the upper left corner (Singapore, Tunisia, Hong Kong). These countries may see reason to critically reexamine their sentencing policies, specifically with regard to the use of imprisonment. From a global perspective, their prison population seems out of proportion with the seriousness of their domestic-crime problems.

Similarly, countries with below-average imprisonment rates and above-average homicide rates—depicted in the bottom right corner—may see reason to reassess their sentencing tariffs, which seem lenient from a global perspective. This group includes Venezuela, Guatemala, and Albania. Most of these countries show below-average scores on the Police Performance Index (shown in Chapter 9). Their below-average imprisonment rates may partly be the result of low effectiveness of their law enforcement agencies in investigating serious crime rather than of lenient sentencing.

In the countries in the upper right corner, such as South Africa, Russia, and several other eastern European and central Asian countries, above-average imprisonment rates are matched by above-average levels of serious crime. This seems also the case in

❖ **Figure 11.3**   Ranking of Countries on Prison Population per 100,000 Population and on Homicide Rates per 100,000 Population

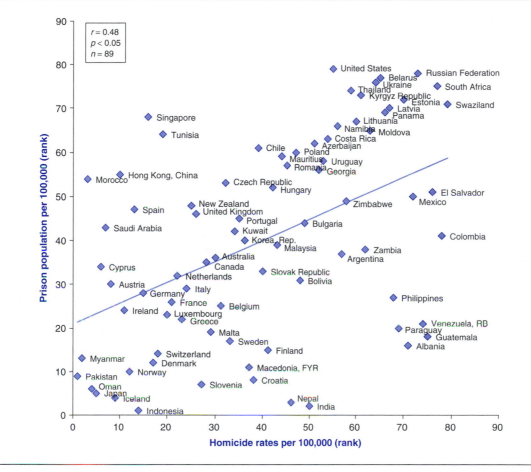

Sources: www.unodc.org; 8th UN Crime Survey; World Prison Population List (Seventh Edition), King's College, London, UK, 2007.

Thailand and in some Caribbean countries (Trinidad and Tobago, and Barbados). The imprisonment rates of these countries would seem driven more by the extent of their domestic-crime problems than by sentencing policies that are unusually severe from a global perspective.

Countries in the bottom left corner combine low imprisonment rates with low levels of violent crime. Almost all are western European countries. Non-Western countries in this group are Japan, Pakistan, and Indonesia. The low level of homicides in Pakistan may have been, however, a statistical artifact caused by underreporting and underrecording.

An Index of Punitiveness

For statistical analyses, a single indicator of the punitivity or severity of criminal policies of countries would be useful. To obtain such a proxy indicator, rank numbers for imprisonment rates (from low to high) were subtracted from homicide rank numbers per country (also from low to high). Countries with higher positions on homicide than on imprisonment rates obtained positive net scores. Such scores reflect that from a global perspective, imprisonment rates in these countries are relatively low considering their homicide rates. Such incongruity possibly indicates relatively mild sentencing policies. Ecuador ranked highest on this index. Of the major countries, Colombia and India scored in the top 10. In these countries, too, relatively high homicides rates are not accompanied by high imprisonment rates.

Countries with higher positions on imprisonment rates than on homicide rates obtained negative values, possibly indicating severe sentencing or punitiveness. Singapore, a country with low homicide rates and a high imprisonment rate, came out as the country with the highest negative score. The United States was ranked 12 out of 108. Japan is the only country whose rank number on imprisonment is exactly the same as the one on homicide (106). From a global perspective, that country's use of imprisonment seems to be perfectly balanced with its level of homicides. Other countries with fairly balanced rates are Australia and Denmark.

The scores of individual countries on this proxy indicator cannot, of course, be taken at face value. Like the country scores on the index of organized crime presented earlier, the scores should be used as a diagnostic tool. High scores should first of all be an inducement for further fact-based analysis. Appendix B shows the rankings of countries on the indicator of punitiveness.

To explore the possible correlates of the degree of punitiveness of countries as measured by discrepancies between ranking on homicide rates and imprisonment rates, we looked at the correlations between this "net ranking," ranging from extremely high positive net values to the highest negative values, and the human development index. This exploration revealed that punitiveness is positively correlated with human development ($r = .33$). In other words, more-affluent nations tend on average to be somewhat less restrained with the use of imprisonment, controlling for levels of homicide. This finding suggests that the extended use of imprisonment is in part a luxury that poor countries cannot afford. This finding explains the puzzling positive link between democratization and more resources for prisons found by Sung (Sung, 2006). While more authoritarian societies may ideologically support extended use of imprisonment, budgetary constraints often prevent them from actually expanding their prison systems. Democratic governments may have reservations about imprisonment but are less constrained to expand prison capacity by lack of funds.

One other explanation for the comparatively extensive use of imprisonment in some developed countries could be a comparatively high prevalence of drug-related prison sentences (UNODC, 2005). Drug consumption tends to be more prevalent in more-affluent countries. Since much drug-related crime is not violent in nature, its prevalence is not adequately reflected in homicide rates. On the other hand, sentences for drug-related offenses show huge variation across developed countries regardless of the prevalence of drug abuse. Longer prison sentences for drug offenses seem based more on political considerations than on the severity of national drug problems.

The most plausible explanation for the link between human development and imprisonment rates seems to be that affluent countries can simply better afford the funding of large prison populations than poorer ones can. In this light, extensive use of imprisonment can be seen as a collective "luxury good." Some of the major nations with disproportionately large prison populations such as the United States and Russia could probably achieve better returns on their investments in security if they reallocated part of their expenditures on prisons to other areas in the security and justice sector such as better, intelligence-led law enforcement, innovative crime prevention, and, last but not least, more generous victim assistance.

❖

SUMMARY POINTS/IN CONCLUSION

• At the latest count, more than 10 million people are detained in prisons or jails worldwide. One of the most striking trends in modern criminal justice is that in spite of newly introduced types of sanctions and experiments with crime prevention, prison populations have persistently grown across the world since 1980. The country with the highest imprisonment rate per 100,000 is the United States (710). This has not always been the case. Thirty years ago, the U.S. imprisonment rate stood at 149, not much higher than that of the United Kingdom at the time.

• Incarceration of offenders can contribute to better crime control. The contribution of incarceration to the recent drop in violent crime in the United States has been estimated as 27%. Costs of prisons are huge though. They can first be expressed in financial terms. The total bill for incarceration for the U.S. taxpayers was $61 billion in 2003 and is still growing (Waller, 2007). Other, more hidden costs are borne by the prisoners and their families. Violence and sexual abuse are rampant in prisons across the world, and so is contamination by HIV/AIDS and other blood-borne diseases. Upon their release, ex-prisoners are often socially and medically handicapped and may erode social control in already vulnerable neighborhoods.

• The rise of prison populations is often portrayed as the inevitable result of rises in violent crime and subsequent popular demand for a tougher, more effective stance of the government. International comparisons bring to light that some governments have given in to these external pressures more than others. Many countries experiencing similarly high rates of serious crime have maintained prison populations that are modest compared to those of the United States or the United Kingdom.

• Across the Western world, levels of crime have recently decreased, regardless of the sizes of national imprisonment rates. Crime has dropped off as steeply as in the United States in countries that have reduced reliance on imprisonment such as Poland, Finland, and France. These comparative findings may give American taxpayers food for thought. According to the latest ICVS findings, popular support for imprisonment is declining, also in the United States. This turnaround in public opinion may create the political space for a critical reexamination of sentencing tariffs introduced in the 1970s that have caused the imprisonment boom.

Notes

1.   Data on prison populations from the UN Crime Surveys and from other international sources as well as from national prison administrations can be found in the World Prison Population List (maintained by Roy Walmsley of King's College, University of London (www.prisonstudies.org) (Walmsley, 2000, 2003, 2007). Figures in the latest World Prison Population List are for 2004 up to October 2006.

2.   A feature of punitiveness as a national characteristic is the retention of capital punishment. Globally, the trend toward abolition continues. The number of completely abolitionist countries was 77 in 2003. The number of countries that can be considered de facto abolitionist has further increased from 33 to 37. The overall number of retentionist countries decreased from 71 to 66. The latter list includes some of the most populous countries in the world: China, Egypt, India, Indonesia, Iran, Japan, Nigeria, Pakistan, South Korea, Thailand, the United States, and Vietnam (Source: United Nations Economic and Social Council E/CN.4/2004/86, January 23, 2004, Commission on Human Rights, Status of the International Covenants on Human Rights, "Question of the death penalty," Report of the Secretary-General submitted pursuant to Commission resolution 2003/67). In 2007, Morocco decided as one of the first Arabic countries to abolish capital punishment. According to Amnesty International, in 2005, 2,148 people were executed worldwide, of which 1,770 were in China, 94 in Iran, 86 in Saudi-Arabia, and 60 in the United States.

3.   Levitt's study is based on an analysis of police-recorded crime in periods following the pardoning of prisoners after local elections. Since local elections often are followed by the appointment of new police chiefs, it is likely that local policing policies show changes after elections (Waller, 2006). Higher rates of police-recorded crimes after local elections may reflect the impact of newly introduced standards for detecting and recording crimes rather than changes in actual crime.

4.   Calculations of the effects of incarceration typically count the numbers of offenses committed by offenders with similar careers that have not been incarcerated. It is assumed that imprisonment has prevented these crimes from happening. This approach ignores the possibility that on major crime markets such as those related to drug trafficking and peddling, arrested offenders are replaced by competitors who will commit similar rates of offenses.

5.   Prison populations are at an extremely high risk to be infected by the HIV virus through the common practice of sharing (unclean) needles for drug injecting and tattooing as well as through unsafe sex, especially sexual abuse among men (Martin et al., 1998). Hygienic conditions may get worse due to overcrowding and budget cuts, and basic medical services are often insufficient to address risks of contamination (Muller et al., 1995). For these reasons, prisons have been called the ideal incubators of the HIV virus. In South Africa, over 40% of all national prisoners are said to be HIV-positive. Double-digit percentages are also reported from Russia, other eastern and central European countries, Brazil, Argentina, Indonesia, and Iran (Aceijas et al., 2004). Within the European Union, Spain reports a 25% and Italy a 17% HIV infection rate among national prison populations (Aceijas et al., 2004). The HIV virus can spread explosively within a prison setting in a period of months. One of the latest penitentiary mini-epidemics took place within a prison in Lithuania in 2003, where

the rate of infection went from zero to 90% within months (UNAIDS/WHO, 2002). In many countries, there is an urgent need for more voluntary HIV testing in prisons and the provision of harm-reduction measures, such as information, condoms, bleach, and, wherever domestically permitted, clean needles and methadone substitution treatment (International Federation of the Red Cross, 2003). The international scientific evidence shows that such measures can stem the spread of the virus in prison settings without unintended negative consequences (WHO/UNAIDS/UNODC, 2004).

PART V

International Perspectives on Crime and Justice

12

Security, Rule of Law, and Sustainable Development

Introductory Remarks

In Chapter 9, we have cast doubt on the common belief that the level of common crime in society is a function of the effectiveness of law enforcement. As discussed there, our Composite Police Performance Index (PPI), integrating both subjective and objective measures of effectiveness, showed only a weak link with overall victimization by common crime ($r = -.32$).[1] Levels of volume crime seem more determined by social macro factors such as urbanization, social inequality, use of antiburglary measures, alcohol abuse, and availability of guns than by the quality of domestic law enforcement and/or the administration of criminal justice. Evidence-based crime reduction is therefore focused on improvements in situational and social crime prevention rather than on more or smarter policing alone.

In earlier chapters, we have also refuted the notion that high levels of crime always go together with poverty. The relationship between economic development and levels of common crime is a complex one. In some respects, rises in common criminality can even be seen as the downside of newly acquired riches of modern society such as cars for private transportation.

In this chapter, we will focus our attention on the relationships between institutional, economic, and social factors and complex crimes such as organized crime and corruption. We will first try to understand the impact of legal institutions on organized crime and grand corruption. Possibly police performance is more key to the control of such complex crimes than to the control of common crime. We will then look at the relationships between organized crime–corruption and sustainable development. It may be the case that common crime does not stem from poverty but that poverty stems from (complex) crime's negative impact on governance.

Legal Institutions and the Level of Complex Crime

Is there less organized crime and corruption where relevant domestic institutions are better funded and functioning better? To empirically explore the links between institutional performance and the levels of complex crime, indicators of performance must be correlated with indicators of complex crime. In previous chapters, we have described our Composite Index of Organized Crime and our Composite Police Performance Index. Scores on these two indices were correlated with each other in the form of a scatterplot. Figure 12.1 presents results of the analysis.

The results are strikingly different from those found for common volume crime. At the macro level, the relationships between police resources and performance and the level of common crime are tenuous. In contrast, the extent of organized crime–related activities is strongly, inversely related to the performance of the police ($r = -.67$, $p < 0.000$, $n = 113$). Where domestic police forces are more effective, the organized crime–corruption nexus is less prevalent.

Our police performance index does not specifically measure the capacity to investigate complex crime. One of the indicators used in the Composite Police Performance Index is the clearance rate for homicides. The investigation of homicides outside the domestic sphere is usually in the hands of specialized units. Countries scoring favorably on the performance index will usually have established elite task forces or units within their police and prosecution services to counter organized crime and corruption. The strong inverse correlation with the organized-crime index suggests that the operations of such units make a difference indeed.[2]

In the countries depicted in the corner at the upper left, scores on the organized-crime index are worse and as well as those on police performance. Organized crime is more rampant here than elsewhere in the world, and the police seem least able to counter the threat. The most problematic countries in these respects are Haiti, where law and order was on the brink of collapse in 2005 and has not yet been fully restored in 2007, and Pakistan, a country without a functioning police organization under control of the central state.

The strong relationship between police performance and organized crime was upheld after controlling for the influence of other explanatory factors such as level of human development (Buscaglia & Van Dijk, 2003). Independently of other factors, organized crime is more prevalent where police are less effective in fighting crime. Similarly, strong relationships were found between police performance and the prevalence of high-level corruption, using indicators collated by the World Bank Institute.

The contradictory finding that police performance is inversely and strongly related to levels of organized crime but only weakly to volume crime suggests that law enforcement performs different functions in the containment of these two types of crime. To effectively reduce volume crime, law enforcement must offset powerful and deeply rooted social causes of crime through deterrence and rehabilitation directed at large pools of juvenile

❖ **Figure 12.1** Country Scores on Composite Police Performance Index and on Composite Index of Organized Crime in the Country

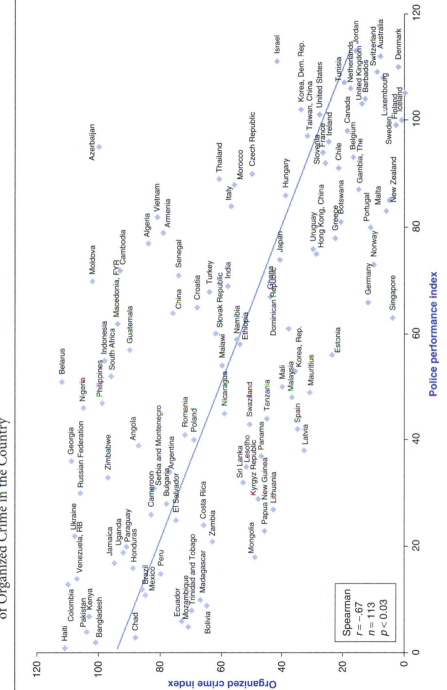

Sources: See Figures 7.4 and 9.12.

delinquents and habitual offenders. With clearance rates for volume crime below 10% in most countries and falling, the contribution of traditional law enforcement to the control of common crime can only be modest, as concluded in Chapter 9.

On theoretical grounds, police units possess better prospects for success with detecting and disrupting criminal organizations. Such types of criminals are easier to target since they carry out their criminal activities over a time span of several years or even decades on a given territory or on specific criminal markets. Their need to launder money, reinvest assets in the licit economy, and secure protection through corrupting public officials offers additional points of entry for criminal investigation. Finally, leaders of organized-crime groups are vulnerable because of their tendency to flaunt their riches to overcome stigma.

The results of both the statistical analyses and case studies of the fight against local Mafias in, for example, Marseille (drugs/pizza connection), New York City (racketeering/Cosa Nostra), Sicily (Mafia), Colombia (drug cartels), Mexico (drug cartels), Hong Kong (triads), and Kosovo (drugs and human trafficking) confirm the great potential of law enforcement and criminal justice in controlling the organized crime–corruption nexus when sustained and comprehensive efforts are made (e.g., Finkenauer, Fuentes, & Ward, 2001; Gonzalez-Ruiz, 2001; Jacobs, 1999; Orlando, 2001; Wilson, 2006).

The analysis of the correlates of organized crime yields different findings from those regarding volume crime in some other respects as well. Unlike conventional volume crime, organized crime is not positively related to the level of urbanization. In fact, the correlation goes in the other direction, with less urbanized countries reporting higher levels of organized crime. As discussed earlier, the relationship between affluence and common crime was found to be complex and, on balance, fairly weak at the country level. Organized crime, however, is clearly inversely correlated with human development. Organized crime is much more prevalent in developing countries and countries with economies in transition than in the more-affluent countries.

Organized Crime and the Rule of Law

Considering the well-documented, crucial role of independent and committed prosecution services and judiciaries in tackling organized crime and corruption (Joly, 2003; Orlando, 2002), special attention was given to the relationship between the rule of law, including perceived independence of the judiciary, and the level of organized crime. As a measure of the rule of law, a composite index was used that was developed by the World Bank Institute (Kaufmann, Kraay, & Mastruzzi, 2004). Figure 12.2 shows the relationship between country values on this index and our composite index indicating national levels of organized crime.

Figure 12.2 shows that the two indices are almost perfectly correlated ($r = -.89$). Manifestations of organized crime are more prevalent in countries where the rule of law is less well assured, and vice versa. There are very few exceptions to this rule.

A separate analysis was made of the relationship between the organized-crime index and the perceived independence of the judiciary specifically (WEF, 2003). The latter indicator is more narrowly defined and shows no conceptual overlap with organized crime. The two variables were found to be almost equally strongly correlated

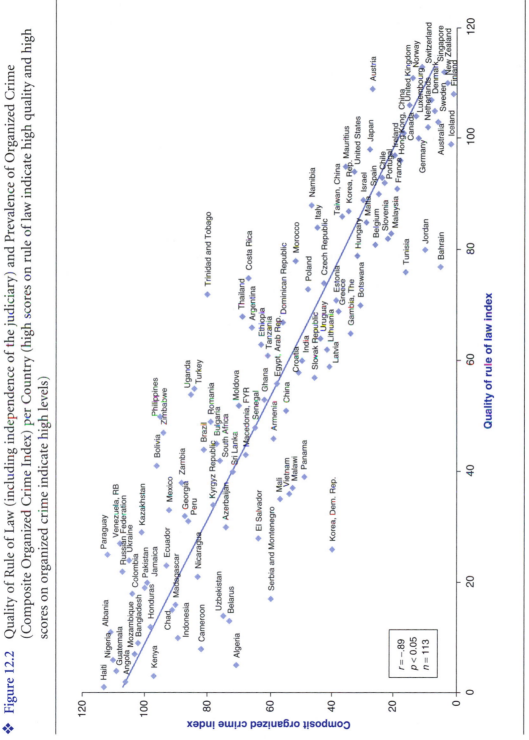

❖ **Figure 12.2** Quality of Rule of Law (including independence of the judiciary) and Prevalence of Organized Crime (Composite Organized Crime Index) per Country (high scores on rule of law indicate high quality and high scores on organized crime indicate high levels)

Sources: For Kaufmann, Kraay, & Mastruzzi, 2004, see www.worldbank.org/wbi/governance/govdata; for COCI, see Figure 7.4.

($r = 0.79$). Multivariate analyses confirmed the relationship between the measure of judicial independence and levels of organized crime. Previous analyses showed furthermore that independence of the judiciary was the single most important predictor of the extent of organized crime (Buscaglia & Van Dijk, 2003; Sung, 2004).

The critical factor determining the extent of organized crime seems to be the quality of institutions responsible for the rule of law, including competent police services and independent courts complying with high standards of professionalism and integrity. These results signify that criminal justice systems probably play a significantly larger role in shaping the phenomenon of organized crime and related high-level corruption than in determining levels of volume crime. Well-performing police services and independent, professional judiciaries seem to make a difference in controlling complex crime. The role of the criminal justice system in fighting common crime has perhaps in the past been somewhat overrated by the public. But in matters of complex crime, including the organized crime–corruption nexus, the importance of criminal justice seems underrated. One possible explanation for the lack of recognition of the role played by specialized police and prosecution units in curbing organized crime may be persistent negative media publicity about alleged corruption and abuse of power by such units. In Mafia-infested countries, much of this publicity is based on deliberate disinformation campaigns from local organized-crime groups and their associates in the media and politics. Even when such units are winning the battles with the Mafia in court, they are often losing it in the media-led public mind.

Rule of Law and Terrorism

Explorative analyses by terrorism experts have yielded indications of a possible negative link between indicators for the rule of law in a country and prevalence of terrorist incidents. Where the rule of law is insufficiently assured, terrorist incidents tend to be more frequent (Gupta, 2001; Schmid, 2005). Gupta's multivariate analysis suggested that terrorism was best explained by the lack of civil and political rights, followed by a high perceived prevalence of corruption. Schmid found a moderately strong relationship between his index of terrorism and a measure of the observance of human rights, ranging from countries with secured rule of law and human rights observance to countries with generalized state repression.[3]

The analyses of Gupta and Schmid were repeated by us using the index of "costs of terrorism for business" from the WEF business executives' surveys. This WEF-based indicator covers more countries than the indices of incidents per country in specialized databases such as that of RAND (WEF, 2003, 2004).[4] As an indicator of the rule of law, we used the World Bank index (Kaufmann, Kraay, & Matruzzi, 2003). Figure 12.3 shows the results in the form of a scatterplot.

Figure 12.3 confirms that terrorism is more common, or perceived to be so, in countries where the rule of law is less well institutionally assured. Outliers are a group of developed countries, including the United States and Israel, that are mainly exposed to international terrorism. The WEF index of perceived costs of terrorism for business refers to costs of both domestic and international terrorism. It seems likely that indices focusing exclusively on domestic terrorism would show even stronger relationships between the quality of the rule of law in countries and terrorism.

❖ **Figure 12.3** Quality of Rule of Law and Perceived Cost of Terrorism per Country (low scores on rule of law indicate high quality and high scores on cost of terrorism indicate high prevalence)

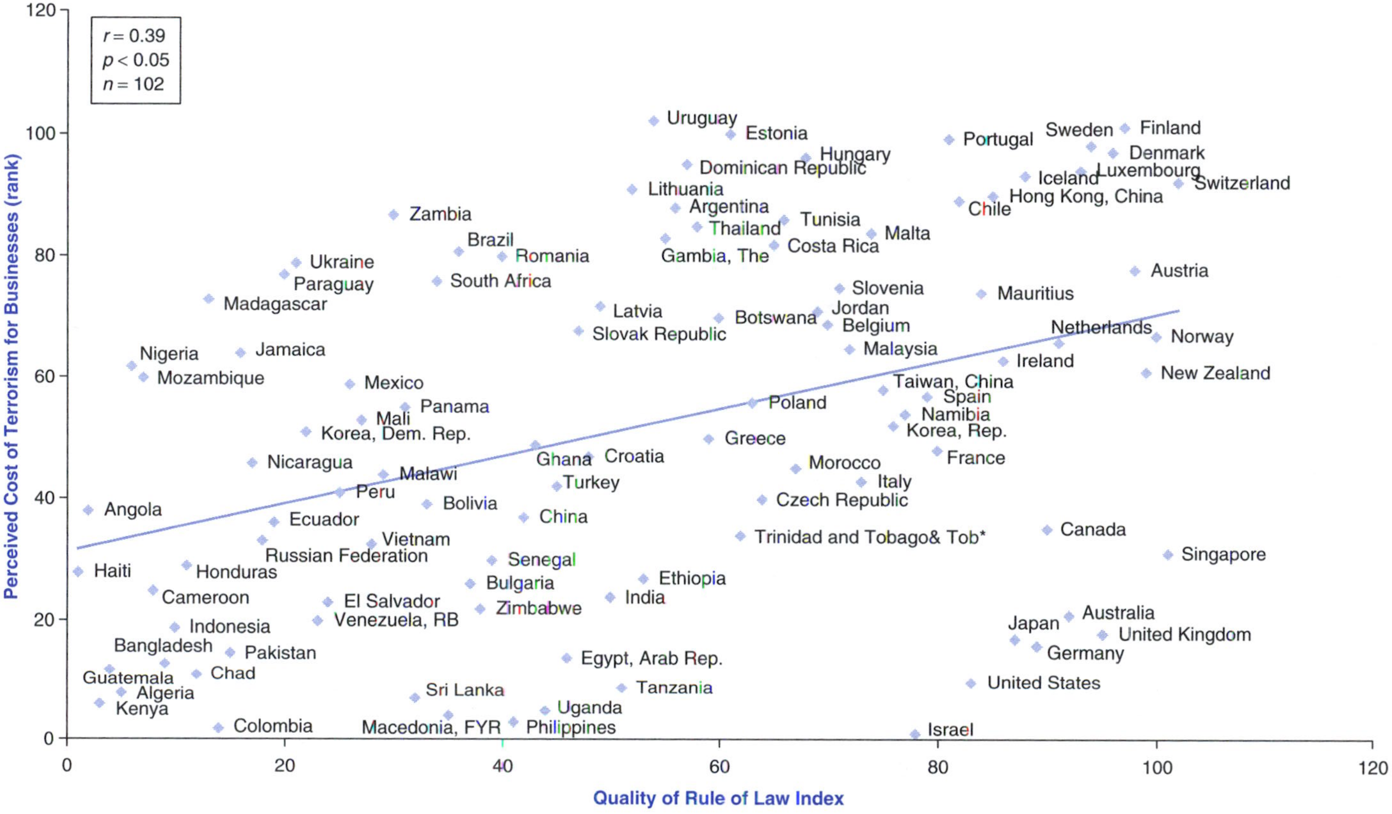

r = 0.39
p < 0.05
n = 102

Perceived Cost of Terrorism for Businesses (rank)

Quality of Rule of Law Index

Sources: WEF, 2003; Kaufmann, Kraay, & Mastruzzi, 2004; see www.worldbank.org/wbi/governance/govdata; and the rule of law index (WBI).

Kaufmann (2005), in his contribution to the World Competitiveness Report 2004–2005, reports on the lack of any clear relationships between the quality of domestic governance and the perceived threat of terrorism. He found negligible correlations between the extent of terrorist threats and either the quality of parliament or police performance, using a single-issue, perception-based indicator for the latter. He concludes that "country-specific institutions and measures can have only a limited impact on diminishing the threat of terrorism." Our own findings concerning the inverse links between rule of law and terrorism are more in line with those of Gupta and Schmid. Like them, we also found moderately strong inverse relationships between the index of perceived terrorism and several indicators of "governance" besides rule of law, such as with the World Bank's Index of Voice and Accountability, a measure of the democratic quality of governance ($r = .31$). Although none of the correlations are as strong as those with organized crime, the results suggest that governance and rule of law matter in the prevention of terrorism too.

Our own analyses also showed a weak negative inverse correlation between our composite Police Performance Index and terrorism ($r = .30$, $p < 0.000$, $n = 101$). In countries with better-performing police forces, according to our index, terrorism is perceived to be less of a threat. This correlation is not strong but nevertheless suggests that effective policing can contribute to the protection of societies against terrorist attacks. In democratic environments, effective policing, respecting human rights, may offer protection against attacks and is part of the solution. In the context of countries with nondemocratic regimes, a strong and effective security sector may on the contrary contribute to repression and violations of human rights. In those countries, heavy-handed policing strategies may fuel political tensions and be part of the problem. For this reason, no strong relationship between police performance and terrorism was to be expected.

Although terrorism, in our opinion, must analytically be clearly distinguished from organized crime, both global threats seem to be facilitated by institutional failures to maintain the rule of law, including through democratic and effective policing. Improvements in the justice and security sector can, in our view, be instrumental in the reduction of both organized crime and terrorist threats. In both Afghanistan and Iraq, the urgency to restore law and order parallel to military action against insurgents has been insufficiently understood. Those responsible for counterterrorism strategies seem to rely mainly on intelligence operations. They ignore the potential contributions of law enforcement and the administration of criminal justice at their peril. We will revisit this policy issue in the concluding chapter.

Trafficking in Persons and Police Performance

Flows or routes of international trafficking of illicit drugs are primarily determined by the geographical position of the main production and consumption countries. The flows of trafficking of persons for sexual or other forms of exploitation are less clearly concentrated. As discussed earlier, the trafficking database of UNODC counts the number of references in public sources to countries as either country of origin, transit country, or country of destination in the analyzed cases (Kangaspunta, 2003). Data presented in Chapter 7 helped to identify the main confirmed countries of origin and main confirmed countries of destination. As could be seen in Table 7.3, the main

❖ **Figure 12.4** National Scores on Demand and Supply Index for Human Trafficking and GDP per Capita

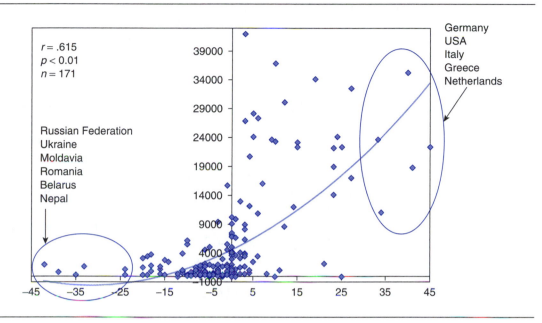

Sources: UNODC, 2006; WEF, 2003.

countries of origin are geographically very different from the countries of destination, with the exception of Thailand, which appears in both categories.

In order to get a clearer insight into the dynamics of the global trade in persons, a comprehensive scale was designed to measure the extent to which countries are either sending or receiving victims of trafficking. In the measure, being a receiving country was counted as a plus and being a sending country was counted as a minus. The scores on the integrated demand (receiving country) and supply (sending country) index for human trafficking were correlated with the GDP per capita (see Figure 12.4).[5]

The results of the analysis confirm that the main countries of origin are poorer, less developed countries in the South, where women and girls have few or no employment prospects.[6] Countries of destination are the most affluent countries in the world where commercial sex industries are booming. As has been extensively documented, most of the victims of human trafficking receive no or only marginal remunerations and return to their home countries without savings and often in bad medical condition (Travnickova et al., 2004; UNICRI, 2004). Many of the victims are economically exploited and find themselves in a situation of coerced servitude. Our global results show how in this area increased opportunities to travel across countries and continents have not diminished economic inequalities but have resulted in the victimization and exploitation of residents from the poorer South by organized-crime groups in the North supported by their criminal counterparts in the South. Human trafficking presents a glaring example of the dark side of globalization.

Although countries of origin are almost exclusively in the world's poorer South, far from all poor countries are involved in this trade. And likewise, many but not all of the most affluent countries are listed as main countries of destination. We were interested to see whether main trading countries differed from others in terms of policing or organized-crime prevalence. We found an inverse relationship between our measures of police performance and the number of times countries are mentioned in open sources as countries of origin or destination of human trafficking in the UNODC database (Kangaspunta, 2003; UNODC, 2006). We also found that, especially among the more-affluent countries, those with high prevalence of organized crime are more likely to be cited as destination countries of trafficked women. The key countries of origin likewise showed significantly higher scores on the organized-crime index than others. These findings indicate that although global economic inequalities explain most of the trafficking patterns, countries with relatively weak police performance and high levels of perceived organized crime are more likely to be involved in these inhuman practices, either as the source country or as the destination country.

The results suggest that the policy debate on trafficking in persons should not focus exclusively on the so-called push factors, such as lack of opportunities for young women in poor countries, or on market-specific pull factors, such as inadequate or poorly enforced antiprostitution laws. Due attention should be given to the role of organized crime and poorly performing, not rarely corrupted law enforcement agencies in the facilitation of this inhuman trade, in countries of origin, transit, and destination (Heikkinen & Lohrmann, 1998; IOM, 1996). To address human trafficking, sustained action against the perpetrators and their protectors is imperative, besides offering adequate protection of and care for the victims. The humanitarian aspects of human trafficking should not blind the international community to the key role that law enforcement has to play in combating the phenomenon. In the field of human trafficking, specialized police officers are uniquely qualified to act as rescuers of victimized persons held in servitude and as protectors of their human rights and safety thereafter.

Good Governance and Development

In "comparative economics," it is now more and more acknowledged that sound legal infrastructures, especially those governing property rights, are a primary determinant of economic performance (Acemoglu & Johnson, 2003).[7] Empirical studies have specifically demonstrated that various dimensions of "good governance" are prerequisites for sustainable economic development (Mauro, 1996). Good governance, including the rule of law, has been found to be a critical success factor for sustainable development (Eiras, 2003; Kaufmann, Kraay, & Mastruzzi, 2003). Some recent studies have confirmed the prominent role of protection of property rights and independent judiciaries for economic success (Barro & Sala-i-Martin, 2004; Feld & Voigt, 2003). In analyses of the World Bank Institute, "state capture"—defined as undue influence on laws, policies, and regulation by special interest groups—and other manifestations of "crony capitalism" or "economic elitism" have been identified as root causes of institutional failure hampering development (Kaufmann, 2004).

The strong statistical relationships between measures of governance and economic growth or performance do not by themselves provide evidence that good institutions promote economic performance. The causal effects might in theory also be the other way around. Perhaps economic performance instigates governments to improve their institutions through more generous funding. There are several arguments why this alternative, second interpretation of the governance growth correlations is less plausible. It should, first of all, be understood that good governance such as independent judiciaries does not require significant expenditures that only rich countries can afford. Independently functioning judiciaries depend more on sound legislation and political will than on available resources. There is supporting empirical evidence for the causal impact of governance on growth. Institutional failures have been found to be correlated to not only current economic performance but also to future economic performance (Knack & Keefer, 1995). Kaufmann and Kraay (2002) have empirically refuted the notion that economic growth generally results in incremental strengthening of legal and institutional arrangements for "good governance." Their results suggest the absence of "virtuous circles" in which higher incomes due to an economic boost and massive development aid lead to further improvements in governance. Experiences in South America and eastern Europe in particular show that higher levels of affluence do not necessarily translate into better governance. In periods of prosperity, established interest groups unduly influencing state policies may grow even more powerful. Higher income levels may therefore actually entrench rather than diminish Mafia-related forms of state failure (Kaufmann, 2004).

By the same token, economic prosperity based on the exploitation of natural resources such as oil or diamonds acts for many developing countries as an economic "curse in disguise." In many cases, resource dependency provokes the capture of the state by corrupt and/or criminal groups and thereby stifles other forms of economic activity.[8] The law and development literature provides several examples of countries where the possession of oil, diamonds, or other natural resources could have resulted in stronger institutions and subsequent lasting economic growth—as has been the case in Botswana—but where the opposite has taken place. The revenues from economic windfalls are more likely to generate rampant corruption and subsequent weakened institutions and diminished economic growth. Examples where such negative side effects seem to have prevailed are Angola, Nigeria, Zambia, Gabon, and Venezuela (McMillan, 2005). Russia also qualifies as a country where necessary institutional reforms are blocked by a corrupted elite feeding itself on abundant natural resources.

The political implications of these analytical results showing that institutions are the driving forces behind economic development—and not the other way around—are huge and still insufficiently understood. According to protagonists of good governance, an improvement in a country of, for example, 6 points on the Transparency International Corruption Perception Index may increase the GDP by more than 20% (Lambsdorff, 2004). The economic consequences of improved judicial infrastructures have also been quantified. When the quality of the rule of law is measured on a scale of 1 to 10, every point of improvement generates between 0.2% and 0.8% additional economic growth per year (Barro & Sala-i-Martin, 2004; Torstensson, 1994). If all African countries would succeed in building up justice and security sectors that match those in Botswana, many of them would soon be known as "African lions." Oil- and population-rich Nigeria could easily become the second economic engine of the sub-Saharan continent besides South Africa if only rampant corruption and crime would be brought under control.

Good Governance, Development, and the Role of Crime

In Chapters 7 and 8, data were presented on the close link between organized crime and corruption. The two phenomena are interlinked to such an extent that an indicator of grand corruption was included in our Composite Index of Organized Crime. In many parts of the world, grand corruption and organized crime are two sides of the same coin. Surprisingly, little attention is given in the law and economics literature just cited to the possible specific role of criminal justice and organized-crime control in the institutional arrangements determining good governance or the lack of it. In this section, we will explore in more detail the links between the organized crime–corruption nexus, functioning justice systems, and sustainable development. We will start with a theoretical cost-benefits assessment of organized crime and then return to our metrics to analyze relationships between criminal justice, organized crime, and economic performance empirically.

On the cost side, high levels of common crime, just as high levels of corruption, add to the immediate costs of doing business in a country. In its 2005 World Development Report, the World Bank sums up its evolving thoughts on the issue: "crime . . . increases the cost of business, whether through direct loss of goods or the costs of taking precautions such as hiring security guards, building fences, or installing burglar alarm systems. In the extreme, foreign firms will decline to invest, and domestic ones will flee the country for a more peaceful locale" (Stone, 2006; World Bank, 2005). In some instances, rampant organized crime may also deter foreign tourists from visiting the country. Security concerns are known to be among the most important considerations for selecting holiday destinations (World Tourism Organization, 1997).

In the business executive opinion surveys of the World Economic Forum, respondents are specifically asked to identify the most important obstacles to doing business in their country. Business executives in many countries list corruption and/or crime and violence as the most or second most important impediments to doing business in their countries (WEF, 2003). This is often the case in countries with comparatively high scores on the index for perceived organized-crime prevalence. These opinions of business leaders working in high-crime countries confirm the negative impact of crime on investments. In recent Investment Climate Surveys, 15% of business executives reported that crime was a major constraint on investment (29% of African executives gave this response) (Brunetti et al., 1997).

In Mafia-infested countries, the costs of crime may go far beyond company losses to "criminal leakage," "loss of customers," or "loss of tourists." In an important revision of the good governance theory, Kaufmann and Kraay (2002) have attributed the negative influence of high-level corruption on development to the intermediary factor of "cronyism," the widespread interference of particular interest groups in rational decision making in the economic domain.[9] Infiltration in the legitimate economy and political process is, as discussed in Chapter 7, a defining characteristic of Mafia-type organizations. If such "crony capitalism" is indeed the main impediment of economic development, organized crime as an especially entrenched form of cronyism may well be at the heart of the governance-related, economic problems of many countries.[10]

The Sicilian economy, for example, seems to have been seriously hampered by the reign of the Mafia over local politics and started to prosper only after the local Mafia bosses were put on the defensive through the maxi-trials and community mobilization (Orlando, 2001).[11] The experience with racketeering in New York City also points to economic revitalization after the defeat of mob-related racketeering in several sectors of the local economy (Jacobs, 2003).

Although organized-crime groups are likely to be part of the problem of crony capitalism, the overall impact of their criminal activities on the economy may not always be exclusively negative. The production and trafficking of illicit commodities can result in considerable profits that are reinvested in the formal and informal economy of countries. Australian criminologist John Walker has estimated the total value of illicit drugs at wholesale value to be at $94 billion (World Drug Report, 2005). This is the equivalent of the export values of the agricultural commodities meat and cereals combined. At retail level, the total value of illicit drugs is estimated at $322 billion. Countries dominating the production and/or trafficking of illicit drugs will obviously benefit economically from their activities on these markets to some extent. Narco dollars generated by the cocaine trade in the Americas are indeed known to have given a significant boost to national economies in Latin America in the 1990s. The total value of illicit drug trafficking, injected annually into the Mexican economy in those years, has been estimated at over $ 25 billion, or 6% of the country's GDP (Gonzalez-Ruiz, 2001). In Tajikistan, heroin trafficking revenues have been estimated as equivalent to 50% of the recorded GDP (Reuter et al., 2004). More recently, estimated revenues from drugs in Afghanistan vary from 30% to as much as 60% of the GDP. There can be no doubt that the heroin trade has fueled the Afghanistan economy as well as the economies of several transit countries since the defeat of the Taliban (World Drug Report, 2004). It is also widely assumed that mini-countries with offshore centers specializing in facilitation of money laundering reap significant economic benefits of such illicit financial services.

To empirically explore these issues at the macro level, the correlations between the composite measure of organized-crime prevalence and indicators of economic development were analyzed. The index for organized-crime prevalence was found to have a moderately strong negative correlation with the Human Development Index ($r = -.49$). The negative relationship between organized-crime prevalence and the GDP per 100,000 population was stronger ($r = -.76$). Figure 12.5 shows the results in the form of a scatterplot.

The results depicted in Figure 12.5 lend empirical support to the hypothesis that, on balance, organized crime is bad for the economy.[12] It may, as in the case of drugs production and trafficking, generate sizeable illegal profits, but it deters investment and, as a virulent form of cronyism, impairs the capacity of countries to experience sustainable economic growth through rational decision making on key markets and in government. Countries where organized-crime groups are powerful are likely to fare worse economically than countries where organized crime plays no significant role, such as the Scandinavian countries, Australia, Germany, and the United States.

❖ Figure 12.5   Prevalence of Organized Crime (Composite Organized-Crime Index) and GDP per Capita (high scores on organized crime indicate high levels and high scores on GDP indicate high GDP)

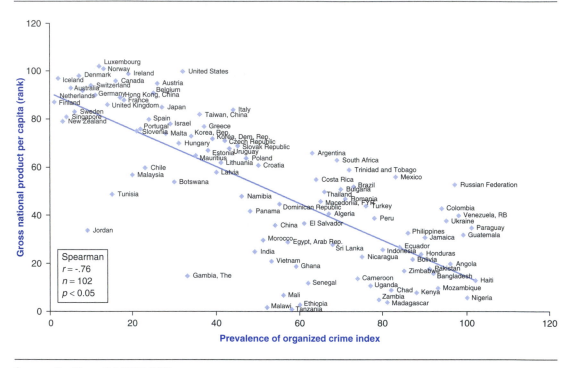

Sources: See Figure 7.4; WEF, 2003.

Case studies of individual countries and territories as varied as the United States (New York), Singapore, Botswana, Jordan, Hong Kong, and Taiwan document the crucial role of proper legal infrastructures and zero tolerance for organized crime and corruption in promoting economic growth (see, e.g., the case studies of New York in Jacobs [1999] and of Taiwan in Lintner [2002]). In Chile, one of the economically best-performing countries in the region, a full-fledged ministry is traditionally tasked with the protection of the interests of the state (Szczaranski, 2002). From a global perspective, such sustained investments in organized-crime–corruption control seem to pay off well in terms of sustainable development.

Organized Crime as a Trojan Horse

The fairly strong inverse correlation between organized crime and collective wealth merits further examination. Although the inverse correlation between organized-crime prevalence and economic wealth is strong, there are, as Figure 12.5 shows, significant outliers. The scatterplot positions some countries with very high levels of organized crime in the middle range for their GDP rather than in the expected low range. This category of economically "overperforming" high-crime countries includes Mexico, Russia, Venezuela, Colombia, and Guatemala. Their relative wealth in spite of rampant organized crime and corruption might point to the positive economic effects of crime-related windfalls. Although none of these countries enjoy the stably high GDP levels of the OECD countries, they might perhaps have been even poorer without the injection of criminally acquired assets. This group of outliers point at the working of complex crimino-economic dynamics that do not show up in simple two-dimensional correlations.

As demonstrated above, organized crime, grand corruption, and rule of law are strongly and inversely related to collective wealth. However, the first three factors are also closely interlinked with each other, and the independent impact of each of them on wealth is difficult to unravel. In order to unbundle the relationships and determine the independent impact of each of these factors on wealth, we tested some multivariate models describing the possible relationships between the four variables. For this purpose, we first carried out a multiple regression analysis with the Composite Organized-Crime Index, the index for corruption (CPI of Transparency International), and the World Bank Index of Rule of Law as independent variables and GDP as the dependent. The three independent variables combined explained 80% of the variance in GDP scores of countries.[13] The strongest negative relationship was that between corruption and GDP ($r = -.77$). The rule of law indicator showed a positive correlation, independently of corruption ($r = .43$). Somewhat surprisingly for a variable with a strong negative correlation with GDP in a simple, two-dimensional model, organized crime was *positively* correlated with GDP, after controlling for the effects of corruption and rule of law. These results were confirmed in an analysis using different operationalizations of some of the key variables.[14]

One theoretically plausible model to explain these results assumes that organized crime leads to both less rule of law and more corruption, which both in turn lead to lower wealth. These indirect effects may fully explain the negative relationship between organized crime and wealth. The direct effect of organized crime on wealth, after controlling for the indirect effects, may disappear or even become positive, as suggested by the outcome of the regression analysis. In the final step in our analysis, we looked at the independent effect of organized crime, rule of law, and corruption on wealth in a structural model representing the mechanisms just described. The model explains 65% of the total variance in the level of wealth and can thus be considered as fairly strong. In the model, the negative relationship between organized crime and wealth does indeed turn into a positive relationship in a multivariate analysis controlling for the strong indirect, negative effects through rule of law and corruption. Figure 12.6 shows the results.

❖ **Figure 12.6**   Results of a Structural Modeling Analysis of the Relationships Between the Prevalence of Organized Crime, Rule of Law, and Corruption and Country Wealth (GDPPC)

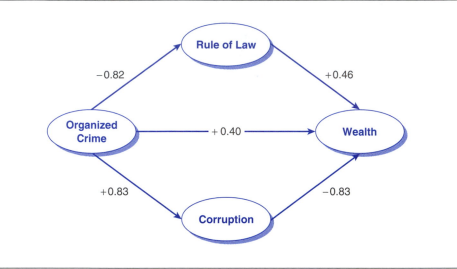

Although this causal model should not be taken at face value—replication studies, using other indicators or testing other structural models, may show somewhat different outcomes—the results confirm the hypothesis that organized crime has a dual impact on economic growth. On one hand, organized crime goes together with compromised state institutions and rampant grand corruption. Organized crime and bad governance mutually reinforce each other. Bad governance is known to hamper economic growth. On the other hand, organized crime brings in considerable profits from criminal activities, which by themselves may give a boost to the economy.[15] This model should not lead to the conclusion that up to a point organized crime can be beneficial for national economies. The overall net effect of organized crime on the economy through weakened governance and rampant corruption is strongly negative, as shown in Figure 12.5. At the macro level, crime does not pay.

The finding that, on balance, significant revenues from drug trafficking or other forms of lucrative crime slow down rather than strengthen economic growth may seem economically puzzling. But this phenomenon is actually just another example of what development economists have called the "resource curse" (McMillan, 2005). As mentioned above, developing countries that are rich in natural resources such as oil or diamonds often experience reduced rather than enhanced economic growth. This is because their institutions are undermined by rampant corruption at the highest level of government fueled by the presence of rich and easy pickings. Some of the main drug-exporting countries seem to suffer from exactly the same predicament. In such countries, drug revenues allow criminal groups to become so wealthy that they can take over control of the institutions and buy the political support of the local populations (Reuter et al., 2004).

After World War II, the Allied Forces allowed local Mafia leaders in Sicily to return to their former positions of authority in the hopes of restoring order and promoting a rapid economic recovery. More recently in Colombia and southern Afghanistan, insurgents were allowed to engage in illicit drug cultivation in exchange for peace. In our view, such accommodating strategies will always prove to be economically disastrous for the countries at issue in the medium and long term. Tolerating Mafia-type activities implies letting the Trojan horse of racketeering and grand corruption into the walls of government. The inevitable deleterious effects on the rule of law and governance will impede sustainable development in the long run as can be witnessed in Sicily to this day. Organized crime tends to erode the integrity of those holding a public office, including those responsible for upholding the rule of law. Where organized-crime groups are powerful, legislation, policymaking, and legal rulings no longer serve the general interest but just the interests of the few. Through the pervasive bias of legislation, policy decisions, and jurisprudence, market efficiencies are undermined and both local and foreign investors lose confidence in the legal and regulatory functions of the state and, consequently, stay away. A national growth strategy based on tolerating organized crime is not just immoral but economically unsound as well. Under such a Mafia-friendly regime, no country will ever achieve sustainable development, least of all an equitable one.

Vicious Crimino-Economic Circles

As shown in Chapter 7, the entrenchment of organized crime in society goes hand in hand with a growth in the shadow economy. When shadow economies make up a large part of the economy, this factor alone can lead to reduced state revenues, which in turn lessens the quality and quantity of publicly provided goods and services, including the administration of justice (the rule of law). Ultimately, a decline in state revenues can lead to an increase in the tax rates and social security contributions for firms and individuals in the official sector, with the consequence of even stronger incentives to participate in the shadow economy (Johnson, Kaufmann, & Zoido-Lobatón, 1998; Schneider & Enste, 2000). From a criminological perspective, poorly funded, weakened public administrations will lead to poor law enforcement and criminal justice, and thus to more opportunities for organized crime, investing its illicit gains mainly in the shadow economies. These crimino-economic chain effects further undermine the capacity of the state to raise the required revenues for an institutional attack on groups involved in organized crime. Poverty, weak states, and organized crime are intertwined, mutually reinforcing evils. They are part of the vicious circles that have kept many developing countries badly governed, lawless, and poor since their independence.

Although levels of affluence have increased in several developing and transitional countries over the past decade, investments in institutions fighting crime and corruption have often lagged behind those in other areas. With the exception of South Africa, criminal justice systems, which provide the indispensable backbone of good governance, are not a spending priority in the developing world, in spite of rising rates of serious crime and widespread concern about rampant corruption. Although problems of crime are a major concern in many developing countries, increased funding of law enforcement and criminal justice cannot be taken for granted, even if economies are growing. In all poorer regions of the world, the professional capacity and integrity of the judiciaries have been in decline. Findings presented in Chapters 9 and 10 on resources for police and judiciaries confirm the absence of virtuous circles in the relationships between the rule of law and affluence. External interventions seem needed.

❖

SUMMARY POINTS/IN CONCLUSION

• The prevalence of organized crime and related forms of grand corruption in countries is inversely related to police performance and indices of the rule of law or independence of the judiciary. These strong correlations suggest that the institutional quality of the justice and security sector is crucially important for the control of complex crimes. Analyses of data on human trafficking show that main countries of origin and destination are on average less well policed and characterized by a relatively high prevalence of organized crime. In strategies tackling human trafficking, a prominent role should be played by improvements in investigation, prosecution of traffickers, and protection of victim/witnesses

• Measures of law enforcement performance and the rule of law are also inversely related to the prevalence of perceived threats of terrorism. Although organized crime and terrorism are separate criminal phenomena, law enforcement and criminal justice seem to be key to their containment.

• There are strong statistical links between levels of organized crime and development. High levels of organized crime go together with economic stagnation. The most plausible interpretation of this link is that rampant organized crime and related grand corruption fosters forms

of crony capitalism undermining the capacity of governments to promote sustainable and equitable development.

• Organized crime may bring in important revenues that can boost economic growth in limited domains. Large-scale organized crime such as opium production in Afghanistan and cocaine production and trafficking in Colombia and Mexico generates undoubtedly enormous revenues. On the downside, organized crime tends to corrupt core institutions, including police forces and judiciaries that are needed for development. Analyses of the impact of organized crime show that Mafia-infested countries are, on balance, economically in dire straits.

• Common crime shows an intrinsic tendency toward stabilization by generating spontaneous countermeasures from key target groups. Households and businesses victimized by crime step up their self-protection measures and demand more law and order from their government. Levels of common crime will therefore normally exhibit a cyclical boom-and-bust pattern: Increasing levels of crime are with some delay matched with increased levels of self-protection, resulting in decreasing levels of crime. No such spontaneous homeostasis can be expected to operate in the case of organized crime. The level of organized crime is more than common crime dependent on the performance of state institutions. If organized crime and corruption reach a certain critical mass, the security and justice sector is contaminated and criminal elites can continue their activities with impunity. By systematically undermining the integrity and credibility of state institutions responsible for the rule of law, the organized crime–corruption nexus resembles the AIDS disease, undermining the social body's vital immunity systems.

• Without a functioning justice system, both the government and civil society are defenseless against rampant crime and corruption, and development is likely to stagnate. In such situations, financial injections from outside are unlikely to spur economic growth and may, in fact, make matters worse by expanding opportunities for looting. If the state itself is criminalized, regeneration requires first and foremost radical transformations in core institutions such as law enforcement and the courts. We will return to this issue in the final chapter.

Notes

1. Kaufmann (2005) reports a very close correlation between a WEF-based measure of the perceived prevalence of common crime and a WEF measure of the perceived quality of the police. This conflicting result may be due to the broad definition of common crime in the WEF questionnaire: "The incidence of common crime and violence (e.g., street muggings, firms being looted) imposes significant costs on businesses." The reference to looting of firms seems to refer to organized crime rather than to common crime. Our analyses showed that the WEF measure for perceived common crime was only weakly related to the overall ICVS victimization rate. The perceptional WEF measure of common crime seems conceptually unclear, and it was therefore not included in our analyses.

2. Low scores on the police performance index do not exclude the existence of sophisticated anti-Mafia units in the police or prosecutorial offices. Examples of such exceptions are Mexico and Colombia.

3. Source: World Conflict and Human Rights Map, 2001/2002, by Interdisciplinary Research Programme on Causes of Human Rights Violations at Leiden University, the Netherlands, Leiden, 2001.

4. As discussed in Chapter 8, RAND's index of terrorism incidents is heavily skewed to a minority of countries most afflicted and therefore technically less well suited to correlation analysis.

5. The country scores are taken from the 2003 version of the UNODC database and may differ somewhat from the updated 2005 version used in Table 7.3.

6. As reported before, the majority of cases in the database relate to cases of trafficking of women and girls for the purpose of sexual exploitation.

7. Acemoglu and Johnson (2003) found in their historical studies that economic wealth is dependent on the quality of historically established institutions, in particular, institutions protecting citizens against expropriations by the government and powerful elites (public law, including criminal law). The historical studies of Acemoglu lead to the hypothesis that criminal justice is key to economic wealth by containing abuses of power deterring investments. From an historical perspective, the current looting of poor developing countries by endogenous criminal elites

may simply be a continuation of previous colonial practices against the backdrop of poorly functioning police and justice systems inherited from the colonial era.

8. "Wealthier countries of the OECD, as well as some in eastern Europe, find themselves in the 'good equilibrium' of relatively low tax and regulatory burden, sizeable revenue mobilization, good rule of law and corruption control, and [relatively] small unofficial economy," according to Johnson, Kaufmann, and Zoido-Lobatón (1998). "By contrast, a number of countries in Latin America and the former Soviet Union exhibit characteristics consistent with a 'bad equilibrium': tax and regulatory discretion and burden on the firm are high, the rule of law is weak, and there is a high incidence of bribery and a relatively high share of activities in the unofficial economy." To this salient conclusion one could add that organized crime is prominently present across countries in Latin America and the former Soviet Union. Rampant organized crime forms part of the bad equilibrium in many developing countries.

9. In some publications sponsored by the World Bank, statistical relationships are presented between common crime and development as evidence that crime and violence in general act as impediments to development (e.g., UNODC, 2007a). There are serious problems with this interpretation. Although crime certainly imposes extra costs on businesses, there are no economic or criminological theories that can explain why high levels of common crime would significantly hamper economic growth, nor are there any clear case studies illustrating how high levels of assault or robbery have reduced development. Ireland, South Africa, and Brazil could be mentioned as high-crime countries with rapidly expanding economies. In many of the World Bank studies, homicide rates are used as the sole indicator of common violent crime. The use of this indicator is unwarranted. There are only weak statistical relationships between homicide rates and other forms of violent crime and no positive relationships between homicide and main forms of property crime. Since homicide rates are fairly strongly correlated with our index of organized crime, the relationships found in World Bank studies between common crime and development might be spurious. The results may in fact confirm the causal relationship between organized crime/corruption and economic stagnation found in many other studies, including our own presented here.

10. In a case study of "cronyism" in a Latin American country by Kaufmann and Kraay (2002), drug cartels and other organized-crime groups are mentioned as key examples of the phenomenon.

11. Moody Financial Certification, a financial analysis agency, upgraded its rating of the city of Palermo to Aa3, meaning excellent, in 2000 at the end of the mayorship of Orlando.

12. The simple correlation between perceived prevalence of organized crime and GDP is moderately strong ($r = .63$). The simple correlations between the Corruption Perception Index of Transparency International and the Rule of Law Index of the World Bank and GDP are even stronger ($r = .83$ and $.77$, respectively).

13. The multiple regression coefficient was $r = .87$.

14. The analysis was repeated using as independent variables the Organized-Crime Perception Index (instead of the Composite Organized-Crime Index); an index for serious corruption, developed by Buscaglia & and Van Dijk (instead of the CPI of TI); and the Rule of Law Index of the World Bank Institute. As a fourth independent, we added the Police Performance Index. The four independent variables combined explained 74% of the variance in GDP scores of countries ($r = .871$). The strongest negative relationship was that between high-level corruption

and GDPPC ($\beta = -.551$). The rule-of-law indicator showed a positive correlation, independently of corruption ($\beta = .363$). Police performance also contributes, independently of the other factors, to GDPPC. Again, the variable representing organized-crime prevalence proved to become positively related to GDP, after controlling for the effects of corruption and rule of law ($\beta = .256$).

15. The positive relationship between organized crime and GDP in a multivariate model may also point to a lack of opportunities for organized crime activities, such as racketeering, in very poor countries.

13

Crime and Justice

The Need for Global Reform

Diagnosing Crime

In this chapter, we will sum up the statistical information and findings presented before and then draw some general policy conclusions on the need for action against crime by the international community. First, the various indices of crime and justice developed throughout the book will be integrated into one composite index of "lawfulness," which will allow a rapid identification of countries where the degree of lawfulness is comparatively high and of those where it leaves something, or much, to be desired. In this section, we will also present for ease of reference criminological x-rays. These "radar pictures" provide summary information on key security and justice indicators that together provide a detailed diagnosis of the situation. We will subsequently try to estimate the total costs of crime to the world community. In this context, we will once again highlight the close links between rule of law and economic performance by showing the relative positions of countries on both lawfulness and the Human Development Index. The results will illustrate the universality of the lawfulness–development link across world regions, regardless of average levels of wealth. In the final section, we will make a plea for global reform of the justice and security sector, in the interest of sustainable development for developing countries and of sustainable global security for all.

A Culture of Lawfulness

As just said, we have constructed a catchall index of justice and security that will be called the "index of lawfulness." The concept of lawfulness is more encompassing than that of the rule of law. For a society to be lawful, it is not sufficient if the state respects the constitution and human rights. It must also address crime problems effectively with the involvement of civil society.[1] The concept of "lawfulness" refers to both the quality of institutions upholding the rule of law and the normative orientation of the public. Ideally, the state and the citizens reinforce each other in efforts to ensure a safe and just society.

In the previous chapters, we presented a series of indicators and indices that capture different aspects of the culture of lawfulness. In Chapters 3, 4, 7, and 8, statistical indicators were presented of aspects of the state of crime in various countries. As discussed in Chapters 2 and 3, the most reliable, comparative measure of common crime is the percentage of the public victimized by it (the ICVS-based overall prevalence rate of victimization). A new composite index of prevalence of organized crime, based on surveys among businesspeople and security experts, and rates of unsolved homicides was presented in Chapter 7. An indicator of street-level corruption, based on survey research into experiences with corruption, was found to be closely correlated with the well-known Corruption Perception Index, published annually by TI, as presented in Chapter 8. In order to include as many countries as possible, we decided to use the ICVS overall victimization rate, the organized-crime perception index, and the corruption perception index of TI as constituting components of a comprehensive index of lawfulness. In Part IV, Chapters 9 and 10, several performance measures were presented of the functioning of the justice and security sector in various countries. One of the key indicators is the newly designed composite Police Performance Index, based on a combination of subjective and objective indicators. Also presented was a composite measure of the rule of law, designed by the World Bank Institute. We decided to include these two indicators in the new index of lawfulness as well.

Our statistical analyses have shown that indicators of organized crime, corruption, police performance, and rule of law are closely related to each other. They are also, though less strongly, related to the indicator of common crime, the ICVS overall victimization rate. Using the scores on these five supplementary measures of the state of crime and justice, a composite index of lawfulness was constructed, covering 158 countries. This comprehensive index reflects both the quality of domestic legislation and legal institutions (the indicators of police performance and the rule of law) as the extent to which nationals are exposed to or involved in the three main types of crime (common crime, organized crime, and corruption). It captures in one single index the main dimensions of the statistical data on levels of crime and justice elaborated throughout this book.

The index was constructed in such a way that high scores reflect comparatively high levels of justice and low levels of crime. Countries were included in the ranking only if at least three or more sources were available. Table 13.1 presents country scores according to this new index.

The country scores are also presented in the form of a global map in Figure 13.1. This map sums up all metrics on crime and justice presented and discussed in the previous chapters.

❖ **Table 13.1**   World Ranking of Countries According to Scores on the Index of Lawfulness, Combining Indicators of Police Performance, Rule of Law, and the Prevalence of Three Main Types of Crime (common crime, organized crime, and corruption)

Twenty-Five Countries With Highest Country Scores (most lawful):

1	Iceland	100.0	10	Netherlands	91.2	19	Barbados	83.5
2	Switzerland	99.1	11	Norway	91.0	20	Chile	83.5
3	Denmark	98.0	12	Austria	90.6	21	Jordan	83.2
4	Finland	97.3	13	Canada	89.8	22	Hong Kong	82.5
5	Luxembourg	97.1	14	United Kingdom	89.8	23	Belgium	82.1
6	Australia	95.5	15	Ireland	85.7	24	Puerto Rico	81.4
7	Sweden	94.3	16	United States	84.7	25	Israel	81.4
8	New Zealand	92.2	17	Malta	84.5			
9	Singapore	92.2	18	Germany	84.1			

Twenty-Five Countries With Moderately High Scores

26	Japan	81.0	73	Poland	56.4	112	Cuba	42.2
27	France	80.9	80	Turkey	52.9	123	Iran	40.3
33	Tunisia	77.7	85	Bulgaria	51.4	125	Nigeria	39.7
34	Botswana	76.9	87	Argentina	50.8	129	Albania	38.9
39	Spain	71.7	88	South Africa	50.8	130	Mexico	37.5
47	Italy	68.5	98	Indonesia	46.3	132	Guatemala	36.3
63	Thailand	59.7	104	Russian Fed.	44.7	133	Colombia	36.2
65	India	58.8	107	Brazil	43.3			
68	China	58.2	109	Algeria	43.2			

Twenty-Five Countries With the Lowest Scores (least lawful)

134	Sierra Leone	35.0	143	Honduras	32.2	152	Sudan	24.7
135	Cote d'Ivoire	34.2	144	Tajikistan	31.8	153	Kenya	23.8
136	Jamaica	34.1	145	Turkmenistan	29.2	154	Pakistan	23.7
137	Eritrea	33.8	146	Venezuela, RB	29.1	155	Bangladesh	20.6
138	Cameroon	33.7	147	Congo, Rep.	28.9	156	Iraq	15.9
139	Angola	33.6	148	Burundi	26.1	157	Congo, Dem Rep	14.5
140	Niger	33.1	149	Myanmar	25.8	158	Haiti	13.7
141	Ecuador	32.5	150	Yemen, Rep.	25.8			
142	Bosnia & Herz.	32.5	151	Chad	25.7			

Cross-Validating the Index

As explained in Chapter 7, one of the indicators of perceived organized-crime prevalence is based on the ratings of an international network of security experts, working for one of the major security consultancy firms (MIG). Similarly, based on the opinions of

❖ **Figure 13.1**   World Map of the Degree of Lawfulness of Countries, Reflecting the State of Security and Crime Across the World According to a Composite Index

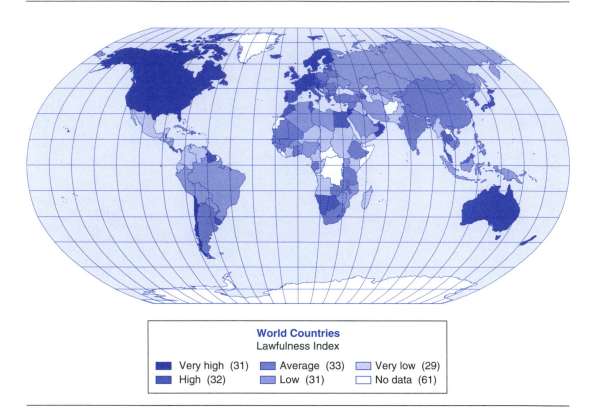

World Countries
Lawfulness Index

■ Very high (31)	■ Average (33)	■ Very low (29)
■ High (32)	■ Low (31)	□ No data (61)

locally based experts, the U.S.-based PRS Group offers country ratings on a variety of risk dimensions to the international business community (www.countrydata.com). One of their risk dimensions is the degree of law and order in a country, assessing "the strength and impartiality of the legal system" and "popular observance of the law." With these two components, the measure captures both the quality of criminal justice responses and the general state of crime. In other words, it provides an alternative composite index of justice and security. As a check on the soundness of our own comprehensive index of lawfulness, we looked at the relationship between the country scores on lawfulness and on the law and order ratings of the PRS Group. The two measures were found to be highly correlated ($r = .79$, $n = 156$). Incorporation of the law and order scores into the lawfulness index does not significantly alter the ranking of individual countries but allows the addition of five new countries. On the basis of the extended index scores, Brunei is included into the category of most lawful countries at place 15, just after Ireland. Added to the least lawful countries is Somalia at place 160, after Bangladesh, and Liberia at place 140, after

Jamaica. For details on the index incorporating the PRS data, see Appendix B. Results presented in the text are based on our own index of lawfulness based on five indicators.

As discussed in the previous chapter, organized crime, police performance, and rule of law are linked to the level of terrorism: Where governance and criminal justice are weak, organized crime is more prevalent and more terrorist attacks are launched. Our index of lawfulness was, in line with these previous findings, correlated with the index of terrorism ($r = .37$). Although the terrorism index was not itself included in the measure of lawfulness, high scores on lawfulness indicate low levels of all types of crime, including terrorism. The index can confidently be used as a rough measure of the state of security and justice in countries in a very broad sense.

Country Profiles at a Glance

Country scores on the index of "lawfulness" provide a first rough indication of the state of security and justice. For a more precise and nuanced diagnosis, the radar pictures presented below show the country's scores on eight key indicators, five indicators of security and three indicators of the state of justice. Country scores are compared to the world mean scores. The five security or crime indicators are the Composite Organized-Crime Index, the ICVS victimization rate by common crime, the rate of homicide, the rate of street-level corruption (integration of ICVS victimization rates and TI corruption barometer), and the perceived prevalence of terrorism. The three indicators of the state of justice are the Police Performance Index, the Rule of Law Index, and, finally, the comprehensive lawfulness index.

Figure 13.2 depicts the radar pictures of the United States and the European Union. Many of the observations concerning these regions and countries made in the previous chapters are summarily reflected in these two pictures. They show, at a glance, that the Unites States and the European Union have similar security and justice profiles in a global perspective. Data contained in Appendix B will allow the reader to make similar diagnoses of the state of security and justice of all other countries. Other crime and justice indicators than the ones chosen here can easily be included as well.

Crime Alert

Radar pictures can also be made that compare scores of two regions or countries with each other. Such pairs of country radars provide useful information to international travelers. In the case of the European Union and United States, there are few differences in the state of crime and justice that travelers may want to be informed about. Cross-Atlantic travelers will normally not be confronted with vastly different crime risks at their place of destination. Americans on their Grand Tour through Europe need not be unduly concerned. Most European countries, including Italy, are three-star destinations in terms of public safety. There are two important exceptions, though. In Europe, American and Canadian travelers will be exposed to risks of pickpocketing that are significantly higher than at home, for example, while enjoying the services of public transport. This is a particularly serious problem when traveling further eastbound on the European continent. Americans may also be unhappily surprised by the lack of integrity in the consumer market and may fall victim to cunning forms of consumer fraud. When reporting a crime to the police, in northern

❖ **Figure 13.2** Radar Pictures of the State of Crime and Justice of the United States and the European Union

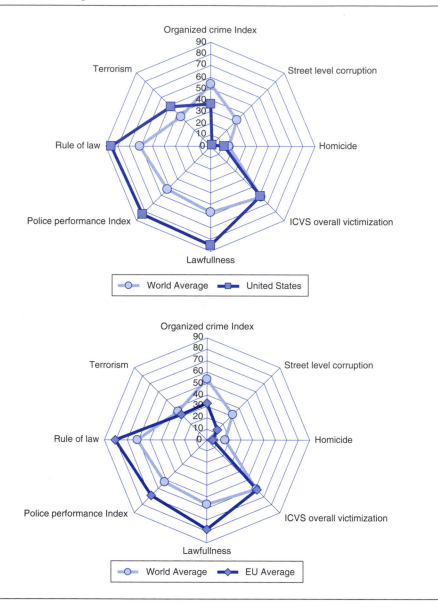

European countries, the reception will be similar to what Americans are used to at home. However, reporting crime incidents to the police may turn out to be a bad experience in southern Europe (Belgium, Greece, France, Spain, Italy, and Portugal) and even more so in eastern Europe. In those countries, most local police officers see all citizens, including crime- reporting victims, as (potential) troublemakers rather than as clients. They will often show little patience with victims speaking only English.

Europeans, in turn, need to be aware that in certain urban and rural areas in the United States, gun ownership is very common. Americans collectively own more than 200 million firearms, or one or two per household. Risk of (gun-related) violence, including lethal violence, is consequently much higher in the United States than anywhere in western or central Europe. Although the chance that a foreign visitor will become the target of a shooting is slight, victimization by gun-related violence is not quite the purely theoretical risk that it is in the European Union, especially in the inner cities of the United States. Also, robberies are more likely to be at gunpoint than anywhere in Europe. And, finally, European tourists should be aware of more punitive sentencing, including for simple possession of soft drugs, like cannabis, in some states.

Costs of Crime: The Global Crime Bill

Traditionally, the discourse on crime and justice is coached in normative terms. Large amounts of crime were seen as primarily a moral problem. Crime statistics in 19th-century France were called "moral statistics." More recently, criminologists and economists have tried to describe the impact of crime in financial or economic terms. The discussion in the previous chapter on the link between security and development reflects this new line of thinking.

According to Brand and Price (2000), the "costs of crime" fall into three main categories of crime:

1. Costs in anticipation of crime (preventive costs)

2. Costs incurred as a direct or indirect consequence of crime/losses of crime (consequential costs)

3. Costs in response to crime (criminal justice expenditures)

Of these three, criminal justice expenditures are easiest to determine by analyzing available state budgets. In the United States, $200 billion was spent on 2.5 million employees in law enforcement, courts, and corrections in 2005 (Waller, 2006). Internationally, data on financial resources for the subsystems of criminal justice are collected through the UN Crime Surveys, as discussed in Chapter 9. Using data from the 7th UN Crime Survey provided by 70 countries, an estimate was made of the total worldwide expenditures on criminal justice (Farrell & Clark, 2004). Global criminal justice expenditure in 1997 was estimated at $360 billion, the equivalent of $424 billion in 2004 prices. According to the latest UN Crime Survey data, expenditures among reporting countries have gone up by more than 10% between 1997 and 2002. Current annual worldwide public expenditures on criminal justice can be estimated at $500 billion, or $0.5 trillion.

The estimated total expenditures on criminal justice of $0.5 trillion can be used as a starting point for a rough estimate of the total global crime bill. Added to this amount should be the estimated costs in anticipation of crime (preventive costs). As discussed, private security industries have boomed almost everywhere. In national studies in the United Kingdom, Canada, Australia, the Netherlands, and the United States, costs of prevention amounted to 50%–70% of criminal justice expenditures (Anderson, 1998; Brand 7 Price, 2000; Brantingham & Eaton, 1998; Mayhew, 2003;

Moolenaar, 2005, 2006). On this basis, total preventive and responsive costs can be tentatively estimated at $0.8 trillion globally ($0.5 trillion for criminal justice plus $0.3 trillion for prevention).

The third item on the global crime bill is the consequential costs of crime. Several studies at the national level have tried to estimate costs incurred as a direct consequence of crime. A Canadian study estimated the direct consequential costs—losses and damages, including medical costs and pain and suffering—as roughly equal to the expenditures on criminal justice and prevention (Brantingham & Eaton, 1998). This fifty-fifty ratio was also found previously in studies in the Netherlands (Van Dijk, Sagel-Grande, & Toornvliet, 2002) and in an Australian study (Mayhew, 2003). On the assumption that this ratio can indeed be universally applied, the total costs of direct consequences of crime worldwide can be estimated at $0.8 trillion. This would yield a global crime bill of $1.6 trillion.

In some estimates of crime costs, researchers have also looked at various indirect consequences such as "shattered lives" or opportunity costs. In the Canadian study of Brantingham and Eaton, such indirect consequential costs were found to be in the same range as direct consequential costs. These calculations led the authors to postulate a "rule of thirds" for total crime costs, with equal parts for direct consequences, indirect consequences, and preventive and criminal justice costs. A recent Dutch study came up with a roughly similar ratio (Moolenaar, 2006). If conservative estimates of indirect consequential costs are added to the equation, the global costs of crime can thus be estimated as $2.4 trillion. This would amount to 7% of the global GDP around 2004. This rough estimate of a global crime bill illustrates the colossal negative impact of crime on today's societies. It also underlines the huge economic significance of more effective policies to reduce crime.[2] If governments and international organizations in conjunction with the private sector would be more effective in preventing and reducing crime, this would be not just a humanitarian value in itself but also would bring significant economic side benefits. It would generate savings for the private and public sectors that could be reallocated to other, more useful purposes. Its contribution to the general well-being would go far beyond the direct benefits of more security and less fear.

In the previous chapter, the argument was made that in many developing countries, organized crime and corruption undermine the rule of law required for sustainable economic growth. Many developing countries would experience much higher annual growth rates if they would be able to put their legal house in order and empower law enforcement and criminal justice to crush criminal elites. If such missed opportunities of economic development are added to the "losses of crime" under the category of indirect consequences, the world's total crime bill would far exceed the estimated $2.4 trillion. In the developing world, it would stimulate sustainable growth and thereby contribute to the elimination of poverty. To highlight the missed opportunities of development through crime prevention, we will demonstrate the crime-development link once more in the following section.

Lawfulness and Human Development

The index of lawfulness is, as was to be expected for the reasons discussed in the previous chapter, strongly related to indices of human development ($r = .72$, $p < 0.000$,

$n = 152$). The correlation between lawfulness and human development is strongest for the group of Western countries ($r = .77$). Within Europe, the correlation is almost perfect ($r = .91$). On the basis of the lawfulness index, the level of human development of individual European countries can be estimated within very small margins. In all other world regions, the correlations between lawfulness and human development are moderately strong to strong.

In Figures 13.3, 13.4, and 13.5, we present a final overview of our analytical results in the form of scatterplots depicting the degree of lawfulness of countries and their level of human development worldwide, for the groups of Western countries and for Latin America. Data for the other world regions are given in Appendix B. The scatterplots visualize once again how closely human development and lawfulness are interrelated. Although the precise causal mechanisms at play are not yet fully understood, improvements on the vertical axis depicting human development seem hard to obtain without concurrent improvements in lawfulness. On the other hand, the potential for achieving increases in wealth through investments in better infrastructures for lawfulness seems enormous.

The North–South "Security Divide"

The results of the epidemiological analyses presented in the previous chapters convey both bad and good news. The good news is that crime rates are no longer increasing everywhere. Evidence from both police records and victimization surveys show significant drops in common crime across the industrialized world. The volume crime epidemics that have plagued Western societies for decades have abated as a result of several social changes such as aging of the population and the stabilization of drug markets. The declines have also resulted from large-scale investments in self-protection and evidence-based crime prevention and control. Several decades of rising crime have mobilized public opinion against crime. This awareness has spurred a powerful countercrime movement of individual and collective responses to crime that is now finally bringing results. In the early 21st century, postindustrialized societies seem to have found the answer to common crime. Internet-based crimes may cause increasing problems, but countermeasures will probably soon become more effective in this domain as well. A considerable body of knowledge on the best ways to reduce volume crime through collaborative efforts of the private and public sectors has been accumulated. This knowledge is now available to the world community at large.

Also on the positive side, our analytical findings suggest that institutional arrangements for the maintenance of the rule of law impact strongly on the extent of organized crime and corruption in a country. Where the rule of law is institutionally assured and law enforcement operates well, the organized crime–corruption nexus is less pronounced, suggesting that well-functioning law enforcement and court systems can contribute significantly to the control of complex crimes such as organized crime and grand corruption. Contrary to widespread defeatist beliefs, our analysis also showed the potential contribution of law enforcement and the rule of law for the prevention of terrorist attacks. Stronger criminal justice systems will help to control organized crime/corruption and prevent terrorism as a bonus.

❖ **Figure 13.3** Scores on the Comprehensive Index of Lawfulness and the Human Development Index by Country (high scores indicate high levels of lawfulness and of human development)

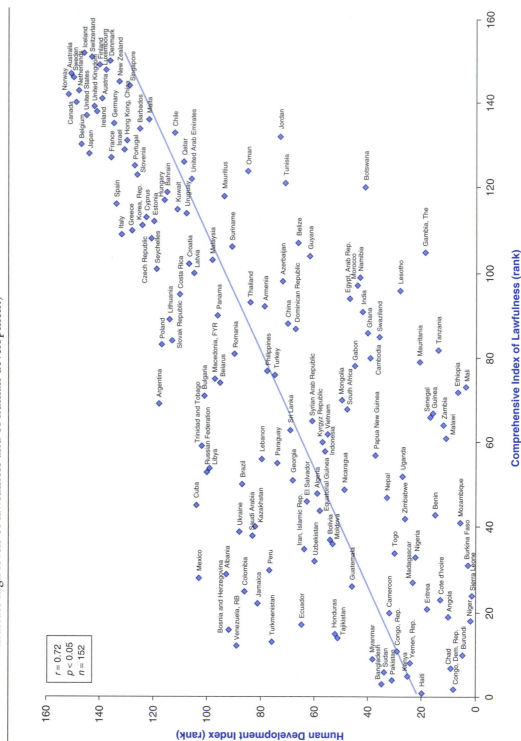

$r = 0.72$
$p < 0.05$
$n = 152$

Source:

❖ **Figure 13.4**   Scores on the Comprehensive Index of Lawfulness and the Human Development Index, in Western Countries

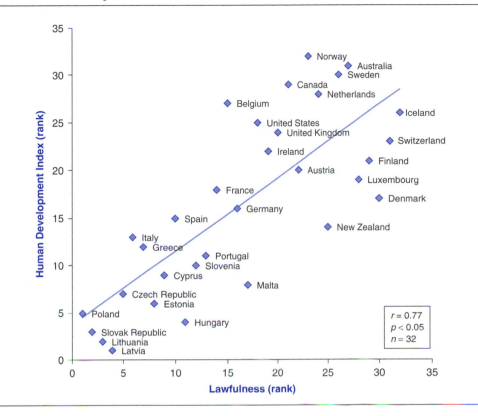

However, most other news from the international crime front is less positive. There are, first of all, few indications of declining crime rates in poorer regions of the world. Available data indicate that violent predatory crime in many developing countries is still trending upward. Macro changes such as urbanization and, paradoxically, greater affluence will not facilitate reductions in the level of common crime in the near term. Many developing countries are likely to mirror the prolonged rises in volume crime experienced in most Western countries during the 1970s and 1980s. Volume crime and rampant violence against both women and men will probably continue to inflict suffering on the rapidly growing urban populations of Latin America, sub-Saharan Africa, and parts of Asia on a huge scale.

Many of the same countries are also confronted with a high prevalence of organized crime and corruption, which interfere with political and legislative processes and hamper sustainable development. The inhabitants of these countries are the collective victims of these types of crime. The burden of crime weighs heavily on the populations of many developing countries both at the individual level and collectively. In the area of crime and public safety, globalization processes have not led to converging trends. On the contrary, a veritable "security divide" between the North and the South has come

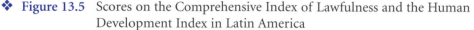

❖ **Figure 13.5** Scores on the Comprehensive Index of Lawfulness and the Human Development Index in Latin America

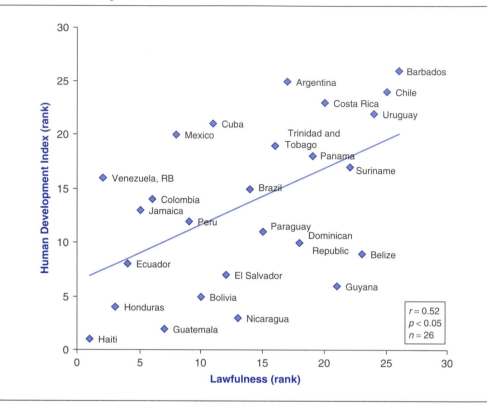

into being. The burden of crime is unequally divided between the developed North and the developing South. A particularly sad element of this divide is the large-scale victimization of young women and men from developing countries by human trafficking for exploitation in sex industries or sweatshops. And, finally, and on the negative side, innocent residents of countries across the world in the North and in the South are increasingly victimized by terrorist acts committed by ideologues with an international, nonsecular agenda. No region is immune from the attacks of international terrorism.

The "Justice Deficit"

Many developing countries face growing crime problems that victimize the national populations and that can easily spill over to other countries as well. Unfortunately, trend data on the operation of criminal justice leave little ground for optimism about the institutional capacities of developing countries to meet their growing crime challenges. In stark contrast to the increasing resources for law enforcement and criminal justice in developed countries, many developing countries have not matched rising crime rates with expanded resources. Even countries that have stepped up investments, such as South Africa, have not been able to prevent steep rises in the workloads of police officers, prosecutors, and judges. Criminal justice systems in many countries of the world are consequently overburdened or even in a state of crisis. The poor success rates of law enforcement sadly reflect their overburdening. In terms of risks to offenders of serious crimes to be arrested and convicted, many developing countries are in a vulnerable position. To recall just one telling statistic: Chances for those committing murder to be convicted are lower than 1 in 10 across sub-Saharan Africa. Similar de facto impunities for perpetrators of serious crimes exist in large parts of Latin America and the Caribbean. Many police forces in developing countries are also reputed for their solicitation of bribes and other criminal practices as a way to jack up their meager salaries.

The resulting low levels of trust among the public and businesspeople further drive down the willingness to cooperate with the police and increase reliance on the services of private security companies. Although the rapid growth of private security is likely to contribute to better control of crime against businesses, the activities of private security firms may not always be in the best interest of the community at large. It will, at any rate, never provide solutions to the security concerns of the poorest and most vulnerable groups in the population.

Court systems, like police forces, are underfunded and overburdened in most developing countries. Perhaps the most disturbing aspect of global trends in criminal justice relates to the tenuous and diminishing integrity of judiciaries. Strong, de facto independent judiciaries are critically important for the effective control of organized crime and corruption. Yet, in large parts of the world, judicial independence from external interference seems to be problematic and to have deteriorated over the past decade rather than improved. In view of the pronounced presence of organized-crime groups and the phenomenon of "state capture" in many countries, such deterioration was perhaps to be expected. Organized-crime groups typically target judges in criminal tribunals and appeals courts with bribery and intimidation in order to protect their criminal interests.

Our analyses of statistical data show, as mentioned, that terrorism is more prevalent in countries where the rule of law is less well assured. Both organized crime and terrorism flourish in countries where institutions for the maintenance of the rule of law—such as independent judiciaries respecting human rights—are weak. In countries where the rule of law is weak, special interest groups are often allowed to plunder public resources. If law enforcement is also weak, such environments form a breeding ground for organized crime. In countries where democratic freedoms and basic rights are curtailed and law enforcement, including by secret security forces, is heavy-handed, there is less space for organized crime outside the government. Instead, grievances of disadvantaged groups against the prevailing economic elites may express themselves in domestic or international terrorism. Weak rule of law, combined with repressive law enforcement and limited opportunities to express political dissent, appears to be the breeding ground of international terrorism.

Security and Justice Reform First

Just as political elites in the West in the 1970s belatedly recognized the need to respond to problems of urban crime, world leaders should now become cognizant of the need to address the multifaceted security problems of the developing world. Functioning justice and security systems are indispensable for the protection of personal security and human rights, especially of vulnerable groups such as women and children. The prevention and control of common crime should urgently be strengthened for humanitarian reasons. Tackling justice and security problems of poor people in developing countries should be recognized as one of the key humanitarian objectives of international cooperation. In many developing countries, victimization by common crime remains the most important threat to human security. Governments such as Japan and Canada that have chosen human security as the guiding principle of their international politics should put justice and security reform higher on their development agendas. Evidence-based crime prevention and victim support should be adapted to special circumstances in developing countries and then implemented on a large scale in the South.

At another level of analysis, justice and security systems are of critical importance for sustainable and equitable development. If the organized crime–corruption nexus is allowed to grow roots in a country, prospects for development are significantly diminished in the medium and long term. Many developing countries are trapped in vicious circles of dysfunctional law enforcement and criminal justice, increasing lawlessness, growing shadow economies, decreasing tax revenues, and economic stagnation. There is an emerging consensus among development experts about the need for governments of developing countries to improve governance as a requirement for receiving foreign aid. In the absence of strong institutional infrastructures, foreign aid reinforces corrupt practices and becomes itself a "resource curse," undermining rather than promoting development (Cooksey, 2002). For this reason, the World Bank and other bilateral foreign aid organizations now rightly consider to stop aid programs in countries where corruption is insufficiently controlled. Withdrawal of aid that is mismanaged or leaking away systematically seems fully justified.

Such withdrawal of aid, however, will not by itself help to solve entrenched institutional problems. Deficiencies in the capacity to control corruption should preferably lead to a reallocation of foreign support focusing on the justice and security sector rather than to withdrawal of aid across the board. The U.S. government has placed governance reform center stage in its new development aid policies. In many countries, it provides technical assistance on legal and judicial reform through its legal attachés and regional programs of the American Bar Association. Canada and several European countries including the United Kingdom and Germany have also expanded their technical assistance in the domain of governance and rule of law. The Organization for Security and Economic Cooperation (OSCE) supports police and judicial reforms across eastern and central Europe and central Asia. To an increasing extent, the World Bank acknowledges that legal and judicial reforms spur economic development and should be actively promoted (World Development Report, 2006).

Unfortunately, too many of these initiatives, programs, and projects, laudable as they are, fall short of real institution building in the areas that really count, that is, the fight against organized crime and high-level corruption. Projects favored by the donors include legal awareness-raising, legal clinics for lawyers and nonlawyers, ethics training of public officials, and promotion of a greater voice for civil interest groups. Among the rule-of-law projects, access to justice and restorative justice are in the forefront.[3] In an otherwise exemplary list of policy recommendations to address crime problems in the Caribbean adopted by UNODC and the World Bank, the emphasis is on juvenile delinquency and domestic violence (UNODC, 2007a). Hardly any attention is given to the need to set up or strengthen law enforcement and prosecutorial institutions that can target the entrenched positions of criminal political elites in the region, for example, in the Dutch Antilles. Perhaps our ranking of regions on organized-crime prevalence, showing the Caribbean on top, should give these international organizations reason to rethink their priorities.

Another approach popular with both donors and recipients is the establishment of anticorruption agencies. There is reason to fear that such projects will have little sustainable impact in developing countries infested with corrupt practices or Mafia-related activities. Extensive legal assistance programs in the 1990s in Russia, for example, were found to have had no lasting impact due to rampant corruption among judges (GAO, 2001). Many of the existing anticorruption bodies, with or without civil society participation, are doomed from the outset for lack of political support at the highest level (Moran, Doig, & Watt, 2001). There seems also little point in awareness-raising, training of low-level officials, or civil society involvement if the political elite of a country are themselves deeply involved in organized crime and corruption. The fight against such evils cannot be relegated to civil society but must primarily be fought by the state itself.

The development community has for far too long neglected the justice and security sector. Now that it has belatedly understood the importance of justice sector reforms, it largely fails, in our view, to set the right priorities. The experience in the developed world in places such as New York and Sicily has taught that preventive action against local Mafias must be accompanied by sustained efforts of law enforcement, prosecution, and the courts. Countering the Mafia, in the words of a former mayor of Palermo (Orlando, 2001), is like a two-wheeled Sicilian cart: With prevention without repression or repression without prevention, no real advances can ever be made in the fight against the Mafia. Without proper protection by the state, business leaders or civil leaders willing to stand up against criminal elites will always be exposed to intimidation. In our view, insufficient attention is given in most good governance and rule-of-law projects to the priority need of establishing anti-Mafia units in police forces and prosecution that can offer protection to those who rebel against the looting of their countries by those in power. There seems little recognition of the fact that in dangerous environments, civic activism or improved "access to justice" must be backed up by "cover fire" from law enforcement and criminal justice to stand any chance of success.

In many countries, strategies against bad practices by state officials will immediately mobilize lethal counterforces. In 2002, the attorney general and minister of justice of Nigeria, Bola Ige, a committed promotor of anticorruption measures in his country, was murdered in his home. Just before his death, he had initiated new investigations into the possibility of repatriating billions of dollars stolen by the Abacha regime. In the same year, the chief prosecutor of Guatemala, Carlos de Leon Argueta, became the target of an assassination attempt when he initiated investigations into the collusion between the army and organized crime. Many other prosecutors were intimidated into resignation. In 2003, the reform-minded prime minister of Serbia, Zoran Djindjic, was killed by powerful organized-crime groups that had operated with near impunity during the Milosovic regime. It seems somehow forgotten that even in the

European Union, the fight against organized crime and corruption led only a decade ago to the brutal killing of the Italian judges Falcone and Borssellino, among many others. The former mayor of Palermo, Leoluca Orlando, was forced to go into hiding with his family to avoid assassination by the Mafia (Orlando, 2001).

Many more examples can be given of preemptive or retributive strikes by Mafia groups against officials or journalists advocating greater lawfulness. In countries such as Mexico and Colombia, police and justice officials are killed on an almost weekly basis by drug syndicates. Gonzalez-Ruiz (2001) gave a grueling account of the kidnapping and killing of Jose Patino Moreno, federal antinarcotics prosecutor of Mexico, by the Tijuana cartel in 2000. At the time of this writing, Samuel Gonzalez-Ruiz, former chief of the Organized Crime Department of the Prosecutorial Office of Mexico, had himself left his country for security reasons. In 2000, a leading journalist in Mozambique, Carlos Cardoso, on the trail of organized-crime activities in his country at the highest political level, was assassinated (Gastrow, 2003). In 2002, Brazilian journalist Tim Lopes was killed while reporting on organized-crime-related abuses in the favelas in Rio de Janeiro (ICHRP, 2003). In 2004, one of Russia's leading investigative journalists, Paul Klebnikov, was liquidated by a "hired hand." In 2005, John Githongo, permanent secretary for ethics and governance in Kenya, decided to flee the country in response to anonymous death threats (*The Economist,* January 28, 2006). And, finally, in 2006, no less than three staff members of the Economic and Financial Crimes Commission of Nigeria were assassinated.

The cases mentioned here are just the tip of the iceberg. The ubiquity of Mafia-related terror should remind international governance reformers that in many parts of the world, promoting ad hoc reform programs to tackle crime or grand corruption is not just naïve but irresponsible as well. The moment such efforts threaten entrenched criminal interests, violent retaliation against the local reformers is a near certainty. No one should be encouraged to enter this battle without proper protection from the state or, in the case of postconflict countries, institutional entities backed by the international community.

In most countries where good governance is missing, it cannot be established without confronting the organized crime–corruption nexus head-on. Such action therefore requires the capacity to carry out criminal investigations using special techniques including adequate witness protection and, most importantly, expedient sentencing of arrested suspects by judges who cannot themselves be bribed or intimidated. This approach has worked in Sicily. More recently in Serbia, the special court for organized crime and corruption could be made operational only after special security measures for judges had been put in place and salaries were tripled.[4] In Romania, anticorruption efforts became serious only after the establishment in 2006 of a well-resourced anticorruption agency with a strong investigative and prosecutorial mandate and a well-paid staff. One of the few success stories of international peace building and postconflict reconstruction is Kosovo. One of the pillars of the international aid provided by the United Nations was a comprehensive program to strengthen the civil police, prosecution, courts, and corrections (Jones et al., 2005). At the core of the Police and Justice pillar were specialized investigative units against organized crime and human trafficking and international criminal judges protected against intimidation by local Mafia dons. Evaluation studies report that in once crime-ridden Kosovo, levels of mob-related homicide and corruption are now below the regional average.

The approach taken in Kosovo contrasts starkly with the slow and fragmented efforts of peace building forces in other postconflict countries to reestablish a functioning criminal justice system. Mr. Paddy Ashdown, looking back on the UN peace-keeping mission in East Timor, made the following observation: "In hindsight, we should have put the establishment of the rule of law first, for everything depends on it: a functioning economy, a free and fair political system, the development of civil society, public confidence in police and courts." Precious little of the lessons learned in Kosovo and Timor were put into practice in Afghanistan and Iraq. In Afghanistan, reconstruction of the security and justice system was never made a top priority, besides half-hearted attempts to stem the production of opium. As I know from personal experience as ad hoc adviser of Minister of Justice Abdul Karimi, 2 years after the international military intervention had been completed, the interim government of President Karzai still had no single prison cell at its disposal. The donor community was reluctant to invest in such a sinister institution as a prison and preferred to be associated with other, more appealing areas such as education, child care, gender equality, and health. In the early years, while several other ministries were already located in beautifully refurbished buildings, the Ministry of Justice of Afghanistan received no concrete support of the donor community at all: It lacked even basic items like office furniture or computers. In 2003, international criminal justice expert Professor Cherif Bassiouni of DePaul University in the United States was appointed by the United Nations High Commissioner of Human Rights to review the situation. He wrote a damning critique of the fragmented and flawed reconstruction of the justice sector in Afghanistan and recommended starting from scratch with the formulation of a master plan. In Iraq, efforts to strengthen the justice system have to date hardly started, although a new highly protected court has belatedly been opened in 2007. Military-type security concerns seem to have dominated the reconstruction agenda from the outset.

As said, anticorruption strategies are currently actively promoted by the development community. However, only rarely is sufficient support given to the indispensable hard edges of such strategies, such as adequately renumerated specialists in law enforcement, prosecution, sentencing, and corrections. It comes as no surprise, then, that independent evaluations of the World Bank projects in Africa make such depressing reading. In many African countries, the fight against corruption is more words than action. Typically, prosecutorial decisions are politically manipulated, and anticorruption commissions are specifically forbidden to initiate criminal proceedings. In fact, many of the newly established anticorruption agencies seem to have deliberately vague and abstract mandates. And even if their mandates are clear and concrete, they are given neither the resources nor the expertise to effectively investigate and prosecute cases of grand corruption (Klein-Haarhuis, 2005). To name and shame just one country, in Angola, where corruption has been called the "only functioning institution in the country" (McMillan, 2005), not a single case of corruption has ever been brought before the courts since independence.

In the sequencing of aid to developing countries, support for the establishment of functioning law enforcement and criminal justice systems should in my view be a top priority. Such prioritization is especially indicated in postconflict situations where organized-crime groups fill power vacuums and perpetuate conflicts and humanitarian crises for profit. Reconstruction and peace building in such countries should be spearheaded by capacity building in the investigation and prosecution of the organized crime–corruption complex. Everywhere else, criminal justice ought to be a top priority of development.

The litmus test for anticorruption or anti-Mafia strategies in vulnerable countries is the actual conviction and punishment of high-ranking public officials, including ministers and ex-ministers of the ruling party. Few if any of the countries listed in this book as the 25 least lawful will pass this test. One of the few African countries with a passable track record is South Africa. It is no coincidence that South Africa boasts a well-resourced specialized antigraft unit within its national police force (called the Scorpions). This unit is well funded, independent, and meets the highest standards of professionalism. It stubbornly prepared the ground for the indictment for corruption of the country's then vice president, Mr. Zuma, and his business associates (subsequently convicted). In the framework of the South Africa Growth Initiative, Harvard economist Stone (2006) advises the government of South Africa to give priority to solving narrowly circumscribed crime problems such as those of small, household-based enterprises. My advice to the South African government to spur growth through criminal justice would be to stop interfering in the operations of the Scorpions. Investors' confidence hinges on the perception of how the government handles growing problems of high-level corruption and not those of petty crime against retailers.

Developments in Nigeria, where in 2004 a well-resourced new anticorruption agency, the Economic and Financial Crimes Commission (EFCC), was established with a strong mandate to investigate, seem also encouraging.[5] So far, 60 convictions of high-ranking officials have been obtained. In the run-up to national elections in 2007, 200 candidates, including many from President Obusanjo's party, have been blacklisted by the commission on account of corrupt practices.[6] Other countries in the region such as Kenya would be well advised to consider copying these African "best practices." The development of good governance should start with a functioning justice and security sector including specialized and well-resourced units targeting high-level corruption and collusion of public officials with organized-crime groups.

Addressing crime requires investments besides political will. In Hong Kong, 0.3% of the total state budget is allocated to the anticorruption agency. The agency employs a staff of over 50 specialized investigators. Many developing countries are hard-pressed to raise the revenues needed to upgrade their law enforcement and justice systems to tackle crime and corruption. The justice and security sectors of poor countries have to compete for resources with other, more politically appealing departments such as education and health. A strong security and justice sector is a hard sell as a spending priority, especially for new democracies. It is a typical case of economically sound but politically unpopular allocation of scarce public resources. This dilemma is eloquently expressed by the current president of Georgia and former minister of justice, Mikhail Saakashvili: "We need first to create elite investigation units—small, well-paid, very well-selected people with help from the FBI and other enforcement agencies to investigate corruption. We cannot do anything economically if we cannot combat corruption. But to combat corruption, the government should be strong, with enough revenue to sustain armed forces, police, security apparatus, and courts. So it's like a catch-22 situation" (cited by Russell Johnston, 2004).

To break the downward spirals of lawlessness and poverty, development strategies should give more priority to strengthening judiciaries and specialized anti-Mafia and antigraft units within law enforcement and prosecution services. In many countries, such units can potentially gain back significant parts of their funding through efforts to trace, freeze, confiscate, and repatriate illicit gains of crime and corruption transferred to Western banks, especially if duly supported by Western authorities and banks in accordance with international conventions.[7]

In parallel, civil society should be empowered to act as guardians of reform and to hold authorities accountable for their performance in upholding the law. Public revenues and spending should be made fully transparent for watchdog institutions. Freedom of the press should be made meaningful through adequate protection of journalists against retaliations. In short, large-scale and sustained support programs are called for to reduce the justice deficit of the South, especially in the difficult field of specialized investigation of complex crimes. Only by reducing the justice deficit can the security divide be narrowed. Only by investing in criminal justice can avenues be opened for sustainable and equitable development.

The UN Millennium Development Goals

In spite of the successes of the UN reconstruction efforts in Kosovo and the advice of Mr. Ashdown, the need of institutional reform in the security and justice sector is conspicuously missing in the UN's own Millennium Development Goals.[8] In the current situation, funding for such reforms is marginal, and security and justice sectors will remain the Cinderellas of International Development Aid. In some countries, notably the United States, projects strengthening law enforcement or prison systems are explicitly excluded from funding by development aid programs. And yet many objectives of development cooperation, including the UN's Millennium Development Goals themselves, will remain sadly out of reach without functioning criminal justice systems capable of effectively addressing common crime, the organized crime–corruption nexus, and terrorism. Development experts monitoring the implementation of the UN's Millennium Project, belatedly, have arrived at the same conclusion in the 2007 State of the Future Report (Glenn & Gordon, 2007).[9]

There is little reason to doubt the potential cost-effectiveness of the proposed institution building. In fact, international "best practices" in tackling crime and corruption show the potential for excellent returns on investment. It should be recalled in this context that, as described in Chapter 10, total resources for criminal justice, especially for prosecution services and courts, are miniscule compared to those for education or health care. Globally, there are less than 10 judges per 100,000 population employed. With small funds, systemwide improvements can be achieved in almost all developing countries. With hindsight, it seems a sadly missed opportunity that strengthening the rule of law itself was not chosen as one of the Millennium Development Goals.

A More Secure World

International cooperation in criminal justice is not only a priority for development reasons. It is, of course, also dictated by the increasingly global nature of conventional and emerging security threats. An increasing number of emerging crimes, such as international terrorism and crimes committed on the World Wide Web, are transnational in nature. The growing internal security problems of many developing countries are likely to spill over into other countries in numerous ways. Increasing numbers of inhabitants of the more-affluent countries spend time traveling to the South for business or vacation. The number of people visiting other countries as tourists is nearing one billion per year. More-affluent nations are at the receiving end of large-scale cyberfraud as well as of criminal trafficking of persons and smuggling of migrants, ineffectively addressed in countries of origin and transit. Organized crime and corruption are often instrumental in the perpetuation of internal conflicts, which prevent state formation. The prolonged absence of functioning core state institutions can have serious global security implications, as shown by the examples of Afghanistan, Colombia, Haiti, and Somalia (Gros, 2003).

The world community is now, as the Secretary General's report *In Larger Freedom* concluded, increasingly at risk of victimization by terrorists using primitive nuclear bombs or other weapons of mass destruction. The seriousness of these emerging global threats underlines the need to fight transnational (organized) crime and related security problems through operational partnerships of competent law enforcement and criminal justice agencies spanning the world. International cooperation in criminal justice is still often perceived by legal dogmatists as a threat to national sovereignty. In reality, the sovereignty of nations is under threat from criminal globalists that no national government on its own can control.

Legal frameworks for international cooperation in law enforcement and judicial matters such as the new UN criminal law conventions against transnational organized crime and corruption have recently been elaborated (Laborde, 2005). A new convention against cybercrime has been under consideration for some years. Such instruments, however, even with close to universal ratification, do not, by themselves, assure effective international cooperation between law enforcement officials and judges (Williams & Vlassis, 2001).[10] Implementation requires political will and sufficient resources (Gros, 2003). In his proposals for reform of the United Nations, the former Secretary General of the UN, Mr. Kofi A. Annan, applauded the ready adoption of the said legal instruments by so many countries but added the following reservation: "However, many of the states parties to these treaties have not implemented them adequately, sometimes because they genuinely lack the capacity to do so" (United Nations, 2005). One of the proposals to governments in Annan's report is "to accede to the conventions on organized crime and corruption, and take all necessary steps to implement them effectively, including by incorporating the provisions of those conventions into national legislation and strengthening criminal justice systems." Elsewhere in the report, states are encouraged to help "each other to strengthen domestic criminal justice systems and rule of law systems."

The UN conventions against transnational organized crime and against corruption contain special provisions on the implementation of the convention through economic development and technical assistance. The UNTOC convention even foresees the creation of a special account to which donor countries can make voluntary contributions through sharing a percentage of proceeds of crime or property confiscated from criminal groups. To date, no follow-up to this provision has been given by any of the state parties.[11] Donor countries, to serve their own security interests, should be ready to give a higher priority in their development aid programs to capacity building in the justice and security sector. To this end, the North should facilitate large-scale investment in crime prevention, law enforcement, and criminal justice capacities in the South, not just out of global solidarity but for reasons of global as well as national security. As is often repeated, today's global crime problems require global solutions. The time has come to turn this notion into a vibrant international reality.[12]

Notes

1. The concept "rule of law"—or "Etat de droit" in French—refers to the institutional and legal capacity of governments to uphold the law, including basic human rights. The concept refers to the relationships between the state and its citizens rather than to the relationships among citizens themselves. The concept of a culture of legality or "culture of lawfulness" is described by Italian scholars as a culture supportive of the rule of law: "Without such a culture, there would almost certainly be more crime. Most people act in a manner consistent with the law because of their expectations that others will behave similarly and that this is best for everyone. In the absence of a culture of lawfulness, many will be freer to satisfy their immediate needs and preferences, even in the presence of elaborate laws. On the other hand, without laws and law enforcement, the culture of lawfulness is, on its own, unlikely to provide for the rule of law. There must be specific processes for rulemaking and rule enforcing. The culture needs enforcement, but the enforcers need the culture" (Godson, 2000).

2. If indirect consequential costs for society are understood in a broader way, the estimated costs become even considerably higher. By looking at a wide range of indirect consequential costs including opportunity costs of victims and offenders, for example, the costs of spending time on taking precautions, Anderson (1999) arrived at a total crime bill of $1 trillion for the United States alone. By comparison, the estimate of a global crime bill of $2.4 trillion seems conservative.

3. In a recent report of the Vera Institute of Justice for the UK Department for International Development (DFID) on justice and security sector reform, much importance is attached to the need of involving civil society and of poverty reduction through access of justice and community safety (Stone et al., 2005). The Canadian International Development Agency stresses similar bottom-up approaches with a focus on governance, human rights, people-centeredness, civil society involvement, locally owned activities, community-based approaches, multisector strategies, and partnerships (Dandurand et al., 2004). In the World Bank's 2006 World Development Report, the emphasis is on promoting equity in development through legal reform rather than on tackling the Mafias of the world by strengthening specialized law enforcement, prosecution, and judicial integrity and protection against intimidation.

4. "The problem of organized crime has deeply shaken Serbian society and threatened its vital functions. As has been the experience of all states confronted with the threat of organized crime, the efficient fight against it requires first of all a well-organized network of specialized state bodies supported by strong media campaigns and fast and efficiently operating courts. It should also be stressed that officials working for these bodies must be well paid and, even more importantly, adequately protected against the serious risks their work entails" (Dulic, 2004).

5. The EFCC of Nigeria also provides invaluable help to European and American investigators, investigating the Nigerian letter scams (www.ultrascan.nl).

6. In the media, doubts have been expressed about the impartiality of the commission, which is said to be used as a means to discredit political opponents of the president.

7. In many developing countries, a considerable portion of the transfer and storing of wealth takes place outside of official financial institutions (for example, the trust-based hawala system of transferring funds). Many developing countries and countries in transition therefore have an urgent need to develop skills and techniques for targeting criminal proceeds that are appropriate to the level of development of their financial systems and law enforcement expertise. This implies a renewed focus on aspects such as basic investigative skills, intelligence-led policing, value-based confiscation, reversal of the onus of proof as regards origin of assets, cross-border currency detection, and other related interventions.

8. In his latest book, Jeffrey Sachs, key adviser on the UN's Development Goals, largely ignores the impact of institutional factors on economic development (Sachs, 2005). In his essays on "clinical economics" analyzing the past or present economic problems of a dozen countries including Russia, Guatemala, and Bolivia, no mention is made of the organized crime–corruption nexus and the need of functioning justice and security sectors to tackle these sociopathological phenomena. In the "clinical economics" of Sachs, some of the most important ills of countries as well as proven cures against them are completely ignored.

9. In an otherwise fairly optimistic overview of global trends, the authors point to the economic and political threat posed by organized crime and corruption: "Transnational organized crime continues to grow in the absence of a comprehensive, integrated global counter strategy. Its total annual income could be well over 2 trillion dollars, giving it more financial resources than all the military budgets worldwide."

10. To counter the growing threat of cybercrime, police forces worldwide employ an estimated 0.5 expert per 100,000 police officers. The number needed to make a dent in the Nigerian scams has been estimated at 16 per 100,000. Besides more personnel, international cooperation needs to be significantly improved (www.ultrascan.nl).

11. At the signing ceremony of the UNTOC in Palermo in December 2000, the minister of justice of Italy formally announced his government's intention to donate in accordance with Article 30 of the UNTOC convention 10% of all confiscated assets of criminal groups in Italy to the UN as a voluntary contribution to the convention's worldwide implementation. To date, Italy has not made any such donation.

12. At the Round Table in Abuja, Nigeria, on October 14, 2005, organized by the African Union and the United Nations Office on Crime and Drugs, a plan of action was adopted to tackle the region's endemic problems of crime (UNODC, 2005) but no real follow up has been given so far.

Appendix A

Data Sources

International Crime Victim Surveys (ICVS)

The International Crime Victim Surveys (ICVS) provide internationally comparable information on victimization by crime through a standard questionnaire. To ensure comparability, all aspects of the methodology have been standardized to the maximum possible extent. The first round of international surveys was done in 14 countries in 1989, providing a first comparable estimate of the level of common crime in 1988. The interviews were done by phone using the CATI (Computer Assisted Telephone Interviewing) technique. That year pilot studies were also done in Indonesia (Surabaja) and Poland (Warsaw). Results were presented in Van Dijk, Mayhew, and Killias (1990). The United Nations Interregional Crime and Justice Research Institute (UNICRI) became involved in 1991 with the aim of providing a wider geographical coverage to the project. Since in most non-Western countries telephone interviewing was not possible, a face-to-face methodology was used for this purpose. For cost reasons, it was agreed that face-to-face surveys would be mainly conducted in the capital (or largest) cities of participating developing countries.

The second round of surveys took place in 1992 with a total of 33 participating countries, including 20 developing or transitional countries where the face-to-face technique was used. The third round of surveys was done in 1996 in 48 countries (36 face-to-face). The fourth round of surveys was done in 2000–2002 with a total of 48 participating countries again, including 30 face-to-face. A fifth round of surveys was conducted in 2004–2005 under the supervision of UNODC, UNICRI, and INTERVICT. Surveys were executed among 18 member states of the European Union by a consortium, consisting of UNICRI, Gallup/Europe, and the Max Planck Institute in Freiburg, Germany, among others, and with partial funding of the European Commission (DG Research). Participation in the 5th sweep was secured with national samples in 28 countries and capital city samples in another 5. The 33 participants included several new entrants such as Bulgaria, Cambodia, Greece, Ireland, Luxembourg, Mozambique, Iceland, Turkey, Mexico, Hong Kong, and Peru. By 2005, over 140 surveys had been done in 78 different countries (in 37 countries nationwide). Over 320,000 citizens have been interviewed in the course of the ICVS so far. Funding for the ICVS has come from a variety of sources. In most developed and middle-income countries, data collection was funded by national ministries or research agencies. Surveys conducted in developing and transitional countries in 1992, 1996, and 2000 were mainly funded by the Dutch Ministry of Development Cooperation. The Dutch Ministry of Justice has over the years been the main contributor to the overhead of the ongoing project. A consortium of research institutes from England/Wales, the US, Canada, Australia and The Netherlands, is planning a repeat of the survey in 2009.

Methodology

The ICVS targets samples of households in which only one respondent age 16 or above is selected for interviewing. National samples include at least 2,000 respondents who are generally interviewed by telephone (CATI). In the countries where this method is not applicable because of insufficient distribution of telephones, face-to-face interviews are generally conducted in the capital city, with samples of 1,000–1,500 respondents. To reduce memory errors in the timing of incidents (forward time-telescoping), respondents are first asked whether they have been victimized in the course of the past 5 years and, if yes, whether it (also) happened during the past calendar year. Victimization percentages relate to incidents that are placed in the last year (for details, see Van Dijk, Manchin, Van Kesteren & Hideg, 2007; Van Dijk, Van Kesteren, & Smit, 2007).

Samples for the ICVS surveys using CATI are based on random-digit dialing of landline phone numbers stratified by local area. Interviews are taken with the member of the household whose birthday is coming up next. Results are weighted for the variables gender, age, household composition, and area. Surveys using face-to-face interviewing in Estonia, Poland, and Japan used randomly selected persons drawn from official national registrations. These samples were also stratified by local area. The surveys in the main cities in developing countries were, as said, done face-to-face. The sample method was tailored to local circumstances, but generally, a multi-stage stratified sample was used.

The average duration of the interview in the CATI-based studies was around 20 minutes. The surveys that were done face-to-face took more time; this interview technique generally takes 30% to 50% longer. In Japan, the interviews lasted on average 50 minutes, due mainly to the elaborate formulations needed in the Japanese language.

The use of different modes of interviewing raises the issue whether this may have compromised comparability of results. Methodological work has shown that, generally speaking, responses to questions on victimization from telephone interviews are similar to those obtained face-to-face (Van Dijk & Mayhew, 1992). This conclusion is based on, among other things, experimental work carried out in the Netherlands comparing CATI-based interviews on a core set of ICVS questions with face-to-face interviews. Both modes of interviewing produced the same prevalence rates. No significant differences in victimization rates were found in a similar ICVS-based experiment in Slovenia. Tests in the course of the NCVS in the United States, however, have demonstrated higher victimization counts in CATI-based interviews than in either face-to-face or telephone interviews. This difference seems to have been caused primarily by better supervision of interviewers in centralized CATI facilities. The available experimental evidence suggests that, *given the same standard of field work*, interview mode does not significantly affect victimization counts (for references, see

❖ **Table A.1**   Countries That Have Participated in the ICVS at Least Once, 1989–2005*

Country (city)	National	Main city	Country (city)	National	Main city
Africa			**West-Central Europe**		
Botswana (Gaborone)		●	Austria (Vienna) *	●	●
Egypt (Cairo)		●	Belgium (Brussels) *	●	●
Lesotho (Maseru)		●	Czech Republic (Prague)		●
Mozambique (Maputo)		●	Denmark (Copenhagen) *	●	●
Namibia (Windhoek)		●	England & Wales (London) *	●	●
Nigeria (Lagos)		●	Estonia	●	●
Republic of South Africa		●	Finland (Helsinki) *	●	●
Swaziland (Mbabane)		●	France (Paris) *	●	●
Tanzania (Dar es Salaam)		●	Germany (Berlin) *	●	●
Tunisia (Tunis)		●	Hungary (Budapest) *	●	●
			Iceland (Reykjavik)	●	
Latin America			Ireland (Dublin) *	●	●
Argentina (Buenos Aires)		●	Italy (Rome) *	●	●
Bolivia (La Paz)		●	Latvia (Riga)		●
Brazil (Rio de Janeiro + Sao Paulo)		●	Lithuania (Vilnius)		●
Colombia (Bogotá)		●	Luxembourg *	●	
Costa Rica (San Jose)	●	●	Malta	●	
Mexico	●		Netherlands (Amsterdam) *	●	●
Panama (Panama city)		●	Northern Ireland (Belfast)	●	●
Paraguay (Asuncion)		●	Norway	●	
Peru (Lima)		●	Poland	●	
			Portugal (Lisbon) *	●	●
Asia			Scotland (Edinburgh)	●	●
Azerbaijan (Baku)		●	Slovak Republic (Bratislava)		●
China (Beijing)		●	Slovenia (Ljubljana)		●
Kyrgyzstan (Bishkek)		●	Spain (Madrid) *	●	●
Hong Kong -SAR China-	●	●	Sweden (Stockholm) *	●	●
India (Mumbai)		●	Switzerland (Zurich) *	●	●
Indonesia (Jakarta)		●	Turkey (Istanbul)		●
Japan	●				
Cambodia (Phnom Penh)		●	**South East Europe**		
Korea (Seoul)		●	Albania (Tirana)		●
Mongolia (Ulaanbaatar)		●	Bulgaria (Sofia)	●	
The Philippines (Manila)		●	Croatia (Zagreb)		●
Papua New Guinea			Georgia (Tbilisi)	●	
			Macedonia (Skopje)		●
North America			Romania (Bucharest)		●
Canada	●		Yugoslavia (Belgrade)		●
United States (New York)	●	●			
			East Europe		
Oceania			Belarus (Minsk)		●
Australia (Sydney)	●	●	Russian Federation		●
New Zealand	●		Ukraine (Kiev)		●

*Most of the ICVS data presented in this report are from urban areas. In case a city is mentioned, the urban data applies to that city. In case a national survey does not mention a city, a selection of people living in cites larger than 100,000 inhabitants have been used.

Van Dijk, Van Kesteren, & Smit, 2007). In the framework of the ICVS, all surveys were supervised by experienced experts receiving methodological guidance from the key coordinators.

The ICVS provides rates of victimization in the previous year by 11 types of common crimes. In the 2005 survey, a question on car vandalism was deleted to create room for other questions such as those on hate crimes. An important secondary objective of the ICVS is to assess attitudes of respondents to crime and justice. Respondents are asked to explain reasons for nonreporting of crimes, thus to provide comparative information on why police statistics do not reflect the full crime picture. Those who have reported victimization to the police are asked to assess the way the police have handled their report. Furthermore, all respondents are asked to assess the performance of the police in preventing and controlling crime in their areas, the use of common crime-prevention measures by their household, and attitudes toward punishment of offenders. More details on methodology and content are given in Van Kesteren, Mayhew, and Nieuwbeerta (2002), Van Dijk, Manchin, Van Kesteren, and Hideg (2007), and Van Dijk, Van Kesteren, and Smit (2007).

Definitions

The standard questionnaire[1] has been translated in to the languages of all participating countries. The questionnaire includes sections on different types of common crime, which are described in colloquial nonlegal language, providing a common definition (see Table A.2).[2] Furthermore, questions on consumer fraud and corruption are included, also accompanied by standard definitions. The questionnaire, as said, also explores whether crimes were reported to the police, reasons for not reporting, attitudes toward the police, fear of crime, use of crime prevention measures, and opinions about sentencing. A complicating factor in the conduct of the ICVS is the tendency of partner organizations to introduce small changes in the questionnaire. Where this had happened, results on such issues were either dismissed for comparative purposes or adjusted. This has, for example, happened with some Australian results from ICVS 2005.

Among the 11 common crimes, some are "household crimes," that is, those that can be seen as affecting the household at large, and respondents report on all incidents known to them. One group of crimes deals with the vehicles owned by the respondent or his or her household, and a second group refers to breaking and entering. A third group refers to victimization experienced by the respondent personally (including corruption and consumer fraud/cheating).

Technical Note on ICVS Data Presentation

Results of the ICVS presented here are mainly based on capital city surveys or, in a few cases, subsamples from populations living in cities of 100,000 inhabitants or more (urban rates). Country rates are based on data from the latest available surveys conducted between 1996 and 2005, occasionally supplemented with data from the ICVS 1992 (five countries). All country rates used in cross-sectional analyses relate to capital city or urban rates to enhance comparability. Trend data, presented in Chapter 6, are

❖ **Table A.2**   ICVS Definitions of 13 Types of Crime

Theft of car	*Have you or other members of your household had any of their cars/vans/trucks stolen?*
Theft from car	*Have you or have members of your household been the victim of a theft of a car radio, or something else that was left in your car, or theft of a part of the car, such as a car mirror or wheel?*
Car vandalism	*Have parts of any of the cars/vans/trucks belonging to your household been deliberately damaged (vandalized)?*
Theft of motorcycle	*Have you or other members of your household had any of their mopeds/scooters/motorcycles stolen?*
Theft of bicycle	*Have you or other members of your household had any of their bicycles stolen?*
Burglary	*Did anyone actually get into your home/residence without permission, and steal or try to steal something? (not including thefts from garages, sheds, or lock-ups)*
Attempted burglary	*Do you have any evidence that someone tried to get into your home/residence unsuccessfully? For example, damage to locks, doors, or windows or scratches around the lock?*
Robbery	*Has anyone stolen something from you by using force or threatening you, or did anybody try to steal something from you by using force or threatening force?*
Theft of personal property	*Apart from theft involving force, there are many other types of theft of personal property, such as pickpocketing or theft of a purse, wallet, clothing, jewelry, or sports equipment. This can happen at one's work, at school, in a pub, on public transport, on the beach, or in the street. Have you personally been the victim of any of these thefts?*
Sexual incidents (women only in most surveys)	*People sometimes grab, touch, or assault others for sexual reasons in a really offensive way. This can happen either at home or elsewhere, for instance, in a pub, the street, at school, on public transport, in cinemas, on the beach, or at one's workplace. Has anyone done this to you?*
Assault/threat	*Have you been personally attacked or threatened by someone in a way that really frightened you, either at home or elsewhere, such as in a pub, in the street, at school, on public transport, on the beach, or at your workplace?*
Consumer fraud	*Were you the victim of a consumer fraud? In other words, has someone—when selling something to you or delivering a service—cheated you in terms of quantity or quality of the goods or services?*
Bribery/corruption	*In some countries, there is a problem of corruption among government or public officials. Has any government official, for instance, a customs officer, a police officer, or inspector in your country, asked you or expected you to pay a bribe for his or her services?*

based on national rates since capital city data on developed countries are not available for the older sweeps of the ICVS. Analyses of the correlates of crime are done on data of the ICVS 1996 and 2000 whereby 1996 and 2000 rates have been averaged if both were available. Data on correlates relate mainly to 2000. Rates of victimization used in these analyses can differ significantly from those used in the descriptive tables that are based on results of the ICVS 2005. Regional rates are based on averaging of rates from individual countries from the region (not weighted for population), and world rates are based on averaging of regional rates (not weighted for population). National sample sizes are 2,000 or more in most countries, with the exception of Luxembourg (850). Urban sample sizes per country are given in Table A.3.

The International Crime Business Survey (ICBS)

The first International Commercial Crime Survey (ICCS) was carried out in 1994 in eight countries (Van Dijk & Terlouw, 1996).[3] The same questionnaire was used in 1997 in Estonia and 1998 in South Africa (Naudee, Prinsloo, & Martins, 1999). A national survey with a very similar questionnaire was also conducted in Australia (Walker, 1994), which was followed by a national survey on the retail sector in 1999 (Taylor & Mayhew, 2002). Two surveys were carried out in southwestern Finland in 1994–1995, mostly based on the same questionnaire (Aromaa & Laitinen, 1994). Between 1995 and 1999, surveys with the same methodology were also replicated in St. Petersburg, Latvia, and Lithuania to address the issue of security of foreign businesses (Aromaa & Lehti, 1996).

The ICCS questionnaire focused mostly on experiences of victimization, information on perceptions, and attitudes toward several aspects of everyday business. However, from the surveys conducted in St. Petersburg and the Baltic countries, it became clear that extortion and corruption were among the most pressing problems of businesses in eastern Europe (Aromaa, 2000). In the late 1990s, the ICCS questionnaire was modified to include more items on extortion and corruption. A second round of the International Crime Business Survey (ICBS)—a new name for the international survey was deemed desirable—was conducted by UNICRI in 2000 in nine central and eastern European countries. The national coordinators appointed for the ICVS in each participating country were also requested to monitor the progress of the ICBS. The role of the national coordinators included ensuring the correctness of the translation/localization of the questionnaires, monitoring of the sampling procedure, and participation in the training of the interviewers. Sampling designs for the ICBS were more complicated than for the ICVS (see Table A.4).

Funding was provided by the Ministries of Justice and Foreign Affairs/ Development Cooperation of the Netherlands and the Ministry of Justice of Hungary.[4] In order to provide for the highest comparability of the results, the fieldwork was contracted to a major international survey company, Gallup/Europe, which used its branches and associates in each participating country. Survey teams received standard training and guidelines for the project, along the lines of training provided for the ICVS. Because of the elevated costs involved, it was decided to limit the surveys to capital cities in each participating country.[5]

(*Text Continues on Page 331*)

Data from the International Crime Victim Surveys, Latest Available Urban Data (main city of inhabitants of cities larger than 100,000)

	2nd sweep-1992-1994		3rd sweep-1995-1998		4th sweep-1999-2003		5th sweep-2004-2006	
	Year of the Survey	Number of Respondents	Year of the Survey	Number of Respondents	Year of the Survey	Number of Respondents	Year of the Survey	Number of Respondents
Albania					2000	1,498		
Argentina							2004	2,533
Australia							2004	1,491
Austria							2005	1,133
Azerbaijan					2000	930		
Belarus					2000	1,520		
Belgium							2005	879
Bolivia			1996	637				
Botswana					2000	1,197		
Brazil					2002	1,400		
Bulgaria					2001	1,245	2004	577
Cambodia								
Canada							2004	765
Colombia					2000	1,016		
Costa Rica			1996	701				
Czech Rep. Republic					2000	1,511		
Denmark							2005	1,053
Egypt	1992	1,000						
England & Wales							2005	874
Estonia							2004	489

(Continued)

❖ Table A.3 (Continued)

	2nd sweep-1992-1994		3rd sweep-1995-1998		4th sweep-1999-2003		5th sweep-2004-2006	
	Year of the Survey	Number of Respondents	Year of the Survey	Number of Respondents	Year of the Survey	Number of Respondents	Year of the Survey	Number of Respondents
Finland							2005	902
France							2005	730
Georgia					2000	1,000	2005	815
Germany							2005	1,073
Greece							2005	1,105
Hungary							2005	2,283
Hong Kong (SAR)								
Iceland							2005	717
India			1996	1,014				
Ireland							2005	1,156
Italy			1996	997			2005	858
Japan							2004	1,263
Kyrgyzstan					2000	1,007		
Latvia					2000	1,010		
Lesotho					2000	1,526		
Lithuania			1996	700				
Macedonia								
Mexico					2002	993	2004	1,392
Mozambique								
Netherlands							2005	772
New Zealand							2004	1,071

	2nd sweep-1992-1994		3rd sweep-1995-1998		4th sweep-1999-2003		5th sweep-2004-2006	
	Year of the Survey	Number of Respondents	Year of the Survey	Number of Respondents	Year of the Survey	Number of Respondents	Year of the Survey	Number of Respondents
Northern Ireland							2005	965
Norway							2004	468
Paraguay			1996	587				
Peru							2005	7,011
Philippines					2000	1,500		
Poland					2000	1,061		
Portugal							2005	1,020
Republic of Korea					2000	2,043		
Romania					2000	1,506		
Russia					2000	1,500		
Scotland							2005	923
Slovenia					2001	513		
South Africa							2004	1,500
Spain							2005	927
Swaziland					2000	1,006		
Sweden							2005	1,114
Switzerland							2005	483
Tanzania	1992	1,002						
Tunisia	1992	1,086						

(Continued)

❖ Table A.3 (Continued)

	2nd sweep-1992-1994		3rd sweep-1995-1998		4th sweep-1999-2003		5th sweep-2004-2006	
	Year of the Survey	Number of Respondents	Year of the Survey	Number of Respondents	Year of the Survey	Number of Respondents	Year of the Survey	Number of Respondents
Turkey					2000	1,509	2005	1,241
Ukraine								
United Kingdom							2005	874
USA							2004	1,010
Yugoslavia			1996	1,094				
Zambia					2000	1,047		
Zimbabwe			1996	1,006				

Source: Intervict, Tilburg University

❖ Table A.4   ICBS 2000. Participating Cities/Countries, Sample Size, and
              Sampling Information

City	Country	Sample Size	Sampling
Tirana	Albania	493	List of business owners and businesses
Minsk	Belarus	316	Random sampling out of the "Directory of partner enterprises founded by members of the Minsk-capital union of entrepreneurs and employers" and the directory "Business Belarus"
Sofia	Bulgaria	532	Sample based on the database of the National Statistical Insititute
Zagreb	Croatia	457	List of companies in the city of Zagreb
Budapest	Hungary	517	Sampling based on the database of the National Statistical Institute (KSH)
Vilnius	Lithuania	525	Random route method
Bucharest	Romania	480	Random selected from three business databases
Moscow	Russia	500	Random sample of Moscow companies' phones out of WA-2 database (about 10,000 companies in Moscow)
Kiev	Ukraine	502	Sample from the latest (1998) State Statistics Committee data

The International Violence Against Women Survey (IVAWS)

The International Violence Against Women Survey (IVAWS) was started in 1997 with the development of a draft questionnaire and methodology. In late 1999, the International Project Team was formed comprising HEUNI, UNICRI, and Statistics Canada. Preparations for pilot studies were commenced in November 2001, with Canada carrying out a 100-respondent pilot study. Other countries followed with pilot studies during 2002, including Argentina, Costa Rica, Denmark, Estonia, Italy, Kazakhstan, Poland, Australia, Indonesia, the Philippines, Serbia, Switzerland, and Ukraine. In early December 2002, the questionnaire was ready for the full-fledged surveys. To date, surveys have been conducted in 10 countries.

The United Nations Survey on Crime Trends and the Operations of Criminal Justice Systems

The Economic and Social Council, in its resolution 1984/48 of May 25, 1984, requested that the Secretary-General maintain and develop a United Nations crime-related database by continuing to conduct surveys of crime trends and operations of criminal justice systems. The major goal of the United Nations Surveys on Crime Trends and the Operations of Criminal Justice Systems is to collect data on the incidence of reported crime and the operations of criminal justice systems with a view to improving the analysis and dissemination of that information globally. The survey results should provide an overview of trends and interrelationships between various parts of the criminal justice system to promote informed decision making nationally and internationally.

The definitions used in the questionnaire are broad enough to be applicable in the varying context of national criminal codes. Data from the eighth (covering 2001–2002) and previous surveys are available at the UNODC Web site (www.unodc.org). The questionnaire is available to download in Arabic, Chinese, English, French, Spanish, and Russian. The ninth survey (covering the years 2003–2004) was launched mid-2005 and has not yet produced results. A critical review of the methodology of the UN Crime Survey by Marilyn Rubin and other researchers of John Jay College, New York, is available on the UNODC Web site. For an overview of participating countries, see Table A.5.

Some Other Technical Matters

Method for Constructing Composite Indices

The following procedure was used to build the composite indices presented throughout the book. First, variables are selected that can be seen as indicators of the construct at issue (e.g., perceived prevalence of organized crime or quality of police performance). Second, the values of countries on these selected variables are rank-ordered. Third, the rank numbers are standardized by dividing them by the highest rank, multiplied by 100. Finally, country scores on the index are calculated by averaging the standardized rank numbers. This formula has been applied in previous work on comparative crime statistics done under the aegis of HEUNI in Helsinki, Finland. For more detail, see Kangaspunta et al. (1998) and Aromaa et al. (2003). For some indices, however, this method was used without applying Step 2. These indices were calculated to a 100% scale without being rank-ordered first. This was done in order to give a more detailed picture of the location of countries on the scale. The composite organized-crime index and the lawfulness index were constructed by the latter method.

Method for Constructing Scatterplots

It should be noted that most scatterplots in this book are constructed on the basis of reversed rank numbers. For both variables presented in a plot, the lowest score is given the lowest rank and the highest score the highest rank. This was done in order to make the pictures easier to understand and to be able to add country labels for as many countries as possible. Some countries are, however, not explicitly named, due to a lack of space in the plot area. Values can be found in Appendix B. In the case of the scatterplot depicting the relationship between bicycle ownership and bicycle theft in Chapter 5, we have used nonranked scores to show the exponential relationship.

Method for Constructing Bar Charts

Two different methods were used for constructing the regional bar charts in this book. In case only a limited number of data were available (<70 observations), the following regions were used: Africa, Asia, eastern Europe, western and central Europe, Canada and

❖ Table A.5   Countries Responding to the UN Survey (1995-2002)-Police Section

Region	Subregion	Country
Africa	East Africa	Mauritius Seychelles Tanzania, United Republic of Uganda
	North Africa	Morocco Tunisia
	Southern, West, and Central Africa	Côte d'Ivoire (Ivory Coast) Lesotho Namibia South Africa Swaziland Zambia Zimbabwe
	Caribbean	Bahamas Barbados Dominica Jamaica
	Central America	Costa Rica El Salvador Guatemala Panama
	North America	Canada Mexico United States of America
	South America	Argentina Bolivia Chile Colombia Paraguay Peru Uruguay Venezuela
Asia	Central Asia and Transcaucasian Countries	Armenia Azerbaijan Georgia Kazakhstan Kyrgyzstan Tajikistan

(Continued)

❖ Table A.5 (Continued)

Region	Subregion	Country
	East and Southeast Asia	China
		Hong Kong, China (SAR)
		Indonesia
		Japan
		Korea, Republic of
		Malaysia
		Myanmar
		Philippines
		Singapore
		Thailand
	Near and Middle East/Southwest Asia	Israel
		Jordan
		Kuwait
		Oman
		Pakistan
		Qatar
		Saudi Arabia
		Yemen
	Southern Asia	India
		Maldives
		Nepal
		Sri Lanka
Europe	Eastern Europe	Belarus
		Moldova, Republic of
		Russian Federation
		Ukraine
	Southeastern Europe	Albania
		Bulgaria
		Croatia
		Macedonia, FYR
		Romania
		Turkey
	Western & Central Europe	Austria
		Belgium
		Cyprus
		Czech Republic
		Denmark
		Estonia
		Finland

Region	Subregion	Country
		France
		Germany
		Greece
		Hungary
		Iceland
		Ireland
		Italy
		Latvia
		Lithuania
		Luxembourg
		Malta
		Netherlands
		Norway
		Poland
		Portugal
		Slovakia
		Slovenia
		Spain
		Sweden
		Switzerland
		United Kingdom
Oceania		Australia
		Fiji
		New Zealand
		Papua New Guinea
		Tonga

the United States (North America; weighted as 1:9), Latin America and the Caribbean (including Mexico), and Oceania (Australia and New Zealand). This is the case for most bar charts with ICVS data. In case data on more countries were available, the following regional division was used: East Africa, North Africa, southern Africa, West and central Africa, the Caribbean, Central America, North America (the United States, Canada, Mexico; unweighted), South America, Central Asia and Transcaucasian countries, East and Southeast Asia, the Near and Middle East (Southwest Asia), southern Asia, eastern Europe, southeastern Europe, western and central Europe, and Oceania (excluding Papua New Guinea). In a few cases, however, the first method was also used for larger data sets. Data on Papua New Guinea that are not available in machine-readable form and have been added on an ad hoc basis were not included in the regional rates for Oceania.

The details on both regional divisions are showed in the tables below:

❖ **Table A.6**   Regional Divisions for Smaller Data Sets*

Africa
Algeria
Angola
Benin
Botswana
Burkina Faso
Burundi
Cameroon
Cape Verde
Central African
    Republic
Chad
Comoros
Congo, Dem. Rep.
Congo, Rep.
Cote d'Ivoire
    (Ivory Coast)
Djibouti
Egypt, Arab Rep.
Equatorial Guinea
Eritrea
Ethiopia
Gabon
Gambia, The
Ghana
Guinea
Guinea-Bissau
Kenya
Lesotho
Liberia
Libya
Madagascar
Malawi
Mali
Mauritania
Mauritius
Morocco
Mozambique
Namibia
Niger
Nigeria
Reunion
Rwanda
Sao Tome and
    Principe

Senegal
Seychelles
Sierra Leone
Somalia
South Africa
Sudan
Swaziland
Tanzania
Togo
Tunisia
Uganda
Zambia
Zimbabwe

USA & Canada**
Canada
USA

Latin America + Caribbean
Antigua and Barbuda
Argentina
Bahamas, The
Barbados
Belize
Bolivia
Brazil
Canada
Chile
Colombia
Costa Rica
Cuba
Dominica
Dominican Republic
Ecuador
El Salvador
Grenada
Guadelupe
Guatemala
Guyana
Haiti
Honduras
Jamaica
Martinique
Mexico
Nicaragua

Panama
Paraguay
Peru
Puerto Rico
Saint Kitts & Nevis
Saint Lucia
Saint Vincent & Grenadines
Suriname
Trinidad and Tobago
Uruguay
Venezuela, RB

Eastern/Southeastern
Europe Vietnam
Albania
Belarus
Bosnia and Herzegovina
Bulgaria
Croatia
Macedonia, FYR
Moldova
Romania
Russian Federation
Serbia and Montenegro
Turkey
Ukraine

Asia
Afghanistan
Armenia
Azerbaijan
Bahrain
Bangladesh
Bhutan
Brunei
Cambodia
China
East Timor
Georgia
Hong Kong, China
India
Indonesia
Iran, Islamic Rep.
Iraq
Israel

Japan
Jordan
Kazakhstan
Korea, Dem. Rep.
Korea, Rep.
Kuwait
Kyrgyz Republic
Lao, PDR
Lebanon
Macao, China
Malaysia
Maldives
Mongolia
Myanmar
Nepal
Oman
Pakistan
Philippines
Qatar
Saudi Arabia
Singapore
Sri Lanka
Syrian Arab
    Republic
Taiwan, China
Tajikistan
Thailand
Turkmenistan
United Arab
    Emirates
Uzbekistan
Vietnam
West Bank and
    Gaza
Yemen, Rep.

Western and
    Central Europe
Andora
Austria
Belgium
Cyprus
Czech Republic
Denmark
Estonia

Finland	Lithuania	Slovenia	Kiribati
France	Luxembourg	Spain	Marshall Islands
Germany	Malta	Sweden	Micronesia
Greece	Monaco	Switzerland	Nauru
Hungary	Netherlands	United Kingdom	New Zealand
Iceland	Norway		Papua New Guinea
Ireland	Poland		Samoa (Western)
Italy	Portugal	**Oceania**	Solomon Islands
Latvia	San Marino	Australia	Tonga
Liechtenstein	Slovak Republic	Fiji	Vanatu

*All regional scores are computed giving each country equal weight, disregarding the size of a country.

**USA and Canada are weighted though as 9:1

❖ Table A.7   Regional Divisions for Bigger Data Sets

East Africa	Lesotho	Guinea-Bissau	Saint Kitts & Nevis
Burundi	Malawi	Liberia	Saint Lucia
Comoros	Mozambique	Mali	Saint Vincent & Grenadines
Djibouti	Namibia	Mauritania	Trinidad and Tobago
Eritrea	Reunion	Niger	
Ethiopia	South Africa	Nigeria	**Central America**
Kenya	Swaziland	Sao Tome and Principe	Belize
Madagascar	Zambia	Senegal	Costa Rica
Mauritius	Zimbabwe	Sierra Leone	El Salvador
Rwanda		Togo	Guatemala
Seychelles	**West & Central Africa**	Sierra Leone	Honduras
Somalia	Benin	Togo	Nicaragua
Tanzania	Burkina Faso		Panama
Uganda	Cameroon	**Caribbean**	
	Cape Verde	Antigua and Barbuda	**North America**
North Africa	Central African	Bahamas, The	Canada
Algeria	Republic	Barbados	Mexico
Egypt, Arab Rep.	Chad	Cuba	United States
Libya	Congo, Dem. Rep.	Dominica	
Morocco	Congo, Rep.	Dominican Republic	**South America**
Sudan	Cote d'Ivoire	Grenada	Argentina
Tunisia	Equatorial Guinea	Guadelupe	Bolivia
	Gabon	Haiti	Brazil
Southern Africa	Gambia, The	Jamaica	Chile
Angola	Ghana	Martinique	Colombia
Botswana	Guinea	Puerto Rico	Ecuador

(Continued)

❖ **Table A.7** (Continued)

Guyana	Mongolia	Nepal	Iceland
Nepal	Myanmar	Sri Lanka	Ireland
Paraguay	Philippines		Italy
Peru	Singapore	**Eastern Europe**	Latvia
Suriname	Taiwan, China	Belarus	Liechtenstein
Uruguay	Thailand	Moldova	Lithuania
Venezuela, RB	Vietnam	Russian Federation	Luxembourg
		Ukraine	Malta
Central Asia	**Near and Middle East**		Monaco
Armenia	**(Southwest Asia)**	**Southeastern Europe**	Netherlands
Azerbaijan	Afghanistan	Albania	Norway
Georgia	Bahrain	Bosnia and Herzegovina	Poland
Kazakhstan	Iran, Islamic Rep.	Bulgaria	Portugal
Kyrgyz Republic	Iraq	Croatia	San Marino
Tajikistan	Israel	Macedonia, FYR	Slovak Republic
Turkmenistan	Jordan	Romania	Slovenia
Uzbekistan	Kuwait	Turkey	Spain
	Lebanon	Serbia and Montenegro	Sweden
East and	Oman		Switzerland
Southeast Asia	Pakistan	**Western and Central**	United Kingdom
Brunei	Qatar	**Europe**	
Cambodia	Saudi Arabia	Andora	**Oceania**
	Syrian Arab Republic	Austria	Australia
China	United Arab	Belgium	Fiji
East Timor	Emirates	Cyprus	Kiribati
Hong Kong, China	West Bank and Gaza	Czech Republic	Marshall Islands
Indonesia	Yemen, Rep.	Denmark	Micronesia
Japan		Estonia	New Zealand
Korea, Dem. Rep.	**Southern Asia**	Finland	Papua New Guinea
Korea, Rep.	Bangladesh	France	Samoa (Western)
Lao, PDR	Bhutan	Germany	Solomon Islands
Macao, China	India	Greece	Tonga
Malaysia	Maldives	Hungary	Vanatu

Notes

1. Downloadable in English from the UNODC Web site http://www.unodc.org/unodc/en/research_icvs.html or www.tilburguniversity.nl/intervict

2. Much attention has been paid to the issue of translation of concepts and terms into the various languages. Regular meetings of survey coordinators from participating countries have facilitated the exercise.

3. Full-fledged surveys in 1994 were conducted in the Czech Republic, France, Germany, Hungary, Italy, the Netherlands, Switzerland, and the United Kingdom. Pilot surveys were also done in Australia, Indonesia, South Africa (Johannesburg), and Spain (Malaga).

4. Funding for the surveys in Albania, Croatia, and Romania was provided by the Dutch Ministry of Justice within the framework of the ICVS/ICBS 2000. Funding for the surveys in Belarus, Bulgaria, Lithuania, Russia, and Ukraine was provided by the Ministry of Foreign Affairs of the Netherlands within the framework of the project "Assessing Violence, Corruption, and Organized Crime in Eastern-Central European Countries." The survey in Hungary was funded by the Hungarian Ministry of Justice within the framework of the joint UNICRI/CICP project Assessment of Corruption in Hungary, a component of the UNODC Global Programme Against Corruption.

5. Another reason for carrying out city rather than national surveys was the lack of systematic information in the participating countries. The same decision was made with the ICVS in central-eastern Europe and developing countries. For more detailed information and technical discussion on the ICVS methodology in developing countries, see Alvazzi del Frate, Zvekic, & Van Dijk (1993), Svekic & Alvazzi del Frate (1995), and Hatalak, Alvazzi del Frate, & Zvekic (2000).

Appendix B

Data Tables

Chapter 2

Data in Figures 2.1, 2.2, 2.3, and 2.4

Country/City	Reporting 9 Crimes Last Year	Burglary	Robbery	Assault & Threat	Police Doing Good Job	Total Recorded Crimes × 100,000 Population	Total Prevalence Victims × 100 Survey Sample
Albania	18	37	16	19	44	168.3	31.7
Argentina	29	33	34	25	37	3,674.6	33.7
Australia	57	86	55		81	4,163.6	32.1
Austria	61	73	48	35	77		
Azerbaijan	25	35	47	31	76	189.9	8.3
Belarus	34	63	40	22	33	1,338.7	23.6
Belgium	63	90	64	37	58	9,421.7	32.8
Bolivia	15	30	14	12			
Botswana	48	70	38	24			
Brazil (Rio)	32	31	24	30			
Brazil (Sao Paolo)	37	31	32	27			
Bulgaria	41	52	32	27		1,822.7	27.2
Cambodia					65		
Canada	46	74	46	37	87	8,025.4	26.9
China					92		
Colombia	23	42	19	18	32	506.4	50, 7
Costa Rica	21	36	20	25			
Croatia					48	2,281.1	14.3
Czech Republic					57	3,650.0	34.1
Denmark	60	82	43	39	79	9,137.7	31.1
Egypt, Arab Rep.					39		
England & Wales	59	88	60	36			
Estonia	42	52	39	26	42	4,218.9	41.2
Finland	48	68	41	23	85	10,005.7	26.6
France	56	77	44	40	62	6,404.6	32.8
Georgia					34		
Germany	52	86	36	24	62		
Greece	45	71	34	22	45		
Hong Kong	24	74	40	33	94		
Hungary	55	76	46	18	69	4,142	32.1
Iceland	36	73	41	30			
India	35	67	52	29			
Ireland	48	85	38	31	81		
Italy	58	78	51	35	57		
Japan	55	63	25	46		2,244.4	15.3
Korea, Rep.					63	3,282.9	20.9
Kyrgyzstan	17	66	19	13			
Latvia	29	71	37	22	28	2,109.9	27.8

Country/City	Reporting 9 Crimes Last Year	Burglary	Robbery	Assault & Threat	Police Doing Good Job	Total Recorded Crimes × 100,000 Population	Total Prevalence Victims × 100 Survey Sample
Lesotho	32	61	27	30		1,282.2	27.7
Lithuania	33	50	44	24	32	2,670.7	31
Luxembourg	48	82	39	29			
Macedonia	37	65	41	33			
Malta	60	77	27	37			
Mexico	19	3	2	2	41		
Mongolia					28		
Mozambique	21	26	13	19	91		
Netherlands	52	92	52	33	70	8,813.6	30.3
New Zealand	59	80	52	44	82		
Northern Ireland	58	88	67	51			
Norway	51	72	59	34	70		
Panama					44	716.3	20.3
Paraguay	26	42	21	43			
Peru	20	41	22	5			
Philippines	14	20	16	25	81	107.3	9.1
Phnom Pehn (Cambodia)	22	17	50	32			
Poland	46	62	38	38	34	3,672.9	29.7
Portugal	54	55	61	22	66	2,145.6	18.7
Prague (Czech Republic)	57	70	45	30			
Republic of Korea	20	36	31	19			
Romania	37	76	32	26	39	1,640.4	24.5
Russia	26	68	30	27	40	2,028.4	26.3
Scotland	57	90	44	53			
Slovenia	52	71	47	34	62	4,159.7	32
South Africa	44	57	38	32	53	5,918.7	36.4
Spain	48	63	48	38	53	2,279.7	18.3
Swaziland	45	83	49	23		4,802.5	44.6
Sweden	58	77	49	35	60	13,836.7	30.4
Switzerland	52	82	45	22	68	3,774.4	22.6
Tanzania					57		
Tunisia					50		
Turkey	44	56	49	18	44		
Uganda						240.6	37.3
Ukrain	21	66	31	21	29	1,118.3	29.1
United Kingdom					76	11,014.4	28.1
United States	48	77	61	43	86	4,118.8	28.4
Yugoslavia	34	72	38	26			
Zambia	38	60	27	23		601.1	34.6
Zimbabwe	33	72	42	15			

Data in Figures 2.5 and 2.6

Region	Recorded Fraud per 100,000 Inhabitants	Fraud Victimization Prevalence %	Recorded Corruption per 100,000 Inhabitants	Corruption Victimization Prevalence %
Africa	73.9	29.7	2.3	16.7
Americas	130.8	17.3	0.1	8.8
Asia	99.7	16.8	0.8	8.1
Europe	278.9	24.0	5.8	12.3
Oceania		9.0		0.5

Notes to Chapter 2 figures

ICVS-based rates in Figures 2.1 to 2.3 are based on surveys conducted in the capital. Rates are based on the last data available (1996, 2000, or 2005). Data for five countries are from the 1992 survey. This approach was taken in order to maximize the number of countries that could be included, especially developing countries. For references to core publications, see Appendix A.

For data in Figure 2.4 on crime per 100,000 population: See 8th UN Crime Survey, 2002, and ICVS, 2000, for victimization rate in cities of 100,000 inhabitants or more.

For data in Figure 2.5 on fraud: See 8th UN Crime Survey, 2002, for police-recorded fraud, and see ICVS, 2000, for victimization rate in cities of 100,000 or more.

For data in Figure 2.6 on corruption: See 8th UN Crime Survey for police-recorded corruption and ICVS, 2000, for corruption victimization rate in cities of 100,000 or more.

For data in Figure 2.7 on total crime: See Van Kesteren, Mayhew, & Nieuwbeerta (2000) for sources of national police data and ICVS, 1989–2000, for victimization data.

Chapter 3

Data in Figures 3.1– 3.13 and in Tables 3.1–3.4

Regions:

Region	Victim of 10 Crimes	Burglary	Attempted Burglary	Pick pocketing	Consumer Fraud	Car Theft	Car Theft Owners	Robbery
Asia	21.2	2.4		6.6	30.8	0.4	1.1	1.3
Western and Central Europe	22.2	2.8		3.6	15.7	1.2	1.7	1.5
Eastern Europe	22.4	2.5		6.5	38.5	0.9	1.9	1.5
North America	23.0	1.9		3.1	12.4	1.5	2.5	2.2
Oceania	23.1	4.8		1.6	7.8	1.3	1.3	1.1
Latin America and Caribbean	33.1	5.4		6.6	19.4	1.4	2.8	6.6
Africa	33.8	8.1		6.7	26.1	1.3	3.7	4.3
World	25.0	4.0		5.2	23.2	1.1	2.0	2.5

Countries:

Country	Victim of 10 Crimes	Burglary	Attempted Burglary	Pick pocketing	Consumer Fraud	Two Car-Related Crimes	Car Theft	Car Theft Owners	Robbery
Albania	31.2	3.1	3.3	7.7	47.9	6.3	1.5	3.5	2.9
Argentina	31.2	2.0	3.4	5.5	20.4	9.0	2.1	3.9	10.0
Australia	13.7	2.2	2.0	2.4		5.4	0.7	0.8	1.1
Austria	17.2	2.8	1.6	3.6	7.9	4.9	0.4	0.5	0.8
Azerbaijan	7.7	0.6	0.7	2.2	36.1	1.4	0.4	1.7	1.6
Belarus	21.7	2.6	2.1	6.7	51.7	8.2	1.0	2.2	1.4
Belgium	20.2	3.1	2.5	3.8	10.0	7.1	0.9	1.1	2.5
Bolivia	38.9	7.7	7.1	11.3	22.3	5.0	0.3	1.3	6.6
Botswana	25.7	6.8	4.0	4.2	23.6	4.3	0.3	1.0	1.8
Brazil	18.4	1.3	1.9	1.8		5.4	2.9	6.0	5.2
Bulgaria	18.0	3.1	4.4	2.5	26.1	4.4	1.7	3.0	1.2
Cambodia	41.3	15.8	7.6	11.3	40.0	4.6	0.2	1.0	1.8
Canada	19.1	1.9	1.9	0.7	7.7	6.7	0.9	1.0	1.0
China		2.3	0.2	4.7	32.3	0.7	0.0	0.6	5.3
Colombia	48.7	6.4	7.9	11.0	32.3	11.4	1.9	3.5	8.6
Costa Rica	43.5	8.5	10.6	6.5	18.6	10.8	1.1	2.4	10.0
Croatia	12.9	1.3	1.1	2.3	29.8	3.8	0.9	1.2	0.6
Czech Republic	31.3	6.7	3.8	5.5	19.6	13.9	2.6	3.5	0.5
Denmark	22.9	2.6	1.2	2.0	15.7	2.3	1.0	1.6	1.2
Egypt, Arab Rep.		2.6	4.4	6.6	48.6	6.8	1.0	3.0	8.4
Estonia	29.3	3.7	2.9	6.5	24.5	8.9	0.6	1.0	2.8
Finland	20.5	4.4	0.5	1.3	5.0	5.0	1.7	2.4	1.4
France	17.8	1.9	2.0	3.1	14.0	3.2	0.2	0.3	1.2

(Continued)

(Continued)

Country	Victim of 10 Crimes	Burglary	Attempted Burglary	Pick pocketing	Consumer Fraud	Two Car-Related Crimes	Car Theft	Car Theft Owners	Robbery
Georgia	22.5	2.6	2.5	8.2	57.3	7.0	0.7	1.7	2.0
Germany	19.3	1.1	1.3	3.0	11.0	4.2	0.4	0.6	1.2
Greece	13.5	1.7	1.9	2.6	24.1	4.0	0.7	0.9	0.7
Hong Kong, China	7.8	0.6	0.4	2.9	21.7	0.5	0.0	0.0	0.4
Hungary	12.6	1.2	1.0	3.7	25.8	2.5	0.4	0.6	1.1
Iceland	26.4	2.2	2.7	2.4	13.6	4.8	1.0	1.1	0.7
India	29.7	1.9	2.9	9.4	39.6	1.8	0.1	0.9	1.2
Indonesia	21.8	5.1	3.7	4.1	11.6	4.1	0.4	0.8	0.5
Ireland	25.7	2.6	4.0	2.6	8.2	8.3	3.0	3.5	1.8
Italy	16.6	1.5	2.1	2.2	7.8	8.5	3.4	3.7	0.7
Japan	10.8	0.7	0.9		1.9	1.4	0.2	0.2	0.4
Korea, Rep.	16.7	4.7	2.8	1.7	11.2	2.6	0.2	0.4	0.3
Kyrgyz Republic	25.6	3.4	1.9	6.0	73.3	5.0	0.7	1.8	1.6
Latvia	25.9	1.9	2.5	6.7	29.2	6.7	0.8	1.9	3.2
Lesotho	27.3	6.6	5.0	4.3	22.4	3.3	0.7	2.6	2.0
Lithuania	29.5	5.7	4.3	5.0	39.3	9.8	1.4	2.1	3.2
Macedonia, FYR	18.4	2.3	1.3	5.7	31.2	7.4	0.4	0.5	1.1
Malta		0.4	0.4	1.1	38.0	18.1	1.7	1.9	
Mexico	22.6	3.5	3.7	0.7	8.5	6.2	1.3	2.6	3.9
Mongolia	40.6	8.0	5.5	17.1	31.6	8.9	0.7	2.0	4.5
Mozambique	37.7	12.6	9.5	8.2	35.8	6.5	1.9	7.5	7.6
Namibia	35.1	8.1	6.0	3.1	19.8	7.6	1.0	1.9	5.0
Netherlands	27.0	2.1	1.8	2.4	7.6	4.7	0.7	1.0	1.1
New Zealand	25.9	4.2	4.1	0.7	7.8	10.1	1.8	1.9	1.1
Nigeria	30.5	4.5	4.4	5.4	29.9	4.0	1.0	2.7	4.6
Norway	21.5	1.9	2.1	3.3	9.1	4.0	1.0	1.2	1.0
Panama	19.0	3.8	3.3	3.1	11.4	6.2	1.0	2.0	0.9
Papua New Guinea		14.4		7.8			4.0	9.8	
Paraguay	34.5	8.2	6.5	7.8	25.5	6.0	1.2	2.0	6.7
Peru	41.0	6.8	13.0	11.4	15.8	4.7	0.3	1.5	7.4
Philippines	9.1	1.2	0.7	2.7	14.6	0.9	0.1	1.3	0.3
Poland	20.7	1.8	1.5	3.5	20.0	6.9	0.8	1.3	2.1
Portugal	9.7	0.7	0.6	1.4	7.7	4.6	2.0	2.6	1.9
Romania	22.6	1.5	1.9	9.0	39.3	7.7	0.1	0.2	0.8
Russian Federation	23.1	1.8	2.5	6.8	46.3	7.1	0.7	1.4	2.4
Serbia and Montenegro	28.7	2.9	2.7	6.7	49.6	10.5	1.4	2.1	1.1
Slovak Republic	32.4	6.4	2.3	9.8	35.3	16.2	1.8	3.0	1.2
Slovenia	26.8	3.5	1.7	2.0	10.2	9.9	0.7	0.8	1.9

Country	Victim of 10 Crimes	Burglary	Attempted Burglary	Pick pocketing	Consumer Fraud	Two Car-Related Crimes	Car Theft	Car Theft Owners	Robbery
South Africa	25.7	5.4	3.6	4.5	10.3	5.6	2.6	7.1	5.5
Spain	13.7	1.1	1.3	3.2	11.6	5.2	1.8	2.3	1.5
Swaziland	43.4	9.4	8.9	8.1	23.1	8.9	2.8	6.3	3.8
Sweden	22.6	2.1	1.3	1.2	13.7	8.5	1.8	2.1	0.7
Switzerland	20.1	2.7	1.7		7.7	2.1	0.2	0.3	1.7
Tanzania	37.6		19.2	1.4	88.8	15.8	2.9	5.7	16.4
Tunisia	35.9	7.2	3.6	11.8	59.5	11.5	1.9	4.8	13.8
Turkey	17.9	4.6	4.1	2.7	11.5	4.3	0.9	2.4	0.9
Uganda	37.3	5.9	7.0	7.6	43.5	6.0	0.3	1.1	
Ukraine	28.9	2.0	2.6	15.2	51.8	5.2	0.7	2.2	2.4
United Kingdom	32.0	4.5	5.1	5.2	12.9	9.1	1.3	2.0	2.6
United States	23.3	1.9	2.4	3.3	12.9	7.2	1.6	2.7	2.3
Zambia	34.4	10.8	6.6	6.7	43.2	3.4	0.8	3.2	2.5
Zimbabwe	46.8	10.7	9.0	16.0	27.0	6.9	0.4	1.2	4.8

See Notes to Chapter 2.

Chapter 4

Data in Figures 4.1-4.5 and in Tables 4.1-4.3

Country	Sexual offences	Assaults	Country	Homicide
Albania	6.7	0.7	Albania[1]	5.7
Argentina	2.1	0.8	Andora[3]	4.7
Australia	4.0	2.4	Argentina[1]	9.5
Austria	1.3	0.7	Armenia[2]	7.2
Azerbaijan	0.2	0.4	Australia[2]	2.8
Belarus	1.8	1.3	Austria[1]	0.8
Belgium	0.2	1.2	Azerbaijan[1]	2.6
Bolivia	1.8	2.0	Bahamas, The[4]	14.9
Botswana	5.0	1.7	Bahrain[3]	1.0
Brazil	1.3	0.9	Barbados[2]	7.5
Bulgaria	0.4	0.9	Belarus[1]	10.0
Cambodia	1.4	1.6	Belgium[1]	1.5
Canada	3.1	1.9	Bolivia[1]	2.8
China	2.0	1.5	Botswana	
Colombia	10.2	2.9	Brazil[4]	23.0
Costa Rica	5.5	1.6	Bulgaria[2]	4.1
Croatia	2.3	0.9	Cambodia	
Czech Republic	1.2	1.1	Canada[1]	1.7
Denmark	3.8	1.6	Chile[2]	1.5
Egypt	9.5	1.6	China	
Estonia	1.4	1.3	Colombia[2]	62.7
Finland	4.3	1.7	Costa Rica[1]	6.4
France	0.5	1.1	Cote d'Ivoire[2]	4.1
Georgia	1.5	0.9	Croatia[1]	1.8
Germany	2.5	1.2	Cuba[4]	6.2
Greece	1.1	0.6	Cyprus[1]	0.3
Hong Kong, China	1.2	0.3	Czech Republic[1]	2.3
Hungary	0.3	0.5	Denmark[1]	1.0
Iceland	2.6	3.0	Dominica[2]	2.7
India	7.0	0.9	Ecuador[4]	15.3
Indonesia	3.3	0.6	Egypt, Arab Rep.	
Ireland	0.8	1.4	El Salvador[1]	31.5
Italy	0.9	0.2	Estonia[2]	10.4
Japan	1.7	.	Fiji[3]	1.6
Korea, Rep.	1.2	0.5	Finland[1]	2.5
Kyrgyz Republic	2.3	2.5	France[2]	1.8
Latvia	0.7	2.0	Georgia[2]	4.8
Lesotho	5.7	2.0	Germany[1]	1.1
Lithuania	3.2	1.4	Greece[2]	0.8
Macedonia, FYR	0.5	1.0	Guatemala[2]	25.5
Mexico	1.7	0.1	Guyana[4]	6.6

Country	Sexual offences	Assaults	Country	Homicide
Mongolia	2.4	2.1	Hong Kong, China[2]	0.6
Mozambique	2.6	2.9	Hungary[1]	2.0
Namibia	4.8	2.5	Iceland[1]	1.4
Netherlands	3.2	1.6	India[2]	3.7
New Zealand	2.4	2.4	Indonesia[1]	1.0
Nigeria	8.8	1.5	Ireland[1]	1.0
Norway	2.3	1.5	Israel[4]	0.5
Panama	0.7	0.8	Italy[1]	1.1
Paraguay	3.2	1.0	Jamaica[2]	33.7
Peru	4.7		Japan[2]	0.5
Philippines	0.3	0.1	Jordan[3]	1.0
Poland	1.8	1.1	Kazakhstan[4]	17.1
Portugal	0.4	0.3	Korea, Rep.[1]	2.0
Romania	0.6	0.6	Kuwait[1]	1.0
Russian Federation	1.3	1.1	Kyrgyz Republic[2]	8.4
Serbia and Montenegro	4.6	2.3	Latvia[1]	9.2
Slovak Republic	0.7	0.6	Lesotho	
Slovenia	2.6	1.6	Lithuania[1]	8.4
South Africa	1.7	5.6	Luxembourg[1]	0.9
Spain	0.7	1.1	Macedonia, FYR[2]	2.3
Swaziland	6.2	3.8	Malaysia[2]	2.4
Sweden	0.8	1.1	Maldives[1]	2.8
Switzerland	3.1	1.0	Malta[1]	1.5
Tanzania	5.5	4.1	Mauritius[2]	2.2
Turkey	2.5	0.2	Mexico[1]	13.0
Tunisia	5.2	1.5	Moldova[1]	8.0
Ukraine	2.2	1.5	Mongolia	
United Kingdom	3.0	2.5	Morocco[1]	0.5
United States	3.5	1.7	Mozambique	
Zambia	5.4	3.1	Myanmar[1]	0.2
Zimbabwe	3.3	5.0	Namibia[1]	6.3
			Nepal[1]	3.4
			Netherlands[1]	1.0
			New Zealand[1]	1.3
			Nicaragua[4]	8.4
			Nigeria	
			Norway[2]	1.1
			Oman[1]	0.6
			Pakistan	0.0
			Panama[1]	9.6
			Papua New Guinea[2]	9.1
			Paraguay[2]	12.0
			Peru[1]	4.2

(Continued)

(Continued)

Notes to appendix chapter 4

The dataset on homicide has been constructed by taking the latest data available from different sources.
[1]UN Survey on Crime Trends and the Operation of Criminal Justice Systems, 8th survey, 2002 data;
[2]Data from UN Survey on Crime Trends and the Operation of Criminal Justice Systems, 7th survey, 2000/1999 data;
[3]Data from UN Survey on Crime Trends and the Operation of Criminal Justice Systems, 6th survey, 1997 data;
[4]Data from WHO data from World Report on Violence and Health 2002. In middle and low-income countries however the WHO data show significantly more cases of homicide than the UN Crime Surveys, 18 and 45 percent respectively. (See: Shaw, M., Van Dijk, J. and Rhomberg, W., 2003) Therefore these data have been adjusted in order to match the UN data.

ICVS - based rates are based on either special city surveys, usually conducted in the capital of countries or on the parts of national surveys that were carried out among respondents in cities of 100.000 or more inhabitants (urban rates). Rates are based on the last available (1996, 2000 or 2005). Data for five countries are from the 1992 survey. This approach was taken in order to maximize the number of countries that could be included, especially developing countries. For references to core publications see appendix A.

Chapter 5

Data in Figures 5.2, 5.3, 5.4, 5.6, 5.10, and 5.11

	Gini Index	Car Crimes	Victimization by 11 Crimes	Bicycle Ownership	Theft of a Bicycle	Ownership of a Firearm	Assault With a Gun	Robbery
Albania		7.0	31.7	54.0	4.6	14	0.5	1.4
Argentina		13.0		62.5	4.1	10	0.1	
Australia	35.2	16.6	32.1	63.2	2.0	4	0.2	
Austria	23.1	12.3	27.0	74.3	3.6	7	0.2	0.2
Azerbaijan	36	2.1	8.3	4.9	0.2	1	0.2	1.6
Belarus	21.7	10.5	23.6	40.1	0.4	6	0.3	1.4
Belgium	25	14.5	32.8	61.7	4.6	14	0.0	1.9
Bolivia	58.9	7.4	40.1	52.9	2.6	9	0.4	6.2
Botswana		5.3	26.4	27.7	1.3	4	0.1	
Brazil	59.1	16.9	48.1	67.8	1.5	9	0.1	13.5
Bulgaria	26.4	12.4	27.2	24.8	1.0	7	0.1	1.5
Cambodia	40.4	5.1	41.5	60.1	5.3	0	0.6	1.8
Canada	31.5	13.3	26.9	74.8	4.0	12	0.0	1.4
China		0.7	21.6	98.0	11.9			
Colombia	57.1	16.4	50.7	60.3	3.4	11	1.0	8.6
Costa Rica	45.9	15.3	45.5	65.3	3.4	19	0.8	10.0
Croatia	29	6.9	14.3	64.7	1.4	12	0.5	0.5
Czech Republic	25.4	17.8	34.1	65.8	4.0	9	0.4	0.5
Denmark	24.7	8.3	31.1	88.8	11.1	5	0.2	1.0
Egypt, Arab Rep.		6.8	27.0	27.4	0.7			
Estonia	37.6	19.2		57.4	5.1			6.3
Finland	25.6	8.8	26.6	88.0	6.6	13	0.0	1.2
France	32.7	19.0	34.5	58.2	2.7	11	0.0	2.3
Georgia	37.1	8.1	23.5	11.8	0.5	7	0.5	2.0
Germany		16.3	29.3	71.0	4.5			
Hungary	24.4	15.5	32.1	58.2	3.6	6	0.1	1.8
India	37.8	2.8	30.5	29.8	1.8	1	0.1	1.2
Indonesia	31.7	4.7	21.4	72.5	2.6	7	0.0	0.7
Italy		18.2	31.4	57.8	3.1			
Japan	24.9	5.2	15.3	83.3	6.6	0	0.0	0.0
Korea, Rep.	31.6	7.8	20.9	42.7	4.9	2	0.0	0.3
Kyrgyz Republic	40.5	5.5	27.4	35.9	1.9	11	0.0	1.6
Latvia	32.4	9.3	27.8	41.8	2.4	4	0.2	3.2
Lesotho	56	3.8	27.7	22.6	.8	15	1.5	2.0
Lithuania	32.4	12.6	31.0	42.6	1.2	7	0.2	3.2
Macedonia, FYR		11.2	21.6	66.5	1.4	13	0.0	
Malta		18.1	23.3	43.4	0.2	17	0.0	
Mongolia	33.2	11.4	41.8	23.8	1.3	8	0.0	4.5
Mozambique	39.6	7.4		22.8	0.8	3	1.3	7.6

(Continued)

(Continued)

	Gini Index	Car Crimes	Victimization by 11 Crimes	Bicycle Ownership	Theft of a Bicycle	Ownership of a Firearm	Assault With a Gun	Robbery
Namibia	32.6	9.6	36.4	38.5	4.0	22	0.8	
Netherlands		12.7	30.3	88.9	11.6	1	0.0	1.1
New Zealand		21.7	36.0	64.9	4.9			
Nigeria	50.6	6.5	32.2	5.9	0.2	2	0.6	4.6
Panama	48.5	8.2	20.3	41.9	1.4	12	1.0	0.9
Paraguay	57.7	8.7	36.3	61.2	4.1	32	0.2	6.7
Philippines	46.2	1.0	9.1	21.3	0.8	3	0.1	0.3
Poland	31.6	17.7	31.7	63.9	3.2	5	0.2	3.0
Romania	28.2	9.7	24.5	19.1	1.2	2	0.2	0.8
Russian Federation	48.7	11.4	26.3	45.9	1.5	8	0.3	2.4
Serbia and Montenegro	14.8		48.3	0.9	28	1.3		
Slovak Republic	19.5	21.2	35.9	66.7	5.5	4	0.4	1.2
Slovenia	28.4	17.6	32.0	81.7	6.2	5	0.5	1.9
South Africa	59.3	8.4	36.4	22.8	1.6	18	4.1	5.4
Spain		22.3	33.1	36.5	0.9			
Swaziland	60.9	11.0	44.6	34.6	2.7	11	0.8	3.8
Sweden	25	13.7	30.4	90.0	6.3	8	0.0	0.9
Switzerland	33.1	6.1	22.6	68.9	5.7	27	0.1	1.2
Tanzania		15.8	37.6	38.4	4.3			
Tunisia		11.5	35.9	39.8	3.8			
Uganda	37.4	6.0	37.3	29.8	0.8	2	0.4	4.5
Ukraine	29	6.0	29.1	25.2	1.0	6	0.1	2.4
United Kingdom	36.1	13.9	34.4	54.5	3.2	1	0.0	1.7
United States	40.8	15.4	30.7	61.9	4.1	34	2.2	1.8
Zambia	52.6	3.8	34.6	22.6	1.2	9	0.6	2.5
Zimbabwe	56.8	8.4	47.5	28.4	1.0	3	0.3	4.8

For full data set on robbery, see Chapter 4.

Data in Figures 5.7 and 5.9

Country	Homicide	Drug-Related Crimes	Spirits Consumption
Australia	1.73	12	1.18
Belgium	1.42	18	1.24
Bulgaria	2.43		2.12
Cyprus	0.39		4.30
Czech Republic	1.64		3.70
Denmark	1.44	8	1.10
Estonia	9.07		1.40
Finland	1.93	14	2.11
France		16	
Germany	0.25	13	2.00
Greece	1.93	20	1.80
Hungary	2.20		3.40
Ireland	1.04	14	2.50
Italy	0.66	23	0.40
Latvia	4.93		5.70
Luxembourg		11	
Netherlands	1.54	26	1.66
New Zealand	0.98		1.44
Norway	0.54		0.80
Poland	2.09		1.70
Portugal	1.70	24	1.40
Romania	3.07		2.50
Russian Federation	12.08		6.20
Slovak Republic	1.34		3.50
Spain	0.19	15	2.40
Sweden	1.41	15	1.00
Switzerland	0.47		1.60
Ukraine	6.7		0.40
United Kingdom		27	

Notes to Appendix Chapter 5

Data on liquor consumption stem from the World Drink Trends Report 2004 (liters of pure alcohol per capital, rates of some countries are estimated). The Gini index provides a measure of the degree of inequality.

ICVS-based rates in Chapter 5 are based on either special city surveys, usually conducted in the capital of countries, or on the parts of national surveys in developed countries that were carried out among respondents in cities of 100,000 or more inhabitants (urban rates). Rates are based on the last available survey up to 2000 (1996-2000). Data for five countries are from the 1992 survey. Overall victimization rates refer to 11 types of crime, including car vandalism (deleted in the 5th sweep). For references to core publications, see Appendix A.

Data in Figure 5.8

	Beer Consumption	Threats & Assaults 2005
Australia	92	3.4
Austria	109	1.8
Belgium	96	3.6
Bulgaria	15	1.7
Canada	69	3.0
Denmark	70	3.3
Estonia	71	2.7
Finland	81	2.2
France	35	2.1
Germany	122	2.7
Greece	39	2.4
Hungary	71	1.2
Iceland	51	5.9
Ireland	147	4.9
Italy	28	0.8
Japan	33	0.4
Luxembourg	108	2.3
Mexico	48	2.2
Netherlands	79	4.3
New Zealand	78	4.9
Norway	52	2.9
Poland	71	3.0
Portugal	59	0.9
Spain	73	1.6
Sweden	56	3.5
Switzerland	56	2.5
United Kingdom	101	5.8
United States	82	4.3

In Figure 5.8, data from the national surveys conducted in the 5th sweep (ICVS 2005) have been used in order to include some new countries in the analysis. Data on beer consumption are from the World Drink Trends 2004 (liters per capita).

Chapter 6

Data in Figure 6.1

Victimization by 10 crimes in the year preceding the survey (national surveys)					
	1st sweep (1989)	2nd sweep (1992)	3rd sweep (1996)	4th sweep (2000)	5th sweep (2004/05)
Johannesburg		32.5	35.8	35.1	23.5
Buenos Aires		40.2	56	31.7	31.2
Australia	23.3	24.0		25.2	17.3
Canada	22.4	24.0	21.8	20.5	17.2
United States	25.0	22.2	21.5	17.6	17.5
European average	16.0	21.8	22.6	20.1	16.8

Data in Figure 6.2

Victimization by contact crimes in the year preceding the survey (national surveys)					
National data	1st sweep (1989)	2nd sweep (1992)	3rd sweep (1996)	4th sweep (2000)	5th sweep (2004/05)
Johannesburg		14	13.7	12.5	9.4
Buenos Aires		13	16.1	13	13.5
Canada	6.2	7.0	6.1	6.5	4.4
United States	7.9	6.5	7.0	4.8	5.5
European average	3.3	5.7	6.1	5.7	4.7

Data in Figure 6.3

Victimization by 10 crimes in the year preceding the survey (national surveys)					
National data	1st sweep (1989)	2nd sweep (1992)	3rd sweep (1996)	4th sweep (2000)	5th sweep (2004/05)
Belgium	13.4	15.2	–	17.5	17.7
Estonia	–	27.6	28.3	26.0	20.2
Finland	13.0	17.2	16.2	16.6	12.7
France	16.4	–	20.8	17.2	12.0
Netherlands	21.9	25.7	26.0	20.2	19.7
Poland	–	24.6	20.5	19.1	15.0
Sweden	–	18.7	22.0	22.6	16.1
Switzerland	13.0	–	21.6	15.6	18.1
United Kingdom	15.0	23.9	24.7	21.8	21.0

Data in Figure 6.4

Victimization by contact crimes in the year preceding the survey (national surveys)					
National data: sweep	1st sweep (1989)	2nd sweep (1992)	3rd sweep (1996)	4th sweep (2000)	5th sweep (2004/05)
Belgium	3.3	3.0	–	4.2	4.3
Estonia	–	7.3	8.4	8.6	4.8
Finland	3.6	6.3	5.6	6.3	3.1
France	2.8	–	4.5	4.9	2.8
Netherlands	4.7	5.3	5.9	5.1	5.2
Poland	–	7.0	5.5	4.4	4.4
Sweden	–	3.3	6.2	5.4	5.3
Switzerland	2.5	–	5.3	3.9	4.4
United Kingdom	2.9	5.2	7.1	7.1	7.3

Data in Figure 6.6

	1995	2000	2005
Asia	3.2	1.8	3.7
Latin America and Caribbean	9.9	8.1	7.4
Africa	7.5	8	7.6
Western and Central Europe	8.6	9.9	13
North America	17.6	24	28.5
Oceania	18.3	31.1	40.7

Data on trends in rates of victimization by burglary per income quartiles; sources: ICVS 1998-2005

	Upper 25%	Above Average	Below Average	Lower 25%
1st sweep	2.4	2.5	2.5	2.6
2nd sweep	2.7	2.5	1.7	2.4
3rd sweep	2.8	1.8	1.7	2.7
4th sweep	2.2	1.9	2.0	2.3
5th sweep	1.7	1.4	1.9	2.3

Data on trends in % use of burglar alarms per income quartiles; sources: ICVS, 1998-2005

Income Levels	Upper 25%	Above Average	Below Average	Lower 25%
1st sweep	18	13	11	11
2nd sweep	12	9	7	7
3rd sweep	22	13	11	8
4th sweep	24	17	13	11
5th sweep	33	23	19	17

Note to data on burglary: Decrease in second sweep caused by adjustment of question in questionnaire.

Data on trends in victimization by joyriding (car recovered) and car theft (not recovered) in Chapter 6

	1st sweep −1989	2nd sweep −1992	3rd sweep −1996	4th sweep −2000	5th sweep −2005
Australia	1.9	2.8	–	1.6	0.9
Belgium	0.5	0.8	–	0.4	0.3
Canada	0.6	1.0	1.2	1.1	0.5
England & Wales	1.4	2.8	1.8	1.4	1.2
Estonia	–	0.6	1.4	0.5	0.3
Finland	0.3	0.7	0.4	–	0.4
France	1.8	–	1.2	1.2	0.4
Netherlands	0.2	0.3	0.2	0.3	0.6
Northern Ireland	1.4	–	1.2	0.9	1.1
Poland	–	0.5	0.4	0.5	0.2
Scotland	0.6	–	1.3	0.5	0.2
Spain	1.1	–	–	–	0.6
United States	1.7	–	1.6	0.4	0.7
Total Joyriding (stolen car was recovered)	1.1	1.2	1.1	0.8	0.6

	1st sweep −1989	2nd sweep 1992	3rd sweep 1996	4th sweep 2000	5th sweep −2005
Australia	0.4	0.4	–	0.3	0.2
Belgium	0.3	0.3	–	0.2	0.2
Canada	0.2	0.3	0.3	0.3	0.2
England & Wales	0.4	0.8	0.7	0.7	0.6
Estonia	–	0.1	0.5	0.4	0.2
Finland	0.1	0.0	0.1	–	0.0
France	0.5	–	0.4	0.5	0.2
Netherlands	0.1	0.2	0.2	0.2	0.4
Northern Ireland	0.3	–	0.3	0.3	0.4
Poland	–	0.2	0.5	0.6	0.4
Scotland	0.2	–	0.3	0.2	0.1
Sweden	–	0.1	0.1	0.0	0.0
United States	0.4	–	0.3	0.1	0.4
Total car theft	0.3	0.3	0.3	0.3	0.3

Chapter 7

Data in Figure 7.8

Country	Eurobarometer Percentage That Agrees Organized Crime Has Infiltrated National Government (2002)	Composite OC: Money Laundering, High-Level Corruption, Unsolved Homicide, Informal Sector, OC Index GAD; WEF; BEEPS
Austria	32	32.5
Belgium	33	31.9
Denmark	13	18.4
Estonia		42.8
Finland	29	10.4
France	52	27.0
Germany	37	20.2
Greece	62	42.4
Hungary		36.1
Ireland	61	27.5
Italy	71	46.8
Luxembourg	29	21.1
Netherlands	49	18.9
Poland		52.4
Portugal	57	30.1
Spain	42	30.8
Sweden	25	18.3
United Kingdom	42	23.9

Data in Figures 7.4, 7.5, and 7.9

Country	High-Level Corruption Index	Organized-Crime Perception Index	Unsolved Homicides	Victim of 11 Crimes	Composite OC Index
Algeria	16.3			31.7	93.9
Argentina	48.5			33.7	59.4
Armenia	35.1	33.1	1.2		
Australia	72.3			32.1	16.8
Austria				27.0	32.5
Azerbaijan	6.1	15.3	0.2	8.3	63.9
Bangladesh	28.3				
Barbados		89.8	0.9		
Belarus	47.4	1.3	1.2	23.6	63.6
Belgium	58.0	87.3	0.1	32.8	31.9
Belize	63.1				
Bolivia	38.5	42.7	1.6	40.1	79.8
Bosnia and Herzegovina	16.7				
Botswana				26.4	35.1
Brazil	43.6			48.1	69.2
Bulgaria	33.8	36.9	2.5	27.2	66.3
Cambodia	30.0				
Cameroon	16.7				
Canada	71.8	86.0	1.0	26.9	25.1
Chile	77.7				
China	28.4				
Colombia	45.6	4.5		50.7	86.8
Costa Rica	40.5	45.9	2.9	45.5	59.7
Croatia	32.8	44.6		14.3	53.9
Czech Republic	49.1	58.0	0.3	34.1	46.3
Denmark	86.6	98.7	0.3	31.1	18.4
Dominican Republic	61.7				
Ecuador	27.6				
Egypt, Arab Rep.	51.6				
El Salvador	60.3	39.5			
Estonia	53.5	80.3	3.0	41.2	42.8
Ethiopia	39.9				
Finland	90.3	99.4	0.9	26.6	10.4
France	74.1	77.1	0.7	34.5	27.0
Georgia	26.2	5.7	0.1	23.5	72.6
Germany	74.1	90.4	0.9		
Ghana	39.9				
Greece	40.2				
Guatemala	73.2				
Haiti	20.0				
Honduras	58.3				

Country	High-Level Corruption Index	Organized-Crime Perception Index	Unsolved Homicides	Victim of 11 Crimes	Composite OC Index
Hong Kong, China	72.7	75.8	0.6		
Hungary	60.6			32.1	36.1
Iceland	77.1	100.0	0.3		
India	47.4	51.0	1.7	30.5	53.8
Indonesia	20.9	17.4	0.1	21.4	74.5
Iran, Islamic Rep.	32.1				
Iraq	5.8				
Ireland	73.1				
Israel	56.5				
Italy	51.5	51.6	0.3		
Japan	43.8	65.0	0.2	15.3	32.7
Jordan	64.4				
Kazakhstan	24.4				
Kenya	16.7				
Korea. Rep.	60.1			20.9	37.4
Kyrgyz Republic	16.4	58.6		27.4	68.2
Latvia	18.2	71.3	5.1	27.8	44.8
Lithuania	56.5			31.0	45.7
Luxembourg	94.9				
Macedonia, FYR		21.0	0.5	21.6	61.0
Madagascar	16.7				
Malawi	79.7				
Malaysia	60.3	67.5	2.4		
Malta		96.2	0.1	23.3	32.7
Mauritius	22.0				
Mexico	36.4	30.6	11.3		
Moldova	6.4	13.4	2.3		
Mozambique				38.0	86.5
Namibia	79.7			36.4	49.3
Netherlands	89.1			30.3	18.9
New Zealand	84.9	96.8	0.5		
Norway		93.6	0.5		
Nicaragua	58.1				
Nigeria	16.4			32.2	91.9
Norway	75.3				
Pakistan	21.0				
Panama	45.8	59.9	6.7	20.3	52.4
Papua New Guinea		60.5	6.4		
Paraguay				36.3	95.7
Peru	48.6				
Philippines	46.0			9.1	78.6
Poland	50.9	43.9	2.3	31.7	52.4
Portugal	67.8	91.7	1.3		
Romania	29.9			24.5	68.5

(Continued)

(Continued)

Country	High-Level Corruption Index	Organized-Crime Perception Index	Unsolved Homicides	Victim of 11 Crimes	Composite OC Index
Russian Federation	11.6	9.6	6.1	26.3	88.2
Saudi Arabia	56.3				
Senegal	79.7				
Serbia and Montenegro				32.3	56.9
Seychelles		73.2	5.1		
Singapore	78.8	97.5	0.7		
Slovak Republic	33.5			35.9	48.0
Slovenia	60.7			32.0	30.0
South Africa	54.5			36.4	66.1
Spain	76.7	70.1	0.9		
Sri Lanka	38.8				
Swaziland		56.7			
Sweden	76.9	98.1	1.2	30.4	18.3
Switzerland	86.6	94.3	0.1	22.6	20.0
Taiwan. China	60.1				
Tanzania	16.7				
Thailand	37.8	49.0	4.6		
Trinidad and Tobago	80.7				
Tunisia	52.9				
Turkey	39.8				
Uganda	52.9			37.3	72.3
Ukraine	7.6	7.6	1.1	29.1	87.4
United Kingdom	81.7	89.2	1.3	34.4	23.9
United States	60.2			30.7	36.4
Uzbekistan	39.0				
Venezuela. RB	28.3	8.9	11.6		
Vietnam	39.4				
West Bank and Gaza	78.3				
Zambia	79.7	47.8	7.9	34.6	73.8
Zimbabwe	9.3	17.8	5.9	47.5	75.2

Notes to Appendix Chapter 7

The Organized Crime Perception Index is based on an average of organized-crime perception figures of WEF, GAD, and BEEPS. Figures based on solely one value (WEF, GAD, or BEEPS) have been removed from the ranking.

The Composite Organized-Crime Index is based on data on the Organized-Crime Perception Index, informal sector (WEF), unsolved homicide (UNODC), high-level corruption (World Bank), and money laundering (WEF). Data that are included in the index have been recalculated by dividing them by the highest score in the data series and multiplying by 100 (/ highest score*100). All data are thus presented on a 100% scale. In these calculations, Albania and Cameroon were not considered to be the highest scores for unsolved homicide, since they were too much removed from the average. They are counted as 100%. For country scores on COCI of all countries, see data Chapter 12 below.

In using the Organized-Crime Perception Index for the calculation of the Composite Organized-Crime Index, data that are solely based on one value (GAD, WEF, or BEEPS, but most of the time just GAD) were used. In the calculation of the Composite OC Index, only figures that are based on at least two values are entered. According to the GAD survey, however, perception of crime is very high in Iraq, the Congo, West Bank and Gaza, and Colombia (all top five). These countries are not included in our index, due to a lack of other values.

Chapter 8

Data in Figures 8.2 and 8.3

Country	Street-Level Corruption
Albania	59.1
Argentina	5.8
Austria	0.7
Azerbaijan	20.8
Belarus	20.6
Belgium	1.2
Bolivia	25.3
Botswana	0.8
Bulgaria	10.3
Cambodia	29.0
Canada	0.9
Colombia	17.2
Costa Rica	11.1
Croatia	12.1
Czech Republic	5.7
Denmark	0.4
Estonia	3.7
Finland	0.1
France	0.8
Georgia	16.8
Germany	0.5
Greece	13.8
Hungary	6.9
Hong Kong, China	0.0
Iceland	0.4
India	23.1
Indonesia	19.5
Ireland	0.1
Italy	0.9
Japan	0.1
Kyrgyz Republic	22.4
Latvia	15.4
Lesotho	19.2
Lithuania	22.9
Macedonia, FYR	7.7
Mexico	17.0
Mongolia	21.3
Mozambique	30.5
Namibia	5.5
Netherlands	0.2

(Continued)

(Continued)

Country	Street-Level Corruption
New Zealand	0.6
Nigeria	29.8
Norway	0.2
Panama	10.5
Paraguay	13.8
Peru	13.7
Philippines	3.6
Poland	15.2
Portugal	1.1
Korea, Rep.	3.4
Romania	19.2
Russian Federation	16.6
Slovak Republic	13.9
Slovenia	1.9
South Africa	15.5
Spain	0.4
Swaziland	17.3
Sweden	0.5
Turkey	7.1
Ukraine	16.2
United Kingdom	0.7
United States	0.4
Serbia and Montenegro	17.4
Zambia	9.8
Zimbabwe	7.2

Data in Figures 8.1 and 8.5

Region	Corruption	Terrorist Incidents	Mean Numbers Terrorist Incidents
Central America	11.1		
Central Asia	19.6	81	10
East Africa	37.1	64	7
East and Southeast Asia	9.4	893	74
Eastern Europe	22.1	232	58
Latin America	16.3	1,191	70
Near and Middle East	6.0	4,812	401
North Africa	18.7	56	11
North America	7.4	90	90
Oceania	0.5	3	2
South Asia	23.1	711	178
Southeastern Europe	19.0	609	
Southern Africa	11.7	30	15
West & Central Africa	38.9	17	7
Western and Central Europe	4.8	2,041	102
World	16.4	883	79

Notes to Appendix Chapter 8

Corruption data are based on ICVS 2000/2002. If no ICVS data are available, Transparency International data are used. These data are positively correlated with the ICVS ($r = 0.75$). On average, ICVS data are 9.9% higher than the Transparency International data. The latter have therefore been adjusted to match ICVS data.

Terrorism data stem from the National Memorial Institute for the Prevention of Terrorism (MIPT) database (online: www.tkb.org). They include both international and domestic incidents.

Data on business costs of terrorism are taken from the World Economic Forum Global Competiveness Report 2003/2004. Data on rule of law and GDP per capita are taken from the World Bank Institute Web site (www.worldbank.org/wbi/governance/pubs).

Chapter 9 Data in Figures 9.6 and 9.7

Region	Police per 100,000	Number of Homicides per 1,000 Police Officers
Asia		5.5
Caribbean	605.1	
Central America	39.0	
Central Asia	356.4	
East Africa	417.9	
East and Southeast Asia	273.2	
Eastern Europe	396.9	
Near and Middle East	770.4	
North Africa	141.6	
North America	334.8	18.8
Oceania	304.2	5.7
South America	290.6	18.5
South Asia	132.0	
Southeastern Europe	354.7	42.5
Southern Africa	154.4	
Western and Central Europe	325.6	6.4
World	326.5	

Data in Figure 9.8

Region	Police per 100,000	Private Police per 100,000
Africa	185	231
Canada	186	273
Central Europe	245	435
Eastern Europe	512	459
Oceania	304	474
South America	492	197
United States	326	533
Western Europe	297	198
World	318	350

Data in Figures 9.13, 9.15, 9.16 and Tables 9.3 and 9.4

	Satisfied With Report	Victim Support 4 Crimes	Victim Support Would Have Been Useful	Victim Support Take-Up Rate
Albania	29	8	22	34.8
Argentina	48	2	46	3.3
Australia	71	6	32	16.1
Austria	48	13	26	38.4
Azerbaijan	56	0	49	0.0

	Satisfied With Report	Victim Support 4 Crimes	Victim Support Would Have Been Useful	Victim Support Take-Up Rate
Belarus	31	4	57	6.3
Belgium	50	13	36	28.2
Bolivia	14	1	70	1.6
Botswana	44	7	53	14.8
Brazil	34		88	
Bulgaria	20	1	13	9.9
Cambodia	49	3	71	3.9
Canada	72	14	27	36.5
Colombia	27	3	37	6.7
Costa Rica	35	3	62	5.0
Croatia	37	3	71	5.0
Czech Republic	46	3	31	8.9
Denmark	75	10	30	26.5
Finland	80	2	32	6.5
France	52	4	38	11.2
Georgia	19	13	83	15.8
Germany		2	27	7.7
Greece		2	64	3.8
Hungary	39	0	43	1.1
Hong Kong (SAR China)		13	42	25.0
Iceland		6	23	21.9
India	58	0	49	
Ireland		6	42	12.7
Italy		3	36	7.4
Indonesia	48	4	37	10.1
Japan	39	8	20	29.8
Korea, Rep.	17			
Kyrgyz Republic	19	4	62	6.0
Latvia	31	3	47	7.3
Lesotho	33	8	64	14.7
Luxemburgh		5	43	10.5
Lithuania	30	4	67	6.0
Macedonia, FYR	42	5	71	7.9
Malta	31	12	68	17.0
Mexico		5	54	8.1
Mongolia	18	1	68	4.0
Mozambique	27	2	54	3.8
Namibia	46	5	51	11.0
Netherlands	71	14	30	34.9
New Zealand		24	36	47.1
Northern Ireland		21	45	36.8
Norway		10	37	23.2
Nigeria	51	7	66	11.0
Panama	29	12	67	16.0
Paraguay	32	2	68	3.0
Peru		1	26	4.7

(Continued)

(Continued)

	Satisfied With Report	Victim Support 4 Crimes	Victim Support Would Have Been Useful	Victim Support Take-Up Rate
Philippines	41	9	53	16.7
Poland	35	4	51	7.8
Portugal		4	70	5.3
Republic of Korea		3	38	7.2
Romania	28	2	67	2.8
Russian Federation	26	1	29	2.9
Scotland		22	42	40.4
Slovak Republic	48	2	67	2.0
Slovenia	49	4	20	16.4
South Africa	40	15		
Spain		3	68	4.4
Swaziland	36	3	38	10.2
Sweden	69	9	39	21.2
Switzerland	71	7	32	18.0
Turkey		2	64	2.9
Uganda	36	7	65	11.0
Ukraine	16	3	36	8.1
United Kingdom	65	16	45	29.6
United States	65	16	38	32.9
Serbia and Montenegro	34	1	66	1.4
Zambia	27	5	80	7.3
Zimbabwe	35	0	71	

Note: Data on victim satisfaction are from the ICVS, 1996-2000 and data on victim support, support useful, and take-up rates are from ICVS, 2005 or latest available.

Data in Figures 9.9, 9.11, and 9.12

Country	Police Performance Index	Total Police Personnel	Police Per 100,000	Private Police per 100,000
Africa	42	183		
Americas	36	308		
Asia	53	363		
Australia	92	304		
Austria	72	305	305	84
Azerbaijan	73	402		
Belgium	71	357	357	178
Bolivia	11	220		
Canada	76	186		
Central America	35	270		
Central Asia and Transcaucasian Countries	52	402		
Chile	71	193		

Country	Police Performance Index	Total Police Personnel	Police Per 100,000	Private Police per 100,000
Costa Rica	30	39		
Croatia	54	446		
Czech Republic	71	458	458	273
Denmark	89	192	192	102
East and Southeast Asia	55	155		
Eastern Europe	60	324		
El Salvador	30	252		
Estonia			265	358
Europe	60	346		
Finland	77	160	160	116
France			211	200
Germany	54	303	303	206
Greece			373	228
Hungary	68	287	287	784
Iceland	83	290		
Ireland			305	511
Italy	67	559	559	96
Japan	60	182		
Latvia	38	442		
Lithuania	31	337	337	287
Luxembourg	86	294		
Malta	66	452		
Mexico	20	492		
Moldova	57	324		
Morocco	68	142		
Netherlands	83	212	212	186
North Africa	71	142		
North America	58	335		
Oceania	63	304		
Panama	37	519		
Philippines	43	141		
Poland	39	259	259	523
Portugal	64	450	450	270
Slovak Republic	50	376	376	387
Slovenia	71	364		
South Africa	46	224		
South America	31	242		
South Asia	31	193		
Southeastern Europe	44	413		
Southern Africa	40	224		
Spain			286	219
Sweden	77	181	181	116
United Kingdom	78	258	258	255
United States	77	326		
Uruguay	60	541		
Venezuela, RB	25	16		
Western and Central Europe	66	341		

Chapters 9, 10, and 11

Data in Table 9.2, Table 10.1, Figure 10.1, Table 11.1, and in final section Chapter 11 (text on punitiveness scale)

Country	Number of Judges per 100,000 Population	Number of Police Officers per 100,000 Population	World Prison Population	Punitiveness Scale
Albania	10.57	380.54	90	36
Algeria			110	
Andora	35.22	232.77	83	38
Angola			36	
Antigua and Barbuda			278	
Argentina	4.74	558.55	107	46
Armenia			135	16
Australia		304.19	115	5
Austria		305.08	100	−27
Azerbaijan	3.73	402.28	217	−34
Bahamas, The		693.77	410	−4
Bahrain	9.68		155	−47
Bangladesh			45	
Barbados	6.74	516.48	367	−21
Belarus	10.20		554	−16
Belgium	23.04	357.50	89	−1
Belize			459	
Benin			81	
Bolivia		219.83	102	13
Bosnia and Herzegovina			59	
Botswana			327	
Brazil			160	36
Brunei			133	
Bulgaria	20.02		134	4
Burkina Faso			23	
Burundi			129	
Cambodia			44	
Cameroon			129	
Canada	6.59	186.28	116	−17
Cape Verde			178	
Central African Republic			110	
Chad			46	
Chile	4.21	193.02	212	−52
China	15.94		117	
Colombia	9.44	215.50	126	56
Comoros			30	

Country	Number of Judges per 100,000 Population	Number of Police Officers per 100,000 Population	World Prison Population	Punitiveness Scale
Congo, Dem. Rep.			38	
Congo, Rep.			38	
Costa Rica	15.25	39.00	229	−16
Cote d'Ivoire			62	48
Croatia	40.22	446.23	59	24
Cuba			297	−22
Cyprus	11.50	618.17	49	−2
Czech Republic	26.62	458.48	170	−30
Denmark	12.41	192.09	64	5
Djibouti			61	
Dominica	8.39	605.00	420	−55
Dominican Republic	6.40		193	
Ecuador			59	89
Egypt, Arab Rep.			121	
El Salvador	9.65	251.66	158	41
Estonia	16.64	265.18	361	−1
Ethiopia	0.15			
Fiji			108	−15
Finland	13.12	160.09	70	31
France	11.50	211.03	93	−1
Gambia, The			32	
Georgia	5.99	218.68	198	−13
Germany	25.34	303.17	98	−14
Ghana			58	
Greece	20.51	373.21	80	−14
Grenada			333	
Guadeloupe			159	
Guatemala	3.36	233.94	71	87
Guinea			37	
Guyana			175	−1
Haiti			53	
Honduras			172	
Hong Kong, China	2.15	496.20	184	−69
Hungary	25.06	286.57	165	−34
Iceland	13.38	289.79	37	23
India			29	55
Indonesia			29	19
Iran, Islamic Rep.			226	
Ireland	2.84	305.32	85	−10
Israel	6.84	424.78	163	−64
Italy	11.81	558.99	100	−16
Jamaica		272.60	176	33
Japan	2.43	182.23	53	0

(Continued)

(Continued)

Country	Number of Judges per 100,000 Population	Number of Police Officers per 100,000 Population	World Prison Population	Punitiveness Scale
Jordan			106	−29
Kazakhstan		464.31	522	−7
Kenya			111	
Kiribati			67	
Korea, Rep.	3.40	191.90	128	−17
Kuwait		1,116.11	102	−23
Kyrgyz Republic	4.80	340.33	390	−18
Latvia	13.47	441.62	352	−4
Lebanon			172	
Lesotho	7.68	101.89	143	
Libya			127	
Liechtenstein			50	
Lithuania	18.28	336.64	266	−5
Luxembourg	16.67	294.37	85	−16
Macao, China			197	
Macedonia, FYR	31.44	483.17	61	31
Madagascar			130	
Malawi			70	
Malaysia	1.53	354.03	125	−9
Maldives		71.37	414	−52
Mali			34	
Malta	8.56	452.39	73	10
Marshall Islands			44	
Martinique			164	
Mauritania			48	
Mauritius	3.66	755.43	214	−42
Mexico		491.79	156	34
Micronesia			34	
Moldova	6.63	323.53	301	−12
Monaco			39	
Mongolia			279	
Morocco		141.62	176	−70
Mozambique			50	
Myanmar	2.36	141.00	118	−48
Namibia	0.69		267	−20
Nepal		192.67	29	55
Netherlands		212.00	100	−22
New Zealand	4.26		155	−37
Nicaragua			143	20
Niger			52	
Nigeria			33	
Norway		247.92	59	12
Oman			81	−16

Country	Number of Judges per 100,000 Population	Number of Police Officers per 100,000 Population	World Prison Population	Punitiveness Scale
Pakistan			59	−7
Panama	8.37	518.88	354	−2
Papua New Guinea	0.29		66	73
Paraguay			75	75
Peru			104	21
Philippines	1.97	141.34	94	45
Poland	20.50	258.98	218	−49
Portugal	13.50	449.80	137	−12
Puerto Rico			378	5
Qatar	9.74		95	
Reunion			143	
Romania	15.65	217.70	200	−32
Russian Federation	46.71		606	−8
Saint Kitts & Nevis			338	
Saint Lucia			243	
Saint Vincent & Grenadines			270	
Samoa (Western)			158	
Sao Tome and Principe			79	
Saudi Arabia	3.23		110	−34
Senegal			54	
Serbia and Montenegro			78	
Seychelles			207	−5
Singapore	2.12	324.22	388	−87
Slovak Republic	23.59	376.39	164	−21
Slovenia	39.41	364.15	56	28
Solomon Islands			31	
South Africa	4.37	224.02	402	7
Spain	8.44		138	−34
Sri Lanka			91	62
Sudan			36	
Suriname			437	
Swaziland	12.48		359	16
Sweden	19.15	180.96	73	25
Switzerland			68	39
Syrian Arab Republic			93	
Taiwan, China			250	
Tajikistan	0.47		159	19
Tanzania		80.32	120	26
Thailand	4.82	354.78	401	−17
Togo			46	
Tonga			106	−4
Trinidad and Tobago			351	5
Tunisia			252	−63

(Continued)

Country	Number of Judges per 100,000 Population	Number of Police Officers per 100,000 Population	World Prison Population	Punitiveness Scale
Turkey	8.68	245.97	92	23
Turkmenistan			489	−21
Uganda			89	60
Ukraine	8.91	470.20	415	−18
United Arab Emirates			250	
United Kingdom	2.25	257.60	141	−21
United States	10.41	326.37	701	−45
Uruguay	13.25	540.70	209	−10
Uzbekistan			184	−15
Vanatu			46	
Venezuela, RB	2.61	15.76	76	85
Vietnam			71	
Yemen, Rep.			83	34
Zambia	10.41	129.50	121	26
Zimbabwe	0.65	162.33	160	7

Notes to Appendix Chapters 9, 10, and 11

The data set on number of judges and police officers has been constructed by using data from the UN Crime Surveys, the latest available from 1997–2002.

The world prison population list has been collated by Roy Wamsley of King's College London (www.prisonstudies.org). The punitiveness scale has been created by subtracting ranks on the prison population by ranks of countries on homicide. The figures presented below show how ranks on prison population and homicide are related per country in a comparative perspective.

Chapters 9, 10

Data in Table 9.2 and Table 10.3; reliability is used in calculation of PPI figures

Country	Police Performance Index	Judicial Independence	Reliability of Police
Algeria	60.40	2.8	4.5
Angola	37.62	2	3.6
Argentina	35.44	1.8	2.6
Armenia	64.81		
Australia	91.65	6.4	6.3
Austria	71.67	5.5	5.7
Azerbaijan	73.42		
Bangladesh	2.97	2.9	2.1
Barbados	79.63		
Belarus	43.62		
Belgium	71.35	5	4.7
Bolivia	11.08	1.7	3.0
Botswana	63.99	5.9	4.8
Brazil	17.65	3.9	3.1
Bulgaria	32.17	2.7	3.1
Cambodia	57.76		
Cameroon	30.69	3	3.3
Canada	76.44	5.5	5.8
Chad	5.45	1.8	2.3
Chile	70.79	4.6	5.1
China	53.47	3.4	4.2
Colombia	24.45	3.1	4.4
Costa Rica	29.94	3.8	3.7
Croatia	53.98	2.7	3.5
Czech Republic	70.53	4.2	3.8
Denmark	88.62	6.4	6.5
Dominican Republic	50.99	3.6	4.1
Ecuador	12.87	1.9	2.7
El Salvador	29.96	2.9	3.9
Estonia	47.74	5.3	4.4
Ethiopia	48.02	2.3	4
Finland	77.05	6.1	6.3
France	71.68	4.4	5.5
Gambia, The	68.32	4.8	4.9
Georgia	37.23		
Germany	54.24	6.1	5.8
Ghana	54.95	4.1	4.3
Greece	62.87	4.7	4.6
Guatemala	47.78	2.2	2.1
Haiti	0.99	1.1	1.4
Honduras	26.73	1.9	3.2

(Continued)

(Continued)

Country	Police Performance Index	Judicial Independence	Reliability of Police
Hong Kong, China	60.30	5.6	6.3
Hungary	67.75	4.9	4.1
Iceland	82.53	6.3	6.3
India	56.19	5.2	4.1
Indonesia	47.36	3.2	3.5
Ireland	74.26	5.2	5.2
Israel	90.59	6.5	5.9
Italy	67.22	4.4	5.2
Jamaica	26.73	4.2	3.2
Japan	59.79	4.7	5.1
Jordan	94.06	5.2	6.2
Kenya	14.70	2.4	2.8
Korea, Dem. Rep.	77.72	4.1	5.3
Korea, Rep.	45.93	4.1	5.3
Kyrgyz Republic	33.41		
Latvia	37.62	4.2	4.5
Lesotho	37.16		
Lithuania	31.49	3.3	3.3
Luxembourg	85.64	5.5	5.7
Macedonia, FYR	51.88	2.3	3.6
Madagascar	16.83	2.4	2.9
Malawi	46.04	4.6	3.9
Malaysia	43.44	4.5	5.6
Mali	43.56	3.4	3.8
Malta	66.09	5.3	5.2
Mauritius	43.56	4.4	3.8
Mexico	19.93	3.3	3.1
Moldova	57.41		
Mongolia	27.17		
Morocco	68.32	3.1	4.9
Mozambique	15.60	2.4	3
Namibia	48.17	4.8	3.2
Netherlands	82.96	6.3	5.2
New Zealand	67.67	6.3	5.8
Nicaragua	40.59	1.6	3.7
Nigeria	40.63	3.5	2.6
Norway	59.54	5.6	5.5
Pakistan	6.93	2.8	2.4
Panama	37.29	2.2	4.1
Papua New Guinea	29.63		
Paraguay	28.05	1.4	2.6
Peru	26.73	1.9	3.2
Philippines	43.17	2.9	2.5
Poland	39.09	3.9	3.4
Portugal	63.71	5.7	5.5

Country	Police Performance Index	Judicial Independence	Reliability of Police
Romania	39.24	2.4	3.2
Russian Federation	33.64	2.5	2.8
Senegal	57.43	3.1	4.4
Serbia and Montenegro	34.47		
Singapore	52.53	5.2	6.5
Slovak Republic	49.65	3.2	3.1
Slovenia	71.16	4.3	4
South Africa	45.70	5.6	2.9
Spain	39.37	3.8	4.7
Sri Lanka	34.65	3.2	3.5
Swaziland	40.08		
Sweden	76.62	6	5.9
Switzerland	87.92	5.9	6
Taiwan, China	74.26	4.7	5.2
Tanzania	40.59	4.6	3.7
Thailand	68.32	4.8	4.9
Trinidad and Tobago	16.83	5.2	2.9
Tunisia	83.17	4.8	5.6
Turkey	54.95	3.7	4.3
Uganda	27.47	3.7	3.3
Ukraine	28.55	2.4	2.6
United Kingdom	78.21	6	5.6
United States	77.49	5.7	6
Uruguay	60.40	4.8	4.5
Venezuela, RB	25.10	1.2	2.1
Vietnam	62.87	3.9	4.6
Zambia	28.49	3.8	3.6
Zimbabwe	35.22	1.7	2.3

Notes to Appendix Chapters 9 and 10

Data on police reliability and judicial independence are taken from the World Economic Forum Global Competiveness Report 2003–2004.

The police performance index comprises 5 variables: (1) Reporting to the police of selected crimes, (2) Were victims satisfied with reporting to the police, (3) Satisfaction with how the police are dealing with crime (all three ICVS 1996–2000), Reliability of police services (WEF, 2004), and (5) Homicide conviction ratio. The last is computed using the number of intentional homicides minus the number of convictions for intentional homicides (8th UN survey).

Appendix Chapter 10

Data in Table 10.1, Figures 10.3, 10.4, and 10.5

Country	Number of Professional Jud/Mag 1999–2004 (UN Crime Survey)	Scores for Perceived Judicial Independence, Results of the WEF Business opinion Surveys, 1999–2005 (trend and average)							Percentage of the Population Preferring a Prison Sentence in Case of a Recidivist Burglar ICVS
		1999	2000	2001	2002	2003	2005	AVERAGE	
Afghanistan									
Albania	9.2						2.8	2.8	46
Algeria						2.8	2.8	2.8	
Andora	35.2								
Angola							2.0		2.0
Antigua and Barbuda									
Argentina	4.7	2.5	2.9	2.7	1.6	1.8	2.2	2.3	54
Armenia							2.1	2.1	
Australia	5.0	6.6	6.7	6.4	6.6	6.4	6.1	6.5	33
Austria		6.2	6.4	6.3	6.0	5.5	5.8	6.0	16
Azerbaijan	3.0						2.8	2.8	24
Bahamas, The									
Bahrain	9.7						3.8	3.8	
Bangladesh				3.0	3.2	2.9	2.7	3.0	
Barbados	6.8								
Belarus	9.8								43
Belgium	23.0	4.5	5.4	5.9	4.7	5.0	5.1	5.1	11
Belize									
Benin							2.4	2.4	
Bhutan									
Bolivia		2.1	2.3	2.0	1.8	1.7	2.2	2.0	39
Bosnia and Herzegovina						2.7	2.7		
Botswana					5.6	5.9	5.3	5.6	57
Brazil			4.6	4.3	4.1	4.2	3.9	3.0	4.0
Brunei									
Bulgaria	16.7	3.6	3.5	3.0	2.9	2.7	2.5	3.0	46
Burkina Faso									
Burundi									
Cambodia							2.3	2.3	64
Cameroon							2.2		2.2
Canada	3.3	6.6	6.5	6.4	6.3	5.5	5.5	6.1	47
Cape Verde									
Central African Republic									

Country	Number of Professional Jud/Mag 1999–2004 (UN Crime Survey)	Scores for Perceived Judicial Independence, Results of the WEF Business opinion Surveys, 1999–2005 (trend and average)							Percentage of the Population Preferring a Prison Sentence in Case of a Recidivist Burglar ICVS
		1999	2000	2001	2002	2003	2005	AVERAGE	
Chad						1.8	1.9	1.9	
Chile	3.7	4.8	4.5	4.3	4.2	4.6	4.1	4.4	
China	14.9	2.9	3.0	3.1	4.4	3.4	3.4	3.4	84
Colombia	9.7	3.3	3.1	3.3	3.4	3.1	3.4	3.3	48
Comoros									
Congo, Dem. Rep.									
Congo, Rep.									
Costa Rica	15.0	4.3	4.8	5.1	4.5	3.8	5.0	4.6	54
Cote d'Ivoire									
Croatia	36.5				2.9	2.7		2.8	19
Cuba									
Cyprus	10.5						5.4	5.4	
Czech Republic	24.3	4.5	4.6	4.0	3.9	4.2	4.3	4.3	26
Denmark	12.4	6.6	6.6	6.5	6.6	6.4	6.2	6.5	19
Djibouti									
Dominica	7.0								
Dominican Republic	6.4			3.6	3.3	3.6	2.4	3.2	
East Timor							2.8	2.8	
Ecuador									
Egypt, Arab Rep.		5.1	5.1	5.2				5.1	66
El Salvador	4.8		3.4	3.6	3.5	3.0	2.9	3.1	3.3
Equatorial Guinea									
Eritrea									
Estonia	16.0			5.1	4.7	5.3	4.7	5.0	29
Ethiopia	0.2					2.3	2.5	2.4	
Fiji	3.4								
Finland	21.0	6.8	6.8	6.6	6.3	6.1	5.9	6.4	13
France	11.3	5.5	4.8	5.7	4.3	4.4	5.1	5.0	12
Gabon									
Gambia, The						4.8	3.4	4.1	
Georgia	5.9						2.4	2.4	16
Germany	25.5	6.5	6.6	6.7	6.2	6.1	6.3	6.4	22
Ghana						4.1	5.0	4.6	
Greece	20.5	4.0	4.8	4.7	4.5	4.7	4.1	4.5	26
Grenada									
Guadeloupe									
Guatemala	3.7								
Guinea									
Guinea-Bissau									

Country	Number of Professional Jud/Mag 1999–2004 (UN Crime Survey)	Scores for Perceived Judicial Independence, Results of the WEF Business opinion Surveys, 1999–2005 (trend and average)							Percentage of the Population Preferring a Prison Sentence in Case of a Recidivist Burglar ICVS
		1999	2000	2001	2002	2003	2005	AVERAGE	
Guyana							2.4	2.4	
Haiti					1.3	1.1		1.2	
Honduras				2.1	2.0	1.9	2.4	2.1	
Hong Kong, China	5.1	5.6	5.6	5.9	5.8	5.6	5.2	5.6	58
Hungary	24.3	5.2	4.9	5.3	4.4	4.9	4.3	4.8	28
Iceland	16.2	5.7	6.1	6.1	6.2	6.3	5.9	6.0	18
India		5.4	5.2	5.3	5.2	5.2	5.3	5.3	64
Indonesia		2.7	2.8	2.8	2.5	3.2	3.2	2.9	62
Iran, Islamic Rep.									
Iraq									
Ireland	2.8	5.7	6.2	6.1	6.0	5.2	6.1	5.9	38
Israel	6.8	6.3	6.5	6.4	5.9	6.5	5.7	6.2	
Italy	13.2	3.8	3.9	4.5	4.5	4.4	3.5	4.1	24
Jamaica				5.0	4.4	4.2	4.1	4.4	
Japan	2.3	5.7	5.8	5.8	4.9	4.7	5.3	5.4	55
Jordan		5.5	4.9	5.5	4.3	5.2	4.7	5.0	
Kazakhstan							2.9	2.9	
Kenya						2.4	2.9	2.7	
Kiribati									
Korea, Dem. Rep.		3.3		3.8	4.3	4.1		3.9	
Korea, Rep.	3.1	3.3	3.8	3.8	4.3	4.1	4.2	3.9	21
Kuwait							5.2	5.2	
Kyrgyz Republic	5.6						1.7	1.7	23
Lao, PDR									
Latvia	14.1			3.3	3.5	4.2	3.5	3.6	48
Lebanon									
Lesotho	7.7								59
Liberia									
Libya									
Liechtenstein									
Lithuania	16.3			2.8	3.1	3.3	2.8	3.0	24
Luxembourg	16.7	6.4	6.8			5.5	6.0	6.2	
Macao, China									
Macedonia, FYR	32.0					2.3	2.3	2.3	41
Madagascar						2.4	2.9	2.7	
Malawi						4.6	4.3	4.5	
Malaysia	1.6	3.8	3.7	3.6	4.2	4.5	5.4	4.2	
Maldives	80.8								
Mali						3.4	3.8	3.6	

(Continued)

(Continued)

Country	Number of Professional Jud/Mag 1999–2004 (UN Crime Survey)	Scores for Perceived Judicial Independence, Results of the WEF Business opinion Surveys, 1999–2005 (trend and average)							Percentage of the Population Preferring a Prison Sentence in Case of a Recidivist Burglar ICVS
		1999	2000	2001	2002	2003	2005	AVERAGE	
Malta	8.6					5.3	5.1	5.2	
Marshall Islands									
Martinique									
Mauritania							3.4	3.4	
Mauritius	3.7	4.8	4.7	5.1	4.9	4.4		4.8	
Mexico		3.6	3.0	3.5	2.8	3.3	3.5	3.3	71
Micronesia									
Moldova	7.9								
Monaco									
Mongolia							2.4	2.4	40
Morocco					3.3	3.1	3.1	3.2	
Mozambique						2.4	2.5	2.5	42
Namibia	0.7				5.2	4.8	4.8	4.9	59
Nauru									
Nepal									
Netherlands		6.6	6.7	6.6	6.4	6.3	6.0	6.4	30
New Zealand	4.3	6.6	6.5	6.4	6.5	6.3	6.0	6.4	40
Nicaragua				2.2	1.9	1.6	1.2	1.7	
Niger									
Nigeria				3.3	3.1	3.5	3.9	3.5	67
Norway		6.0	6.0	6.2	5.8	5.6	6.0	5.9	24
Oman									
Pakistan	0.0					2.8	2.6	2.7	
Panama	8.3			3.1	2.5	2.2	2.5	2.6	57
Papua New Guinea	0.3								
Paraguay				2.3	2.0	1.4	1.4	1.8	58
Peru		2.5	1.9	2.0	2.3	1.9	2.0	2.1	56
Philippines	2.0	3.3	3.7	3.7	3.4	2.9	2.7	3.3	76
Poland	20.5	4.7	4.2	5.0	3.7	3.9	3.4	4.2	11
Portugal	13.2	5.5	5.2	5.1	6.0	5.7	5.6	5.5	15
Puerto Rico									
Qatar	9.4						5.4	5.4	
Reunion									
Romania	14.9			3.3	2.7	2.4	2.6	2.8	49
Russian Federation	46.0	2.8	3.1	2.9	2.5	2.5	2.3	2.7	38
Rwanda									
Saint Kitts & Nevis									
Saint Lucia									

Country	Number of Professional Jud/Mag 1999–2004 (UN Crime Survey)	Scores for Perceived Judicial Independence, Results of the WEF Business opinion Surveys, 1999–2005 (trend and average)							Percentage of the Population Preferring a Prison Sentence in Case of a Recidivist Burglar ICVS
		1999	2000	2001	2002	2003	2005	AVERAGE	
Saint Vincent & Grenadines									
Samoa (Western)									
San Marino									
Sao Tome and Principe									
Saudi Arabia	3.2								
Senegal						3.1		3.1	
Seychelles									
Sierra Leone									
Singapore	2.4	4.9	5.4	5.7	5.1	5.2	5.4	5.3	
Slovak Republic	22.9	4.2	4.0	4.0		3.2	3.3	3.7	36
Slovenia	41.6			4.4	5.0	4.3	4.0	4.4	29
Solomon Islands									
Somalia									
South Africa	3.9	4.8	5.3	5.7	5.6	5.6	4.9	5.3	76
Spain	8.4	5.0	5.5	5.0	4.1	3.8	3.8	4.5	20
Sri Lanka				4.1	4.9	3.2	3.0	3.8	
Sudan									
Suriname									
Swaziland	3.9								62
Sweden	17.6	6.2	6.2	6.5	5.6	6.0	4.8	5.9	28
Switzerland		6.3	6.2	6.5	5.7	5.9	6.1	6.1	11
Syrian Arab Republic									
Taiwan, China		4.5	4.2	4.3	4.0	4.7	4.3	4.3	
Tajikistan	0.5						3.0	3.0	
Tanzania						4.6	4.8	4.7	75
Thailand	3.7	4.4	4.5	4.7	4.6	4.8	4.4	4.6	
Togo									
Tonga	0.0								
Trinidad and Tobago			4.2	5.2	5.2	3.8	4.6		
Tunisia					5.0	4.8	4.8	4.9	56
Turkey	8.6	3.6	4.2	3.9	3.0	3.7	3.6	3.7	53
Turkmenistan									
Uganda						3.7	3.8	3.8	
Ukraine	8.7	3.0	2.9	2.3	2.2	2.4	2.3	2.5	34

(Continued)

(Continued)

Country	Number of Professional Jud/Mag 1999–2004 (UN Crime Survey)	Scores for Perceived Judicial Independence, Results of the WEF Business opinion Surveys, 1999–2005 (trend and average)							Percentage of the Population Preferring a Prison Sentence in Case of a Recidivist Burglar ICVS
		1999	2000	2001	2002	2003	2005	AVERAGE	
United Arab Emirates							4.2	4.2	
United Kingdom	2.2	6.3	6.4	6.3	6.2	6.0	6.0	6.2	44
United States	8.2	5.9	5.8	6.1	5.7	5.7	5.5	5.8	47
Uruguay	44.9			5.3	5.2	4.8	5.2	5.1	
Uzbekistan									
Vanatu									
Venezuela, RB	2.2	2.5	2.0	1.7	1.3	1.2	1.3	1.7	
Vietnam		4.2	3.9	3.7	3.3	3.9	3.4	3.7	
West Bank and Gaza									
Yemen, Rep.									
Serbia and Montenegro							2.5	2.5	42
Zambia	10.4					3.8		3.8	71
Zimbabwe	0.5	5.4	4.7	2.6	1.8	1.7	2.1	3.1	79

Appendix Chapter 11

Data in Table 11.3

Country	Average Recorded Homicides 1998–2002 (UN Crime Survey)	Prison Population in 2002/03 (Walmsley)	Country	Average Recorded Homicides 1998–2002 (UN Crime Survey)	Prison Population in 2002/03 (Walmsley)
Afghanistan			Luxembourg	1.1	81
Albania	13.6	69	Macao, China		
Algeria		110	Macedonia, FYR	2.2	61
Andora			Madagascar		130
Angola		36	Malawi		70
Antigua and Barbuda			Malaysia	2.6	125
Argentina	6.4	115	Maldives		
Armenia	3.6		Mali		34
Australia	1.6	115	Malta	1.5	72
Austria	0.8	100	Marshall Islands		
Azerbaijan	4.0	226	Martinique		
Bahamas, The			Mauritania		
Bahrain			Mauritius	2.7	214
Bangladesh		45	Mexico	15.1	164
Barbados	7.9		Micronesia		
Belarus	10.2	535	Moldova	9.6	256
Belgium	1.6	86	Monaco		
Belize			Mongolia		279
Benin			Morocco	0.5	180
Bhutan			Mozambique		50
Bolivia	3.3	102	Myanmar	0.2	67
Bosnia and Herzegovina			Namibia	6.3	267
Botswana		327	Nauru		
Brazil		160	Nepal	3.0	30
Brunei			Netherlands	1.3	102
Bulgaria	3.4	134	New Zealand	1.3	155
Burkina Faso			Nicaragua		143
Burundi			Niger		
Cambodia		44	Nigeria		33
Cameroon		129	Norway	0.9	59
Canada	1.4	115	Oman	0.6	55
Cape Verde			Pakistan	0.1	59
Central African Republic	110		Panama	10.5	353
Chad		46	Papua New Guinea	9.4	
Chile	2.3	224	Paraguay	13.3	75

(Continued)

(Continued)

Country	Average Recorded Homicides 1998–2002 (UN Crime Survey)	Prison Population in 2002/03 (Walmsley)	Country	Average Recorded Homicides 1998–2002 (UN Crime Survey)	Prison Population in 2002/03 (Walmsley)
China		117	Peru		104
Colombia	60.5	126	Philippines	11.0	94
Comoros			Poland	3.3	214
Congo, Dem. Rep.			Portugal	2.0	137
Congo, Rep.			Puerto Rico		
Costa Rica	5.9	229	Qatar	0.4	
Cote d'Ivoire	4.1		Reunion		
Croatia	2.2	59	Romania	2.8	200
Cuba			Russian Federation	20.3	606
Cyprus	0.6	106	Rwanda		
Czech Republic	1.7	177	Saint Kitts & Nevis		
Denmark	1.1	64	Saint Lucia		
Djibouti			Saint Vincent & Grenadines		
Dominica	8.3		Samoa (Western)		
Dominican Republic		193	San Marino		
East Timor			Sao Tome and Principe		
Ecuador		62	Saudi Arabia	0.7	131
Egypt, Arab Rep.			Senegal		54
El Salvador	44.4	165	Serbia and Montenegro		78
Equatorial Guinea					
Eritrea			Seychelles	8.1	
Estonia	13.4	361	Sierra Leone		
Ethiopia			Singapore	1.0	338
Fiji			Slovak Republic	2.4	103
Finland	2.4	68	Slovenia	1.4	56
France	1.2	93	Solomon Islands		
Gabon			Somalia		
Gambia, The		32	South Africa	58.3	402
Georgia	4.6	198	Spain	1.0	138
Germany	1.0	94	Sri Lanka		91
Ghana			Sudan		
Greece	1.3	80	Suriname		
Grenada		53	Swaziland	89.3	359
Guadeloupe		29	Sweden	1.7	70
Guatemala	26.7	71	Switzerland	1.1	68
Guinea		58	Syrian Arab Republic		
Guinea-Bissau					
Guyana		175			
Haiti		351			

Country	Average Recorded Homicides 1998–2002 (UN Crime Survey)	Prison Population in 2002/03 (Walmsley)	Country	Average Recorded Homicides 1998–2002 (UN Crime Survey)	Prison Population in 2002/03 (Walmsley)
Honduras		172	Taiwan, China		250
Hong Kong, China	0.9	184	Tajikistan		
Hungary	2.5	170	Tanzania		120
Iceland	0.9	37	Thailand	8.2	401
India	3.8	29	Togo		
Indonesia	1.0	29	Tonga		
Iran, Islamic Rep.			Trinidad and Tobago		
Iraq					
Ireland	0.9	85	Tunisia	1.1	252
Israel		163	Turkey		92
Italy	1.3	98	Turkmenistan		
Jamaica	33.9		Uganda		89
Japan	0.6	54	Ukraine	10.1	415
Jordan		107	United Arab Emirates		
Kazakhstan					
Kenya		111	United Kingdom	1.3	137
Kiribati			United States	6.1	701
Korea, Dem. Rep.			Uruguay	4.7	209
Korea, Rep.	2.0	125	Uzbekistan		
Kuwait	1.8	127	Vanatu		
Kyrgyz Republic	8.7	390	Venezuela, RB	21.0	76
Lao, PDR			Vietnam		71
Latvia	10.6	357	West Bank and Gaza		
Lebanon			Yemen, Rep.	4.6	
Liberia			Zambia	9.4	121
Libya			Zimbabwe	6.9	160
Liechtenstein					
Lithuania	8.4	293			

Appendix Chapter 12

Data in Figures 12.1 and 12.2 (WEF measure costs of crime and violence is referred to in introductory remarks)

Country	PPI Police Performance Index	Composite OC Index Composite OC: Money Laundering, High-Level Corruption, Unsolved Homicide, Informal Sector, OC Index GAD; WEF; BEEPS	World Bank Rule of Law	World Economic Forum Business Costs of Crime and Violence	GDP per Capita (PPP), 2002
Afghanistan			–		
Albania		93.9	−0.918		
Algeria	60	63.4	−1.103	4.7	5,536
Andora					
Angola	38	87.9	−1.225	2.7	2,053
Antigua and Barbuda					
Argentina	35	59.4	0.319	2.5	10,954
Armenia	65	56.3	−0.146		
Australia	92	16.8	1.596	6.2	27,756
Austria	72	32.5	1.812	6.1	28,611
Azerbaijan	73	63.9	−0.563		
Bahamas, The			0.563		
Bahrain		15.3	0.665		
Bangladesh	3	84.7	−0.929	2.8	1,736
Barbados	80		0.411		
Belarus	44	63.6	−0.876		
Belgium	71	31.9	0.797	5	26,695
Belize			0.088		
Benin			−0.422		
Bhutan			–		
Bolivia	11	79.8	−0.355	3.8	2,360
Bosnia and Herzegovina			−1.108		
Botswana	64	35.1	0.502	5.3	8,244
Brazil	18	69.2	−0.222	2.5	7,156
Brunei			1.252		
Bulgaria	32	66.3	−0.150	2.8	6,909
Burkina Faso			−0.350		
Burundi			−0.881		

(Continued)

(Continued)

Country	PPI Police Performance Index	Composite OC Index Composite OC: Money Laundering, High-Level Corruption, Unsolved Homicide, Informal Sector, OC Index GAD; WEF; BEEPS	World Bank Rule of Law	World Economic Forum Business Costs of Crime and Violence	GDP per Capita (PPP), 2002
Cambodia	58		−0.235		
Cameroon	31	71.7	−1.015	2.6	1,712
Canada	76	25.1	1.549	5.4	28,699
Cape Verde			0.088		
Central African Republic			−		
Chad	5	75.0	−0.827	2.9	1,008
Chile	71	30.6	1.086	4.8	9,561
China	53	55.5	−0.040	4.3	4,475
Colombia	24	86.8	−0.783	2.9	6,068
Comoros			−		
Congo, Dem. Rep.			−2.153		
Congo, Rep.			−1.435		
Costa Rica	30	59.7	0.553	3.5	8,470
Cote d'Ivoire			−0.335		
Croatia	54	53.9	0.146	4.3	9,967
Cuba			0.115		
Cyprus			0.928		
Czech Republic	71	46.3	0.543	4.7	15,148
Denmark	89	18.4	1.691	6.3	29,975
Djibouti			−0.235		
Dominica					
Dominican Republic	51	55.8	0.380	4.8	6,197
East Timor					
Ecuador	13	75.1	−0.721	2.8	3,357
Egypt, Arab Rep.		56.2	0.128	4.7	3,701
El Salvador	30	59.0	−0.656	2.5	4,675
Equatorial Guinea			−1.204		
Eritrea			−		
Estonia	48	42.8	0.507	4.8	11,712
Ethiopia	48	58.9	0.269	4.7	724
Fiji			−0.495		
Finland	77	10.4	1.736	6.6	25,859
France	72	27.0	1.077	4.9	26,151

Country	PPI Police Performance Index	Composite OC Index Composite OC: Money Laundering, High-Level Corruption, Unsolved Homicide, Informal Sector, OC Index GAD; WEF; BEEPS	World Bank Rule of Law	World Economic Forum Business Costs of Crime and Violence	 GDP per Capita (PPP), 2002
Gabon			−0.525		
Gambia, The	68	36.7	0.274	5.4	1,723
Georgia	37	72.6	−0.494		
Germany	54	20.2	1.483	6.3	26,324
Ghana	55	57.4	−0.014	4.1	2,050
Greece	63	42.4	0.496	5.5	18,184
Grenada					
Guadeloupe			−		
Guatemala	48	91.6	−1.106	1.7	3,927
Guinea			−0.762		
Guinea–Bissau			−1.615		
Guyana			−0.140		
Haiti	1	100.0	−1.495	2	1,578
Honduras	27	83.4	−0.895	2	2,520
Hong Kong, China	60	26.7	1.333	6.5	26,235
Hungary	68	36.1	0.706	4.8	13,129
Iceland	83	12.5	1.469	6.3	29,614
India	56	53.8	0.160	5.5	2,571
Indonesia	47	74.5	−0.918	3.7	3,138
Iran, Islamic Rep.			−0.364		
Iraq			−1.844		
Ireland	74	27.5	1.395	4.5	32,960
Israel	91	33.7	0.966	6.5	19,382
Italy	67	46.8	0.861	4.8	25,570
Jamaica	27	83.4	−0.728	1.9	3,774
Japan	60	32.7	1.422	5.4	25,650
Jordan	94	19.4	0.708	6.4	4,106
Kazakhstan		83.8	−0.590		
Kenya	15	82.8	−1.220	2.2	992
Kiribati					
Korea, Dem. Rep.	78	44.1	−0.667	5.4	16,465
Korea, Rep.	46	37.4	0.943	5.4	16,465
Kuwait			0.907		

(Continued)

(Continued)

Country	PPI Police Performance Index	Composite OC Index Composite OC: Money Laundering, High-Level Corruption, Unsolved Homicide, Informal Sector, OC Index GAD; WEF; BEEPS	World Bank Rule of Law	World Economic Forum Business Costs of Crime and Violence	GDP per Capita (PPP), 2002
Gabon			−0.525		
Gambia, The	68	36.7	0.274	5.4	1,723
Georgia	37	72.6	−0.494		
Germany	54	20.2	1.483	6.3	26,324
Ghana	55	57.4	−0.014	4.1	2,050
Greece	63	42.4	0.496	5.5	18,184
Grenada					
Guadeloupe			−		
Guatemala	48	91.6	−1.106	1.7	3,927
Guinea			−0.762		
Guinea–Bissau			−1.615		
Guyana			−0.140		
Haiti	1	100.0	−1.495	2	1,578
Honduras	27	83.4	−0.895	2	2,520
Hong Kong, China	60	26.7	1.333	6.5	26,235
Hungary	68	36.1	0.706	4.8	13,129
Iceland	83	12.5	1.469	6.3	29,614
India	56	53.8	0.160	5.5	2,571
Indonesia	47	74.5	−0.918	3.7	3,138
Iran, Islamic Rep.			−0.364		
Iraq			−1.844		
Ireland	74	27.5	1.395	4.5	32,960
Israel	91	33.7	0.966	6.5	19,382
Italy	67	46.8	0.861	4.8	25,570
Jamaica	27	83.4	−0.728	1.9	3,774
Japan	60	32.7	1.422	5.4	25,650
Jordan	94	19.4	0.708	6.4	4,106
Kazakhstan		83.8	−0.590		
Kenya	15	82.8	−1.220	2.2	992
Kiribati					
Korea, Dem. Rep.	78	44.1	−0.667	5.4	16,465
Korea, Rep.	46	37.4	0.943	5.4	16,465
Kuwait			0.907		
Kyrgyz Republic	33	68.2	−0.468		

Country	PPI Police Performance Index	Composite OC Index Composite OC: Money Laundering, High-Level Corruption, Unsolved Homicide, Informal Sector, OC Index GAD; WEF; BEEPS	World Bank Rule of Law	World Economic Forum Business Costs of Crime and Violence	GDP per Capita (PPP), 2002
Lao, PDR			−1.204		
Latvia	38	44.8	0.155	4.6	8,965
Lebanon			0.262		
Lesotho	37		−0.240		
Liberia			−1.289		
Libya			−1.113		
Liechtenstein					
Lithuania	31	45.7	0.180	3.9	10,015
Luxembourg	86	21.1	1.621	6.1	56,546
Macao, China			−		
Macedonia, FYR	52	61.0	−0.256	2.9	6,262
Madagascar	17	74.8	−0.825	3.4	735
Malawi	46	55.2	−0.409	4.3	586
Malaysia	43	29.2	0.834	6	8,922
Maldives			−		
Mali	44	56.1	−0.465	5.4	878
Malta	66	32.7	0.864	6	17,344
Marshall Islands					
Martinique			−		
Mauritania			−0.558		
Mauritius	44	39.4	1.279	4.9	10,530
Mexico	20	75.0	−0.474	2.7	8,707
Micronesia					
Moldova	57	61.3	−0.019		
Monaco					
Mongolia	27		0.039		
Morocco	68	55.1	0.678	5	3,767
Mozambique	16	86.5	−1.046	2.5	1,237
Myanmar			−0.839		
Namibia	48	49.3	0.954	3.1	6,410
Nauru					
Nepal			−0.558		
Netherlands	83	18.9	1.584	4.7	27,275
New Zealand	68	12.8	1.824	5.6	20,455

(Continued)

(Continued)

Country	PPI Police Performance Index	Composite OC Index Composite OC: Money Laundering, High-Level Corruption, Unsolved Homicide, Informal Sector, OC Index GAD; WEF; BEEPS	World Bank Rule of Law	World Economic Forum Business Costs of Crime and Violence	GDP per Capita (PPP), 2002
Nicaragua	41	71.8	−0.726	3.7	2,510
Niger			−1.144		
Nigeria	41	91.9	−1.097	2.9	851
Norway	60	22.1	1.833	6	36,047
Oman			1.077		
Pakistan	7	83.7	−0.760	3.3	2,014
Panama	37	52.4	−0.392	3.6	5,972
Papua New Guinea	30		−0.307		
Paraguay	28	95.7	−0.695	2.5	4,419
Peru	27	72.6	−0.522	3.1	4,924
Philippines	43	78.6	−0.078	3.2	4,021
Poland	39	52.4	0.538	3.9	10,187
Portugal	64	30.1	1.083	6.3	17,808
Puerto Rico			0.771		
Qatar			1.269		
Reunion			−		
Romania	39	68.5	−0.088	4	6,326
Russian Federation	34	88.2	−0.722	3.5	7,926
Rwanda			−1.204		
Saint Kitts & Nevis					
Saint Lucia					
Saint Vincent & Grenadines					
Samoa (Western)					
San Marino					
Sao Tome and Principe			−		
Saudi Arabia			0.494		
Senegal	57	59.1	−0.097	3.2	1,535
Seychelles					
Sierra Leone			−0.906		
Singapore	53	14.1	1.939	6.6	23,393
Slovak Republic	50	48.0	0.134	4.6	12,426
Slovenia	71	30.0	0.825	5.6	17,748
Solomon Islands			−		
Somalia			−1.495		

Country	PPI Police Performance Index	Composite OC Index Composite OC: Money Laundering, High-Level Corruption, Unsolved Homicide, Informal Sector, OC Index GAD; WEF; BEEPS	World Bank Rule of Law	World Economic Forum Business Costs of Crime and Violence	GDP per Capita (PPP), 2002
Serbia and Montenegro	34	56.9	−0.806		
South Africa	46	66.1	−0.351	2.4	10,132
Spain	39	30.8	1.032	4.3	20,697
Sri Lanka	35	63.6	−0.361	4	3,447
Sudan			−1.346		
Suriname			−0.730		
Swaziland	40		−0.062		
Sweden	77	18.3	1.623	6.1	25,315
Switzerland	88	20.0	1.996	6.3	28,359
Syrian Arab Republic			−0.291		
Taiwan, China	74	40.5	0.928	5.7	23,420
Tajikistan			−1.335		
Tanzania	41	57.0	0.161	3.6	557
Thailand	68	61.0	0.413	5.7	6,788
Togo			−0.799		
Tonga					
Trinidad and Tobago	17	68.9	0.514	2.8	9,114
Tunisia	83	24.3	0.648	5.6	6,579
Turkey	55	72.1	−0.010	5.7	6,176
Turkmenistan			−0.971		
Uganda	27	72.3	−0.013	3.2	1,354
Ukraine	29	87.4	-0.707	3.8	4,714
United Arab Emirates			0.767		
United Kingdom	78	23.9	1.689	4.9	25,672
United States	77	36.4	1.254	5.5	35,158
Uruguay	60	46.7	0.270	4.9	12,118
Uzbekistan		64.1	−0.870		
Vanatu					
Venezuela, RB	25	89.6	−0.662	1.9	5,226
Vietnam	63	55.4	−0.437	4.2	2,240
West Bank and Gaza			1.222		
Yemen, Rep.			−1.008		
Zambia	28	73.8	−0.402	3.7	806
Zimbabwe	35	75.2	−0.146	3.2	1,993

Chapter 12

Data in Figures 12.2, 12.3, 12.4, and 12.5

Country	Business Costs of Terrorism	Rule of Law	GDP per Capita 2002
Albania		−0.918	
Algeria	3.4	−1.103	5,536
Angola	4.9	−1.225	2,053
Argentina	5.7	0.319	10,954
Armenia		−0.146	
Australia	4.2	1.596	27,756
Austria	5.5	1.812	28,611
Azerbaijan		−0.563	
Bahamas, The		0.563	
Bahrain		0.665	
Bangladesh	3.8	−0.929	1,736
Barbados		0.411	
Belarus		−0.876	
Belgium	5.4	0.797	26,695
Belize		0.088	
Benin		−0.422	
Bolivia	4.9	−0.355	2,360
Bosnia and Herzegovina		−1.108	
Botswana	5.4	0.502	8,244
Brazil	5.6	−0.222	7,156
Brunei		1.252	
Bulgaria	4.5	−0.150	6,909
Burkina Faso		−0.350	
Burundi		−0.881	
Cambodia		−0.235	
Cameroon	4.4	−1.015	1,712
Canada	4.7	1.549	28,699
Cape Verde		0.088	
Chad	3.6	−0.827	1,008
Chile	5.7	1.086	9,561
China	4.8	−0.040	4,475
Colombia	2.1	−0.783	6,068
Congo, Dem. Rep.		−2.153	
Congo, Rep.		−1.435	
Costa Rica	5.6	0.553	8,470
Cote d'Ivoire		−0.335	
Croatia	5.1	0.146	9,967
Cuba		0.115	
Cyprus		0.928	
Czech Republic	4.9	0.543	15,148

Country	Business Costs of Terrorism	Rule of Law	GDP per Capita 2002
Denmark	6	1.691	29,975
Djibouti		−0.235	
Dominican Republic	5.9	0.380	6,197
Ecuador	4.7	−0.721	3,357
Egypt, Arab Rep.	3.8	0.128	3,701
El Salvador	4.3	−0.656	4,675
Equatorial Guinea		−1.204	
Estonia	6.3	0.507	11,712
Ethiopia	4.5	0.269	724
Fiji		−0.495	
Finland	6.3	1.736	25,859
France	5.1	1.077	26,151
Gabon		−0.525	
Gambia, The	5.6	0.274	1,723
Georgia		−0.494	
Germany	4	1.483	26,324
Ghana	5.1	−0.014	2,050
Greece	5.1	0.496	18,184
Guatemala	3.7	−1.106	3,927
Guinea		−0.762	
Guinea–Bissau		−1.615	
Guyana		−0.140	
Haiti	4.5	−1.495	1,578
Honduras	4.5	−0.895	2,520
Hong Kong, China	5.7	1.333	26,235
Hungary	5.9	0.706	13,129
Iceland	5.8	1.469	29,614
India	4.3	0.160	2,571
Indonesia	4.1	−0.918	3,138
Iran, Islamic Rep.		−0.364	
Iraq		−1.844	
Ireland	5.3	1.395	32,960
Israel	1.7	0.966	19,382
Italy	5	0.861	25,570
Jamaica	5.3	−0.728	3,774
Japan	4	1.422	25,650
Jordan	5.4	0.708	4,106
Kazakhstan		−0.590	
Kenya	3.1	−1.220	992
Korea, Dem. Rep.	5.1	−0.667	16,465
Korea, Rep.	5.1	0.943	16,465
Kuwait		0.907	
Kyrgyz Republic		−0.468	

(Continued)

(Continued)

Country	Business Costs of Terrorism	Rule of Law	GDP per Capita 2002
Lao, PDR		−1.204	
Latvia	5.4	0.155	8,965
Lebanon		0.262	
Lesotho		−0.240	
Liberia		−1.289	
Libya		−1.113	
Lithuania	5.7	0.180	10,015
Luxembourg	5.8	1.621	56,546
Macedonia, FYR	2.7	−0.256	6,262
Madagascar	5.4	−0.825	735
Malawi	5	−0.409	586
Malaysia	5.3	0.834	8,922
Mali	5.1	−0.465	878
Malta	5.6	0.864	17,344
Mauritania		−0.558	
Mauritius	5.4	1.279	10,530
Mexico	5.2	−0.474	8,707
Moldova		−0.019	
Mongolia		0.039	
Morocco	5	0.678	3,767
Mozambique	5.2	−1.046	1,237
Myanmar		−0.839	
Namibia	5.1	0.954	6,410
Nepal		−0.558	
Netherlands	5.3	1.584	27,275
New Zealand	5.2	1.824	20,455
Nicaragua	5	−0.726	2,510
Niger		−1.144	
Nigeria	5.2	−1.097	851
Norway	5.3	1.833	36,047
Oman		1.077	
Pakistan	3.9	−0.760	2,014
Panama	5.1	−0.392	5,972
Papua New Guinea		−0.307	
Paraguay	5.5	−0.695	4,419
Peru	4.9	−0.522	4,924
Philippines	2.5	−0.078	4,021
Poland	5.1	0.538	10,187
Portugal	6.2	1.083	17,808
Puerto Rico		0.771	
Qatar		1.269	
Romania	5.5	−0.088	6,326
Russian Federation	4.6	−0.722	7,926

Country	Business Costs of Terrorism	Rule of Law	GDP per Capita 2002
Rwanda		−1.204	
Saudi Arabia		0.494	
Senegal	4.5	−0.097	1,535
Serbia and Montenegro		−0.806	
Sierra Leone		−0.906	
Singapore	4.5	1.939	23,393
Slovak Republic	5.3	0.134	12,426
Slovenia	5.4	0.825	17,748
Somalia		−1.495	
South Africa	5.4	−0.351	10,132
Spain	5.1	1.032	20,697
Sri Lanka	3.1	−0.361	3,447
Sudan		−1.346	
Suriname		−0.730	
Swaziland		−0.062	
Sweden	6.1	1.623	25,315
Switzerland	5.7	1.996	28,359
Syrian Arab Republic		−0.291	
Taiwan, China	5.1	0.928	23,420
Tajikistan		−1.335	
Tanzania	3.5	0.161	557
Thailand	5.6	0.413	6,788
Togo		−0.799	
Trinidad and Tobago	4.6	0.514	9,114
Tunisia	5.6	0.648	6,579
Turkey	4.9	−0.010	6,176
Turkmenistan		−0.971	
Uganda	3	−0.013	1,354
Ukraine	5.4	−0.707	4,714
United Arab Emirates		0.767	
United Kingdom	4	1.689	25,672
United States	3.5	1.254	35,158
Uruguay	6.6	0.270	12,118
Uzbekistan		−0.870	
Venezuela, RB	4.1	−0.662	5,226
Vietnam	4.5	−0.437	2,240
West Bank and Gaza		1.222	
Yemen, Rep.		−1.008	
Zambia	5.6	−0.402	806
Zimbabwe	4.2	−0.146	1,993

Chapter 13

Data in Figures 13.1, 13.2, 13.3, 13.4, 13.5, and 13.6

Country	Lawfulness	Human Development Index 2002
Albania	38.88	0.78
Algeria	43.22	0.70
Angola	33.59	0.38
Antigua and Barbuda		0.80
Argentina	50.83	0.85
Armenia	59.57	0.75
Australia	95.48	0.95
Austria	90.61	0.93
Azerbaijan	62.00	0.75
Bahamas, The		0.82
Bahrain	75.25	0.84
Bangladesh	20.56	0.51
Barbados	83.52	0.89
Belarus	52.25	0.79
Belgium	82.09	0.94
Belize	67.54	0.74
Benin	41.94	0.42
Bhutan		0.54
Bolivia	40.95	0.68
Bosnia and Herzegovina	32.47	0.78
Botswana	76.91	0.59
Brazil	43.34	0.78
Brunei		0.87
Bulgaria	51.43	0.80
Burkina Faso	39.45	0.30
Burundi	26.11	0.34
Cambodia	54.05	0.57
Cameroon	33.67	0.50
Canada	89.81	0.94
Cape Verde		0.72
Central African Republic		0.36
Chad	25.72	0.38
Chile	83.50	0.84
China	58.21	0.75
Colombia	36.19	0.77
Comoros		0.53
Congo, Dem. Rep.	14.52	0.37
Congo, Rep.	28.87	0.49
Costa Rica	60.02	0.83
Cote d'Ivoire	34.20	0.40
Croatia	63.80	0.83

Country	Lawfulness	Human Development Index 2002
Cuba	42.23	0.81
Cyprus	71.60	0.88
Czech Republic	68.20	0.87
Denmark	98.04	0.93
Djibouti		0.45
Dominica		0.74
Dominican Republic	58.01	0.74
East Timor		0.44
Ecuador	32.50	0.74
Egypt, Arab Rep.	59.77	0.65
El Salvador	42.29	0.72
Equatorial Guinea	42.21	0.70
Eritrea	33.84	0.44
Estonia	70.06	0.85
Ethiopia	51.49	0.36
Fiji		0.76
Finland	97.34	0.94
France	80.95	0.93
Gabon	53.44	0.65
Gambia, The	66.81	0.45
Georgia	43.41	0.74
Germany	84.07	0.93
Ghana	57.99	0.57
Greece	69.02	0.90
Grenada		0.75
Guatemala	36.33	0.65
Guinea	50.42	0.43
Guinea-Bissau		0.35
Guyana	66.13	0.72
Haiti	13.75	0.46
Honduras	32.21	0.67
Hong Kong, China	82.47	0.90
Hungary	72.99	0.85
Iceland	100.00	0.94
India	58.76	0.60
Indonesia	46.32	0.69
Iran, Islamic Rep.	40.32	0.73
Iraq	15.92	
Ireland	85.73	0.94
Israel	81.38	0.91
Italy	68.46	0.92
Jamaica	34.10	0.76
Japan	81.03	0.94
Jordan	83.17	0.75
Kazakhstan	41.08	0.77

(Continued)

(Continued)

Country	Lawfulness	Human Development Index 2002
Kenya	23.79	0.49
Korea, Dem. Rep.	70.01	
Korea, Rep.	69.74	0.89
Kuwait	71.65	0.84
Kyrgyz Republic	46.95	0.70
Lao, PDR		0.53
Latvia	62.79	0.82
Lebanon	45.44	0.76
Lesotho	60.76	0.49
Libya	45.16	0.79
Lithuania	58.50	0.84
Luxembourg	97.12	0.93
Macedonia, FYR	52.36	0.79
Madagascar	36.56	0.47
Malawi	46.99	0.39
Malaysia	64.20	0.79
Maldives		0.75
Mali	51.98	0.33
Malta	84.50	0.88
Mauritania	54.04	0.47
Mauritius	73.43	0.79
Mexico	37.51	0.80
Moldova	40.68	0.68
Mongolia	51.28	0.67
Morocco	61.36	0.62
Mozambique	41.14	0.35
Myanmar	25.79	0.55
Namibia	62.49	0.61
Nepal	42.47	0.50
Netherlands	91.19	0.94
New Zealand	92.23	0.92
Nicaragua	43.31	0.67
Niger	33.14	0.29
Nigeria	39.69	0.47
Norway	91.00	0.96
Oman	79.98	0.77
Pakistan	23.71	0.50
Panama	58.61	0.79
Papua New Guinea	45.97	0.54
Paraguay	45.26	0.75
Peru	39.33	0.75
Philippines	53.05	0.75
Poland	56.44	0.85
Portugal	80.44	0.90
Puerto Rico	81.44	

Country	Lawfulness	Human Development Index 2002
Qatar	80.61	0.83
Romania	54.14	0.78
Russian Federation	44.67	0.80
Rwanda		0.43
Saint Kitts & Nevis		0.84
Saint Lucia		0.78
Saint Vincent & Grenadines		0.75
Samoa (Western)		0.77
Sao Tome and Principe		0.65
Saudi Arabia	41.04	0.77
Senegal	49.84	0.44
Serbia and Montenegro	45.98	
Seychelles	62.93	0.85
Sierra Leone	34.99	0.27
Singapore	92.19	0.90
Slovak Republic	57.33	0.84
Slovenia	79.39	0.90
Solomon Islands		0.62
South Africa	50.76	0.67
Spain	71.67	0.92
Sri Lanka	47.69	0.74
Sudan	24.72	0.51
Suriname	67.51	0.78
Swaziland	57.62	0.52
Sweden	94.28	0.95
Switzerland	99.12	0.94
Syrian Arab Republic	49.42	0.71
Taiwan, China	75.84	
Tajikistan	31.80	0.67
Tanzania	56.31	0.41
Thailand	59.68	0.77
Togo	39.89	0.50
Tonga		0.79
Trinidad and Tobago	46.84	0.80
Tunisia	77.65	0.75
Turkey	52.87	0.75
Turkmenistan	29.21	0.75
Uganda	44.20	0.49
Ukraine	41.05	0.78
United Arab Emirates	77.78	0.82
United Kingdom	89.80	0.94
United States	84.66	0.94
Uruguay	71.60	0.83
Uzbekistan	39.66	0.71
Vanatu		0.57

(Continued)

(Continued)

Country	Lawfulness	Human Development Index 2002
Venezuela, RB	29.07	0.78
Vietnam	47.57	0.69
West Bank and Gaza	40.83	
Yemen, Rep.	25.76	0.48
Zambia	48.19	0.39
Zimbabwe	41.55	0.49

Data in Figures 13.1, 13.2, 13.3, 13.4, 13.5, and 13.6

Country	Lawfulness Rank With Law & Order	Country	Lawfulness Rank Without Law & Order
Iceland	1	Iceland	1
Denmark	2	Switzerland	2
Luxembourg	3	Denmark	3
Finland	4	Finland	4
Switzerland	5	Luxembourg	5
Australia	6	Australia	6
Sweden	7	Sweden	7
Norway	8	New Zealand	8
Netherlands	9	Singapore	9
Austria	10	Netherlands	10
Canada	11	Norway	11
Singapore	12	Austria	12
United Kingdom	13	Canada	13
Ireland	14	United Kingdom	14
Brunei	15	Ireland	15
New Zealand	16	United States	16
United States	17	Malta	17
Malta	18	Germany	18
Germany	19	Barbados	19
Chile	20	Chile	20
Barbados	21	Jordan	21
Belgium	22	Hong Kong, China	22
Israel	23	Belgium	23
Qatar	24	Puerto Rico	24
Japan	25	Israel	25
France	26	Japan	26
Oman	27	France	27
Portugal	28	Qatar	28
Hong Kong, China	29	Portugal	29
Puerto Rico	30	Oman	30
Jordan	31	Slovenia	31
Tunisia	32	United Arab Emirates	32
Slovenia	33	Tunisia	33
Bahrain	34	Botswana	34
Taiwan, China	35	Taiwan, China	35
Bahamas, The	36	Bahrain	36
Cyprus	37	Mauritius	37
United Arab Emirates	38	Hungary	38
Kuwait	39	Spain	39
Botswana	40	Kuwait	40
Korea, Dem. Rep.	41	Uruguay	41
Spain	42	Cyprus	42

(Continued)

(Continued)

Country	Lawfulness Rank With Law & Order	Country	Lawfulness Rank Without Law & Order
Mauritius	43	Estonia	43
Korea, Rep.	44	Korea, Dem. Rep.	44
Hungary	45	Korea, Rep.	45
Czech Republic	46	Greece	46
Greece	47	Italy	47
Estonia	48	Czech Republic	48
Italy	49	Belize	49
Croatia	50	Suriname	50
Gambia, The	51	Gambia, The	51
Belize	52	Guyana	52
Latvia	53	Malaysia	53
Namibia	54	Croatia	54
Morocco	55	Seychelles	55
Uruguay	56	Latvia	56
Malaysia	57	Namibia	57
Seychelles	58	Azerbaijan	58
Suriname	59	Morocco	59
Azerbaijan	60	Lesotho	60
Egypt, Arab Rep.	61	Costa Rica	61
Costa Rica	62	Egypt, Arab Rep.	62
China	63	Thailand	63
Tanzania	64	Armenia	64
India	65	India	65
Lesotho	66	Panama	66
Lithuania	67	Lithuania	67
Slovak Republic	68	China	68
Syrian Arab Republic	69	Dominican Republic	69
Ethiopia	70	Ghana	70
Guyana	71	Swaziland	71
Poland	72	Slovak Republic	72
Armenia	73	Poland	73
Turkey	74	Tanzania	74
Panama	75	Romania	75
Swaziland	76	Cambodia	76
Romania	77	Mauritania	77
Thailand	78	Gabon	78
Belarus	79	Philippines	79
Bulgaria	80	Turkey	80
Mongolia	81	Macedonia, FYR	81
Cambodia	82	Belarus	82
Mauritania	83	Mali	83
Dominican Republic	84	Ethiopia	84
Ghana	85	Bulgaria	85

Country	Lawfulness Rank With Law & Order	Country	Lawfulness Rank Without Law & Order
Gabon	86	Mongolia	86
Saudi Arabia	87	Argentina	87
Macedonia, FYR	88	South Africa	88
Vietnam	89	Guinea	89
Mali	90	Senegal	90
Zambia	91	Syrian Arab Republic	91
Lebanon	92	Zambia	92
Libya	93	Sri Lanka	93
Argentina	94	Vietnam	94
Senegal	95	Malawi	95
Moldova	96	Kyrgyz Republic	96
Philippines	97	Trinidad and Tobago	97
South Africa	98	Indonesia	98
Cuba	99	Serbia and Montenegro	99
Russian Federation	100	Papua New Guinea	100
Nicaragua	101	Lebanon	101
Sri Lanka	102	Paraguay	102
Serbia and Montenegro	103	Libya	103
Uganda	104	Russian Federation	104
Kazakhstan	105	Uganda	105
Guinea	106	Georgia	106
Malawi	107	Brazil	107
Iran, Islamic Rep.	108	Nicaragua	108
Indonesia	109	Algeria	109
Burkina Faso	110	Nepal	110
Kyrgyz Republic	111	El Salvador	111
Ukraine	112	Cuba	112
Algeria	113	Equatorial Guinea	113
Trinidad and Tobago	114	Benin	114
El Salvador	115	Zimbabwe	115
Togo	116	Mozambique	116
Sierra Leone	117	Kazakhstan	117
Papua New Guinea	118	Ukraine	118
Brazil	119	Saudi Arabia	119
Zimbabwe	120	Bolivia	120
Georgia	121	West Bank and Gaza	121
Paraguay	122	Moldova	122
Mozambique	123	Iran, Islamic Rep.	123
Bolivia	124	Togo	124
Nepal	125	Nigeria	125
Equatorial Guinea	126	Uzbekistan	126
Peru	127	Burkina Faso	127
Benin	128	Peru	128

(Continued)

(Continued)

Country	Lawfulness Rank With Law & Order	Country	Lawfulness Rank Without Law & Order
Guinea-Bissau	129	Albania	129
West Bank and Gaza	130	Mexico	130
Mexico	131	Madagascar	131
Uzbekistan	132	Guatemala	132
Albania	133	Colombia	133
Madagascar	134	Sierra Leone	134
Angola	135	Cote d'Ivoire	135
Nigeria	136	Jamaica	136
Cote d'Ivoire	137	Eritrea	137
Guatemala	138	Cameroon	138
Jamaica	139	Angola	139
Liberia	140	Niger	140
Ecuador	141	Ecuador	141
Cameroon	142	Bosnia and Herzegovina	142
Venezuela, RB	143	Honduras	143
Eritrea	144	Tajikistan	144
Niger	145	Turkmenistan	145
Colombia	146	Venezuela, RB	146
Myanmar	147	Congo, Rep.	147
Bosnia and Herzegovina	148	Burundi	148
Tajikistan	149	Myanmar	149
Honduras	150	Yemen, Rep.	150
Congo, Rep.	151	Chad	151
Sudan	152	Sudan	152
Pakistan	153	Kenya	153
Turkmenistan	154	Pakistan	154
Yemen, Rep.	155	Bangladesh	155
Kenya	156	Iraq	156
Burundi	157	Congo, Dem. Rep.	157
Chad	158	Haiti	158
Bangladesh	159		
Somalia	160		
Haiti	161		
Iraq	162		
Congo, Dem. Rep.	163		

Appendix Chapter 13

Data in Figure 13.4

Country	Lawfulness Combining Indicators of Police Performance, Rule of Law, and of the Prevalence of Various Types of Crime	UNDP Human Development Index 2002
Afghanistan		
Albania	39	0.78
Algeria	43	0.70
Andora		
Angola	34	0.38
Antigua and Barbuda		0.80
Argentina	51	0.85
Armenia	60	0.75
Australia	95	0.95
Austria	91	0.93
Azerbaijan	62	0.75
Bahamas, The		0.82
Bahrain	75	0.84
Bangladesh	21	0.51
Barbados	84	0.89
Belarus	52	0.79
Belgium	82	0.94
Belize	68	0.74
Benin	42	0.42
Bhutan		0.54
Bolivia	41	0.68
Bosnia and Herzegovina	32	0.78
Botswana	77	0.59
Brazil	43	0.78
Brunei		0.87
Bulgaria	51	0.80
Burkina Faso	39	0.30
Burundi	26	0.34
Cambodia	54	0.57
Cameroon	34	0.50
Canada	90	0.94
Cape Verde		0.72
Central African Republic		0.36
Chad	26	0.38
Chile	83	0.84
China	58	0.75

(Continued)

(Continued)

Country	Lawfulness Combining Indicators of Police Performance, Rule of Law, and of the Prevalence of Various Types of Crime	UNDP Human Development Index 2002
Colombia	36	0.77
Comoros		0.53
Congo, Dem. Rep.	15	0.37
Congo, Rep.	29	0.49
Costa Rica	60	0.83
Cote d'Ivoire	34	0.40
Croatia	64	0.83
Cuba	42	0.81
Cyprus	72	0.88
Czech Republic	68	0.87
Denmark	98	0.93
Djibouti		0.45
Dominica		0.74
Dominican Republic	58	0.74
East Timor		0.44
Ecuador	33	0.74
Egypt, Arab Rep.	60	0.65
El Salvador	42	0.72
Equatorial Guinea	42	0.70
Eritrea	34	0.44
Estonia	70	0.85
Ethiopia	51	0.36
Fiji		0.76
Finland	97	0.94
France	81	0.93
Gabon	53	0.65
Gambia, The	67	0.45
Georgia	43	0.74
Germany	84	0.93
Ghana	58	0.57
Greece	69	0.90
Grenada		0.75
Guadeloupe		
Guatemala	36	0.65
Guinea	50	0.43
Guinea-Bissau		0.35
Guyana	66	0.72
Haiti	14	0.46
Honduras	32	0.67
Hong Kong, China	82	0.90

Country	Lawfulness Combining Indicators of Police Performance, Rule of Law, and of the Prevalence of Various Types of Crime	UNDP Human Development Index 2002
Hungary	73	0.85
Iceland	100	0.94
India	59	0.60
Indonesia	46	0.69
Iran, Islamic Rep.	40	0.73
Iraq	16	
Ireland	86	0.94
Israel	81	0.91
Italy	68	0.92
Jamaica	34	0.76
Japan	81	0.94
Jordan	83	0.75
Kazakhstan	41	0.77
Kenya	24	0.49
Kiribati		
Korea, Dem. Rep.	70	
Korea, Rep.	70	0.89
Kuwait	72	0.84
Kyrgyz Republic	47	0.70
Lao, PDR		0.53
Latvia	63	0.82
Lebanon	45	0.76
Lesotho	61	0.49
Liberia		
Libya	45	0.79
Liechtenstein		
Lithuania	59	0.84
Luxembourg	97	0.93
Macao, China		
Macedonia, FYR	52	0.79
Madagascar	37	0.47
Malawi	47	0.39
Malaysia	64	0.79
Maldives		0.75
Mali	52	0.33
Malta	85	0.88
Marshall Islands		
Martinique		
Mauritania	54	0.47
Mauritius	73	0.79

(Continued)

(Continued)

Country	Lawfulness	UNDP
	Combining Indicators of Police Performance, Rule of Law, and of the Prevalence of Various Types of Crime	Human Development Index 2002
Mexico	38	0.80
Micronesia		
Moldova	41	0.68
Monaco		
Mongolia	51	0.67
Morocco	61	0.62
Mozambique	41	0.35
Myanmar	26	0.55
Namibia	62	0.61
Nauru		
Nepal	42	0.50
Netherlands	91	0.94
New Zealand	92	0.92
Nicaragua	43	0.67
Niger	33	0.29
Nigeria	40	0.47
Norway	91	0.96
Oman	80	0.77
Pakistan	24	0.50
Panama	59	0.79
Papua New Guinea	46	0.54
Paraguay	45	0.75
Peru	39	0.75
Philippines	53	0.75
Poland	56	0.85
Portugal	80	0.90
Puerto Rico	81	
Qatar	81	0.83
Reunion		
Romania	54	0.78
Russian Federation	45	0.80
Rwanda		0.43
Saint Kitts & Nevis		0.84
Saint Lucia		0.78
Saint Vincent & Grenadines		0.75
Samoa (Western)		0.77
San Marino		
Sao Tome and Principe		0.65
Saudi Arabia	41	0.77
Senegal	50	0.44

Country	Lawfulness Combining Indicators of Police Performance, Rule of Law, and of the Prevalence of Various Types of Crime	UNDP Human Development Index 2002
Serbia and Montenegro	46	
Seychelles	63	0.85
Sierra Leone	35	0.27
Singapore	92	0.90
Slovak Republic	57	0.84
Slovenia	79	0.90
Solomon Islands		0.62
Somalia		
South Africa	51	0.67
Spain	72	0.92
Sri Lanka	48	0.74
Sudan	25	0.51
Suriname	68	0.78
Swaziland	58	0.52
Sweden	94	0.95
Switzerland	99	0.94
Syrian Arab Republic	49	0.71
Taiwan, China	76	
Tajikistan	32	0.67
Tanzania	56	0.41
Thailand	60	0.77
Togo	40	0.50
Tonga		0.79
Trinidad and Tobago*	47	0.80
Tunisia	78	0.75
Turkey	53	0.75
Turkmenistan	29	0.75
Uganda	44	0.49
Ukraine	41	0.78
United Arab Emirates	78	0.82
United Kingdom	90	0.94
United States	85	0.94
Uruguay	72	0.83
Uzbekistan	40	0.71
Vanatu		0.57
Venezuela, RB	29	0.78
Vietnam	48	0.69
West Bank and Gaza	41	
Yemen, Rep.	26	0.48
Zambia	48	0.39
Zimbabwe	42	0.49

For data in the radars:

See Appendix **Chapter 3** for data on ICVS total (11 crimes)

See Appendix **Chapter 7** for data on the composite organized-crime index

See Appendix **Chapter 8** for data on (business costs of) terrorism

See Appendix **Chapter 8** for data on corruption

See Appendix **Chapter 9** for data on the police performance index

See Appendix **Chapter 12** for data on the rule of law

See Appendix **Chapter 13** for data on lawfulness

Notes to Chapter 13

[1]Data on human development stem from the Human Development Reports of United Nations Development Programme (United Nations, 2002b).

[2]The Lawfulness Index is based on data on corruption perception (Transparency International), organized-crime perception (composed of data from WEF, GAD, and BEEPS), rule of law (World Bank Institute), police performance (ICVS), and victims of common crimes (ICVS).

[3]Data that are included in the index have been recalculated by dividing them by the highest score in the data series and multiplying them by 100. All data are thus presented on a 100% scale.

[4]Revised lawfulness index, including scores on PRS Group's Law and Order Measure (online: www.CountryData.com)

References

Abrahemsen, R., & Williams, M. C. (2005). *The globalization of private security. Country report: Nigeria.* Aberystwyth: University of Wales.

Aceijas, C., Stimson, G., & Hickman, M. (2004). *Review of injecting drug users and HIV infection in prisons in developing and transitional countries.* London: Imperial College. Online: http://www.idurefgroup.org.

Acemoglu, D., & Johnson, S. (2003, July). Unbundling institutions. Working paper, MIT. Also in *The Journal of Political Economy, 79,* 5. Online: http://papers.ssrn.com/abstract.

Adamoli, S., Di Nicola, A., Savona, E. U., & Zoffi, P. (1998). *Organized crime around the world.* Helsinki: HEUNI.

Adler, F. (1983). *Nations not obsessed with crime.* Comparative Criminal Law Project Publication Series, Vol. 15. Littleton, CO: Fred B. Rothman.

Adler, F., Mueller, G. O. W., & Laufer, W. S. (1998). *Criminology.* Boston: McGraw-Hill.

Aebi, M. F., Killias, M., & Tavares, C. (2001). Comparing crime rates: Confronting the ICVS, the European sourcebook of crime and criminal justice statistics and Interpol statistics. In H. Kury (Ed.), *International comparison of crime and victimization: The ICVS.* International Studies in Social Science, Vol. 2. Willowdale, ON: De Sitter Publications.

Afrobarometer. (2004). *Afrobarometer round 2: Compendium of comparative results from a 15-country survey.* Working paper No. 34, March 2004.

Altbeker, A. (2005). Puzzling statistics: Is South Africa really the world's crime capital? *Crime Quarterly, 11.* Online: www.iss.org.za/pubs/Crime

Alvazzi del Frate, A. (2003). The voice of victims of crime. *Forum on Crime and Society, 3,* 127–141.

Alvazzi del Frate, A. (2004). The international crime business survey. Findings from nine Central-Eastern European cities. *European Journal on Criminal Policy and Research, 10,* 137–161.

Alvazzi del Frate, A., Bule, J., Van Kesteren, J., & Patrignani, A. (2003). *Strategic plan of the police of the Republic of Mozambique. Results of surveys on victimization and police performance.* Turin: UNICRI Publications.

Alvazzi del Frate, A., & Van Kesteren, J. (2001). The ICVS in the developing world. In H. Kury (Ed.), *International comparison of crime and victimization: The ICVS.* Willowdale, ON: De Sitter Publications.

Alvazzi del Frate, A., & Van Kesteren, J. (2004). *Criminal victimization in urban Europe.* Turin: UNICRI Publications.

Alvazzi del Frate, A., Zvekic, U., & Van Dijk, J. J. M. (Eds.). (1993). *Understanding crime: Experiences of crime and crime control.* Rome: UNICRI Publications.

Anderson, D. A. (1999). The aggregate burden of crime. *Journal of Law and Economics, 42,* 611–643.

Angers, L. (2004). Combating cyber-crime: National legislation as a prerequisite to international cooperation. In E. U. Savona (Ed.), *Crime and technology. New frontiers for regulation, law enforcement and research.* Dordrecht, The Netherlands: Springer.

Aos, S., et al. (2001). *The comparative costs and benefits of programs to reduce crime.* Olympia: Washington State Institute for Public Policy. Online: www.wa.gov/wsipp.

Arlacchi, P. (1993). *Men of dishonor: Inside the Sicilian Mafia. An account of Antonino Calderone.* New York: William Morrow.

Aromaa, K. (2000). Organized crime and business security. In O. Hatalak, A. Alvazzi del Frate, & U. Zvekic (Eds.), *Surveying crime: A global approach.* Rome: ISTAT/UNICRI.

Aromaa, K., & Laitinen, A. (1994). Business security in South-Western Finland. In K. Aromaa & A. Laitinen (Eds.), *Juvenile delinquency and business security.* Helsinki, Finland: Ministry of the Interior, Police Department.

Aromaa, K., & Lehti, M. (1996). *Foreign companies and crime in eastern Europe.* Helsinki, Finland: National Research Institute of Legal Policy, Publication No. 135.

Aromaa, K., Leppa, S., Nevala, S., & Ollus, N. (Eds.). (2003). *Crime and criminal justice systems in Europe and North America 1995–1997.* Helsinki: HEUNI.

AUCERT. (2006). *2006 Australian Computer Crime and Security Survey.*

Barro, R. J., & Sala-i-Martin, X. (2004). *Economic growth* (2nd ed.). Cambridge, MA; London: MIT Press.

Bartelet, R. (2004). *Self-reported juvenile delinquency in England and Wales, The Netherlands, and Spain.* Helsinki, Finland: European Institute for Crime Prevention and Control.

Bauer, L, & Owens, S. D. (2004). Justice expenditure and employment in the United States, 2001. *Bureau of Justice Statistics Bulletin.* Washington, DC: U.S. Department of Justice, Bureau of Justice Statistics.

BEEPS. (1996). *Business Environment and Enterprise Performance Survey.* World Bank and the EBRD. Online: http://info.worldbank.org/governance/beeps1996/

Beirne, P. (1993). *Inventing criminology. Essays on the rise of "homo criminalis."* Albany: State University of New York Press.

Belknap, J. E. (1989). The economics-crime link. *Criminal Justice Abstracts, 21,* 1.

Bennett, R. R. (1991). Development and crime: A cross-national time-series analysis of competing models. *Sociological Quarterly, 32,* 343–363.

Bennett, T., Holloway, K., & Williams, T. (2001). *Drug use and offending: Summary results from the first year of the NEW-ADAM research programme.* London: Home Office Findings, No. 148.

Bezlov, T. (2005). *Crime trends in Bulgaria: Police statistics and victimization surveys.* Sofia, Bulgaria: Center for the Study of Democracy.

Biebesheimer, C., & Payne, J. M. (2001). *IDB experience in justice reform: Lessons learned and elements for policy formulation.* Washington, DC: Inter-American Development Bank.

Blickman, T. (2005). The ecstasy industry in The Netherlands in a global perspective. In P. Van Duyne, K. Von Lampe, J. J. M. Van Dijk, & J. L. Newell (Eds.), *The organized crime economy: Managing crime markets in Europe.* Nijmegen, The Netherlands: Wolf Legal Publishers.

Block, R. (1993). Measuring victimization risk: The effects of methodology, sampling and fielding. In A. Alvazzi del Frate, U. Zvekic, & J. J. M. Van Dijk (Eds.), *Understanding crime: Experiences of crime and crime control.* Rome: UNICRI Publications.

Blumstein, A. (1993). Making rationality relevant. *Criminology, 31,* 1–16.

Blumstein, A., & Wallman, J. (2000). *The crime drop in America.* New York: Cambridge University Press.

Boutelier, J. C. J. (2004). *The safety utopia: Contemporary discontent and desire as to crime and punishment.* Dordrecht, the Netherlands: Kluwer.

Braithwaite, J. (1989). *Crime, shame, and integration.* Cambridge, UK: Cambridge University Press.

Brand, S., & Price, R. (2000). *The economic and social costs of crime.* Home Office Research Study 217. London: Home Office.

Brantingham, P., & Easton, T. (1998). *The costs of crime, who pays and how much?* Fraser Institute Critical Issues Bulletin. Vancouver, BC: Fraser Institute.

Brunetti, A., Kisunko, G., & Weder, B. (1997). *Institutional obstacles for doing business. Data description and methodology of a worldwide private sector survey.* World Bank Policy Research Working Paper No. 1759. Washington, DC: The World Bank.

Bureau of Justice Statistics. (1998). *Alcohol and crime. An analysis of national data on the prevalence of alcohol involvement in crime.* U.S. Department of Justice. Washington, DC: Bureau of Justice Statistics.

Burton, P., Du Plessis, A., Leggett, T., Louw, A., Mistry, D., & Van Vuuren, H. (2004). *National victims of crime survey South Africa 2003.* Monograph No. 101. Pretoria, South Africa: Institute for Security Studies.

Buscaglia, E., & Van Dijk, J. J. M. (2003). Controlling organized crime and corruption in the public sector. *Forum on Crime and Society, 3,* 3–35.

Buvinic, M., Morrison, A., & Shifter, M. (1999). *Violence in Latin America and the Caribbean: A framework for action.* Technical Study. Washington, DC: Sustainable Development Department. Inter-American Development Bank.

Caranza, E., & Solana, E. (2004). ILANUD. Paper drafted at the request of UNICRI as input to a document on *Trends in Crime and Justice* submitted by UNICRI/UNODC at the United Nations Eleventh Congress on Crime Prevention and Criminal Justice in Bangkok, Thailand, 2005.

Centre for Crime and Justice Studies. (2005). *Crime and social exclusion.* Factsheet. Accessed January 5, 2005. London: King's College. Online: http://www.crimeinfo.org.uk/servlet/factsheetservlet?command=view factsheet&factsheetid=54&category=factsheets.

Chockalingam, K. (2003). Victimization by crime in four large cities in southern India. *Forum on Crime and Society, 3,* 117–127.

Clarke, R. V. (1992). *Situational crime prevention: Successful case studies.* Albany, NY: Harrow and Heston.

Clarke, R. V. (1995). Situational crime prevention. In M. Tonry & D. P. Farrington (Eds.), *Building a safer society: Strategic approaches to crime prevention. Crime and Justice: A Review of Research, 19,* 91–150. Chicago: University of Chicago Press.

Clarke, R. V. (1999). *Hot products: Understanding, anticipating and reducing demand for stolen goods.* Police Research Series, Paper 112. London: Home Office Research Development and Statistics Directorate.

Clarke, R. V., & Homel, R. (1997). A revised classification of situational crime prevention techniques. In S. P. Lab (Ed.), *Crime prevention at a crossroads* (pp. 17–27). Cincinnati, OH: Anderson.

Coalition 2000. (2005). Anti-corruption reforms in Bulgaria. Sofia, Bulgaria: Center for the Study of Democracy. Online: coalition2000@online.bg.

Cohen, L. E., & Felson, M. (1979). Social change and crime rate trends: A routine activity approach. *American Sociological Review, 44,* 588–608.

Collier, P., & Hoeffler, A. (2001). *Greed and grievance in civil war.* Washington, DC: Post Conflict Unit, World Bank.

Cook, P. (1987). Robbery violence. *Journal of Criminal Law and Criminology, 70,* 357–376.

Cook, P. J., & Khmilevska, N. (2005). Cross-national patterns in crime rates. In M. Tonry & D. Farrington (Eds.), *Crime and justice.* Vol. 33. Chicago: University of Chicago Press.

Cooksey, B. (2002). Can aid agencies really help combat corruption? *Forum on Crime and Society, 2*(1), 45–57. Vienna: UNODC.

Costa, A. M. (2002). Institutional failures, organized crime and their global security implications. In *Tackling cross border crime. Challenges of international development cooperation.* Bonn, Germany: InWEnt, Development Policy Forum.

Council of Europe. (2004, December 23). *Organized crime situation report 2004: Focus on the threat of cybercrime.* Strasbourg: Council of Europe.

Crawford, A., & Goodey, J. (2000). *Integrating a victim perspective within criminal justice.* Aldershot, UK: Darmouth/Ashgate: International Debates.

Cusson, M. (1990). *Croissance et decroissance du crime.* Presses Universitaires de France.

Dandurand, Y., Griffith, C. T., & Chin, V. (2004*). Towards a programming framework for development assistance in the justice and security sector.* Discussion note—America branch. Ottawa, ON: Canadian International Development Agency.

David, P. (2004). *Technical cooperation in strengthening the rule of law in Latin America: Applicability of United Nations standards and norms in crime prevention and criminal justice to facilitate access to justice.* UNODC. Expert Group Meeting, Vienna, Austria, December 10, 2003.

De Waard, J. (1999). The private security industry in international perspective. *European Journal on Criminal Policy and Research, 7*(2), 143–174.

Dulic, D. (Ed.). (2005). *Human security indicators in Serbia.* Belgrade, Serbia: Philo (in Serbian with an English summary).

Dunlap, R. W. (1997). Asian home invasion robbery. *Journal of Contemporary Criminal Justice, 13,* 309–319.

Dutch National Rapporteur on THB. (2005). *Trafficking in human beings—Third report of the Dutch National Rapporteur.* The Hague: Bureau NRM.

Eck, J. E. (2002). Preventing crime at places. In L. W. Sherman, D. P. Farrington, B. C. Welsh, & D. L. MacKenzie (Eds.), *Evidence-based crime prevention* (pp. 207–265). New York: Routledge.

Eck, J. E., & Maguire, E. R. (2005). Have changes in policing reduced violent crime? An assessment of the evidence. In A. Blumstein & J. Wallman (Eds.), *The crime drop in America.* New York: Cambridge University Press.

Economist, The. (2005). *Pocket world in figures.* London: Profile Books.

Eiras, A. I. (2003, March 7). Make the rule of law a necessary condition for the millennium challenge account. In *The heritage foundation backgrounder.* Washington, DC: Heritage Foundation.

Ernst &Young. (2004). *Fraud, the unmanaged risk.* 8th Global Survey. Online: www.ey.com/southafrica.

Eurobarometer. (2003, May). *Public safety, exposure to drug-related problems and crime.* Report prepared for the European Commission by the European Opinion Research Group (EORG).

European Sourcebook of Crime & Criminal Justice Statistics. (2006). The Hague: WODC/Boom Juridische Uitgevers.

European Sourcebook of Crime & Criminal Justice Statistics. (2003). The Hague: WODC/Boom Juridische Uitgevers.

EUROPOL. (2003). *European Union Organized-Crime Report,* Open Version, December 2003. Online: http://europa.eu.int.

EUROPOL. (2004). *European Union Organized-Crime Report,* Open Version, December 2004.

Fajnzylber, P. (1997, September 26). *What causes crime and violence?* Office of the Chief Economist Latin America and the Caribbean. Washington, DC: The World Bank.

Fajnzylber, P., Lederman, D., & Loayza, N. (2000). Crime and violence: An economic perspective. *Economia, 1*, 219–302.

Farrell, G., & Clark, K. (2004). *What does the world spend on criminal justice?* Helsinki: HEUNI Paper, No 20. HEUNI.

Farrell, G., & Pease, K. (2001). *Repeat victimization.* Crime prevention studies, Vol. 12. Monsey, NY: Criminal Justice Press.

Farrington, D. P., & Jolliffe, D. (2005). Cross-national comparisons of crime rates in four countries. In M. Tonry & D. P. Farrington (Eds.), *Crime and punishment in Western countries, 1980–1999,* Crime and Justice. Chicago: University of Chicago Press.

Farrington, D. P., Langan, P. A., & Tonry, M. (2004, September). *Cross-national studies in crime and justice.* U.S. Department of Justice, Office of Justice Programs, Bureau of Justice Statistics. Washington, DC.

Farrington, D. P., Petrosino, A., & Welsh, B. C. (2001). Systematic reviews and cost-benefit analyses of correctional interventions. *Prison Journal, 81,* 339–359.

Farrington, D. P., & Welsh, B. C. (2002). *Effects of improved street lighting on crime: A systematic review.* Home Office Research Study, No. 251. London: Home Office.

Farrington, D. P., & Welsh, B. C. (2003). Family-based prevention of offending: A meta-analysis. *Australian and New Zealand Journal of Criminology, 36,* 127–151.

Feld, L. P., & Voigt, S. (2003). Economic growth and judicial independence: Cross-country evidence using a new set of indicators. *European Journal of Political Economy, 19,* 497–527.

Felson, M. (1997). *Crime and everyday life* (2nd ed.). Thousand Oaks, CA: Pine Forge Press/SAGE.

Felson, M., & Clarke, R. V. (1998). Opportunity makes the thief. Practical theory for crime prevention. In *Police Research Series, Paper 98. Policing & Reducing Crime.* London: Home Office.

Felson, R.B., Pare, P.-P., & Haber, K. (2006). *Firearms and fisticuffs: Region, race, and adversary effects on assault.* Paper of the American Society of Criminology, Los Angeles, CA.

Fijnaut, C., & Paoli, L. (2004). *Organized crime in Europe. Concepts, patterns, and control policies in the European Union and beyond.* Studies on Organized Crime, Vol. 1.4. Dordrecht, the Netherlands: Springer.

Finckenauer, J., Fuentes, J. R., & Ward, G. L. (2001). Mexico and the United States of America: Neighbors confront drug trafficking. *Forum on Crime and Society, 1,* 1–19.

Finckenauer, J. O., & Waring, E. J. (1998). *Russian Mafia in America: Immigration, culture, and crime.* Boston: Northeastern University Press.

Fitzgerald, J. (2002). The war against crime: Is the tide beginning to turn? In *South Africa: The Good News.* Cape Town, South Africa.

Foglesong, T. (2005). *Regional variation in public perceptions of organized crime in the Balkans.* Center on Organized Crime in Southeast Europe, Vera Institute of Justice, May 15, 2005.

Freel, R., & French, B. (2006). *Perceptions of crime: Findings of the 2005 Northern Ireland Crime survey.* Belfast: Statistics and Research Agency.

Friday, P. C., Ren, X., Weitekamp, E., Kerner, H.-J., & Taylor, T. (2005). *A Chinese birth cohort: Theoretical implications.* National Institute of Justice, Office of Justice Programs, U.S. Department of Justice (Award number 199IJCX0048). Charlotte: University of North Carolina–Charlotte.

Gastrow, P. (2003). *Penetrating state and business. Organized crime in Southern Africa,* Volume One. Pretoria: Institute for Security Studies.

Gauthier, A., Hicks, D., Sansfacon, D., & Salel, L. (1999). *Hundred crime prevention programmes to inspire action across the world.* Montreal, QU: International Centre for Crime Prevention. Online: www.crime-prevention-intl.org.

Gilling, D. (1997). *Crime prevention, theory, policy, and politics.* London: UCL Press.

Glenn, J. C., & Gordon, T. J. (2007). *State of the Future.* Washington, DC: Millenium Project.

Godson, R. (2000). *The role of civil society in countering organized crime: Global implications of the Palermo, Sicily, Renaissance.* UNODC/The Sicilian Renaissance Institute, Cita di Palermo, Palermo, December 14, 2000.

Gonczöl, K. (2004). *Hungarian National Strategy for Social Crime Prevention.* Paper for ICPC 10th Anniversary Colloquium in Paris (ICPC, Montreal).

Gonzalez-Ruiz, S. (2001). Fighting drug cartels on the Mexico–United States border. *Forum on Crime and Society, 1,* 19–31.

Goodey, J. (2005). *Victims and victimology. Research, policy, and practice.* Longman Criminology Series. Pearson Longman.

Gorman, R. F. (2001). *Great debates at the United Nations. An encyclopaedia of fifty key items, 1945–2000.* Westport, CT: Greenwood Press.

Goudriaan, H. (2004). Reporting to the police in Western countries: A theoretical analysis of the effects of social context. In *Justice Quarterly, 21*(4), 933–969.

Greenwood, P. W., Model, K. E., Rydell, C. P., & Chiesa, J. (1996). *Diverting children from a life of crime: Measuring costs and benefits.* Santa Monica, CA: RAND.

Groenhuysen, M. S. (1999). Victims' rights in the criminal justice system: A call for more comprehensive implementation theory. In J. J. M. Van Dijk, R. Van Kaam, & J. Wemmers (Eds.), *Caring for crime victims.* Monsey, NY: Criminal Justice Press.

Gros, J.-G. (2003). Trouble in paradise: Crime and collapsed states in the age of globalization. *British Journal of Criminology, 43,* 63–80.

Gruszczynska, B. (2001). Victimization, crime, and social factors in post-socialist countries. In H. Kury (Ed.), *International comparison of crime and victimization: The ICVS.* Willowdale, ON: De Sitter Publications.

Gruszczynska, B., & Gruszczynski, M. (2005). Crime in enlarged Europe: Comparison of crime rates and victimization risks. *Transition Studies Review, 12,* 1337–1345.

Guo, T. (1999). Private security in China: A note on recent developments. *Security Journal, 12*(4), 43–46.

Gupta, D. K. (2001). *Rule of law and terrorism.* Paper, San Diego State University, San Diego, CA.

Haarhuis, C. M. K., & Leeuw, F. L. (2004). Fighting governmental corruption: The new World Bank program evaluated. *Journal of International Development, 16,* 4, 547–561.

Haen-Marshall, I. (1998). Operation of the criminal justice system. In K. Kangaspunta, M. Joutsen, & N. Ollus (Eds), *Crime and criminal justice in Europe and North America 1990–1994.* New York: Criminal Justice Press.

Hatalak, O., Alvazzi Del Frate, A., & Zvekic, U. (Eds.). (2000). *Surveying crime: A global approach.* Rome: ISTAT/UNICRI.

Heidensohn, F. (2002). Gender and crime. In M. Maguire, R. Morgan, & R. Reiner (Eds.), *Oxford handbook of criminology.* Oxford, UK: Oxford University Press.

Heikkinen, H., & Lohrmann, R. (1998, October). *Involvement of organized crime in the trafficking in migrants.* International Organization on Migration. Online: http://migration.ucdavis.edu/rs/printfriendly.php?id=54_0_3_0.

Hepburn, L. M., & Hemenway, D. (2004). Firearm availability and homicide: A review of the literature. *Aggression and Violent Behavior, 9,* 417–440.

Hicks, D. (1998). Thinking about organized crime prevention. *Journal of Contemporary Criminal Justice, 14,* 325–350.

Hicks, D., & Sansfacon, D. (1999). *Preventing residential burglaries and home invasions.* Montreal, QU: International Centre for the Prevention of Crime.

Hobbs, D. (1995). *Bad business: Professional crime in modern Britain.* Oxford, UK: Oxford University Press.

Homel, P., Webb, B., Tilley, N., & Nutley, S. (2003, April). *Investing to deliver. Reviewing the implementation of the UK crime reduction programme.* London: Home Office.

Hope, T. (1995). Community crime prevention. In M. Tonry & D. P. Farrington (Eds.), *Building a safer society: Strategic approaches to crime prevention. Crime and Justice: A Review of Research, 19,* 21–89. Chicago: University of Chicago Press.

Hope, T. (2007). Has the British crime survey reduced crime? In M. Hough & M. Maxfield (Eds.), *Surveying crime in the XXI century.* Proceedings of a conference marking the 25th anniversary of the British Crime Survey. Devon, England: Criminal Justice Press/Willan.

Howard, G. J., & Smith, T. R. (2003). Understanding cross-national variations of crime rates in Europe and North America. In K. Aromaa, S. Leppa, S. Nevala, & N. Ollus (Eds.), *Crime and criminal justice systems in Europe and North America, 1995–1997.* Helsinki: HEUNI.

Human Rights Watch. (2004). *Prisons in Latin America.* Online: http://www.hrw.org

Human Security Report. (2005). *Part II, Human Security Audit.* Online: http://www.humansecurityreport.info.

Hysi, V. (2000). Future criminological research in Albania. In A. Alvazzi Del Frate, O. Hatalak, & U. Zvekics (Eds.), *Surveying crime: A global perspective.* Essays, No 7. Rome: UNICRI/ISTAT.

IC3 Internet Crime Report. (2005). January 1, 2005–December 31, 2005.

Institute of Criminology and Social Prevention (ICSI). (2004, April). *Trafficking in women: The Czech Republic perspective.* Prague, Czech Republic.

International Crime Threat Assessment. (2000). Prepared by the Government Interagency Working Group in support of and pursuant to the President's International Crime Control Strategy. Washington, DC.

International Federation of Red Cross and Red Crescent Societies. (2003). *Spreading the light of science: Guidelines on harm reduction related to injecting drug use.* Geneva.

International Labor Office (ILO). (2005). *A global alliance against forced labor.* Global Report. Geneva: ILO.

International Organization for Migration (IOM). (1996, June). Organized crime moves into migrant trafficking. *Trafficking in Migrants: Quarterly Bulletin.* Geneva, Switzerland.

Intomart GfK. (2005). Wat gaat u daar aan doen? (*What are you going to do about it?*). Unpublished lecture in Dutch by Tom Van Dijk, director of policy research, Intomart GfK, the Netherlands.

Jacobs, J. B. (1999). *Gotham unbound. How New York City was liberated from the grip of organized crime.* New York: New York University Press.

Jacobs, J. B. (2003). Preventing organized crime. In H.-J. Albrecht & C. Fijnaut, *The containment of transnational organized crime.* Kriminologische Forschungsberichte. Freiburg: Max Planck Institute for Foreign and International Criminal Law.

Jamieson, A. (2000). *The Antimafia: Italy's fight against organized crime.* London: Macmillan Press.

Johnson, S., Kaufmann, D., & Zoido-Lobatón, P. (1998). Regulatory discretion and the unofficial economy. *The American Economic Review, 88,* 387–392.

Johnston, R. (2004). The legislative approach to fighting corruption. In *Global Action Corruption. The Merida Papers.* United Nations Office on Drugs and Crime, Vienna.

Joly, E. (2003). *Est-ce dans ce monde-là que nous voulons vivre?* Paris, France: Editions des Arènes.

Jones, S., Wilson, J. M., Rathmel, A., & Riley, K. J. (2005). *Establishing law and order after conflict.* MG-374. Santa Monica, CA: RAND.

Joutsen, M. (2004). From criminology to applied comparative criminology: Life as a peripatetic comparativist. In J. Winterdijk & L. Cao (Eds.), *Lessons from international/comparative criminology/criminal justice.* Willowdale, ON: De Sitter Publications.

Junger-Tas, J., Ribeaud, D., & Cruyff, M. J. L. F. (2004). Juvenile delinquency and gender. *European Journal of Criminology, 1,* 333–377.

Kangaspunta, K (2000). Secondary analysis of integrated sources of data. In Alvazzi del Frate et al. (Eds.), *Surveying crime: A global perspective.* Rome: UNICRI/ISTAT.

Kangaspunta, K. (2003). Mapping the inhuman trade: Preliminary findings of the database on trafficking in human beings. *Forum on Crime and Society, 3,* 81–105.

Kangaspunta, K., Joutsen, M., & Ollus, N. (1998). *Crime and criminal justice in Europe and North America 1990–1994.* New York: Criminal Justice Press.

Karmen, A. (2000). *New York murder mystery: The true story behind the crime crash of the 1990s.* New York: New York University Press.

Kaufmann, D. (2004). Governance redux: The empirical challenge. In X. Sala-i-Martin (Ed.), *World Economic Forum. The global competitiveness report 2003–2004.* New York: Oxford University Press.

Kaufmann, D. (2005). Corruption, governance, and security: Challenges for the rich countries of the world. In A. Lopez-Claros (Ed.), *World Economic Forum. The global competitiveness report 2004–2005.* New York: Oxford University Press.

Kaufmann, D., & Kraay, A. (2002). Growth without governance. *Economia, 3,* 169–215. Online: http://www.worldbank.org/wbi/governance/pubs/growthgov.html

Kaufmann, D., Kraay, A., & Mastruzzi, M. (2004). *Governance matters III: Governance indicators for 1996–2002.* Policy Research Working Paper 3106. Washington, DC: World Bank. Online: http://www.worldbank.org/wbi/governance/pubs/govmatters3.html.

Kereszi, C. (2004). *Human safety in central and eastern Europe.* Unpublished paper, commissioned by UNODC.

Kershaw, C., Chivite-Matthews, N., Thomas, C., & Aust, R. (2001). *The 2001 British crime survey.* Home Office Statistical Bulletin 18/01. London: Home Office.

Kenney, D. J., & Finckenauer, J. O. (1995). *Organized crime in America.* Belmont, CA: Wadsworth Publishing Company.

Killias, M. (1993). Gun ownership, suicide, and homicide: An international perspective. In A. Alvazzi del Frate, U. Zvekic, &. J. J. M.Van Dijk (Eds.), *Understanding crime: Experiences of crime and crime control.* Rome: UNICRI Publication.

Killias, M., & Aebi, M. F. (2000). Crime trends in Europe from 1990 to 1996: How Europe illustrates the limits of the American experience. *European Journal on Criminal Policy and Research, 8,* 43–63.

Killias, M., Simonin, M., & Du Puy, J. (2005). *Violence experienced by women in Switzerland over their lifespan.* Bern: Stampfli.

Killias, M., Van Kesteren, J., & Rindlisbacher, M. (2001, October). Guns, violent crime, and suicide in 21 countries. *Canadian Journal of Criminology,* 429–448.

Knack, S., & Keefer, P. (1995), Institutions and economic performance: Cross-country tests using alternative institutional measures. *Economics and Politics, 7,* 207–227.

Krajewski, K. (2004). Crime and criminal justice in Poland. *European Journal of Criminology, 1,* 377–407.

Kurian, G. T. (1998). *Fitzroy Dearborn book of world rankings* (pp. 314–321). London: Fitzroy Dearborn.

Kury, H. (2001). *International comparison of crime and victimization: The ICVS.* International Studies in Social Science, Vol. 2. Willowdale, ON: De Sitter Publications.

Laborde, J.-P. (2005). *Etat de droit et crime organisée.* Paris: edition Dalloz.

LaFree, G. (1999). A summary and review of cross-national comparative studies of homicide. In D. Smith & M. A. Zahn (Eds.), *Homicide studies: A sourcebook of social research.* Thousand Oaks, CA: Sage.

LaFree, G., & Drass, K. (2001). Are national crime trends converging? Evidence for homicide victimization rates, 1956 to 1994. Paper, University of Maryland/University of Nevada.

LaFree, G., & Tseloni, A. (2006, May). Democracy and crime: A multilevel analysis of homicide trends in forty-four countries, 1950–2000. *Annals of the American Academy of Political and Social Science, 605.*

Lambsdorff, J. (2000). Transparency international corruption index. In A. Alvazzi del Frate & G. Pasqua (Eds.), *Responding to the challenges of corruption.* Proceedings of the UNICRI-ISPAC International Conference. Rome-Milan: UNICRI Publication.

Lambsdorff, J. (2005). Corruption perception index 2004. Transparency International. *Global Corruption Report 2005.* London: Yeomans Press.

Langan, P., & Levin, D. (2002). *Recidivism of prisoners released in 1994.* Bureau of Justice Statistics Special Report. Washington, DC: U.S. Department of Justice, Office of Justice Programs.

Langseth, P. (Ed.) (2002). *Anti-corruption toolkit.* Vienna: United Nations Office on Drugs and Crime (UNODC).

Langseth, P., & Mohammed, A. (2002). *Strengthening judicial integrity and capacity in Nigeria.* Vienna: UNODCCP.

Lauw, A. & Schonteich, M. (2001). Playing the numbers game: Promises and crime statistics. In J. Steinberg (Ed.), *Crime wave: The South African underworld and its foes.* Witswatersrand, South Africa: Witswatersrand University Press.

Laycock, G. (2001). *Scientists or politicians—Who has the answer to crime?* Lecture delivered on April 26, 2001, University College London, The Jill Dando Institute of Crime Science, London.

Lehti, M. (2003). *Trafficking in women and children in Europe.* Helsinki: HEUNI.

Lenke, L. (1990). *Alcohol and criminal violence—Time series analyses in a comparative perspective.* Stockholm: Almqvist and Wiksell.

Levi, M. (2002). The organization of serious crime. In M. Maguire, R. Morgan, & R. Reine (Eds.), *Oxford handbook of criminology.* Oxford, UK: Oxford University Press.

Levi, M., & Maguire, M. (2004). Reducing and preventing organized crime: An evidence-based critique. *Crime, Law, and Social Change, 41.*

Levitt, S. (1996). The effect of prison population size on crime rates: Evidence from prison overcrowding litigation. *Quarterly Journal of Economics, 111,* 319–352.

Levitt, S., & Dubner, S. J. (2006). *Freakonomics.* London: Penguin Books.

Lintner, B. (2002). *Blood brothers. Crime, business and politics in Asia.* Crows Nest, New South Wales: Allen & Unwin.

Lipsey, M. W., & Wilson, D. B. (2001). *Practical meta-analysis.* Thousand Oaks, CA: Sage.

Lipton, D., Martinson, R., & Wilks, J. (1975). *The effectiveness of correctional treatment: A survey of treatment evaluation studies.* New York: Praeger.

Lott, J. (1998). *More guns, less crime: Understanding crime and gun control laws.* Chicago: University of Chicago Press.

Louw, A., & Lynch, J. P. (1993). Secondary analysis of international crime survey data. In A. Alvazzi del Frate, U. Zvekic, &. J. J. M. Van Dijk (Eds.), *Understanding crime: Experiences of crime and crime control.* Rome: UNICRI Publication.

Lurigio, A. J., Skogan, W. G., & Davis, R. C. (1990). *Victims of crime: Problems, policies, and programs.* Newbury Park, CA: Sage.

Lynch, J. P. (2006). Problems and promises of victimization surveys for cross-national research. *Crime and Justice.* Vol 34. Chicago: University of Chicago Press.

MacKenzie, D. L. (2002). Reducing the criminal activities of known offenders and delinquents: Crime prevention in the courts and corrections. In L. W. Sherman, D. P. Farrington, B. C. Welsh, & D. L. MacKenzie (Eds.), *Evidence-based crime prevention* (pp. 330–404). New York: Routledge.

Maguire, M. (2002). Crime statistics: The "data explosion" and its implications. In M. Maguire, R. Morgan, & R. Reiner (Eds.), *Oxford handbook of criminology.* Oxford, UK: Oxford University Press.

Makkai, T., & McGregor, K. (2003). *Drug use monitoring in Australia: 2002 annual report on drug use among police detainees.* Research and Public Policy Series No. 47, Australian Institute of Criminology, Canberra.

Manning, P. (2006). The United States of America. In T. Jones & T. Newburn (Eds.), *Plural policing: A comparative perspective.* London: Routledge.

Martin, V., Cayla, J. A., & Moris, M. L. (1998). Predictive factors of HIV-infection in injecting drug users upon incarceration. *European Journal of Epidemiology, 14*, 327–331.

Mauro, P. (1996, September). *The effects of corruption on growth, investment, and government expenditure.* IMF working paper.

Mawby, R. I. (1999). *Policing across the world: Issues for the twenty-first century.* London: UCL Press.

Mawby, R. I. (2001). *Burglary.* Crime and Society Series. Devon, UK: William Publishing.

Mayhew, P. (2003, April). *Counting the costs of crime in Australia.* Australian Institute of Criminology. Trends & Issues in Crime and Criminal Justice. No. 247.

Mayhew, P. (2003). Operation of the criminal justice system. In K. Aromaa, S. Leppa, S. Nevala, & N. Ollus (Eds.), *Crime and criminal justice systems in Europe and North America 1995–1997.* Helsinki: HEUNI.

Mayhew, P., Clarke, R. V., & Elliot, D. (1989). Motorcycle theft, helmet legislation, and displacement. *Howard Journal, 28,* 1–8.

Mayhew, P., & Van Dijk, J. J. M. (1997). *Criminal victimization in eleven industrialized countries. Key findings from the 1996 international crime victims' survey.* The Hague: WODC.

McConnell. (2000). *Cybercrime . . . and punishment? Archaic laws threaten global information.* McConnell International LLC. Online: www.mcconnellinternational.com.

McMillan, J. (2005). *The main institution in the country is corruption: Creating transparency in Angola.* CDDRL, Stanford Institute on international studies (http://cddrl.stanford.edu).

Merchant International Group Limited (MIG). (2004). *Gray-area dynamics, organized crime figures 2004.* Special analysis commissioned by UNICRI .

Mesquita Neto, de P. (2004). *Criminal justice in transition in Latin America.* Original paper commissioned by UNODC.

Miller, M., Azrael, D., & Hemenway, D. (2002). Household firearm ownership levels and homicide rates across US regions and states, 1988–1997. *American Journal of Public Health, 92,* 1988–1993.

Mirrlees-Black, C., & Ross, A. (1995). *Crimes against retail and manufacturing premises.* London: Home Office, RPU.

Moffatt, M. S., Weatherburn, W., & Donnelly, D. J. (2005). What caused the recent drop in property crime? In *Crime and Justice Bulletin: Contemporary Issues in Crime and Justice.* Sydney, Australia/New South Wales: Bureau of Criminal Statistics and Research.

Moolenaar, D. (2006). Expenditure on crime in the Netherlands. In A. Eggen & W. van der Heide (Eds.), *Criminaliteit en Rechtshandhaving 2004; ontwikkelingen en samenhangen.* Den Haag: WODC/CBS (online: www.ministerievanjustitite.nl:8080/b-organ/wodc/publications/wodc 205 website.pdf).

Moran, J., Doig, A., & Watt, D. (2001). Managing anti-corruption agencies. In *Forum on Crime and Society, (11)*1, 69–89.

Morree, L. (2004). *Panoramic overview of private security industry in the 25 member states of the European Union.* Brussels: CoESS/Uni-Europa (online: www.coess.org).

Mouzos, J., & Makkai, T. (2004). *Women's experiences of male violence. Findings of the Australian component of the international violence against women survey (IVAWS).* Canberra: Australian Institute of Criminology, Research and Public Policy Series No. 56.

National Crime Prevention. (1999). *Pathways to prevention, developmental and early intervention approaches to crime in Australia,* edited by R. Hommel et al., Attorney-General's Department, Canberra.

Naudé, C. M. B. (1994). *South African businesses as victims of crime: Summary of research findings.* Pretoria: University of South Africa, Department of Criminology.

Naudé, C. M. B., & Prinsloo, J. H. (2002). Crime victimization in southern Africa. The unique status of the ICVS. In P. Nieuwbeerta (Ed.), *Crime victimization in comparative perspective.* The Hague: Boom Juridische Uitgevers.

Naudé, C. M. B., Prinsloo, J. H., & Ladikos A. (2006). *Experiences of crime in thirteen African countries: Results from the International Crime Victim Survey.* Turin: UNICRI (www.unicit.it).

Naudé, C. M. B., Prinsloo, J. H., & Martins, J. H. (1999). *Crimes against the South African business sector* (draft report). Pretoria: University of South Africa.

Naylor, R. T. (2002). *Wages of crime: Black markets, illegal finance, and the underworld economy.* Ithaca: Cornell University Press.

Neapolitan, J. (1995). Differing theoretical perspectives and cross-national variations in thefts in less developed nations. In *International Criminal Justice Review, 5,* 17–31.

Nevala, S. (2003). *The International Violence Against Women Surveys.* Helsinki: European Institute for Crime Prevention and Control.

Newman, G. (Ed.) (1999). United Nations. *Global report on crime and justice*. United Nations Office for Drug Control and Crime Prevention, Center for International Crime Prevention. New York: Oxford University Press.

Newman, G., & Howard, G. J. (1999). Resources in criminal justice. In G. Newman (Ed.), *Global report on crime and justice*. United Nations Office for Drug Control and Crime Prevention, Center for International Crime Prevention. New York: Oxford University Press.

Neumayer, E. (2003). Good policy can lower violent crime: Evidence from a cross-national panel of homicide rates, 1980–1997. *Journal of Peace Research, 40,* 619–640.

Nieuwbeerta, P. (2002). *Crime victimization in comparative perspective. Results from the international crime victims survey, 1989–2000.* The Hague: Boom Juridische Uitgevers.

Ogata, S., & Sen, A. (2003). *Human security now, protecting and empowering people.* New York: Human Security Commission, United Nations. Online: www. humansecurity-chs.org.

O'Malley, P., & Sutton, A. (1997). *Crime prevention in Australia.* Sydney: The Federation Press.

Orlando, L. (2001). *Fighting the Mafia; and renewing Sicilian culture.* San Francisco: Encounter Books.

Pare, P.-P. (2006). *Income inequality and crime across nations reexamined.* Thesis, Pennsylvania State University.

Pelton, R. Y. (2003). *The world's most dangerous places.* New York: HarperCollins.

Pfeiffer, C. (2004, February 16). *Victim assistance and support in Lower Saxony: A multifaceted approach based on empirical findings.* Criminological Research Institute of Lower Saxony (transcript keynote lecture at seminar on victim support and the police in Hanover).

Philipson, T. J., & Posner, R. A. (1996). The economic epidemiology of crime. *Journal of Law and Economics, 34,* 405–433.

Pluchinsky, D., Armond de, P., & Sprinzak, E. (2004). The classic politically-motivated non–state groups. In *Chemical and Biological Arms Control Institute.* Lawrence Livermore National Laboratories, n.d.

Poole-Robb, S., & Bailey, A. (2003). *Risky business. Corruption, fraud, terrorism & other threats to global business.* London: Kogan Page Ltd.

PricewaterhouseCoopers (2005). *Global Economic Crime Survey 2005,* in collaboration with Martin Luther University, Economy and Crime Research Center.

Prinsloo, J., & Naudé, C. M. B. (2001). Organized crime and corruption in Southern Africa. *International Journal of Comparative Criminology, 1,* 65–90.

Quimet, M. (2002). Explaining the American and Canadian crime drop in the 1990s. *Canadian Journal of Criminology, 44,* 33–50.

Reichel, P. L. (1992, 1994). *Comparative criminal justice systems. A topical approach* (1st ed. & 2nd ed.). Englewood Cliffs, NJ: Prentice-Hall.

Reiner, R. (1995). Myth vs. modernity: Reality and unreality in the English model of policing. In J. P. Brodeur (Ed.), *Comparisons in policing: An international perspective* (pp. 16–48). Avebury, England: Aldershot.

Reuter, P. (1987). Racketeering in legitimate industries. Santa Monica, CA: RAND Publication Series.

Reuter, P., et al. (2004). *Mitigating the effects of illicit drugs on development. Potential roles for the World Bank.* Rand Corporation project memorandum series. PM-1645-PSJ-1. Prepared for the World Bank.

Rosenbaum, D. P. (1986). *Community crime prevention: Does it work?* Beverly Hills, CA: Sage.

Rossow, I. (2001). Drinking and violence: A cross-cultural comparison of alcohol consumption and homicide rates in fourteen European countries. *Addiction, 96.*

Rubin, M. (2006). *Assessing the reliability of UN and Interpol crime statistics: A John Jay College analysis.* Paper, American Society of Criminology, Los Angeles.

Rubin, M., & Walker, M. C. (2004, November 3–4). *Cross-national comparisons of rape rates: Problems and issues.* Paper prepared for ECE-UNODC Meeting on Crime Statistics. Geneva.

Rubio, M. (2001). Homicide, kidnapping, and armed conflict in Colombia. *Forum on Crime and Society, 1,* 55–69.

Sachs, J. (2005). *The end of poverty: How we can make it happen in our lifetime.* London: Penguin Group.

Sanders, A., & Young, R. (2002). From suspect to trial. In M. Maguire, R. Morgan, & R. Reiner (Eds.), *The Oxford handbook of criminology.* Oxford, UK: Oxford University Press.

Savona, E. U., & Mignone, M. (2004). The fox and the hunters: How IC technologies change the crime race. In E. U. Savona (Ed.), *Crime and technology. New frontiers for regulation, law enforcement, and research.* Dordrecht, the Netherlands: Springer.

Schaerf, W. (2003), *Non-state justice systems in Southern Africa: How should governments respond.* Mimeo: Institute for Criminology, University of Cape Town.

Schmid, A. (200, December 6–8). Links between terrorist and organized crime networks: Emerging patterns and trends. In D. Vlassis (Ed.), *Trafficking: Networks and logistics of transnational crime and international terrorism*. Proceedings of the International Conference on "Trafficking: Networks and Logistics of Transnational Crime and International Terrorism." Courmayeur Mont Blanc, Italy.

Schmid, A. (2004). Statistics on terrorism, the challenge of measuring trends in global terrorism. *Forum in Crime and Society, 4*, 49–71.

Schneider, A. L. (1978). *Portland forward record check of crime: Victims' final report.* Washington, DC: U.S. Government Printing Office.

Schneider, F. (2004). *The size of the shadow economies of 145 countries all over the world: First results over period 1999–2003.* Online: http://www.econ.jku.at/Schneider.

Schneider, F., & Erntse, D. (2000). *Shadow economies around the world: Size, causes, and consequences.* IMF Working Paper, WP00/26.

Schonteich, M. (2003). *Crime statistics, patterns, and trends.* Open Society Justice Initiative, Lecture at UNICRI, April 2004 (unpublished).

Schweinart, L. (2004). *The High/Scope Perry Preschool Study through age 40: Summary, conclusions, and frequently asked questions.* Ypsilanti, MI: High/Scope Press.

Sebba, L. (1996). *Third parties, victims, and the criminal justice system.* Columbus, OH: State University Press.

SECI. (2004, September 22–23). Southeast European Cooperative Initiative. Regional Center for Combating Trans-Border Crime. *Evaluation Report 2004. Operation Mirage.* Report prepared for the 11th SECI Center THB Task Force Meeting, Pioana Brasov, Romania.

SECI. (2005, September 22–23). Southeast European Cooperative Initiative. Regional Center for Combating Trans-Border Crime. *Report on Human Trafficking and Migrant Smuggling,* Report prepared for the 12th SECI Center Mirage Task Force Meeting, Bucharest, Romania.

Shapland, J., Wilmore, J., & Duff, P. (1985). Victims in the criminal justice system. *Cambridge Studies in Criminology, 53.* Hants, England: Gower Publishing Company Limited.

Shaw, M. (2002). *Crime and policing in post-apartheid South Africa. Transforming under fire.* London: Hurst & Company.

Shaw, M. (2003). *Crime as business, business as crime: West African criminal networks in Southern Africa.* Johannesburg: SAIIA (www.wits.ac.za/saiia).

Shaw, M., Van Dijk, J., & Rhomberg, W. (2003). Determining global trends in crime and justice: An overview of results from the United Nations surveys of crime trends and operations of criminal justice systems. *Forum on Crime and Society, 3,* 35–65.

Shelley, L. (1981). *Crime and modernization: The impact of industrialization and urbanization on crime.* Carbondale: Southern Illinois University.

Shepherd, J., & Sivarajasingam, V. (2005). Injury research explains conflicting violence trends. In www.injuryprevention.com.

Sherman, L. W., & Eck, J. E. (2002). Policing for crime prevention. In L. W. Sherman, D. P. Farrington, B. C. Welsh, & D. L. MacKenzie (Eds.), *Evidence-based crime prevention.* New York: Routledge.

Sherman, L. W., Gottfredson, D. C., MacKenzie, D. L., Eck, J. E., Reuter, P., & Bushway, S. D. (1997). *Preventing crime: What works, what doesn't, what's promising.* Washington, DC: National Institute of Justice, U.S. Department of Justice.

Shikita, M., & Morosowa, H. (2005, April). The long-awaited enactment of a victim's right law in Japan. In E. Vetere & P. David (Eds.), *Victims of crime and abuse of power: Festschrift in Honor of Irene Melup.* Bangkok, 11th Congress on Crime Prevention and Criminal Justice, United Nations, New York.

Skogan, W. (1984). Reporting crimes to the police: The status of world research. *Journal of Research in Crime and Delinquency, 21,* 113–137.

Sloan, J. H., et al. (1988). Handgun regulations, crime, assaults and homicide: A tale of two cities. *New England Journal of Medicine, 319,* 1256–1262.

Soares, R. (2005). Measuring corruption: Validating subjective surveys of perceptions. *Global Corruption Report 2005,* Tranparency International.

Spelman, W. (2006). The limited importance of prison expansion. In A. Blumstein & J. Wallman (Eds,), *The crime drop in America.* New York: Cambridge University Press.

Stangeland, P. (1995). *The crime puzzle: Crime patterns and crime displacement in southern Spain.* Malaga: Muguel Gòmez Ediciones, IAIC.

Stone, C. (2006), *Crime, justice, and growth in South Africa: Towards a plausible contribution from criminal justice to economic growth.* Center for International Development at Harvard University, CID Working Paper No.131.

Stone, C., Miller, J., Thorton, M., & Trone, J. (2005). *Supporting security, justice, and development: Lessons for a new era. Report for UK DFID.* New York: Vera Institute of Justice.

Stoyanov, B. (2000). The corruption monitoring system of coalition 2000 and the results from its implementation. In A. Alvazzi del Frate & G. Pasqua (Eds.), *Responding to the challenges of corruption.* Proceedings of the UNICRI-ISPAC International Conference. Rome: UNICRI.

Strang, H., & Sherman, L. (2004, November). *Protocol for a Campbell collaboration systemic review: Campbell collaboration systemic review: Effects of face-to-face restorative justice for personal victims of crime, draft 4.* See http://www.campbellcollaboration.org/doc-pdf/restorativejusticeprot.pdf

Sung, H.-E. (2004). State failure, economic failure, and predatory organized crime: A comparative analysis. *Journal of Research in Crime and Delinquency, 41,* 111–129.

Sung, H.-E. (2005). Gender and corruption: In search of better evidence. In *Global Corruption Report 2005.* Transparency International. London: Pluto Press. Online: gcr@transparency.org

Sung, H.-E. (2006, May). Democracy and criminal justice in cross-national perspective: From crime control to due process. *Annals of the American Academy of Political and Social Science, 605.*

Swamy, A., Knack, S., Lee, Y., & Azfar, O. (2001). Gender and corruption. *Journal of Development Economics, 64,* 25–55.

Szczaranski, C. (2002). *Testimonios, el bisel del espejo: Mi ventana.* Edebe, Santiago de Chile: Editorial Don Bosco S.A.

Taylor, B., Brownstein, H. H., Parry, C., Plüddemann, A., Makkai, T., Bennett, T., & Holloway, K. (2003). Monitoring the use of illicit drugs in four countries through the international arrestee drug abuse monitoring (I-Adam) program. *Criminal Justice, 3,* 269–286.

Taylor, N., & Mayhew, P. (2002). *Patterns of victimization among small retail businesses.* Trends and Issues, Crime and Criminal Justice, No. 221. Canberra: Australian Institute of Criminology.

Thoumi, F. (2002). Can the United Nations support "objective" and unhampered illicit drug policy research? *Crime, Law, and Social Change, 38,* 161–183.

Tjaden, P., & Thoennes, N. (2000). *Extent, nature, and consequences of intimate partner violence: Findings from the national violence against women survey.* Washington, DC: U.S. Department of Justice.

Tonry, M., & Farrington, D. P. (1995). Building a safer society: Strategic approaches to crime prevention. In *Crime and Justice: A Review of Research, 19.* Chicago: University of Chicago Press.

Tonry, M., & Farrington, D. P. (2005). Crime and punishment in Western Countries, 1980–1999. *Crime and Justice: A Review of Research, 33.* Chicago: University of Chicago Press.

Tornudd, P. (1997). Fifteen years of decreasing prisoner rates in Finland. In *Prison population in Europe and North America: Problems and solutions.* Helsinki, Finland: Ministry of Justice.

Torstensson, J. (1994). Property rights and economic growth: An empirical study. *Kyklos, 47,* 231–247.

Trafficking in Persons Report. (2005, June). U.S. State Department.

Transparency International. The Coalition Against Corruption. (2002). *Annual report 2002.* United Kingdom: Yeomans Press.

Transparency International. The Coalition Against Corruption. (2003). *Annual report 2003.* United Kingdom: Yeomans Press.

Transparency International. The Coalition Against Corruption. (2004a). *Annual Report 2004.* United Kingdom: Yeomans Press.

Transparency International. (2004b, December 9). *Report on the global corruption barometer 2004.*

Travis, J. (2000). *Building knowledge about crime and justice in the global age: Infrastructure first.* Address to the Fifth Biennial Conference of International Perspectives on Crime, Justice, and Public Order. Washington, DC: The Urban Institute.

Travis, J. (2005). *But they all come back: Rethinking the challenges of prisoner reentry.* Washington, DC: The Urban Institute Press.

Travis, J., Solomon, A. L., & Waul, M. (2001). *From prison to home.* Washington, DC: The Urban Institute.

Travnickova, I., Luptakova, M., Necada, V., Preslickova, H., & Trdlicova, K. (2004). *Trafficking in women: The Czech Republic perspective.* Prague: Institute of Criminology and Social Prevention.

Uggen, C., Manza, J., & Thompson, M. (2006, May). Citizenship, democracy, and the civic reintegration of criminal offenders. In S. Karstedt & G. LaFree (Eds), *Democracy, crime, and justice. Annals of the American Academy of Political and Social Science, 605.*

UNICEF/Innocenti. (2003). A. Rossi (Ed.), *Trafficking in human beings, especially women and children, in Africa.* Florence: Unicef Innocenti Research Centre.

UNICRI. (2004). *Trafficking of Nigerian girls to Italy.* Turin, Italy: UNICRI.

United Kingdom, House of Commons, Home Affairs Committee (2004–2005). *Rehabilitation of offenders.* First Report of Session 2004–2005, Vols. I and II. Stationary Office, London.

United Nations. (1980). Department of International Economic and Social Affairs. *Patterns of urban and rural population growth.* Population Studies, No. 68. New York.

United Nations. (1995). *Compendium of human settlement statistics* (5th Issue). New York.

United Nations. (1999). *Global report on crime and justice.* G. Newman (Ed.), United Nations Office for Drug Control and Crime Prevention, Centre for International Crime Prevention. New York: Oxford University Press.

United Nations. (2001). *International instruments related to the prevention and suppression of international terrorism.* New York.

United Nations. (2002). Economic and Social Affairs. *World population ageing.* New York.

United Nations. (2003). *Human security now.* United Nations Commission on Human Security. New York.

United Nations. (2004). *Challenges and change, a more secure world: Our shared responsibility.* Report of the Secretary-General's High-level Panel on Threats. New York.

United Nations. (2004). Department of Economic and Social affairs, Population Division, *World population prospects: The 2004 revision highlights.* New York.

United Nations. (2004, January 23). Economic and Social Council (E/CN.4/2004/86), Commission on Human Rights, Status of the International Covenants on Human Rights, *Question of the death penalty.* Report of the Secretary-General submitted pursuant to Commission Resolution 2003/67.

United Nations. (2005). *Corruption, compendium of international legal instruments on corruption.* United Nations Office on Drugs and Crime. Vienna, New York.

United Nations. (2005). *In larger freedom, towards development, security and human rights for all.* Report of the Secretary-General. New York.

United Nations. (2006). *In-depth study on all forms of violence against women.* Report of the Secretary-General, New York, United Nations (A/61/122/Add.1.).

United Nations Development Program. (2002a). *Justice and security sector reform. BCPR's programmatic approach.* UNDP.

United Nations Development Program. (2002b). *Human Development Report 2002,* Oxford, UK: Oxford University Press.

United Nations International Drug Control Program. (UNDCP). (1997). *World Drug Report.* Oxford, UK: Oxford University Press.

United Nations Office on Drugs and Crime (UNODC) and Department of Public Service and Administration, Republic of South Africa (DPSA). (2003). *Country corruption assessment report.* South Africa. Online: www.unodc.org

United Nations Office on Drugs and Crime (UNODC). (2004). *World drug report.* New York.

United Nations Office on Drugs and Crime (UNODC). (2005a). *Crime and development in Africa.* Vienna.

United Nations Office on Drugs and Crime (UNODC). (2005b). *Rule of law and protection of the most vulnerable— Why fighting crime can assist development in Africa.*

United Nations Office on Drugs and Crime (UNODC). (2005c). *Transnational organized crime in the Central Asian region* (unpublished).

United Nations Office on Drugs and Crime (UNODC). (2005d). *World drug report.* Vienna.

United Nations Office on Drugs and Crime (UNODC). (2006). *Trafficking in persons: Global patterns.* Vienna.

United Nations Office on Drugs and Crime (UNODC). (2007, March). *Crime and development in Central America: Caught in the cross-fire.* Vienna.

United Nations Office on Drugs and Crime (UNODC) and Department of Public Service and Administration, Republic of South Africa (DPSA). (2003). *Country corruption assessment report.* South Africa. Online: www.unodc.org

United Nations Office on Drugs and Crime (UNODC) and Latin America and Caribbean Region of the World Bank. (2007). *Crime, violence, and development: Trends, costs, and policy options in the Caribbean.* Vienna.

United States of America. (2004). *Trafficking in persons report.* Washington, DC: U.S. State Department. Online: http://www.state.gov/g/tip/rls/tiprpt/2004/

U.S. General Accounting Office. (2001). Former Soviet Union; U.S. rule of law assitance has limited impact. Washington, DC.

Van de Bunt , H., & Van der Schoot, C. R. A. (2003). *Prevention of organized crime: A situational approach.* Den Haag: WODC, Ministerie van Justitie.

Van der Heide, W., & Eggen, A., Th. J. (2003). *Criminaliteit en rechtshandhaving 2001. Ontwikkelingen en samenhangen.* Meppel, the Netherlands: Boom Juridische Uitgevers.

Van Dijk, J. J. M. (1982). Die bereitschaft des opfers zur anzeige: Eine funktion der strafverfolgungspolitik? In H. J. Schneider (Ed.), *Das verbrechensopfer in der strafrechtshilfe.* De Gruyter.

Van Dijk, J. J. M. (1986). Responding to crime: Reflections on the reactions of victims and non-victims to the increase in petty crime. In E. Fattah (Ed.), *From crime policy to victim policy* (pp. 156–166). London: Macmillan.

Van Dijk, J. J. M. (1992). Als de dag van gisteren: Over de betrouwbaarheid van het slachtofferverhaal (*On the reliability of the victims account*). *Justitiele Verkenningen, 18,* 47–66.

Van Dijk, J. J. M. (1994a). Opportunities for crime: A test of the rational-interactionist model. In *Crime and Economy. Reports presented to the 11th Criminological Colloquium.* Criminological Research, Vol. XXXII. Council of Europe Publishing, 1995.

Van Dijk, J. J. M. (1994b). Understanding crime rates: On the interactions between the rational choices of victims and offenders. *British Journal of Criminology, 34,* 105–121.

Van Dijk, J. J. M. (1999). The experience of crime and justice. In G. Newman (Ed.), *Global report on crime and justice.* United Nations Office for Drug Control and Crime Prevention, Centre for International Crime Prevention. New York: Oxford University Press.

Van Dijk, J. J. M. (2000). Implications of the international crime victims survey for a victim perspective. In A. Crawford & J. Goodey (Eds.), *Integrating a victim perspective within criminal justice.* Aldershot, UK: Darmouth/Ashgate.

Van Dijk, J. J. M. (2005, April). Benchmarking legislation on crime victims: The UN victims declaration of 1985. In E. Vetere & P. David (Eds.), *Victims of crime and abuse of power: Festschrift in honor of Irene Melup.* Bangkok, 11th Congress on Crime Prevention and Criminal Justice. United Nations, New York.

Van Dijk, J. J. M. (2007). The International crime victims survey and complementary measures of corruption and organized crime. In M. Hough & M. Maxfield (Eds.), *Surveying crime in the XXI century, Proceedings of a conference marking the 25th anniversary of the British crime Survey.* Criminal Justice Press/Willan.

Van Dijk, J. J. M. (2008). Mafia markers: Assessing the prevalence of organized crime and its impact upon societies. *Trends in Organized Crime* (forthcoming in first issue).

Van Dijk, J. J. M., & Kangaspunta, K. (2000). Piecing together the cross-national crime puzzle. *National Institute of Justice Journal.* U.S. Department of Justice. Office of Justice Programs. Washington, DC: National Institute of Justice.

Van Dijk, J. J. M., Manchin, R., Van Kesteren, J., & Hideg, G. (2007). The burden of crime in the EU, key findings of the EU/International Crime Victim Survey 2005. Turin: UNICRI; Brussels: Gallup/Europe.

Van Dijk, J. J. M., & Mayhew, P. (1992). *Criminal victimization in the industrialized world.* Key findings of the 1989 and 1992 International Crime Surveys. The Hague: Ministry of Justice, the Netherlands.

Van Dijk, J. J. M., Mayhew, P., & Killias, M. (1990). *Experiences of crime across the world.* Key Findings from the 1989 International Crime Survey. Deventer: Kluwer Law and Taxation Publishers.

Van Dijk, J. J. M., & Nevala, S. (2002). Intercorrelations of crime. In P. Nieuwbeerta (Ed.), *Crime victimization in international perspective.* The Hague: Boom Juristische Uitgevers.

Van Dijk, J. J. M., Sagel-Grande, H. I., & Toornvliet, L. G. (2002). *Actuele criminologie.* Vierde, herziene druk. The Hague: Sdu Uitgevers.

Van Dijk, J. J. M., Shaw, M., & Buscaglia, E. (2002). The TOC convention and the need for comparative research: Some illustrations from the work of the UN center for international crime prevention. In: H.-J. Albrecht & C. Fijnaut (Eds.), *The containment of transnational organized crime. Comments on the UN Convention of December 2000.* Freiburg: Max Planck Institut für Ausländisches und Internationales Strafrecht.

Van Dijk, J. J. M., & Steinmetz, C. D. (1980). *The RDC victim surveys, 1973–1979.* No. 35. The Hague: Research and Documentation Centre, Ministry of Justice, the Netherlands.

Van Dijk, J. J. M., & Terlouw, G. J. (1996). An international perspective of the business community as victims of fraud and crime. *Security Journal, 7,* 157–167.

Van Dijk, J. J. M., & Toornvliet, L. G. (1996, November 21). *Towards a Eurobarometer of public safety* (pp. 1–12). Paper at seminar on the prevention of urban delinquency linked to drugs dependence, European Commission, Brussels.

Van Dijk, J. J. M., Van Kesteren, J., & Smit, P. (2007). Criminal victimization in global perspective: Key findings of the ICVS 2004–2005 and the EU ICS. Meppel: Boom Legal Publishers; and The Hague: Research and Documentation Center, Ministry of Justice.

Van Duyne, P. C., Von Lampe, K., Van Dijk, J. J. M., & Newell, J. L. (Eds.). (2005). *The organized crime economy: Managing crime markets in Europe.* Nijmegen: Wolf Legal Publishers.

Van Kesteren, J. N. (2005, March 15). Some results on firearms ownership from the International Crime Victim Survey. Presentation held at the COST meeting: *European Firearms Violence Data: Limitations and Research Opportunities,* organized by Small Arms Survey, Geneva.

Van Kesteren, J. N. (2006, August 19–26). *Hate crime in Europe: Results from the 2005 EU/ICS (ICVS)*. Paper presented at the International Symposium of the World Society of Victimology, Orlando, Florida.

Van Kesteren, J. N., Mayhew, P., & Nieuwbeerta, P. (2000). *Criminal victimization in seventeen industrialized countries*. Key findings from the 2000 International Crime Victims Survey. The Hague: Onderzoek en beleid, No. 187. Ministry of Justice, WODC.

Van Steden R., & Sarre, R. (2007). The growth of privatized policing: Some cross-national data and comparisons. Amsterdam: Free University of Amsterdam (article to be published).

Van Velthoven, B. C. J. (2005). *The value of the judicial infrastructure for the Dutch economy*. Report published by the Netherlands Council for the Judiciary, The Hague.

Vermeulen, G. (Ed.) (2004). *Missing and sexually exploited children in the enlarged EU: Epidemiological data in the new member states*. Antwerp: Maklu.

Vetere, E, & David, P. (Eds.) (2005, April). *Victims of crime and abuse of power: Festschrift in honor of Irene Melup*. Bangkok, 11th Congress on Crime Prevention and Criminal Justice. United Nations, New York.

Walker, J. (1994). *The first Australian national survey of crimes against businesses*. Canberra: Australian Institute of Criminology.

Waller, I. (2006). *Less law, more order: The truth about reducing crime*. West Point, NY: Praeger.

Waller, I., & Sansfacon, D. (2000). *Investing wisely in crime prevention: International experiences*. Montreal, QU: ICPC.

Walmsley, R. (2000). *World prison population list*. In Research Findings No. 116. Home Office Research, Development and Statistics Directorate. London, UK.

Walmsley, R. (2003). Global incarceration and prison trends. *Forum on Crime and Society, 3. Vienna: UNODC*.

Walmsley, R. (2007). *World Prison Population List* (7th ed.). International Center for Prison Studies. London: King's College.

Weatherburn, D., Hua, J., & Moffatt, S. (2006). *How much crime does prison stop?* Crime and Justice Bulletin, No. 93. NSW Bureau of Crime Statistics and Research.

Webb, B. (1997). Steering column locks and motor vehicle theft: Evaluations from three countries. In R.V. Clarke (Ed.), *Situational crime prevention: Successful case studies* (2nd ed.). Monsey, NY: Willan Publishing.

Wellford, C. F., Pepper, J. V., & Petrie, C. V. (2004). *Firearms and violence: A critical review*. Washington, DC: The National Academies Press.

Welsh, B. C. (2003). Community-based approaches to preventing delinquency and crime: Promising results and future directions. *Japanese Journal of Sociological Criminology, 28,* 7–24.

Welsh, B. C. (2004). *Proven practices to prevent crime*. Department of Criminal Justice, University of Massachusetts, Original paper prepared for UNODC.

Welsh, B. C., & Farrington, D. P. (2000). Monetary costs and benefits of crime prevention programs. *Crime and Justice: A Review of Research, 27,* 305–361. Chicago: University of Chicago Press.

Welsh, B. C., & Farrington, D. P. (2004). Evidence-based crime prevention: The effectiveness of CCTV. *Crime Prevention and Community Safety, 6.*

Welsh, B. C., & Hoshi, A. (2002). Communities and crime prevention. In L. W. Sherman, D. P. Farrington, B. C. Welsh, & D. L. MacKenzie (Eds.), *Evidence-based crime prevention* (pp. 165–197). New York: Routledge.

Welsh, B. C., & Irving, M. H. (2005). Crime and punishment in Canada, 1980–1999. In M. Tonry & D. P. Farrington (Eds.), *Crime and Justice: A Review of Research, 33.* Chicago: University of Chicago Press.

Wemmers, J. A. (1995). *Victims in the criminal justice system: A study into the treatment of victims and its effects on their attitudes and behavior*. Amsterdam: Kugler Publications.

Williams, P., & Vlassis, D. (Eds.) (2001). *Combating transnational organized crime: Concepts, activities, and responses*. London: Frank Cass.

Wilsem, J. Van. (2003). *Crime and context. The impact of individual, neighborhood, city, and country characteristics on victimization*. Doctoral Dissertation, Katholieke Universiteit Nijmegen. ICS.

Wilson, J. M. (2006, May). Law and order in an emerging democracy: Lessons from the reconstruction of Kosovo's police and justice system. *Annals of the American Academy of Political and Social Science, 605.*

Wilson, J. Q., & Herrnstein, R. J. (1995). *Crime and human nature*. New York: Simon & Schuster.

Wintemut, G. J. (2005). Guns and gun violence. In A. Blumstein & J. Wallman, *The crime drop in America*. Cambridge, UK: Cambridge University Press.

World drink trends. (2004). World Advertising Research Center. Published in association with Commissie Gedistilleerd (Commission for Distilled Spirits).

World Bank. (2004, October). *Post-conflict peace-building in Africa: The challenges of socio-economic recovery and development*. World Bank Africa Region Working Paper Series, No. 76.

World Bank. (2005). *World development report: Doing business in 2005.* Washington, DC: World Bank.

World Economic Forum. (2003). *The Global Competitiveness Report 2002–2003.* New York: Oxford University Press.

World Economic Forum. (2004). *The Global Competitiveness Report 2003–2004.* New York: Oxford University Press.

World Economic Forum. (2005). *The Global Competitiveness Report 2004–2005.* Hampshire, UK: Palgrave Macmillan.

World Health Organization. (2002). *World report on violence and health.* Geneva: WHO.

World Health Organization. (2004). *The economic dimensions of interpersonal violence.* Geneva: WHO.

World Health Organization. (2005). *WHO multi-country study on women's health and domestic violence against women.* Geneva: WHO.

World Health Organization/UNAIDS/UNODC. (2004). *Policy brief: Reduction of HIV transmission in prisons. Evidence for action on HIV/AIDS and injecting drug use.* Geneva: WHO.

World Tourism Organization. (1997). *Tourist safety and security. Practical measures for destinations.* Madrid: WTO.

World Travel and Tourism Council. (2004). *Sub-Saharan Africa: Travel and tourism forging ahead.* London: WTTC.

Yodanis, C. L. (2004). Gender inequality, violence against women, and fear: A cross-national test of the feminist theory of violence against women. *Journal of Interpersonal Violence, 19,* 655–675.

Zhang, S., & Chin, K.-L. (2001). Chinese human smuggling in the United States of America. *Forum on Crime and Society, 1,* 31–53.

Zhang, X. (2001). The emergence of "black society" crime in China. *Forum on Crime and Society, 1,* 53–73.

Zimring, F. E., & Hawkins, G. (1997). *Crime is not the problem.* New York: Oxford University Press.

Zvekic, U. (1998). *Criminal victimization in countries in transition.* Rome: UNICRI.

Zvekic, U., & Alvazzi del Frate, A. (1995). *Criminal victimization in the developing world.* Rome: UNICRI.

Zvekic, U., & Weatherburn, D. J. (1994). *Crime and criminal justice information in Papua New Guinea.* UNICRI Issues and Report, No.3. Rome: UNICRI.

Index

About the Author

After a career as a professor in criminology and policy adviser at the Ministry of Justice in the Netherlands, **Jan Van Dijk** joined the United Nations Office of Drugs and Crime in 1998 and served in several senior positions, including as Officer in Charge of the Centre of International Crime Prevention. He currently holds the Pieter Van Vollenhoven Chair in Victimology and Human Security at Tilburg University, the Netherlands. He served as President of The World Society of Victimology from 1997 until 2000 and received the Stephen Schafer Award of the National Organization of Victim Assistance in the United States for his contributions to the international victims' rights movement.